A Step-by-Step Approach to Using the SAS® System for Univariate and Multivariate Statistics

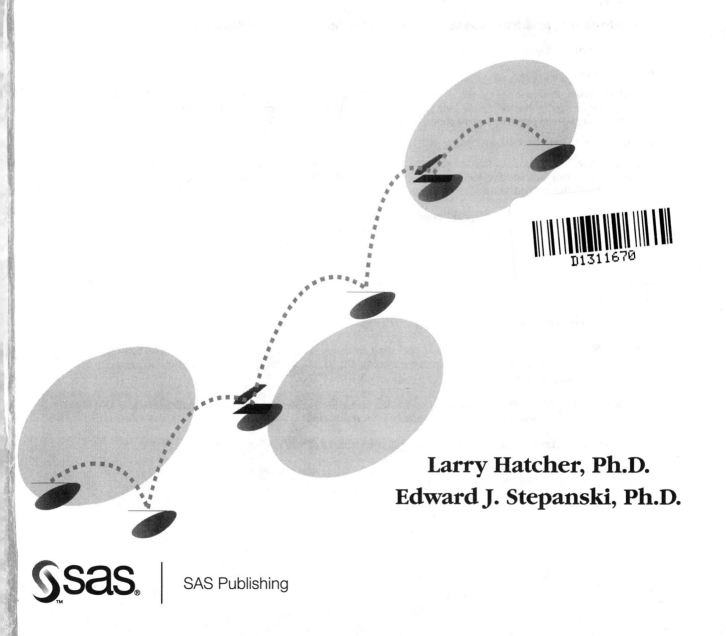

Larry Hatcher, Ph.D.
Edward J. Stepanski, Ph.D.

§sas. | SAS Publishing

Comments or Questions?

The authors assume complete responsibility for the technical accuracy of the content of this book. If you have any questions about the material in this book, please write to the authors at this address:

> SAS Institute Inc.
> Books by Users
> Attn: Larry Hatcher and Edward J. Stepanski
> SAS Campus Drive
> Cary, NC 27513

If you prefer, you can send e-mail to sasbbu@sas.com with "comments for Larry Hatcher and Edward J. Stepanski" as the subject line, or you can fax the Books by Users program at (919) 677-4444.

The correct bibliographic citation for this manual is as follows: Hatcher, Larry, and Edward J. Stepanski. *A Step-by-Step Approach to Using the SAS® System for Univariate and Multivariate Statistics,* Cary, NC: SAS Institute Inc., 1994. 552 pp.

A Step-by-Step Approach to Using the SAS® System for Univariate and Multivariate Statistics

1st printing, July 1994
2nd printing, March 1996
3rd printing, September 1997
4th printing, January 1999
5th printing, May 2001

Note that text corrections may have been made at each printing.

SAS Publishing provides a complete selection of books and electronic products to help customers use SAS software to its fullest potential. For more information about our e-books, CD-ROMs, hardcopy books, and Web-based training, visit the SAS Publishing Web site at www.sas.com/pubs or call 1-800-727-3228.

The Institute is a private company devoted to the support and further development of its software and related services.

Contents

ACKNOWLEDGMENTS

This book began as a handout for a statistics course and never would have progressed beyond that stage were it not for the encouragement of my colleague, Heidar Modaresi and my department chair, Mel Goldstein. In particular, Mel has my thanks for making every possible accommodation in my teaching schedule to allow time for this book. Thanks also to my colleagues Bill Murdy and Reid Johnson who answered many statistical questions, and to my secretary Cathy Carter who performed countless helpful tasks.

I began work on this text during a sabbatical at Bowling Green State University in 1990. My thanks to Joe Cranny, who was chair of the Psychology Department at BGSU at the time, and who helped make the sabbatical possible.

All of the SAS Institute people with whom I worked were very encouraging, generous with their time, and helpful in their comments as they reviewed and edited this book. These include David Baggett, Jennifer Ginn, Jeff Lopes, Blanche Phillips, Jim Ashton, and Cathy Maahs-Fladung. It was a pleasure to work with one and all.

Finally, my wife Ellen was unrelentingly supportive and understanding throughout the entire writing and editing process. I could not have done it without her.

L. H.

viii

Using This Book

Purpose

This book provides you with virtually everything you need to know to input data and to perform the statistical analyses that are most commonly used in research in the social sciences. *A step-by-step approach to using the SAS system for univariate and multivariate statistics* shows you how to

- key data
- choose the correct statistic
- perform the analysis
- interpret the results
- prepare tables, figures, and text that summarize the results according to the guidelines of the *Publication manual of the American Psychological Association* (the most widely-used format in the social science literature).

Audience

This text is designed to be useful to students and researchers whose background in statistics may be very weak. An introductory chapter reviews basic concepts in statistics and research methods. The chapters on data input and statistical analysis assume that the reader has absolutely no familiarity with the SAS System; all programming concepts are taught at an introductory level. The chapters that deal with specific statistics clearly describe the circumstances under which it is appropriate to analyze a data set with the statistic of interest. Finally, each chapter provides at least one detailed example of how the researcher should key data, prepare the SAS program, and interpret the results for a representative research problem. Even users whose only exposure to data analysis was an elementary statistics course taken years previously should be able to use this guide to perform statistical analyses successfully.

Organization

Although no single text can discuss *every* statistical procedure, this book covers the statistics that are most commonly used in research in psychology, sociology, marketing, organizational behavior, political science, communication, and the other social sciences. Material covered in each chapter is summarized as follows:

Chapter 1: Basic Concepts in Research and Data Analysis

reviews fundamental issues in research methodology and statistics. This chapter defines and discusses the differences between concepts such as *variables* and *values*, *quantitative variables* and *classification variables*, *experimental research* and *nonexperimental research*, and *descriptive analysis* and *inferential analysis*. Chapter 1 also describes the various scales of measurement (e.g., nominal, ordinal, and so on) and covers the basic issues in hypothesis testing. After completing this chapter, you should be familiar with the fundamental issues and terminology of data analysis, and you will be prepared to begin learning about the SAS System in subsequent chapters.

Chapter 2: Introduction to SAS Programs, SAS Logs, and SAS Output

introduces three elements that you will work with when using the SAS System: the SAS program, the SAS log, and the SAS output file. Chapter 2 presents a simple SAS program along with the log and output files produced by the program. By the conclusion of this chapter, you will understand the steps that you need to follow to submit SAS programs and review the results of those programs.

Chapter 3: Data Input

shows you how to key data and write the statements that create a SAS data set. This chapter provides instructions on inputting data with either the CARDS statement or the INFILE statement, and it shows you how information may be read either as raw data or as a correlation or covariance matrix. By the conclusion of the chapter, you should be prepared to input any type of data that is commonly encountered in social science research.

Chapter 4: Working with Variables and Observations in SAS Data Sets

shows you how to modify a data set so that existing variables are transformed or recoded or so that new variables are created. Chapter 4 shows you how to write statements that eliminate unwanted observations from a data set so you can perform analyses on only a specified subgroup or on subjects that have no missing data. This chapter also demonstrates the correct use of arithmetic operators, IF-THEN control statements, and comparison operators. After completing this chapter, you will know how to transform variables and perform analyses on data from specific subgroups of subjects.

Chapter 5: Exploring Data with PROC MEANS, PROC FREQ, PROC PRINT, and PROC UNIVARIATE

discusses the use of four procedures:

- PROC MEANS, which may be used to calculate means, standard deviations, and other descriptive statistics for quantitative variables
- PROC FREQ, which may be used to construct frequency distributions
- PROC PRINT, which allows you to create a printout of the raw data set
- PROC UNIVARIATE, which allows you to prepare stem-and-leaf plots to test for normality.

By the conclusion of the chapter, you will understand how these procedures may be used to screen data for errors as well as to obtain simple descriptive statistics for the research article.

Chapter 6: Measures of Bivariate Association

discusses procedures that may be used to test the significance of the relationship between two variables. Chapter 6 also gives guidelines for choosing the correct statistic based on the level of measurement used to assess the two variables. After completing this chapter, you will know how to use

- PROC PLOT to prepare bivariate scattergrams
- PROC CORR to compute Pearson correlations and Spearman correlations
- PROC FREQ to perform the chi-square test of independence.

Chapter 7: *t* Tests: Independent Samples and Paired Samples

shows you how to key data and prepare SAS programs that perform an independent-samples *t* test using the TTEST procedure or a paired-samples *t* test using the MEANS procedure. This chapter introduces a fictitious study designed to test a hypothesis based on the investment model (Rusbult, 1980), a theory of interpersonal attraction. With respect to the independent samples *t* test, the chapter shows how to use a folded form of the *F* statistic to determine whether the equal-variances or unequal-variances *t* test is appropriate for a given analysis. The chapter also provides a structured set of guidelines for interpreting the output from PROC TTEST and for summarizing the results of the analysis. With respect to the paired-samples *t* test, Chapter 7 shows how to create the necessary difference scores and how to test the mean difference score for statistical significance. By the chapter's conclusion, you will know when it is appropriate to perform either the independent-samples *t* test or the paired-samples *t* test, and you will understand what steps to follow in performing each analysis.

Chapter 8: One-Way ANOVA with One Between-Groups Factor

shows you how to key data and prepare SAS programs that perform a one-way analysis of variance (ANOVA) using the GLM procedure. Chapter 8 focuses on the *between-groups* design in which each subject is exposed to only one condition under the independent variable. This chapter also describes the use of a multiple comparison procedure (Tukey's HSD test). By the chapter's conclusion, you should be able to

- identify the conditions under which this analysis is appropriate
- prepare the necessary SAS program to perform the analysis
- review the SAS log and the output for errors
- prepare tables and text that summarize the results of your analysis.

Chapter 9: Factorial ANOVA with Two Between-Groups Factors

shows you how to key data and prepare SAS programs that perform a two-way ANOVA using the GLM procedure. This chapter focuses on factorial designs with two *between groups* factors, meaning that each subject is exposed to only one condition under each independent variable. The chapter provides guidelines for interpreting results that do not display a significant interaction, and it provides separate guidelines for interpreting results that do display a significant interaction. After completing this chapter, you should be able to determine whether the interaction is significant and to summarize the results involving main effects in the case of a nonsignificant interaction. For significant interactions, you should be able to display the interaction in a figure and perform tests for simple effects.

Chapter 10: Multivariate Analysis of Variance (MANOVA) with One Between-Groups Factor

shows you how to key data and prepare SAS programs that perform a one-way multivariate analysis of variance (MANOVA) using the GLM procedure. MANOVA may be viewed as an extension of ANOVA that allows for the inclusion of multiple criterion variables in a single test. This chapter focuses on the between-groups design in which each subject is exposed to only one condition under the independent variable. By the completion of this chapter, you should be able to summarize both significant and nonsignificant MANOVA results.

Chapter 11: One-Way ANOVA with One Repeated-Measures Factor

shows you how to key data and prepare SAS programs that perform a one-way repeated-measures ANOVA using the GLM procedure with the REPEATED statement. This chapter focuses on *repeated-measures* designs in which each subject is exposed to every condition under the independent variable. After completing this chapter, you should understand the

- necessary conditions for performing a valid repeated-measures ANOVA
- alternative analyses to use when the validity conditions are not met
- strategies for minimizing sequence effects.

Chapter 12: Factorial ANOVA with Repeated-Measures Factors and Between-Groups Factors

shows you how to key data and prepare SAS programs that perform a two-way mixed-design ANOVA using the GLM procedure and the REPEATED statement. This chapter provides guidelines for the hierarchical interpretation of the analysis along with an alternative method of performing the analysis that allows for use of a variety of post-hoc tests using SAS/STAT software. By the end of this chapter, you should be able to interpret the results of analyses both with and without significant interactions.

Chapter 13: Multiple Regression

shows you how to perform multiple-regression analysis to investigate the relationship between a continuous criterion variable and multiple continuous predictor variables. Chapter 13 describes the different components of the multiple regression equation and discusses the meaning of R^2 and other results from a multiple-regression analysis. The chapter also shows how bivariate correlations, multiple-regression coefficients, and uniqueness indices may be reviewed to assess the relative importance of predictor variables. After completing the chapter, you should be able to use PROC CORR and PROC REG to conduct the analysis, and you should be able to summarize the results of a multiple-regression analysis in tables and in text.

Chapter 14: Principal Component Analysis

provides an introduction to principal component analysis, which is a variable-reduction procedure similar to factor analysis. This chapter offers guidelines regarding the necessary sample size and recommended number of items per component. The chapter also analyzes fictitious data from two studies to illustrate these procedures. By the end of the chapter, you should be able to determine the correct number of components to retain, interpret the rotated solution, create factor scores, and summarize the results.

Note: This chapter deals only with the creation of orthogonal (uncorrelated) components; oblique (correlated) solutions are covered in the exploratory factor analysis chapter from *A step-by-step approach to using the SAS system for factor analysis and structural equation modeling* (Hatcher, 1994), a companion volume.

Chapter 15: Assessing Scale Reliability with Coefficient Alpha

shows how PROC CORR may be used to compute the coefficient-alpha reliability index for a multiple-item scale. This chapter reviews basic issues regarding the assessment of reliability and describes the circumstances under which a measure of internal consistency reliability is likely to be high. The chapter also analyzes fictitious questionnaire data to demonstrate how the results of PROC CORR can be used to perform an item analysis, thereby improving the reliability of the scale. After completing this chapter, you should understand how to construct multiple-item scales that are likely to have high reliability coefficients, and you should be able to use PROC CORR to assess and improve the reliability of your scales.

Appendix A: Choosing the Correct Statistic

provides a structured approach for choosing the correct statistical procedure to use when analyzing data. This approach bases the choice of a specific statistic upon the number and scale of the criterion (dependent) variables in the study considered in conjunction with the number and scale of the predictor (independent) variables. The chapter groups commonly used statistics into three tables based upon the number of criterion and predictor variables in the analysis.

Appendix B: Data Sets

provides data sets used in Chapters 13-15.

Appendix C: Critical Values of the *F* Distribution

provides tables that show critical values of the *F* distribution with alpha levels of .05, .01, and .001.

References

American Psychological Association (1987). *Publication manual of the American Psychological Association, third edition*. Washington, D.C.: American Psychological Association.

Hatcher, L. (1994). *A step-by-step approach to using the SAS system for factor analysis and structural equation modeling*. Cary, NC: SAS Institute Inc.

Rusbult, C. E. (1980). Commitment and satisfaction in romantic associations: A test of the investment model. *Journal of Experimental Social Psychology, 16,* 172-186.

Chapter 1

BASIC CONCEPTS IN RESEARCH
AND DATA ANALYSIS

Overview. This chapter reviews basic concepts and terminology from research design and statistics. It describes the different types of variables that may be analyzed, as well the scales of measurement with which these variables are assessed. The chapter reviews the differences between nonexperimental and experimental research, as well as the differences between descriptive and inferential analyses. Finally, basic concepts in hypothesis testing are presented. After completing this chapter, you should be familiar with the fundamental issues and terminology of data analysis, and will be prepared to begin learning about the SAS System in subsequent chapters.

Introduction: A Common Language for Researchers

Research in the social sciences is a diverse topic. In part, this is because the social sciences represent a wide variety of *disciplines* including (but not limited to) psychology, sociology, political science, anthropology, communication, education, management, and economics. Further complicating matters is the fact that, within each discipline, researchers can use a number of very different *methods* to conduct research. These methods may include unobtrusive observation, participant observation, case studies, interviews, focus groups, surveys, ex post facto studies, laboratory experiments, and field experiments.

Despite this diversity in methods used and topics investigated, most social science research still shares a number of common characteristics. Regardless of field, most research involves an investigator gathering data and performing analyses to determine what the data mean. In addition, most social scientists use a common language in conducting and reporting their research: researchers in psychology and management speak of "testing null hypotheses" and "obtaining significant *p* values."

The purpose of this chapter is to review some of the fundamental concepts and terms that are shared across the social sciences. You should familiarize (or refamiliarize) yourself with this material before proceeding to the subsequent chapters, as most of the terms introduced here will be referred to again and again throughout the text. If you are currently taking your first course in statistics, this chapter provides an elementary introduction; if you have already completed a course in statistics, it provides a quick review.

Steps to Follow when Conducting Research

The specific steps to follow when conducting research depend, in part, on the topic of investigation, where the researchers are in their overall program of research, and other factors. Nonetheless, it is accurate to say that much research in the social sciences follows a systematic course of action that begins with the statement of a research question and ends with the researcher drawing conclusions about a null hypothesis. This section describes the research process as a planned sequence that consists of the following six steps:

1. Developing a statement of the research question
2. Developing a statement of the research hypothesis
3. Defining the instrument (e.g., questionnaire, unobtrusive measures)
4. Gathering the data
5. Analyzing the data
6. Drawing conclusions regarding the hypothesis

The preceding steps are illustrated here with reference to a fictitious research problem. Imagine that you have been hired by a large insurance company to find ways of improving the productivity of its insurance agents. Specifically, the company would like you to find ways to increase the dollar amount of insurance policies sold by the average agent. You will therefore begin a program of research to identify the determinants of agent productivity.

The research question. The process of research often begins with an attempt to arrive at a clear statement of the **research question** (or questions). The research question is a statement of what you hope to have learned by the time you have completed the program of research. It is good practice to revise and refine the research question several times to ensure that you are very clear about what it is you *really* want to know.

For example, in the present case, you might begin with the question "What is the difference between agents who sell much insurance and agents who sell little insurance?" An alternative question might be "What variables have a causal effect on the amount of insurance sold by agents?" Upon reflection, you may realize that the insurance company really only wants to know what things *management* can do to cause the agents to sell more insurance. This may eliminate from consideration certain personality traits or demographic variables that are not under management's control, and substantially narrow the focus of the research program. This narrowing, in turn, leads to a more specific statement of the research question such as "What variables under the control of management have a causal effect on the amount of insurance sold by agents?" Once you have defined the research question more clearly, you are in a better position to develop a good hypothesis that provides an answer to the question.

The hypothesis. A **hypothesis** is a statement about the predicted relationships among events or variables. A good hypothesis in the present case might identify which *specific* variable will have a causal effect on the amount of insurance sold by agents. For example, an hypothesis might predict that the agents' level of training will have a positive effect on the amount of insurance sold. Or it might predict that the agents' level of motivation will positively affect sales.

In developing the hypothesis, you may be influenced by any of a number of sources: an existing theory, some related research, or even personal experience. Let's assume that you have been influenced by **goal-setting theory**. This theory states, among other things, that higher levels of work performance are achieved when difficult work-related goals are set for employees. Drawing on goal-setting theory, you now state the following hypothesis: "The difficulty of the goals that agents set for themselves is positively related to the amount of insurance they sell."

Notice how this statement satisfies our definition for an hypothesis, as it is a statement about the relationship between two variables. The first variable can be labelled Goal Difficulty, and the second can be labelled Amount of Insurance Sold. This relationship is illustrated in Figure 1.1:

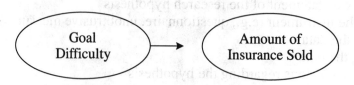

Figure 1.1 Hypothesized Relationship Between Goal Difficulty and Amount of Insurance Sold

The same hypothesis could also be stated in a number of other ways. For example, the following hypothesis makes the same basic prediction: "Agents who set difficult goals for themselves sell greater amounts of insurance than agents who do not set difficult goals."

Notice that these hypotheses have been stated in the present tense. It is also acceptable to state hypotheses in the past tense. For example, the preceding could have been stated, "Agents who set difficult goals for themselves sold greater amounts of insurance than agents who did not set difficult goals."

You should also note that these two hypotheses are quite broad in nature. In many research situations, it is helpful to state hypotheses that are more specific in the predictions they make. A more specific hypothesis for the present study might be "Agents who score above 60 on the Smith Goal Difficulty Scale will sell greater amounts of insurance than agents who score below 40 on the Smith Goal Difficulty Scale."

Defining the instrument, gathering data, analyzing data, and drawing conclusions. With the hypothesis stated, you may now test it by conducting a study in which you gather and analyze some relevant data. **Data** may be defined as a collection of scores obtained when a subject's characteristics and/or performance are assessed. For example, you may choose to test your hypothesis by conducting a simple correlational study: you may identify a group of 100 agents and determine

(a) the difficulty of the goals that have been set for each agent

(b) the amount of insurance sold by each agent.

Different types of instruments may be used to obtain different types of data. For example, you may use a questionnaire to assess goal difficulty, but rely on company records for measures of insurance sold. Once the data are gathered, each agent will have one score indicating the difficulty of his or her goals, and a second score indicating the amount of insurance that he or she has sold.

With the data gathered, you analyze them to see if the agents with the more difficult goals did, in fact, sell more insurance. If yes, the study lends some support to your hypothesis; if no, it fails to provide support. In either case, you could draw conclusions regarding the tenability of your hypotheses, and would have made some progress toward answering your research question. The information learned in the current study may stimulate new questions or new hypotheses for subsequent studies, and the cycle would repeat. For example, if you obtained support for your hypothesis with the current correlational study, you may choose to follow it up with a study using a different method, perhaps an experimental study (the difference between these methods is described later). Over time, a body of research evidence would accumulate, and researchers would be able to review this body to draw general conclusions about the determinants of insurance sales.

Variables, Values, and Observations

Variables. When discussing data, one often speaks in terms of variables, values, and observations. For the type of research discussed here, a **variable** refers to some specific characteristic of a subject which may assume one or more different values. For the subjects in the study just described, Amount of Insurance Sold is an example of a variable: some subjects had sold a lot of insurance, and others had sold less. A different variable was Goal Difficulty: some subjects had more difficult goals, while others had less difficult goals. Subject Age was a third variable, while subject Sex (male or female) was yet another.

Values. A **value**, on the other hand, refers to either a subject's relative standing on a quantitative variable, or a subject's classification within a classification variable. For example, Amount of Insurance Sold is a quantitative variable which may assume a large number of values: one agent may sell $2,000,000 worth of insurance in one year, one may sell $100,000 worth, and another may sell $0 worth. Age is another quantitative variable which may assume a wide variety of values. In the sample studied, these values may have ranged from a low of 22 years (for the youngest agent) to a high of 64 years (for the oldest agent).

Quantitative variables versus classification variables. You can see that, in both of these examples, a given value is a type of score that indicates where the subject stands on the variable of interest. The word "score" is an appropriate substitute for the word value in these cases because both Amount of Insurance Sold and Age are **quantitative variables**: variables in which numbers serve as values.

A different type of variable is a **classification variable** or, alternatively, **qualitative variable** or **categorical variable**. With classification variables, different values represent different groups to which the subject may belong. Sex is a good example of a classification variable, as it may assume only one of two values: a subject is classified as either male or female. Race is an example of a classification variable which may assume a larger number of values: a subject may be classified as Caucasian, African American, Asian American, or as belonging to a large number of other groups. Notice why these variables are classification variables and not quantitative variables. The values only represent group membership; they do not represent a characteristic that some subjects possess in greater quantity than others.

Observational units. In discussing data, researchers often make references to **observational units**, which may be defined as the individual subjects (or other objects) which serve as the source of the data. Within the social sciences, a *person* usually serves as the observational unit under study (although it is also possible to use some other entity such as an individual school or organization as the observational unit). In this text, the person is used as the observational unit in all examples. Researchers often refer to the number of **observations** (or **cases**) included in their data set, and this simply refers to the number of subjects who were studied.

For a more concrete illustration of the concepts discussed so far, consider the following data set:

Table 1.1

Insurance Sales Data

Observation	Name	Sex	Age	Goal Difficulty Scores	Rank	Sales
1	Bob	M	34	97	2	$598,243
2	Walt	M	56	80	1	$367,342
3	Jane	F	36	67	4	$254,998
4	Susan	F	24	40	3	$80,344
5	Jim	M	22	37	5	$40,172
6	Mack	M	44	24	6	$0

The preceding table reports information about six research subjects: Bob, Walt, Jane, Susan, Jim, and Mack; therefore, the data set includes six observations. Information about a given observation (subject) appears as a **row** running left to right across the table. The first **column** of the data set (running vertically) indicates the observation number, and the second column reports the name of the subject who constitutes that observation. The remaining five columns report information on the five research variables under study. The "Sex" column reports subject sex, which may assume one of two values: "M" for male and "F" for female. The "Age" column reports the subject's age in years. The "Goal Difficulty Scores" column reports the subject's score on a fictitious goal difficulty scale: assume that each participant completed a 20-item questionnaire which assessed the difficulty of his or her work goals. Depending on how they respond to the questionnaire, subjects receive a score which may range from a low of 0 (meaning that the subject's work goals are quite easy) to a high of 100 (meaning that they are quite difficult). The "Rank" column shows how the subjects were ranked by their supervisor according to their overall effectiveness as agents. A rank of 1 represents the most effective agent, and a rank of 6 represents the least effective. Finally, the "Sales" column reveals the amount of insurance sold by each agent (in dollars) during the most recent year.

The preceding example illustrates a very small data set with six observations and five research variables (Sex, Age, Goal Difficulty, Rank, and Sales). One variable is a classification variable (Sex), while the remainder are quantitative variables. The numbers or letters which appear within a column represent some of the values which can be assumed by that variable.

Scales of Measurement

One of the most important schemes for classifying a variable involves its **scale of measurement**. Researchers generally discuss four different scales of measurement: nominal, ordinal, ratio, and interval. Before analyzing a data set, it is important to determine which scales of measurement were used, because certain types of statistical procedures require certain scales of measurement. For example, one-way analysis of variance generally requires that the independent variable be a nominal-level variable and the dependent variable be an interval-level or ratio-level variable. In this text, each chapter that deals with a specific statistical procedure indicates what scale of measurement is required with the variables under study. Then, you must decide whether your variables meet these requirements.

Nominal scales. A nominal scale is a classification system that places people, objects, or other entities into mutually exclusive categories. A variable measured using a nominal scale is a classification variable: it simply indicates the group to which each subject belongs. The examples of classification variables provided earlier (e.g., Sex and Race) also serve as examples of nominal-level variables: they tell us which group a subject belongs to but they do not provide any quantitative information about the subjects. That is, the Sex variable might tell us that some subjects are males and other are females, but it does not tell us that some subjects possess more of a specific characteristic relative to others. The remaining three scales of measurement, however, provide some quantitative information.

Ordinal scales. Values on an ordinal scale represent the rank order of the subjects with respect to the variable being assessed. For example, the preceding table includes one variable called Rank which represents the rank-ordering of the subjects according to their overall effectiveness as agents. The values on this ordinal scale represent a *hierarchy of levels* with respect to the construct of "effectiveness": we know that the agent ranked 1 was perceived as being more effective than the agent ranked 2, that the agent ranked 2 was more effective than the one ranked 3, and so forth.

Caution: An ordinal scale has a serious limitation in that equal differences in scale values do not necessarily have equal quantitative meaning. For example, notice the following rankings:

Rank	Name
1	Walt
2	Bob
3	Susan
4	Jane
5	Jim
6	Mack

Notice that Walt was ranked 1 while Bob was ranked 2. The difference between these two rankings is 1 (because 2 – 1 = 1), so there is one unit of difference between Walt and Bob. Now notice that Jim was ranked 5 while Mack was ranked 6. The difference between these two rankings is also 1 (because 6 – 5 = 1), so there is also 1 unit of difference between Jim and Mack. Putting the two together, the difference in ranking between Walt and Bob is equal to the difference in ranking between Jim and Mack. But does this mean that the difference in *overall effectiveness* between Walt and Bob is equal to the difference in overall effectiveness between Jim and Mack? Not necessarily. It is possible that Walt was just barely superior to Bob in effectiveness, while Jim was substantially superior to Mack. These rankings reveal very little about the quantitative differences between the subjects with regard to the underlying construct (effectiveness, in this case). An ordinal scale simply provides a rank order of who is better than whom.

Interval scales. With an interval scale, equal differences between scale values do have equal quantitative meaning. For this reason, it can be seen that the interval scale provides more quantitative information than the ordinal scale. A good example of an interval scale is the Fahrenheit scale used to measure temperature. With the Fahrenheit scale, the difference between 70 degrees and 75 degrees is equal to the difference between 80 degrees and 85 degrees: The units of measurement are equal throughout the full range of the scale.

However, the interval scale also has an important limitation: It does not have a true zero point. A **true zero point** means that a value of zero on the scale represents zero quantity of the construct being assessed. It should be obvious that the Fahrenheit scale does not have a true zero point: when the thermometer reads 0 degrees, that does not mean that there is absolutely no heat present in the environment.

Researchers in the social sciences often assume that many of their man-made variables are measured on an interval scale. For example, in the preceding study involving insurance agents, you would probably assume that scores from the goal difficulty questionnaire constitute an interval-level scale; that is, you would likely assume that the difference between a score of 50 and 60 is approximately equal to the difference between a score of 70 and 80. Many researchers would also assume that scores from an instrument such as an intelligence test are also measured at the interval level of measurement.

On the other hand, some researchers are skeptical that instruments such as these have true equal-interval properties, and prefer to refer to them as **quasi-interval** scales. Disagreements concerning the level of measurement achieved with such instruments continues to be a controversial topic within the social sciences.

At any rate, it is clear that there is no true zero point with either of the preceding instruments: a score of 0 on the goal difficulty scale does not indicate the complete absence of goal difficulty, and a score of 0 on an intelligence test does not indicate the complete absence of intelligence. A true zero point may be found only with variables measured on a ratio scale.

Ratio scales. Ratio scales are similar to interval scales in that equal differences between scale values have equal quantitative meaning. However, ratio scales also have a true zero point which gives them an additional property: With ratio scales, it is possible to make meaningful statements about the ratios between scale values. For example, the system of inches used with a common ruler is an example of a ratio scale. There is a true zero point with this system, in that zero inches does in fact indicate a complete absence of length. With this scale, it is possible to make meaningful statements about ratios. It is appropriate to say that an object four inches long is twice as long as an object two inches long. Age, as measured in years, is also on a ratio scale: a 10-year-old house is twice as old as a 5-year-old house. Notice that it is not possible to make these statements about ratios with the interval-level variables discussed above. One would not say that a person with an IQ of 160 is twice as intelligent as a person with an IQ of 80, as there is no true zero point with that scale.

Although ratio-level scales may be easiest to find when one considers the physical properties of objects (e.g., height and weight), they are also common in the type of research discussed in this manual. For example, the study discussed previously included the variables for age and amount of insurance sold (in dollars). Both of these have true zero points, and are measured as ratio scales.

Basic Approaches to Research

Nonexperimental research. Much research can be described as being either nonexperimental or experimental in nature. In **nonexperimental research** (also called **nonmanipulative** or **correlational research**), the researcher simply studies the naturally occurring relationship between two or more naturally occurring variables. A **naturally occurring variable** is a variable which is *not* manipulated or controlled by the researcher; it is simply measured it as it normally exists.

The insurance study described previously is a good example of nonexperimental research in that you simply measured two naturally occurring variables (goal difficulty and amount of insurance sold) to determine whether they were related. If, in a different study, you investigated the relationship between IQ and college grade point average (GPA), this would also be an example of nonexperimental research.

With nonexperimental designs, researchers often refer to criterion variables and predictor variables. A **criterion variable** is an outcome variable which may be predicted from one or more predictor variables. The criterion variable is often the main focus of the study in that it is the outcome variable mentioned in the statement of the research problem. In our example, the criterion variable is Amount of Insurance Sold.

The **predictor variable**, on the other hand, is that variable used to predict values on the criterion. In some studies, you may even believe that the predictor variable has a causal effect on the criterion. In the insurance study, for example, the predictor variable was Goal Difficulty. Because you believed that Goal Difficulty may positively affect insurance sales, you conducted a study in which Goal Difficulty was the predictor and Sales was the criterion. You do not necessarily have to believe that there is a causal relationship between two variables to conduct a study such as this; however, you may simply be interested in determining whether it is possible to predict one variable from the other.

You should note here that nonexperimental research that investigates the relationship between just two variables generally provides relatively weak evidence concerning cause-and-effect relationships. The reasons for this can be seen by reviewing the study on insurance sales. If the psychologist conducts this study and finds that the agents with the more difficult goals also tend to sell more insurance, does that mean that having difficult goals *caused* them to sell more insurance? Not necessarily. You can argue that selling a lot of insurance increases the agents' self-confidence, and that this causes them to set higher work goals for themselves. Under this second scenario, it was actually the insurance sales which had a causal effect on Goal Difficulty.

As this example shows, with nonexperimental research it is often possible to obtain a single finding which is consistent with a number of contradictory causal explanations. Hence, a strong inference that "variable A had a causal effect variable B" is seldom possible when you conduct simple correlational research with just two variables. To obtain stronger evidence of cause and effect, researchers generally either analyze the relationships between a larger number of variables using sophisticated statistical procedures that are beyond the scope of this text (such as path analysis), or drop the nonexperimental approach entirely and instead use experimental research methods. The nature of experimental research is discussed in the following section.

Experimental research. Most **experimental research** can be identified by three important characteristics:

- Subjects are randomly assigned to experimental conditions.

- The researcher manipulates an independent variable.

- Subjects in different experimental conditions are treated similarly with regard to all variables except the independent variable.

To illustrate these concepts, assume that you conduct an experiment to test the hypothesis that goal difficulty positively affects insurance sales. Assume that you identify a group of 100 agents who will serve as subjects. You randomly assign 50 agents to a "difficult goal" condition. Subjects in this group are told by their superiors to make at least 25 cold calls (sales calls) to potential policy-holders per week. The other 50 agents have been randomly assigned to the "easy goal" condition. They have been told to make just 5 cold calls to potential policy holders per week. The design of this experiment is illustrated in Figure 1.2.

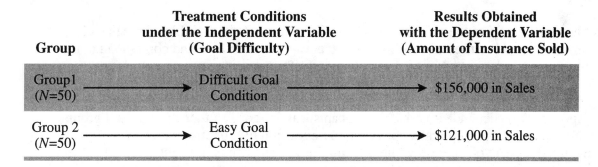

Group	Treatment Conditions under the Independent Variable (Goal Difficulty)	Results Obtained with the Dependent Variable (Amount of Insurance Sold)
Group1 (*N*=50)	Difficult Goal Condition	$156,000 in Sales
Group 2 (*N*=50)	Easy Goal Condition	$121,000 in Sales

Figure 1.2   Design of the Experiment Used to Assess the Effects of Goal Difficulty

After one year, you determine how much new insurance each agent has sold that year. Assume that the average agent in the difficult goal condition sold $156,000 worth of new policies, while the average agent in the easy goal condition sold just $121,000 worth.

It is possible to use some of the terminology associated with nonexperimental research when discussing this experiment. For example, it would be appropriate to continue to refer to Amount of Insurance Sold as being a criterion variable, because this is the outcome variable of central interest. You could also continue to refer to Goal Difficulty as the predictor variable because you believe that this variable will predict sales to some extent.

Notice however, that Goal Difficulty is now a somewhat different variable. In the nonexperimental study, Goal Difficulty was a naturally occurring variable which could take on a wide variety of values (whatever score the subject received on the goal difficulty questionnaire). In the present experiment, however, Goal Difficulty is a **manipulated variable**, which means that you (as the researcher) determined what value of the variable would be assigned to each subject. In the experiment, Goal Difficulty could assume only one of two values: subjects were either in the difficult goal group or the easy goal group. Therefore, Goal Difficulty is now a classification variable, assessed on a nominal scale.

Although it is acceptable to speak of predictor and criterion variables within the context of experimental research, it is more common to speak in terms of independent variables and dependent variables. The **independent variable** (abbreviated IV) is that variable whose values (or levels) are selected by the experimenter to determine what effect the independent variable has on the dependent variable. The independent variable is the experimental counterpart to a predictor variable. A **dependent variable** (abbreviated DV), on the other hand, is some aspect of the subject's behavior which is assessed to reflect the effects of the independent variable. The dependent variable is the experimental counterpart to a criterion variable. In the present experiment, Goal Difficulty is the independent variable, while Sales is the dependent variable. Remember that the terms predictor variable and criterion variable may be used with almost any type of research, but that the terms independent and dependent variable should be used only with experimental research.

Researchers often refer to the different **levels of the independent variable**. These levels are also referred to as **experimental conditions** or **treatment conditions** and correspond to the different groups to which a subject may be assigned. The present example includes two experimental conditions: a difficult goal condition, and an easy goal condition.

With respect to the independent variable, you can speak in terms of the experimental group versus the control group. Generally speaking, the **experimental group** receives the experimental treatment of interest, while the **control group** is an equivalent group of subjects that does not receive this treatment. The simplest type of experiment consists of just one experimental group and one control group. For example, the present study could have been redesigned so that it consisted of an experimental group that was assigned the goal of making 25 cold calls (the difficult goal condition), and a control group in which no goals were assigned (the no goal condition). Obviously, you can expand the study by creating more than one experimental group. You could do this in the present case by assigning one experimental group the difficult goal of 25 cold calls and the second experimental group the easy goal of just 5 cold calls.

Descriptive Versus Inferential Statistical Analysis

To understand the difference between descriptive and inferential statistics, you must first understand the difference between populations and samples. A **population** is the *entire collection* of a carefully defined set of people, objects, or events. For example, if the insurance company in question employed 10,000 insurance agents in the U.S., then those 10,000 agents would constitute the population of agents hired by that company. A **sample**, on the other hand, is a *subset* of the people, objects, or events selected from that population. For example, the 100 agents used in the experiment described earlier constitute a sample.

Descriptive analyses. A **parameter** is a descriptive characteristic of a population. For example, if you assessed the average amount of insurance sold by all 10,000 agents in this company, the resulting average would be a parameter. To obtain this average, of course, you would first need to tabulate the amount of insurance sold by each and every agent. In calculating this mean, you are engaging in descriptive statistical analysis. **Descriptive** statistical analysis focuses on the exhaustive measurement of population characteristics: You define a population, assess each member of that population, and arrive at some form of summary value (such as a mean or standard deviation).

Most people think of populations as being very large groups, such as "all of the people in the U.S." However, a group does not have to be large to be a population, it only has to be the *entire collection* of the people or things being studied. For example, a teacher may define as a population all 23 students taking an English course, and then calculate the average score of these students on a measure of class satisfaction. The resulting average would be a parameter.

Inferential analyses. A **statistic**, on the other hand, is a numerical value which is computed from a sample, and either describes some characteristic of that sample such as the mean, or is used to make inferences about the population from which the sample is drawn. For example, if you were to compute the average amount of insurance sold by your sample of 100 agents, that average would be a statistic because it summarizes a specific characteristic of the sample. Remember that the word "statistic" is generally associated with samples, while "parameter" is generally associated with populations.

In contrast to descriptive statistics, **inferential** statistical analysis involves using information from a sample to make inferences, or estimates, about the population. For example, assume that you need to know how much insurance is sold by the average agent in the company. It may not be possible to obtain the necessary information from all 10,000 agents and then calculate a mean. An alternative would be to draw a random (and ideally representative) sample of 100 agents and determine the average amount sold by this subset. If this group of 100 sold an average of $179,322 worth of policies last year, then your "best guess" of the amount of insurance sold by all 10,000 agents would likewise be $179,322. Here, you have used characteristics of the sample to make inferences about characteristics of the population. Using some simple statistical procedures, you could even put confidence intervals around the estimate which would allow you to make statements such as "there is a 95% chance that the actual population mean lies somewhere between $172,994 and $185,650." This is the real value of inferential statistical procedures: they allow you to review information obtained from a relatively small sample, and then make inferences about a much larger population.

Hypothesis Testing

Most of the procedures described in this manual are inferential procedures that allow you to test specific hypotheses about the characteristics of populations. As an illustration, consider the simple experiment described earlier in which 50 agents were assigned to a difficult goal condition and 50 other agents to an easy goal condition. Assume that, after one year, the difficult-goal agents had sold an average of $156,000 worth of insurance, while the easy-goal agents had sold only $121,000 worth. On the surface, this would seem to support your hypothesis that difficult goals cause agents to sell more insurance. But can you be sure of this? Even if goal setting had no effect at all, you would not really expect the two groups of 50 agents to sell exactly the same amount of insurance: one group would sell somewhat more than the other due to chance alone. The difficult-goal group did sell more insurance, but did it sell *enough* more to make you confident that the difference was due to your manipulation?

What's more, one could easily argue that you don't really even *care* about the amount of insurance sold by these two small samples. What really matters is the amount of insurance sold by the larger populations which they represent. The first population could be defined as "the population of agents who are assigned difficult goals" and the second would be "the population of agents who are assigned easy goals." Your real research question involves the issue of whether the first population sells more than the second. This is where hypothesis testing comes in.

Types of inferential tests. Generally speaking, there are two types of tests conducted when using inferential procedures: tests of group differences and tests of association. With a **test of group differences**, you typically want to know whether two populations differ with respect to their mean scores on some criterion variable. The present experiment would lead to a test of group differences, because you want to know whether the average amount of insurance sold in the population of difficult-goal agents is different from the average amount sold in the population of easy-goal agents. A different example of a test of group differences might involve a study in which the researcher wants to know whether Caucasian Americans, African Americans, and Asian Americans differ with respect to their mean scores on a locus of control scale. Notice that in both cases, two or more distinct populations are being compared with respect to their mean scores on a single criterion variable.

With a **test of association**, on the other hand, you are working with a single population of individuals and wish to know whether there is a relationship between two or more variables within this population. Perhaps the best-known test of association involves testing the significance of a correlation coefficient. Assume that you have conducted a simple correlational study in which you asked 100 agents to complete the 20-item goal difficulty questionnaire. Remember that, with this questionnaire, subjects could receive a score which may range from a low of 0 to a high of 100. You could then correlate these goal difficulty scores with the amount of insurance sold by the agents that year. Here, the goal difficulty scores constitute the predictor variable, while the amount of insurance sold serves as the criterion. Obtaining a strong positive correlation between these two variables would mean that the more difficult the agents' goals, the more insurance they tended to sell. Notice why this would be called a test of association: you are determining whether there is an association, or *relationship*, between the predictor and criterion variables. Notice also that there is only one population being studied; there is no experimental manipulation which creates a difficult-goal population versus an easy-goal population.

For the sake of completeness, it is worth mentioning that there are some relatively sophisticated procedures that also allow you to perform a third type of test: whether the association between two variables is the same across two or more populations. Analysis of covariance (ANCOVA) is one procedure that allows such a test. For example, you may form a hypothesis that the association between self-reported goal difficulty and insurance sales is stronger in the population of agents assigned difficult goals than it is in the population assigned easy goals. To test this hypothesis, you might randomly assign a group of insurance agents to either an easy-goal condition or a difficult-goal condition (as described earlier). Each agent could complete the 20-item self-report goal difficulty scale, and then be exposed to the appropriate treatment.

Subsequently, you could record each agent's sales. Analysis of covariance would allow you to determine whether the relationship between questionnaire scores and sales is stronger in the difficult-goal population than it is in the easy-goal population (ANCOVA would also allow you to test a number of additional hypotheses). Although analysis of covariance is beyond the scope of this text, interested readers are referred to Littell, Freund, and Spector (1991) for instructions on how it may be performed using the SAS System.

Types of hypotheses. Two different types of hypotheses are relevant to most statistical tests. The first is called the null hypothesis, which is often abbreviated as H_0. The **null hypothesis** is a statement that, in the population(s) being studied, there are either (a) *no differences* between the group means, or (b) *no relationships* between the measured variables. For a given statistical test, either (a) or (b) will apply, depending on whether one is conducting a test of group differences or a test of association.

With a test of group differences, the null hypothesis states that, in the population, there are no differences between any of the groups being studied with respect to their mean scores on the criterion variable. In the experiment in which a difficult-goal condition is being compared to an easy-goal condition, the following null hypothesis might be used:

H_0: In the population, individuals assigned difficult goals do not differ from individuals assigned easy goals with respect to the mean amount of insurance sold.

This null hypothesis can also be expressed with symbols in the following way:

H_0: $M_1 = M_2$

where

      H_0 represents null hypothesis
      M_1 represents mean sales for the difficult-goal population
      M_2 represents mean sales for the easy-goal population.

In contrast to the null hypothesis, you will also form an alternative hypothesis (H_1) which states the opposite of the null. The **alternative hypothesis** is a statement that there *is a difference* between the means, or that there *is a relationship* between the variables, in the population(s) being studied.

Perhaps the most common alternative hypothesis is a **nondirectional alternative hypothesis**. With a test of group differences, a nondirection alternative hypothesis predicts that the means for the various populations will differ, but makes no specific prediction as to which mean will be relatively high and which will be relatively low. In the preceding experiment, the following nondirectional null hypothesis might be used:

H_1: In the population, individuals assigned difficult goals differ from individuals assigned easy goals with respect to the mean amount of insurance sold.

This alternative hypothesis can also be expressed with symbols in the following way:

H_1: $M_1 \neq M_2$

In contrast, a **directional alternative hypothesis** makes a more specific prediction regarding the expected outcome of the analysis. With a test of group differences, a directional alternative hypothesis not only predicts that the population means differ, but also predicts which population means will be relatively high and which will be relatively low. Here is a directional alternative hypothesis for the preceding experiment:

H_1: The average amount of insurance sold is higher in the population of individuals assigned difficult goals than in the population of individuals assigned easy goals.

This hypothesis may be symbolically represented with the following:

H_1: $M_1 > M_2$

Had you believed that the easy-goal population would sell more insurance, you would have replaced the "greater than" symbol ($>$) with the "less than" symbol ($<$), as follows:

H_1: $M_1 < M_2$

Null and alternative hypotheses are also used with tests of association. For the study in which you correlated goal-difficulty questionnaire scores with the amount of insurance sold, you might have used the following null hypothesis:

H_0: In the population, the correlation between goal difficulty scores and the amount of insurance sold is zero.

You could state a nondirectional alternative hypothesis that corresponds to this null hypothesis in this way:

H_1: In the population, the correlation between goal difficulty scores and the amount of insurance sold is not equal to zero.

Notice that the preceding is an example of a nondirectional alternative hypothesis because it does not specifically predict whether the correlation is positive or negative, only that it is not zero. A directional alternative hypothesis, on the other hand, might predict a positive correlation between the two variables. You could state such a prediction as follows:

H_1: In the population, the correlation between goal difficulty scores and the amount of insurance sold is greater than zero.

There is an important advantage associated with the use of directional alternative hypotheses compared to nondirectional hypotheses. Directional hypotheses allow researchers to perform *one-sided* statistical tests (also called one-tail tests), which are relatively powerful. Here, "powerful" means that one-sided tests are more likely to find significant differences between group means (for example) when differences really do exist. In contrast, nondirectional hypotheses allow only *two-sided* statistical tests (also called two-tail tests) which are less powerful.

Because they lead to more powerful tests, directional hypotheses are generally preferred over nondirectional hypotheses. However, directional hypotheses should be stated only when they can be justified on the basis of theory, prior research, or some other grounds. For example, you should state the directional hypothesis that "The average amount of insurance sold is higher in the population of individuals assigned difficult goals than in the population of individuals assigned easy goals" only if there are theoretical or empirical reasons to believe that the difficult-goal group will indeed score higher on insurance sales. The same should be true when you specifically predict a positive correlation rather than a negative correlation (or vice versa).

The *p* value. Hypothesis testing, in essence, is a process of determining whether you can reject your null hypothesis with an acceptable level of confidence. When analyzing data with the SAS System, you will review the SAS output for two pieces of information which are critical for this purpose: the obtained statistic, and the probability (*p*) value associated with that statistic. For example, consider the experiment in which you compared the difficult-goal group to the easy-goal group. One way to test the null hypothesis associated with this study would be to perform an independent samples *t* test. When the data analysis for this study has been completed, you would review a *t* statistic and its corresponding *p* value. The *p* value indicates the probability that one would obtain the present results if the null hypothesis were true. If the *p* value is very small, you will reject the null hypothesis.

For example, assume that you obtain a *t* statistic 0.14 and a corresponding *p* value of .90. This *p* value indicates that there are 90 chances in 100 that you would obtain a *t* statistic of 0.14 (or larger) if the null hypothesis were true. Because this probability is so high, you would report that there is very little evidence to refute the null hypothesis. In other words, you would fail to reject your null hypothesis, and would instead conclude that there is not sufficient evidence to find a statistically significant difference between the two groups.

On the other hand, assume that the research project instead produces a *t* value of 8.45 and a corresponding *p* value of .001. The *p* value of .001 indicates that there is only one chance in 1000 that you would obtain a *t* value of 8.45 (or larger) if the null hypothesis were true. This is so unlikely that you can be fairly confident that the null hypothesis is *not* true. You would therefore reject the null hypothesis and conclude that the two populations do, in fact, differ on mean sales. In rejecting the null hypothesis, you have tentatively accepted the alternative hypothesis.

Technically, the *p* value does not really provide the probability that the null hypothesis is true. Instead, it provides the probability that you would obtain the present results (the present *t* statistic, in this case) if the null hypothesis were true. This may seem like a trivial difference, but it is important that you not be confused by the meaning of the *p* value.

Notice that you were able to reject the null hypothesis only when the *p* value was a fairly small number (.001, in the above example). But how small must a *p* value be before you can reject the null hypothesis? A *p* value of .05 seems to be the most commonly accepted cutoff. Typically, when researchers obtain a *p* value *larger* than .05 (such as .13 or .37), they will fail to reject the null hypothesis, and will instead conclude that the differences or relationships being studied were not statistically significant. When they obtain a *p* value *smaller* than .05 (such as .04 or .002 or .0001), they will reject the null and conclude that differences or relationships being studied were statistically significant. The .05 level of significance is not an absolute rule that must be followed in all cases, but it should be serviceable for most types of investigations likely to be conducted in the social sciences.

Fixed effects versus random effects. Experimental designs can be represented as mathematical models, and these models may be described as fixed-effects models, random-effects models, or mixed-effects models. The use of these terms refers to the way that the levels of the independent variable (or predictor variable) were selected.

When the researcher arbitrarily selects the levels of the independent variable, the independent variable is called a **fixed-effects factor**, and the resulting model is a **fixed-effects model**. For example, assume that in the current study you arbitrarily decided that the subjects in your easy-goal condition would be told to make just 5 cold calls per week, and that the subjects in the difficult-goal condition would be told to make 25 cold calls per week. In this case, you have *fixed* (arbitrarily selected) the levels of the independent variable. Your experiment therefore represents a fixed-effects model.

In contrast, when the researcher randomly selects levels of the independent variable from a population of possible levels, the independent variable is called a **random-effects factor**, and the model is a **random-effects model**. For example, assume that you have determined that the number of cold calls that an insurance agent could possibly place in one week ranges from 0 to 45. This range represents the population of cold calls that you could possibly research. Assume that you use some random procedure to select two values from this population (perhaps by drawing numbers from a hat). Following this procedure, the values 12 and 32 are drawn. In conducting your study, one group of subjects is assigned to make at least 12 cold calls per week, while the second is assigned to make 32 calls. In this instance, your study represents a random-effects model because the levels of the independent variable were randomly selected, not fixed.

Most research in the social sciences involves fixed-effects models. As an illustration, assume that you are conducting research on the effectiveness of hypnosis in reducing anxiety among subjects who suffer from phobias. Specifically, you wish to perform an experiment that compares the effectiveness of 10 sessions of relaxation training versus 10 sessions of relaxation training plus hypnosis. In this study, the independent variable might be labelled something like Type of Therapy. Notice that you did not randomly select these two treatment conditions from the population of all possible treatment conditions; you knew which treatments you wished to compare, and designed the study accordingly. Therefore, your study represents a fixed-effects model.

To provide a nonexperimental example, assume that you were to conduct a study to determine whether Caucasian Americans score significantly higher than African Americans on internal locus of control. The predictor variable in your study would be Race, while the criterion variable would be scores on some index of locus of control. In all likelihood, you would have arbitrarily chosen "Caucasian American" versus "African American" as the groups under your predictor variable because you are particularly interested in these two races; you did not randomly select these groups from all possible races. Therefore, the study is again an example of a fixed-effects model.

Of course, random-effects factors do sometimes appear in social science research. For example, in a repeated-measures investigation (in which repeated measures on the criterion variable are taken from each subject), subjects are viewed as a random-effects factor (assuming that they have been randomly selected). Some studies include both fixed-effects factors and random-effects factors. The resulting models are called **mixed-effects models**.

This distinction between fixed versus random effects has important implications for the types of inferences that may be drawn from statistical tests. When analyzing a fixed-effects model, you can generalize the results of the analysis only to the specific levels of the independent variable that were manipulated in that study. This means that if you arbitrarily selected 5 cold calls versus 25 cold calls for your two treatment conditions, once the data are analyzed you may draw conclusions only about the population of agents assigned 5 cold calls versus the population assigned 25 cold calls.

On the other hand, if you randomly selected two values for your treatment conditions (say 12 versus 32 cold calls) from the population of possible values, your model is a random-effects model. This means that you may draw conclusions about the entire population of possible values that your independent variable could assume; these inferences would not be restricted to just the two treatment conditions investigated in the study. In other words, you could draw inferences about the relationship between the population of the possible number of cold calls that agents may be assigned, and the criterion variable (insurance sales).

Conclusion

Regardless of discipline, researchers need a common language to use when discussing their work with others. This chapter has reviewed the basic concepts and terminology of research that will be referred to throughout this text. Now that you can speak the language, you are ready to move on to Chapter 2, where you will learn how to submit a simple SAS program.

References

Littell, R. C., Freund, R. J. & Spector, P. C. (1991). *SAS system for linear models, third edition.* Cary, NC: SAS Institute Inc.

Yaremko, R. M., Harari, H., Harrison, R. C., & Lynn, E. (1982). *Reference handbook of research and statistical methods in psychology: For students and professionals.* New York: Harper & Row.

Chapter 2

INTRODUCTION TO SAS® PROGRAMS, SAS® LOGS, AND SAS® OUTPUT

Overview. This chapter describes the three types of files that you will work with while using the SAS System: the SAS program, the SAS log, and the SAS output file. It presents a very simple SAS program, along with the log and output files produced by that program. This chapter provides the big picture regarding the steps you need to follow when performing data analyses with the SAS System.

Introduction: What is the SAS System?

The SAS System is a modular, integrated, and hardware-independent system of software. It is a particularly powerful tool for social scientists because it allows them to easily perform virtually *any* type of statistical analysis that may be required in the course of conducting social science research. The SAS System is comprehensive enough to perform the most sophisticated multivariate analyses, but is so easy to use that even undergraduates can perform simple analyses after only a short period of instruction.

In a sense, the SAS System may be viewed as a library of prewritten statistical algorithms. By submitting a short SAS program, you can access a prewritten procedure from the library and use it to analyze a set of data. For example, below are the SAS statements used to call up the algorithm that calculates Pearson correlation coefficients:

```
PROC CORR    DATA=D1;
   RUN;
```

The preceding statements will cause the SAS System to compute the Pearson correlation between all numeric variables in your data set. Being able to call up complex procedures with such a simple statement is what makes this system so powerful and so easy to use. By contrast, if you had to prepare your own programs to compute Pearson correlations by using a programming language such as FORTRAN or BASIC, it would require many statements, and there would be many opportunities for error. By using the SAS System instead, most of the work has already been completed, and you are able to focus on the *results* of the analysis rather than on the *mechanics* of obtaining those results.

Where is the SAS System installed? SAS Institute's computer software products are installed at over 25,000 sites in 112 countries. Approximately two-thirds of the installations are in business locations, 15% are government sites, and 18% are education sites. It is estimated that the Institute's software products are used by over three million people worldwide.

Three Types of SAS System Files

Subsequent chapters of this manual will provide details on how to write a SAS program: how to handle the DATA step, how to request specific statistical procedures, and so forth. This chapter however, simply presents a short SAS program and will discuss the output that is created by the program. Little elaboration will be offered. The purpose of this chapter is to provide a very general sense of what it is to submit a SAS program and interpret the results. You are encouraged to copy the program that appears in the following example, submit it for analysis, and verify that the resulting output matches the output reproduced here. This exercise will provide you with the big picture of what it is use the SAS System, and this perspective will facilitate learning the programming details presented later.

Briefly, you will work with three types of "files" when using the SAS System: One file contains the SAS program, one contains the SAS log, and one contains the SAS output. The following sections discuss the differences between these files.

The SAS Program

A SAS program consists of a set of statements written by the researcher or programmer. These statements provide the SAS System with the data to be analyzed, tell it about the nature of these data, and indicate which statistical analyses should be performed on the data.

With older computer systems, these statements were punched onto cards, usually with one statement per card. The cards were then read by a computer and the program was executed. Today, however, the use of *physical* cards has largely been phased out. With modern computer systems, the statements are almost always now typed as *card images* (or *data lines*) in a file in the computer's memory.

This section illustrates a simple SAS program by analyzing some fictitious data from a fictitious study. Assume that six high school students have taken the *Scholastic Assessment Test* (SAT). This test provides two scores for each student: a score on the SAT verbal test, and a score on the SAT math test. With both tests, scores may range from 200 to 800, with higher scores indicating higher levels of aptitude.

Assume that you now wish to obtain some simple descriptive statistics regarding the six students' scores on these two tests. For example, what is their *average* score on the SAT verbal test? On the SAT math test? What is the *standard deviation* of the scores on the two tests?

To perform these analyses, you prepare the following SAS program:

DATA step

```
DATA D1;
INPUT   SUBJECT   SATV   SATM;
CARDS;
1 520 490
2 610 590
3 470 450
4 410 390
5 510 460
6 580 350
;
```

PROC step

```
PROC MEANS   DATA=D1;
   VAR   SATV   SATM;
   RUN;
```

The preceding shows that a SAS program consists of two parts: a **DATA step**, which is used to read data and create a SAS data set, and a **PROC step**, which is used to process or analyze the data. The differences between these steps are described in the next two sections.

The DATA step. In the DATA step, programming statements create and/or modify a SAS data set. Among other things, these statements may

- provide a name for the data set
- provide a name for the variables to be included in the data set
- provide the actual data to be analyzed.

In the preceding program, the DATA step begins with the DATA statement, and ends with the semicolon that immediately precedes the PROC MEANS statement.

The first statement of the preceding program begins with the word DATA, and specifies that the SAS System should create a data set to be called D1. The next line contains the INPUT statement, which indicates that three variables will be contained in this data set. The first variable will be called SUBJECT, and this variable will simply provide a subject number for each student. The second variable will be called SATV (for the SAT verbal test), and the third will be called SATM (for the SAT math test).

The CARDS statement indicates that card images containing your data will appear on the following lines. The first line after the CARDS statement contains the data (test scores) for subject 1. You can see that this first data line contains the numbers 520 and 490, meaning that subject 1 received a score of 520 on the SAT verbal test and a score of 490 on the SAT math test. The next data line shows that subject 2 received a score of 610 for the SAT verbal and a score of 590 for the SAT math, and so forth. The semicolon after the last data line signals the end of the data.

The PROC step. In contrast to the DATA step, the PROC step includes programming statements that request specific statistical analyses of the data. For example, the PROC step might request that correlations be performed between all quantitative variables, or might request that a *t* test be performed. In the preceding example, the PROC step consists of the last three lines of the program.

The first line after the DATA step is the PROC MEANS statement. This requests that the SAS System use a procedure called MEANS to analyze the data. The MEANS procedure computes means, standard deviations, and some other descriptive statistics for numeric variables in the data set. Immediately after the words PROC MEANS are the words DATA=D1. This tells the system that the data to be analyzed are in a data set named D1 (remember that D1 is the name of the data set just created).

Following the PROC MEANS statement is the VAR statement, which includes the names of two variables: SATV and SATM. This requests that the descriptive statistics be performed on just SATV (SAT verbal test scores) and SATM (SAT math test scores).

Finally, the last line of the program is the RUN statement that signals the end of the PROC step. If a SAS program requests multiple PROCs (procedures), you have two options for using the RUN statement:

- You may place a separate RUN statement following each PROC statement

- You may place a single RUN statement following the last PROC statement

> **What is the single most common programming error?** For new users of the SAS System, the single most common error probably involves leaving off a required semicolon (;). Remember that every SAS statement must end with a semicolon (in the preceding program, notice that the DATA statement ends with a semicolon, as does the INPUT statement, the CARDS statement, the PROC MEANS statement, and the RUN statement). When you obtain an error in running a SAS program, one of your first things you should do is look over the program for missing semicolons.

The preceding program is a complete SAS program. However, with a few computer systems it may be necessary to add JCL (job control language) lines at the beginning and end of the SAS program. Different JCL is required by different systems, and the staff of your computer facility can show you what JCL you must use with your SAS programs. As an illustration, the preceding program appears here with JCL added:

```
//SMITH JOB IPSYC,SMITH
// EXEC SAS
DATA D1;
    INPUT  SUBJECT  SATV  SATM;
CARDS;
1 520 490
2 610 590
3 470 450
4 410 390
5 510 460
6 580 350
;
PROC MEANS    DATA=D1;
   VAR  SATV  SATM;
   RUN;
/*EOF
```

The first two lines and the last line of this program are examples of JCL. Remember that if JCL is required with your system, only the staff at your computer facility can show you the exact JCL you will need.

What editor will I use to write my SAS program? An **editor** is an application program that allows you to create lines of text such as the lines that constitute a SAS program. If you are working on a mainframe or midrange computer system, you may have a variety of editors that you can use to write your SAS programs; simply ask the appropriate staff at your computer facility.

For many users, it is wise to use the SAS Display Manager to edit SAS programs. The **SAS Display Manager** is an integrated system that allows users to create and edit SAS programs, submit them for interactive analysis, and view the results on their screens. This application is available at most locations where the SAS System is installed (including personal computers).

Once you have submitted the preceding program for analysis, the SAS System will create two types of files reporting the results of the analysis. One file is called the **SAS log**, or **log file** in this text. This file contains notes, warnings, error messages, and other information related to the execution of the SAS program. The other file is referred to as the **SAS output file**. The SAS output file contains the results of the statistical analyses requested in the SAS program.

The SAS log and output files are created in different ways on different computer systems. With personal computers, the log and output files usually appear in immediate memory, and may be printed or saved as permanent files on a hard drive or floppy disk if the user desires. With some mainframe and midrange systems, the log and output files are created by the system as separate computer files in the researcher's computer account. Users must then open these files to review the results of their analyses. With still other systems, the files are printed on paper as soon are the SAS program is executed.

The SAS Log

The SAS log is a listing of notes and messages that will help you verify that your SAS program was executed successfully. Specifically, the log provides:

- a reprinting of the SAS program that was submitted

- a listing of notes indicating how many variables and observations are contained in the data set

- a listing of any errors made in writing the SAS program.

Log 2.1 provides a reproduction of the SAS log for the preceding program:

```
16:10 Monday, April 11, 1994

NOTE: Copyright(c) 1989 by SAS Institute Inc., Cary, NC USA.
NOTE: SAS (r) Proprietary Software Release 6.07   TS304
      Licensed to WINTHROP UNIVERSITY, Site 0008647001.

NOTE: Running on VAX Model 6000-510 Serial Number 12000003.


Welcome to the new SAS System, Release 6.07.

This message is seen by users when the NEWS option is specified.
You can replace this message with your own by editing the NEWS file.

Changes and enhancements available in SAS Release 6.07 are documented
in the online Host Help.

1               OPTIONS   LINESIZE=80   PAGESIZE=60   NODATE;
2
3               DATA D1;
4                  INPUT   SUBJECT   SATV   SATM;
5               CARDS;

NOTE: The data set WORK.D1 has 6 observations and 3 variables.

12                 ;
13              PROC MEANS    DATA=D1;
14                 VAR SATV SATM;
15                 RUN;

NOTE: The PROCEDURE MEANS printed page 1.

NOTE: SAS Institute Inc., SAS Campus Drive, Cary, NC USA 27513-2414
```

Log 2.1: SAS Log for the Preceding Program

Notice that the statements constituting the SAS program are assigned line numbers, and are reproduced in the SAS log. The data lines are not normally reproduced as part of the SAS log unless they are specifically requested.

About halfway down the log, a note indicates that your data set contains 6 observations and 3 variables. You would check this note to verify that the data set contains all of the variables that you intended to input (in this case 3), and that it contains data from all of your subjects (in this case 6). So far, everything appears to be correct.

If you had made any errors in writing the SAS program, there also would have been ERROR messages in the SAS log. Often, these error messages provide you with some help in determining what was wrong with the program. For example, a message may indicate that SAS was expecting a program statement which was not included. Whenever you encounter an error message, read it carefully and review all of the program statements that preceded it. Often, the error appears in the program statements which immediately precede the error message, but in other cases the error may be hidden much earlier in the program.

If more than one error message is listed, do not panic; there still may be only one error. Sometimes a single error will cause a large number of error messages.

Once the error or errors have been identified, you must revise the original SAS program and resubmit it for analysis. After processing is complete, review the new SAS log to see if the errors have been eliminated. If the log indicates that the program ran correctly, you are free to review the results of the analyses in the SAS output file.

The SAS Output File

The SAS output file contains the results of the statistical analyses requested in the SAS program. Because the program in the previous example requested the MEANS procedure, the corresponding output file will contain means and other descriptive statistics for the variables analyzed. In this text, the SAS output file is sometimes referred to as the **lis file**. "Lis" is used as an abbreviation for "listing of results."

The following is a reproduction of the SAS output file that would be produced from the preceding SAS program:

```
Variable   N          Mean        Std Dev       Minimum        Maximum
-----------------------------------------------------------------------
SATV       6     516.6666667    72.5718035    410.0000000    610.0000000
SATM       6     455.0000000    83.3666600    350.0000000    590.0000000
-----------------------------------------------------------------------
```

Output 2.1: Results of the MEANS Procedure

Below the heading "Variable", the SAS System prints the names of each of the variables being analyzed. In this case, the variables are called SATV and SATM. To the right of the heading SATV, descriptive statistics for the SAT verbal test may be found. Figures for the SAT math test appear to the right of SATM.

Below the heading "N", the number of cases analyzed is reported. The average score on each variable is reproduced under "Mean", and standard deviations appear in the column headed "Std Dev". Minimum and maximum scores for the two variables appear in the remaining two columns. You can see that the mean score on the SAT verbal test was 516.67, and the standard deviation of these scores was 72.57. For the SAT math test, the mean was 455.00, and the standard deviation was 83.37.

The statistics included in the preceding output are printed by default. Later in this text, you will learn that there are many additional statistics that you can request as options with PROC MEANS.

Conclusion

Regardless of the computing environment in which you work, the basics of using the SAS System remain the same: you prepare the SAS program, submit it for analysis, and review the resulting log and output files to gain insight into your data. This chapter has provided a quick overview of how the system is used; you are now ready to move on to Chapter 3, where the fundamentals of creating SAS data sets are introduced.

DATA INPUT

Overview. This section shows how to create a SAS data set. A SAS data set contains the information (independent variables, dependent variables, survey responses, etc.) that is analyzed using SAS procedures such as PROC MEANS or PROC GLM. The chapter begins with a simple illustrative example in which a SAS data set is created using the CARDS statement. In subsequent sections, additional guidelines show how to input the different types of data that are most frequently encountered in social science research.

Introduction: Inputting Questionnaire Data Versus Other Types of Data

This chapter shows how to create SAS data sets in a number of different ways, and it does this by illustrating how to input the type of data that are often obtained through **questionnaire research**. This type of research generally involves distributing structured questionnaires to a sample of subjects, and asking them to respond by circling or checking fixed responses. For example, subjects may be asked to indicate the extent to which they agree or disagree with a set of items by checking a 7-point scale in which 1 represents "strongly disagree", and 7 represents "strongly agree".

Because this chapter (and much of the entire text, for that matter) focuses on questionnaire research, some readers may be concerned that it will not be useful for analyzing data that are obtained using different methods. This concern is understandable, because the social sciences are so diverse, and so many different *types* of variables are investigated in social science research. These variables might be as different as "the number of aggressive acts performed by a child", "rated preferences for laundry detergents", or "levels of serotonin in the frontal lobes of chimpanzees".

However, because of the generality and flexibility of the basic principles of this discussion, you can expect, upon completing this chapter, to be prepared to input virtually any type of data obtained in social science research. The same may be said for the remaining chapters of this text: Although this book emphasizes the analysis of questionnaire data, the concepts taught here can be readily applied to different types of data. This fact should become clear as the mechanics of using the SAS System are presented.

This text emphasizes the analysis of questionnaire data for two reasons. First, for better or for worse, many social scientists rely on questionnaire data in conducting their research. By focusing on this method, this text provides examples that will be meaningful to the single largest subgroup of readers. Second, questionnaire data often creates special input and analysis problems that are not generally encountered with other research methods (e.g., large numbers of variables, "check all that apply" variables). This text addresses some of the more common of these difficulties.

Keying Data: An Illustrative Example

Before data can be input and analyzed by the SAS System, they must be keyed in some systematic way. There are a number of different approaches to keying data, but to keep things simple, this chapter presents only the fixed format approach. With the **fixed format** method, each variable is assigned to a specific column (or set of columns) in the data set. The fixed format method has the advantage of being very general: You can use it for almost any type of research problem. An additional advantage is that researchers are probably less likely to make errors in inputting data if they stick to this format.

In the following example of how to key data, you will actually key some fictitious data from a fictitious study. Assume that you have developed a survey to measure attitudes toward *volunteerism*. A copy of the survey appears here:

Volunteerism Survey

Please indicate the extent to which you agree or disagree with each of the following statements. You will do this by circling the appropriate number to the left of that statement. The following format shows what each response number stands for:

```
5 = Agree Strongly
4 = Agree Somewhat
3 = Neither Agree nor Disagree
2 = Disagree Somewhat
1 = Disagree Strongly
```

For example, if you "Disagree Strongly" with the first question, circle the "1" to the left of that statement. If you "Agree Somewhat," circle the "4," and so on.

```
-------------
 Circle Your
  Response
-------------
```

1 2 3 4 5   1.   I feel a personal responsibility to help needy
                  people in my community.

1 2 3 4 5   2.   I feel I am personally obligated to help homeless
                  families.

1 2 3 4 5   3.   I feel no personal responsibility to work with poor
                  people in my town.

1 2 3 4 5   4.   Most of the people in my community are willing to
                  help the needy.

1 2 3 4 5   5.   A lot of people around here are willing to help
                  homeless families.

1 2 3 4 5   6.   The people in my town feel no personal
                  responsibility to work with poor people.

1 2 3 4 5   7.   Everyone should feel the responsibility to perform
                  volunteer work in their communities.

What is your age in years? _____

Further assume that you administer this survey to 10 subjects. For each of these individuals, you also obtain their IQ scores.

You then key your data as a file in a computer. All of the survey responses and information about subject 1 appear on the first line of this file. All of the survey responses and information about subject 2 appear on the second line of this file, and so forth. You keep the data lined up properly, so that responses to question 1 appear in column 1 for *all* subjects, responses to question 2 appear in column 2 for all subjects, and so forth. When you key in this fashion, your data set should look like this:

```
2234243 22  98  1
3424325 20 105  2
3242424 32  90  3
3242323  9 119  4
3232143  8 101  5
3242242 24 104  6
4343525 16 110  7
3232324 12  95  8
1322424 41  85  9
5433224 19 107 10
```

You can think of the preceding as a matrix of data consisting of 10 rows and 17 columns. The rows run horizontally (from left to right), and each row represents data for a different subject. The columns run vertically (up and down). For the most part, a given column represents a different variable that you measured or created (although, in some cases, a given variable is more than one column wide; more on this later).

For example, look at the last column in the matrix: the vertical column on the right side which goes from 1 (at the top) to 10 (at the bottom). This column codes the Subject Number variable. In other words, this variable simply tells us *which subject's* data are included on that line. For the top line, the value of Subject Number is 1, so you know that the top line includes data for subject 1; the second line down has the value 2 in the subject number column, so this second line down includes data for subject number 2, and so forth.

The *first* column of data includes subject responses to survey question 1. It can be seen that subject 1 circled a "2" in response to this item, while subject 2 circled a "3." The *second* column of data includes subjects responses to survey question 2, the *third* column codes question 3, and so forth. After keying responses to question 7, you left column 8 blank. Then, in columns 9 and 10, you keyed in each subjects' age. We can see that subject 1 was 22 years old, while subject 2 was 20 years old. You left column 11 blank, and then keyed the subjects' IQs in columns 12, 13, and 14 (IQ can be a 3-digit number, so it required three columns to key it). You left column 15 blank, and keyed subject numbers in columns 16 and 17.

The following table presents a brief coding guide to summarize how you keyed your data.

Column	Variable Name	Explanation
1	V1	Responses to survey question 1
2	V2	Responses to survey question 2
3	V3	Responses to survey question 3
4	V4	Responses to survey question 4
5	V5	Responses to survey question 5
6	V6	Responses to survey question 6
7	V7	Responses to survey question 7
8	(blank)	(blank)
9-10	AGE	Subject's age in years
11	(blank)	(blank)
12-14	IQ	Subject's IQ score
15	(blank)	(blank)
16-17	NUMBER	Subject's number

Guides similar to this will be used throughout this text to explain how data sets are arranged, so a few words of explanation are in order. This table simply identifies the specific columns in which variable values are keyed. For example, the first line of the preceding table indicates that in column 1 of the data set, the values of a variable called V1 are stored, and this variable includes responses to question 1. The next line shows that in column 2, the values of variable V2 are stored, and this variable includes responses to question 2. The remaining lines of the guide are interpreted in the same way. You can see, therefore, that it is necessary to read down the lines of this table to learn what is in each column of the data set.

A few important notes about how you should key data that you will analyze using SAS:

- **Make sure that you key the variables in the correct column**. For example, make sure that the data are lined up so that responses to question 6 always appear in column 6. If a subject happened to leave question 6 blank, then you should leave column 6 blank when you are keying your data (leave this column blank by simply striking the space bar on your keyboard). Then go on to type the subject's response to question 7 in column 7. Do *not* key a zero if the subject didn't answer a question; simply leave the space blank.

  It is also acceptable to key a period (.) instead of a blank space to represent missing data. When using this convention, if a subject has a missing value on a variable, key a single period in place of that missing value. If this variable happens to be more than one column wide, you should still key just one period. For example, if the variable occupies columns 12-14 (as does IQ in the table), key just one period in column 14; do not key three periods in columns 12, 13, and 14.

- **Right-justify numeric data**. You should shove over numeric variables to the right side of the columns in which they appear. For example, IQ is a 3-digit variable (it could assume values such as 112 or 150). However, the IQ score for many individuals is a 2-digit number (such as 99 or 87). Therefore, the 2-digit IQ scores should appear to the right side of this 3-digit column of values. A correct example of how to right-justify your data follows:

```
 99
109
100
 87
118
```

The following is *not* right-justified, and so is less preferable:

```
99
109
100
87
118
```

There are exceptions to this rule. For example, if numeric data contain decimal points, it is generally preferable to align the decimal points when keying the data, so that the decimal points appear in the same column. If there are no values to the right of the decimal point for a given subject, you may key zeros to the right of the decimal point. Here is an example of this approach:

```
  3.450
 12.000
  0.133
144.751
  0.000
```

The preceding data set includes scores for five subjects on just one variable. Assume that scores on this variable could range from 0.000 to 200.000. Subject 1 had a score of 3.45, subject 2 had a score of 12, and so forth. Notice that the scores have been keyed so that the decimal points are aligned in the same vertical column.

Notice also that, if a given subject's score does not include any digits to the right of the decimal point, zeros have been added. For example, subject 2 has a score of 12. However, this subject's score has been keyed as 12.000 so that it is easier to line it up with the other scores.

Technically, it is not always necessary to align subject data in this way in order to include it in a SAS data set. However, arranging data in such an orderly fashion generally decreases the likelihood of making an error when entering the data.

• **Left-justify character data**. Remember that character variables may include letters of the alphabet. In contrast to numeric variables, you should typically left-justify character variables. This means that you shoved over entries to the left, rather than the right.

For example, imagine that you are going to key two character variables for each subject. The first variable will be called FIRST, and this variable will include each subect's first name. You will key this variable in columns 1-15. The second variable will be called LAST, and will include each subject's LAST name. You will key this variable in columns 16-25. Data for five subjects are reproduced here:

```
Francis        Smith
John           Wolf
Jean           Adams
Alice          OConnel
```

The preceding shows that the first subject was named Francis Smith, the second was named John Wolf, and so forth. Notice that the value "Francis" has been shoved over to the left side of the columns that include the FIRST variable (columns 1-15) The same is true for "John", as well as the remaining first names. In the same way, "Smith" has been shoved over to the left side of the columns that include the LAST variable (columns 16-25). The same is true for the remaining last names.

• **The use of blank columns can be helpful but is not necessary**. Recall that, when you keyed your data, you left a blank column between V7 and the AGE variable, and another blank column between AGE and IQ. Leaving blank columns between variables can be helpful because it makes it easier for you to look at your data and see if something is keyed out of place. However, leaving blank columns is not necessary for the SAS System to accurately read your data, so this approach is optional.

Inputting Data Using the CARDS Statement

Now that you know how to key your data, you are ready to learn about the SAS statements that actually allow the computer to *read* the data and put them into a SAS data set. There are a variety of ways that you can input data, but this text focuses on only two: the use of the **CARDS statement** (which allows you to include the data lines within the SAS program itself), and the use of the **INFILE statement** (which allows you to include the data lines within an external file).

There are also a number of different *styles* of input that may be used when reading data. The "style of input" refers to the type of instructions that you provide concerning the location and format of your variables. Although the SAS System allows for list input, column input, and formatted input, this text presents only the formatted input style because of its ability to easily handle many different types of data sets. For additional information regarding styles of input, see *SAS language and procedures: usage, version 6, first edition* (particularly Chapter 3), as well as *SAS language: reference, version 6, first edition* (particularly Chapter 9).

Here is the general form for inputting data using the CARDS statement and the formatted input style:

```
DATA data-set-name;
   INPUT  #line-number   @column-number   (variable-name)   (column-width.)
                         @column-number   (variable-name)   (column-width.)
                         @column-number   (variable-name)   (column-width.) ;
CARDS;
keyed data are placed here
;
PROC name-of-desired-statistical-procedure      DATA=data-set-name ;
   RUN;
```

The following example shows a SAS program to analyze the preceding data set. In the following example, the numbers on the far left side are *not* actually part of the program. They are simply provided so that it will be easy to refer to specific lines of the program in explaining the meaning of the program in subsequent sections.

```
1         DATA D1;
2            INPUT    #1   @1   (V1)       (1.)
3                          @2   (V2)       (1.)
4                          @3   (V3)       (1.)
5                          @4   (V4)       (1.)
6                          @5   (V5)       (1.)
7                          @6   (V6)       (1.)
8                          @7   (V7)       (1.)
9                          @9   (AGE)      (2.)
10                         @12  (IQ)       (3.)
11                         @16  (NUMBER)   (2.)    ;
12        CARDS;
13        2234243 22  98  1
14        3424325 20 105  2
15        3242424 32  90  3
16        3242323  9 119  4
17        3232143  8 101  5
18        3242242 24 104  6
19        4343525 16 110  7
20        3232324 12  95  8
21        1322424 41  85  9
22        5433224 19 107 10
23        ;
24
25        PROC MEANS    DATA=D1;
26           RUN;
```

A few important notes about these data input statements:

- **The DATA statement**. Line 1 from the preceding program included the DATA statement, where the general form is:

      DATA data-set-name;

  In this case, you gave your data set the name D1, so the statement read

      DATA D1;

- **DATA set names and variable names**. The preceding paragraph stated that your data set was assigned the name D1 on line 1 of the program. In lines 2-11 of the program, the data set's variables are assigned names such as V1, V2, AGE, and IQ.

  You are free to assign a data set or a variable any name you like as long as it conforms to the following rules:

  - It must begin with a letter (rather than a number).
  - It may be no more than 8 characters long.
  - It may contain no special characters such as "*" or "#".
  - It may contain no blank spaces.

  Although the preceding data set was named D1, it could have been given any of an almost infinite number of other names. Below are examples of some other acceptable names for SAS data sets:

      SURVEY
      SURVEY1
      RESEARCH
      VOLUNT

- **The INPUT statement**. The INPUT statement has the following general form:

      INPUT #line-number @column-number (variable-name) (column-width.)
                           @column-number (variable-name) (column-width.)
                           @column-number (variable-name) (column-width.) ;

  Compare this general form to the actual INPUT statement that appears on lines 2-11 of the preceding SAS program, and note the values which were filled in to read your data. In the actual program, the word INPUT appears on line 2 and tells SAS that the INPUT statement has begun; the SAS System assumes that all of the instructions that follow are data input directions *until* it reads a semicolon (;). At that semicolon, the INPUT statement ends. In the actual program, the semicolon appears at the end of line 11.

- **Line number directions**. To the right of the word INPUT is the following:

      #line-number

This tells SAS what line it should read from to find specific variables. This is important because in some cases there may be two or more lines of data for *each* subject. There will be more on this type of situation in a later section. For the present data, however, the situation is fairly simple: there was only one line of data for each subject, so your program includes the following line number direction (from line 2 of the actual program):

      INPUT   #1

Technically, it is not really necessary to include line number directions when there is only one line of data for each subject (as in the present case). In this text, however, line number directions appear for the sake of consistency.

- **Column location, variable name, and column width directions**. To the right of the line number directions, you place the column location, variable name, and column width directions. The general form for this is as follows:

      @column-number   (variable-name)   (column-width.)

Where `column-number` appears above, you key the number of the column in which a specific variable appears. If the variable occupies more than one column (such as IQ in columns 12, 13, and 14), you should key the number of the column in which it *begins* (e.g., column 12). Where `variable-name` appears, you will key the name that you have given to that variable. And where `column-width` appears, you will key how many columns are occupied by that variable. In the case of the preceding data, the first variable was V1, which appeared in column 1, and was only one column wide. The actual program, therefore, provides the following column location directions (from line 2):

      @1   (V1)   (1.)

The preceding line tells SAS the following: "Go to column 1. In that column you will find a variable called V1. It is 1 column wide."

IMPORTANT: Note that you must follow the column width with a period, so in this case the column width is (1.). It is important that you include this period; later you will learn how the period provides information about decimal places in a data set.

Now that variable V1 has been read, you must give SAS the directions needed to read the remaining variables in the data set. The entire completed INPUT statement appears as follows. Note that the line number directions are given only once because all of these variables come from the same line (for a given subject). However, there are different column directions for the different variables. Note also how the column width is different for AGE, IQ, and NUMBER:

```
INPUT    #1    @1    (V1)        (1.)
               @2    (V2)        (1.)
               @3    (V3)        (1.)
               @4    (V4)        (1.)
               @5    (V5)        (1.)
               @6    (V6)        (1.)
               @7    (V7)        (1.)
               @9    (AGE)       (2.)
               @12   (IQ)        (3.)
               @16   (NUMBER)    (2.)    ;
```

IMPORTANT: Notice the semicolon which appears after the column width entry for the last variable (NUMBER). You must always end your input statement with a semicolon in this way. It is easy to make the mistake of leaving off this semicolon, so always check for this semicolon when you get an error message following the INPUT statement.

- **The CARDS or DATALINES statement**. The CARDS statement goes after the INPUT statement, and tells SAS that the raw data are to follow. Don't forget the semicolon after the word CARDS. In the preceding program, the CARDS statement appeared on line 12.

It is also possible to use the newer DATALINES statement in place of the CARDS statement. The same rules concerning placement of the data and semicolons also apply with the DATALINES statement.

- **The data lines**. The data lines, of course, are the lines that contain the subject's values on the numeric and/or character variables. In the preceding program, these appear on lines 13-22.

The data lines should begin on the very next line after the CARDS (or DATALINES) statement; there should be no blank lines. These data lines begin on line 13 in the preceding program. On the very first line after the last of the data lines (line 23, in this case), you should add another semicolon to let SAS know that the data have ended. Do *not* place this semicolon at the end of the last line of data (that is, on the *same line* as the data), as this may cause an error.

With respect to the data lines, the most important thing to remember is that you must key a given variable in the column that your INPUT statement says it is in. For example, if your input statement contains the following line:

```
@9    (AGE)    (2.)
```

then make sure that the variable AGE really is a 2-digit number keyed in columns 9 and 10.

- **PROC and RUN statements**. There is little to say about PROC and RUN statements at this time because most of the remainder of the text will be concerned with using SAS System procedures. Suffice it to say that a PROC statement asks SAS to perform some statistical analysis. To keep things simple, this section uses a procedure called PROC MEANS. PROC MEANS asks SAS to calculate means, standard deviations, and some other descriptive statistics for numeric variables. The preceding program includes the PROC MEANS statement on line 25.

In most cases, your program will end with a RUN statement. In the preceding program, the RUN statement appears on line 26. A RUN statement executes any previously entered SAS statements, and RUN statements are typically placed after every PROC. If your program includes a number of PROC statements in sequence, it is acceptable to place just one RUN statement after the final PROC.

If you submitted the preceding program for analysis, PROC MEANS would produce the results presented in Output 3.1:

Variable	N	Mean	Std Dev	Minimum	Maximum
V1	10	3.0000000	1.0540926	1.0000000	5.0000000
V2	10	2.6000000	0.8432740	2.0000000	4.0000000
V3	10	3.2000000	0.7888106	2.0000000	4.0000000
V4	10	2.6000000	0.8432740	2.0000000	4.0000000
V5	10	2.9000000	1.1972190	1.0000000	5.0000000
V6	10	2.6000000	0.9660918	2.0000000	4.0000000
V7	10	3.7000000	0.9486833	2.0000000	5.0000000
AGE	10	20.3000000	10.2745641	8.0000000	41.0000000
IQ	10	101.4000000	9.9241568	85.0000000	119.0000000
NUMBER	10	5.5000000	3.0276504	1.0000000	10.0000000

Output 3.1: Results of the MEANS Procedure

Additional Guidelines

Inputting string variables with the same prefix and different numeric suffixes. In this section, **prefix** refers to the first part of a variable's name, while a **suffix** refers to the last part. For example, think about our variables V1, V2, V3, V4, V5, V6, and V7. These are multiple variables with the same prefix (V) and different numeric suffixes (1, 2, 3, 4, 5, 6, and 7).

Variables such as this are sometimes referred to as **string variables**. Earlier, this chapter provided one way of inputting these variables, and this original INPUT statement is reproduced here:

```
INPUT    #1    @1    (V1)       (1.)
               @2    (V2)       (1.)
               @3    (V3)       (1.)
               @4    (V4)       (1.)
               @5    (V5)       (1.)
               @6    (V6)       (1.)
               @7    (V7)       (1.)
               @9    (AGE)      (2.)
               @12   (IQ)       (3.)
               @16   (NUMBER)   (2.)    ;
```

However, with string variables named in this way, there is a much easier way of writing the INPUT statement. You could have written it in this way:

```
INPUT    #1    @1    (V1-V7)    (1.)
               @9    (AGE)      (2.)
               @12   (IQ)       (3.)
               @16   (NUMBER)   (2.)    ;
```

The first line of this INPUT statement gives SAS the following directions: "Go to line #1. There, go to column 1. Beginning in column 1 you will find variables V1 through V7. Each variable is 1 column wide." With this second INPUT statement, SAS will read the data in exactly the same way that it would have using the original input statement.

As an additional example, imagine you had a 50-item survey instead of a 7-item survey. You called your variables Q1, Q2, Q3, and so forth instead of V1, V2, V3, and so forth. You keyed your data in the following way:

Column	Variable Name	Explanation
1-50	Q1-Q50	Responses to survey questions 1-50
51	(blank)	(blank)
52-53	AGE	Subject's age in years
54	(blank)	(blank)
55-57	IQ	Subject's IQ score
58	(blank)	(blank)
59-60	NUMBER	Subject's number

You could use the following INPUT to read these data:

```
INPUT    #1    @1     (Q1-Q50)   (1.)
               @52    (AGE)      (2.)
               @55    (IQ)       (3.)
               @59    (NUMBER)   (2.)   ;
```

Inputting character variables. This text deals with basically two types of variables: numeric variables and character variables. A **numeric variable** consists entirely of numbers–it contains no letters. For example, all of your variables from the preceding data set were numeric variables: V1 could assume only the values of 1, 2, 3, 4, or 5. Similarly, AGE could take on only numeric values. On the other hand, a **character variable** may consist of either numbers or alphabetic characters (letters), or both.

The following is the data set introduced earlier in this chapter. Remember that responses to the seven questions of the Volunteerism Survey are keyed in columns 1-7 of this data set, AGE is keyed in columns 9-10, IQ is keyed in columns 12-14, and subject number is in columns 16-17.

```
2234243 22  98   1
3424325 20 105   2
3242424 32  90   3
3242323  9 119   4
3232143  8 101   5
3242242 24 104   6
4343525 16 110   7
3232324 12  95   8
1322424 41  85   9
5433224 19 107  10
```

None of the preceding variables were character variables, but you could easily add a character variable to this data set. For example, you could determine the sex of each subject and create a new variable called SEX which codes the subjects' gender. If a subject were male, SEX would assume the value "M." If a subject were female, SEX would assume the value "F." In the following, the new SEX variable appears in column 19 (the last column):

```
2234243 22  98   1 M
3424325 20 105   2 M
3242424 32  90   3 F
3242323  9 119   4 F
3232143  8 101   5 F
3242242 24 104   6 M
4343525 16 110   7 F
3232324 12  95   8 M
1322424 41  85   9 M
5433224 19 107  10 F
```

You can see that subjects 1 and 2 were males, while subjects 3, 4, and 5 were females, and so forth.

IMPORTANT: You must use a special command within the INPUT statement to input a character variable. Specifically, in the column width region for the character variable, precede the column width with a dollar sign ("$"). For the preceding data set, you would use the following INPUT statement (note the dollar sign in the column width region for the SEX variable):

```
INPUT    #1    @1    (V1-V7)    (1.)
               @9    (AGE)      (2.)
               @12   (IQ)       (3.)
               @16   (NUMBER)   (2.)
               @19   (SEX)      ($1.)   ;
```

Using multiple lines of data for each subject. Very often a researcher obtains so much data from each subject that it is impractical to key all of the data on just one line. For example, imagine that you administer a 100-item questionnaire to a sample, and that you plan to key responses to question 1 in column 1, responses to question 2 in column 2, and so forth. Following this process, you are likely to run into difficulty, because you will need 100 columns to key all responses from a given subject, but most computer monitors allow only around 79 columns. If you continue keying data past column 79, your data are likely to wrap around or appear in some way that makes it difficult to verify that you are keying a given value in the correct column.

In situations in which you require a very large number of columns for your data, it is often best to divide each subject's data so that they appear on more than one line (in other words, it is often best to have multiple lines of data for each subject). To do this, it is necessary to modify your INPUT statement somewhat.

To illustrate, assume that you have obtained two additional variables for each subject in your study: their SAT verbal test scores and SAT math test scores. You decide to key your data so that there are two lines of data for each subject. On line 1 for a given subject, you key V1 through V7, AGE, IQ, NUMBER, and SEX (as above). On line 2 for that subject, you key SATV (the SAT verbal test score) in columns 1 through 3, and you key SATM (the SAT math test score) in columns 5 through 7:

```
2234243 22  98  1 M
520 490
3424325 20 105  2 M
440 410
3242424 32  90  3 F
390 420
3242323  9 119  4 F

3232143  8 101  5 F

3242242 24 104  6 M
330 340
4343525 16 110  7 F

3232324 12  95  8 M

1322424 41  85  9 M
380 410
5433224 19 107 10 F
640 590
```

It can be seen that the SATV score for subject 1 was 520, and the SATM score was 490.

IMPORTANT: When a given subject has no data for a variable which would normally appear on a given line, your data set must still include a line for that subject, even if it is blank. For example, subject 4 is only 9 years old, so she has not yet taken the SAT, and obviously does not have any SAT scores to key. Nonetheless, you still had to include a second line for subject 4, even though it was blank. Notice that blank lines also appear for subjects 5, 7, and 8, who were also too young to take the SAT.

Be warned that, with some text editors, it is necessary to create these blank lines by pressing the *return* key, thus creating a "hard" carriage return; with these editors, simply using the directional arrows on the keypad may not create the necessary hard return. This is especially true when keying data with PCs and ASCII files, but is less likely to be a problem when working on a mainframe computer. Problems in reading the data are also likely to occur if tabs have been used; it is generally best to avoid the use of tabs or other hidden codes when keying data.

The following coding guide tells us where each variable appears. Notice that this guide indicates the *line* on which a variable is located, as well as which *column* in which it is located.

Line	Column	Variable Name	Explanation
1	1-7	V1-V7	Survey questions 1-7
	8	(blank)	(blank)
	9-10	AGE	Subject's age in years
	11	(blank)	(blank)
	12-14	IQ	Subject's IQ score
	15	(blank)	(blank)
	16-17	NUMBER	Subject's number
	18	(blank)	(blank)
	19	SEX	Subject's sex
2	1-3	SATV	SAT-Verbal test score
	5-7	SATM	SAT-Math test score

IMPORTANT: When there are multiple lines of data for each subject, the INPUT statement must indicate which line a given variable is on. This is done with the line number command ("#") which was introduced earlier. You could use the following INPUT statement to read the preceding data set:

```
INPUT   #1   @1    (V1-V7)    (1.)
             @9    (AGE)      (2.)
             @12   (IQ)       (3.)
             @16   (NUMBER)   (2.)
             @19   (SEX)      ($1.)
        #2   @1    (SATV)     (3.)
             @5    (SATM)     (3.)   ;
```

This INPUT statement tells SAS to begin at line #1 for a given subject, to go to column 1 and find variables V1 through V7. It continues to tell SAS where it will find each of the other variables located on line #1, as before. After reading the SEX variable, SAS is told to move on to line #2. There, it is to go to column 1, and find the variable SATV, which is 3 columns wide. The variable SATM then begins in column 5, and is also 3 columns wide. Obviously, it is theoretically possible to have any number of lines of data for each subject, as long as you use these line number directions correctly.

Creating decimal places for numeric variables. Assume that you have determined the high school grade point ratios (GPRs) for a sample of 5 subjects. You could create a SAS data set containing these GPRs using the following program:

```
1        DATA D1;
2           INPUT   #1   @1   (GPR)    (4.);
3        CARDS;
4        3.56
5        2.20
6        2.11
7        3.25
8        4.00
9        ;
10       PROC MEANS    DATA=D1;
11          RUN;
```

The INPUT statement tells SAS to go to line 1, column 1, and find a variable called GPR which is 4 columns wide. Within the data set itself, values of GPR were keyed using a period as a decimal point, with two digits to the right of the decimal point.

This same data set could have been keyed and input in a slightly different way. For example, what if the data had been keyed without a decimal point, as follows?

```
356
220
211
325
400
```

It is still possible to have SAS insert a decimal point where it belongs, in front of the last two digits in each number. You do this in the column width command of the INPUT statement. With this column width command, you indicate how many columns the variable occupies, key a period, and then indicate how many columns of data should appear to the right of the decimal place. In the present case, the preceding GPR variable was only 3 columns wide, and two columns of data should have appeared to the right of the decimal place. So you would modify the SAS program in the following way (notice the column width command):

```
 1          DATA D1;
 2             INPUT   #1   @1   (GPR)   (3.2);
 3          CARDS;
 4          356
 5          220
 6          211
 7          325
 8          400
 9          ;
10          PROC MEANS   DATA=D1;
11             RUN;
```

Inputting "check all that apply" questions as multiple variables. A "check all that apply" question is a special type of questionnaire item that is often used in social science research. These items generate data that must be input in a special way. The following is an example of a "check all that apply" item that could have appeared on your volunteerism survey:

```
Below is a list of activities.  Please place a check mark next to
any activity that you have engaged in in the past six months.


Check here
-----


_____  1. Did volunteer work at a shelter for the homeless.
_____  2. Did volunteer work at a shelter for battered women.
_____  3. Did volunteer work at a hospital or hospice.
_____  4.  Did volunteer work for any other community agency or
            organization.
_____  5. Donated money to the United Way.
_____  6. Donated money to a church-sponsored charity.
_____  7. Donated money to any other charitable cause.
```

An inexperienced researcher might think of the preceding as a single question with seven possble responses, and try to key the data in a single column in the data set (say, in column 1). But this would lead to big problems: what would you key in column 1 if a subject checked more than one category?

One way out of this difficulty is to treat the seven possible responses above as seven different questions. When keyed, each of these questions will be treated as a separate variable and will appear in a separate column. For example, whether or not a subject checked activity 1 may be coded in column 1; whether the subject checked activity 2 may be coded in column 2, and so forth.

Researchers may code these variables by placing any values they like in these columns, but you should key a zero ("0") if the subject did not check that activitiy, and a one ("1") if the subject did check it. Why code the variables using zeros and ones? The reason is that this makes it easier to perform some types of analyses that you may later wish to perform. A variable that may assume only two values is called a **dichotomous variable**, and the process of coding dichotomous variables with ones and zeros is known as **dummy coding**.

Once a dichotomous variable has been dummy coded, it can be analyzed using a variety of SAS System procedures such as PROC CORR, which computes Pearson product-moment correlations between quantitative variables. Once a dichotomous variable has been dummy-coded, it is possible to compute the Pearson correlation between it and other numeric variables using PROC CORR. Similarly, you can use PROC REG to perform **multiple regression analysis**, a procedure that allows one to assess the nature of the relationship between a single criterion variable and multiple predictor variables. Once again, if a dichotomous variable has been appropriately dummy-coded, it can be used as a predictor variable in a multiple regression analysis. For these and other reasons, it is good practice to code dichotomous variables using zeros and ones.

The following coding guide summarizes how you could key responses to the preceding question:

Line	Column	Variable Name	Explanation
1	1-7	V1-V7	Responses regarding activities 1 through 7. For each activity, a 0 was recorded if the subject did not check the activity, and a 1 was recorded if the subject did check it.

When subjects have responded to a "check all that apply" item, it is often best to analyze the resulting data with the FREQ procedure. PROC FREQ indicates the raw number of people who appear in each category (in this case, PROC FREQ will indicate the number of people who did not check a given activity versus the number who did). It also provides percent of people who appear in each category, along with some additional information.

The following program inputs some fictitious data and requests frequency tables for each activity using PROC FREQ:

```
1          DATA D1;
2             INPUT    #1   @1   (V1-V7)    (1.);
3          CARDS;
4          0010000
5          1011111
6          0001001
7          0010000
8          1100000
9          ;
10         PROC FREQ     DATA=D1;
11            TABLES V1-V7;
12            RUN;
```

Data for the first subject appears on line 4 of the program. Notice that a one is keyed in column 3 for this subject, indicating that he or she did perform activity 3 ("did volunteer work at a hospital or hospice"), and that zeros are recorded for the remaining six activities, meaning that the subject did not perform those activities. The data keyed for subject 2 on line 5 shows that this subject performed all of the activities except for activity 2.

Inputting a Correlation or Covariance Matrix

There are times when, for reasons of either necessity or convenience, you may choose to analyze a correlation matrix or covariance matrix rather than raw data. The SAS System allows you to input such a matrix as data, and some (but not all) SAS System procedures may then be used to analyze the data set. For example, a correlation or covariance matrix can be analyzed using PROC REG, PROC FACTOR, or PROC CALIS, along with some other procedures.

Inputting a correlation matrix. This type of data input is sometimes necessary when a researcher obtains a correlation matrix from an earlier study (perhaps from an article published in a research journal) and wishes to perform further analyses on the data. You could input the published correlation matrix as a SAS System data set and analyze it in the same way you would analyze raw data.

For example, imagine that you have read an article that tested a social psychology theory called the *investment model* (Rusbult, 1980). The investment model identifies a number of variables that are believed to influence a person's satisfaction with and commitment to a romantic relationship. The following are short definitions for the variables that constitute the investment model:

Commitment: The person's intention to remain in the relationship

Satisfaction: The person's affective (emotional) response to the relationship

Rewards: The number of good things or benefits associated with the relationship

Costs: The number of bad things or hardships associated with the relationship

Investment size: The amount of time, energy, and personal resources put into the relationship

Alternative value: The attractiveness of one's alternatives to the relationship (e.g., attractiveness of alternative romantic partners)

One interpretation of the investment model predicts that commitment to the relationship is determined by satisfaction, investment size, and alternative value, while satisfaction with the relationship is determined by rewards and costs. The predicted relationships between these variables are portrayed in Figure 3.1:

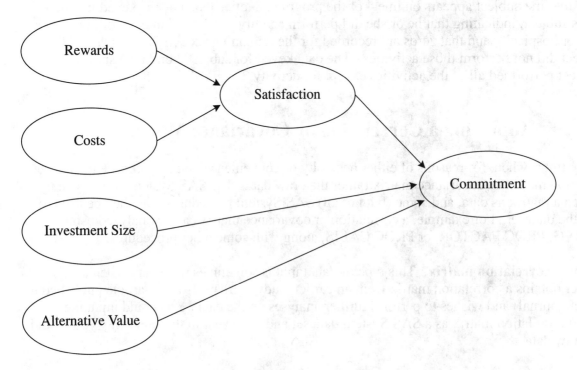

Figure 3.1: Predicted Relationships between Investment Model Variables

Assume that you have read an article that reports an investigation of the investment model, and that the article included the following (fictitious) table:

Table 3.1

Standard Deviations and Intercorrelations for All Variables

| | | | Intercorrelations | | | | | |
Variable	SD	1	2	3	4	5	6
1. Commitment	2.3192	1.0000					
2. Satisfaction	1.7744	.6742	1.0000	.			
3. Rewards	1.2525	.5501	.6721	1.0000			
4. Costs	1.4086	-.3499	-.5717	-.4405	1.0000		
5. Investments	1.5575	.6444	.5234	.5346	-.1854	1.0000	
6. Alternatives	1.8701	-.6929	-.4952	-.4061	.3525	-.3934	1.0000

Note: N = 240.

Armed with this information, you may now create a SAS data set that includes just these correlations and standard deviations. Here are the necessary data input statements:

```
1        DATA D1(TYPE=CORR) ;
2          INPUT _TYPE_ $ _NAME_ $ V1-V6 ;
3          LABEL
4              V1 ='COMMITMENT'
5              V2 ='SATISFACTION'
6              V3 ='REWARDS'
7              V4 ='COSTS'
8              V5 ='INVESTMENTS'
9              V6 ='ALTERNATIVES' ;
10         CARDS;
11         N    .   240    240    240    240    240    240
12         STD  .   2.3192 1.7744 1.2525 1.4086 1.5575 1.8701
13         CORR V1  1.0000 .      .      .      .      .
14         CORR V2  .6742  1.0000 .      .      .      .
15         CORR V3  .5501  .6721  1.0000 .      .      .
16         CORR V4  -.3499 -.5717 -.4405 1.0000 .      .
17         CORR V5  .6444  .5234  .5346  -.1854 1.0000 .
18         CORR V6  -.6929 -.4952 -.4061 .3525  -.3934 1.0000
19         ;
```

The following shows the general form for this DATA step; the statements assume that six variables are to be analyzed. The program would, of course, be modified if the analysis involved a different number of variables.

```
1          DATA data-set-name(TYPE=CORR) ;
2            INPUT _TYPE_ $ _NAME_ $ variable-list ;
3            LABEL
4               V1 ='long-name'
5               V2 ='long-name'
6               V3 ='long-name'
7               V4 ='long-name'
8               V5 ='long-name'
9               V6 ='long-name' ;
10         CARDS;
11         N       .    n        n        n        n        n        n
12         STD     .    std      std      std      std      std      std
13         CORR  V1   1.0000     .        .        .        .        .
14         CORR  V2     r      1.0000     .        .        .        .
15         CORR  V3     r        r      1.0000     .        .        .
16         CORR  V4     r        r        r      1.0000     .        .
17         CORR  V5     r        r        r        r      1.0000     .
18         CORR  V6     r        r        r        r        r      1.0000
19           ;
```

where

variable-list = List of variables (V1, V2, etc.).

long-name = Full name for the given variable (this will be used to label the variable when it appears in certain parts of the SAS output; if this is not desired, you can omit the entire LABEL statement).

n = Number of observations contributing to the correlation matrix. Each correlation in this matrix should be based on the same observations (and hence the same number of observations); this will automatically be the case if the matrix is created using the NOMISS option with PROC CORR, as discussed in Chapter 6.

std = Standard deviation obtained for each variable. Technically, these standard deviations are not needed if you are performing an analysis on the *correlation* matrix. However, if you wish to instead perform an analysis on a variance-covariance matrix, then the standard deviations are required so that the SAS System can convert the correlation matrix into a variance-covariance matrix.

r = Correlations between the variables.

The observations that appear on lines 11-18 in the preceding program are easiest to understand if you think of the observations as a matrix with eight rows and eight columns. The first column in this matrix (running vertically) contains the _TYPE_ variable (notice that the INPUT statement tells SAS that the first variable it will read is a character variable named "_TYPE_"). If an "N" appears as a value in this _TYPE_ column, then the SAS System knows that sample sizes will appear on that line. If an "STD" appears as a value in the _TYPE_ column, then the system knows that standard deviations will appear on that line. Finally, if a "CORR" appears as a value in the _TYPE_ column, the system knows that correlation coefficients will appear on that line.

The second column in this matrix contains short names for the manifest variables. These names should appear only on the CORR lines; periods (for missing data) should appear where the N and STD lines intersect with this column.

Looking at the matrix from the other direction, you see eight rows running horizontally. The first row is the N row (or "line") which should contain

- the N symbol.
- a period for the missing variable name.
- the sample sizes for the variables, each separated by at least one blank space. The preceding program shows that the sample size was 240 for each variable.

The STD row (or line) should contain

- the STD symbol.
- the period for the missing variable name.
- the standard deviations for the variables, each separated by at least one blank space. If the STD line is omitted from a correlation matrix, the analysis can only be performed on correlations, not on covariances.

Finally, where rows 3-8 intersect with columns 3-8, the correlation coefficients should appear. The coefficients themselves appear below the diagonal, ones should appear on the diagonal, and periods appear above the diagonal (where the correlation coefficients would again appear if this were a full matrix). Be very careful in keying these correlations; one missing period can cause an error in reading the data.

You can see that the columns of data in this matrix are lined up in a fairly neat fashion. Technically, this neatness was not really required, as this INPUT statement is in free format. However, you should try to be equally neat when preparing your matrix, as this will minimize the chance of leaving out an entry and causing an error.

Inputting a covariance matrix. The procedure for inputting a covariance matrix is very similar to that used with a correlation matrix. An example is presented here:

```
 1        DATA D1(TYPE=COV) ;
 2          INPUT _TYPE_ $ _NAME_ $ V1-V6 ;
 3          LABEL
 4              V1 ='COMMITMENT'
 5              V2 ='SATISFACTION'
 6              V3 ='REWARDS'
 7              V4 ='COSTS'
 8              V5 ='INVESTMENTS'
 9              V6 ='ALTERNATIVES' ;
10        CARDS;
11        N      .      240      240      240      240      240      240
12        COV   V1  11.1284     .        .        .        .        .
13        COV   V2   5.6742   9.0054     .        .        .        .
14        COV   V3   4.5501   3.6721   6.8773     .        .        .
15        COV   V4  -3.3499  -5.5717  -2.4405  10.9936     .        .
16        COV   V5   7.6444   2.5234   3.5346  -4.1854   7.1185     .
17        COV   V6  -8.6329  -3.4952  -6.4061   4.3525  -5.3934   9.2144
18        ;
```

Notice that the DATA statement now specifies TYPE=COV rather than TYPE=CORR. The line providing standard deviations is no longer needed, and has been removed. The matrix itself now provides variances on the diagonal and covariances below the diagonal, and the beginning of each line now specifies COV to indicate that this is a covariance matrix. The remaining sections are identical to those used to input a correlation matrix.

Inputting Data Using the INFILE Statement Rather than the CARDS Statement

When working with a very large data set with many lines of data, it may be more convenient to input data using the INFILE statement rather than the CARDS statement. This involves

- adding an INFILE statement to your program
- placing your data lines in a second computer file, rather than in the computer file that contains your SAS program
- deleting the CARDS statement from your SAS program.

Your INFILE statement should appear *after* the DATA statement, but *before* the INPUT statement. The general form for a SAS program using the INFILE statement is as follows:

```
DATA data-set-name;
   INFILE  'name-of-data-file' ;
   INPUT  #line-number    @column-number   (variable-name)   (column-width.)
                          @column-number   (variable-name)   (column-width.)
                          @column-number   (variable-name)   (column-width.) ;

PROC name-of-desired-statistical-procedure    DATA=data-set-name;
   RUN;
```

Notice that the above is identical to the general form for a SAS program presented earlier, except an INFILE statement has been added, and the CARDS statement and data lines have been deleted.

To illustrate the use of the INFILE statement, consider Dr. Smith's volunteerism study. The data set itself is reproduced here:

```
2234243 22   98   1 M
3424325 20  105   2 M
3242424 32   90   3 F
3242323  9  119   4 F
3232143  8  101   5 F
3242242 24  104   6 M
4343525 16  110   7 F
3232324 12   95   8 M
1322424 41   85   9 M
5433224 19  107  10 F
```

If you were to input these data using the INFILE statement, you would key the data in a separate computer file, giving the file any name you like. Assume, in this case, that the preceding data file is named "VOLUNT."

Note: You must key these data lines beginning on line 1 of the computer file--do *not* leave any blank lines at the top of the file. Similarly, there should be no blank lines at the end of the file (unless a blank line is appropriate because of missing data for the last subject).

Once the data are keyed and saved in the file called VOLUNT, you could key the SAS program itself in a separate file. Perhaps you would give this file a name such as SURVEY.SAS. A SAS program which would input the preceding data and calculate means for the variables appears here:

```
1          DATA D1;
2             INFILE 'VOLUNT';
3             INPUT    #1    @1    (V1-V7)    (1.)
4                            @9    (AGE)      (2.)
5                            @12   (IQ)       (3.)
6                            @16   (NUMBER)   (2.)
7                            @19   (SEX)      ($1.)   ;
8
9          PROC MEANS    DATA=D1;
10            RUN;
```

Controlling the Size of the Ouput and
Log Pages with the OPTIONS Statement

Although it is not really related to the topic of data input, the OPTIONS statement is introduced at this point in the text so that you can modify the size of your output pages and log pages, if necessary. For example, when printing your output on a 132-character printer, you may wish to modify your output so that each line may be up to 120-characters long. When working with a printer with a smaller platen width, however, you may wish to produce output that is less than 120 characters in length. The OPTIONS statement allows you to do this.

Here is the general form of the OPTIONS statement that will allow you to control the maximum number of characters and lines that appear on each page in output and log files:

```
OPTIONS    LINESIZE=x    PAGESIZE=y ;
```

With the preceding general form, "x" = the maximum number of characters that you wish to appear on each line, and "y" = the maximum number of lines that you wish to appear on each page. The values that you specify for LINESIZE= may range from 64 through 256. The values that you specify for PAGESIZE= may range from 15 through 32,767.

For example, to request output and log files in which each line may be up to 80 characters long and each page may contain up to 60 lines, use the following OPTIONS statement as the first line of your program:

```
OPTIONS    LINESIZE=80    PAGESIZE=60;
```

To request output and log files with lines that are up to 120 characters long, use the following:

```
OPTIONS   LINESIZE=120   PAGESIZE=60;
```

Conclusion

The material presented in this chapter has prepared you to input most of the types of data that are normally encountered in social science research. However, even when the data have been successfully input, they are not necessarily ready to be analyzed. Perhaps you have input raw data, and need to transform the data in some way before they can be analyzed. This is often the case with questionnaire data, as responses to multiple questions are often summed or averaged to create new variables to be analyzed. Or perhaps you have input data from a large and heterogenous sample, and wish to perform analyses on only a subgroup of that sample (such as the female, but not the male, respondents). In these situations, some form of *data manipulation* or *data subsetting* are called for, and the following chapter shows how to do this.

References

Rusbult, C. E. (1980). Commitment and satisfaction in romantic associations: A test of the investment model. *Journal of Experimental Social Psychology, 16*, 172-186.

SAS Institute Inc., (1989). *SAS language and procedures: usage, version 6, first edition*. Cary, NC: SAS Institute Inc.

SAS Institute Inc., (1990). *SAS language: reference, version 6, first edition*. Cary, NC: SAS Institute Inc.

60

Chapter 4

WORKING WITH VARIABLES AND OBSERVATIONS IN SAS® DATA SETS

Overview. This chapter shows how to modify a data set so that existing variables are transformed or recoded or so that new variables are created. The chapter shows how to eliminate unwanted observations from a data set so you can perform analyses only on a specified subgroup or on subjects that have no missing data. This chapter also shows the correct use of arithmetic operators, IF-THEN control statements, and comparison operators. Finally, the chapter shows how to concatenate and merge existing data sets to create new data sets.

Introduction: Manipulating, Subsetting, Concatenating, and Merging Data

Very often, researchers obtain a data set in which the data are not yet in a form appropriate for analysis. For example, imagine that you are conducting research on job satisfaction. Perhaps you wish to compute the correlation between subject age and a single index of job satisfaction. You administer to 200 employees a 10-item questionnaire that assesses job satisfaction, and you key their responses to the 10 individual questionnaire items. You now need to add together each subject's response to those 10 items to arrive at a single composite score that reflects that subject's overall level of satisfaction. This computation is very easy to perform by including a number of data-manipulation statements in the SAS program. **Data-manipulation** statements are SAS statements that transform the data set in some way. They may be used to recode reversed variables, create new variables from existing variables, and perform a wide range of other tasks.

At the same time, your original data set may contain observations that you do not wish to include in your analyses. Perhaps you administered the questionnaire to hourly as well as nonhourly employees, and you wish to analyze only data from the hourly employees. In addition, you may wish to analyze data only from subjects who have usable data on all of the study's variables. In these situations, you may include data-subsetting statements to eliminate the unwanted people from the sample. **Data-subsetting** statements are SAS statements that eliminate unwanted observations from a sample, so that only a specified subgroup is included in the resulting data set.

In other situations, it may be necessary to concatenate or merge data sets before you can perform the analyses you desire. When you **concatenate** data sets, you combine two previously existing data sets that contain data on the same variables but from different subjects. The resulting concatenated data set contains aggregate data from all subjects. In contrast, when you **merge** data sets, you combine two data sets that involve the same subjects but contain different variables. For example, assume that data set D1 contains variables V1 and V2, while data set D2 contains variables V3 and V4. Assume further that both data sets have a variable called ID (identification number) that will be used to merge data from the same subjects. Once D1 and D2 have been merged, the resulting data set (D3) contains V1, V2, V3, and V4 as well as ID.

The SAS programming language is so comprehensive and flexible that it can perform virtually any type of manipulation, subsetting, concatenating, or merging task imaginable. A complete treatment of these capabilities would easily fill a book; therefore it is beyond the scope of this text. However, this chapter reviews some basic statements that can be used to solve a wide variety of problems that are commonly encountered in social science research (particularly in research that involves the analysis of questionnaire data). Readers needing additional help should consult *SAS language and procedures: usage, version 6, first edition* and *SAS language: reference, version 6, first edition*.

Placement of Data Manipulation and Data Subsetting Statements

The use of data manipulation and data subsetting statements are illustrated here with reference to the fictitious study described in the preceding chapter. In that chapter, you were asked to imagine that you had developed a 7-item questionnaire dealing with volunteerism, as shown in the following example.

Volunteerism Survey

Please indicate the extent to which you agree or disagree with each of the following statements. You will do this by circling the appropriate number to the left of that statement. The following format shows what each response number stands for:

```
        5 = Agree Strongly
        4 = Agree Somewhat
        3 = Neither Agree nor Disagree
        2 = Disagree Somewhat
        1 = Disagree Strongly
```

For example, if you "Disagree Strongly" with the first question, circle the "1" to the left of that statement. If you "Agree Somewhat," circle the "4," and so on.

```
--------------
 Circle Your
  Response
--------------
```

1 2 3 4 5   1. I feel a personal responsibility to help needy people in my community.

1 2 3 4 5   2. I feel I am personally obligated to help homeless families.

1 2 3 4 5   3. I feel no personal responsibility to work with poor people in my town.

1 2 3 4 5   4. Most of the people in my community are willing to help the needy.

1 2 3 4 5   5. A lot of people around here are willing to help homeless families.

1 2 3 4 5   6. The people in my town feel no personal responsibility to work with poor people.

1 2 3 4 5   7. Everyone should feel the responsibility to perform volunteer work in their communities.

What is your age in years? _____

Assume that you administer this survey to a number of subjects, and you also obtain information concerning sex, IQ scores, SAT verbal test scores, and SAT math test scores for each of the subjects. Once the data are keyed, you may wish to write a SAS program that includes some data-manipulation or data-subsetting statements to transform the raw data. But where within the SAS program should these statements appear?

In general, these statements should only appear somewhere within the *DATA step*. Remember that the DATA step begins with the DATA statement and ends as soon as the SAS System encounters a procedure. This means that if you prepare the DATA step, end the DATA step with a procedure, and then place some manipulation or subsetting statements immediately after the procedure, you will receive an error.

To avoid this error (and keep things simple), place your data-manipulation and data-subsetting statements in only two locations within a SAS program:

- immediately following the INPUT statement

- immediately following the creation of a new data set.

Immediately following the INPUT statement. The first of the two preceding guidelines indicates that the statements may be placed immediately following the INPUT statement. This guideline is illustrated by again referring to the study on volunteerism. Assume that you prepare the following SAS program to analyze data obtained in your study. In the following program, lines 11 and 12 indicate where you can place data-manipulation or data-subsetting statements in that program. (To conserve space, only some of the data lines are reproduced in the program.)

```
1       DATA D1;
2          INPUT    #1    @1    (V1-V7)    (1.)
3                          @9    (AGE)      (2.)
4                          @12   (IQ)       (3.)
5                          @16   (NUMBER)   (2.)
6                          @19   (SEX)      ($1.)
7                    #2    @1    (SATV)     (3.)
8                          @5    (SATM)     (3.)    ;
9
10
11      place data-manipulation statements and
12      data-subsetting statements here
13
14      CARDS;
15      2234243 22   98   1 M
16      520 490
17      3424325 20 105    2 M
18      440 410
19         .
```

```
20          .
21
22          5433224 19 107 10 F
23          640 590
24          ;
25
26          PROC MEANS   DATA=D1;
27              RUN;
```

Immediately after creating a new data set. The second guideline for placement provides another option regarding where you may place data-manipulation or data-subsetting statements: They may also be placed immediately following program statements that create a new data set. A new data set may be created at virtually any point in a SAS program (even after procedures have been requested).

At times, you may want to create a new data set so that, initially, it is identical to an existing data set (perhaps the one created with a preceding INPUT statement). If data-manipulation or data-subsetting statements follow the creation of this new data set, the new set displays the modifications requested by those statements.

To create a new data set which is identical to an existing data set, the general form is

```
DATA  new-data-set-name;
   SET  existing-data-set-name;
```

To create such a data set, use the following statements:

```
    DATA D2;
        SET D1;
```

These lines told the SAS System to create a new data set called D2 and to make this new data set identical to D1. Now that a new set has been created, you are free to write as many manipulation and subsetting statements as you like. However, once you write a procedure, that effectively ends the DATA step, and you cannot write any more manipulation or subsetting statements beyond that point (unless you create another data set later in the program).

The following is an example of how you might write your program so that the manipulation and subsetting statements follow the creation of the new data set:

```
1         DATA D1;
2             INPUT   #1    @1    (V1-V7)    (1.)
3                           @9    (AGE)      (2.)
4                           @12   (IQ)       (3.)
5                           @16   (NUMBER)   (2.)
6                           @19   (SEX)      ($1.)
```

```
7                    #2    @1    (SATV)    (3.)
8                          @5    (SATM)    (3.)   ;
9
10      CARDS;
11      2234243 22   98   1 M
12      520 490
13      3424325 20 105   2 M
14      440 410
15         .
16         .
17
18      5433224 19 107 10 F
19      640 590
20      ;
21
22      DATA D2;
23         SET D1;
24
25      place data manipulation statements and
26      data subsetting statements here
27
28      PROC MEANS  DATA=D2;
29         RUN;
```

The SAS System creates two data sets according to the preceding program: D1 contains the original data, and D2 is identical to D1 except for any modifications requested by the data-manipulation and data-subsetting statements.

Notice that the MEANS procedure in line 28 requests the computation of some simple descriptive statistics. It is clear that these statistics are performed on the data from data set D2 because DATA=D2 appears in the PROC MEANS statement. If the statement instead specified DATA=D1, the analyses would have instead been performed on the original data set.

The INFILE statement versus the CARDS statement. The preceding program illustrates the use of the CARDS statement rather than the INFILE statement, but the guidelines regarding the placement of data-modifying statements are the same regardless of which approach is followed. The data-manipulation or data-subsetting statement should either immediately follow the INPUT statement *or* the creation of a new data set. When a program is written using the INFILE statement rather than the CARDS statement, data-manipulation and subsetting statements should appear after the INPUT statement but before the first procedure. For example, if your data are keyed into an external file called VOLUNTEER.DAT, you can write the following program. Notice where the manipulation and subsetting statements are placed.

```
 1    DATA D1;
 2       INFILE 'VOLUNTEER.DAT';
 3       INPUT    #1    @1    (V1-V7)    (1.)
 4                      @9    (AGE)      (2.)
 5                      @12   (IQ)       (3.)
 6                      @16   (NUMBER)   (2.)
 7                      @19   (SEX)      ($1.)
 8                #2    @1    (SATV)     (3.)
 9                      @5    (SATM)     (3.)   ;
10
11       place data manipulation statements and
12       data subsetting statements here
13
14       PROC MEANS    DATA=D1;
15          RUN;
```

In the preceding program, the data-modifying statements again come immediately after the INPUT statement but before the first procedure, consistent with earlier recommendations.

Data Manipulation

Data manipulation involves performing some type of transformation on one or more variables in the DATA step. This section discusses several types of transformations that are frequently required in social science research: such as creating duplicate variables with new variable names, creating new variables from existing variables, recoding reversed items, and using IF-THEN/ELSE statements, along with some related procedures.

Creating duplicate variables with new variable names. Suppose you give a variable a certain name when it is input, but then you want the variable to have a different, perhaps more *meaningful* name when it appears later in the SAS program or in the SAS output. This can easily be accomplished with a statement written according to the following general form:

```
new-variable-name  =  existing-variable-name;
```

For example, in the preceding data set, the first 7 questions are given variables names of V1 through V7. Item 1 in the questionnaire says "I feel a personal responsibility to help needy people in my community." In the INPUT statement, this item was given a SAS variable name V1, which is not very meaningful. RESNEEDY, which stands for "responsible for the needy," is a more meaningful name. Similarly, RESHOME is more meaningful than V2, and NORES is more meaningful than V3.

One way to rename an existing variable is to create a new variable that is identical to the existing variable and assign a new, more meaningful name to this new variable. The following program renames V1, V2, and V3 in this way.

Note: This and later examples show only a portion of the entire program. However, enough of the program appears to illustrate where the remaining statements should be placed.

```
15           .
16           .
17
18        5433224 19 107 10 F
19        640 590
20        ;
21
22        DATA D2;
23           SET D1;
24
25        RESNEEDY  = V1;
26        RESHOME   = V2;
27        NORES     = V3;
28
29        PROC MEANS    DATA=D2;
30           RUN;
```

Line 25 tells SAS to create a new variable called RESNEEDY and to set it identical to the existing variable, V1. Variables RESNEEDY and V1 now have identical data, but RESNEEDY has a more meaningful name, which will facilitate the reading of printouts when statistical analyses are performed later.

Note: When developing a new variable name, conform to the rules for naming SAS variables discussed in Chapter 3 (e.g., begins with a letter, can be no longer than 8 characters, etc.). Also, note that each statement that creates a duplicate of an existing variable must end with a semicolon.

Duplicating variables versus renaming variables. Technically, the previous program did not really rename variables V1, V2, and V3. Rather, the program created duplicates of these variables and assigned new names to the duplicate variables. Therefore, the resulting data set contains both the original variables under their old names (V1, V2, and V3) as well as the duplicate variables under their new names (RESNEEDY, RESHOME, and NORES). If, for some reason, you literally need to rename the existing variables so that the old variable names no longer exist in the data set, you might consider using the RENAME statement. For details on the RENAME statement, see Chapter 9 of *SAS language: reference*.

Creating new variables from existing variables. It is often necessary to perform mathematical operations on existing variables and use the results to create a new variable. With SAS, the following symbols may be used in arithmetic operations:

+ (addition)
- (subtraction)
* (multiplication)
/ (division)
= (equals)

When writing formulas, you should make heavy use of parentheses. Remember that operations enclosed within parentheses are performed first, and operations outside of the parentheses are performed later. To create a new variable by performing mathematical operations on existing variables, use the following general form:

```
new-variable-name  =  formula-including-existing-variables;
```

For example, two existing variables in your data set are SATV (SAT verbal test scores) and SATM (SAT math test scores). Suppose you wanted to create a new variable called SATCOMB. This variable includes each subject's combined SAT score. For a given subject, you need to add together that person's SATV score and SATM score; therefore, the SATCOMB value for that subject is the sum of the values for SATV and SATM. The program repeats this operation for each subject in the sample, using just one statement:

```
SATCOMB = (SATV + SATM);
```

The preceding statement tells SAS to create a new variable called SATCOMB and set it equal to the sum of SATV and SATM.

Suppose you wanted to calculate, for a given subject, the *average* of that subject's SATV and SATM scores. The new variable is called SATAVG. The program repeats this operation for each subject in the sample using the following statement:

```
SATAVG = (SATV + SATM) / 2;
```

The preceding statement tells SAS to create a new variable called SATAVG by adding together the values of SATV and SATM then dividing this sum by 2. The resulting quotient is that subject's score for SATAVG. You can also arrive at the same result by using two statements instead of one, as shown here:

```
SATCOMB = (SATV + SATM);
SATAVG  = SATCOMB/2;
```

Very often, researchers need to calculate the average of a subject's responses to several items on a questionnaire. For example, look at items 1 and 2 in the questionnaire shown previously. Both items seem to be measuring the subject's sense of personal responsibility to help the needy.

Rather than analyze responses to the items separately, it may be more useful to calculate (for a given subject) the average of his or her responses to those items. This average could then serve as that subject's score on some "personal responsibility" variable. For example, consider the following:

```
RESPONS = (V1 + V2) / 2;
```

The preceding statement tells SAS to create a new variable called RESPONS by adding together a given subject's scores for V1 and V2 then dividing the resulting sum by 2. The resulting quotient is that subject's score for RESPONS.

Note: When creating new variables in this fashion, be sure that all variables on the right side of the equals sign are *existing* variables. This means that they already exist in the data set, either because they are listed in the INPUT statement or because they were created with earlier data-manipulation statements.

Priority of operators in compound expressions. A SAS expression (for example, a formula) that contains just one operator is known as a **simple expression**. The following statement contains a simple expression. Notice that there is only one operator (+ sign) to the right of the = sign:

```
RESPONS = V1 + V2;
```

In contrast, a **compound expression** is one that contains more than one operator. A compound expression is illustrated in the following example; notice that several different operators appear to the right of the = sign:

```
RESPONS = V1 + V2 - V3 / V4 * V5;
```

When an expression contains more than one operator, the SAS System follows a set of rules that determine which operations are performed first, which are performed second, and so forth. The rules that pertain to mathematical operators (+, -, /, and *) are summarized here:

- Multiplication and division operators (* and /) have equal priority, and they are performed first.

- Addition and subtraction operators (+ and -) have equal priority, and they are performed second.

One point made in the preceding rules is that multiplication and division are performed prior to addition or subtraction. For example, consider the following statement:

```
RESPONS = V1 + V2 / V3;
```

Since division has priority over addition, the operations in the preceding statement would be executed in this sequence:

- V2 would first be divided by V3

- The resulting quotient would then be added to V1.

Notice that the division is performed first, even though the addition appears earlier in the formula (reading from left to right).

But what if multiple operators that have equal priority appear in the same statement? In this situation, the SAS System reads the formula from left to right, and performs the operations in that sequence. For example, consider the following:

```
RESPONSE = V1 + V2 - V3;
```

The preceding expression contains only addition and subtraction, operations that have equal priority. The SAS System therefore reads the statement from left to right: First, V1 is added to V2; then V3 is subtracted from the resulting sum.

Because different priority is given to different operators, it is unfortunately very easy to write a statement that results in operations being performed in some sequence other than the intended sequence. For example, imagine that you want to create a new variable called RESPONS. Each subject's score for RESPONS is created by adding the subject's values for V1, V2, and V3 and by dividing this sum by 3. Imagine further that you attempt to achieve this with the following statement:

```
RESPONS = V1 + V2 + V3 / 3;
```

The preceding statement will not create RESPONS in the manner that you intended. Because division has priority over addition, the SAS System performs the operations in the following order:

1. V3 is divided by 3
2. The resulting quotient is then added to V1 and V2.

Obviously, this is not what you intended.

To avoid mistakes such as this, it is important to use parentheses when writing formulas. Because operations that are included inside parentheses are performed first, the use of parentheses gives you control over the sequence in which operations are executed. For example, the following statement creates RESPONS in the way originally intended because the lower priority operations (adding together V1 plus V2 plus V3) are now included within parentheses:

```
RESPONSE = (V1 + V2 + V3) / 3;
```

This statement tells the SAS System to add together V1 plus V2 plus V3; whatever the sum is, divide it by 3.

This section has provided a brief introduction the priority of a few of the operators that can be used with the SAS System. To learn about the priority for other operators (such as exponentiation or comparison operators), see Chapter 10 of *SAS language: reference.*

Recoding reversed variables. Very often, a questionnaire contains a number of reversed items. A **reversed item** is a question stated so that its meaning is the opposite of the meaning of the other items in that group. For example, consider the meaning of the following items from the volunteerism survey:

```
1  2  3  4  5      1.  I feel a personal responsibility to help
                       needy people in my community.

1  2  3  4  5      2.  I feel I am personally obligated to help
                       homeless families.

1  2  3  4  5      3.  I feel no personal responsibility to work
                       with poor people in my town.
```

In a sense, all of these questions are measuring the same thing: whether the subject feels some sense of personal responsibility to help the needy. Items 1 and 2 are stated so that the more strongly you agree with the statement, the stronger is your sense of personal responsibility. This means that scores of 5 indicate a strong sense of responsibility and scores of 1 indicate a weak sense of responsibility. However, item 3 is a *reversed* item. It is stated so that the more strongly you agree with it, the weaker is your sense of personal responsibility. Here, scores of 1 indicate a strong sense of responsibility and scores of 5 indicate a weak sense of responsibility (which is just the reverse of items 1 and 2).

It would be nice if all three items were consistent so that scores of 5 always indicate a strong sense of responsibility and scores of 1 always indicate a weak sense of responsibility. This requires that you recode item 3 so that people who actually circle 5 are given, instead, a score of 1; people who actually circle 4, are given, instead, a score of 2; people who actually circle 2 are given a score of 4; and people who actually circle 1 are given a score of 5. This can be done very easily with the following statement:

```
V3 = 6 - V3;
```

The preceding statement tells SAS to create a new version of the variable V3, then take the number 6 and subtract from it the subject's existing (old) score for V3. The result is the subject's new score for V3. Notice that with this statement, if a person's old score for V3 was 5, his or her new score is, in fact, 1; if the old score was 1, the new score is 5, and so forth.

The general form for this recoding statement is as follows:

```
existing-variable  =  constant  -  existing-variable;
```

The constant is always equal to the number of response points on your survey plus 1. For example, the volunteerism survey included 5 response points: people could circle "1" for "Disagree Strongly" all the way through "5" for "Agree Strongly." It was a 5-point scale, so the constant was 5 + 1 = 6. What would the constant be if the following 7-point scale had been used instead?

> 7 = Agree Very Strongly
> 6 = Agree Strongly
> 5 = Agree Somewhat
> 4 = Neither Agree nor Disagree
> 3 = Disagree Somewhat
> 2 = Disagree Strongly
> 1 = Disagree Very Strongly

It would be 8 because 7 + 1 = 8, and the recoding statement would read

```
V3 = 8 - V3;
```

Where **should the recoding statements go?** In most cases, reversed items should be recoded *before* other data manipulations are performed on them. For example, assume that you want to create a new variable called RESPONS, which stands for "personal responsibility." With this scale, higher scores indicate higher levels of perceived personal responsibility. For a given subject, his or her score on this scale is the average of his or her responses to items 1, 2, and 3 from the survey. Because item 3 is a reversed item, it is important that it be recoded before it is added in with items 1 and 2 in calculating this scale score. Therefore, the correct sequence of statements is as follows:

```
V3 = 6 - V3;
RESPONS = (V1 + V2 + V3) / 3;
```

The following sequence is *not* correct:

```
RESPONS = (V1 + V2 + V3) / 3;
V3 = 6 - V3;
```

Using IF-THEN control statements. An IF-THEN control statement allows you to make sure that operations are performed on a given subject's data only if certain conditions are true regarding that subject. The following comparison operators may be used with IF-THEN statements:

```
    =     is equal to
   NE     is not equal to
GT or >   is greater than
   GE     is greater than or equal to
LT or <   is less than
   LE     is less than or equal to
```

The general form for an IF-THEN statement is as follows:

```
IF  expression  THEN  statement ;
```

The expression usually consists of some comparison involving existing variables. The statement usually involves some operation performed on existing variables or new variables. For example, assume that you want to create a new variable called SATVGRP for "SAT-verbal group." This variable will be created so that

- if you do not know what a subject's SAT verbal test score is, that subject will have a score of "." (for "missing data").

- if subject's score is under 500 on the SAT verbal test, the subject will have a score of 0 for SATVGRP.

- if the subject's score is 500 or greater on the SAT verbal test, the subject will have a score of 1 for SATVGRP.

Assume that the variable SATV already exists in your data set and that it contains each subject's score for the SAT verbal test. You can use it to create the new variable SATVGRP by writing the following statements:

```
SATVGRP = .;
IF SATV LT 500 THEN SATVGRP = 0;
IF SATV GE 500 THEN SATVGRP = 1;
```

The preceding statements tell the SAS System to create a new variable called SATVGRP and begin by setting everyone's score as equal to "." (missing). If a subject's score for SATV is less than 500, then set his or her score for SATVGRP equal to 0. If a subject's score for SATV is greater than or equal to 500, then set his or her score for SATVGRP equal to 1.

Using ELSE statements. In reality, you can perform the preceding operations more efficiently by using the ELSE statement. The general form for using the ELSE statement, in conjunction with the IF-THEN statement, is presented as follows:

```
IF  expression  THEN  statement  ;
   ELSE  IF  expression  THEN  statement;
```

The ELSE statement provides alternative actions that the SAS System may take if the original IF expression is not true. For example, consider the following:

```
1     SATVGRP = .;
2     IF SATV LT 500 THEN SATVGRP = 0;
3     ELSE  IF SATV GE 500 THEN SATVGRP = 1;
```

The preceding tells the SAS System to create a new variable called SATVGRP and initially assign all subjects a value of "missing." If a given subject has an SATV score less than 500, the system assigns that subject a score of 0 for SATVGRP. Otherwise, if the subject has an SATV score greater than or equal to 500, then the system assigns that subject a score of 1 for SATVGRP.

Obviously, the preceding statements are identical to the earlier statements that created SATVGRP, except that the word ELSE has been added to the beginning of the third line. In fact, these two approaches actually result in assigning exactly the same values for SATVGRP to each subject. So what, then, is the advantage of including the ELSE statement? The answer has to do with efficiency. When an ELSE statement is included, the actions specified in that statement are executed only if the expression in the preceding IF statement is not true.

For example, consider the situation in which subject 1 has a score for SATV that is less than 500. Line 2 in the preceding statements assigns that subject a score of 0 for SATVGRP. The SAS System then ignores line 3 (because it contains the ELSE statement), thus saving computer time. If line 3 did not contain the word ELSE, the SAS System would have executed the line, checking to see whether the SATV score for subject 1 is greater than or equal to 500 (which is actually unnecessary, given what was learned in line 2).

A word of caution regarding missing data is relevant at this point. Notice that line 2 of the preceding program assigns subjects to group 0 (under SATVGRP) if their values for SATV are less than 0. Unfortunately, a value of "missing" (that is, a value of ".") for SATV is viewed as being less than 500 (actually, it is viewed as being less than 0) by the SAS System. This means that subjects with missing data for SATV are assigned to group 0 under SATVGRP by line 2 of the preceding program. This is not desirable.

To prevent this from happening, you may rewrite the program in the following way:

```
1     SATVGRP = .;
2     IF SATV GE 200 AND SATV LT 500 THEN SATVGRP = 0;
3     ELSE  IF SATV GE 500 THEN SATVGRP = 1;
```

Line 2 of the program now tells the SAS System to assign subjects to group 0 only if their values for SATV are both greater than or equal to 200 and less than 500. This modification to the line involves the use of the conditional AND statement, which is discussed in greater detail in the following section.

Finally, remember that the ELSE statement should only be used in conjunction with a preceding IF statement. In addition, remember to always place the ELSE statement *immediately* following the relevant IF statement.

Using the conditional statements AND and OR. As the preceding section suggests, you can also use the conditional statement AND within an IF-THEN statement or an ELSE statement. For example, consider the following:

```
SATVGRP = .;
IF SATV GT 400 AND SATV LT 500 THEN SATVGRP = 0;
ELSE IF SATV GE 500 THEN SATVGRP = 1;
```

The second statement in the preceding program tells SAS that if SATV is greater than 400 and less than 500, then give this person a score for SATVGRP of 0. This means that subjects are given a value of 0 *only* if they are both over 400 and under 500. What happens to people who have a score of 400 or less for SATV? They are given a value of "." for SATVGRP. That is, they are classified as having missing data for SATVGRP. This is because they (along with everyone else) were given a value of "." in the first statement, and neither of the later statements replaces that "." with 0 or 1. However, for people over 400, one of the later statements replaces the "." with either 0 or 1.

You can also use the conditional statement OR within an IF-THEN statement or an ELSE statement. For example, assume that you have a variable in your data set called ETHNIC. With this variable, subjects were assigned the value 5 if they were Caucasian, 6 if they were African-American, or 7 if they were Asian-American. Assume that you now wish to create a new variable called MAJORITY. Subjects will be assigned a value of 1 for this variable if they are in the majority group (i.e., if they are Caucasians), and they will be assigned a value of 0 for this variable if they are in a minority group (if they are either African-Americans or Asian-Americans). The creation of this variable can be achieved with the following statements:

```
MAJORITY=.;
IF ETHNIC = 5 THEN MAJORITY = 1;
ELSE IF ETHNIC = 6 OR ETHNIC = 7 THEN MAJORITY = 0;
```

In the preceding statements, all subjects are first assigned a value of "missing" for MAJORITY. If their value for ETHNIC is 5, their value for MAJORITY changes to 1 and the SAS System ignores the following ELSE statement. If their value for ETHNIC is not 5, then the SAS System moves on to the ELSE statement. There, if the subject's value for ETHNIC is either 6 or 7, the subject is assigned a value of 0 for MAJORITY.

Working with character variables. When working with character variables (variables in which the values consists of letters rather than numbers), you must enclose values within single quotation marks in the IF-THEN and ELSE statements. For example, suppose you want to create a new variable called SEXGRP. With this variable, males are given a score of 0, and females are given a score of 1. The variable SEX already exists in your data set, and it is a character variable in which males are coded with the letter M and females are coded with the letter F. You can create the new SEXGRP variable using the following statements:

```
SEXGRP = .;
IF SEX = 'M' THEN SEXGRP = 0;
ELSE IF SEX = 'F' THEN SEXGRP = 1;
```

Using the IN operator. The IN operator makes it easy to determine whether a given value is among a specified list of values. Because of this, a single IF statement including the IN operator can perform comparisons that could otherwise require a large number of IF statements. The general form for using the IN operator is as follows:

```
IF  variable  IN (value-1,value-2, ...value-n)  THEN  statement;
```

Notice that each value in the preceding list of values must be separated by a comma.

For example, assume that you have a variable in your data set called MONTH. The values assumed by this variable are the numbers 1 through 12. With these values, 1 represents January, 2 represents February, 3 represents March, and so forth. Assume that these values for MONTH indicate the month in which a given subject was born, and that you have data for 100 subjects.

Imagine that you now wish to create a new variable called SEASON. This variable will indicate the season in which each subject was born. Subjects are assigned values for SEASON according to the following guidelines:

- Subjects are assigned a value of 1 for SEASON if they were born in January, February, or March (months 1, 2, or 3);

- Subjects are assigned a value of 2 for SEASON if they were born in April, May, or June (months 4, 5, or 6);

- Subjects are assigned a value of 3 for SEASON if they were born in July, August, or September (months 7, 8, or 9), and

- Subjects are assigned a value of 4 for SEASON if they were born in October, November, or December (months 10, 11, or 12).

One way to create the new SEASON variable involves using four IF-THEN statements, as shown here:

```
SEASON = .;
IF   MONTH = 1   OR MONTH = 2   OR MONTH = 3   THEN   SEASON = 1;
IF   MONTH = 4   OR MONTH = 5   OR MONTH = 6   THEN   SEASON = 2;
IF   MONTH = 7   OR MONTH = 8   OR MONTH = 9   THEN   SEASON = 3;
IF   MONTH = 10 OR MONTH = 11 OR MONTH = 12 THEN   SEASON = 4;
```

However, the same results can be achieved somewhat more easily by using the IN operator within the IF-THEN statements, as shown here:

```
SEASON = .;
IF   MONTH IN (1,2,3)    THEN SEASON = 1;
IF   MONTH IN (4,5,6)    THEN SEASON = 2;
IF   MONTH IN (7,8,9)    THEN SEASON = 3;
IF   MONTH IN (10,11,12) THEN SEASON = 4;
```

In the preceding example, all variable values are numbers. However, the IN operator may also be used with character variables. As always, it is necessary to enclose all character variable values within single quotation marks. For example, assume that MONTH is actually a character variable that assumes values such as "Jan," "Feb," "Mar," and so forth. Assume further that SEASON assumes the values "Winter," Spring," Summer," and "Fall." Under these circumstances, the preceding statements would be modified in the following way:

```
SEASON = '.';
IF   MONTH IN ('Jan', 'Feb', 'Mar')   THEN SEASON = 'Winter';
IF   MONTH IN ('Apr', 'May', 'Jun')   THEN SEASON = 'Spring';
IF   MONTH IN ('Jul', 'Aug', 'Sep')   THEN SEASON = 'Summer';
IF   MONTH IN ('Oct', 'Nov', 'Dec')   THEN SEASON = 'Fall';
```

Data Subsetting

Using a simple subsetting statement. Often, it is necessary to perform an analysis on only a subset of the subjects who are included in the data set. For example, you may wish to review the mean survey responses provided by just the female subjects. A subsetting IF statement may be used to accomplish this, and the general form is presented here:

```
DATA  new-data-set-name;
   SET  existing-data-set-name;
IF  comparison;

PROC  name-of-desired-statistical-procedure    DATA=new-data-set-name;
   RUN;
```

The comparison described in the preceding statements generally includes some existing variable and at least one comparison operator. The following statements allow you to calculate the mean survey responses for only the female subjects.

```
15          .
16          .
17
18      5433224 19 107 10 F
19      640 590
20      ;
21
22      DATA D2;
23          SET D1;
24
25          IF SEX = 'F';
26
27      PROC MEANS    DATA=D2;
28          RUN;
```

The preceding statements tell SAS to create a new data set called D2 and to make it identical to D1. However, the program keeps a subject's data only if SEX has a value of F. Then the program executes the MEANS procedure for the data which are retained.

Using comparison operators. All of the comparison operators described previously can be used in a subsetting IF statement. For example, consider the following:

```
DATA D2;
   SET D1;

   IF SEX = 'F' AND AGE GE 65;

PROC MEANS    DATA=D2;
   RUN;
```

The preceding statements analyze only data from women who are 65 or older.

Eliminating observations with missing data for some variables. One of the most common difficulties encountered by researchers in the social sciences is the problem of missing data. Briefly, **missing data** involves not having scores for all variables for all subjects in a data set. This section discusses the problem of missing data, and shows how a subsetting IF statement may be used to deal with it.

Assume that you administer your volunteerism survey to 100 subjects, and you use their scores to calculate a single volunteerism score for each subject. You also obtain a number of additional variables regarding the subjects. The SAS names for the study's variables and their descriptions are as follows:

VOLUNT: Subject scores on the volunteerism questionnaire, where higher scores reveal greater intention to engage in unpaid prosocial activities.

SATV: Subject scores on the verbal subtest of the Scholastic Assessment Test.

SATM: Subject scores on the math subtest of the Scholastic Assessment Test.

IQ: Subject scores on a standard intelligence test.

Assume further that you obtained scores for VOLUNT, SATV, and SATM for all 100 of the subjects. However, due to a recordkeeping error, you were able to obtain IQ scores for only 75 of the subjects.

You now wish to analyze your data using a procedure called multiple regression (this procedure is covered in a later chapter; you do not need to understand multiple regression to understand the points to be made here, however). In Analysis #1, VOLUNT is the criterion variable, and SATV and SATM are the predictor variables. The multiple regression equation for Analysis #1 is represented in the following PROC REG statement:

Analysis #1:

```
PROC REG   DATA=D1;
   MODEL VOLUNT  =  SATV   SATM ;
   RUN;
```

When you review the results of the analysis, note that the analysis is based on 100 subjects. This makes sense because you had complete data on all of the variables included in this analysis.

In Analysis #2, VOLUNT is again the criterion variable, but this time the predictor variables will include SATV and SATM as well as IQ. The equation for Analysis #2 is as follows:

Analysis #2:

```
PROC REG   DATA=D1;
   MODEL VOLUNT  =  SATV   SATM   IQ;
   RUN;
```

When you review the results of analysis #2, however, you see that you have encountered a problem. The SAS output indicates that the analysis is based on only 75 subjects. At first you may not understand this because you know that there are 100 subjects in the data set. But then you remember that you did not have complete data for one of the variables. You had values for the IQ variable for only 75 subjects. The REG procedure (and many other SAS procedures) includes in the analysis only those subjects who have complete data for *all* of the variables being analyzed with that procedure. For Analysis #2, this means that any subject with missing data for IQ will be eliminated from the sample. Twenty-five subjects had missing data for IQ and were therefore eliminated.

Why were these 25 subjects not eliminated from Analysis #1? Because that analysis did not involve the IQ variable. It only involved VOLUNT, SATV, and SATM, and all 100 subjects had complete data for those three variables.

In a situation such as this, you have a number of options with respect to how you might perform these analyses and summarize the results for publication. One option is to retain the results described previously. You could report that you performed one analysis on all 100 subjects and a second analysis on just the 75 subjects who had complete data for the IQ variable.

This approach might leave you open to criticism, however. The beginning of your research paper probably reported demographic characteristics for all 100 subjects (how many were female, mean age, etc.). However, you may not have a section providing demographics for the subgroup of 75. This might lead readers to wonder if the subgroup differed in some important way from the aggregate group.

There are statistical reasons that this approach might cause problems as well. For example, you might wish to test the significance of the difference between the R^2 value obtained from Analysis #1 and the R^2 value obtained from Analysis #2. (This test is described in Chapter 13, "Multiple Regression.") When performing this test, it is important that both R^2 values be based on exactly the same subjects in both analyses. This is obviously not the case in your study, as 25 of the subjects used in Analysis #1 were not used in Analysis #2.

In situations such as this, you are usually better-advised to ensure that every analysis you perform is performed on exactly the same sample of people. This means that, in general, any subject who has missing data for variables to be included in any (reported) analysis should be deleted from the sample before the analyses are performed. In your case, therefore, it is best to see to it that both Analysis #1 and Analysis #2 are performed on only those 75 subjects who had complete data for all four variables (VOLUNT, SATV, SATM, and IQ). Fortunately, this may easily be done using a subsetting IF statement.

With the SAS System, a missing value is represented in the computer's memory with a period (a "."). You can take advantage of this fact to eliminate any subject with missing data for any variable being analyzed. For example, consider the following subsetting IF statement:

```
DATA D2;
   SET D1;
IF VOLUNT NE . AND SATV NE . AND
   SATM   NE . AND IQ   NE . ;
```

The preceding statements tell the system to

  1) create a new data set named D2, and make it an exact copy of D1;

  2) retain a subject in this new data set *only* if (for that subject)

     • VOLUNT is not equal to missing

     • SATV is not equal to missing

     • SATM is not equal to missing

     • IQ is not equal to missing.

In other words, the system creates a new data set named D2. That new data set contains only the 75 subjects who have complete data for all four variables of interest. You may now specify DATA=D2 in all SAS procedures, with the result that all analyses will be performed on exactly the same 75 subjects.

The following SAS program shows where these statements should be placed:

```
14          .
15          .
16          .
17
18          5433224 19 107 10 F
19          640 590
20          ;
21
22          DATA D2;
23             SET D1;
24
25          IF VOLUNT NE . AND SATV NE . AND
26             SATM   NE . AND IQ   NE . ;
27
28          PROC REG    DATA=D2;
29             MODEL VOLUNT =   SATV   SATM ;
30             RUN;
31
32          PROC REG    DATA=D2;
33             MODEL VOLUNT =   SATV   SATM   IQ ;
34             RUN;
```

Obviously, the subsetting IF statement must appear in the program before the procedures that request the modified data set (data set D2, in this case).

How should I key missing data? If you are keying data and come to a subject with missing data for some variable, you do not need to record a "." to represent the missing data . As long as your data are being input using the CARDS statement and the conventions discussed here, it is acceptable to simply leave that column (or those columns) blank by hitting the space bar on your keyboard. The SAS System, however, will internally give that subject a missing data value (a ".") for the concerned variable. In some cases, however, it may be useful to key a "." for variables with missing data, as this may make it easier to keep your place when keying information.

When using a subsetting IF statement to eliminate subjects with missing data, exactly *which* variables should be included in that statement? In most cases, it should be those variables–and only those variables–that are ultimately discussed in the published article. This means that you may not know exactly which variables to include until you actually begin analyzing the data. For example, imagine that you conduct your study and obtain data for the following number of subjects for each of the following variables:

Variable	Number of Subjects with Valid Data for This Variable
VOLUNT	100
SATV	100
SATM	100
IQ	75
AGE	10

As before, you obtained complete data for all 100 subjects for VOLUNT, SATV, and SATM, and you obtained data for 75 subjects on IQ. But notice the last variable. You obtained information concerning the subjects' age for only 10 subjects. What would happen if you included the variable AGE in the subsetting IF statement, as shown here?

```
IF VOLUNT NE . AND SATV NE . AND
   SATM   NE . AND IQ   NE . AND  AGE  NE  . ;
```

This IF statement causes the system to eliminate from the sample anyone who does not have complete data for all five variables. Since only 10 subjects have values for the AGE variable, you know that the resulting data set includes no more than 10 subjects. Obviously, this sample is too small for most statistical procedures. At this point, you have to decide whether to gather more data or forget about doing any analyses with the AGE variable.

In summary, one approach for identifying those variables to be included in the subsetting if statement is to

- perform some initial analyses

- decide which variables will be included in the final analyses (for the published paper)

- include all of those variables in the subsetting IF statement

- perform again all analyses on this reduced data set so that all analyses reported in the paper are performed on exactly the same sample.

Of course, there will sometimes be circumstances in which it is neither necessary nor desirable that all analyses be performed on exactly the same group of subjects. The purpose of the research, along with other considerations, should determine when this is appropriate.

A More Comprehensive Example

Often, a single SAS program will contain a large number of data-manipulation and subsetting statements. Consider the following example, which makes use of the INFILE statement rather than the CARDS statement:

```
1    DATA D1;
2        INFILE 'VOLUNTEER.DAT' ;
3        INPUT    #1    @1    (V1-V7)    (1.)
4                       @9    (AGE)      (2.)
5                       @12   (IQ)       (3.)
6                       @16   (NUMBER)   (2.)
7                       @19   (SEX)      ($1.)
8                 #2    @1    (SATV)     (3.)
9                       @5    (SATM)     (3.)   ;
10
11       DATA D2;
12          SET D1;
13
14       V3 = 6 - V3;
15       V6 = 6 - V6;
16       RESPONS = (V1 + V2 + V3) / 3;
17       TRUST   = (V4 + V5 + V6) / 3;
18       SHOULD = V7;
19
20       PROC MEANS    DATA=D2;
21          RUN;
22
23       DATA D3;
24          SET D2;
25          IF SEX = 'F';
26
27       PROC MEANS    DATA=D3;
28          RUN;
29
30       DATA D4;
31          SET D2;
32          IF SEX = 'M';
33
34       PROC MEANS    DATA=D4;
35          RUN;
```

In the preceding program, lines 11 and 12 create a new data set called D2 and set it identical to D1. All of the data-manipulation commands which appear between those lines and PROC MEANS on line 20 are performed on this data set called D2. Notice that a new variable called

TRUST is created on line 17. TRUST is the average of a subject's responses to items 4, 5, and 6. Look over these items on the volunteerism survey to see why the name TRUST makes sense. On line 18, variable V7 is duplicated, and the resulting new variable is called SHOULD. Why does this make sense? PROC MEANS appears on line 20, so the means and other descriptive statistics are calculated for all of the quantitative variables in the most recently created data set, which is D2. This includes all of the variables input in data set D1 as well as the new variables which were just created.

In lines 22 through 26, a new data set called D3 is created. A given subject's responses are retained in this data set only if that subject is a female. Notice that the SET statement sets D3 equal to D2 rather than D1. This way, the newly created variables (such as TRUST and SHOULD) appear in this all-female data set. In lines 30 through 32, a new data set called D4 is created, and it is also set equal to D2 (not D3). This new data set contains data only from males.

After this program is submitted for analysis, the SAS output contains three tables of means. The first table is based on lines 1-21, and gives the means based on all subjects. The second table is based on lines 23-28 and gives the means based on the responses of females. The third table is based on lines 30-35, and is based on the responses of males.

Concatenating and Merging Data Sets

The techniques taught to this point in this chapter are designed to help you transform data within a single data set (e.g., to recode a variable within a single data set). However, very often you need to perform transformations that involve combining more than one data set to create a new data set. For example, **concatenating** involves creating a new data set by combining two or more previously existing data sets. With concatenation, the same variables typically appear in both of the previously existing data sets, but the two sets contain data from *different subjects*. By concatenating the two previously existing sets, you create a new set that contains data from all subjects.

In contrast, **merging** involves combining data sets in a different way. With merging, each of the previously existing data sets typically contain data from the same subjects. However, the different, previously existing sets usually contain different *variables*. By merging these sets, you can create a single new data set that contains all of the variables found in the previously existing data sets. For example, assume that you conduct a study with 100 subjects. Data set A contains each subject's age, while data set B contains questionnaire responses from the same 100 subjects. By merging data sets A and B, you can create a new data set called C which, again, contains just 100 observations. A given observation in data set C contains a given subject's age as well as the questionnaire responses made by that same subject. Now that the data sets are merged, it is possible to correlate subject age with responses to the questionnaire (for example). This could not be done when AGE was in one data set and the questionnaire responses were in another.

The following section discusses the basics of concatenating and merging SAS data sets. For additional details and related procedures, see Chapters 4 and 9 of *SAS language: reference* as well as Chapters 14, 15, and 17 of *SAS language and procedures: usage*.

Concatenating data sets. Imagine that you are conducting research that involves the Scholastic Assessment Test (SAT). You obtain data from four subjects: John, Sally, Fred, and Emma. You key information about these four subjects into a SAS data set called A. This data set contains three variables:

- NAME, which contains the subject's first name

- SATV, which contains the subject's score on the SAT verbal test

- SATM, which contains the subject's score on the SAT math test.

The contents of data set A appear in Table 4.1. You can see that John has a score of 520 for SATV and a score of 500 for SATM, Sally had a score of 610 for SATV and 640 for SATM, and so forth.

Table 4.1

Contents of Data Set A

NAME	SATV	SATM
John	520	500
Sally	610	640
Fred	490	470
Emma	550	560

Imagine that later you create a second data set called B that contains data from four different subjects: Susan, James, Cheri, and Will. Values for these subjects for SATV and SATM appear in Table 4.2.

Table 4.2

Contents of Data Set B

NAME	SATV	SATM
Susan	710	650
James	450	400
Cheri	570	600
Will	680	700

Assume that you would like to perform some analyses on a single data set that contains scores from all eight of these subjects. But you encounter a problem. The values in data set A were keyed differently than the values of data set B, making it impossible to read data from both sets with a single INPUT statement. For example, perhaps you keyed SATV in columns 10-12 in data set A, but keyed it in columns 11-13 in data set B. Because the variable was keyed in different columns in the two data sets, it is not possible to write a single INPUT statement that will input this variable (assuming that you use a formatted input approach).

One way around this problem is to input A and B as separate data sets and then concatenate them to create a single data set that contains all eight observations. You can then perform your analyses on the new data set. The following is the general form for concatenating multiple data sets into a single data set:

```
DATA  new-data-set-name;
     SET  data-set-1  data-set-2 ... data-set-n;
```

In the present situation, you wish to concatenate just two data sets (A and B) to create a new data set named C. This could be done in the following statements:

```
    DATA C;
       SET A B;
```

The entire program follows that places these statements in context. This program

- inputs data set A

- inputs data set B

- concatenates A and B to create C

- uses PROC PRINT to print the contents of data set C (PROC PRINT will be discussed in greater detail in Chapter 5 of this text).

```
1       DATA  A;
2          INPUT  #1   @1   (NAME)   ($7.)
3                       @10  (SATV)   (3.)
4                       @14  (SATM)   (3.)   ;
5       CARDS;
6       John       520 500
7       Sally      610 640
8       Fred       490 470
9       Emma       550 560
10      ;
11
12      DATA  B;
13         INPUT  #1   @1   (NAME)   ($7.)
14                      @11  (SATV)   (3.)
15                      @15  (SATM)   (3.)   ;
16      CARDS;
17      Susan      710 650
18      James      450 400
19      Cheri      570 600
20      Will       680 700
21      ;
22
23      DATA  C;
24         SET  A  B;
25
26      PROC PRINT   DATA=C
27         RUN;
```

In the preceding program, data set A is input in program lines 1-10, and data set B is input in lines 12-21. In lines 23-24, the two data sets are concatenated to create data set C. In lines 26-27, PROC PRINT is used to print the contents of data set C, and the results of this procedure are reproduced as Output 4.1. The results of Output 4.1 show that data set C contains eight observations: the four observations from data set A along with the four observations from data set B. To perform additional statistical analyses on this combined data set, you would simply specify DATA=C in the PROC statement of your SAS program.

```
OBS     NAME     SATV     SATM

 1      John     520      500
 2      Sally    610      640
 3      Fred     490      470
 4      Emma     550      560
 5      Susan    710      650
 6      James    450      400
 7      Cheri    570      600
 8      Will     680      700
```

Output 4.1: Results of Performing PROC PRINT on Data Set C

Merging data sets. As was stated earlier, you would normally merge data sets when

- you are working with two data sets

- both data sets contain information for the same subjects, but one data set contains one set of variables, while the other data set contains a different set of variables.

Once these two data sets have been merged, you will have a single data set that contains all of these variables. Having all the variables in one set allows you to assess the relationships between the variables, should you wish to do so.

As an illustration, assume that your sample consists of just four subjects: John, Sally, Fred, and Emma. Assume that you have obtained the social security number for each of these subjects, and that these numbers are included in a SAS variable named SOCSEC in both previously existing data sets. In data set D, you have SAT verbal test scores and SAT math test scores for these subjects (represented as SAS variables SATV and SATM, respectively). In data set E, you have college cumulative grade point average for the same four subjects (represented as GPA). Table 4.3 and Table 4.4 shows the content of these two data sets.

Table 4.3

Contents of Data Set D

NAME	SOCSEC	SATV	SATM
John	232882121	520	500
Sally	222773454	610	640
Fred	211447653	490	470
Emma	222671234	550	560

Table 4.4

Contents of Data Set E

NAME	SOCSEC	GPA
John	232882121	2.70
Sally	222773454	3.25
Fred	211447653	2.20
Emma	222671234	2.50

Assume that, in conducting your research, you would like to compute the correlation between SATV and GPA (let's forget for the moment that you really shouldn't perform a correlation using such a small sample!). On the positive side, computing this correlation should be possible because you do have values for these two variables for all four of your subjects. On the negative side however, you will not be able to compute this correlation until both variables appear in the same data set. Therefore, it will be necessary to merge the variables contained in data sets D and E.

There are actually two ways of merging data sets. Perhaps the simplest way is the one-to-one merging approach. With **one-to-one merging**, observations are simply merged according to their order of appearance in the data sets. For example, imagine that you were to merge data sets D and E using one-to-one merging. In doing this, the SAS System would take the first observation from data set D and pair it with the first observation from data set E, and the result would become the first observation in the new data set (data set F). If the observations in data sets D and E were in exactly the correct sequence, this method would work fine. Unfortunately, if any of the observations were out of sequence, or if one data set contained more observations than another, then this approach could result in the incorrect pairing of observations. For this reason, this text recommends a different strategy for merging: the match-merging approach, described next. For users who are interested in learning more about one-to-one merging, consult Chapters 4 and 9 of *SAS language: reference* or Chapter 17 of *SAS language and procedures: usage*.

Match-merging seems to be the method that is least likely to produce undesirable results. With **match-merging**, both data sets must contain a common variable, so that values for this common variable can be used to combine observations from the two previously existing data sets into observations for the new data set. For example, consider data sets D and E from Table 4.3 and Table 4.4. The variable SOCSEC appears in both of these data sets, so it is a common variable. When the SAS System uses match-merging to merge these two data sets according to values on SOCSEC, it will

- read the social security number for the first subject in data set D

- look for a subject in data set E who has the same social security number

- merge the information from that subject's observation in data set D with his or her information from data set E (if it finds a subject in data set E with the same social security number)

- combine the information into a single observation in the new data set, F.

- repeat this process for all subjects.

As the preceding suggests, the variable that you use as your common variable must be chosen very carefully. Ideally, each subject should be assigned a *unique value* for this common variable. This means that no two subjects should have the same value for the common variable. This objective should be achieved when social security numbers are used as the common variable, because no two people are given the same social security number.

The SAS program for match-merging data sets is somewhat more complex than the program for concatenating data sets. In part, this is because both previously existing data sets must be sorted according to values for the common variable prior to merging. This means that the observations must be rearranged in ascending order with respect to values for the common variable. Fortunately, this is easy to do with PROC SORT, a SAS System procedure that allows you to sort variables. This section shows how PROC SORT can be used to achieve this.

The general form for match-merging two previously existing data sets is presented as follows:

```
PROC SORT  DATA=data-set-1;
   BY  common-variable;
   RUN;
```

```
PROC SORT  DATA=data-set-2;
   BY  common-variable;
   RUN;


DATA  new-data-set-name;
   MERGE  data-set-1  data-set-2;
   BY  common-variable;
   RUN;
```

To illustrate, assume that you wish to match-merge data sets D and E from Table 4.3 and Table 4.4. To do this, use SOCSEC as the common variable. In the following program, these two data sets are input, sorted, and then merged using the match-merge approach:

```
1       DATA  D;
2          INPUT  #1   @1   (NAME)   ($7.)
3                       @9   (SOCSEC) (9.)
4                       @19  (SATV)   (3.)
5                       @23  (SATM)   (3.)   ;
6       CARDS;
7       John     232882121 520 500
8       Sally    222773454 610 640
9       Fred     211447653 490 470
10      Emma     222671234 550 560
11      ;
12
13
14      DATA  E;
15         INPUT  #1   @1   (NAME)   ($7.)
16                      @9   (SOCSEC) (9.)
17                      @19  (GPA)    (4.)   ;
18      CARDS;
19      John     232882121 2.70
20      Sally    222773454 3.25
21      Fred     211447653 2.20
22      Emma     222671234 2.50
23      ;
24
25      PROC SORT  DATA=D;
26         BY  SOCSEC;
27         RUN;
28
```

```
29      PROC SORT  DATA=E;
30         BY  SOCSEC;
31         RUN;
32
33      DATA  F;
34         MERGE  D  E;
35         BY  SOCSEC;
36         RUN;
37
38      PROC PRINT  DATA=F;
39         RUN;
```

In the preceding program, data set D was input in lines 1-11, and data set E was input in lines 14-23. In lines 25-31, both data sets were sorted according to values for SOSEC, and the two data sets were merged according to values of SOSEC in lines 33-36. Finally, the PROC PRINT on lines 38-39 requests a printout of the raw data contained in the new data set.

Output 4.2 contains the results of PROC PRINT, which printed the raw data now contained in data set F. You can see that each observation in this new data set now contains the merged data from the two previously existing data sets D and E. For example, the line for the subject named Fred now contains his scores on the verbal and math sections of the SAT (which came from data set D), as well as his grade point average score (which came from data set E). The same is true for the remaining subjects. It would now be possible to correlate SATV with GPA, if that analysis were desired.

OBS	NAME	SOCSEC	SATV	SATM	GPA
1	Fred	211447653	490	470	2.20
2	Emma	222671234	550	560	2.50
3	Sally	222773454	610	640	3.25
4	John	232882121	520	500	2.70

Output 4.2: Results of Performing PROC PRINT on Data Set F

Notice that the observations in Output 4.2 are not in the same order in which they appeared in tables 4.3 and 4.4. This is because they have now been sorted according to values for SOCSEC by the PROC SORT statements in the preceding SAS program.

Conclusion

After completing this chapter, you should be prepared to modify data sets, isolate subgroups of subjects for analysis, and perform other tasks that are often required when performing empirical research in the social sciences. At this point, you should be prepared to move on to the stage of analyzing data to determine what they *mean*. Some of the most simple statistics for this purpose (descriptive statistics and related procedures) are covered in the following chapter.

References

SAS Institute Inc. (1990). *SAS language: reference, version 6, first edition.* Cary, NC: SAS Institute Inc.

SAS Institute Inc. (1989). *SAS language and procedures: usage, version 6, first edition.* Cary, NC: SAS Institute Inc.

Chapter 5

EXPLORING DATA WITH PROC MEANS, PROC FREQ, PROC PRINT, AND PROC UNIVARIATE

Overview. This chapter illustrates the use of four procedures: PROC MEANS, which may be used to calculate means, standard deviations, and other descriptive statistics for quantitative variables, PROC FREQ, which may be used to construct frequency distributions, PROC PRINT, which may be used to create a printout of the raw data set, and PROC UNIVARIATE, which may be used to test for normality and produce stem-and-leaf plots. Once data are keyed, these procedures can be used to screen for errors, test statistical assumptions, and obtain simple descriptive statistics to be reported in the research article.

Introduction: Why Perform Simple Descriptive Analyses?

The procedures discussed in this chapter are useful for (at least) three important purposes. The first purpose involves the concept of data screening. **Data screening** is the process of carefully reviewing the data to ensure that they were keyed correctly and are being read correctly by the computer. Before conducting any of the more sophisticated analyses to be described in this manual, you should carefully screen your data to make sure that you are not analyzing "garbage": numbers that were accidently punched while keying, impossible values on variables that no one could have obtained, numbers which were keyed in the wrong column, and so forth. The process of data screening does not guarantee that your data are correct, but it does increase the likelihood.

Second, these procedures are useful because they allow you to explore the shape of your data distribution. Among other things, understanding the shape of your data will help you choose the appropriate measure of central tendency (i.e., the mean versus the median). In addition, some statistical procedures require that sample data be drawn from a normally-distributed population, or at least that the sample data do not display a *marked* departure from normality. You can use the procedures discussed here to produce graphic plots of the data, as well as test the null hypothesis that the data are from a normal population.

Finally, the nature of an investigator's research question itself may require the use of a procedure such as PROC MEANS or PROC FREQ to obtain a desired statistic. For example, if your research question is "what is the average age at which women married in 1991?" you could obtain data from a representative sample of women who married in that year, analyze their ages with PROC MEANS, and review the results to determine the mean age.

Similarly, in almost any research article it is desirable to report demographic information about the sample. For example, if a study is performed on a sample that includes subjects from a variety of demographic groups, it is desirable to report the percent of subjects of each gender, the percent of subjects by race, the mean age, and so forth. You can also use PROC MEANS and PROC FREQ to obtain this information.

Example: A Revised Volunteerism Survey

To help illustrate these procedures, assume that you conduct a scaled-down version of your study on volunteerism. You construct a new questionnaire which asks just one question related to helping behavior. The questionnaire also contains an item that assesses subject sex, and another that determines the subject's class in college (e.g., freshman, sophomore). A reproduction of the questionnaire follows:

```
Please indicate the extent to which you agree or disagree with the
following statement:

  1  "I feel a personal responsibility to help needy people in my
     community." (please check your response below)

     (5) _____ Agree Strongly
     (4) _____ Agree Somewhat
     (3) _____ Neither Agree nor Disagree
     (2) _____ Disagree Somewhat
     (1) _____ Disagree Strongly


  2. Your sex (please check one):

     (F) _____ Female
     (M) _____ Male


  3. Your classification as a college student:

     (1) _____ Freshman
     (2) _____ Sophomore
     (3) _____ Junior
     (4) _____ Senior
     (5) _____ Other
```

Notice that this instrument has been printed so that keying the data will be relatively simple. With each variable, the value which will be keyed appears to the left of the corresponding subject response. For example, with question 1 the value "5" appears to the left of "Agree Strongly". This means that the number "5" will be keyed for any subject checking that response. For subjects checking "Disagree Strongly", a "1" will be keyed. Similarly, notice that, for question 2, the letter "F" appears to the left of "Female", so an "F" will be keyed for subjects checking this response.

The following format is used when keying the data:

COLUMN	VARIABLE NAME	EXPLANATION
1	RESNEEDY	Responses to question 1: Subject's perceived responsibility to help the needy
2	(blank)	(blank)
3	SEX	Responses to question 2: Subject's sex
4	(blank)	(blank)
5	CLASS	Responses to question 3: Subject's classification as a college student

You administer the questionnaire to 14 students. The following is the entire SAS program used to analyze the data, including the raw data:

```
1       DATA D1;
2           INPUT   #1   @1   (RESNEEDY)   (1.)
3                        @3   (SEX)        ($1.)
4                        @5   (CLASS)      (1.)    ;
5       CARDS;
6       5 F 1
7       4 M 1
8       5 F 1
9         F 1
10      4 F 1
11      4 F 2
12      1 F 2
13      4 F 2
14      1 F 3
15      5 M
16      4 F 4
17      4 M 4
18      3 F
19      4 F 5
20      ;
```

```
21          PROC MEANS    DATA=D1;
22             VAR RESNEEDY CLASS;
23             RUN;
24          PROC FREQ    DATA=D1;
25             TABLES SEX CLASS RESNEEDY;
26             RUN;
27          PROC PRINT    DATA=D1;
28             VAR RESNEEDY SEX CLASS;
29             RUN;
```

The data obtained from the first subject appears on line 6 of the preceding program. This subject has a value of "5" on the RESNEEDY variable (indicating that she checked "Agree Strongly"), has a value of "F" on the SEX variable (indicating that she is a female), and has a value on "1" on the CLASS variable (indicating that she is a freshman).

Notice that there are some missing data in this data set. On line 9 in the program, you can see that this subject indicated that she was a female freshman, but did not answer question 1. That is why the corresponding space in column 1 is left blank. In addition, there appears to be missing data for the CLASS variable on lines 15 and 18. Missing data are common in research of this nature (questionnaire research).

Computing Descriptive Statistics with PROC MEANS

You can use PROC MEANS to analyze quantitative (numeric) variables. For each variable analyzed, it provides the following information:

- The number of useful cases on which calculations were performed (abbreviated "N" in the output)

- The mean

- The standard deviation

- The minimum (smallest) value observed

- The maximum (largest) value observed

These statistics are produced by default, and some additional statistics (to be described later) may also be requested as an option.

Here is the general form for PROC MEANS:

```
PROC MEANS   DATA=data-set-name
             option-list
             statistic-keyword-list ;
  VAR  variable-list  ;
  RUN;
```

The PROC MEANS statement. The PROC MEANS statement begins with "PROC MEANS" and ends with a semicolon. It is recommended (and on some platforms it is required) that the statement should also specify the name of the data set to be analyzed with the DATA= option.

The "option-list" appearing in the preceding program indicates that you can request a number of options with PROC MEANS, and a complete list of these appears in the *SAS procedures guide* (1990). Some options especially useful for social science research are:

MAXDEC=N
> Specifies the maximum number of decimal places (digits to the right of the decimal point) to be used when printing results; possible range is 0 to 8.

VARDEF=divisor
> Specifies the devisor to be used when calculating variances and covariances. Two possible divisors are:

> > VARDEF=DF   Divisor is the degrees of freedom for the analysis: $(n–1)$. This is the default.

> > VARDEF=N   Divisor is the number of observations, n.

The "statistic-keyword-list" appearing in the program indicates that you can request a number of statistics to replace the default output. Some statistics that may be of particular value in social science research include the following; see the *SAS procedures guide* (1990) for a more complete listing:

NMISS
> The number of observations in the sample that displayed missing data for this variable.

RANGE
> The range of values displayed in the sample.

SUM
> The sum.

CSS
> The corrected sum of squares.

USS
> The uncorrected sum of squares.

VAR   The variance

STDERR   The standard error of the mean.

SKEWNESS   The skewness displayed by the sample. **Skewness** refers to the extent to which the sample distribution departs from the normal curve because of a long "tail" on one side of the distribution. If the long tail appears on the right side of the sample distribution (where the higher values appear), it is described as being **positively skewed**. If the long tail appears on the left side of the distribution (where the lower values appear), it is described as being **negatively skewed**.

KURTOSIS   The kurtosis displayed by the sample. **Kurtosis** refers to the extent to which the sample distribution departs from the normal curve because it is either peaked or flat. If the sample distribution is relatively peaked (tall and skinny), it is described as being **leptokurtic**. If the distribution is relatively flat, it is described as being **platykurtic**.

T   The obtained value of Student's *t* test for testing the null hypothesis that the population mean is zero.

PRT   The *p* value for the preceding *t* test; that is, the probability of obtaining a *t* value this large or larger if the population mean were zero.

To illustrate the use of these options and statistic keywords, assume that you wish to use the MAXDEC option to limit the printing of results to two decimal places, use the VAR keyword to request that the variances of all quantitative variables be printed, and use the KURTOSIS keyword to request that the kurtosis of all quantitative variables be printed. You could do this with the following PROC MEANS statement:

```
   PROC MEANS    DATA=D1   MAXDEC=2   VAR   KURTOSIS ;
```

The VAR statement. Here again is the general form of the statements requesting the MEANS procedure, including the VAR statement:

```
PROC MEANS   DATA=data-set-name
             option-list
             statistic-keyword-list ;
   VAR   variable-list   ;
   RUN;
```

In the place of "variable-list" in the preceding VAR statement, you may list the quantitative variables to be analyzed. Each variable name should be separated by at least one blank space. If no VAR statement is used, SAS will perform PROC MEANS on all of the quantitative variables in the data set. This is true for many other SAS procedures as well, as explained in the following note:

What happens if I do not include a VAR statement? For many SAS System procedures, failure to include a VAR statement causes the system to perform the requested analyses on *all* variables in the data set. For data sets with a large number of variables, leaving off the VAR statement may therefore unintentionally result in a very long output file.

The program used to analyze your data set included the following statements; RESNEEDY and CLASS were specified in the VAR statement so that descriptive statistics would be calculated for both variables:

```
PROC MEANS    DATA=D1;
   VAR RESNEEDY CLASS;
   RUN;
```

Variable	N	Mean	Std Dev	Minimum	Maximum
RESNEEDY	13	3.6923077	1.3155870	1.0000000	5.0000000
CLASS	12	2.2500000	1.4222262	1.0000000	5.0000000

Output 5.1: Results of the MEANS Procedure

Reviewing the output. Output 5.1 contains the results created by the preceding program. Before doing any more sophisticated analyses, you should always perform PROC MEANS on each quantitative variable and carefully review the output to ensure that everything looks right. Under the heading "Variable" is the name of each variable being analyzed. The statistics for that variable appear to the right of the variable name. Below the heading "N" is the number of valid cases, or useful cases, on which calculations were performed. Notice that, in this instance, calculations were performed on only 13 cases for RESNEEDY. This may come as a surprise, because the data set actually contains 14 cases. However, recall that one subject did not respond to this question (question 1 on the survey). It is for this reason that N is equal to 13 rather than 14 for RESNEEDY in these analyses.

You should next review the mean for the variable, to verify that it is a reasonable number. Remember that, with question 1, responses could range from 1 (for "Disagree Strongly") to 5 (for "Agree Strongly"). Therefore, the mean response should be somewhere between 1.00 and 5.00 for the RESNEEDY variable. If it is outside of this range, you will know that some type of error has been made. In the present case the mean for RESNEEDY is 3.69, which is within the predetermined range, so everything looks correct so far.

Using the same reasoning, it is wise to next check the column headed "Minimum". Here you will find the lowest value on RESNEEDY which appeared in the data set. If this is less than 1.00, you will again know that some type of error was made, because 1 was the lowest value that could have been assigned to a subject. On the printout, the minimum value is 1.00, which indicates no problems. Under "Maximum", the largest value observed for that variable is reported. This should not exceed 5.00, because 5 was the largest score a subject could obtain on item 1. The reported maximum value is 5.00, so again it looks like there were no obvious errors in keying the data or writing the program.

Once you have reviewed the results for RESNEEDY, you should also inspect the results for CLASS. If any of the observed values are out of bounds, you should carefully review the program for programming errors, and the data set for miskeyed data. In some cases, you may choose to use PROC PRINT to print out the raw data set because this makes the review easier. PROC PRINT is described later in this chapter.

Creating Frequency Tables with PROC FREQ

The FREQ procedure produces frequency distributions for quantitative variables as well as classification variables. For example, you may use PROC FREQ to determine the percent of subjects who "agreed strongly" with a statement on a questionnaire, the percent who "agreed somewhat," and so forth.

The PROC FREQ and TABLES statements. The general form for the procedure is as follows:

```
PROC FREQ   DATA=data-set-name;
   TABLES variable-list  /  options;
   RUN;
```

In the TABLES statement, you list the names of the variables to be analyzed, with each name separated by at least one blank space. Below are the PROC FREQ and TABLES statements from the program presented earlier in this chapter (analyzing data from the volunteerism survey):

```
   PROC FREQ   DATA=D1;
      TABLES SEX CLASS RESNEEDY;
      RUN;
```

Reviewing the output. These statements will cause the SAS System to create three frequency distributions: one for the SEX variable, one for CLASS, and one for RESNEEDY. A reproduction of this output appears in Output 5.2.

```
                                   Cumulative  Cumulative
      SEX    Frequency   Percent   Frequency    Percent
      ----------------------------------------------------
      F          11       78.6        11         78.6
      M           3       21.4        14        100.0



                                   Cumulative  Cumulative
    CLASS    Frequency   Percent   Frequency    Percent
    ------------------------------------------------------
      1           5       41.7         5         41.7
      2           3       25.0         8         66.7
      3           1        8.3         9         75.0
      4           2       16.7        11         91.7
      5           1        8.3        12        100.0

               Frequency Missing = 2




                                    Cumulative  Cumulative
  RESNEEDY   Frequency   Percent    Frequency    Percent
  --------------------------------------------------------
      1           2       15.4          2         15.4
      3           1        7.7          3         23.1
      4           7       53.8         10         76.9
      5           3       23.1         13        100.0

               Frequency Missing = 1
```

Output 5.2: Results of the FREQ Procedure

Output 5.2 shows that the variable name for the variable being analyzed appears on the far left side of the frequency distribution, just above the dotted line. The values assumed by the variable appear below this variable name. The first distribution provides information about the SEX variable, and below the word "SEX" appear the values "F" and "M." Information about female subjects appears to the right of "F", and information about males appears to the right of "M". When reviewing a frequency distribution, it is useful to think of these different values as representing categories to which a subject may belong.

Under the heading "Frequency", the output indicates the number of individuals who belong in a given category. Here, you can see that 11 subjects were female, while 3 were male. Below

"Percent", the percent of subjects in each category appears. The table shows that 78.6% of the subjects were female, while 21.4% were male.

Under "Cumulative Frequency" is the number of observations that appear in the current category plus all of the preceding categories. For example, the first (top) category for SEX was "female". There were 11 subjects in that category, so the cumulative frequency was 11. The next category was "male", and there were 3 subjects in that category. The cumulative frequency for the "male" category was therefore 14 (because 11 + 3 = 14). In the same way, the "Cumulative Percent" category provides the percent of observations that appear in the current category plus all of the preceding categories.

The next table presents results for the CLASS variable. Notice that just below this table appears "Frequency Missing = 2". This indicates that there were missing data for two subjects on the CLASS variable, a fact that may be verified by reviewing the data as they appear in the preceding program: CLASS values are blank for two subjects. The existence of two missing values means that there are only 12 valid cases for the CLASS variable. In support of this, the "Cumulative Frequency" column shows an ultimate value (at the bottom of table) of only 12.

If no subject appears in a given category, the value representing that category will not appear in the frequency distribution at all. This is demonstrated with the third table, which presents the frequency distribution for the RESNEEDY variable. Notice that, under the "RESNEEDY" heading, you may find only the values "1", "3", "4", and "5". The value "2" does not appear because none of the subjects checked "Disagree Somewhat" for question 1.

How do I include missing data in my frequency table? By default, missing values are not printed as values in the frequency table, and do not go into the calculation of the percentages, cumulative frequencies, or cumulative percentages. However, it is possible to include missing values in the table by including the MISSPRINT option in the TABLES statement. In the resulting table, missing values will be identified with a period ("."). In addition, it is also possible to request that missing values be included in the computation of statistics by including the MISSING option in the TABLES statement. An example of statements requesting these options is:

```
PROC FREQ   DATA=D1;
   TABLES SEX CLASS RESNEEDY  /  MISSPRINT   MISSING;
   RUN;
```

Printing Raw Data with PROC PRINT

PROC PRINT can be used to create a printout of your raw data as it exists in the computer's internal memory. The output of PROC PRINT shows each subject's value on each of the variables requested. You may use this procedure with both quantitative variables and classification variables. The general form is:

```
PROC PRINT    DATA=data-set-name;
  VAR  variable-list  ;
  RUN;
```

In the variable list, you may request any variable that has been specified in the INPUT statement, as well as any new variable which has been created from existing variables. If you do not include the VAR statement, then all existing variables will be printed. The program presented earlier in this chapter included the following PROC PRINT statements:

```
      PROC PRINT    DATA=D1;
         VAR RESNEEDY SEX CLASS;
         RUN;
```

These statements produce Output 5.3.

OBS	RESNEEDY	SEX	CLASS
1	5	F	1
2	4	M	1
3	5	F	1
4	.	F	1
5	4	F	1
6	4	F	2
7	1	F	2
8	4	F	2
9	1	F	3
10	5	M	.
11	4	F	4
12	4	M	4
13	3	F	.
14	4	F	5

Output 5.3: Results of the PRINT Procedure

The first column of output is headed "OBS" for "observation." This variable is created by SAS to give an observation number to each subject. The second column provides the raw data for the RESNEEDY variable, the third column displays the SEX variable, and the last displays the CLASS variable. The output shows that observation 1 (subject 1) displayed a value of 5 on RESNEEDY, was a female, and displayed a value of 1 on the CLASS variable. Notice that SAS prints periods where missing values appeared.

PROC PRINT is helpful for verifying that your data are keyed correctly, and that SAS is reading the data correctly. It is particularly useful for studies with a large number of variables such as when you use a questionnaire with a large number of questions. In these situations, it is often difficult to visually inspect the data as they exist in the SAS program file. In the SAS program file, subject responses are often keyed immediately adjacent to each other, making it difficult, for example, to determine just which number represents question 24 as opposed to question 25. When the data are printed using PROC PRINT, however, the variables are separated from each other and are clearly labeled with their variable names.

After keying questionnaire data, you should compare the results of PROC PRINT with several of the questionnaires as they were actually filled out by subjects. Verify that a subject's responses on the PROC PRINT output correspond to the original responses on the questionnaire. If not, it is likely that mistakes were made in either keying the data or in writing the SAS program.

Testing for Normality with PROC UNIVARIATE

The normal distribution is a symmetrical, bell-shaped theoretical distribution of values. The shape of the normal distribution is portrayed in Figure 5.1.

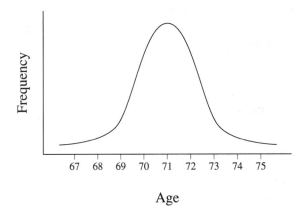

Figure 5.1: The Normal Distribution

To understand the distribution in Figure 5.1, assume that you are interested in conducting research on people who live in retirement communities. Imagine for a moment that it is possible to assess the age of every person in this population. To summarize this distribution, you prepare a figure similar to Figure 5.1: the variable AGE is plotted on the horizontal axis, and the frequency of persons at each age is plotted on the vertical axis. Figure 5.1 suggests that many of your subjects are around 71 years of age, since the distributions of ages "peaks" near the age of 71. This suggests that the mean of this distribution will likely be somewhere around 71. Notice also that most of your subjects' ages are between 67 (near the lower end of the distribution) and 75 (near the upper end of the distribution). This is the approximate range of ages that we would expect for persons living in a retirement community.

Why test for normality? Normality is an important concept in data analysis because there are at least two problems that may result when data are not normally distributed. The first problem is that markedly non-normal data may lead to incorrect conclusions in inferential statistical analyses. Many inferential procedures are based on the assumption that the sample of observations was drawn from a normally distributed population. If this assumption is violated, the statistic may give misleading findings. For example, the independent groups *t* test assumes that both samples in the study were drawn from normally distributed populations. If this assumption is violated, then performing the analysis may cause you to incorrectly reject the null hypothesis (or incorrectly fail to reject the null hypothesis). Under these circumstances, you should instead analyze the data using some procedure that does not assume normality (perhaps some nonparametric procedure).

The second problem is that markedly non-normal data may have a biasing effect on correlation coefficients, as well as more sophisticated procedures that are based on correlation coefficients. For example, assume that you compute the Pearson correlation between two variables. If one or both of these variables are markedly non-normal, this may cause your obtained correlation coefficient to be much larger (or much smaller) than the actual correlation between these variables in the population. Your obtained correlation is, essentially, just garbage. To make matters worse, many sophisticated data analysis procedures (such as principal component analysis) are actually performed on a matrix of correlation coefficients. If some or all of these correlations are distorted due to departures from normality, then the results of the analyses may again be misleading. For this reason, many experts recommend that researchers routinely check their data for major departures from normality prior to performing sophisticated analyses such as principal component analysis (e.g., Rummel, 1970).

Departures from normality. Assume that you draw a random sample of 18 subjects from your population of persons living in retirement communities. There are a wide variety of ways that your data may display a departure from normality.

Figure 5.2 shows the distribution of ages in two samples of subjects drawn from the population of retirees. This figure is somewhat different from Figure 5.1 because the distributions have been "turned on their sides" so that age is now plotted on the vertical axis rather than on the horizontal axis (this is so that these figures will be more similar to the stem-and-leaf plots produced by PROC UNIVARIATE, discussed in a later section) . Each small circle in a given distribution of Figure 5.2 represents one subject. For example, in the distribution for Sample A, you can see that there is one subject at age 75, one subject at age 74, two subjects at age 73, three subjects at age 72, and so forth. The ages of the 18 subjects in Sample A range from a low of 67 to a high of 75.

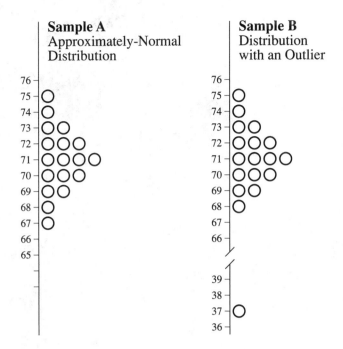

Figure 5.2: Sample with an Approximately Normal Distribution and a Sample with an Outlier

The data in Sample A form an approximately normal distribution (called *approximately normal* because it is difficult to form a perfectly normal distribution using a small sample of just 18 cases). An inferential test (discussed later) will show that Sample A does not demonstrate a significant departure from normality. Therefore, it would probably be appropriate to include the data in Sample A in an independent samples *t* test, for example.

In contrast, there are problems with the data in Sample B. Notice that its distribution is very similar to that of Sample A, except that there is an outlier at the lower end of the distribution. An **outlier** is an extreme value that differs substantially in size from the other values in the distribution. In this case, the outlier represents a subject whose age is only 37. Obviously, this person's age is markedly different from that of the other subjects in your study. Later, you will see that this outlier causes the data set to demonstrate a significant departure from normality, making the data inappropriate for some statistical procedures. When you observe an outlier such as this, it is important to determine whether it should be either corrected or simply deleted from the data set. Obviously, if the outlier exists because an error was made in keying the data, it should be corrected.

A sample may also depart from normality because it displays kurtosis. **Kurtosis** refers to the peakedness of the distribution. The two samples displayed in Figure 5.3 demonstrate different types of kurtosis:

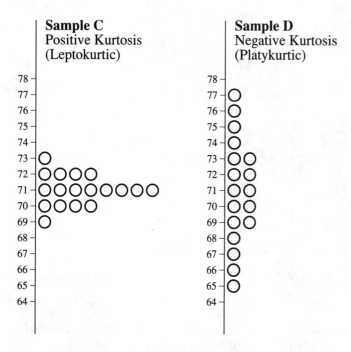

Figure 5.3: Samples Displaying Positive versus Negative Kurtosis

Sample C in Figure 5.3 displays **positive kurtosis**, which means that the distribution is relatively peaked (tall and skinny) rather than flat. Notice that, with Sample C, there are a relatively large number of subjects who cluster around the central part of the distribution (around age 71). This is what makes the distribution peaked (relative to Sample A, for example). Distributions with positive kurtosis are also called **leptokurtic**.

In contrast, Sample D in the same figure displays **negative kurtosis**, which means that the distribution is relatively flat. Flat distributions are sometimes also described as being **platykurtic**.

In addition to kurtosis, distributions may also demonstrate varying degrees of **skewness**, or sidedness. A distribution is skewed if the tail on one side of the distribution is longer than the tail on the other side. The distributions in Figure 5.4 show two different types of skewness:

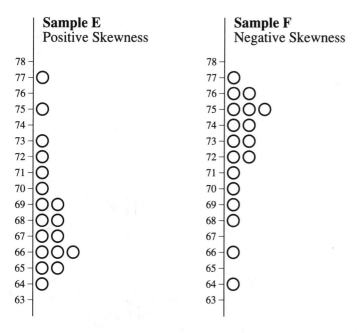

Figure 5.4: Samples Displaying Positive versus Negative Skewness

Consider Sample E in Figure 5.4. Notice that the biggest number of subjects in this distribution tend to cluster around the age of 66. The tail of the distribution that stretches above 66 (from 67 to 77) is relatively long, while the tail of the distribution that stretches below 66 (from 65 to 64) is relatively short. Clearly, this distribution is skewed. A distribution is said to display **positive skewness** if the longer tail of a distribution points in the direction of *higher* values. You can see that Sample E displays positive skewness, because its longer tail points toward larger numbers such as 75, 77, and so forth.

On the other hand, if the longer tail of a distribution points in the direction of lower values, the distribution is said to display **negative skewness.** You can see that Sample F of Figure 5.4 displays negative skewness because in that sample the longer tail points downward, in the direction of lower values (such as 66 and 64).

General form for PROC UNIVARIATE. Like the MEANS procedure, PROC UNIVARIATE provides a number of descriptive statistics for quantitative variables, including the mean, standard deviation, kurtosis, and skewness. However, PROC UNIVARIATE has the added advantage of also printing a significance test for the null hypothesis that the data come from a normally distributed population. The procedure also provides plots that will help you understand the shape of your sample's distribution, along with additional information that will help you understand *why* your data depart from normality (if, indeed, they do). This text describes just a few of the features of PROC UNIVARIATE; for a complete listing, see the *SAS procedures guide* (1990).

Here is the general form for the PROC UNIVARIATE statements that produce the output discussed in this chapter:

```
PROC UNIVARIATE   DATA=data-set-name   NORMAL   PLOT;
   VAR variable-list;
   ID identification-variable;
   RUN;
```

In the preceding program, the NORMAL option requests a significance test for the null hypothesis that the sample data are from a normally distributed population. The Shapiro-Wilk statistic is printed for samples of 2000 or less; for larger samples the Kolmogorov statistic is printed. See Chapter 42 of the *SAS procedures guide* (1990) for details.

The PLOT option of the preceding program produces a stem-and-leaf plot, a box plot, and a normal probability plot, each of which is useful for understanding the shape of the sample's distribution. This text shows how to interpret the stem-and-leaf plot; see Schlotzhauer and Littell (1991) for guidance in interpreting box plots and normal probability plots.

The names of the variables to be analyzed should be listed in the VAR statement. The ID statement is optional, and is useful for identifying outliers. PROC UNIVARIATE prints an "extremes" table that lists the five largest and five smallest values in the data set. These values are identified by the identification variable listed in the ID statement. For example, assume that AGE (subject age) is listed in the VAR statement, and SOCSEC (for subject social security number) is listed in the ID statement. PROC UNIVARIATE will print the social security numbers for the subjects with the five largest and five smallest values on AGE. This should make it easier to identify the specific subject who contributes an outlier to your data set (this use of the extremes table is illustrated here).

Results for an approximately normal distribution. For purposes of illustration, assume that you wish to analyze the data that are illustrated as Sample A of Figure 5.2 (the approximately normal distribution). You prepare a SAS program in which subject age is keyed in a variable called AGE, and subject identification numbers are keyed in a variable called SUBJECT. Here is the entire program that will input these data and analyze them using PROC UNIVARIATE:

```
1           DATA D1;
2              INPUT    #1    @1    (SUBJECT)    (2.)
3                             @4    (AGE)        (2.)    ;
4           CARDS;
5            1 72
6            2 69
7            3 75
8            4 71
9            5 71
10           6 73
11           7 70
12           8 67
13           9 71
14          10 72
15          11 73
16          12 68
17          13 69
18          14 70
19          15 70
20          16 71
21          17 74
22          18 72
23           ;
24          PROC UNIVARIATE    DATA=D1    NORMAL    PLOT;
25             VAR AGE;
26             ID SUBJECT;
27             RUN;
```

The preceding program requests that PROC UNIVARIATE be performed on the variable AGE. Values of the variable SUBJECT will be used to identify outlying values of AGE in the extremes table.

With LINESIZE=80, the preceding program would produce two pages of output. This output would contain:

- a **moments table** that includes the mean, standard deviation, variance, skewness, kurtosis, and normality test, along with other statistics

- a **quantiles table** that provides the mode, median, 25th percentile, 75th percentile, and related information

- an **extremes table** that provides the five highest values and five lowest values on the variable being analyzed

- a stem-and-leaf plot, box plot, and normal probability plot.

Output 5.4 includes the moments table, quantiles table, and extremes table for the analysis of Sample A.

```
                              Univariate Procedure

Variable=AGE


                                  Moments

           N                  18   Sum Wgts               18
           Mean               71   Sum                  1278
           Std Dev      2.057983   Variance         4.235294
           Skewness            0   Kurtosis         -0.13576
           USS             90810   CSS                    72
           CV           2.898568   Std Mean         0.485071
           T:Mean=0     146.3702   Pr>|T|             0.0001
           Num ^= 0           18   Num > 0                18
           M(Sign)             9   Pr>=|M|            0.0001
           Sgn Rank         85.5   Pr>=|S|            0.0001
           W:Normal      0.98356   Pr<W               0.9666


                             Quantiles(Def=5)

           100% Max           75        99%             75
            75% Q3            72        95%             75
            50% Med           71        90%             74
            25% Q1            70        10%             68
             0% Min           67         5%             67
                                         1%             67

           Range              8
           Q3-Q1              2
           Mode              71


                                 Extremes

           Lowest      ID      Highest      ID
               67(      8)          72(     18)
               68(     12)          73(      6)
               69(     13)          73(     11)
               69(      2)          74(     17)
               70(     15)          75(      3)
```

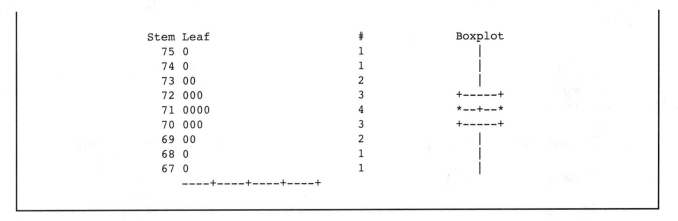

```
Stem Leaf                       #            Boxplot
   75 0                         1               |
   74 0                         1               |
   73 00                        2               |
   72 000                       3            +-----+
   71 0000                      4            *--+--*
   70 000                       3            +-----+
   69 00                        2               |
   68 0                         1               |
   67 0                         1               |
      ----+----+----+----+
```

Output 5.4: Tables from PROC UNIVARIATE for Sample A

On the far-left side of Output 5.4, the note "Variable=AGE" indicates that AGE is the name of the variable being analyzed by PROC UNIVARIATE. The moments table is the first table reproduced in Output 5.4. On the upper-left side of the moments table is the heading "N", and to the right of this you can see that the analysis was based on 18 observations. Below "N" are the headings "Mean" and "Std Dev"; to the right of these you can see that the mean and standard deviation for AGE were 71 and 2.06, respectively.

To the right of "Skewness" you can see that the skewness statistic for AGE is zero. In interpreting the skewness statistic, keep in mind the following:

- A skewness value of zero means that the distribution is not skewed; in other words, this means that the distribution is symmetrical, that neither tail is longer than the other.

- A positive skewness value means that the distribution is positively skewed, that the longer tail points toward higher values in the distribution (as with Sample E of Figure 5.4).

- A negative skewness value means that the distribution is negatively skewed, that the longer tail points toward lower values in the distribution (as with Sample F of Figure 5.4).

Since the AGE variable of Sample A displays a skewness value of zero, we know that neither tail is longer than the other in this sample.

A closer look at the moments table of Output 5.4 shows that it actually consists of two columns of statistics. The column on the left provides statistics such as the sample size, the mean, the standard deviation, and so forth. The column on the right contains headings such as "Sum Wgts", "Sum", and "Variance". Notice that in this right-hand column, the fourth entry down has the heading "Kurtosis" (this appears just below "Variance"). To the right of "Kurtosis", you can see that the kurtosis statistic for AGE is –0.13576, which rounds to –.14. When interpreting this kurtosis statistic, keep in mind the following:

- A kurtosis value of zero means that the distribution displays no kurtosis; in other words, the distribution is neither relatively peaked nor is it relatively flat, compared to the normal distribution.

- A positive kurtosis value means that the distribution is relatively peaked, or leptokurtic.

- A negative kurtosis value means that the distribution is relatively flat, or platykurtic.

The small negative kurtosis value of –.14 in Output 5.4 indicates that Sample A is slightly flat, or platykurtic.

The last entry in the left column of the moments table (headed "W:Normal") provides the Shapiro-Wilk statistic that tests the null hypothesis that the sample data were drawn from a normally distributed population. To the right of "W:Normal", you can see that the value for this statistic is 0.98356. To the immediate right of this statistic is its corresponding p value. This p value appears as the last entry in the right column of the moments table, to the right of the heading "Pr<W". In the present case, the p value is 0.9666. Remember that this statistic tests the null hypothesis that the sample data are from a normal distribution. This p value is very large at .9666, meaning that there are 9,666 chances in 10,000 that you would obtain the present results if the data were drawn from a normal population. In other words, it is very likely that you would obtain the present results if the sample were from a normal population. Because this statistic gives so little evidence to reject the null hypothesis, you can tentatively accept it, and assume that the sample was drawn from a normally-distributed population (this makes sense when you review the shape of the distribution of Sample A in Figure 5.2: the sample data clearly display an approximately normal distribution). In general, you should reject the null hypothesis of normality only when the p value is less than .05.

Results for a distribution with an outlier. The data of Sample A in Figure 5.2 displayed an approximately normal distribution. For purposes of contrast, assume that you now use PROC UNIVARIATE to analyze the data of Sample B from Figure 5.2. You will remember that Sample B was similar in shape to sample A, except that Sample B contained an outlier: the lowest value in Sample B was 37, which was an extremely low score compared to the other values in the sample (if necessary, turn back to Figure 5.2 at this time to verify this).

The raw data from Sample B follow. Columns 1-2 contain values of SUBJECT, the subject identification number, and columns 4-5 contain AGE values. Notice that these data are identical to those of Sample A, except for subject 8. In Sample A, subject 8's age was listed as 67; in Sample B, it is listed as 37.

```
 1 72
 2 69
 3 75
 4 71
 5 71
 6 73
 7 70
 8 37
 9 71
10 72
11 73
12 68
13 69
14 70
15 70
16 71
17 74
18 72
```

When analyzed with PROC UNIVARIATE, the preceding data would again produce two pages of output. Some of the results of this analysis are presented in Output 5.5.

```
                         Univariate Procedure

Variable=AGE

                             Moments

                N               18   Sum Wgts           18
                Mean      69.33333   Sum              1248
                Std Dev   8.267584   Variance     68.35294
                Skewness  -3.90499   Kurtosis     16.03325
                USS          87690   CSS              1162
                CV         11.9244   Std Mean     1.948688
                T:Mean=0  35.57949   Pr>|T|         0.0001
                Num ^= 0        18   Num > 0            18
                M(Sign)          9   Pr>=|M|        0.0001
                Sgn Rank      85.5   Pr>=|S|        0.0001
                W:Normal  0.458479   Pr<W           0.0001
```

```
                            Quantiles(Def=5)

            100%  Max          75         99%          75
             75%  Q3           72         95%          75
             50%  Med          71         90%          74
             25%  Q1           70         10%          68
              0%  Min          37          5%          37
                                           1%          37

            Range             38
            Q3-Q1              2
            Mode             71


                              Extremes

         Lowest      ID        Highest     ID
             37(       8)          72(      18)
             68(      12)          73(       6)
             69(      13)          73(      11)
             69(       2)          74(      17)
             70(      15)          75(       3)


    Stem Leaf                        #         Boxplot
       7 5                           1            |
       7 0001111222334              13         +-----+
       6 899                         3            +
       6
       5
       5
       4
       4
       3 7                           1            *
         ----+----+----+----+
    Multiply Stem.Leaf by 10**+1
```

Output 5.5: Tables from PROC UNIVARIATE for Sample B

By comparing the moments table of Output 5.5 (for Sample B) to that of Output 5.4 (for Sample A) you can see that the inclusion of the outlier has had a dramatic effect on some of the descriptive statistics for AGE. The mean of Sample B is now 69.33, down from the mean of 71 found for Sample A. More dramatic is the effect that the outlier has had on the standard deviation. With the approximately normal distribution, the standard deviation was only 2.05; with the outlier included, the standard deviation was much larger at 8.27.

Output 5.5 shows that the skewness index for Sample B is –3.90. A negative skewness index such as this is just what you would expect: the outlier has, in essence, created a long tail that points toward the lower values in the AGE distribution, and you will remember that this normally results in a negative skewness index.

Output 5.5 shows that the test for normality for Sample B results in a Shapiro-Wilk statistic of .458479 (to the right of "W:Normal") and a corresponding *p* value of .0001 (to the right of "Pr<W"). Because this *p* value is below .05, you reject the null hypothesis, and tentatively conclude that Sample B was not drawn from a normally distributed population. In other words, you can conclude that Sample B displays a statistically significant departure from normality.

The extremes table for Sample B appears just below the quantiles table in Output 5.5. On the left side of the extremes table, below the heading "Lowest", PROC UNIVARIATE prints the lowest values observed for the variable specified in the VAR statement (AGE, in this case). Here, you can see that the lowest values were 37, 68, 69, 69, and 70. To the immediate right of each value (appearing within parentheses) is the subject identification number for the subject who contributed that value to the data set. The subject identification variable is the variable specified in the ID statement (SUBJECT, in this case). Reviewing these values in parentheses shows you that subject 8 contributed the AGE value of 37, subject 12 contributed the AGE value of 68, and so forth. Compare the results in this extremes table with the actual raw data (reproduced earlier) to verify that these are in fact the specific subjects who provided these values on AGE.

On the right side of the extremes table, similar information is provided, although in this case it is provided for the five *highest* values observed in the data set. Under the heading "Highest" (and reading from the bottom up), you can see that the highest value on age was 75, and it was provided by subject 3, the next highest value was 74, provided by subject 17, and so forth.

This extremes table is useful for quickly identifying the specific subjects who have contributed outliers to a data set. For example, in the present case you were able to determine immediately that it was subject 8 who contributed the low outlier on AGE. Using the extremes table may be unnecessary when working with a very small data set (as in the present situation), but it can be invaluable when dealing with a large data set. For example, if you know that you have an outlier in a data set with 1,000 observations, the extremes table can immediately identify the subject who contributed the outlier. This will save you the tedious chore of examining data lines for each of the 1,000 observations individually.

Understanding the stem-and-leaf plot. A stem-and-leaf plot provides a visual representation of your data, using conventions somewhat similar to those used with Figures 5.2, 5.3, and 5.4. Output 5.6 provides the stem-and-leaf plot for Sample A (the approximately-normal distribution):

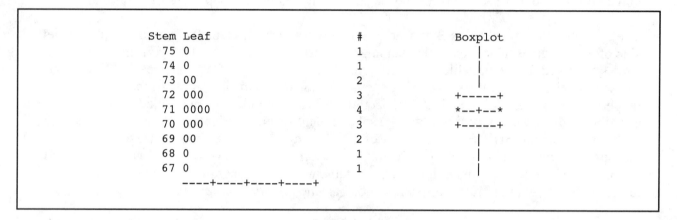

```
          Stem Leaf                        #          Boxplot
           75 0                            1            |
           74 0                            1            |
           73 00                           2            |
           72 000                          3         +------+
           71 0000                         4         *--+--*
           70 000                          3         +------+
           69 00                           2            |
           68 0                            1            |
           67 0                            1            |
              ----+----+----+----+
```

Output 5.6: Stem-and-Leaf Plot from PROC UNIVARIATE for Sample A (Approximately Normal Distribution)

To understand a stem-and-leaf plot, it is necessary to think of a given subject's score on AGE as consisting of a "stem" and a "leaf." The **stem** is that part of the value that appears to the left of the decimal point, and the **leaf** consists of that part that appears to the right of the decimal point. For example, subject 8 in Sample A had a value on AGE of 67.0 For this subject, the stem is 67 (because it appears to the left of the decimal point), and the leaf is 0 (because it appears to the right). Subject 12 had a value on age of 68.0, so the stem for this value is 68, and the leaf is again 0.

In the stem-and-leaf plot of Output 5.6, the vertical axis (running up and down) plots the various stems that could be encountered in the data set (these appear under the heading "Stem"). Reading from the top down, these stems are 75, 74, 73, and so forth. Notice that at the very bottom of the plot is the stem 67. To the right of this stem appears a single leaf (a single 0). This means that there was only one subject in Sample A with a stem-and-leaf of 67.0 (that is, a value on AGE of 67.0). Move up one line, and you see the stem 68. To the right of this, again one leaf appears (that is, one zero appears), meaning that only one subject had a score on AGE of 68.0. Move up an additional line, and you see the stem 69. To the right of this, two leaves appear (that is, two zeros appear). This means that there were two subjects with a stem-and-leaf of 69.0 (two subjects with values on AGE of 69.0). Continuing up the plot in this fashion, you can see that there were three subjects with at age 70, four subjects at age 71, three at age 72, two at age 73, one at 74, and one at 75.

On the right side of the stem-and-leaf plot appears a column headed "#". This column prints the number of observations that appear at each stem. Reading from the bottom up, this column again confirms that there was one subject with a score on age of 67, one with a score of 68, two with a score of 69, and so forth.

Reviewing the stem-and-leaf plot of Output 5.6 shows that its shape is very similar to the shape portrayed for Sample A in Figure 5.2. This is to be expected, since both figures use similar conventions and both describe the data of Sample A. In Output 5.6, notice that the shape of the distribution is symmetrical: neither tail is longer than the other. This, too, is to be expected, since Sample A demonstrated zero skewness.

In some cases, the stem-and-leaf plot produced by UNIVARIATE will be somewhat more complex than the one reproduced in Output 5.6. For example, Output 5.7 includes the stem-and-leaf plot produced by Sample B from Figure 5.2 (the distribution with an outlier). Consider the stem-and-leaf at the very bottom of this plot. The stem for this entry is 3, and the leaf is 7, meaning that the stem-and-leaf is 3.7. Does this mean that some subject had a score on AGE of 3.7? Not at all.

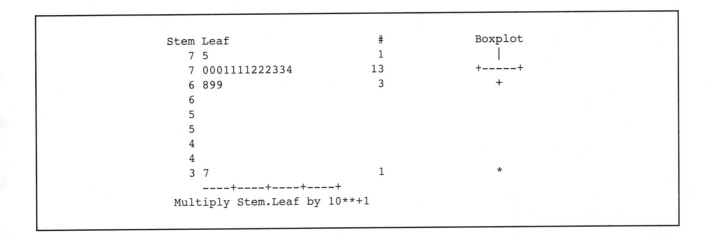

```
     Stem Leaf                      #            Boxplot
       7 5                          1               |
       7 0001111222334            13           +-----+
       6 899                       3               +
       6
       5
       5
       4
       4
       3 7                         1               *
          ----+----+----+----+
       Multiply Stem.Leaf by 10**+1
```

Output 5.7: Stem-and-Leaf Plot from PROC UNIVARIATE for Sample B (Distribution with Outlier)

Notice the note at the bottom of this plot, which says "Multiply Stem.Leaf by 10**+1". This means "Multiply the stem-and-leaf by 10 raised to the first power." 10 raised to the first power, of course, is merely 10. This means that to find a subject's *actual* value on AGE, you must multiply a stem-and-leaf for that subject by 10.

For example, consider what this means for the stem-and-leaf at the bottom of this plot. This stem-and-leaf was 3.7. To find the actual score that corresponds to this stem-and-leaf, you would perform the following multiplication:

```
3.7 X 10 = 37
```

This means that, for the subject who had a stem-and-leaf of 3.7, the actual value of AGE was 37.

Move up one line in the plot, and you come to the stem "4". However, note that there are no leaves for this stem, which means that there were no subjects with a stem of 4.0. Reading up the plot, note that no leaves appear until you reach the stem "6". The leaves on this line suggest that there was one subject with a stem-and-leaf of 6.8, and two subjects with a stem-and-leaf of 6.9. Multiply these values by 10 to determine their actual values on AGE:

```
6.8 X 10 = 68
6.9 X 10 = 69
```

Move up an additional line, and note that there are actually two stems for the value 7. The first stem (moving up the plot) includes stem-and-leaf values from 7.0 through 7.4, while the next stem includes stem-and-leaf values from 7.5 through 7.9. Reviewing values in these rows, you can see that there are three subjects with a stem-and-leaf of 7.0, four with a stem-and-leaf of 7.1, and so forth.

The note at the bottom of the plot told you to multiply each stem-and-leaf by 10 raised to the first power. However, sometimes this note will tell you to multiply by 10 raised to a different power. For example, consider the following note:

```
Multiply Stem.Leaf by 10**+2
```

This note tells you to multiply by 10 raised to the second power, or 100. Notice what some of the actual values on AGE would have been if this note had appeared (needless to say, such large values would not have made sense for the AGE variable):

```
6.8 X 100 = 680
6.9 X 100 = 690
```

All of this multiplication probably seems somewhat tedious at this point, but there is a simple rule that you can use to ease the interpretation of the note that sometimes appears at the bottom of a stem-and-leaf plot. With respect to this note, remember that the power to which 10 is raised indicates the *number of decimal places* you should move the decimal point in the stem-and-leaf. Once you have moved the decimal point this number of spaces, your stem-and-leaf will represent the actual value that you are interested in. For example, consider the following note:

```
Multiply Stem.Leaf by 10**+1
```

This note tells you to multiply the stem-and-leaf by 10 raised to the power of one; in other words, move the decimal point *one space to the right*. Imagine that you start with a stem-and-leaf of 3.7. Moving the decimal point one space to the right results in an actual value on AGE of 37. If you begin with a stem-and-leaf of 6.8, this becomes 68.

On the other hand, consider if the plot had included this note:

```
Multiply Stem.Leaf by 10**+2
```

It would have been necessary to move the decimal point *two* decimal spaces to the right. In this case, a stem-and-leaf of 3.7 would become 370; 6.8 would become 680 (again, these values would not make sense for the AGE variable; they are used only for purposes of demonstration). Finally, remember that, if no note appears at the bottom of the plot, it is not necessary to move the decimal points in the stem-and-leaf values at all.

Results for distributions demonstrating skewness. Output 5.8 provides some results from the PROC UNIVARIATE analysis of Sample E from Figure 5.4. You will recall that this sample demonstrated a positive skew.

```
                        Univariate Procedure

Variable=AGE


                              Moments

        N                    18   Sum Wgts              18
        Mean           68.77778   Sum                 1238
        Std Dev        3.622731   Variance        13.12418
        Skewness       0.869826   Kurtosis        0.110096
        USS               85370   CSS             223.1111
        CV             5.267299   Std Mean        0.853886
        T:Mean=0       80.54679   Pr>|T|            0.0001
        Num ^= 0             18   Num > 0               18
        M(Sign)               9   Pr>=|M|           0.0001
        Sgn Rank           85.5   Pr>=|S|           0.0001
        W:Normal       0.929487   Pr<W              0.1944


                          Quantiles(Def=5)

        100% Max             77      99%              77
         75% Q3              71      95%              77
         50% Med             68      90%              75
         25% Q1              66      10%              65
          0% Min             64       5%              64
                                     1%              64

        Range                13
        Q3-Q1                 5
        Mode                 66


                             Extremes

        Lowest    ID        Highest    ID
           64(     7)          71(     11)
           65(    15)          72(      6)
           65(    10)          73(     16)
           66(    14)          75(     13)
           66(     8)          77(      1)
```

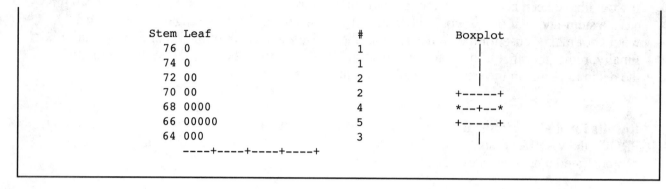

```
      Stem Leaf                     #             Boxplot
        76 0                        1               |
        74 0                        1               |
        72 00                       2               |
        70 00                       2            +------+
        68 0000                     4            *--+--*
        66 00000                    5            +------+
        64 000                      3               |
           ----+----+----+----+
```

Output 5.8: Tables and Stem-and-Leaf Plot from PROC UNIVARIATE for Sample E (Positive Skewness)

Remember that when the approximately normal distribution was analyzed, it displayed a skewness index of zero. In contrast, note that the skewness index for Sample E in Output 5.8 is 0.869826, which rounds to .87. This positive skewness index is what you would expect, given the positive skew of the data. The skew is also reflected in the stem-and-leaf plot that appears in Output 5.8: notice the relatively long tail that points in the direction of higher values for age (such as 74 and 76).

Although this sample displays a positive skew, it does not display a significant departure from normality. In the moments table of Output 5.8, you can see that the Shapiro-Wilk statistic (to the right of "W:Normal") is .93; its corresponding *p* value (to the right of "Pr<W") is .1944. Because this *p* value is greater than .05, you may not reject the null hypothesis that the data were drawn from a normal population. With small samples such as the one investigated here, this test is not very powerful (that is, is not very sensitive). This is why the sample was not found to display a significant departure from normality, even though it was clearly skewed.

For purposes of contrast, Output 5.9 presents the results of an analysis of Sample F from Figure 5.4. Sample F displayed a negative skew, and this is reflected in the skewness index of −.87 that appears in Output 5.9. Once again, the Shapiro-Wilk test at the bottom of the moments table shows that the sample does not demonstrate a significant departure from normality.

```
                           Univariate Procedure

Variable=AGE


                               Moments

                N             18   Sum Wgts          18
                Mean     72.22222  Sum             1300
                Std Dev  3.622731  Variance     13.12418
                Skewness -0.86983  Kurtosis     0.110096
                USS         94112  CSS          223.1111
                CV        5.01609  Std Mean     0.853886
                T:Mean=0 84.58064  Pr>|T|         0.0001
```

```
          Num ^= 0          18   Num > 0            18
          M(Sign)            9   Pr>=|M|        0.0001
          Sgn Rank        85.5   Pr>=|S|        0.0001
          W:Normal    0.929487   Pr<W           0.1944


                      Quantiles(Def=5)

        100% Max       77        99%        77
         75% Q3        75        95%        77
         50% Med       73        90%        76
         25% Q1        70        10%        66
          0% Min       64         5%        64
                                  1%        64

        Range          13
        Q3-Q1           5
        Mode           75


                         Extremes

          Lowest    ID      Highest    ID
             64(    11)       75(     13)
             66(     2)       75(     18)
             68(    10)       76(     12)
             69(     8)       76(     14)
             70(     5)       77(      7)


      Stem Leaf                      #         Boxplot
        76 000                       3            |
        74 00000                     5         +-----+
        72 0000                      4         *--+--*
        70 00                        2         +-----+
        68 00                        2            |
        66 0                         1            |
        64 0                         1            |
           ----+----+----+----+
```

Output 5.9: Tables and Stem-and-Leaf Plot from PROC UNIVARIATE for Sample F (Negative Skewness)

The stem-and-leaf plot of Output 5.9 reveals a long tail that points in the direction of lower values for AGE (such as 64 and 66). This, of course, is the type of plot that you would expect for a negatively skewed distribution.

Conclusion

Regardless of what other statistical procedures you use in an investigation, you should always *begin* the data analysis process by performing the simple analyses described here. This will help ensure that the data set and program do not contain any errors that, if left unidentified, could lead to incorrect conclusions and even to ultimate retractions of published findings. Once the data have survived this initial screening, you may move forward to the more sophisticated procedures described in the remainder of this text.

References

Rummel, R. J. (1970). *Applied factor analysis*. Evanston, IL: Northwestern University Press.

SAS Institute Inc. (1990). *SAS procedures guide, version 6, third edition*. Cary, NC: SAS Institute Inc.

Schlotzhauer, S. D. & Littell, R. C. (1991). *SAS system for elementary statistical analysis*. Cary, NC: SAS Institute Inc.

Chapter 6

MEASURES OF BIVARIATE ASSOCIATION

> **Overview**: This chapter discusses procedures that you can use to test the significance of the relationship between two variables. Recommendations are made for choosing the correct statistic based on the level of measurement used to assess the two variables. The chapter shows how to use PROC PLOT to prepare bivariate scattergrams, how to use PROC CORR to compute Pearson correlations and Spearman correlations, and how to use PROC FREQ to perform the chi-square test of independence.

Introduction: Significance Tests versus Measures of Association

A **bivariate relationship** involves the relationship between just two variables. For example, if you conduct an investigation in which you study the relationship between SAT verbal test scores and college grade point average (GPA), you are studying a bivariate relationship.

There are a large number of statistical procedures that you can use to investigate bivariate relationships. These procedures may provide a test of statistical significance, a measure of association, or both. **A test of statistical significance** allows you to test hypotheses about the relationship between the variables in the population. For example, the Pearson correlation coefficient allows you to test the null hypothesis that the correlation between the two interval-level variables is zero in the population. In a study, you may draw a sample of 200 subjects and determine that the Pearson correlation between the SAT verbal test and GPA is .35 for this sample. You may then use this finding to test the null hypothesis that the correlation between SAT-verbal and GPA is zero in the population. The resulting test may prove to be significant at $p < .001$. This p value suggests that there is less than 1 chance in 1,000 of obtaining a sample correlation of .35 or larger if the null hypothesis were true. You therefore reject the null hypothesis, and conclude that the correlation is probably not equal to zero in the population.

In addition to serving as a test of statistical significance, a Pearson correlation may also serve as a measure of association. A **measure of association** reflects the strength of the relationship between two variables (regardless of the statistical significance of the relationship). For example, the absolute value of a Pearson correlation coefficient reveals something about how strongly the two variables are related. A Pearson correlation may range from –1.00 through 0.00 through +1.00, with larger absolute values indicative of stronger relationships. For example, a correlation of 0.00 indicates no relationship between the variables, a correlation of .20 (or –.20) indicates a weak relationship, and a correlation of .90 (or –.90) indicates a strong relationship (a later section provides more detailed guidelines for interpreting Pearson correlations).

Choosing the Correct Statistic

Levels of Measurement

When investigating the relationship between two variables, it is important to use the appropriate bivariate statistic, given the nature of the two variables being studied. In choosing this statistic, you must pay particular attention to the level of measurement used to assess the two variables. This section briefly reviews the various levels of measurement that were discussed in Chapter 1 of this text; the following section will show how you can use the scale of measurement to identify the right statistic for a given research problem.

Chapter 1 described the four levels of measurement used with variables in social science research: nominal, ordinal, interval, and ratio. A variable measured on a **nominal scale** is a *classification* variable: it simply indicates the group to which a subject belongs. For example, "race" is a nominal-level variable: A subject may be classified as being African-American, Asian-American, Caucasian, and so forth.

A variable measured on an **ordinal scale** is a *ranking* variable. An ordinal variable indicates which subjects have more of the construct being assessed, and which subjects have less. For example, if all students in a classroom were ranked with respect to verbal ability so that the best student was assigned the value "1", the next-best student was assigned the value "2", and so forth, this ranking variable would be assessed at the ordinal level. However, ordinal scales have a limitation in that equal differences in scale value do not necessarily have equal quantitative meaning. This means that the difference in verbal ability between student #1 and student #2 is not necessarily the same as the difference in ability between student #2 and student #3.

With an **interval scale** of measurement, equal differences in scale values do have equal quantitative meaning. For example, imagine that you develop a test of verbal ability. Scores on this test may range from 0 through 100, with higher scores reflecting greater ability. If the scores on this test are truly on an interval scale, then the difference between a score of 60 and a score of 70 should be equal to the difference between a score of 70 and a score of 80. In other words, the units of measurement should be the same throughout the full range of the scale. Nonetheless, an interval-level scale does not have a true zero-point. Among other things, this means that a score of zero on the test does not necessarily indicate a complete absence of verbal ability.

Finally, a **ratio scale** has all of the properties of an interval scale and also has a true zero-point. This makes it possible to make meaningful statements about the ratios between scale values. For example, body weight is assessed on a ratio scale: a score of "0 pounds" indicates no body weight at all. With this variable, it is possible to state that "a person who weighs 200 pounds is twice as heavy as a person who weighs 100 pounds." Other examples of ratio-level variables include age, height, and income.

A Table of Appropriate Statistics

Once you have identified the level of measurement at which your variables are assessed, it is a relatively simple matter to determine the correct statistic for analyzing the relationship between these variables; this section presents a figure to make this task easier. First, however, be warned that the actual situation is a bit more complex than the figure suggests. This is because when two variables are assessed at a given level of measurement, there may actually be more than one statistic that can be used to investigate the relationship between those variables. In keeping with the relatively narrow scope of this text, however, this chapter presents only a few of the options that are available to you (in general, this chapter emphasizes what are probably the most commonly used statistics). To learn about additional procedures and the special conditions under which they may be appropriate, consult a more comprehensive statistics textbook such as Hays (1988).

Figure 6.1 identifies some of the statistics that may be appropriate for pairs of variables assessed at given levels of measurement. The vertical columns of the figure indicate the scales of measurement used to assess the predictor variable of the pair, while the horizontal rows indicate the scale used to assess the criterion (or predicted) variable. The appropriate statistic for a given pair of variables is identified where a given row and column intersect.

Predictor Variable

Criterion Variable		Nominal-Level	Ordinal-Level	Interval-Level	Ratio-Level
	Ratio-Level	ANOVA	Spearman Correlation	Pearson Correlation or Spearman Correlation	Pearson Correlation or Spearman Correlation
	Interval-Level	ANOVA	Spearman Correlation	Pearson Correlation or Spearman Correlation	
	Ordinal-Level	Kruskal-Wallis Test	Spearman Correlation		
	Nominal-Level	Chi-Square Test			

Figure 6.1: Statistics for Pairs of Variables

The chi-square test of independence. For example, at the intersection of a nominal-level predictor variable and a nominal-level criterion variable, the figure indicates that an appropriate statistic may be the chi-square test (short for "chi-square test of independence"). To illustrate this situation, imagine that you are conducting research that investigates the relationship between place of residence and political party membership. Assume that you have hypothesized that people who live in the midwestern states of the United States are more likely to belong to the Republican party, relative to those who live in the east or those who live in the west. To test this hypothesis, you gather data on two variables for each of 1,000 subjects. The first variable is "place of residence," and each subject is coded as living either in the east, the midwest, or the west of the United States. It should be clear that place of residence is therefore a nominal-level variable that can assume one of three values. The second variable is "party membership," and each subject is coded as either being a republican, a democrat, or other. Obviously, party membership is also a nominal-scale variable that also may assume just one of three values.

If you analyzed your data with a chi-square test of independence and obtained a significant value of chi-square, this would tell you that there is a relationship between place of residence and party membership. Close inspection of the two-way classification table that is produced in the course of this analysis (to be discussed later) would then tell you whether those in the midwest were, in fact, more likely to be republicans.

The Spearman correlation coefficient. Figure 6.1 shows that, where an ordinal-level predictor intersects with an ordinal-level criterion, the Spearman correlation coefficient is recommended. As an illustration, imagine that an author has produced a book that has ranked the 100 largest universities in the U.S. from best to worst, so that the best school was ranked #1, the second best was ranked #2, and so forth. In addition to providing an overall ranking for the institutions, the author also ranked them from best to worst with respect to a number of specific criteria such as "intellectual environment," "prestige," "quality of athletic programs," and so forth. Assume that you have formed the hypothesis that the universities' overall rankings will demonstrate a strong positive correlation with the rankings of the quality of their athletic programs.

To test this hypothesis, you compute the correlation between two variables: their overall rankings, and the rankings of their athletic programs. Both of these variables are clearly on an ordinal scale, because both merely tell you about the ordinal rankings of the universities. For example, the athletic program variable may tell you that university #1 has a better program than university #2, but it does not tell you *how much* better. Because both variables are on an ordinal scale, it is appropriate to analyze the relationship between them with the Spearman correlation coefficient.

The Pearson correlation coefficient. Finally, Figure 6.1 shows that, when both the predictor and criterion are assessed on either the interval- or ratio-level of measurement, the Pearson correlation coefficient may be appropriate. For example, assume that you wish to test the hypothesis that income is positively correlated with age. That is, you predict that older people will tend to have more income than younger people. To test this hypothesis, you obtain data from 200 subjects on two variables. The first variable is AGE, which is simply the subject's age in years. The second variable is INCOME: the subject's annual income in dollars. It may assume values such as $0, $10,000, $1,200,000, and so forth.

You know that both variables in this study are assessed on a ratio scale, because with both variables equal intervals have equal quantitative meaning, and both variables have a true zero point (i.e., zero years of age and zero dollars of income). Because both variables are on a ratio scale, you may compute a Pearson correlation to assess the nature of the relationship between them (this assumes that certain other assumptions for the statistic have been met; these assumptions are discussed in a later section and are also summarized in an appendix at the end of this chapter).

Other statistics. The statistics identified on the diagonal of the figure are the statistics to be used when both predictor and criterion variable are assessed on the same level of measurement (for example, you should use the chi-square test when both variables are nominal-level variables). The situation becomes a bit more complex when one variable is assessed at one level of measurement, and the second variable is assessed at a different level. For example, when the criterion variable is interval-level and the predictor variable is nominal-level, the appropriate procedure is ANOVA (for "analysis of variance"). This chapter discusses only three of the statistics identified in Figure 6.1: the Pearson correlation coefficient, the Spearman correlation coefficient, and the chi-square test of independence. With respect to the remaining statistics, ANOVA is covered in later chapters of this text, and the Kruskal-Wallis test is not covered in this text at all, but is described by other documentation for the SAS System. For information on the Kruskal-Wallis test, consult Schlotzhauer and Littell's (1987) *SAS system for elementary statistical analysis* as well as Chapter 30 in the *SAS/STAT user's guide, version 6, volume 2*.

Exceptions to Figure 6.1. Remember that Figure 6.1 presents only *some* of the statistics that may be appropriate for a given combination of variables, and there will be many exceptions to the general guidelines that it illustrates. For example, the figure assumes that all nominal-level variables assume only a relatively small number of values (perhaps 2-6), and all ordinal-, interval-, and ratio-level variables are *continuous*, taking on a large number of values. When these conditions do not hold, the correct statistic may differ from the one indicated by the table. For example, in some cases ANOVA may be the appropriate statistic when both criterion and predictor variables are assessed on a ratio level. This would be the case when conducting an experiment in which the criterion variable is "number of errors on a memory task" (a ratio-level variable), and the predictor is "amount of caffeine administered: 0 mg. versus 100 mg. versus 200 mg." In this case, the predictor variable (amount of caffeine administered) is clearly assessed on a ratio-level, but the correct statistic is ANOVA because this predictor takes on such a small number of values (just three). As you read about the examples of research throughout this text, you will begin to develop a better sense of how to take these factors into account when choosing the correct statistic for a given study.

Conclusion

The purpose of this section was to provide a simple strategy for choosing the correct measure of bivariate association for conditions that are frequently encountered in social science research. The following section reviews information about the Pearson correlation coefficient, and shows how to use PROC PLOT to view scattergrams to verify that the relation between two variables is linear. This and subsequent sections also provide a more detailed discussion of the three statistics that are emphasized in this chapter: the Pearson correlation, the Spearman correlation, and the chi-square test of independence. For each, the text provides an example of a study for which the statistic would be appropriate, shows how to prepare the data and the necessary SAS program, and shows how to interpret the output.

Pearson Correlations

When to Use

You can use the Pearson product-moment correlation coefficient (symbolized as r) to assess the nature of the relationship between two variables when both variables are assessed on either an interval- or ratio-level of measurement. It is further assumed that both variables should include a relatively large number of values; for example, you would not use this statistic if one of the variables could assume only three values.

It would be appropriate to compute a Pearson correlation to investigate the nature of the relationship between SAT verbal test scores and grade point average (GPA). SAT verbal is assessed on an interval-level of measurement, and may assume a wide variety of values (possible scores range from 200 through 800). Grade point ratio is also assessed on an interval level, and may also assume a wide variety of values from 0.00 through 4.00.

In addition to interval- or ratio-scale measurement, the statistic also assumes that the observations have been drawn from normally-distributed populations. When one or both variables display a markedly non-normal distribution (for example, when one or both variables are marked skewed), it may be more appropriate to analyze the data with the Spearman correlation coefficient. A later section of this chapter discusses the Spearman coefficient; summarized assumptions of both the Pearson and Spearman correlations appear in an appendix at the end of this chapter.

Interpreting the Coefficient

To more fully understand the nature of the relationship between the two variables studied, it is necessary to interpret two characteristics of a Pearson correlation coefficient. First, the **sign of the coefficient** tells you whether there is a positive relationship or a negative relationship between the two variables. A **positive correlation** indicates that as values on one variable increase, values on the second variable also increase. A positive correlation is illustrated in Figure 6.2, which shows the relationship between SAT verbal test scores and GPA in a fictitious sample of data.

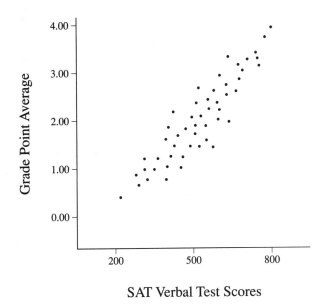

Figure 6.2: A Positive Correlation

You can see that subjects who received low scores on the predictor variable (SAT verbal) also received low scores on the criterion variable (GPA); at the same time, subjects who received high scores on SAT verbal also received high scores on GPA. The two variables may therefore be said to be positively correlated.

With a **negative correlation**, on the other hand, as values on one variable increase, values on the second variable decrease. For example, you might expect to see a negative correlation between SAT verbal test scores and the number of errors that subjects make on a vocabulary test: The students with high SAT verbal scores tend to make few mistakes, and the students with low SAT scores tend to make many mistakes. This relationship is illustrated with fictitious data in Figure 6.3.

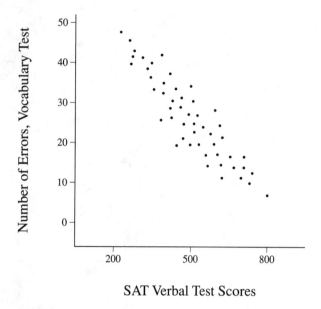

Figure 6.3: A Negative Correlation

The second characteristic of a correlation coefficient is its **size**: the greater the absolute value of a correlation coefficient, the stronger the relationship between the two variables. Pearson correlation coefficients may range in size from −1.00 through 0.00 through +1.00. Coefficients of 0.00 indicate no relationship between the two variables. For example, if there were zero correlation between SAT scores and GPA, then knowing a person's SAT score would tell you nothing about what his or her GPA is likely to be. In contrast, correlations of −1.00 or +1.00 indicate perfect relationships. For example, if the correlation between SAT scores and GPA were 1.00, it would mean that knowing someone's SAT score would allow you to predict his or her GPA with perfect accuracy. In the real world, however, SAT scores are not that strongly related to GPA, so you would expect the correlation between them to be less than 1.00.

The following is an approximate guide for interpreting the strength of the relationship between two variables, based on the absolute value of the coefficient:

```
±1.00 = Perfect correlation
 ±.80 = Strong correlation
 ±.50 = Moderate correlation
 ±.20 = Weak correlation
 ±.00 = No correlation
```

Remember that one considers the *absolute value* of the coefficient in interpreting its size. This is to say that a correlation of −.50 is just as strong as a correlation of +.50, a correlation of −.75 is just as strong as a correlation of +.75, and so forth.

Linear versus Nonlinear Relationships

The Pearson correlation is appropriate only if there is a linear relationship between the two variables. There is a **linear relationship** between two variables when their scattergram follows the form of a straight line. For example, it is possible to draw a straight line through the center of the scattergram presented in Figure 6.4, and this straight line fits the pattern of the data fairly well. This means that there is a linear relationship between SAT verbal test scores and GPA.

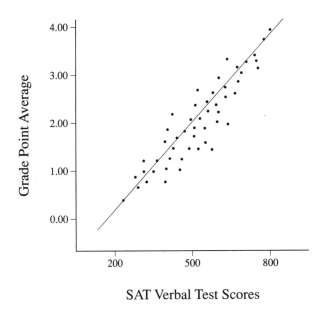

Figure 6.4: A Linear Relationship

In contrast, there is a **nonlinear relationship** between two variables if their scattergram does not follow the form of a straight line. For example, imagine that you have constructed a test of creativity and have administered it to a large sample of college students. With this test, higher scores reflect higher levels of creativity. Imagine further that you obtain the SAT verbal test scores for these students, plot their SAT scores against their creativity scores, and obtain the scattergram presented in Figure 6.5.

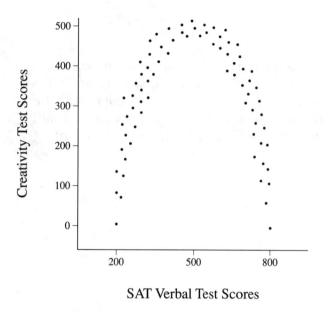

Figure 6.5: A Nonlinear Relationship

The scattergram in Figure 6.5 reveals a nonlinear relationship between SAT scores and creativity. It shows that

- students with low SAT scores tend to have low creativity scores
- students with moderate SAT scores tend to have high creativity scores
- students with high SAT scores tend to have low creativity scores.

It is not possible to draw a good-fitting straight line through the data points of Figure 6.5; this is why we say that there is a *nonlinear* (or perhaps a *curvilinear*) relationship between SAT scores and creativity scores.

When one uses the Pearson correlation to assess the relationship between two variables involved in a nonlinear relationship, the resulting correlation coefficient usually *underestimates* the actual strength of the relationship between the two variables. For example, computing the Pearson correlation between the SAT scores and creativity scores presented in Figure 6.5 might result in a coefficient of .10, which would indicate only a very weak relationship between the two variables. However, there is clearly a fairly strong relationship between SAT scores and creativity. The figure shows that if you know what someone's SAT score is, you can predict with good accuracy what his or her creativity score will be.

The implication of all this is that you should always verify that there is a linear relationship between two variables before computing a Pearson correlation for those variables. One of the easiest ways of verifying that the relationship is linear is to prepare a scattergram similar to those presented in the preceding figures. Fortunately, this is very easy to do using the SAS System's PLOT procedure.

Producing Scattergrams with PROC PLOT

Here is the general form for requesting a scattergram with the PLOT procedure:

```
PROC PLOT   DATA=data-set-name;
   PLOT    criterion-variable*predictor-variable ;
   RUN;
```

The variable listed as the "criterion-variable" in the preceding program will be plotted on the vertical axis, and the "predictor-variable" will be plotted on the horizontal axis.

To illustrate this procedure, imagine that you have conducted a study dealing with the *investment model*, a theory of commitment in romantic associations (Rusbult, 1980). The investment model identifies a number of variables that are believed to influence a person's commitment to a romantic association. **Commitment** refers to the subject's intention to remain in the relationship. These are some of the variables that are predicted to influence subject commitment:

Satisfaction: The subject's affective response to the relationship

Investment size: The amount of time and personal resources that the subject has put into the relationship

Alternative value: The attractiveness of the subject's alternatives to the relationship (e.g., the attractiveness of alternative romantic partners)

Assume that you have developed a 16-item questionnaire to measure these four variables. The questionnaire is administered to 20 subjects who are currently involved in a romantic relationship, and the subjects are asked to complete the instrument while thinking about their relationship. When they have completed the questionnaire, it is possible to use their responses to compute four scores for each subject. First, each subject receives a score on the *commitment scale*. Higher values on the commitment scale reflect greater commitment to the relationship. Each subject also receives a score on the *satisfaction scale*, where higher scores reflect greater satisfaction with the relationship. Higher scores on the *investment scale* mean that the subject believes that he or she has invested a great deal of time and effort in the relationship. Finally, with the *alternative value scale* higher scores mean that it would be attractive to the respondent to find a different romantic partner.

Once the data have been keyed, you can use the PLOT procedure to prepare scattergrams for various combinations of variables. The following SAS program inputs some fictitious data and requests that a scattergram be prepared in which commitment scores are plotted against satisfaction scores:

```
1       DATA D1;
2          INPUT    #1   @1    (COMMIT)    (2.)
3                        @4    (SATIS)     (2.)
4                        @7    (INVEST)    (2.)
5                        @10   (ALTERN)    (2.)      ;
6       CARDS;
7       20 20 28 21
8       10 12  5 31
9       30 33 24 11
10       8 10 15 36
11      22 18 33 16
12      31 29 33 12
13       6 10 12 29
14      11 12  6 30
15      25 23 34 12
16      10  7 14 32
17      31 36 25  5
18       5  4 18 30
19      31 28 23  6
20       4  6 14 29
21      36 33 29  6
22      22 21 14 17
23      15 17 10 25
24      19 16 16 22
25      12 14 18 27
26      24 21 33 16
27      ;
28      PROC PLOT    DATA=D1;
29         PLOT COMMIT*SATIS;
30         RUN;
```

In the preceding program, scores on the commitment scale are keyed in columns 1-2, and are given the SAS variable name COMMIT. Similarly, scores on the satisfaction scale are keyed in columns 4-5, and are given the name SATIS; scores on the investment scale appear in columns 7-8 and are given the name INVEST; and scores on the alternative value scale appear as the last column of data, and are given the name ALTERN.

The data for the 20 subjects appear on lines 7-26 in the program. There is one line of data for each subject.

Line 28 of the program requests the PLOT procedure, specifying that the data set to be analyzed is data set D1. The PLOT command on line 29 specifies COMMIT as the criterion variable and SATIS as the predictor variable for this analysis. The results of this analysis appear in Output 6.1.

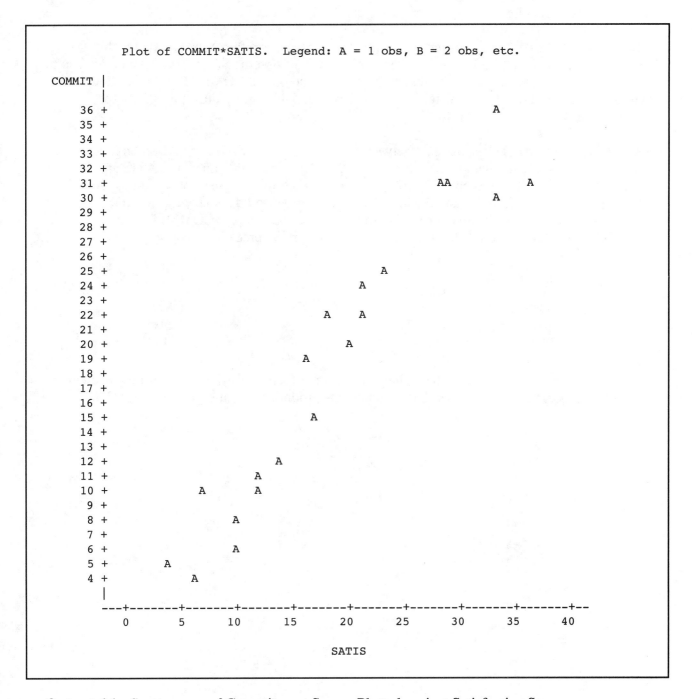

Output 6.1: Scattergram of Commitment Scores Plotted against Satisfaction Scores

Notice that, in this output, the criterion variable (COMMIT) is plotted on the vertical axis, while the predictor variable (SATIS) is plotted on the horizontal axis. The shape of the scattergram shows that there is a linear relationship between SATIS and COMMIT. This can be seen from the fact that it would be possible to draw a good-fitting straight line through the center of the scattergram. Given that the relationship is linear, it seems safe to proceed with the computation of a Pearson correlation for this pair of variables.

The general shape of the scattergram also suggests that there is a fairly strong relationship between the two variables: Knowing where a subject stands on the SATIS variable allows you to predict, with some accuracy, where that subject will stand on the COMMIT variable. Later, you will compute the correlation coefficient for these two variables to see just how strong the relationship is.

Output 6.1 shows that the relationship between SATIS and COMMIT is *positive:* large values on SATIS are associated with large values on COMMIT, and small values on SATIS are associated with small values on COMMIT. This makes intuitive sense: you would expect that the subjects who are highly satisfied with their relationships would also be highly committed to those relationships. To illustrate a negative relationship, you can plot COMMIT against ALTERN. To do this, include the following statements in the preceding program:

```
PROC PLOT    DATA=D1;
   PLOT COMMIT*ALTERN;
   RUN;
```

These statements are identical to the earlier statements, except that ALTERN has now been specified as the predictor variable. These statements produce the scattergram presented in Output 6.2.

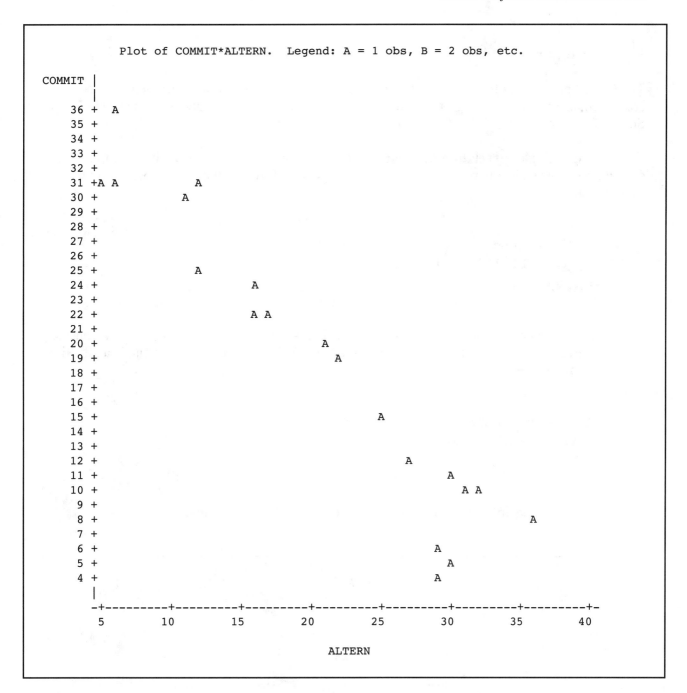

Output 6.2: Scattergram of Commitment Scores Plotted against Alternative Value Scores

Notice that the relationship between these two variables is *negative*. This is as you would expect: it makes intuitive sense that subjects who indicate that the alternatives to their current romantic partner are attractive would not be terribly committed to the current partner. The relationship between ALTERN and COMMIT also appears to be linear; it is therefore appropriate to assess the strength of the relationship between these variables with the Pearson correlation coefficient.

Computing Pearson Correlations with PROC CORR

The CORR procedure offers a number of options regarding what *type* of coefficient will be computed, as well as a number of options regarding the *way* they will appear on the printed page. Some of these options are discussed here.

Computing a single correlation coefficient. In some instances, you may wish to compute the correlation between just two variables. Here is the general form for the statements that will accomplish this:

```
PROC CORR   DATA=data-set-name   options;
   VAR   variable1   variable2;
   RUN;
```

The choice of which variable is "variable1" and which is "variable2" is arbitrary. For a concrete example, assume that you want to compute the correlation between commitment and satisfaction. These are the required statements:

```
   PROC CORR   DATA=D1;
      VAR COMMIT SATIS;
      RUN;
```

The preceding results in a single page of output, reproduced here as Output 6.3:

```
                      Correlation Analysis

               2 'VAR' Variables:  COMMIT    SATIS


                      Simple Statistics

Variable         N        Mean     Std Dev         Sum      Minimum      Maximum

COMMIT          20    18.60000    10.05459   372.00000      4.00000     36.00000
SATIS           20    18.50000     9.51177   370.00000      4.00000     36.00000
```

```
Pearson Correlation Coefficients / Prob > |R| under Ho: Rho=0 / N = 20

                           COMMIT            SATIS

          COMMIT          1.00000          0.96252
                          0.0              0.0001

          SATIS           0.96252          1.00000
                          0.0001           0.0
```

Output 6.3: Computing the Pearson Correlation between Commitment and Satisfaction

The first part of Output 6.3 presents simple descriptive statistics for the variables being analyzed. This allows you to verify that everything looks right: that the correct number of cases were analyzed, that no variables were out of bounds, and so forth. The names of the variables appear below the "Variable" heading, and the statistics for the variables appear to the right of the variable names. These descriptive statistics show that 20 subjects provided usable data for the COMMIT variable, that the mean for COMMIT was 18.6 and the standard deviation was 10.05. It is always important to review the "Minimum" and "Maximum" columns to verify that no impossible scores appear in the data. With COMMIT, the lowest possible score was 4 and the highest possible score was 36. The "Minimum" and "Maximum" columns of Output 6.3 show that no observed values were beyond these bounds, thus providing no evidence of miskeyed data (again, these proofing procedures do not *guarantee* that no errors were made in keying data, but they are useful for identifying some types of errors). Since the descriptive statistics provide no obvious evidence of keying or programming mistakes, you are now free to review the correlations themselves.

The bottom half of Output 6.3 provides the correlations requested in the VAR statement. There are actually four correlation coefficients in the output because your statement requested that the system compute every possible correlation between the variables COMMIT and SATIS. This caused SAS to compute the correlation between COMMIT and SATIS, between SATIS and COMMIT, between COMMIT and COMMIT, and between SATIS and SATIS.

The correlation between COMMIT and COMMIT appears in the upper-left corner of the matrix of correlation coefficients in Output 6.3. You can see that the correlation between these variables is 1.00, and this makes sense, because the correlation of any variable with itself is always equal to 1.00. Similarly, in the lower-right corner, you see that the correlation between SATIS and SATIS is also 1.00.

The correlation you are actually interested in appears where the column headed COMMIT intersects with the row headed SATIS. The top number in the "cell" where this column and row intersect is .96252, which is the Pearson correlation between COMMIT and SATIS. You may round this to .96.

Just below the correlation is the *p* value associated with the correlation. This is the *p* value obtained from a test of the null hypothesis that the correlation between COMMIT and SATIS is zero in the population. More technically, the *p* value gives us the probability that you would obtain a sample correlation this large (or larger) if the correlation between COMMIT and SATIS were really zero in the population. For the present correlation of .96, the corresponding *p* value is .0001. This means that, given your sample size, there is only 1 chance in 10,000 of obtaining a correlation of .96 or larger if the population correlation were really zero. You may therefore reject the null hypothesis, and tentatively conclude that COMMIT is related to SATIS in the population. (The alternative hypothesis for this statistical test is that the correlation is not equal to zero in the population; this alternative hypothesis is two-sided, which means that it does not predict whether the population correlation is positive or negative, only that it is not equal to zero.)

Determining sample size. The size of the sample used in computing the correlation coefficient may appear in one of two places on the output page. First, if all correlations in the analysis were based on the same number of subjects, the sample size appears only once on the page, in the line above the matrix of correlations. This line appears just below the descriptive statistics. In Output 6.3 the line says

```
Pearson Correlation Coefficients / Prob > |R| under Ho: Rho=0 / N = 20
```

The "N =" portion of this output indicates the sample size. In Output 6.3, the sample size was 20.

However, if one is requesting correlations between several different pairs of variables, it is possible that some correlations will be based on more subjects than others (due to missing data). In this case, the sample size will be printed for each individual correlation coefficient. Specifically, the sample size will appear immediately just below the correlation coefficient and its associated *p* value, following this format:

```
correlation
p value
N
```

Computing all possible correlations for a set of variables. Here is the general form for computing all possible Pearson correlations for a set of variables:

```
PROC CORR    DATA=data-set-name    options;
   VAR    variable-list;
   RUN;
```

Each variable name in the preceding "variable-list" should be separated by at least one space. For example, assume that you now wish to compute all possible correlations for the variables COMMIT, SATIS, INVEST, and ALTERN. The statements that request these correlations are as follows:

```
PROC CORR    DATA=D1;
    VAR COMMIT SATIS INVEST ALTERN;
    RUN;
```

The preceding program produced the output reproduced here as Output 6.4:

```
                        Correlation Analysis

        4 'VAR' Variables:  COMMIT    SATIS     INVEST    ALTERN


                        Simple Statistics

Variable        N        Mean      Std Dev        Sum      Minimum      Maximum

COMMIT         20     18.60000    10.05459    372.00000    4.00000     36.00000
SATIS          20     18.50000     9.51177    370.00000    4.00000     36.00000
INVEST         20     20.20000     9.28836    404.00000    5.00000     34.00000
ALTERN         20     20.65000     9.78869    413.00000    5.00000     36.00000


    Pearson Correlation Coefficients / Prob > |R| under Ho: Rho=0 / N = 20

                  COMMIT          SATIS          INVEST          ALTERN

   COMMIT        1.00000         0.96252        0.71043        -0.95604
                  0.0            0.0001         0.0004          0.0001


   SATIS         0.96252         1.00000        0.61538        -0.93355
                  0.0001          0.0            0.0039         0.0001


   INVEST        0.71043         0.61538        1.00000        -0.72394
                  0.0004          0.0039          0.0            0.0003


   ALTERN       -0.95604        -0.93355       -0.72394         1.00000
                  0.0001          0.0001          0.0003          0.0
```

Output 6.4: Computing All Possible Pearson Correlations

You can interpret the correlations and *p* values in this output in exactly the same way as with the preceding output. For example, to find the correlation between INVEST and COMMIT, you find the cell where the row for INVEST intersects with the column for COMMIT. The top number in this cell is .71043, which is the Pearson correlation between these two variables. Just below this correlation coefficient is the *p* value of .0004, meaning that there are only 4 chances in 10,000 of observing a sample correlation this large if the population correlation is really zero. In other words, the observed correlation is statistically significant.

Notice that the pattern of the correlations supports some of the predictions of the investment model: commitment is positively related to satisfaction and investment size, and is negatively related to alternative value. With respect to strength, the correlations range from being moderately strong to very strong (remember, however, that these data are fictitious).

> **What happens if I omit the VAR statement?** It is possible to run PROC CORR without the VAR statement; this causes every possible correlation to be computed between all quantitative variables in the data set. Use caution in doing this: with very large data sets, leaving off the VAR statement may result in a very long printout.

Computing correlations between subsets of variables. By using the WITH statement in the SAS program, it is possible to compute correlations between one subset of variables and a second subset of variables. The general form is as follows:

```
PROC CORR   DATA=data-set-name   options;
   VAR   variables-that-will-appear-as-columns;
   WITH  variables-that-will-appear-as-rows;
   RUN;
```

Any number of variables may appear in the VAR statement, and any number of variables may also appear in the WITH statement. To illustrate, assume that you want to prepare a matrix of correlation coefficients in which there is one column of coefficients, representing the COMMIT variable, and there are three rows of coefficients representing the SATIS, INVEST, and ALTERN variables. The following statements create this matrix:

```
PROC CORR   DATA=D1;
   VAR  COMMIT;
   WITH SATIS INVEST ALTERN;
   RUN;
```

Output 6.5 presents the results generated by this program. Obviously, the correlations in this output are identical to those obtained in Output 6.4, although the Output 6.5 is more compact. This is why it is often wise to use the WITH statement in conjunction with the VAR statement, as this can produce smaller and more manageable printouts than may be obtained if you use only the VAR statement.

```
                         Correlation Analysis

              3 'WITH' Variables:   SATIS    INVEST    ALTERN
              1 'VAR'  Variables:   COMMIT


                         Simple Statistics

Variable        N        Mean     Std Dev        Sum     Minimum      Maximum

SATIS          20     18.50000     9.51177    370.00000     4.00000     36.00000
INVEST         20     20.20000     9.28836    404.00000     5.00000     34.00000
ALTERN         20     20.65000     9.78869    413.00000     5.00000     36.00000
COMMIT         20     18.60000    10.05459    372.00000     4.00000     36.00000


     Pearson Correlation Coefficients / Prob > |R| under Ho: Rho=0 / N = 20

                                       COMMIT

                       SATIS          0.96252
                                      0.0001

                       INVEST         0.71043
                                      0.0004

                       ALTERN        -0.95604
                                      0.0001
```

Output 6.5: Computing Pearson Correlations for Subsets of Variables

Options used with PROC CORR. The following items are some of the PROC CORR options that you might find especially useful when conducting social science research. Remember that the option names should appear before the semicolon that ends the PROC CORR statement:

ALPHA

Prints coefficient alpha (a measure of scale reliability) for the variables listed in the VAR statement. Chapter 15 of this text deals with coefficient alpha in greater detail.

COV

> Prints covariances between the variables. This is useful when you need a variance-covariance table, rather than a table of correlations.

KENDALL

> Prints Kendall's tau-b coefficient, a measure of bivariate association for variables assessed at the ordinal level.

NOMISS

> Drops from the analysis any observation (subject) with missing data on any of the variables listed in the VAR statement. Using this option ensures that all correlations will be based on exactly the same observations (and, therefore, on the same *number* of observations).

NOPROB

> Prevents the printing of *p* values associated with the correlations.

RANK

> For each variable, reorders the correlations from highest to lowest (in absolute value) and prints them in this order.

SPEARMAN

> Prints Spearman correlations, which are appropriate for variables measured on an ordinal level. Spearman correlations are discussed in the following section.

Spearman Correlations

When to Use

Spearman's rank-order correlation coefficient (symbolized as r_s) may be appropriate under a variety of circumstances. First, you can use Spearman correlations when both variables are assessed on an ordinal level of measurement. It is also correct when one variable is an ordinal-level variable, and the other is an interval- or ratio-level variable.

However, it may also be appropriate to use the Spearman correlation when both variables are on an interval or ratio scale. The Spearman coefficient is a **distribution-free test**: among other things, a distribution-free test is one that makes no assumption concerning the shape of the distribution from which the sample data were drawn. For this reason, researchers sometimes compute Spearman correlations when one or both of the variables are interval- or ratio-level but are markedly non-normal (e.g., skewed), making a Pearson correlation inappropriate. The Spearman correlation is less useful than a Pearson correlation when both variables are truly normal, but it is more useful when one or both variables are non-normal.

The SAS System computes a Spearman correlation by converting both variables to ranks and computing the correlation between the ranks. The resulting correlation coefficient may range from -1.00 through $+1.00$, and is interpreted in the same way that the Pearson correlation coefficient is interpreted.

Computing Spearman Correlations with PROC CORR

Here is the general form for computing a Spearman correlation between two variables; notice that this is identical to the form used to compute Pearson correlations, except that you specify the option SPEARMAN in the PROC CORR statement (if you did not specify the SPEARMAN option, the program would have again produced Pearson correlations, since Pearson correlations are the default output):

```
PROC CORR   DATA=data-set-name   SPEARMAN   options;
   VAR   variable1   variable2;
   RUN;
```

To illustrate this statistic, assume that a teacher has administered a test of creativity to 10 students at Time 1. After reviewing the results, she ranks her students from 1 to 10, with "1" representing the "most creative student," and "10" representing the "least creative student." Two months later, at Time 2, she repeats the process, arriving at a slightly different set of rankings. She now wants to determine the correlation between her rankings made at Time 1 and Time 2. The data (rankings) are clearly on an ordinal level of measurement, so the correct statistic is the Spearman rank-order correlation coefficient.

This is the entire program that will input the fictitious data and compute the Spearman correlation:

```
1       DATA D1;
2          INPUT  #1   @1   (TEST1)   (2.)
3                       @4   (TEST2)   (2.)  ;
4       CARDS;
5        1  2
6        2  3
7        3  1
8        4  5
9        5  4
10       6  6
11       7  7
12       8  9
13       9 10
14      10  8
15       ;
16      PROC CORR   DATA=D1   SPEARMAN;
17         VAR TEST1 TEST2
18         RUN;
```

This program results in the output reproduced here as Output 6.6. Notice that the output's format is identical to that observed with the Pearson correlations in Output 6.4, except that the heading above the matrix of correlations indicates that Spearman correlations have been printed. Correlation coefficients and *p* values are interpreted in the usual way.

```
                          Correlation Analysis

                2 'VAR' Variables:  TEST1     TEST2


                          Simple Statistics

Variable          N      Mean    Std Dev     Median    Minimum    Maximum

TEST1            10    5.50000   3.02765    5.50000    1.00000   10.00000
TEST2            10    5.50000   3.02765    5.50000    1.00000   10.00000
```

```
Spearman Correlation Coefficients / Prob > |R| under Ho: Rho=0 / N = 10

                        TEST1                TEST2

        TEST1         1.00000              0.91515
                       0.0                  0.0002

        TEST2         0.91515              1.00000
                       0.0002               0.0
```

Output 6.6: Computing the Spearman Correlation between Test 1 and Test 2

When requesting Spearman correlations, the VAR and WITH statements are used in the same way as when computing Pearson correlations. That is:

- Using only the VAR statement results in the printing of all possible correlations for the listed variables.

- Combining the VAR with the WITH statement results in the printing of correlations for subsets of variables.

- Leaving these statements off results in the printing of all possible correlations for all numeric variables.

The Chi-Square Test of Independence

When to Use

The chi-square test of independence (sometimes called the chi-square test of association or homogeneity) is appropriate when both variables are assessed on a nominal level of measurement; that is, when both variables are *classification* variables. Theoretically, either of the variables may have any number of categories, but in practice the number of categories is usually relatively small, perhaps 2-10.

The Two-Way Classification Table

The nature of the relationship between two nominal-level variables is easiest to understand using a **two-way classification** table. This is a table in which the rows represent the categories of one variable, while the columns represent the categories of the second variable. This two-way classification table is important because, once it has been prepared, it is possible to review the number of observations that appear in the various cells of the table to see if there is any pattern that would indicate some relationship between the two variables, as well as perform a chi-square test of independence to see if there is any evidence that the variables are related in the population.

For example, assume that you want to prepare a table that plots one variable that contains two categories against a second variable with three categories. The general form for such a table appears in Figure 6.6:

Column Variable

	column 1	column 2	column 3
row 1	$cell_{11}$	$cell_{12}$	$cell_{13}$
row 2	$cell_{21}$	$cell_{22}$	$cell_{23}$

Row Variable

Figure 6.6: General Form for a Two-Way Classification Table

The point at which a row and column intersects is called a **cell**, and each cell is given a unique subscript. The first number in this subscript indicates *row* to which the cell belongs, and the second number indicates *column* to which the cell belongs. So the general form for cell subscripts is "$cell_{rc}$," where r = row and c = column. This means that $cell_{21}$ is at the intersection of row 2 and column 1, $cell_{13}$ is at the intersection of row 1 and column 3, and so forth. One of the first steps in performing a chi-square test of independence is to determine exactly how many subjects fall into each of the cells of the classification table (that is, how many subjects appear in each subgroup). The pattern shown by these subgroups will help you understand whether the two classification variables are related to one another.

An Example

To make this a bit more concrete, assume that you are a university administrator preparing to purchase a large number of new personal computers for three of the schools that constitute your university: the School of Arts and Science, the School of Education, and the School of Business. For a given school, you may purchase either IBM compatible computers or Macintosh computers, and you need to know which type of computer the students within each school tend to prefer.

In general terms, your research question is "Is there a relationship between the following two variables: (a) school of enrollment, and (b) computer preference?" The chi-square test of independence will help answer this question. If this test shows that there is a relationship between the two variables, you may review the two-way classification table to see which type of computer most students in each of the three schools prefer.

To answer this question, you draw a representative sample of 370 students from the 8,000 students that constitute the three schools. Each student is given a short questionnaire that asks just two questions:

```
1.  In which school are you enrolled? (Circle one):

    a. School of Arts and Sciences.

    b. School of Business.

    c. School of Education.


2.  Which type of computer do you prefer that we purchase for your
    school?  (circle one):

    a.  IBM compatible.

    b.  Macintosh.
```

These two questions constitute the two nominal-level variables for your study: Question 1 allows you to create a "school of enrollment" variable that may take on one of three values (Arts & Science, Business or Education), while question 2 allows you to create a "computer preference" variable that may take on one of two values (IBM compatible or Macintosh). Clearly these are *nominal-level* variables, as they merely indicate group membership, and provide no quantitative information.

You may now prepare a two-way classification table that plots preference against school; this table (with fictitious data) appears as Figure 6.7. Notice that, in the table, computer preference is the row variable, in that row 1 represents students who preferred IBM compatibles, while row 2 represents students who preferred Macintosh. In the same way, you can see that school of enrollment is the column variable:

School of Enrollment

	Arts & Sciences	Business	Education
IBM Compatible	$n=30$	$n=100$	$n=20$
Macintosh	$n=60$	$n=40$	$n=120$

(row label at left: **Computer Preference**)

Figure 6.7: Two-Way Classification Table Plotting Computer Preference against School of Enrollment

Figure 6.7 reveals the number of students who appear in each cell of the classification table. For example, the first row of the table shows that, among those students who preferred IBM compatibles, 30 were Arts and Science students, 100 were Business students, and 20 were Education majors.

Remember that the purpose of the study was to determine whether there is any relationship between the two variables, to determine whether school of enrollment is related to computer preference. This is just another way of saying, "If you know what school a student is enrolled in, does that help you predict what type of computer that student is likely to prefer?" In the present case, the answer to this question is easiest to find if you review the table just one column at a time. For example, review just the Arts and Sciences column of the table. Notice that most of the students ($n = 60$) preferred Macintosh computers, while fewer ($n = 30$) preferred IBM compatibles. The column for the Business students shows just the opposite trend, however: most business students ($n = 100$) preferred IBM compatibles. Finally, the pattern for the Education students was similar to that of the Arts and Sciences students, in that the majority ($n = 120$) preferred Macintosh.

In short, there appears to be a relationship between school of enrollment and computer preference, with Business students preferring IBM compatibles, and Arts and Sciences and Education students preferring Macintoshes. But this is just a trend that you observed in the *sample*. Is this trend strong enough to allow you to conclude that the variables are probably related in the *population* of 8,000 students? To determine this, you must conduct the chi-square test of independence.

Tabular versus Raw Data

You may use the SAS System to compute the chi-square test of independence regardless of whether you are dealing with tabular data or raw data. When you are working with **raw data**, you are working with data that have not been summarized or tabulated in any way. For example, imagine that you have administered your questionnaire to 370 students, and have not yet tabulated their responses; you merely have 370 completed questionnaires. In this situation, you are working with raw data.

On the other hand, **tabular data** are data that have been summarized in a table. For example, imagine that it was actually another researcher who administered this questionnaire, summarized subject responses in a two-way classification table (similar to Figure 6.7), and provided this completed table in a published article. In this case you are dealing with tabular data.

In computing the chi-square statistic, there is no real advantage to using one form of data rather than another, although you will generally have a lot less data to key if your data are already in tabular form. The following section shows how to input the data and request the chi-square statistic for tabular data; a subsequent section deals with raw data.

Computing Chi-Square from Tabular Data

Inputting tabular data. Very often, the data to be analyzed with a chi-square test of independence have already been summarized in a two-way classification table such as in Figure 6.7. In these situations, you must create a special type of INPUT statement to read the data. Here is the general form:

```
DATA    data-set-name;
   INPUT    row-variable-name         $
            column-variable-name      $
            number-variable-name  ;
CARDS;
row-value    column-value    number-in-cell
row-value    column-value    number-in-cell
row-value    column-value    number-in-cell
  .
  .
  .
;
```

The INPUT statement in this program tells SAS that the data set includes three variables, and the names of these three variables are symbolized as "row-variable-name", "column-variable-name", and "number-variable-name". The first variable is a character variable that codes the rows of the classification table (in the present study, the "row-variable" was "computer preference"). The second variable is a character variable that codes the *columns* of the table (here, the "column-variable" was "school of enrollment"). Finally, the third variable (symbolized as "number-variable-name") is a quantitative variable that codes how many subjects appear in a given cell. (You will give specific names to these variables in the program to be presented shortly.)

The preceding program is in *free format*, meaning that it did not tell SAS exactly which column in the CARDS section each variable is located in. However, this should not cause any problems as long as you remember to separate each value in the CARDS section by at least one blank space, and do not accidently skip any values in the CARDS section.

Each line of data in the CARDS section corresponds to just one of the cells in the classification table. In the preceding general form, the "number-in-cell" in the CARDS section represents the number of subjects in that cell. Therefore, the number of data lines in the CARDS section will be equal to the number of cells in the two-way classification table. The present classification table included six cells, so there will be six data lines in the CARDS statement.

This is the actual data input step for inputting the tabular data presented in the two-way classification table of Figure 6.7:

```
1        DATA D1;
2           INPUT    PREF      $
3                    SCHOOL    $
4                    NUMBER    ;
5
6        CARDS;
7        IBM    ARTS     30
8        IBM    BUS     100
9        IBM    ED       20
10       MAC    ARTS     60
11       MAC    BUS      40
12       MAC    ED      120
13        ;
```

The preceding INPUT statement tells SAS that the data set contains just three variables for each line of data. The first variable is a character variable named PREF (coding student preferences, the row-variable), the second is a character variable named SCHOOL (coding the student's school, the column-variable), and the third variable is a numeric variable called NUMBER (indicating how many students appear in a given cell). Compare the INPUT statement from the preceding program to the INPUT statement from the general form presented earlier to verify that you understand what each variable name stands for.

The CARDS portion of the program includes six lines of data, one for each cell. The first cell represents those students who preferred IBM compatibles and were in the School of Arts and Sciences. The value for NUMBER on this line shows that there were 30 subjects in this cell. The next line shows that there were 100 subjects who preferred IBM compatibles and were in the School of Business, and so forth. You should compare the six lines of data to the six cells of Figure 6.6 to verify how the data were coded.

Computing chi-square with PROC FREQ using tabular data. By now, you may be wondering why there is so much emphasis on preparing a two-way classification table when you want to perform a chi-square test of independence. This is necessary because computing chi-square involves determining the **observed frequencies** in each cell of the table (the number of observations that actually appear in each cell), and comparing these to the **expected frequencies** in each cell of the table (the number of observations that you would expect to appear in each cell if the row variable and the column variable were completely unrelated). Now that your two-way classification table has been completed and input, you may request the actual chi-square statistic.

Here is the general form for a SAS program that creates a two-way classification table for two nominal-level variables when the data have been input in tabular form. The options used with these statements (described after the program) allow you to request a chi-square test of independence, along with additional information.

```
PROC FREQ    DATA=data-set-name;
   TABLES    row-variable-name*column-variable-name    /    options ;
   WEIGHT    number-variable-name;
   RUN;
```

These are some of the options for the TABLES statement that may be especially useful in social science research:

ALL

Requests several significance tests (including the chi-square test of independence) and measures of bivariate association. Although several statistics are printed, not all will be appropriate for a given analysis; the choice of the correct statistic will depend on the level of measurement used with the variables along with other considerations.

CHISQ

Requests the chi-square test of independence, and prints a number of measures of bivariate association based on chi-square.

EXACT

Prints Fisher's exact test. This is printed automatically for 2 X 2 tables (provided the CHISQ option is specified), but must be specifically requested for other tables.

EXPECTED

Prints the expected cell frequencies; that is, the cell frequencies that would be expected if the two variables were in fact independent (unrelated). This is a very useful option for determining the *nature* of the relationship between the two variables.

MEASURES

Requests several measures of bivariate association, along with their asymptotic standard errors. These include the Pearson and Spearman correlation coefficients, gamma, Kendall's tau-b, Stuart's tau-c, symmetric lambda, asymmetric lambda, uncertainty coefficients, as well as other measures. Again, some of these indices will not be appropriate for a given study. All of these measures are printed if you request the ALL option.

To illustrate, here is a complete SAS program that reads tabular data, creates a two-way classification table, and prints the statistics requested by the ALL option (including chi-square):

```
1      DATA D1;
2         INPUT   PREF      $
3                 SCHOOL    $
4                 NUMBER    ;
5
6      CARDS;
7      IBM   ARTS    30
8      IBM   BUS    100
9      IBM   ED      20
10     MAC   ARTS    60
11     MAC   BUS     40
12     MAC   ED     120
13     ;
14     PROC FREQ   DATA=D1;
15        TABLES   PREF*SCHOOL   /   ALL;
16        WEIGHT   NUMBER;
17        RUN;
```

The preceding TABLES statement requests that PREF be the row-variable and SCHOOL be the column-variable in the printed table. This request is followed by a slash, the ALL option, and a semicolon.

In the WEIGHT statement, you provide the name of the variable that codes the number of subjects in each cell. In this case, you specify the variable NUMBER.

The two-way classification table produced by this program appears here as Output 6.7:

```
                    TABLE OF PREF BY SCHOOL

          PREF         SCHOOL

          Frequency|
          Percent  |
          Row Pct  |
          Col Pct  |ARTS    |BUS     |ED      |   Total
          ---------+--------+--------+--------+
          IBM      |     30 |    100 |     20 |    150
                   |   8.11 |  27.03 |   5.41 |  40.54
                   |  20.00 |  66.67 |  13.33 |
                   |  33.33 |  71.43 |  14.29 |
          ---------+--------+--------+--------+
          MAC      |     60 |     40 |    120 |    220
                   |  16.22 |  10.81 |  32.43 |  59.46
                   |  27.27 |  18.18 |  54.55 |
                   |  66.67 |  28.57 |  85.71 |
          ---------+--------+--------+--------+
          Total          90      140      140      370
                       24.32    37.84    37.84   100.00
```

Output 6.7: Two-Way Classification Table Requested by PROC FREQ

In the 2 X 3 classification table reproduced in Output 6.7, the name of the row variable (PREF) appears in the upper-left corner. The label for each row appears on the far-left side of the appropriate row: the first row (labelled IBM) represents the subjects who preferred IBM compatibles, and the second row (labelled MAC) represents subjects who preferred Macintoshes.

The name of the column-variable (SCHOOL) appears above the three columns, and each column in turn is headed with its label: column 1 represents the Arts and Sciences students, column 2 represents the Business students, and column three represents the Education students.

Where a given row and column intersect, information regarding the subjects in that cell is provided. Within each cell the following information is provided (in this sequence):

1. The "Frequency," or the raw number of subjects in the cell.

2. The "Percent," or the percent of subjects in that cell relative to the total number of subjects (the number of subjects in the cell divided by the total number of subjects).

3. The "Row Pct," or the percent of subjects in that cell, relative to the number of subjects in that row. For example, there are 30 subjects in the IBM ARTS cell, and 150 subjects in the IBM row. Therefore, the row percent for this cell is 30 / 150 = 20%.

4. The "Col Pct," or the percent of subjects in that cell, relative to the number of subjects in that column. For example, there are 30 subjects in the IBM ARTS cell, and 90 subjects in the ARTS column. Therefore, the column percent for this cell is 30 /90 = 33.33%.

In the present study, it is particularly revealing to review the classification table just one column at a time, and to pay particular attention to the last entry in each cell: the "column percent." First, consider the ARTS column. The column percent entries show that only 33.33% of the Arts and Sciences students preferred IBM compatibles, while 66.67% preferred Macintoshes. Next, consider the BUS column, which shows the reverse trend: 71.43% of the Business students preferred IBM compatibles while only 28.57 percent preferred Macintoshes. Finally, the trend of the Education students in the ED column is similar to that for the Arts and Sciences students: only 14.29% preferred IBM compatibles, while 85.71% preferred Macintoshes.

These percentages reinforce the suspicion that there is a relationship between school of enrollment and computer preference. But is the relationship statistically significant? To answer this, you must consult the chi-square test of independence, which (along with other information) is reproduced in Output 6.8.

```
          STATISTICS FOR TABLE OF PREF BY SCHOOL

Statistic                        DF     Value        Prob
--------------------------------------------------------------
Chi-Square                        2     97.385       0.000
Likelihood Ratio Chi-Square       2    102.685       0.000
Mantel-Haenszel Chi-Square        1     16.981       0.000
Phi Coefficient                          0.513
Contingency Coefficient                  0.456
Cramer's V                               0.513

Statistic                               Value        ASE
--------------------------------------------------------------
Gamma                                    0.355       0.071
Kendall's Tau-b                          0.229       0.048
Stuart's Tau-c                           0.257       0.054

Somers' D C|R                            0.267       0.056
Somers' D R|C                            0.196       0.042

Pearson Correlation                      0.215       0.048
Spearman Correlation                     0.242       0.051
```

```
        Lambda Asymmetric C|R                  0.348      0.044
        Lambda Asymmetric R|C                  0.400      0.061
        Lambda Symmetric                       0.368      0.044

        Uncertainty Coefficient C|R            0.129      0.023
        Uncertainty Coefficient R|C            0.206      0.037
        Uncertainty Coefficient Symmetric      0.158      0.029

        Sample Size = 370
```

Output 6.8: Chi-Square Test of Independence and Other Statistics Requested by the ALL Option

The chi-square test of independence appears as the first statistic in the table. It tests the null hypothesis that, in the population, the two variables are independent, or unrelated. When the null hypothesis is true, expect the value of chi-square to be relatively small; the stronger the relationship between the two variables in the sample, the larger chi-square will be.

Output 6.8 shows that the obtained value of chi-square was 97.385, with 2 degrees of freedom. The degrees of freedom for the chi-square test are calculated as:

$$df = (r-1)(c-1)$$

where

   r = number of categories for the row variable, and
   c = number of categories for the column variable.

For the current analysis, the row variable (PREF) had two categories, and column variable (SCHOOL) had three categories, so the degrees of freedom are calculated as:

$$
\begin{aligned}
df &= (2-1)(3-1) \\
&= (1)(2) \\
&= 2
\end{aligned}
$$

At 97.385, the obtained value of chi-square was quite large, given the degrees of freedom. The probability value, or *p* value, for this chi-square statistic is printed below the heading "Prob" in Output 6.8. This *p* value is less than .0001, meaning that there is less than one chance in 10,000 of obtaining a chi-square value of this size (or larger) if the variables were independent in the population. You may therefore reject the null hypothesis, and tentatively conclude that school of enrollment is related to computer preferences.

Computing Chi-Square from Raw Data

Inputting raw data. If the data to be analyzed are in raw form (that is, if the data have not already been summarized in a two-way classification table), you can input them following the procedures discussed in Chapter 3. For example, if the preceding questionnaire had been administered to the 370 subjects, you could key their data according to the following guide:

Column	Variable Name	Explanation
1-4	SCHOOL	School of enrollment, coded:
		ARTS = "Arts and Sciences"
		BUS = "Business"
		ED = "Education"
5	(blank)	(blank)
6-8	PREF	Computer preference, coded:
		IBM = "IBM compatible"
		MAC = "Macintosh"

The entire data input step, including a small portion of the sample data, is presented here:

```
1       DATA D1;
2          INPUT   #1   @1   (SCHOOL)   ($4.)
3                       @6   (PREF)     ($3.)    ;
4       CARDS;
5       ARTS IBM
6       BUS  IBM
7       BUS  MAC
8       ED   IBM
9       .
10      .
11      .
12      ED   MAC
13      ARTS MAC
14      BUS  IBM
15      ;
```

The fictitious data for the subjects begin on line 5, and there is one line of data for each subject. You can see that the first subject was an Arts and Sciences student, and preferred an IBM compatible, the second student was a Business student, and also preferred an IBM compatible, and so forth. For this program, there would be 370 lines of data, because there were 370 subjects.

The preceding program specified SCHOOL and PREF as *character* variables with values such as ARTS and MAC, but it also would have been possible to code them as *numeric* variables. For example, SCHOOL could have been coded so that 1 = Arts and Sciences, 2 = Business, and 3 = Education. You could have proceeded with the analysis in the usual fashion, although you would then have to make a record to remember exactly which group is represented by these numerical values, or use the VALUES statement of PROC FORMAT to attach meaningful value labels (such as "ARTS" and "BUS") to the variable categories when they are printed. For the latter approach, consult Chapter 18 in the *SAS procedures guide* (1990).

Computing chi-square with PROC FREQ using raw data. Here is the general form of the statements that request a chi-square test of independence (along with other statistics) when the data are input in raw form:

```
PROC FREQ    DATA=data-set-name;
   TABLES    row-variable*column-variable    /    options ;
   RUN;
```

This general form is identical to the general form used with tabular data, except that the WEIGHT statement has been deleted. The full program (including a portion of the data) to compute the chi-square test with raw data is presented here:

```
1        DATA D1;
2            INPUT   #1   @1   (SCHOOL)   ($4.)
3                         @6   (PREF)     ($3.)    ;
4        CARDS;
5        ARTS IBM
6        BUS   IBM
7        BUS   MAC
8        ED    IBM
9        .
10       .
11       .
12       ED    MAC
13       ARTS MAC
```

```
14        BUS    IBM
15        ;
16        PROC FREQ    DATA=D1;
17            TABLES    PREF*SCHOOL    /    ALL;
18            RUN;
```

From this point forward, the analysis proceeds in exactly the same fashion as when the data set was based on tabular data: you can request the same options, and you can interpret the results in exactly the same way.

Special Notes Regarding the Chi-Square Test

Using Fisher's exact test for 2 X 2 tables and larger tables. A 2 X 2 table is one that contains just two rows and two columns. A two-way classification table for a chi-square study will be a 2 X 2 table if there are just two values for the row-variable, and just two values for the column-variable. For example, imagine that you modified the preceding computer preference study so that there were just two values for the computer preference variable (IBM compatible and Macintosh), as before, but just two values for the school of enrollment variable (Arts and Sciences and Business). The two-way classification table that would result from this modified study would resemble the one portrayed in Figure 6.7, except that the column for the School of Education would be eliminated. The resulting table is called a 2 X 2 table because it consists of just two rows (IBM versus Macintosh) and two columns (Arts & Sciences versus Business).

When analyzing a 2 X 2 classification table, it is best to use *Fisher's exact test* rather than the standard chi-square test of independence. This test is printed automatically whenever a 2 X 2 table is analyzed and you request the CHISQ option. In the SAS output, consult the *p* value that appears to the right of the heading "Fisher's Exact test (2-Tail)." This estimates "the probability of observing a table that gives at least as much evidence of association as the one actually observed, given that the null hypothesis is true" (*SAS procedures guide, version 6, third edition*, 1990, p. 339). In other words, when this *p* value for Fisher's exact test is less than .05, you may reject the null hypothesis that the two nominal-scale variables are independent in the population, and may conclude that they are in fact related.

In some situations, Fisher's exact test may also be appropriate for larger classification tables (i.e., for tables with more than 2 rows and/or columns). This will be the case when the sample size is small and the sample size per degree of freedom is less than 5. With larger classification tables, you must specifically request the Fisher's exact test by specifying the EXACT option in the TABLES statement. See the *SAS procedures guide, version 6, third edition*, pp. 356-357 (1990) for details.

Minimum cell frequencies. The chi-square test may not be valid if the observed frequency in any of the cells is zero, or if the expected frequency in any of the cells is less than five (use the EXPECTED option with the TABLES statement to compute expected cell frequencies). When these minimums are not met, consider gathering additional data or perhaps combining similar categories of subjects in order to increase cell frequencies.

Conclusion

Bivariate associations are the simplest types of associations studied, and the statistics presented here (the Pearson correlation, the Spearman correlation, and the chi-square test of independence) are appropriate for investigating most types of bivariate relationships likely to be encountered in the social sciences. With these relatively simple procedures behind you, you are now ready to proceed to the *t* test, the one-way analysis of variance, and other tests of group differences.

Appendix: Assumptions Underlying the Tests

Assumptions Underlying the Pearson Correlation Coefficient

- **Interval-level measurement**. Both the predictor and criterion variables should be assessed on an interval or ratio level of measurement.

- **Random sampling**. Each subject in the sample will contribute one score on the predictor variable, and one score on the criterion variable. These pairs of scores should represent a random sample drawn from the population of interest.

- **Linearity**. The relationship between the criterion variable and the predictor variable should be linear. This means that, in the population, the mean criterion scores at each value of the predictor variable should fall on a straight line. The Pearson correlation coefficient is not appropriate for assessing the strength of the relationship between two variables involved in a curvilinear relationship.

- **Bivariate normal distribution.** The pairs of scores should follow a bivariate normal distribution; that is, scores on the criterion variable should form a normal distribution at each value of the predictor variable. Similarly, scores of the predictor variable should form a normal distribution at each value of the criterion variable. When scores represent a bivariate normal distribution, they form an *elliptical scattergram* when plotted (i.e, their scattergram is shaped like a football: fat in the middle and tapered on the ends).

Assumptions Underlying the Spearman Correlation Coefficient

• **Ordinal-level measurement**. Both the predictor and criterion variables should be assessed on an ordinal level of measurement. However, interval- or ratio-level variables are sometimes analyzed with the Spearman correlation coefficient when one or both variables are markedly skewed.

Assumptions Underlying the Chi-Square Test of Independence

• **Nominal-level measurement**. Both variables should be assessed on a nominal scale.

• **Random sampling**. Subjects contributing data should represent a random sample drawn from the population of interest.

• **Independent cell entries**. Each subject should appear in only one cell. The fact that a given subject appears in one cell should not affect the probability of another subject appearing in any other cell.

• **Expected frequencies of at least 5**. When analyzing a 2 X 2 classification table, no cell should display an expected frequency of less than 5. With larger tables (e.g, 3 X 4 tables), no more than 20% of the cells should have expected frequencies less than 5.

References

Hays, W. L. (1988). *Statistics, fourth edition*. New York: Holt, Rinehart, and Winston.

SAS Institute Inc. (1990). *SAS procedures guide, version 6, third edition*. Cary, NC: SAS Institute Inc.

SAS Institute Inc. (1989). *SAS/STAT user's guide, version 6, fourth edition, volume 2*. Cary, NC: SAS Institute Inc.

Schlotzhauer, S.D. & Littell, R. C. (1987). *SAS system for elementary statistical analysis*. Cary, NC: SAS Institute Inc.

Chapter 7

t TESTS: INDEPENDENT SAMPLES
AND PAIRED SAMPLES

Overview. This chapter describes the differences between the independent-samples *t* test and the paired-samples *t* test, and shows how to perform both types of analyses. It develops an example of a research design that would provide data appropriate for a *t* test. With respect to the independent-samples test, the chapter shows how to write the necessary program using PROC TTEST, determine whether the equal-variances or unequal variances *t* test is appropriate, and interpret the results. With respect to the paired-samples test, it provides examples of paired-samples research designs, discusses problems with these designs, and shows how to perform the analysis using PROC MEANS.

Introduction: Two Types of *t* Tests

A *t* test is appropriate when your analysis involves a single predictor variable that is measured on a nominal scale and assumes only two values, and a single criterion variable that is measured on an interval or ratio scale. This is usually viewed as a test of group differences. For example, when experimental condition is the predictor variable and scores on an attitude scale are the criterion variable, you may want to know whether there was a significant difference between the experimental group and the control group with respect to their mean attitude scores. A *t* test can help determine this.

There are actually two types of *t* tests that are appropriate for different experimental designs. First, the **independent-samples *t* test** is appropriate if the observations obtained under one treatment condition are independent of (unrelated to) the observations obtained under the other treatment condition. For example, imagine that you draw a random sample of subjects, and randomly assign each subject to either Condition 1 or Condition 2 in your experiment. After manipulating the independent variable, you determine scores on the attitude scale for subjects in the two conditions, and use an independent-samples *t* test to determine whether the mean attitude score is significantly higher for the subjects in Condition 1 than for the subjects in Condition 2. The independent-samples *t* test was appropriate here because the observations (attitude scores) in Condition 1 were completely unrelated to the observations in Condition 2: Condition 1 consisted of one group of people, and Condition 2 consisted of a different group of people who were not related to, or affected by, the people in Condition 1.

The second type of test is the **paired-samples *t* test.** This statistic is appropriate if each observation in Condition 1 is paired in some meaningful way with a corresponding observation in Condition 2. There are a number of ways that this pairing can be achieved. For example, imagine that you draw a random sample of subjects, and decide that each subject will provide two attitude scores: one score after being exposed to Condition 1, and a second score after being exposed to Condition 2. In a sense, you still have two samples of observations (the sample from Condition 1 versus that from Condition 2), but the observations from the two samples are now *related*. This means, for example, that if a given subject scored relatively high on the attitude scale under Condition 1, that subject will probably also score relatively high under Condition 2.

Therefore, in analyzing the data, it makes sense to pair each subject's score from Condition 1 with his or her score from Condition 2. Because of this pairing, a paired-samples *t* statistic is calculated differently than an independent-samples *t* statistic.

This chapter is divided into two major sections. The first deals with the independent-samples *t* test, and the second deals with the paired-samples test. These sections provide additional examples of situations in which the two procedures may be appropriate.

Earlier, you read that a *t* test is appropriate when the analysis involves a nominal-scale predictor variable and an interval/ratio-scale criterion. A number of additional assumptions should also be met for the test to be valid (e.g., the samples must be drawn from normal distributions), and these assumptions are summarized in an appendix at the end of this chapter. When these assumptions are violated, consider using a nonparametric statistic instead. For help, consult Chapter 30 in the *SAS/STAT user's guide, volume 2* (1989).

The Independent-Samples *t* Test

Example: A Test of the Investment Model

The use of the independent-samples *t* test will be illustrated by testing a hypothesis that could be derived from the investment model (Rusbult, 1980). As discussed in earlier chapters, the investment model identifies a number of variables that are predicted to affect a subject's commitment to romantic relationships (as well as to some other types of relationships). **Commitment** can be defined as the subject's intention to remain in the relationship and to maintain the relationship. One version of the investment model predicts that commitment will be affected by four variables: rewards, costs, investment size, and alternative value. These variables are briefly defined below:

Rewards:	The number of "good things" that the subject associates with the relationship; the positive aspects of the relationship
Costs:	The number of "bad things" or hardships associated with the relationship
Investment Size:	The amount of time and personal resources that the subject has "put into" the relationship
Alternative value:	The attractiveness of the subject's alternatives to the relationship (e.g., the attractiveness of alternative romantic partners)

At least four testable hypotheses could be derived from the investment model as it was described here: (a) rewards have a causal effect on commitment; (b) costs have a causal effect on commitment; (c) investment size has a causal effect on commitment; (d) alternative value has a causal effect on commitment. If you were ambitious, you might design a single study that tests all four of these hypotheses simultaneously. Such a study would be quite complex, however; to keep things simple, this chapter focuses on testing only the first hypothesis: the prediction that the level of rewards affects commitment.

Rewards refer to the positive aspects of the relationship. Your relationship would score high on rewards if your partner were physically attractive, intelligent, kind, fun, rich, and so forth. Your relationship would score low on rewards if your partner were unattractive, unintelligent, unfeeling, dull, and so forth. It can be seen that the hypothesized relationship between rewards and commitment makes good intuitive sense: an increase in rewards *should* result in an increase in commitment. The predicted relationship between these variables is illustrated with Figure 7.1:

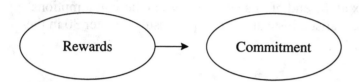

Figure 7.1: Hypothesized Causal Relationship between Rewards and Commitment.

There are any number of ways that you might test the hypothesis that rewards have a causal effect on commitment. One approach would involve a type of **role-playing** procedure: Subjects could be given written descriptions of different fictitious romantic partners, and asked to rate their likely commitment to these partners. The descriptions could be manipulated so that a given fictitious partner could be described as a "high-reward" partner to one group of subjects, and as a "low-reward" partner to a second group of subjects. If the hypothesis concerning the relationship between rewards and commitment is correct, you would expect to see higher commitment scores for the high-reward partner. This part of the chapter describes a fictitious study that utilizes just such a procedure, and tests the relevant null hypothesis using an independent-samples *t* test.

The Study

Assume that you have drawn a sample of 20 subjects, and have randomly assigned 10 subjects to serve in a high-reward condition and 10 to serve in a low-reward condition. Regardless of group, all subjects were given a packet of materials, and the following instructions appeared on the first page:

```
In this study, we are asking that you engage in a role-playing
activity.  Imagine that you are single:  not married and not
involved in any romantic relationship.  You will read descriptions
of 10 different "partners" (people with whom you might be involved
in a romantic relationship).  For each description, imagine that
you are involved in a romantic relationship with that person.
Think about what it would be like to date that person, given
his/her positive features, negative features, and other
considerations.  After you have thought about it, rate how
committed you would be to maintaining your romantic relationship
with that person.  Each "partner" is described on a separate sheet
of paper, and at the bottom of each sheet there are four items
with which you can rate your commitment to that particular
relationship.
```

On the following 10 pages were the descriptions of the 10 partners, with each partner described on a separate page. The paragraph describing a given partner provided information about the extent to which the relationship with that person was rewarding and costly. It also provided information relevant to the investment size and alternative value associated with the relationship.

The dependent variable. The dependent variable in this study was "subject commitment to a specific romantic partner." It would be ideal if you could arrive at a single score that indicates how committed a given subject is to a given partner. High scores on this variable would reveal that the subject is highly committed to the partner, and low scores would indicate the opposite. This section describes one way that you could use rating scales to arrive at such a score.

At the bottom of the sheet that described a given partner, the subject was provided with four items that used a 9-point rating format. The subject was asked to respond to these items to indicate the strength of his or her commitment to the partner described on that page. The items used in making these ratings are presented here:

PLEASE RATE YOUR COMMITMENT TO THIS PARTNER BY CIRCLING YOUR
RESPONSE TO EACH OF THE FOLLOWING ITEMS:

How committed are you to remaining in this relationship?

> Not at all   1 2 3 4 5 6 7 8 9   Extremely
> Committed   Committed

How likely is it that you will maintain this relationship?

> Definitely Plan   1 2 3 4 5 6 7 8 9   Definitely
> Not to Maintain   Plan to
>   Maintain

How likely is it that you will break up with this partner soon?

> Extremely   1 2 3 4 5 6 7 8 9   Extremely
> Likely   Unlikely

"I feel totally committed to this partner."

> Disagree   1 2 3 4 5 6 7 8 9   Agree
> Strongly   Strongly

Notice that, with each of the preceding items, circling a higher response number (closer to "9") reveals a higher level of commitment to the relationship. For a given partner, the subject's responses to these four items were summed to arrive at a final commitment score for that partner. This score could range from a low of 4 (if the subject had circled the "1" on each item) to a high of 36 (if the subject had circled the "9" on each item). These scores will serve as the dependent variable in your study.

Manipulating the independent variable. The independent variable in this study was "level of rewards associated with a specific romantic partner." This independent variable was manipulated by varying the descriptions of the partners that were shown to the two treatment groups.

The partner descriptions given to the high-reward group were identical to those given to the low-reward group, but this was true only for the first 9 descriptions. For partner 10, there was an important difference between the descriptions provided to the two groups. The sheet given to the high-reward group described a relationship with a relatively high level of rewards, and the one given to the low-reward group described a relationship with a relatively low level of rewards. Below is the description seen by subjects in the high-reward condition:

```
PARTNER 10:  Imagine that you have been dating partner 10 for
about 1 year, and you have put a great deal of time and effort
into this relationship.  There are not very many attractive
members of the opposite sex where you live, so it would be
difficult to replace this person with someone else.  Partner 10
lives in the same neighborhood as you, so it is easy to see
him/her as often as you like.  This person enjoys the same
recreational activities that you enjoy, and is very good-looking.
```

Notice how the preceding description provides information relevant to the four investment model variables discussed earlier. The first sentence provides information dealing with investment size ("...you have put a great deal of time and effort into this relationship."), and the second sentence deals with alternative value ("There are not very many attractive members of the opposite sex where you live..."). The third sentence indicates that this is a low-cost relationship because "...it is easy to see him or her as often as you like." In other words, there are no hardships associated with seeing this partner (if the descriptions said that the partner lives in a distant city, this would have been a high-cost relationship).

However, it is the last sentence in this description that you are most interested in, because this last sentence describes the level of rewards associated with the relationship. The relevant sentence is "This person enjoys the same recreational activities that you enjoy, and is very good-looking," and it is this statement that establishes partner 10 as a high-reward partner for the subjects in the high-reward group.

In contrast, consider the description of partner 10 given to the low-reward group. Notice that it is identical to the description given to the high-reward group with regard to the first three sentences. The last sentence, however, deals with rewards, so this last sentence is different for the low-reward group. It describes a low-reward relationship:

PARTNER 10: Imagine that you have been dating partner 10 for about 1 year, and you have put a great deal of time and effort into this relationship. There are not very many attractive members of the opposite sex where you live, so it would be difficult to replace this person with someone else. Partner 10 lives in the same neighborhood as you, so it is easy to see him/her as often as you like. This person does not enjoy the same recreational activities that you enjoy, and is not very good-looking.

Notice that partner 10 is the *only partner that you are really interested in.* You will analyze the subjects' ratings of their commitment to partner 10, and will simply disregard their responses to the first 9 partners (the first 9 were only included to give the subjects some practice at the task before coming to 10).

Also notice the logic behind these experimental procedures: both groups of subjects were treated in exactly the same way with respect to everything except the independent variable. For the first 9 partners, the descriptions were completely identical in the two groups. Even the description of partner 10 was identical with respect to everything except the level of rewards associated with the relationship. Therefore, if the subjects in the high-reward group are significantly more committed to partner 10 than the subjects in the low-reward group, you can be reasonably confident that it was the level of reward manipulation that affected their commitment ratings. It would be difficult to explain the results in any other way.

In summary, you began your investigation with a group of 20 subjects. You randomly assigned 10 to the high-reward condition, and 10 to the low-reward condition. After they completed their task, you disregarded their responses to the first 9 partners, but recorded their responses to partner 10. These responses are the subject of the following analysis.

Writing the SAS Program

Remember that an independent-samples *t* test is appropriate for comparing two samples of observations. It allows you to determine whether there is a significant difference between the two samples with respect to their mean scores on this criterion. More technically, it allows you to test the null hypothesis that, in the population, there is no difference between the two groups with respect to their mean scores on the criterion. This section shows how to write a SAS program with PROC TTEST to test this null hypothesis for the current fictitious study.

There was one predictor variable in this study, and it was "level of reward." This variable could assume one of two values: subjects were either in the high-reward group, or in the low-reward group. Since this variable simply codes group membership, you know that it is measured on a nominal scale. In coding the data, you will give subjects a score of "1" if they were in the high-reward condition, and a score of "0" (zero) if they were in the low-reward condition. You will need a short SAS variable name for this variable, so call it REWGRP (which stands for "reward group").

There was one criterion variable in this study, and it was "commitment": the subjects' ratings of how committed they would be to a relationship with partner 10. When keying the data, you would simply key the sum of the rating numbers that have been circled by the subject in responding to partner 10. This variable could assume values from 4 through 36, and was measured on an interval scale. Give it the SAS variable name of COMMIT.

The general form for the SAS program to perform an independent-samples *t* test is as follows:

```
PROC TTEST    DATA=data-set-name;
   CLASS    predictor-variable;
   VAR      criterion-variables;
   RUN;
```

Here is the entire program--including the DATA step--to analyze some fictitious data from the preceding study.

```
 1        DATA D1;
 2           INPUT  #1  @1  (REWGRP)  (1.)
 3                      @3  (COMMIT)  (2.)  ;
 4        CARDS;
 5        0 12
 6        0 10
 7        0 15
 8        0 13
 9        0 16
10        0  9
11        0 13
12        0 14
13        0 15
14        0 13
15        1 25
16        1 22
17        1 27
18        1 24
19        1 22
```

```
20          1 20
21          1 24
22          1 23
23          1 22
24          1 24
25          ;
26
27          PROC TTEST   DATA=D1;
28              CLASS REWGRP;
29              VAR COMMIT;
30              RUN;
```

Notes Regarding the SAS Program

Each line of data contains responses for one subject. Assume that you key your data using the following format:

Line	Column	Variable Name	Explanation
1	1	REWGRP	Codes group membership, so that 0 = low-reward condition, and 1 = high-reward condition
	2	(blank)	(blank)
	3-4	COMMIT	Commitment ratings obtained when subjects rated partner 10

The classification variable, REWGRP, was coded using zeros and ones, but the choice of these values was arbitrary; you could code using different numbers. If you prefer, you could even use character values such as "L" to code the low-reward condition, and "H" to code the high-reward condition.

The criterion variable, COMMIT, was a 2-digit variable because it could take on a value as high as 36, a 2-digit number. Data from the 10 low-reward subjects were keyed first (in lines 5-14), and were followed by data from the 10 high-reward subjects (in lines 15-24). It was not really necessary to sort the data from the two groups in this way, however: Data from low-reward and high-reward subjects could have been keyed in a random sequence.

Remember to always follow the CLASS statement with the name of the study's predictor variable; in other words, always follow it with the name of the nominal-scale variable that indicates group membership (REWGRP, in this case). It may be helpful to remember that CLASS stands for "classification variable," which is another way of saying "nominal-scale variable."

In contrast, always follow the VAR statement with the name of the interval-level or ratio-level variable that serves as the study's criterion (COMMIT, in this case). You can list more than one criterion variable, and a separate *t* test will be performed for each.

Results From the SAS Output

Output 7.1 presents the results obtained from the preceding program. The name of the criterion variable (COMMIT, in this case) appears to the right of the word "Variable" on the left side of the output. The name of the predictor variable (REWGRP) appears just below "Variable."

```
                              TTEST PROCEDURE

Variable: COMMIT

REWGRP        N          Mean       Std Dev    Std Error     Minimum      Maximum
          ---------------------------------------------------------------------------
    0        10    13.00000000    2.21108319   0.69920590    9.00000000   16.00000000
    1        10    23.30000000    1.94650684   0.61553951   20.00000000   27.00000000


Variances          T      DF     Prob>|T|
          ---------------------------------------
Unequal      -11.0569    17.7     0.0001
Equal        -11.0569    18.0     0.0000

For H0: Variances are equal, F' = 1.29     DF = (9,9)     Prob>F' = 0.7103
```

Output 7.1: Results of PROC TTEST: Significant Differences Observed

The output is divided into two sections. The top section provides information regarding the two groups: the number of observations in each group, their mean scores on the criterion variable, and so forth. The bottom half of the output provides the results of the *t* test for the null hypothesis that the means of the two groups do not differ in the population. The following section offers a systematic approach for interpreting this output.

Steps in Interpreting the Output

1. Make sure that everything looks right. As was stated previously, the name of your nominal-level predictor variable should appear below "Variable" on the left side of the output. Under the name of this predictor variable should be the values used to code the two conditions. In this case, the values were "0" for the low-reward group and "1" for the high-reward group. To the right of these values the TTEST procedure prints simple descriptive statistics for the criterion variable, COMMIT. You can see that, for the low-reward group, the sample size was 10, the mean score on COMMIT was 13, the standard deviation was 2.21, the standard error was 0.70, the minimum observed value was 9, and the maximum observed value was 16. Corresponding statistics for the high-reward group may be found to the right of the value "1".

You should carefully review each of these figures to verify that they are within the expected range. For example, in this case you would want to verify that data for 10 subjects were in fact observed for each group. In addition, the "Minimum" and "Maximum" columns are particularly useful for identifying errors: the way the COMMIT variable was constructed, it could assume possible values between 4 and 36. The observed minimum and maximum values (as reported in the output) are within these bounds, so there is no obvious evidence that an error was made in keying the data or in writing the INPUT statement.

2. Determine which *t* statistic is appropriate. Output 7.1 shows that the TTEST procedure actually provides two *t* statistics, but only one of these will be relevant for a given analysis. The first *t* statistic (under the heading "T" and to the right of "Unequal") is the approximate *t* statistic which is based on the assumption that the variances in the two samples are not equal . The second *t* statistic (also under the heading "T" but to the right of "Equal") is the standard *t* statistic which is based on the assumption that the variances are equal. So which *t* statistic should be reported?

Fortunately, the TTEST procedure automatically performs a folded form of the *F* statistic (symbolized as *F'*) that tests the equality of the variances in the two samples. The results of this test are reported on the last line of output from the TTEST procedure, which is reproduced here:

```
For HO:  Variances are equal, F' = 1.29    DF = (9,9)    PROB > F' = 0.7103
```

This analysis begins with the null hypothesis that, in the population, there is no difference between the low-reward subjects and the high-reward subjects with respect to their *variances* on the commitment variable. It computes a special *F* test--the *F'* test--to test this hypothesis. If the *p* value for the resulting *F'* test is less than .05, you will reject the null hypothesis of no differences and conclude that the variances are *unequal*. If the *p* value is greater than .05, you will tentatively conclude that the variances are *equal*.

For the present analysis, the *F'* value was only 1.29 with a corresponding *p* value of .7103 (this *p* value appears to the right of "Prob>F'"). This means that the probability of obtaining an *F'* this large or larger when the population variances are equal was quite large--it was .7103. You therefore fail to reject the null hypothesis of equal variances, and tentatively conclude that the variances are equal. This means that you will interpret the equal variances *t* statistic, which appears to the right of the word "Equal" in Output 7.1 (if the PROB > F' had been less than .05, you would have interpreted the *t* statistic to the right of the word "Unequal").

In summary, when the PROB > F' is nonsignificant (greater than .05), report the *t* test based on equal variances. When the PROB > F' is significant (less than .05), report the *t* test based on unequal variances.

3. Review the appropriate *t* statistic and its associated probability value. The bottom half of the output provides the information that is of primary interest: The obtained *t* statistic along with its corresponding degrees of freedom and probability value. As was discussed in the preceding section, you will review the equal-variances *t* statistics in the current analysis.

In the column headed with a "T", and to the right of the word "Equal", you can see that the obtained *t* statistic is –11.06, which is quite large. It is associated with 18 degrees of freedom, and under "Prob > I T I" you can see that the *p* value associated with this *t* is 0.00000 (technically, the *p* value for this test is not *really* zero; because the *p* value output of the TTEST procedure goes to only five decimal places, it is clear that the *p* value for this analysis is actually a very small number, perhaps 0.000001 or 0.0000001).

But what does this *p* value really mean? This *p* value is the *probability that you would obtain a t statistic this large or larger (in absolute magnitude) if the null hypothesis were true*.

You can state the null hypothesis tested in this study as follows: "In the population, there is no difference between the low-reward group and the high-reward group with respect to their mean scores on the commitment variable." Symbolically, the null hypothesis can be represented in this way:

$$M_1 = M_2$$

where M_1 = mean commitment score for the population of people in the high-reward condition, and M_2 = mean commitment score for the population of people in the low-reward condition.

If this null hypothesis were true, you should have obtained a *t* statistic somewhat close to zero. In contrast, however, your obtained *t* statistic was –11.06, which is much larger (in its absolute magnitude) than you would expect if the null hypothesis were true. In fact, given the degrees of freedom for this test, the TTEST procedure indicates that the probability of getting a *t* this large was only 0.0000. Remember that, anytime you obtain a *p* value less than .05, you reject the null hypothesis, and because your obtained *p* value is so small in this case, you are able to reject the null hypothesis of no population differences in commitment. You may therefore conclude that there probably is a difference in mean commitment between the population of people in the high-reward condition and the population of people in the low-reward condition.

4. Review the sample means. The significant *t* statistic indicates that the two populations are probably different from each other, but which population is *higher* on the commitment variable? To determine this, you review the output under the column headed "Mean." To the right of the value "0", and under the heading "Mean", you see that the low-reward group had a mean score of 13.00 on commitment (remember that the value "0" coded the low-reward subjects). To the right of the value "1", and under the heading "Mean", you see that the high-reward group had a mean score of 23.00. It is therefore clear that, as you predicted, the high-reward group demonstrates a higher level of commitment compared to the low-reward group.

Summarizing the Results of the Analysis

In performing an independent-samples *t* test, the following format can be used to summarize the research problem and results:

> A) Statement of the problem
> B) Nature of the variables
> C) Statistical test
> D) Null hypothesis (H_0)
> E) Alternative hypothesis (H_1)
> F) Obtained statistic
> G) Obtained probability (*p*) value
> H) Conclusion regarding the null hypothesis
> I) Figure representing the results
> J) Formal description of results for a paper

As an illustration, a summary of the preceding analysis, according to this format, follows:

A) Statement of the problem: The purpose of this study was to determine whether there was a difference between people in a high-reward relationship and people in a low-reward relationship with respect to their mean commitment to the relationship.

B) Nature of the variables: This analysis involved two variables. The predictor variable was level of rewards, which was measured on a nominal scale and could assume two values: a low-reward condition (coded as 0), and a high-reward condition (coded as 1). The criterion variable was commitment, which was measured on an interval scale.

C) Statistical test: Independent-samples *t* test.

D) Null hypothesis (H_0): $M_1 = M_2$. In the population, there is no difference between people in a high-reward relationship and people in a low-reward relationship with respect to their mean levels of commitment.

E) Alternative hypothesis (H_1): $M_1 \neq M_2$. In the population, there is a difference between people in a high-reward relationship and people in a low-reward relationship with respect to their mean levels of commitment.

F) Obtained statistic: $t = -11.06$.

G) Obtained probability (p) value: $p < .0001$.

H) Conclusion regarding the null hypothesis: Reject the null hypothesis.

I) Figure representing the results:

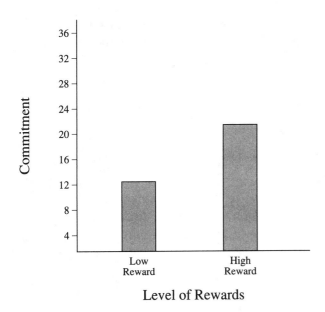

Figure 7.2: Mean Levels of Commitment Observed for Subjects in High-Reward versus Low-Reward Condition (Significant Differences Observed)

J) Formal description of results for a paper: Most chapters of this text show you how to summarize the results of an analysis in a way that would be appropriate if you were preparing a paper to be submitted for publication in a scholarly research journal. These summaries generally follow the format recommended in the *Publication Manual of The American Psychological Association* (1983), a format required by many journals in the social sciences. Here is an example of how the current results could be summarized according to this format:

> Results were analyzed using an independent-samples $\underline{t}$ test. This analysis revealed a significant difference between the two groups, $\underline{t}(18) = -11.06$; $\underline{p} < .001$. The sample means are displayed in Figure 7.2, which shows that subjects in the high-reward condition scored significantly higher on commitment than did subjects in the low-reward condition (for high-reward group, $\underline{M} = 23.30$, $\underline{SD} = 1.95$; for low-reward group, $\underline{M} = 13.00$, $\underline{SD} = 2.21$).

An Example with Nonsignificant Differences

Obviously, researchers do not always obtain significant results when performing investigations such as the one described here. This section repeats the analyses reported previously, this time using fictitious data that will result in a nonsignificant *t* test. The conventions for summarizing nonsignificant results are then presented.

Program and output. Below is a reproduction of the SAS program presented earlier in the chapter. In the following program, however, the data have been modified so that the two groups will not differ significantly on mean levels of commitment.

```
1          DATA D1;
2             INPUT  #1  @1   (REWGRP)   (1.)
3                        @3   (COMMIT)   (2.)   ;
4          CARDS;
5          0 23
6          0 22
7          0 25
8          0 19
9          0 24
10         0 20
11         0 22
12         0 22
13         0 23
14         0 27
15         1 25
16         1 22
17         1 27
18         1 24
19         1 22
20         1 20
21         1 24
22         1 23
23         1 22
24         1 24
25         ;
26
27         PROC TTEST   DATA=D1;
28            CLASS REWGRP;
29            VAR COMMIT;
30            RUN;
```

Simply "eyeballing" the data reveals that very similar commitment scores seem to be displayed by subjects in the two conditions. Nonetheless, a formal statistical test is required to determine whether significant differences exist. The results of the program analyzing the preceding data appear as Output 7.2.

```
                          TTEST PROCEDURE

Variable: COMMIT

REWGRP        N        Mean      Std Dev    Std Error     Minimum      Maximum
-------------------------------------------------------------------------------
    0        10   22.70000000   2.31180545  0.73105707  19.00000000  27.00000000
    1        10   23.30000000   1.94650684  0.61553951  20.00000000  27.00000000


Variances          T       DF      Prob>|T|
----------------------------------------------
Unequal      -0.6278     17.5      0.5382
Equal        -0.6278     18.0      0.5380

For H0: Variances are equal, F' = 1.41    DF = (9,9)    Prob>F' = 0.6166
```

Output 7.2: Results of PROC TTEST: Nonsignificant Differences Observed

Remember that the first step in this analysis is to determine whether the equal-variances *t* test or the unequal variances *t* test is appropriate. The *F'* test reported at the bottom of the output is 1.41, and its corresponding *p* value is .6166. Because this *p* value is greater than .05, you may not reject the null hypothesis of equal variances in the population. This means that it is appropriate to refer to the equal-variances *t* test.

The equal-variances *t* statistic appears under the heading "T" in Output 7.2, and to the right of "Equal". This equal-variances *t* statistic is quite small at –0.63. The *p* value for this *t* statistic is quite large at 0.5380. Obviously, this *p* value is greater than the standard cutoff of .05, meaning that the *t* statistic is nonsignificant. These results mean that you may not reject the null hypothesis of equal population means on commitment. In other words, you conclude that there is not a significant difference between mean levels of commitment in the two samples.

Summarizing the results of the analysis. For this analysis, the statistical interpretation format would appear as follows. (**Note:** Since this is the same study, you would complete items A through E in exactly the same way as earlier.):

F) Obtained statistic: *t* = –0.63.

G) Obtained probability (*p*) value: *p* = .5380.

H) Conclusion regarding the null hypothesis: Fail to reject the null hypothesis.

I) Figure representing the results:

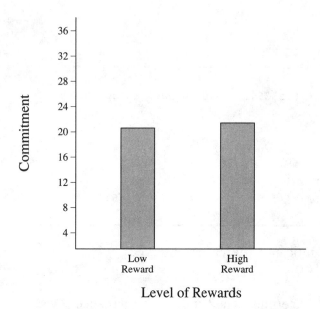

Figure 7.3: Mean Levels of Commitment Observed for Subjects in High-Reward versus Low-Reward Condition (Nonsignificant Differences Observed)

J) Formal description of results for a paper:

> Results were analyzed using an independent-samples t test. This analysis failed to reveal a significant difference between the two groups, t(18) = -0.63; p = .538. The sample means are displayed in Figure 7.3, which shows that subjects in the high-reward condition demonstrated scores on commitment which were quite similar to those shown by subjects in the low-reward condition (for high-reward group, M = 23.30, SD = 1.95; for low-reward group, M = 22.70, SD = 2.31).

The Paired-Samples *t* Test

Paired-Samples versus Independent-Samples

The paired-samples *t* test (sometimes referred to as the *correlated-samples t* test or *matched-samples t* test) is somewhat similar to the independent-samples test in that both procedures involve comparing two samples of observations, and determining whether the mean of one sample is significantly higher than the mean of the other. With the independent-samples procedure, the two groups of scores are completely independent: an observation in one sample is not related to any observation in the other sample. In experimental research, this is normally achieved by drawing a random sample of subjects, and randomly assigning each subject to either condition 1 or condition 2. Because each subject contributes data under only one condition, the two samples are empirically independent.

With the paired-samples procedure, in contrast, each score in one sample is *paired* in some meaningful way with a score in the other sample. There are a number of ways that this may be achieved, and the following examples illustrate some of the most commonly used approaches. One word of warning: the following fictitious studies merely illustrate paired sample designs, and do not necessarily represent sound designs from the perspective of internal or external validity; problems with some of these designs are reviewed in a later section.

Examples of Paired-Samples Research Designs

Each subject is exposed to both treatment conditions. Earlier sections of this chapter described a role playing experiment in which level of reward was manipulated to see how it affected subjects' level of commitment to a romantic relationship. The procedure used in that study required that each subject review 10 "paper people" and rate his or her commitment to each fictitious romantic partner. The dependent variable in the investigation was the rated amount of commitment that the subjects displayed toward partner 10. The independent variable was manipulated by varying the description of partner 10 that was provided to the subjects: subjects in the "high-reward" condition read that partner 10 had several positive attributes, while subjects in the "low-reward" condition read that partner 10 did not have these attributes. This study was as an independent-samples study because each subject was assigned to either a high-reward condition or a low-reward condition (but no subject was ever assigned to *both* conditions).

You could easily modify this investigation so that it would instead follow a paired-samples research design. You could do this by conducting the study with only one group of subjects (rather than two), and having each subject rate partner 10 twice: once after reading the low-reward version of partner 10, and a second time after reading the high-reward version of partner 10.

It would be appropriate to analyze the data resulting from such a study using the paired-samples *t* test because it would be possible to meaningfully pair observations obtained under the two conditions. For example, subject 1's rating of partner 10 under the low-reward condition could be paired with his or her rating of partner 10 under the high-reward condition, subject 2's rating of partner 10 under the low-reward condition could be paired with his or her rating of partner 10 under the high-reward condition, and so forth. Table 7.1 shows how the resulting data could be arranged in tabular form:

Table 7.1

Fictitious Data from a Study Using a Paired Samples Procedure

Subject	Commitment Ratings of Partner 10	
	Low-Reward Condition	High-Reward Condition
John	9	20
Mary	9	22
Tim	10	23
Susan	11	23
Maria	12	24
Fred	12	25
Frank	14	26
Edie	15	28
Jack	17	29
Shirley	19	31

Remember that your dependent variable is still the commitment ratings for partner 10. For subject 1 (John) you have obtained two scores on this dependent variable: a score of 9 obtained in the low-reward condition, and a score of 20 obtained in the high-reward condition. This is what it means to have the scores *paired* in a meaningful way: John's score in the low-reward condition has been paired with his score from the high-reward condition. The same is true for the remaining subjects.

Subjects are matched. The preceding study used a type of **repeated measures** approach: only one sample of subjects participated, and repeated measurements on the dependent variable (commitment) were taken from each subject. That is, each subject contributed one score under the low-reward condition, and a second score under the high-reward condition.

A different approach could have used a type of **matching procedure**. With a matching procedure, a given subject provides data under only one experimental condition; however, each subject is matched with a different subject who provides data under the other experimental condition. The subjects are matched on some variable that is expected to be related to the dependent variable, and the matching is done prior to the manipulation of the independent variable.

For example, imagine that it is possible to administer an "emotionality scale" to subjects, and that prior research has shown that scores on this scale are strongly correlated with scores on romantic commitment (the dependent variable in your study). You could administer this emotionality scale to 20 subjects, and use their scores on the scale to match them; that is, to place them in pairs according to their similarity on the emotionality scale.

For example, scores on the emotionality scale may range from a low of 100 to a high of 500. Assume that John scores 111 on this scale, and William scores 112. Because their scores are very similar, you pair them together, and they become subject pair 1. Tim scores 150 on this scale, and Fred scores 149. Because their scores are very similar, you also pair them together as subject pair 2. Table 7.2 shows how you could arrange these fictitious pairs of subjects:

Table 7.2

Fictitious Data from a Study Using a Matching Procedure

		Commitment Ratings of Partner 10	
Subject Pair		Low-Reward Condition	High-Reward Condition
Subject pair 1	(John and William)	8	19
Subject pair 2	(Tim and Fred)	9	21
Subject pair 3	(Frank and Jack)	10	21
Subject pair 4	(Howie and Jim)	10	23
Subject pair 5	(Andy and Floyd)	11	24
Subject pair 6	(Walter and Rich)	13	26
Subject pair 7	(James and Denny)	14	27
Subject pair 8	(Reuben and Joe)	14	28
Subject pair 9	(Mike and Peter)	16	30
Subject pair 10	(George and Dave)	18	32

Within a subject pair, one subject is randomly assigned to the low-reward condition, and one is assigned to the high-reward condition. Assume that, for each of the subject pairs in Table 7.2, the person listed first had been randomly assigned to the low condition, and the person listed second had been assigned to the high condition. The study then proceeds in the usual way, with subjects rating the various paper people.

Table 7.2 shows that John saw partner 10 in the *low-reward* condition, and provided a commitment rating of 8; William saw partner 10 in the *high-reward* condition, and provided a commitment score of 19. In analyzing the data, you pair John's score on the commitment variable with William's score on commitment; the same will be true for the remaining subject pairs. A later section shows how to write a SAS program that does this.

When should the matching take place? Remember that subjects are placed together in pairs on the basis of some matching variable *before the independent variable is manipulated;* they are *not* placed together in pairs on the basis of their scores on the dependent variable. In the present case, subjects were placed in pairs based on the similarity of their scores on the emotionality scale. Later, the independent variable was manipulated and their commitment scores were recorded. Although they are not paired on the basis of their scores on the dependent variable, the researcher normally hopes that their scores on the dependent variable will be correlated; more on this in a later section.

Pretest and posttest measures are taken. Consider now a different type of research problem. Assume that an educator believes that taking a foreign language course causes an improvement in critical thinking skills among college students. To test the hypothesis, she administers a test of critical thinking skills to a single group of college students at two points in time: A pretest is administered at the beginning of the semester (prior to taking the language course), and a posttest is administered at the end of the semester (after completing the course). The data obtained from the two administrations appear in Table 7.3:

Table 7.3

Fictitious Data from Study Using a Pretest-Posttest Procedure

	Scores on Test of Critical Thinking Skills	
Subject	Pretest	Posttest
John	34	55
Mary	35	49
Tim	39	59
Susan	41	63
Maria	43	62
Fred	44	68
Frank	44	69
Edie	52	72
Jack	55	75
Shirley	57	78

You can analyze these data using the paired-samples *t* test because you can pair together the various scores in a meaningful way: You can pair each subject's score on the pretest with his or her score on the posttest. When the data are analyzed, the results will indicate whether there was a significant increase in critical thinking scores over the course of the semester.

Problems with the Paired Samples Approach

Some of the studies described in the preceding section utilize fairly weak experimental designs. This means that, even if you had conducted the studies, you may not have been able to draw firm conclusions from the results because alternative explanations could be offered for those results.

For example, consider the first investigation in which each subject was exposed to both the low-reward version of partner 10 as well as the high-reward version of partner 10. If you designed this study poorly, it might suffer any of a number of confoundings. For example, what if you designed the study so that each subject rated the low-reward version first, and the high-reward version second? If you then analyzed the data and found that higher commitment ratings were observed for the high-reward condition, you would not know whether to attribute this finding to the manipulation of the independent variable (level of rewards) or to **order effects**: the possibility that the order in which the treatments were presented influenced scores on the dependent variable. For example, it is possible that subjects tend to give higher ratings to partners that are rated later in serial order; if this is the case, the higher ratings observed for the high-reward partner may simply reflect such an order effect.

The third study described previously (which investigated the effects of a language course on critical thinking skills) also displays a weak experimental design: the single-group, pretest-posttest design. Assume that you administer the test of critical thinking skills to the students at the beginning and again at the end of the semester. Assume further that you observe a significant increase in their skills over this time period. This would be consistent with your hypothesis that the foreign language course helps develop critical thinking skills.

Unfortunately, this would very likely not be the *only* reasonable explanation for the findings. Perhaps the improvement was simply due to the process of **maturation**: changes that naturally take place in people as they age. Perhaps the change is simply due to the general effects of being in college, independent of the effects of the foreign language course. Because of the weak design used in this study, you will probably never be able to draw firm conclusions about what was really responsible for the students' improvement.

This is not to argue that researchers should never obtain the type of data that can be analyzed using the paired-samples *t* test. For example, the second study described previously (the one using the matching procedure) was reasonably sound and may have provided interpretable results. The point here is that research involving paired-samples must be designed very carefully to avoid the sorts of problems discussed here. You can deal with most of these difficulties through the appropriate use of counterbalancing, control groups, and other strategies. The problems inherent in repeated measures and matching designs, along with the procedures that may be used to handle these problems, are discussed in Chapter 11: *One-Way ANOVA with One Repeated-Measures Factor*, and Chapter 12: *Factorial ANOVA with Repeated-Measures Factors and Between-Group Factors*.

When to Use the Paired Samples Approach

When conducting a study that involves two treatment conditions, you will often have the choice of using either the independent-samples approach or the paired-samples approach. A number of considerations will influence your decision to use one design rather than the other. One of the most important considerations is the extent to which the paired-samples procedure will result in a more sensitive test; that is, the extent to which the paired-samples approach will make it more likely to detect significant differences when they actually do exist.

It is important to understand that the paired-samples *t* test has one important weakness when it comes to test sensitivity: the paired-samples test has only *one half* the degrees of freedom as are associated with an equivalent independent-samples test (a later section shows how to compute these degrees of freedom). Because the paired-samples approach has fewer degrees of freedom, it must display a larger *t* value to attain statistical significance (compared to the independent-samples *t* test).

Then why use this approach? Because, under the right circumstances, the paired-samples approach results in a smaller standard error of the mean (the denominator in the formula used to compute the *t* statistic). Other factors held equal, a smaller standard error results in a more sensitive test.

However, there is a catch: the paired-samples approach will result in a smaller standard error only if scores on the two sets of observations are positively correlated with one another. This concept is easiest to understand with reference to the pretest-posttest study described previously. Table 7.4 again reproduces the fictitious data obtained in this study:

Table 7.4

Fictitious Data from Study Using a Pretest-Posttest Procedure

	Scores on Test of Critical Thinking Skills	
Subject	Pretest	Posttest
John	34	55
Mary	35	49
Tim	39	59
Susan	41	63
Maria	43	62
Fred	44	68
Frank	44	69
Edie	52	72
Jack	55	75
Shirley	57	78

Notice that, in Table 7.4, scores on the pretest appear to be positively correlated with scores on the posttest. That is, subjects who obtained relatively low scores on the pretest (such as John) also tended to obtain relatively low scores on the posttest; similarly, subjects who obtained relatively high scores on the pretest (such as Shirley) also tended to obtain relatively high scores on the posttest. This shows that although the subjects may have displayed a general improvement in critical thinking skills over the course of the semester, their ranking relative to one another remained relatively constant. The subjects with the lowest scores at the beginning of the term still tended to have the lowest scores at the end of the term.

The situation described here is the type of situation that makes the paired-samples *t* test the optimal procedure. Because pretest scores are correlated with posttest scores, the paired-samples approach should yield a fairly sensitive test.

The same logic applies to the other studies described previously. For example, Table 7.5 again reproduces the data obtained from the study in which subjects were assigned to pairs based on matching criteria:

Table 7.5

<u>Fictitious Data from a Study Using a Matching Procedure</u>

	Commitment Ratings of Partner 10	
Subject Pair	Low-Reward Condition	High-Reward Condition
Subject pair 1 (John and William)	8	19
Subject pair 2 (Tim and Fred)	9	21
Subject pair 3 (Frank and Jack)	10	21
Subject pair 4 (Howie and Jim)	10	23
Subject pair 5 (Andy and Floyd)	11	24
Subject pair 6 (Walter and Rich)	13	26
Subject pair 7 (James and Denny)	14	27
Subject pair 8 (Reuben and Joe)	14	28
Subject pair 9 (Mike and Peter)	16	30
Subject pair 10 (George and Dave)	18	32

Again, there appears to be a correlation between scores obtained in the low-reward condition and those obtained in the high-reward condition. This is apparently because subjects were first placed into pairs based on the similarity of their scores on the emotionality scale, and the emotionality scale is predictive of how subjects respond to the commitment scale. For example, both John and William (pair 1) display relatively low scores on commitment, presumably because they both scored low on the emotionality scale that was initially used to match them. Similarly, both George and Dave (subject pair 10) scored relatively high on commitment, presumably because they both scored high on emotionality.

This illustrates why it is so important to select *relevant* matching variables when using a matching procedure. There is a correlation between the two commitment variables above because (presumably) emotionality is related to commitment. If you had instead assigned subjects to pairs based on some variable that is not related to commitment (such as, say, subject shoe size), the two commitment variables would not be correlated, and the paired-samples *t* test would not provide a more sensitive test. Under those circumstances, you would achieve more power by instead using the independent-samples *t* test and capitalizing on the greater degrees of freedom.

Example: An Alternative Test of the Investment Model

The remainder of this chapter shows how to write SAS programs that perform paired-samples *t* tests, and how to interpret the results. The first example is based on the first fictitious study described earlier, which investigated the effect of levels of reward on commitment to a romantic relationship. The investigation included 10 subjects, and each subject rated partner 10 twice: once after reviewing the low-reward version of partner 10, and once after reviewing the high-reward version. Table 7.6 reproduces the data obtained from the subjects:

Table 7.6

Fictitious Data from the Investment Model Study

	Commitment Ratings of Partner 10	
Subject	Low-Reward Condition	High-Reward Condition
John	9	20
Mary	9	22
Tim	10	23
Susan	11	23
Maria	12	24
Fred	12	25
Frank	14	26
Edie	15	28
Jack	17	29
Shirley	19	31

These data were keyed according to the following format:

Line	Column	Variable Name	Explanation
1	1-2	LOW	Commitment ratings obtained when the subjects rated the low-reward version of partner 10
	3	(blank)	(blank)
	4-5	HIGH	Commitment ratings obtained when the subjects rated the high-reward version of partner 10

Notice from the preceding format that no variable codes "group membership" or "treatment condition". Instead, two variables include commitment ratings: one variable includes commitment ratings obtained when subjects reviewed the low-reward version of partner 10, and the second variable includes commitment ratings obtained when they reviewed the high-reward version.

Writing the SAS program. A paired-samples *t* test is performed by creating a **difference score** variable, and determining whether the average difference score is significantly different from zero. If the average difference score is significantly different from zero, you conclude that your independent variable had a significant effect on the dependent variable (assuming that the study was well-designed and certain other conditions hold).

In the present study, this difference score variable is created by starting with a subject's commitment score obtained in the high-reward condition, and subtracting from it his or her commitment score obtained in the low-reward condition. You can do this using the following equation:

        Difference score = Commitment 1 - Commitment 2

where

        Commitment 1 = commitment scores obtained in the high-reward
                        condition

        Commitment 2 = commitment scores obtained in the low-reward
                        condition.

If a subject's commitment score from the high-reward condition is approximately equal to his or her commitment score from the low-reward condition, the resulting difference score is approximately equal to zero. This suggests that the subject's level of commitment was not affected by the level of reward manipulation. If none of the subjects are affected by the manipulation (on the average), then the average difference score across the subjects should be approximately equal to zero. Therefore, if the average difference score is not significantly different from zero, you will fail to reject the null hypothesis, and will instead conclude that the manipulation had no effect on mean level of commitment.

On the other hand, assume that your manipulation *does* have the expected effect on commitment. This would mean that, for most subjects, the commitment ratings obtained under the high-reward condition would tend to be higher than the commitment ratings under the low-reward condition. Subtracting low-reward commitment scores from high-reward commitment scores under these circumstances would tend to produce positive difference scores (rather than zero or negative difference scores). Therefore, if your manipulation has the predicted effect, the average difference score should be both positive and significantly different from zero. This is important to remember when you review the results of your analyses later.

The preceding shows that you must do three things to perform a paired-samples *t* test: (a) input your data, (b) create the necessary difference score variable, and (c) determine whether the average difference score is significantly different from zero. The following SAS program statements input the data from Table 7.6:

```
1        DATA D1;
2          INPUT   #1    @1    (LOW)    (2.)
3                        @4    (HIGH)   (2.)    ;
4        DIFF = HIGH - LOW;
5        CARDS;
6          9 20
7          9 22
8         10 23
9         11 23
10        12 24
11        12 25
12        14 26
13        15 28
14        17 29
15        19 31
16        ;
```

Lines 1-3 of the preceding program are fairly standard in the way that they input the variables LOW and HIGH. The equation in line 4 creates the difference score variable (named DIFF) needed for the analysis. This equation instructs SAS to create a new variable named DIFF, then, for each subject, to subtract his or her score on LOW from his or her score on HIGH. SAS then stores the resulting difference as that subject's score on DIFF. With the difference score variable created, you are now ready to perform the necessary statistical analyses.

Here is the general form for the SAS statements to perform a paired-samples *t* test:

```
PROC MEANS;
   VAR variable1 variable2;
   RUN;


PROC MEANS    N MEAN STDERR T PRT;
   VAR difference-score-variable;
   RUN;
```

In the preceding, "variable1" and "variable2" are the variables that include scores on the dependent variable under the two treatment conditions. In the present study, they correspond to the variables LOW and HIGH, respectively.

The preceding general form includes two PROC MEANS statements. The first PROC MEANS computes simple descriptive statistics for variable1 and variable2. This allows you to check the data for possible errors in keying or in writing the input statement. It also provides the means and standard deviations for variable1 and variable2.

The second PROC MEANS uses options to request a number of statistics for the difference score variable. Most important, it requests the *t* statistic that will allow you to test the null hypothesis that the average difference score is zero in the population. These options are:

N   The number of observations having nonmissing values on the difference score variable (i.e., the number of difference scores included in the analysis)

MEAN   The mean difference score

STDERR   The standard error of the mean for the difference scores (the standard deviation of the sampling distribution of means of difference scores)

T   Student's *t* statistic for testing the null hypothesis that the mean difference score is zero in the population

PRT   The *p* value for the preceding *t* statistic (the probability of obtaining a *t* this large or larger if the population difference score really is zero)

The following is the entire program--including the DATA step--to analyze the fictitious data from Table 7.6. Notice how the actual variable names LOW, HIGH, and DIFF appear in the appropriate locations in lines 17-23.

```
1          DATA D1;
2             INPUT   #1   @1   (LOW)   (2.)
3                          @4   (HIGH)  (2.)    ;
4          DIFF = HIGH - LOW;
5          CARDS;
6           9 20
7           9 22
8          10 23
9          11 23
10         12 24
11         12 25
12         14 26
13         15 28
14         17 29
15         19 31
16         ;
17         PROC MEANS;
18            VAR LOW HIGH;
19            RUN;
20
21         PROC MEANS    N MEAN STDERR T PRT;
22            VAR DIFF;
23            RUN;
```

Interpreting the SAS Output. Output 7.3 presents the results obtained from the preceding program. The first page of output provides results for the PROC MEANS performed on LOW and HIGH. You should review the results on this page first to verify that everything ran as expected. Under the column headed "N", you see that there were 10 observations for both variables. This is as expected, since there were 10 subjects providing data in the study. Under the column headed "Mean", you can see that the average commitment score in the low-reward condition was 12.8, while the average in the high-reward condition was 25.1. Subjects have therefore displayed higher levels of commitment for the high-reward version of partner 10, consistent with your hypothesis (later, you will determine whether these differences are statistically significant).

```
                            The SAS System                            1

    Variable   N        Mean        Std Dev      Minimum      Maximum
    ------------------------------------------------------------------
    LOW        10    12.8000000    3.3928028    9.0000000    19.0000000
    HIGH       10    25.1000000    3.4140234   20.0000000    31.0000000
    ------------------------------------------------------------------
```

```
            Analysis Variable : DIFF


        N         Mean     Std Error           T   Prob>|T|
        ------------------------------------------------------
        10    12.3000000    0.2134375   57.6281181    0.0001
        ------------------------------------------------------
```

Output 7.3: Results of the Paired Samples *t* Test, Investment Model Study

Earlier in the chapter, you learned that possible scores on the commitment scale can range from 4 to 36. You may now review the values in the "Minimum" and "Maximum" columns of output page 1 to verify that no observed values fell outside of this range (values exceeding these limits could indicate an error in keying data or in writing the input statement). The output shows that observed scores on LOW range from 9 to 19, and that observed scores on HIGH range from 20 to 31. These values fall within your expected range, so there is no obvious evidence of errors. With this done, you are now free to review the output results relevant to your null hypothesis.

Page 2 of output 7.3 provides results pertaining to the difference score variable, DIFF. You can see that the average score on DIFF was 12.3. Given the way that this variable was created, a positive value on DIFF indicates that, on the average, scores on HIGH tended to be higher than scores on LOW. The direction of this difference is consistent with your prediction that higher rewards are associated with greater levels of commitment. You may now review the results of the *t* test to determine whether this mean difference score is significantly different from zero.

The *t* statistic in a paired-samples *t* test is computed using the following formula:

$$t = \frac{M_d}{SE_d}$$

where

M_d = the mean difference score

SE_d = the standard error of the mean for the difference scores (the standard deviation of the sampling distribution of means of difference scores).

The fourth column in the PROC MEANS table in Output 7.3 contains the relevant *t* statistic, under the heading "T". This *t* value of approximately 57.63 was obtained by dividing the mean difference score (under the heading "Mean") by the standard error of the mean (under the heading "Std Error"). The *t* statistic had an associated *p* value of 0.0001 (under the heading "Prob>|T|"). This *p* value was much lower than the standard cutoff of .05, indicating that the mean difference score of 12.3 was significantly different from zero. You may therefore reject the null hypothesis that the population difference score was zero, and may conclude that the mean commitment score of 25.1 observed with the high-reward version of partner 10 was significantly higher than the mean score of 12.8 observed with low-reward version of partner 10. In other words, you may tentatively conclude that the level of reward manipulation had an effect on rated commitment.

The degrees of freedom associated with this t test are equal to $N-1$, where N = the number of pairs of observations in the study. This is analogous to saying that N is equal to the number of difference scores that are analyzed. If the study involves taking repeated measures from a single sample of subjects, N will be equal to the number of subjects. However, if the study involves two sets of subjects who are matched to form subject pairs, N will be equal to the number of subject *pairs* (which will be one-half the total number of subjects).

The present study involved taking repeated measures from a single sample of 10 subjects. Therefore, $N = 10$ in this study, and the degrees of freedom are equal to $10 - 1$, or 9.

Summarizing the results of the analysis. You could summarize the results of the present analysis following the same format used with the independent groups t test, as presented earlier in this chapter (e.g., statement of the problem, nature of the variables). Figure 7.4 illustrates the mean commitment scores obtained under the two conditions manipulated in the present study:

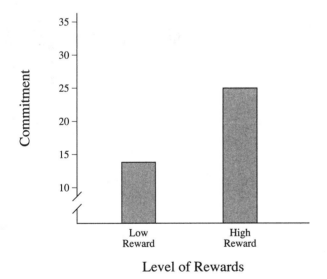

Figure 7.4: Mean Levels of Commitment Observed for Subjects in High-Reward versus Low-Reward Conditions, Paired Samples Design

You could describe the results of the analysis in a paper in the following way:

> Results were analyzed using a paired-samples t test. This analysis revealed a significant difference between mean levels of commitment observed in the two conditions, t(9) = 12.3; p < .001. The sample means are displayed in Figure 7.4, which shows that mean commitment scores were significantly higher in the high-reward condition (M = 25.1, SD = 3.41) than in the low-reward condition (M = 12.8, SD = 3.39).

Example: A Pretest-Posttest study

An earlier section presented the hypothesis that taking a foreign language course will cause an improvement in critical thinking skills among college students. To test this hypothesis, assume that you conducted a study in which a single group of college students took a test of critical thinking skills both before and after completing a semester-long foreign language course. The first administration of the test constituted the study's pretest, and the second administration constituted the posttest. Table 7.7 again reproduces the data obtained in the study:

Table 7.7

Fictitious Data from Study Using a Pretest-Posttest Procedure

	Scores on Test of Critical Thinking Skills	
Subject	Pretest	Posttest
John	34	55
Mary	35	49
Tim	39	59
Susan	41	63
Maria	43	62
Fred	44	68
Frank	44	69
Edie	52	72
Jack	55	75
Shirley	57	78

You could key the data for this study according to the following format:

Line	Column	Variable Name	Explanation
1	1-2	PRE	Scores on the test of critical thinking skills obtained at the first administration
	3	(blank)	(blank)
	4-5	POST	Scores on the test of critical thinking skills obtained at the second administration

Here is the general form for the PROC MEANS statements to perform a paired-samples *t* test using data obtained from a study using a pretest-posttest design:

```
PROC MEANS;
   VAR pretest posttest;
   RUN;

PROC MEANS   N MEAN STDERR T PRT;
   VAR difference-score-variable;
   RUN;
```

Notice that these statements are identical to the general form statements presented earlier in this chapter, except that the "pretest" and "posttest" variables have been substituted for "variable1" and "variable2," respectively.

The following is the entire SAS program to input the data from Table 7.7 and perform a paired-samples *t* test.

```
1        DATA D1;
2            INPUT  #1   @1   (PRE)   (2.)
3                        @4   (POST)  (2.)   ;
4        DIFF = POST - PRE;
5        CARDS;
6        34 55
7        35 49
```

```
 8          39 59
 9          41 63
10          43 62
11          44 68
12          44 69
13          52 72
14          55 75
15          57 78
16          ;
17          PROC MEANS;
18             VAR PRE POST;
19             RUN;
20
21          PROC MEANS    N MEAN STDERR T PRT;
22             VAR DIFF;
23             RUN;
```

The preceding program results in the analysis of just three variables: PRE, each subject's score on the pretest; POST, each subject's score on the posttest; and DIFF, the difference score variable that was created by subtracting each subject's score on PRE from his or her score on POST. Here, SAS creates DIFF when it reads line 4 of the program.

Given the way DIFF was created in the preceding program, a positive mean score on DIFF would indicate that the average posttest score was higher than the average pretest score. Such a finding would be consistent with your hypothesis that the foreign language course would cause an improvement in critical thinking skills. If the average score on DIFF is not significantly different from zero, however, your hypothesis would receive no support (again, remember that any results obtained from the present study would be difficult to interpret with confidence, given the lack of an appropriate control group).

You can interpret the results from the preceding program in the same manner as with Example 1, earlier. In the interest of space, those results do not appear again here.

Conclusion

The *t* test is one of the most commonly used statistics in the social sciences, in part because some of the simplest investigations involve the comparison of just two treatment conditions. When an investigation involves more than two conditions however, the *t* test is no longer appropriate, and you should generally replace it with the *F* test obtained from an analysis of variance (ANOVA). The simplest ANOVA procedure--the one-way ANOVA with one between-groups factor--is the topic of the following chapter.

Appendix: Assumptions Underlying the *t* Test

Assumptions Underlying the Independent-Samples *t* Test

- **Level of measurement**. The criterion variable should be assessed on an interval or ratio level of measurement. The predictor variable should be a nominal-level variable that includes just two categories (two groups).

- **Independent observations**. A given observation should not be dependent on any other observation in either group. In an experiment, you would normally achieve this by drawing a random sample and randomly assigning each subject to only one of the two treatment conditions. This assumption would be violated if a given subject contributed scores on the criterion variable under both treatment conditions. The independence assumption is also violated when one subject's behavior influences another subject's behavior within the same condition. For example, if subjects are given experimental instructions in groups of five, and are allowed to interact in the course of providing scores on the criterion variable, it is likely that their scores will not be independent; each subject's score is likely to be affected by the other subjects in that group. In these situations, scores from the subjects constituting a given group of five should be averaged, and these average scores should constitute the unit of analysis. None of the tests discussed in this text are robust against violations of the independence assumption.

- **Random sampling**. Scores on the criterion variable should represent a random sample drawn from the populations of interest.

- **Normal distributions**. Each sample should be drawn from a normally-distributed population. If each sample contains over 30 subjects, the test is robust against moderate departures from normality.

- **Homogeneity of variance**. To use the equal-variances *t* test, you should draw the samples from populations with equal variances on the criterion. If the null hypothesis of equal population variances is rejected, you should use the unequal-variances *t* test.

Assumptions Underlying the Paired-Samples *t* Test

- **Level of measurement**. The criterion variable should be assessed on an interval or ratio level of measurement. The predictor variable should be a nominal-level variable that includes just two categories.

- **Paired observations**. A given observation appearing in one condition must be paired in some meaningful way with a corresponding observation appearing in the other condition. You can accomplish this by having each subject contribute one score under condition 1, and a separate score under condition 2. Observations could also be paired by using a matching procedure to create the sample.

- **Independent observations**. A given subject's score in one condition should not be affected by any other subject's score in either of the two conditions. It is, of course, acceptable for a given subject's score in one condition to be dependent upon his or her *own score* in the other condition. This is another way of saying that it is acceptable for subjects' scores in condition 1 to be correlated with their scores in condition 2.

- **Random sampling**. Subjects contributing data should represent a random sample drawn from the populations of interest.

- **Normal distribution for difference scores**. The differences in paired scores should be normally distributed. These difference scores are normally created by beginning with a given subject's score on the dependent variable obtained under one treatment condition, and subtracting from it that subject's score on the dependent variable obtained under the other treatment condition. It is not necessary that the individual dependent variables be normally distributed, as long as the distribution of difference scores is normally distributed.

- **Homogeneity of variance**. The populations represented by the two conditions should have equal variances on the criterion.

References

American Psychological Association (1983). *Publication manual of the american psychological association, third edition.* Washington, D.C.: American Psychological Association.

Rusbult, C. E. (1980). Commitment and satisfaction in romantic associations: A test of the investment model. *Journal of Experimental Social Psychology, 16,* 172-186.

SAS Institute Inc. (1989). *SAS/STAT user's guide, version 6, fourth edition, volume 2.* Cary, NC: SAS Institute Inc.

Chapter 8

ONE-WAY ANOVA WITH
ONE BETWEEN-GROUPS FACTOR

Overview. In this chapter you learn how to key data and prepare SAS programs that perform a one-way analysis of variance (ANOVA) using the GLM procedure. This chapter focuses on the *between-groups* design, in which each subject is exposed to only one condition under the independent variable. The use of a multiple comparison procedure (Tukey's HSD test) is described, and guidelines for summarizing the results of the analysis in tables and text are provided.

Introduction: The Basics of One-Way ANOVA, Between-Groups Design

One-way analysis of variance (ANOVA) is appropriate when an analysis involves:

INDEPENDENT VARIABLE;

- a single predictor variable that is measured on a nominal scale and may assume two or more values

DEPENDENT VARIABLE:

- a single criterion variable that is measured on an interval or ratio scale.

In the preceding chapter (Chapter 7: "*t* Tests: Independent Samples and Paired Samples"), you learned about the independent samples *t* test, which you can use to determine whether there is a significant difference between two groups of subjects with respect to their scores on an interval- or ratio-scale criterion variable. But what if you are conducting a study in which you must compare more than just two groups? In those situations, it is often appropriate to instead analyze your data using a one-way ANOVA.

The analysis that this chapter describes is called *one-way* ANOVA because you use it to analyze data from studies in which there is only one predictor variable (or independent variable). In contrast, Chapter 9 of this text ("Factorial ANOVA with Two Between-Groups Factors") will present a statistical procedure that is appropriate for studies with two predictor variables.

The Aggression Study

To illustrate a situation for which one-way ANOVA might be appropriate, imagine that you are conducting research on aggression in children. Assume that a review of prior research has led you to believe that consuming sugar causes children to behave more aggressively. You therefore wish to conduct a study that will test the following hypothesis:

> The amount of sugar consumed by eight-year-old children has a positive effect on the levels of aggression that they subsequently display.

To test your hypothesis, you conduct an investigation in which each child in a group of 60 children is assigned to one of three treatment conditions. Assignments are made in the following way:

- 20 children are assigned to the "0 grams of sugar" treatment condition.

- 20 children are assigned to the "20 grams of sugar" treatment condition.

- 20 children are assigned to the "40 grams of sugar" treatment condition.

The independent variable in the study is "the amount of sugar consumed." You manipulate this variable by controlling the amount of sugar that is contained in the lunch that each child receives. In this way, you ensure that the children in the "0 grams of sugar" group are actually consuming 0 grams of sugar, that the children in the "20 grams of sugar" group are actually consuming 20 grams, and so forth.

The dependent variable in the study is "level of aggression" displayed by each child. To measure this variable, a pair of observers watches each child for a set period of time each day after lunch. These observers tabulate the number of aggressive acts performed by each child during this time. The total number of aggressive acts performed by a child over a two-week period serves as that child's score on the dependent variable.

You can see that the data from this investigation are appropriate for a one-way ANOVA because:

* the study involves a single predictor variable which is measured on a nominal scale (i.e., "amount of sugar consumed")

* the predictor variable assumes more than two values (i.e., the "0-gram" group, the "20-gram" group, and the "40-gram" group)

* the study involves a single criterion variable (number of aggressive acts) which is measured on an interval or ratio scale.

Between-Groups Designs versus Repeated-Measures Designs

The research design that this chapter discusses is referred to as a **between-groups** design because each subject appears in only one group, and comparisons are made *between* different groups of subjects. For example, in the experiment just described, a given subject is assigned to just one treatment condition (such as the 20-gram group), and provides data on the dependent variable from only that specific treatment condition.

A distinction, therefore, is made between a between-groups design and a repeated-measures design. With a **repeated-measures** design, a given subject provides data under each of the treatment conditions used in the study (it is called a "repeated-measures" design because each subject provides repeated measurements on the dependent variable).

In short, a one-way ANOVA with one between-groups factor is directly comparable to the independent-samples *t* test from the last chapter. The main difference is that you can use a *t* test to compare just two groups, while you can use a one-way ANOVA to compare two or more groups. In the same way, a one-way ANOVA with one repeated-measures factor is very similar to the paired-samples *t* test from the last chapter. Again, the main difference is that you can use a *t* test to analyze data from just two treatment conditions, but you can use a repeated-measures ANOVA with data from two or more treatment conditions (the repeated-measures ANOVA is covered in Chapter 11: "One-Way ANOVA with One Repeated-Measures Factor").

Multiple Comparison Procedures

When you analyze data from an experiment with a between-groups ANOVA, you can state the null hypothesis as follows:

> In the population, there is no difference between the various treatment conditions with respect to their mean scores on the dependent variable.

For example, with the preceding study on aggression, you might state a null hypothesis that, in the population, there is no difference between the 0-gram group, the 20-gram group, and the 40-gram group with respect to the mean number of aggressive acts performed. This null hypothesis could be represented symbolically in this way:

$$M_1 = M_2 = M_3$$

where M_1 represents the mean level of aggression shown by the 0-gram group, M_2 represents mean aggression shown by the 20-gram group, and M_3 represents mean aggression shown by the 40-gram group.

When you analyze your data, the SAS System's PROC GLM will test this null hypothesis by computing an F statistic. If the F statistic is sufficiently large (and the p value associated with the F is sufficiently small), you may reject the null hypothesis. In rejecting the null, you tentatively conclude that, in the population, at least one of the three treatment conditions differs from at least one other treatment condition on the measure of aggression.

However, this leads to a problem: which pairs of treatment groups are significantly different from one another? There are many possibilities. Perhaps the 0-gram group is different from the 40-gram group, but is not different from the 20-gram group. Perhaps the 20-gram group is different from the 40-gram group, but is not different from the 0-gram group. Perhaps all three groups are significantly different from one another.

Faced with this problem, researchers routinely rely on **multiple comparison procedures**: statistical tests used in studies with more than two groups to help determine which pairs of groups are significantly different from one another. Several different multiple comparison procedures are available with the SAS System's PROC GLM, including Duncan's multiple-range test, the Scheffe test, and the Student-Newman-Keuls test. This chapter shows how to request and interpret Tukey's studentized range test, sometimes called Tukey's HSD test (for "honestly significant difference"). The Tukey test is especially useful when the various treatment groups in the study have unequal numbers of subjects (which is often the case). For a description of the various multiple comparison tests that are available with PROC GLM, see the section on "Comparison of Means" in Chapter 24, "The GLM Procedure," *SAS/STAT user's guide, version 6, fourth edition, volume 2* (1989).

Statistical Significance versus the Magnitude of the Treatment Effect

This chapter also shows how to calculate the R^2 statistic from the output provided in an analysis of variance. In an ANOVA, R^2 represents the percent of variance in the criterion that is accounted for by variability in the predictor variable. In a true experiment, you can view R^2 as an index of the magnitude of the treatment effect. It is a measure of the strength of the relationship between the predictor and the criterion. Values of R^2 may range from 0 through 1, with values closer to 0 indicating a weak relationship between the predictor and criterion, and values closer to 1 indicating a stronger relationship.

For example, assume that you conduct the preceding study on aggression in children. If your independent variable (amount of sugar consumed by the children) has a very weak effect on the level of aggression displayed by the children, R^2 will be a small value, perhaps .02 or .04. On the other hand, if your independent variable has a very strong effect on their level of aggression, R^2 will be a larger value, perhaps .20 or .40 (exactly how large R^2 must be to be considered "large" will depend on a good number of factors that are beyond the scope of this chapter).

It is good practice to report R^2 or some other measure of the magnitude of the effect in a published paper because researchers like to draw a distinction between results that are merely statistically significant versus those that are truly meaningful. The problem is that very often researchers obtain results that are statistically significant, but not meaningful in terms of the magnitude of the treatment effect. This is especially likely to happen when conducting research with a very large sample. When the sample is very large (say, several hundred subjects), you may obtain results that are statistically significant even though your independent variable has a very weak effect on the dependent variable (this is because many statistical tests become very sensitive to minor group differences when the sample is large).

For example, imagine that you conduct the preceding aggression study with 500 children in the 0-gram group, 500 children in the 20-gram group, and 500 children in the 40-gram group. It is possible that you would analyze your data with a one-way ANOVA, and obtain an F value that is significant at $p < .05$. Normally, this might lead you to rejoice. But imagine that you then calculate R^2 for this effect, and learn that R^2 is only .03. This means that only 3% of the variance in aggression is accounted for by the amount of sugar consumed. Obviously, your manipulation has had a very weak effect. Even though your independent variable is statistically significant, most researchers would argue that it does not account for a meaningful amount of variance in children's aggression.

This is why it is helpful to always provide a measure of the magnitude of the treatment effect (such as R^2) along with your test of statistical significance. In this way, your readers will always be able to assess whether your results are truly meaningful in terms of the strength of the relationship between the predictor variable and the criterion.

Example with Significant Differences between Experimental Conditions

To illustrate one-way ANOVA, imagine that you will replicate the study that investigated the effect of rewards on commitment in romantic relationships (this study was described in Chapter 7). To give the study an added twist, however, in this investigation you will use three experimental conditions instead of the two experimental conditions described in the last chapter.

Recall that the preceding chapter hypothesized that the rewards that people experience in a romantic relationship will have a causal effect on their commitment to those relationships. You tested this prediction by conducting an experiment with 20 subjects. All 20 subjects were asked to engage in a role-playing task: to read the descriptions of 10 potential romantic partners. For each partner, the subjects imagined what it would be like to date this person, and rated how committed they would be to a relationship with that person. For the first 9 partners, every subject saw exactly the same description. There were some important differences with respect to partner 10, however:

- Half of the subjects had been assigned to a "high-reward" condition, and these subjects were told that partner 10 "...enjoys the same recreational activities that you enjoy, and is very good looking."

- The other half of the subjects were assigned to the "low-reward" condition, and were told that partner 10 "...does not enjoy the same recreational activities that you enjoy, and is not very good looking."

You are now going to repeat this experiment using essentially the same procedure used before, but this time you will add a third experimental condition called the "mixed-reward" condition. Here is the description of partner 10 which will be read by subjects assigned to this group:

```
PARTNER 10:  Imagine that you have been dating partner 10 for about 1
year, and you have put a great deal of time and effort into this
relationship.  There are not very many attractive members of the
opposite sex where you live, so it would be difficult to replace this
person with someone else.  Partner 10 lives in the same neighborhood as
you, so it is easy to see him/her as often as you like.  Sometimes this
person seems to enjoy the same recreational activities that you enjoy,
and sometimes he/she does not.  Sometimes partner 10 seems to be very
good looking, and sometimes he/she does not.
```

Notice that the first three sentences of the preceding description are identical to the descriptions read by subjects in the low-reward and high-reward conditions in the experiment described in the preceding chapter. These three sentences deal with investment size, alternative value, and costs, respectively. However, the last two sentences deal with rewards, and they are different from the sentences dealing with rewards in the other two conditions. In this mixed-reward condition, partner 10 is portrayed as being something of a mixed bag: sometimes he/she is rewarding to be around, and sometimes he/she is not.

The purpose of the present study is to determine how this new mixed-reward version of partner 10 will be rated. Will this version be rated more positively than the version provided in the low-reward condition? Will it be rated more negatively than the version provided in the high-reward condition?

To conduct this study, you begin with a total sample of 18 subjects. You randomly assign 6 to the high-reward condition, and they read the high-reward version of partner 10, as it was described in the chapter on *t* tests. You randomly assign 6 subjects to the low-reward condition, and they read the low-reward version of partner 10. Finally, you randomly assign 6 to the mixed-reward condition, and they read the mixed-reward version just presented. As was the case in the previous investigation, you analyze subjects' ratings of how committed they would be to a relationship with partner 10 (and ignore their ratings of the other 9 partners).

You can see that this study is appropriate for analysis with a one-way ANOVA, between groups design because:

- it involves a single predictor variable assessed on a nominal scale (type of rewards)

- it involves a single criterion variable assessed on an interval scale (rated commitment)

- it involves three treatment conditions (low-reward, mixed-reward, and high-reward), making it inappropriate for analysis with an independent-groups *t* test.

The following section shows how to write a program in which PROC GLM analyzes some fictitious data from this study using a one-way ANOVA with one between-groups factor.

Writing the SAS Program

There was one predictor variable in this study, "type of rewards." For purposes of writing the program, you will assign subjects a score of "3" if they were in the high-reward condition, a score of "2" if they were in the mixed-reward condition, and a score of "1" if they were in the low-reward condition. You need a short SAS variable name for this variable, so you call it REWGRP (which stands for "reward group").

There was one criterion variable in this study, "commitment": the subjects' rating of how committed they would be to a relationship with partner 10. This variable was actually based on the sum of subject responses to four questionnaire items described in the last chapter. This variable could assume values from 4 through 36, and was measured on an interval scale. You give it a SAS variable name of COMMIT.

There are a number of ways to perform a one-way ANOVA with the SAS System. In fact, there is even a procedure called PROC ANOVA which is specifically for analyis of variance. However, this manual presents the use of PROC GLM instead. PROC GLM is more appropriate to use when some of your experimental groups have more subjects than other experimental groups. Statistics textbooks sometimes refer to these situations as studies with **unequal cells** or studies with an **unbalanced design**. PROC GLM is appropriate for either balanced or unbalanced designs.

Earlier, you learned that you may use a multiple comparison procedure when your ANOVA reveals significant results, and you want to determine which pairs of groups are significantly different. The program provided here includes a statement to request Tukey's HSD test so that, if the overall ANOVA is significant, the multiple comparison tests will be included in the output, ready for interpretation. However, remember that you should only interpret a multiple comparison test if the *F* for the overall ANOVA is significant.

This is the general form for the SAS program that performs a one-way ANOVA followed by Tukey's HSD Test:

```
PROC GLM  DATA=filename;
   CLASS  predictor-variable;
   MODEL  criterion-variable = predictor-variable;
   MEANS  predictor-variable / TUKEY;
   MEANS  predictor-variable;
   RUN;
```

Here is the entire program--including the DATA step--to analyze some fictitious data from the preceding study:

```
1          DATA D1;
2             INPUT  #1  @1  (REWGRP)  (1.)
3                        @3  (COMMIT)  (2.)   ;
4          CARDS;
5          1 13
6          1 06
7          1 12
8          1 04
9          1 09
10         1 08
11         2 33
12         2 29
13         2 35
14         2 34
15         2 28
16         2 27
17         3 36
18         3 32
19         3 31
20         3 32
```

```
21          3 35
22          3 34
23          ;
24
25          PROC GLM DATA=D1;
26              CLASS REWGRP;
27              MODEL COMMIT = REWGRP;
28              MEANS REWGRP / TUKEY;
29              MEANS REWGRP;
30              RUN;
```

Notes Regarding the SAS Program

The data in the preceding program were keyed so that there is one line of data for each subject. They were keyed according to the following format:

Line	Column	Variable Name	Explanation
1	1	REWGRP	Codes group membership, so that 1 = low-reward condition 2 = mixed-reward condition 3 = high-reward condition
	2	(blank)	(blank)
	3-4	COMMIT	Commitment ratings obtained when subjects rated partner 10

You can see that it was necessary to create just two columns of variables to perform the ANOVA. The first column of data (in column 1) included each subject's score on REWGRP, the variable that coded group membership. REWGRP was coded using 1's, 2's, and 3's, but you could have used any numbers (or even letters, such as L's, M's, and H's).

The second column of data (in columns 3-4) included subject scores on the commitment variable, COMMIT. COMMIT was a 2-digit variable because it could take on a value as high as 36, a 2-digit number. All values on COMMIT were keyed as two-digit numbers, putting a zero in front of a single digit number where appropriate (e.g., 06, 09). Using zeros in this fashion can make it easier to keep your place when keying multiple-digit variables.

In the program, data for the 6 low-reward subjects were keyed in lines 5-10, data for the 6 mixed-reward subjects were keyed in lines 11-16, and data for the 6 high-reward subjects were keyed in lines 17-22. It is not necessary to separate data for the three groups in this way, however; you could have keyed the data in a random sequence if desired.

The PROC GLM step that requests the analysis of variance appears in lines 25-30 of the program. The CLASS statement on line 26 specifies the name of the nominal-scale predictor variable for the analysis. In this analysis, REWGRP is the predictor.

The MODEL statement appears in line 27 of the program. With the MODEL statement, the name of the interval-level or ratio-level criterion variable should appear to the left of the "=" sign, and the name of the nominal-level predictor should appear to the right. If you wish, you may list more than one criterion variable to the left of the "=" sign, and separate ANOVAs will be performed for each. However, do not list more than one predictor variable to the right of the "=" sign, or the analysis performed will not be a one-way ANOVA.

The MEANS statement on line 28 requests that the Tukey HSD test be performed on the data. The second MEANS statement (on line 29) merely requests that the mean commitment scores for the three treatment groups be printed.

Results from the SAS Output

With LINESIZE=80 and PAGESIZE=60 in the OPTIONS statement, the preceding program would produce four pages of output. The contents of each page are summarized here:

- Page 1 provides class level information and the number of observations in the data set.

- Page 2 provides the analysis of variance table.

- Page 3 provides the results of the Tukey HSD test.

- Page 4 provides the means and standard deviations requested by the second MEANS statement.

The output created by the program is reproduced here as Output 8.1.

```
                          The SAS System                          1

                   General Linear Models Procedure
                      Class Level Information

                   Class     Levels    Values

                   REWGRP        3      1 2 3


            Number of observations in data set = 18
```

2

General Linear Models Procedure

Dependent Variable: COMMIT

Source	DF	Sum of Squares	Mean Square	F Value	Pr > F
Model	2	2225.3333333	1112.6666667	122.12	0.0001
Error	15	136.6666667	9.1111111		
Corrected Total	17	2362.0000000			

R-Square	C.V.	Root MSE	COMMIT Mean
0.942139	12.40464	3.0184617	24.333333

Source	DF	Type I SS	Mean Square	F Value	Pr > F
REWGRP	2	2225.3333333	1112.6666667	122.12	0.0001

Source	DF	Type III SS	Mean Square	F Value	Pr > F
REWGRP	2	2225.3333333	1112.6666667	122.12	0.0001

3

General Linear Models Procedure

Tukey's Studentized Range (HSD) Test for variable: COMMIT

NOTE: This test controls the type I experimentwise error rate, but
generally has a higher type II error rate than REGWQ.

Alpha= 0.05 df= 15 MSE= 9.111111
Critical Value of Studentized Range= 3.673
Minimum Significant Difference= 4.5266

Means with the same letter are not significantly different.

Tukey Grouping		Mean	N	REWGRP
A		33.333	6	3
A				
A		31.000	6	2
B		8.667	6	1

```
                                                                    4

                 General Linear Models Procedure

        Level of          ------------COMMIT-----------
        REWGRP       N        Mean              SD

           1         6      8.6666667       3.44480285
           2         6     31.0000000       3.40587727
           3         6     33.3333333       1.96638416
```

Output 8.1: Results of One-Way ANOVA: Significant Differences Observed

Steps in Interpreting the Output

1. Make sure that everything looks right. Page 1 of the PROC GLM output provides class level information for the analysis. Verify that the name of your predictor variable appears under the heading "Class". Under the heading "Levels", the output should indicate how many experimental groups were included in your study (in this case 3). Under the heading "Values", the output should indicate the specific numbers or letters that you used to code this predictor variable (in this case, the values were 1, 2, and 3). Finally, the last line indicates the number of observations in the data set. The present example used 3 groups with 6 subjects each, for a total of $N = 18$. If any of this does not look right, you probably made an error in either keying your data or writing your INPUT statement.

Page 2 of the output provides the analysis of variance table. Near the top of page 2 on the left side, the name of the criterion variable should appear to the right of the heading "Dependent Variable:". In this case, the dependent variable is COMMIT. Below this heading is the ANOVA summary table.

The first column of this table is headed "Source", and below the heading "Source" are three subheadings: "Model", "Error", and "Corrected Total". Look to the right of the heading "Corrected Total", and under the column headed "DF". In this case, you will see the number "17". This number represents the corrected total degrees of freedom. This number should always be equal to $N - 1$, where N represents the total number of subjects for whom you have a complete set of data. In this study, N was 18, and $18 - 1 = 17$, so it looks like everything is correct so far. (A **complete set of data** means the number of subjects for whom you have scores on both the predictor variable and the criterion variable .)

The means for the three experimental groups are found on page 3 of the output. Toward the bottom half of the page, the third column from the right is headed "Mean". Below this heading are the group means. Notice that, in this case, they range from 8.667 through 33.333. Remember that your subjects used a scale which could range from 4 through 36, so these group means are reasonable. If these means had taken on values such as 0.21 or 88.3, it would probably mean that you had made an error in either keying the data, or writing the INPUT statements.

2. Review the appropriate *F* statistic and its associated *p* value. Once you have verified that there are no obvious errors in the output, you may review your results. First you should review the *F* statistic from the ANOVA to see if you can reject the null hypothesis. You can state the null hypothesis for the present study as follows: In the population, there is no difference between the high-reward group, the mixed-reward group, and the low-reward group with respect to mean commitment. Symbolically, you can represent the null hypothesis this way:

$$M_1 = M_2 = M_3$$

where M_1 is the mean commitment score for the population of people in the low-reward condition, M_2 is the mean commitment score for the population of people in the mixed-reward condition, and M_3 is the mean commitment score for the population of people in the high-reward condition.

You will generally use the degrees of freedom, sum of squares, *F* value, and *p* value associated with the type III sum of squares. This is an important point to make because when you actually run a program, the output that you obtain will provide two ANOVA summary tables at the bottom of page 2. The first summary table provides the results using something called the "type I sum of squares", and it has the following headings:

```
DF        Type I SS        Mean Square        F Value        PR > F
```

Below this, you will see results for a second ANOVA table which uses the "type III sum of squares," and it has the following headings:

```
DF        Type III SS        Mean Square        F Value        PR > F
```

The *F* statistic appropriate to test your null hypothesis appears toward the bottom of page 2, in the section that provides the type III sum of squares. Notice that there is a heading called "Source", which stands for "source of variation." Below this heading you will find the name of your predictor variable, which in this case is REWGRP. To the right, you will find an ANOVA summary table using the type III sum of squares.

In this ANOVA summary table at the bottom of the page, look to the right of the word REWGRP. Under the heading "DF", you see that there are 2 degrees of freedom associated with the predictor variable. The degrees of freedom associated with a predictor are equal to $k - 1$, where *k* represents the number of experimental groups. Under the heading "Type III SS", you find the sum of squares associated with your predictor variable, REWGRP, which in this case is 2225.33. Under the heading "F Value" you find the *F* statistic appropriate for the test of your null hypothesis. In this case, $F = 122.12$, which is very large. The last heading is "Pr > F", which gives you the probability of obtaining an *F* this large or larger if the null hypothesis were true. In the present case, this *p* value is very small: less than 0.0001. When a *p* value is less than .05, you may reject the null hypothesis, so in this case the null hypothesis of no population differences is rejected. In other words, you conclude that there is a significant effect for the type of rewards independent variable.

3. Prepare your own version of the ANOVA summary table. Before moving on to interpret the sample means for the three experimental groups, you should prepare your own version of the ANOVA summary table. All of the information that you need either is presented on page 2 of the output, or you can easily calculate it by hand.

Table 8.1 provides the completed ANOVA summary table for the current analysis:

Table 8.1

ANOVA Summary Table for Study Investigating the Relationship Between Type of Rewards and Commitment

Source	df	SS	MS	F	R^2
Type of rewards	2	2225.33	1112.67	122.12 *	.94
Within groups	15	136.67	9.11		
Total	17	2362.00			

Note: N = 18.

* p < .001

In completing this table, you should first summarize the information associated with the predictor variable, type of rewards. On the bottom of page 2 of Output 8.1, look to the right of the name of the predictor variable (REWGRP, in this case). Here you find the results associated with the type III sum of squares. Remember that all of the information related to "type of rewards" in Table 8.1 must come from this section of the output which deals with the type III sum of squares. Under "DF", find the between-groups degrees of freedom, which is 2 in this case. Note where these degrees of freedom are placed in Table 8.1: they appear in the column headed "df", to the right of "Type of rewards".

On the output, next find the sum of squares associated with REWGRP under the heading "Type III SS". This value (2225.33) goes under "SS" in Table 8.1.

Next in Table 8.1, under the heading <u>MS</u>, you find the mean square associated with REWGRP. This mean square is also known as the "mean square between groups." It is calculated by PROC GLM using this simple formula:

$$\text{MS}_{\text{between groups}} = \frac{\texttt{Type III SS}}{\texttt{DF}} = \frac{2225.33}{2} = 1112.67$$

In the above formula, Type III SS represents the type III sum of squares associated with REWGRP, and DF represents the degrees of freedom associated with REWGRP. This mean square has already been calculated by PROC GLM, and appears in Output 8.1 under the heading "Mean Square". It should appear in Table 8.1 under "<u>MS</u>".

Next, find the F statistic appropriate for the test of your null hypothesis. This will again be on page 2 of Output 8.1, under the heading "F Value", and to the right of "REWGRP". This statistic is 122.12, and is placed under the heading "<u>F</u>" in Table 8.1.

Under the heading "PR > F" from Output 8.1, find the p value associated with this F. However, you will not have a separate column in Table 8.1 for this p value. Instead, you can simply mark the F value with an asterisk in superscript (*) to indicate that the F is statistically significant. At the bottom of the table, you place a note that indicates the level of significance attained by this F value. In this case, the output indicated that $p = 0.0001$. This value is less than 0.001, so attach a note at the bottom of the table that indicates that the effect for type of reward was significant at the $p < .001$ level:

        * p < .001

If the F value had been significant at the .01 level, your note would have looked like this:

        * p < .01

If the F value had been significant at the .05 level, your note would have looked like this:

        * p < .05

If the F value had not been statistically significant, you would not have put an asterisk next to it or placed a note at the bottom of the table.

Finally, you need to calculate the R^2 for this predictor variable. As was mentioned before, the R^2 statistic indicates the percent of variance in the criterion (commitment) which is accounted for by the predictor (type of reward). The formula for R^2 is also very simple:

$$R^2 = \frac{\texttt{Type III SS}}{\texttt{Corrected Total Sum of Squares}}$$

In the above formula, Type III SS represents the type III sum of squares associated with REWGRP, and Corrected Total Sum of Squares represents the total sum of squares from the analysis. This total sum of squares appears on page 2 of Output 8.1, to the right of the heading, "Corrected Total", and under the heading, "Sum of Squares". Here, the appropriate figures from page 2 of Output 8.1 have been inserted in the formula:

$$R^2 = \frac{\text{Type III SS}}{\text{Corrected Total Sum of Squares}} = \frac{2225.33}{2362.00} = .94$$

With $R^2 = .94$, this indicates that 94% of the variance in commitment is accounted for by the "type of rewards" independent variable. This is a very high value of R^2, much higher than you are likely to obtain in an actual investigation (remember that the present data are fictitious).

If you look closely at Output 8.1, you will notice that the R^2 value is already presented on page 2, just below the ANOVA summary table. Nevertheless, this chapter still advises that you calculate R^2 values by hand because, depending on the type of analysis that you do, the output of PROC GLM will not always provide the R^2 value that you are actually interested in. This is particularly true when you have more than one predictor variable. Therefore, it is good practice to ignore the R^2 provided in the output, and instead calculate it by hand.

Now that you have filled in the line headed "Type of rewards" in Table 8.1, you will fill in the line headed "Within groups". This line deals with the error variance in your sample, and everything you need appears on page 2 of Output 8.1 to the right of the heading, "Error" . Under "DF" on the output, you can see that there are 15 degrees of freedom associated with this estimate of error variance. Note where this goes in Table 8.1: where the column headed "df" intersects with the row headed "Within groups."

Under the heading "Sum of Squares" on page 2 of Output 8.1, you can see that the sum of squares associated with the error term is 136.67. This term is transferred to its corresponding spot in Table 8.1 in the column headed "SS".

Finally, under the heading "Mean Square" on the output, you can see that the mean square error (also called the mean square within groups) is 9.11. This term is transferred to Table 8.1, in the column headed "MS".

The last line in Table 8.1 deals with the total variability in the data set. You will find all of the information that you need on page 2 of Output 8.1, to the right of the heading, "Corrected Total". Under the heading "DF", you can see that 17 degrees of freedom are associated with the total variance estimate. This goes in Table 8.1 under the heading "df", to the right of the heading, "Total". Under the "Sum of Squares" heading on the output, you find that the total sum of squares is 2362.00. Note that this appears in Table 8.1 in the column headed "SS".

Place a note at the bottom of the table to indicate the size of the total sample, and your own version of the ANOVA summary table is now complete.

4. Review the sample means and the results of the multiple comparison procedure.

Because the *F* statistic was significant, you reject the null hypothesis of no differences in population means. Instead, you tentatively accept the alternative hypothesis that at least one of the population means is different from at least one of the other population means. However, since you have three experimental conditions, you now have a new problem: which of these groups is significantly different from the others? To answer this question, you have performed a multiple comparison procedure called Tukey's HSD test. The results of this analysis appear on page 3 of Output 8.1.

About halfway down this table, it says "Alpha = 0.05". This means that if any of the groups are significantly different from the others, they will be different with a significance level of *p* < .05.

On the bottom half of the table there are four columns of figures. The last column always represents your predictor variable (which, in this case, is REWGRP). Below the REWGRP heading you find the values used to code the experimental conditions. In this case, you used the value of 3, 2, and 1, which coded the high-reward, mixed-reward, and low-reward conditions, respectively. To the left of the REWGRP column is a column headed "N". This column indicates how many subjects were in each condition. In the present case, there were 6 subjects in each group. To the left of the "N" column is a column headed "Mean", which provides the mean scores for the three groups on the criterion variable (the commitment variable in this study). You can see that the high-reward group had a mean commitment score of 33.3, the mixed-reward group had a mean score of 31.00, and the low-reward group had a mean score of 8.7.

Finally, to the left of the "Mean" column is the column headed "Tukey Grouping." It is this column that tells you which groups are significantly different from which. The rules to use here are simple:

- Two groups that are identified by the same letter are not significantly different from each other.

- Two groups that are identified by different letters are significantly different from each other.

For example, notice that group 3 is identified with the letter "A" in the grouping column, while group 1 is identified with the letter "B". This means that groups 3 and 1 are significantly different from each other on commitment (notice how different their means are). Similarly, groups 2 and 1 are also identified by different letters, so they are also significantly different. However, groups 3 and 2 are both identified by the same letter, "A". Therefore, groups 3 and 2 are not significantly different from each other.

NOTE: Remember that you should review the results of a multiple comparison procedure only if the *F* value from the preceding ANOVA summary table is statistically significant. If the *F* for the predictor variable is nonsignificant, then ignore the results of this Tukey HSD test.

5. **Summarize the results of the analysis.** When performing a one-factor ANOVA, you can use the following format to summarize the results of your analysis:

A) Statement of the problem
B) Nature of the variables
C) Statistical test
D) Null hypothesis (H_o)
E) Alternative hypothesis (H_1)
F) Obtained statistic
G) Obtained probability (p) value
H) Conclusion regarding the null hypothesis
I) ANOVA summary table
J) Figure representing the results

An example summary follows:

A) Statement of the problem: The purpose of this study was to determine whether there was a difference between people in a high-reward relationship, people in a mixed-reward relationship, and people in a low-reward relationship with respect to their commitment to the relationship.

B) Nature of the variables: This analysis involved two variables. The predictor variable was types of reward, which was measured on a nominal scale and could assume three values: a low-reward condition (coded as 1), a mixed-reward condition (coded as 2), and a high-reward condition (coded as 3). The criterion variable represented subjects' commitment, which was measured on an interval/ratio scale.

C) Statistical test: One-way ANOVA, between-groups design.

D) Null hypothesis (H_0): $M_1 = M_2 = M_3$; In the population, there is no difference between subjects in a high-reward relationship, subjects in a mixed-reward relationship, and subjects in a low-reward relationship with respect to their mean commitment scores.

E) Alternative hypothesis (H_1): In the population, there is a difference between at least two of the following three groups with respect to their mean commitment scores: subjects in a high-reward relationship, subjects in a mixed-reward relationship, and subjects in a low-reward relationship.

F) Obtained statistic: $F = 122.12$.

G) Obtained probability (p) value: $p = .0001$.

H) Conclusion regarding the null hypothesis: Reject the null hypothesis.

I) ANOVA Summary Table: See Table 8.1.

J) Figure representing the results:

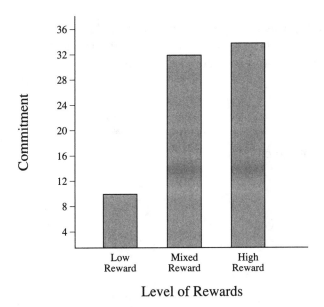

Figure 8.1: Mean Levels of Commitment Observed for Subjects in Low-Reward, Mixed-Reward, and High-Reward Conditions (Significant Differences Observed)

Formal Description of Results for a Paper

You could use the following approach to summarize this analysis for a paper in a scholarly journal:

> Results were analyzed using a one-way ANOVA, between-groups design. This analysis revealed a significant effect for type of rewards, $F(2,15) = 122.12$; $p < .001$. The sample means are displayed in Figure 8.1. Tukey's HSD test showed that subjects in the high-reward and mixed-reward conditions scored significantly higher on commitment than did subjects in the low-reward condition ($p < .05$). There were no significant differences between subjects in the high-reward condition and subjects in the mixed-reward condition.

Example with Nonsignificant
Differences between Experimental Conditions

In this section you repeat the preceding analysis, but this time you perform it on a data set that was designed to provide nonsignificant results. This will help you learn how to interpret and summarize results when there are no significant differences between the groups.

Data for the New Analysis

Here is the data set to be analyzed in this section of the chapter:

```
        CARDS;
        1  15
        1  17
        1  10
        1  19
        1  16
        1  18
        2  14
        2  17
        2  16
        2  18
        2  11
        2  12
        3  17
        3  20
        3  14
        3  16
        3  16
        3  17
        ;
```

Remember that the first column of data (in column 1) of the preceding data set represents each subject's score on REWGRP, the type of rewards independent variable, the second column of data (in columns 3-4) represents each subject's score on COMMIT, the commitment dependent variable.

Results from the SAS Output

If the preceding data set were analyzed using the PROC GLM program presented earlier, it would again produce four pages of output, with the same type of information on each page. The output from this analysis is reproduced here as Output 8.2.

```
                          The SAS System                              1

                   General Linear Models Procedure
                     Class Level Information

                   Class     Levels    Values

                   REWGRP       3       1 2 3


            Number of observations in data set = 18
```

```
                                                                      2


                   General Linear Models Procedure

Dependent Variable: COMMIT
                                 Sum of        Mean
Source                 DF        Squares       Square    F Value    Pr > F

Model                   2     12.11111111    6.05555556    0.83     0.4553

Error                  15    109.50000000    7.30000000

Corrected Total        17    121.61111111

             R-Square          C.V.        Root MSE       COMMIT Mean

             0.099589        17.18492      2.7018512        15.722222


Source                 DF     Type I SS    Mean Square   F Value    Pr > F

REWGRP                  2     12.11111111    6.05555556    0.83     0.4553

Source                 DF     Type III SS   Mean Square   F Value    Pr > F

REWGRP                  2     12.11111111    6.05555556    0.83     0.4553
```

3

```
                    General Linear Models Procedure

            Tukey's Studentized Range (HSD) Test for variable: COMMIT

        NOTE: This test controls the type I experimentwise error rate, but
                  generally has a higher type II error rate than REGWQ.

                      Alpha= 0.05  df= 15  MSE= 7.3
                  Critical Value of Studentized Range= 3.673
                   Minimum Significant Difference= 4.0518

        Means with the same letter are not significantly different.

                Tukey Grouping          Mean       N   REWGRP

                        A              16.667       6   3
                        A
                        A              15.833       6   1
                        A
                        A              14.667       6   2
```

4

```
                    General Linear Models Procedure

            Level of        ------------COMMIT-----------
            REWGRP     N        Mean              SD

               1       6     15.8333333       3.18852108
               2       6     14.6666667       2.80475786
               3       6     16.6666667       1.96638416
```

Output 8.2: Results of One-Way ANOVA: Nonsignificant Differences Observed

Page 1 of the Output 8.2 provides the class level information, which again shows that the class variable (REWGRP) includes three levels. In addition, page 1 shows that the analysis is again based on 18 observations.

Page 2 of Output 8.2 provides the analysis of variance table. Again, you are most interested in the information that appears at the very bottom of the page, in the section that provides information related to the type III sum of squares. Under the heading "F Value", you can see that this analysis resulted in an *F* statistic of only 0.83, which is quite small. Under "Pr > F", you can see that the probability value associated with this *F* is .455. Because this *p* value is greater than .05, you fail to reject the null hypothesis, and instead conclude that the types of reward independent variable did not have a significant effect on rated commitment.

Page 3 of Output 8.2 provides the results of the Tukey HSD test, but you will not interpret these results since the *F* for the ANOVA was nonsignificant. It is, however, interesting to note that the Tukey test indicates that the three groups were not significantly different from each other; notice how all three groups are identified by the same letter ("A").

Finally, page 4 of Output 8.2 provides the mean scores on commitment for the three groups. You can see that there is little difference between these means: all three groups display an average score on COMMIT between 14 and 17. This is what you would expect with nonsignificant differences. You can use the means from this table to prepare a figure that illustrates the results graphically.

Summarizing the Results of the Analysis

This section summarizes the present results according to the statistical interpretation format presented earlier. However, since the same hypothesis is being tested, items A through E would be completed in exactly the same way that they were completed earlier. Therefore, only items F through J are presented here:

F) Obtained statistic: $F = 0.83$.

G) Obtained probability (p) value: $p = .46$.

H) Conclusion regarding the null hypothesis: Fail to reject the null hypothesis.

I) ANOVA summary table:

Table 8.2

ANOVA Summary Table for Study Investigating the Relationship Between Type of Rewards and Commitment

Source	df	SS	MS	F	R^2
Type of rewards	2	12.11	6.06	0.83	.10
Within groups	15	109.50	7.30		
Total	17	121.61			

Note. N = 18.

J) Figure representing the results:

Figure 8.2: Mean Levels of Commitment Observed for Subjects in Low-Reward, Mixed-Reward, and High-Reward Conditions (Nonsignificant Differences Observed)

Formal Description of Results for a Paper

You could summarize the results from the present analysis in the following way for a published paper:

```
      Results were analyzed using a one-way ANOVA, between-
groups design.  This analysis failed to reveal a
significant effect for type of rewards, F(2, 15)  =  0.83,
p  = .455 .  The sample means are displayed in Figure 8.2,
which shows that the three experimental groups demonstrated
similar scores on commitment.
```

Understanding the Meaning of the *F* Statistic

An earlier section mentioned that you obtain significant results in an analysis of variance when the *F* statistic produced in the ANOVA assumes a relatively large value. This section explains why this is so.

The meaning of the F statistic may be easier to understand if you think about it in terms of what results would be expected if the null hypothesis were true. If there really were no differences between the three groups with respect to their population means, you would expect to obtain an F statistic somewhere close to "1.00". In the first analysis, the obtained F was much larger than 1.00, and while it is possible to obtain an F of 122.12 when the population means are equal, it is extremely unlikely. In fact, SAS calculated that the probability was less than or equal to 0.0001 (that is the p value found on the output). Therefore, you rejected the null hypothesis of no population differences.

But why do you expect an F value of 1.00 when the population means are equal? And why do you expect an F value greater than 1.00 when the population means are not equal? To understand this, you must understand how the F statistic is calculated. The formula for the F statistic is as follows:

$$F = \frac{MS_{\text{between groups}}}{MS_{\text{within groups}}}$$

The numerator in this ratio is $MS_{\text{between groups}}$, which represents the "mean square between groups." This is a measure of variability which is influenced by two sources of variation: error variability, plus variability due to the differences in the population means. The denominator in this ratio is $MS_{\text{within groups}}$, which represents the "mean square within groups." This is a measure of variability which is influenced by only one source of variation: error variability. For this reason, the $MS_{\text{within groups}}$ is sometimes referred to as the MS_{error}.

Now you can see why the F statistic should be larger than 1.00 when there are differences in population means (when the null hypothesis is incorrect). Consider the following alternative formula for the F statistic:

$$F = \frac{MS_{\text{between groups}}}{MS_{\text{within groups}}} = \frac{\text{Error variability plus variability due to differences in the population means}}{\text{Error variability}}$$

If the population means are different, that means that your predictor variable (types of reward) has had an effect on commitment. Therefore the numerator of the F ratio contains two sources of variation: both error variability plus variability due to the differences in the population means. The denominator ($MS_{\text{within groups}}$), however, was influenced by only one source of variance: error variability. It is clear that both the numerator and the denominator are influenced by error variability, but the numerator is affected by an additional source of variance, so the numerator should be larger than the denominator. And whenever the numerator is larger than the denominator in a ratio, the resulting quotient should be greater than 1.00. That is why you expect to see an *F* value greater than 1.00 when there are differences between the population means. And that is why you will reject the null hypothesis of no population differences when you obtain a sufficiently large *F* statistic.

In the same way, you can also see why the *F* statistic should be approximately equal to 1.00 when there are no differences in population means (when the null hypothesis is correct). Under these circumstances, your predictor variable (level of rewards) is having no effect on commitment. Therefore, the $MS_{\text{between groups}}$ will not be influenced by variability due to differences between the population means. Instead, it will be influenced only by error variability. So the formula for the *F* statistic reduces to the following:

$$F = \frac{MS_{\text{between groups}}}{MS_{\text{within groups}}} = \frac{\text{Error variability}}{\text{Error variability}}$$

Obviously, the number representing the numerator in this formula is going to be fairly close to the number representing the denominator. And whenever a numerator in a ratio is approximately equal to the denominator in that ratio, the resulting quotient should be fairly close to 1.00. Hence, when a predictor variable has no effect on the criterion variable, you expect an *F* statistic close to 1.00.

Conclusion

The one-way analysis of variance is one of the most flexible and widely-used procedures in the social sciences. It allows you to test for significant differences between groups, and its applicability is not limited to studies with just two groups (as the *t* test is limited). However, an even more flexible procedure is the *factorial* analysis of variance. Factorial ANOVA allows you to analyze data from studies in which more than one independent variable is manipulated. Not only does this allow you to test more than one hypothesis in a single study, but it also allows you to investigate an entirely different type of effect called an "interaction." Factorial analysis of variance is introduced in the following chapter.

Appendix: Assumptions Underlying One-Way ANOVA with One Between-Groups Factor

- **Level of measurement.** The criterion variable should be assessed on an interval- or ratio-level of measurement. The predictor variable should be a nominal-level variable (a categorical variable) that includes two or more categories.

- **Independent observations.** A given observation should not be dependent on any other observation in any group (for a more detailed explanation of this assumption, see Chapter 7).

- **Random sampling**. Scores on the criterion variable should represent a random sample drawn from the populations of interest.

- **Normal distributions**. Each group should be drawn from a normally-distributed population. If each group contains over 30 subjects, the test is robust against moderate departures from normality.

- **Homogeneity of variance**. The populations represented by the various groups should have equal variances on the criterion. If the number of subjects in the largest group is no more than 1.5 times greater than the number of subjects in the smallest group, the test is robust against violations of the homogeneity assumption (Stevens, 1986).

References

SAS Institute Inc. (1989). *SAS/STAT user's guide, version 6, fourth edition, volume 2*. Cary, NC: SAS Institute Inc.

Stevens, J. (1986). *Applied multivariate statistics for the social sciences*. Hillsdale, N.J.: Lawrence Erlbaum Associates.

Chapter 9

FACTORIAL ANOVA WITH TWO BETWEEN-GROUPS FACTORS

> **Overview.** This chapter shows how to key data and prepare SAS programs that perform a two-way ANOVA using the GLM procedure. This chapter focuses on factorial designs with two *between-groups* factors, meaning that each subject is exposed to only one condition under each independent variable. Guidelines are provided for interpreting results that do not display a significant interaction, and separate guidelines are provided for interpreting results that do display a significant interaction. For significant interactions, you see how to display the interaction in a figure and how to perform tests for simple effects.

Introduction to Factorial Designs

The preceding chapter described a simple experiment in which you manipulated a single independent variable, type of rewards. Because there was a single independent variable in that study, it was analyzed using a one-way ANOVA.

But imagine that there were actually two independent variables that you wanted to manipulate. In this situation, you might think that it would be necessary to conduct two separate experiments, one for each independent variable, but you would be wrong. In many cases, it is possible to manipulate both independent variables in a single study.

The research design used in these studies is called a factorial design. In a **factorial design**, two or more independent variables are manipulated in a single study so that the treatment conditions represent all possible combinations of the various levels of the independent variables.

In theory, a factorial design might include any number of independent variables. In practice, however, it generally becomes impractical to use many more than three or four. This chapter illustrates factorial designs that include just two independent variables, and thus may be analyzed using a two-way ANOVA. More specifically, this chapter deals with studies that include two predictor variables, both measured on a nominal scale, as well as a single criterion variable which is assessed on an interval or ratio scale.

The Aggression Study

To illustrate the concept of factorial design, imagine that you are interested in conducting a study that investigates aggression in eight-year-old children. Here, aggression is defined as any verbal or behavioral act performed with the intention of hurting another person. You want to test the following two hypotheses:

- Boys will display higher levels of aggression than girls.

- The amount of sugar consumed will have a positive effect on levels of aggression.

You perform a single investigation to test these two hypotheses. The hypothesis that you are most interested in is the second hypothesis, the hypothesis that consuming sugar will cause children to behave more aggressively. You will test this hypothesis by actually manipulating the amount of sugar that a group of school children consume at lunch time. Each day for two weeks, one group of children will receive a lunch that contains no sugar at all (this is the 0 grams of sugar group). A second group will receive a lunch that contains a moderate amount of sugar (20 grams), and a third group will receive a lunch that contains a large amount of sugar (40 grams). Each child will then be observed after lunch, and a pair of judges will tabulate the number of aggressive acts that the child commits. The total number of aggressive acts committed by each child over the two-week period will result in the dependent variable in the study.

You begin with a sample of 60 children: 30 boys and 30 girls. The children are randomly assigned to treatment conditions in the following way:

- 20 children are assigned to the "0 grams of sugar" treatment condition.

- 20 children are assigned to the "20 grams of sugar" treatment condition.

- 20 children are assigned to the "40 grams of sugar" treatment condition.

In making these assignments, you make sure that there are equal numbers of boys and girls in each treatment condition. For example, you verify that, of the 20 children in the "0 grams" group, 10 are boys and 10 are girls.

The Factorial Design Matrix

The factorial design of this study is illustrated in Figure 9.1. You can see that this design is represented by a matrix that consists of two rows (running horizontally) and three columns (running vertically):

Predictor A:
Amount of Sugar Consumed

	Level A1: 0 Grams	Level A2: 20 Grams	Level A3: 40 Grams
Level B1: Males	10 Subjects	10 Subjects	10 Subjects
Level B2: Females	10 Subjects	10 Subjects	10 Subjects

Predictor B: Subject Sex

Figure 9.1: Experimental Design Used in Aggression Study

When an experimental design is represented in a matrix such as this, it is easiest to understand if you focus on just one aspect of the matrix at a time. For example, consider just the three vertical columns of Figure 9.1. The three columns are headed "Predictor A: Amount of Sugar Consumed," so, obviously, these columns represent the various levels of the sugar consumption independent variable. The first column represents the 20 subjects in level A1 (the subjects who received 0 grams of sugar), the second column represents the 20 subjects in level A2 (who received 20 grams), and the last column represents the 20 subjects in level A3 (who received 40 grams).

Now consider just the two horizontal rows of Figure 9.1. These rows are headed "Predictor B: Subject Sex." The first row is headed "Level B1: Males," and this row represents the 30 subjects who were male. The second row is headed "Level B2: Females," and represents the 30 subjects who were female.

It is common to refer to a factorial design as an "*r* X *c*" design, in which "*r*" represents the number of rows in the matrix, and "*c*" represents the number of columns. The present study is an example of a 2 X 3 factorial design, because it has two rows and three columns. If it included four levels of sugar consumption rather than three, it would be referred to as a 2 X 4 factorial design.

You can see that this matrix consists of six different cells. A **cell** is the location in the matrix where the row for one independent variable intersects with the column for a second independent variable. For example, look at the cell where the row named B1 (males) intersects with the column headed A1 (0 grams). The entry "10 Subjects" appears in this cell, which means that there were 10 subjects who experienced this particular combination of "treatments" under the two independent variables. More specifically, it means that there were 10 subjects who were both (a) male, and (b) given 0 grams of sugar ("treatments" appears in quotation marks in the preceding sentence because "subject sex" is obviously not a true independent variable that is *manipulated* by the researcher; it is merely a predictor variable).

Now look at the cell in which the row labeled B2 (females) intersects with the column headed A2 (20 grams). Again, the cell contains the entry "10 Subjects," which means that there was a different group of 10 children who experienced the treatments of (a) being female, and (b) being given 20 grams of sugar. You can see that there was a separate group of 10 children assigned to each of the six cells of the matrix.

Earlier, it was said that a factorial design involves two or more independent variables being manipulated so that the treatment conditions represent all possible combinations of the various levels of the independent variables, and Figure 9.1 illustrates this concept. You can see that the six cells of the figure represent every possible combination of sex and amount of sugar consumed: males are observed under every level of sugar consumption, and the same is true for females.

Some Possible Results from a Factorial ANOVA

Factorial designs are popular in social science research for a variety of reasons. One reason is that they allow you to test for several different types of effects in a single investigation. Later, this section will illustrate the nature of these effects.

First, however, it is important to note one drawback that is associated with factorial designs: they sometimes produce results that can be difficult to interpret, compared to the results that are produced in a one-way ANOVA. Fortunately, however, this task of interpretation can be made much easier if you first prepare a figure that plots the results of the factorial study. This first section shows how this can be done.

Figure 9.2 presents one type of figure that is often used to illustrate the results of a factorial study. Notice that, with this figure, scores on the criterion variable (level of aggression displayed by the children) are plotted on the vertical axis that runs up and down. Remember that groups that appear higher on this vertical axis are displaying higher mean levels of aggression.

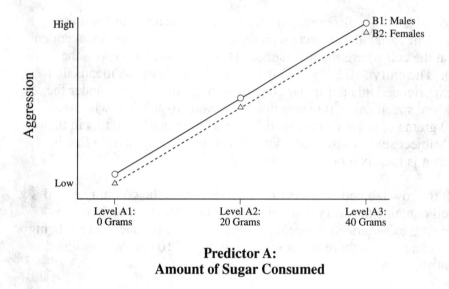

Figure 9.2: A Significant Main Effect for Predictor A (Amount of Sugar Consumed) Only

The three levels of predictor variable A (amount of sugar consumed) are plotted on the horizontal axis (the axis that runs left to right). The point at the left represents group A1 (who received 0 grams of sugar), the middle point represents group A2 (the 20-gram group), and the point at the right represents group A3 (the 40-gram group).

The two levels of predictor variable B (subject sex) are identified by drawing two different lines in the body of the figure itself. Specifically, the mean scores on aggression displayed by the males (level B1) are illustrated with small circles connected by a solid line, while the mean scores on aggression displayed by the females (level B2) are displayed by small triangles connected by a broken line.

In summary, the important points to remember when interpreting the figures in this chapter are as follows:

- The possible scores on the criterion variable are represented on the vertical axis.

- The levels of predictor A are represented as points on the horizontal axis.

- The levels of predictor B are represented by drawing different lines within the figure itself.

With this foundation, you are now ready to learn about the different types of effects that are observed in a factorial design, and how these effects appear when they are plotted in this type of figure.

Significant Main Effects

When a predictor variable (or independent variable) in a factorial design displays a significant **main effect**, it means that, in the population, there is a difference between at least two of the levels of that predictor variable with respect to mean scores on the criterion variable. In a one-way analysis of variance there is essentially just one main effect: the main effect for the study's independent variable. However, in a factorial design, there will be one main effect possible for each predictor variable included in the study.

For example, the preceding study on aggression included two predictor variables: amount of sugar consumed and subject sex. This means that, in analyzing data from this investigation, it is possible to obtain any of the following outcomes related to main effects:

- A significant main effect for just predictor A (amount of sugar consumed)

- A significant main effect for just predictor B (subject sex)

- A significant main effect for both predictor A and B

- No significant main effects at all

This section will describe these effects, and show what they look like when plotted in a figure.

A significant main effect for predictor A. Figure 9.2 shows a possible main effect for predictor A: "Amount of Sugar Consumed" (to save space, we will henceforth refer to this as the "sugar consumption" variable). Notice that a relatively low mean level of aggression was displayed by subjects in the 0-gram condition of the sugar consumption predictor variable. When you look above the heading "Level A1", you can see that both the boys (represented with a small circle) and the girls (represented with a small triangle) display relatively low scores on aggression. However, a somewhat higher level of aggression was demonstrated by subjects in the 20-gram condition: When you look above "Level A2", you can see that both boys and girls display a somewhat higher level of aggression. Finally, an even higher level of aggression was displayed by subjects in the 40-gram condition: when you look above "Level A3", you can see that both boys and girls in this group display fairly high levels of aggression. In short, this trend shows that there was a main effect for the sugar consumption variable.

This leads to an important point. When a figure representing the results of a factorial study displays a significant main effect for predictor variable A, it will demonstrate both of the following characteristics:

- The lines for the various groups are parallel.

- At least one line segment displays a relatively steep angle.

The first of the two conditions--that the lines should be parallel--ensures that the two predictor variables are not involved in an interaction. This is important, because you normally will not interpret a significant main effect for a predictor variable if that predictor variable is involved in an interaction. In Figure 9.2, you can see that the lines for the two groups in the present study (the solid line for the boys and the broken line for the girls) are parallel to one another. This suggests that there probably is not an interaction between sex and sugar consumption in the present study (the concept of interaction will be explained in greater detail later in the section titled "A Significant Interaction").

The second condition--that at least one line segment should display a relatively steep angle--can be understood by again referring to Figure 9.2. Notice that the line segment that begins at level A1 (the 0-gram condition) and extends to level A2 (the 20-gram condition) is not horizontal; it displays upward angle. Obviously, this is because the aggression scores for the 20-gram group were higher than the aggression scores for the 0-gram group. When you obtain a significant effect for the predictor A variable in your study, you should expect to see this type of angle. Similarly, you can see that the line segment that begins at A2 and continues to A3 also displays an upward angle, also consistent with a significant effect for the sugar consumption variable.

Remember that these guidelines are merely intended to help you understand what a main effect *looks like* when it is plotted in a figure such as Figure 9.2. To determine whether this main effect is statistically *significant*, it will of course be necessary to review the results of the analysis of variance, to be discussed later.

A significant main effect for predictor B. You would expect to see a different pattern in a figure if the main effect for the other predictor variable (predictor B) were significant. Earlier, you learned that predictor A was represented in a figure by plotting three points on the horizontal axis. In contrast, you learned that predictor B was represented by drawing different lines within the body of the figure itself: one line for each level of predictor B. In the present study, predictor B was the subject sex variable, so a solid line was used to represent mean scores from the male subjects, and a dotted line was used to represent mean scores from the female subjects.

When predictor B is represented in a figure by plotting separate lines for its various levels, a significant main effect for that variable is revealed when the figure displays both of the following:

• The lines for the various groups are parallel.

• At least two of the lines are relatively *separated* from each other.

For example, a main effect for predictor B in the current study is represented by Figure 9.3. Consistent with the two preceding points, the two lines in Figure 9.3 are parallel to one another (indicating that there is no interaction between sex and sugar consumption), and separated from one another. Regarding this separation, notice that, in general, the males tend to score higher on the measure of aggression compared to the females. What is more, notice that this tends to be true regardless of how much sugar the subjects consume. Figure 9.3 shows the general trend that you would expect when there is a main effect for predictor B only:

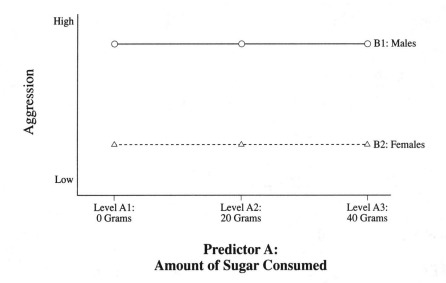

Figure 9.3: A Significant Main Effect for Predictor B (Subject Sex) Only

A significant main effect for both predictor variables. It is possible to obtain significant effects for both predictor A and predictor B in the same investigation. When there is a significant effect for both predictor variables, you should see all of the following:

- The lines for the various groups are parallel (indicating no interaction).

- At least one line segment displays a relatively steep angle (indicating a main effect for predictor A).

- At least two of the lines are relatively separated from each other (indicating a main effect for predictor B).

Figure 9.4 shows what the figure might look like under these circumstances:

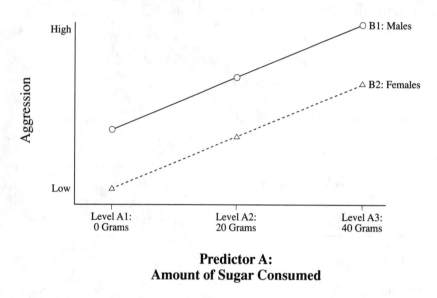

Figure 9.4: Significant Main Effects for Both Predictor A (Amount of Sugar Consumed) and Predictor B (Subject Sex)

No main effects. Figure 9.5 shows what a figure might look like if there were main effects for neither predictor A nor predictor B. Notice that the lines are parallel (indicating no interaction), none of the line segments displays a relatively steep angle (indicating no main effect for predictor A), and the lines are not separated (indicating no main effect for predictor B):

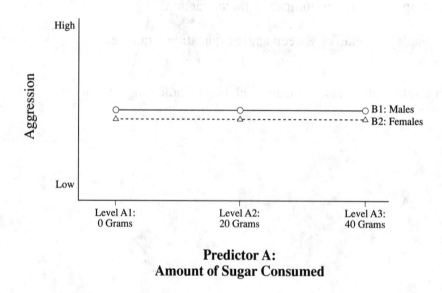

Figure 9.5: A Nonsignificant Interaction, and Nonsignificant Main Effects

A Significant Interaction

The concept of an **interaction** can be defined in a number of ways. For example, with respect to experimental research (in which you are actually manipulating independent variables), the following definition could be used:

> *An interaction is a condition in which the effect of one independent variable on the dependent variable is different at different levels of the second independent variable.*

On the other hand, when conducting nonexperimental research (in which you are simply measuring naturally occurring variables rather than manipulating independent variables), it could be defined in this way:

> *An interaction is a condition in which the relationship between one predictor variable and the criterion is different at different levels of the second predictor variable.*

These definitions are admittedly somewhat abstract at first reading, but the concept of interaction is much easier to grasp by once again referring to a figure. For example, Figure 9.6 displays a significant interaction between sugar consumption and subject sex in the present study. Notice that the lines for the two groups are no longer parallel: the line for the male subjects now displays a somewhat steeper angle, compared to the line for the females. This is the key characteristic of a figure that displays a significant interaction: lines that are not parallel.

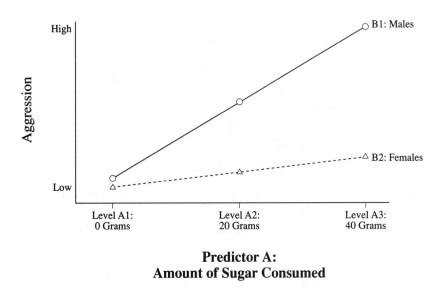

Figure 9.6: A Significant Interaction Between Predictor A (Amount of Sugar Consumed) and Predictor B (Subject Sex)

Notice how the relationships of Figure 9.6 are consistent with the definition for interaction: the relationship between one predictor variable (sugar consumption) and the criterion (aggression) is different at different levels of the second predictor variable (subject sex). More specifically, the figure shows that the relationship between sugar consumption and aggression is relatively *strong* for the male subjects: Consuming larger quantities of sugar results in dramatic increases in aggression among the male subjects (notice that the boys who consumed 40 grams of sugar displayed much higher levels of aggression than the boys who consume 0 or 20 grams). In contrast, the relationship between sugar consumption and aggression is relatively *weak* among the female subjects (notice that the line for the females is fairly "flat"; there is little difference in aggression between the girls who consumed 0 grams versus 20 grams versus 40 grams of sugar).

Figure 9.6 shows why you would normally not interpret main effects when an interaction is significant. To understand why, consider this: Would it make sense to say that there is a main effect for sugar consumption in the study illustrated by Figure 9.6? Probably not. It is clear that sugar consumption does seem to have an effect on aggression among boys, but the figure suggests that sugar consumption probably does not have any real meaningful effect on aggression among girls. To say that there is a main effect for sugar consumption might mislead readers into believing that sugar causes aggression in all children in pretty much the same way (which it apparently does not). Clearly, whether sugar causes aggression depends on the child's sex. In this situation, it would make more sense to instead do the following:

- Note that there was a significant interaction between sugar consumption and subject sex.

- Prepare a figure (like Figure 9.6) that illustrates the nature of the interaction.

- Test for simple effects.

Testing for simple effects is similar to testing for main effects, but is done one group at a time. For example, in the preceding analysis, you would test for simple effects by first dividing your data into two groups: data from the male subjects would be separated from data from the female subjects. With this done, you would perform an analysis to determine whether sugar consumption has a simple effect on aggression among just the male subjects (and you would probably find that this simple effect is significant). Finally, you would perform a separate test to determine whether sugar consumption has a simple effect on aggression among just the female subjects (and you would probably find that this simple effect is not significant). A later section shows how you can use the SAS System to perform these tests for simple effects.

To summarize, an interaction means that the relationship between one predictor variable and the criterion is different at different levels of the second predictor variable. When an interaction is significant, you should interpret your results in terms of *simple* effects, rather than main effects.

Example with a Nonsignificant Interaction

To illustrate how a two-way ANOVA is performed, assume that you will modify the earlier study that investigated the effect of rewards on commitment in romantic relationships. In Chapter 8, "One-Way ANOVA with One Between-Groups Factor," only one independent variable was manipulated, and this variable was called "type of rewards." In this chapter, however, there will be two independent variables: Independent variable A will be "type of rewards," while independent variable B will be "type of costs."

In the study presented in Chapter 8, subjects read descriptions of a fictitious "partner 10" and rated how committed they would be to a relationship with that person. One independent variable (called "type of rewards") was manipulated, and this variable consisted of three experimental conditions. Subjects were assigned to either the low-reward condition, the mixed-reward condition, or the high-reward condition. This variable was manipulated by varying the description of partner 10 which was provided to the subject:

- Subjects in the low-reward condition were told to assume that this partner "...does not enjoy the same recreational activities that you enjoy, and is not very good looking."

- Subjects in the mixed-reward condition were told to assume that "...Sometimes this person seems to enjoy the same recreational activities that you enjoy, and sometimes he/she does not. Sometimes partner 10 seems to be very good looking, and sometimes he/she does not."

- Subjects in the high-reward condition were told that this partner "...enjoys the same recreational activities that you enjoy, and is very good looking."

These same manipulations will be used in the present study. In a sample of 30 subjects, one third will be assigned to a low-reward condition, one third to a mixed-reward condition, and one-third to a high-reward condition. This "type of reward" factor will serve as independent variable A.

However, in this study, you will also manipulate a second predictor variable (independent variable B) at the same time. The second independent variable will be called "type of costs," and it will consist of two experimental conditions. One half of the subjects (the "low-cost" group) will be told to assume that they are in a relationship that does not create significant personal hardships. Specifically, when they read the description of partner 10, it will say "Partner 10 lives in the same neighborhood as you, so it is easy to see him/her as often as you like." The other half of the subjects (the "high-cost" group) will be told to imagine that they are in a relationship that does create significant personal hardships. When they read the description of partner 10, it will say "Partner 10 lives in a distant city, so it is difficult and expensive to visit with him/her."

Your study now has two independent variables. Independent variable A is type of rewards, and it has three levels (or conditions). Independent variable B is type of costs, and it has two levels. The factorial design used in the study is illustrated in Figure 9.7.

Type of Rewards

	Low Reward (1)	Mixed Reward (2)	High Reward (3)
Low Cost (1)	5 Subjects (Cell 1-1)	5 Subjects (Cell 1-2)	5 Subjects (Cell 1-3)
High Cost (2)	5 Subjects (Cell 2-1)	5 Subjects (Cell 2-2)	5 Subjects (Cell 2-3)

Type of Costs

Figure 9.7: Experimental Design Used in Investment Model Study

The preceding 2 X 3 matrix shows that there are two independent variables, that one independent variable has 2 levels, and that the other has 3 levels. There were a total of 30 subjects who were divided into six cells, or subgroups. Each cell contains 5 subjects. Each horizontal row in the figure (running from left to right) represents a different level of the type of costs independent variable. There were 15 subjects in the low-cost condition, and 15 in the high-cost condition. Each vertical column in the figure (running from top to bottom) represents a different level of the type of rewards independent variable. There were 10 subjects in the low-reward condition, 10 in the mixed-reward condition, and 10 in the high-reward condition.

It is strongly advised that you prepare a figure like this whenever you conduct a factorial study, as this will make it easier to key your data correctly. Notice that the cell designator (the cell number, such as "1-1," "2-3," etc.) indicates which experimental condition a given subject experienced under each of the two independent variables. The first number in the designator indicates which level under type of costs was experienced, and the second number indicates which level under type of rewards was experienced. For example, the designator "1-1" for cell 1-1 indicates that the subject was in condition 1 (the low-cost condition) under type of costs, and also in condition 1 (the low-reward condition) under type of rewards. This means that all five subjects in this subgroup read that partner 10 lives in the same town as the subject (low-cost), but is not very good-looking (low-reward), among other things.

On the other hand, the designator "2-3" for cell 2-3 indicates that the subject was in condition 2 (the high-cost condition) under type of costs, and was in condition 3 (the high-reward condition) under type of rewards. This means that all five subjects in this subgroup read that partner 10 lives in a distant city (high-cost), but is very good-looking (high-reward), among other things. Similar reasoning applies in interpreting the designators for the other 4 cells in the figure.

When working with these cell designators, remember that the number for the row always comes first, and the number for the column always comes second. This means that the cell at the intersection of row 2 and column 1 should be identified with the designator 2-1, not 1-2.

Writing the SAS Program

Creating the SAS data set. There were two predictor variables in this study (type of rewards and type of costs) and one criterion variable (commitment). This means that each of your subjects will have a score on three variables. First, with the variable REWGRP, you will indicate which experimental condition this subject experienced under the type of rewards independent variable. Each subject will be given a score of either 1, 2, or 3, depending on which condition he/she was in. Second, with the variable COSTGRP, you will indicate which condition the subject experienced under the type of costs independent variable. Each subject will be given a score of either 1 or 2, depending on which experimental condition he/she was in. Finally, with the variable COMMIT, you will record the subject's rated commitment to the relationship with partner 10. That is, you will simply key the number that is the sum of the subjects' responses to the four questionnaire items that measure commitment to partner 10.

The data are keyed so that there is one line of data for each subject. Assume that you key your data using the following format:

Line	Column	Variable Name	Explanation
1	1	COSTGRP	Codes group membership, so that 1 = low-cost condition, and 2 = high-cost condition
	2	(blank)	(blank)
	3	REWGRP	Codes group membership, so that 1 = low-reward condition, 2 = mixed-reward condition, and 3 = high-reward condition
	4	(blank)	(blank)
	5-6	COMMIT	Commitment ratings obtained when subjects rated partner 10

Remember that there are actually 30 subjects in your study. However, to save space, assume for the moment that there are only 12 subjects: 2 subjects in cell 1-1, 2 subjects in cell 1-2, and so forth. Here is what the data set might look like if it were keyed according to the preceding format:

```
 1          1 1 08
 2          1 1 07
 3          1 2 13
 4          1 2 17
 5          1 3 36
 6          1 3 31
 7          2 1 09
 8          2 1 10
 9          2 2 15
10          2 2 18
11          2 3 35
12          2 3 29
```

Remember that the numbers on the far left are simply line numbers; they are not actually a part of the data set. In the data set itself, the first vertical column of numbers (in column 1) codes the COSTGRP variable. Notice that the subjects who appear in lines 1-6 of the preceding data set have a score of "1" on COSTGRP, indicating that they were in the low-cost condition. In contrast, the subjects on lines 7-12 of the preceding data set have a score of "2" on COSTGRP, indicating that they were in the high-cost condition.

The second column of numbers (in column 3) codes REWGRP. For example the two subjects from lines 1-2 of the preceding program have scores of "1" on REWGRP (indicating that they were in the low-reward condition), the two subjects from lines 3-4 have scores of "2" on REWGRP (indicating that they were in the mixed-reward condition), and the two subjects from lines 5-6 have scores of "3" on REWGRP (indicating that they were in the high-reward condition).

Finally, the last column of data in the data set (in columns 5-6) codes COMMIT, commitment scores from the subjects. Assume that, with this variable, scores could range from 4 to 36, with higher scores representing higher levels of commitment to partner 10. You can see that the subject from line 1 had a score of "08" on COMMIT, the subject from line 2 had a score of "07," and so forth.

This approach to keying data for a two-way ANOVA is particularly useful because it provides a quick way of determining which cell (from the factorial design matrix) a given subject is in. For example, the first two columns of data for the subject from line 1 provide the values "1" and "1"; this tells you that this subject is in cell 1-1. Similarly, the first two columns for the subject from line 5 are "1" and "3"; this tells you that this subject is in cell 1-3. The data in the preceding data set were sorted so that subjects in the same cell were grouped together, but your data do not actually have to be sorted in this fashion to be analyzed with PROC GLM.

Testing for significant effects with PROC GLM. Here is the general form for the PROC GLM step needed to perform a two-way ANOVA, and follow it up with Tukey's HSD test:

```
PROC GLM DATA= filename;
   CLASS  predictorA  predictorB;
   MODEL  criterion-variable = predictorA  predictorB predictorA*predictorB;
   MEANS  predictorA  predictorB  / TUKEY;
   MEANS  predictorA  predictorB  predictorA*predictorB;
   RUN;
```

This is the entire program, including the DATA step, needed to analyze some fictitious data from the preceding study:

```
1          DATA D1;
2             INPUT  #1  @1  (COSTGRP)  (1.)
3                        @3  (REWGRP)   (1.)
4                        @5  (COMMIT)   (2.)  ;
5          CARDS;
6          1 1 08
7          1 1 13
8          1 1 07
9          1 1 14
10         1 1 07
11         1 2 19
12         1 2 17
13         1 2 20
14         1 2 25
15         1 2 16
16         1 3 31
17         1 3 24
18         1 3 37
19         1 3 30
20         1 3 32
21         2 1 09
22         2 1 14
23         2 1 05
24         2 1 14
25         2 1 16
26         2 2 22
27         2 2 18
28         2 2 20
```

```
29          2 2 19
30          2 2 21
31          2 3 24
32          2 3 33
33          2 3 24
34          2 3 26
35          2 3 31
36          ;
37
38          PROC GLM DATA=D1;
39              CLASS REWGRP COSTGRP;
40              MODEL COMMIT = REWGRP COSTGRP REWGRP*COSTGRP;
41              MEANS REWGRP COSTGRP / TUKEY;
42              MEANS REWGRP COSTGRP REWGRP*COSTGRP;
43              RUN;
```

Notes Regarding the SAS Program

The GLM procedure is requested on line 38. In line 39, both REWGRP and COSTGRP are listed as classification variables.

The MODEL statement on line 40 specifies COMMIT as the criterion variable and lists three predictor terms: REWGRP, COSTGRP, and REWGRP*COSTGRP. The last term (REWGRP*COSTGRP) is the interaction term in the model. You create this interaction term by simply typing the names of your two predictor variables, connected by an asterisk (and no blank spaces).

The program includes two MEANS statements. The MEANS statement on line 41 requests that the Tukey multiple comparison procedure be used with predictor variables REWGRP and COSTGRP (do not list the interaction term in this MEANS statement). The MEANS statement on line 42 requests that means be printed for all levels of REWGRP and COSTGRP. You should include the interaction term in this MEANS statement, so that you will obtain means for each of the six cells from the study's factorial design.

Steps in Interpreting the Output

With LINESIZE=80 and PAGESIZE=60 in the OPTIONS statement, the preceding program would produce five pages of output. The information that appears on each page is summarized here:

- Page 1 provides class level information and the number of observations in the data set.

- Page 2 provides the ANOVA summary table from the GLM procedure.

- Page 3 provides the results of the Tukey multiple comparison procedure for the REWGRP independent variable.

- Page 4 provides the results of the Tukey multiple comparison procedure for the COSTGRP independent variable.

- Page 5 provides three tables that summarize the means observed for the various groups that constitute the study:

    - The first table provides the means observed at each level of REWGRP.

    - The second table provides the means observed at each level of COSTGRP.

    - The third table provides the means observed for each of the six cells in the study's factorial design.

The results produced by the preceding program are reproduced here as Output 9.1:

```
                        The SAS System                              1

                  General Linear Models Procedure
                     Class Level Information

                  Class     Levels    Values

                  REWGRP       3      1 2 3

                  COSTGRP      2      1 2


          Number of observations in data set = 30
```

```
                                                                    2

                  General Linear Models Procedure

Dependent Variable: COMMIT
                              Sum of          Mean
Source                DF      Squares        Square    F Value    Pr > F

Model                  5    1746.2666667   349.2533333    24.42    0.0001

Error                 24     343.2000000    14.3000000

Corrected Total       29    2089.4666667

           R-Square          C.V.        Root MSE         COMMIT Mean

           0.835748        19.03457      3.7815341          19.866667
```

Source	DF	Type I SS	Mean Square	F Value	Pr > F
REWGRP	2	1711.6666667	855.8333333	59.85	0.0001
COSTGRP	1	0.5333333	0.5333333	0.04	0.8485
REWGRP*COSTGRP	2	34.0666667	17.0333333	1.19	0.3212

Source	DF	Type III SS	Mean Square	F Value	Pr > F
REWGRP	2	1711.6666667	855.8333333	59.85	0.0001
COSTGRP	1	0.5333333	0.5333333	0.04	0.8485
REWGRP*COSTGRP	2	34.0666667	17.0333333	1.19	0.3212

3

General Linear Models Procedure

Tukey's Studentized Range (HSD) Test for variable: COMMIT

NOTE: This test controls the type I experimentwise error rate, but
generally has a higher type II error rate than REGWQ.

Alpha= 0.05 df= 24 MSE= 14.3
Critical Value of Studentized Range= 3.532
Minimum Significant Difference= 4.2233

Means with the same letter are not significantly different.

Tukey Grouping	Mean	N	REWGRP
A	29.200	10	3
B	19.700	10	2
C	10.700	10	1

4

General Linear Models Procedure

Tukey's Studentized Range (HSD) Test for variable: COMMIT

NOTE: This test controls the type I experimentwise error rate, but
generally has a higher type II error rate than REGWQ.

Alpha= 0.05 df= 24 MSE= 14.3
Critical Value of Studentized Range= 2.919
Minimum Significant Difference= 2.8499
Means with the same letter are not significantly different.

Tukey Grouping	Mean	N	COSTGRP
A	20.000	15	1
A			
A	19.733	15	2

5

General Linear Models Procedure

Level of REWGRP	N	------------COMMIT----------- Mean	SD
1	10	10.7000000	3.88873016
2	10	19.7000000	2.58413966
3	10	29.2000000	4.49196814

Level of COSTGRP	N	------------COMMIT----------- Mean	SD
1	15	20.0000000	9.59166305
2	15	19.7333333	7.56369776

Level of REWGRP	Level of COSTGRP	N	------------COMMIT----------- Mean	SD
1	1	5	9.8000000	3.42052628
1	2	5	11.6000000	4.50555213
2	1	5	19.4000000	3.50713558
2	2	5	20.0000000	1.58113883
3	1	5	30.8000000	4.65832588
3	2	5	27.6000000	4.15932687

Output 9.1: Results of Two-Way ANOVA Performed on Investment Model Data, Nonsignificant Interaction

The fictitious data set analyzed in this section was designed so that the interaction term would be nonsignificant. When the interaction is nonsignificant, interpreting the results of a two-factor ANOVA is very similar to interpreting the results of a one-factor ANOVA. Therefore, many of the instructions provided in the chapter on one-way ANOVA (Chapter 8) will not be repeated here ("making sure page 1 looks right," etc.). Instead, this section will focus on some issues that are relevant only to a two-factor ANOVA. The steps to follow in interpreting the output are discussed next.

1. Determine whether the interaction term is statistically significant. Two-factor ANOVA allows you to test for three types of effects: (a) the main effect of predictor A (type of rewards, in this case), (b) the main effect of predictor B (type of costs), and (c) the interaction of predictor A and predictor B. Remember that you may interpret a main effect only if the interaction is nonsignificant. One of your first steps must be to determine whether the interaction is significant.

You can do this by looking at the analysis of variance results, which appear on page 2 of Output 9.1 (as before, look in the section that provides the "Type III SS"). Toward the bottom left of page 2, you see the heading "Source", as you did with the one-way ANOVA. However, in this case, you see three entries under "Source", indicating that there are three sources of variation in your data: (a) REWGRP, (b) COSTGRP, and (c) REWGRP*COSTGRP. The last entry, REWGRP*COSTGRP, is the interaction term that you are interested in. If this interaction is significant, it suggests that the relationship between one predictor and the criterion variable is different at different levels of the second predictor. In the present case, the interaction is associated with 2 degrees of freedom, a value approximately 34.07 for the type III sum of squares, a mean square of 17.03, an F value of 1.19, and a corresponding p value of .321. Remember that you generally view a result as being statistically significant only if the p value is less than .05. Since this p value of .321 is larger than .05, you conclude that there is no interaction between the two independent variables. You are therefore free to proceed with your review of the two main effects.

2. Determine if either of the two main effects are statistically significant. A two-way ANOVA allows you to test two null hypotheses concerning main effects. The null hypothesis for the type of rewards predictor may be stated as follows:

> In the population, there is no difference between the high-reward group, the mixed reward-group, and the low-reward group with respect to mean scores on the commitment variable.

The F statistic to test this null hypothesis can again be found toward the bottom of page 2 in Output 9.1. To the right of the heading "REWGRP", you can see that this effect is associated with 2 degrees of freedom, a value of 1711.67 for the type III sum of squares, a mean square of 855.83, an F value of 59.85, and a p value of 0.0001. With such a small p value, you can clearly reject the null hypothesis of no main effect for type of rewards. Later, you will review the results of the Tukey test to see which groups (low-reward, high-reward, etc.) are significantly different from which.

The null hypothesis for the type of costs independent variable may be stated in a similar fashion:

> In the population, there is no difference between the high-cost group and the low-cost group with respect to mean scores on the commitment variable.

The appropriate F statistic is once again found toward the bottom of page 2. To the right of the word "COSTGRP", you see that this effect is associated with 1 degree of freedom, a value of 0.53 for the type III sum of squares, a mean square of 0.53, an F value of 0.04, and a p value of

.849. This *p* value is greater than .05; therefore you may not reject the null hypothesis, and will instead conclude that there is not a significant main effect for type of costs.

3. Prepare your own version of the ANOVA summary table. You will use the information from page 2 of Output 9.1 to prepare the ANOVA summary table for the analysis. That table is reproduced here as Table 9.1.

Table 9.1

ANOVA Summary Table for Study Investigating the Relationship between Type of Rewards, Type of Costs, and Commitment (Nonsignificant Interaction)

Source	df	SS	MS	F	R^2
Type of rewards (A)	2	1711.66	855.83	59.85 *	.82
Type of costs (B)	1	0.53	0.53	0.04	.00
A X B Interaction	2	34.07	17.03	1.19	.02
Within groups	24	343.20	14.30		
Total	29	2089.47			

Note. N = 30.

* p < .001

On page 2 of Output 9.1, to the right of the word "REWGRP*COSTGRP", you will find information concerning the study's interaction term. In your own ANOVA summary table (such as Table 9.1), this will appear on the line headed "A X B Interaction". As was the case with one-way ANOVA, look to the right of the word "Error" to find the information needed for the "Within Groups" line of your table, and look to the right of the words "Corrected Total" to find the information needed for the "Total" line of your table.

In the preceding chapter, you learned that R^2 is a measure of the strength of the relationship between a predictor variable and a criterion variable. In a one-way ANOVA, R^2 tells you what percent of variance in the criterion is accounted for by the study's predictor variable. In a two-way ANOVA, R^2 indicates what percent of variance is accounted for by each predictor variable, as well as by their interaction term.

As was the case in the earlier chapter, you will have to perform a few hand calculations to compute these R^2 values. To calculate R^2 for a given effect, divide the type III sum of squares associated with that effect by the corrected total sum of squares. For example, to calculate the R^2 value for the type of rewards main effect, you would take the appropriate terms from page 2 of Output 9.1 (or Table 9.1) and substitute them in the formula for R^2, as is done here:

$$R^2 = \frac{\text{TYPE III SS}}{\text{CORRECTED TOTAL SUM OF SQUARES}} = \frac{1711.66}{2089.47} = .82$$

4. Review the sample means and the results of the multiple comparison procedures. If a given main effect is statistically significant, you may review the Tukey test results for that main effect. Do this in the same way you would if this had been a one-way ANOVA. The results of the Tukey test for the present analysis are presented on pages 3 and 4 of Output 9.1. In this analysis, the type of rewards effect was significant, and the Tukey results on page 3 of Output 9.1 show that all three experimental groups were significantly different from each other, with the high-reward group showing the highest commitment scores, the mixed-reward group the next highest, and the low-reward group the lowest (Chapter 8 showed how to interpret the Tukey test).

The results of the Tukey test for the type of costs main effect appear on page 4 of Output 9.1. However, the type of costs main effect was not statistically significant, and so the Tukey results for that effect will not be interpreted. Technically, it would not really have been necessary to review the results of this multiple comparison procedure even if the type of costs main effect had been significant. This is because COSTGRP consisted of only two groups, which means that you would not need a multiple comparison procedure to determine which "pairs" of groups were significantly different.

5. Summarize the results of your analyses. In performing a two-way ANOVA, you should use the same statistical interpretation format as was used with one-way ANOVA:

A) Statement of the problem
B) Nature of the variables
C) Statistical test
D) Null hypothesis (H_0)
E) Alternative hypothesis (H_1)
F) Obtained statistic
G) Obtained probability (p) value
H) Conclusion regarding the null hypothesis
I) ANOVA summary table
J) Figure representing the results

However, with two-way ANOVA, it would be possible to perform this summary three times, since it is possible to test three null hypotheses in this study:

- The hypothesis of no interaction (which would be stated, "in the population, there is no interaction between type of rewards and type of costs in the prediction of commitment scores")

- The hypothesis of no main effect for predictor A (type of rewards)

- The hypothesis of no main effect for predictor B (type of costs)

Because you should be fairly familiar with this format at this time, it will not be completed again at this point.

Formal Description of Results for a Paper

Below is one approach that could be used to summarize the results of the preceding analysis in a scholarly paper:

> Results were analyzed using two-way ANOVA, with two between-groups factors. This analysis revealed a significant main effect for type of rewards, $F(2, 24) = 59.85$; $p < .001$. The sample means are displayed in Figure 1. Tukey's HSD test showed that subjects in the high-reward condition scored significantly higher on commitment than did subjects in the mixed-reward condition, who, in turn, scored significantly higher than subjects in the low-reward condition ($p < .05$). The main effect for type of costs proved to be nonsignificant, $F(1, 24) = 0.04$; $p = .849$. The interaction between type of rewards and type of costs also proved to be nonsignificant $F(2, 24) = 1.19$; $p = .321$.

Example with a Significant Interaction

When the interaction term is statistically significant, it is necessary to follow a different procedure in interpreting the results. In most cases, this will consist of plotting the interaction in a figure, and determining which of the simple effects are significant. This section shows how to do this.

For example, assume that the preceding study with 30 subjects is repeated, but that this time the analysis is performed on the following data set:

```
 5        CARDS;
 6        1 1 08
 7        1 1 13
 8        1 1 04
 9        1 1 11
10        1 1 05
11        1 2 17
12        1 2 12
13        1 2 20
14        1 2 14
15        1 2 16
16        1 3 31
17        1 3 24
18        1 3 37
19        1 3 30
20        1 3 32
21        2 1 16
22        2 1 10
23        2 1 25
24        2 1 15
25        2 1 14
26        2 2 21
27        2 2 13
28        2 2 16
29        2 2 12
30        2 2 17
31        2 3 18
32        2 3 23
33        2 3 19
34        2 3 18
35        2 3 18
36        ;
```

Analyzing this data set with the program presented earlier would again result in five pages of output, with the same type of information appearing on each page. The results of the analysis of this data set are reproduced here as Output 9.2:

```
                         The SAS System                              1

                  General Linear Models Procedure
                     Class Level Information

                   Class    Levels    Values

                   REWGRP      3       1 2 3

                   COSTGRP     2       1 2


            Number of observations in data set = 30
```

```
                                                                     2



               General Linear Models Procedure

Dependent Variable: COMMIT
                            Sum of         Mean
Source              DF      Squares        Square     F Value    Pr > F

Model                5    1370.9666667   274.1933333   17.60     0.0001

Error               24     374.0000000    15.5833333

Corrected Total     29    1744.9666667

             R-Square         C.V.        Root MSE        COMMIT Mean

             0.785669       22.38699      3.9475731       17.633333


Source              DF     Type I SS     Mean Square    F Value    Pr > F

REWGRP               2    882.46666667   441.23333333    28.31     0.0001
COSTGRP              1     12.03333333    12.03333333     0.77     0.3883
REWGRP*COSTGRP       2    476.46666667   238.23333333    15.29     0.0001

Source              DF    Type III SS    Mean Square    F Value    Pr > F

REWGRP               2    882.46666667   441.23333333    28.31     0.0001
COSTGRP              1     12.03333333    12.03333333     0.77     0.3883
REWGRP*COSTGRP       2    476.46666667   238.23333333    15.29     0.0001
```

```
                                                                    3
                General Linear Models Procedure

      Tukey's Studentized Range (HSD) Test for variable: COMMIT

  NOTE: This test controls the type I experimentwise error rate, but
        generally has a higher type II error rate than REGWQ.

          Alpha= 0.05  df= 24  MSE= 15.58333
        Critical Value of Studentized Range= 3.532
        Minimum Significant Difference= 4.4087

  Means with the same letter are not significantly different.

      Tukey Grouping          Mean      N  REWGRP

             A               25.000     10  3

             B               15.800     10  2
             B
             B               12.100     10  1
```

```
                                                                    4
                General Linear Models Procedure

      Tukey's Studentized Range (HSD) Test for variable: COMMIT

  NOTE: This test controls the type I experimentwise error rate, but
        generally has a higher type II error rate than REGWQ.

          Alpha= 0.05  df= 24  MSE= 15.58333
        Critical Value of Studentized Range= 2.919
        Minimum Significant Difference= 2.975

  Means with the same letter are not significantly different.

      Tukey Grouping          Mean      N  COSTGRP

             A               18.267     15  1
             A
             A               17.000     15  2
```

```
                                                                  5
              General Linear Models Procedure

      Level of            ------------COMMIT-----------
      REWGRP       N        Mean                SD

        1          10     12.1000000        6.08184913
        2          10     15.8000000        3.11982906
        3          10     25.0000000        7.00793201

      Level of            ------------COMMIT-----------
      COSTGRP      N        Mean                SD

        1          15     18.2666667       10.3679910
        2          15     17.0000000        4.0355563

  Level of   Level of          ------------COMMIT-----------
  REWGRP     COSTGRP      N        Mean                SD

    1          1          5      8.2000000        3.83405790
    1          2          5     16.0000000        5.52268051
    2          1          5     15.8000000        3.03315018
    2          2          5     15.8000000        3.56370594
    3          1          5     30.8000000        4.65832588
    3          2          5     19.2000000        2.16794834
```

Output 9.2: Results of Two-Way ANOVA Performed on Investment Model Data, Significant Interaction

Steps in Interpreting the Output for the Omnibus Analysis

This most recent data set was constructed so as to produce a significant interaction between type of rewards and type of costs. The steps to be followed in interpreting this interaction are as follows:

1. Determine if the interaction term is statistically significant. The analysis of variance table for the current analysis appears on page 2 of Output 9.2 As before, you will interpret the information that appears toward the bottom of the page, in the section that provides the type III sum of squares. The interaction term is the REWGRP*COSTGRP term that appears as the very last line on output page 2. You must first determine whether this interaction term is significant before reviewing any other results.

The last line of output page 2 shows that the REWGRP*COSTGRP interaction term displays an *F* value of 15.29 which, with 2 and 24 degrees of freedom, is associated with a *p* value of 0.0001. The interaction therefore is clearly significant, and because of this, you will not interpret the main effects for REWGRP or COSTGRP. Instead, you will plot the interaction and test for simple effects.

2. Plot the interaction. Interactions are easiest to understand when they are represented in a figure that plots the means for each of the cells that appear in the study's factorial design. The factorial design used in the current study involved a total of six cells (this design was presented in Figure 9.7). The mean commitment scores for these six cells are presented on page 5 of Output 9.2.

There are actually three tables of means on page 5 of this output. The first table provides the means for each level of REWGRP, the second table provides the means for each level of COSTGRP, and the third table provides the means for the six cells that represent every possible combination of REWGRP and COSTGRP. It is this third table that will be used to create the figure.

The first line of the third table provides the mean score displayed by the cell that was coded with a "1" on REWGRP and a "1" on COSTGRP. Given the values that were used in coding levels of REWGRP and COSTGRP, you therefore know that the first line provides the mean for the subjects who experienced the "low-reward" condition under REWGRP and the "low-cost" condition under COSTGRP. Notice that this line shows that this subgroup displayed a mean score on COMMIT of 8.20.

The second line of the table provides the mean score displayed by the cell that was coded with a "1" on REWGRP and a "2" on COSTGRP. Given the values that were used to code the variables, you therefore know that this second line provides data for the subjects who experienced the "low-reward" condition under REWGRP and the "high-cost" condition under COSTGRP. Notice that this line shows that this subgroup displayed a mean score on COMMIT of 16.00. The remaining lines in the table can be read in the same way.

It is very difficult to understand a two-way interaction by simply reviewing cell means from a table, such as the third table in output page 5. Interactions are much easier to understand if the means are instead plotted in a figure. Therefore, the cells means from Output 9.2 have been plotted in Figure 9.8.

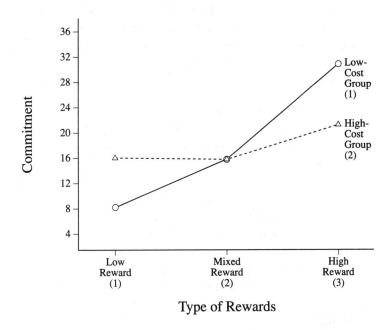

Figure 9.8: Mean Levels of Commitment as a Function of the Interaction between Type of Rewards and Type of Costs

The vertical axis in Figure 9.8 is labelled "Commitment," to convey that this figure plots mean commitment scores. Notice that scores may range from a low of 4 to a high of 36.

The two different lines that appear in Figure 9.8 represent the two different conditions under independent variable B (the type of costs independent variable). The solid line represents means commitment scores displayed by the low-cost group, and the dotted line represents mean commitment scores from the high-cost group.

The horizontal axis of the figure labels the three conditions under independent variable A (the type of rewards independent variable). For example, directly above the label "Low Reward," you see the mean scores displayed by subjects in the low reward condition. Notice that two mean scores are plotted: a small circle plots the mean commitment scores of subjects who were in the "low reward/low cost" cell, and a small triangle plots the mean commitment scores of subjects who were in the "low reward/high cost" cell. The same system was used to plot mean scores for subjects in the remaining cells.

When there is an interaction between two variables, it means that at least two of the line segments in the resulting figure are not parallel to each other. You can see that this is the case in Figure 9.8. Notice that the line for the low-cost group (the solid line) displays a steeper angle than is displayed by the line for the high-cost group (the dotted line). This suggests that the type of rewards independent variable had a stronger effect on the low-cost group, compared to the high cost group. Another way of putting it is to say that type of costs moderates the relationship between type of rewards and commitment.

This figure is also useful for again illustrating the definition for **interaction**. Earlier, it was said that an interaction involves a situation in which the effect of one independent variable on the dependent variable is different at different levels of the second independent variable. In Figure 9.8, you can see that the effect of the rewards independent variable on commitment is stronger in the low-cost group than it is in the high-cost group.

Preparing a figure that plots an interaction (such as Figure 9.8) can be a confusing undertaking. For this reason, this section presents structured, step-by-step guidelines that should make the task easier. The following guidelines describe how to begin with the cells means from page 5 of Output 9.2, and transform them into the figure represented in Figure 9.8:

1. Label the vertical axis with the name of the criterion variable (in this case, commitment). On this same axis, provide some midpoints of scores which were possible. In Figure 9.8, this was done by using the midpoints of 4, 8, 12, and so forth.

2. Label the horizontal axis with the name of predictor A (type of rewards, in this case). On the same axis, provide one midpoint for each level of this independent variable, and label these midpoints. For this variable, this was done by creating three midpoints labeled low-reward (1), mixed-reward (2), and high-reward (3).

3. Now draw some small circles on the figure to indicate the mean commitment scores of just those subjects in the low-cost group. First, plot the mean of the subjects who were in the low-cost group under the type of costs predictor, and were also in the low-reward group under the type of rewards predictor. Go to the means provided on page 5 of Output 9.2, and find the entry for the group that is coded with a "1" under "COSTGRP" (1 stands for "low-cost") and is also coded with a "1" under "REWGRP" (1 stands for "low-reward"). It turns out that this is the first entry, and the mean COMMIT score for this subgroup was 8.20. Therefore, go to the figure and draw a small circle that is directly above the "low-reward" midpoint, and directly to the right of the where 8.20 would be on the COMMITMENT axis.

   Next, plot the mean of the subjects who were in the low cost/mixed reward subgroup. On output page 5, find the entry for the subgroup that is coded with a "1" under "COSTGRP" and a "2" under "REWGRP". This is the third entry down, and their mean commitment score was 15.80. Therefore, draw a small circle that is directly above the "mixed-reward" midpoint, and to the right of where 15.80 would be on the COMMITMENT axis. Finally, find the mean for the low cost/high reward subgroup, coded with a "1" under "COSTGRP" and a "3" under "REWGRP". This is the fifth entry in the table, and the mean for this subgroup is 30.80. The circle representing this score goes above the high-reward midpoint on the figure. As a final step, draw a solid line connecting these three circles.

4. Now repeat this procedure, except that this time you will draw small triangles to represent the scores of just those subjects in the high-cost group. Remember that these are the subgroups coded with a "2" under "COSTGRP". The mean for the high-cost/low-reward group is 16.00, and it is the second entry in the table on page 5 of Output 9.2. To represent this score, a small triangle is drawn above the "low-reward" midpoint in the figure. The mean for the high cost/mixed reward subgroup is 15.80, and the mean for the high-cost/high-reward subgroup is 19.20. Note where triangles were drawn on the figure to represent these means. Once all three triangles are in place, they are connected with a dotted line. With this done, the figure is now complete.

Using this system, you will know that whenever you see a solid line connecting circles, you are looking at mean commitment scores from subjects in the low-cost group, and whenever you see a dotted line connecting triangles, you are looking at mean commitment scores from the high-cost group.

Testing for Simple Effects

When there is a **simple effect** for independent variable A at a given level of independent variable B, it means that there is a significant relationship between independent variable A and the dependent variable at *that level* of independent variable B. As was stated earlier, the concept of a simple effect is perhaps easiest to understand by again referring to Figure 9.8.

First, consider the solid line (the line representing the low-cost group) in Figure 9.8. This line displays a relatively steep angle, suggesting that there may be a significant relationship between rewards and commitment for the subjects in the low-cost group. In other words, there may be a significant simple effect for rewards at the low-cost level of the "type of costs" independent variable.

Now consider the dotted line in the same figure, which represents the high-cost group. This line displays an angle that is less steep than the angle displayed by the solid line. It is impossible to tell by simply "eyeballing" the data in this way, but this may mean that there is not a simple effect for rewards at the high-cost level of the "type of costs" independent variable.

Testing for simple effects is fairly straightforward. In simplified terms, this procedure involves dividing your sample into two groups (the low-cost group and the high-cost group); using only the low-cost group, performing a one-way ANOVA in which the predictor is type of rewards and the criterion is commitment; and using only the high-cost group, performing another one-way ANOVA where the predictor is type of rewards and the criterion is commitment.

In truth, the preceding description actually oversimplifies the process of testing for simple effects. The actual process is actually slightly more complicated, because you must use a special error term in computing the *F* tests of interest, rather than the *F* term that is provided with the one-way ANOVAs. The meaning of this will be explained shortly, after first presenting the SAS program that is necessary to test for simple effects.

Writing the SAS program. The general form for the SAS program that will allow the testing of simple effects is now presented:

```
PROC GLM    DATA=data-set-name;
   CLASS  predictorA  predictorB;
   MODEL  criterion-variable = predictorA  predictorB predictorA*predictorB;
   MEANS  predictorA  predictorB  / TUKEY;
   MEANS  predictorA  predictorB  predictorA*predictorB;
   RUN;

PROC SORT   DATA=data-set-name;
   BY predictorB;
   RUN;

PROC GLM;
   CLASS  predictorA;
   MODEL  criterion-variable = predictorA;
   MEANS  predictorA / TUKEY;
   MEANS  predictorA;
   BY     predictorB;
   RUN;
```

Here are the actual statements needed to test for simple effects with the present study:

```
1          PROC GLM DATA=D1;
2             CLASS REWGRP COSTGRP;
3             MODEL COMMIT = REWGRP COSTGRP REWGRP*COSTGRP;
4             MEANS REWGRP COSTGRP / TUKEY;
5             MEANS REWGRP COSTGRP REWGRP*COSTGRP;
6             RUN;
7
8          PROC SORT DATA=D1;
9             BY COSTGRP;
10            RUN;
11
```

```
12          PROC GLM DATA=D1;
13              CLASS REWGRP;
14              MODEL COMMIT = REWGRP;
15              MEANS REWGRP / TUKEY;
16              MEANS REWGRP;
17              BY COSTGRP;
18              RUN;
```

Lines 1-6 of the preceding program request the standard "omnibus" two-way ANOVA, identical to that performed earlier. Lines 8-10 request that SAS sort the data by the variable COSTGRP, so that all subjects with a COSTGRP score of 1 are together, and all subjects with a COSTGRP score of 2 are together. Lines 12 through 18 ask for a standard one-way ANOVA with REWGRP as the predictor. However, line 17 asks SAS to perform this ANOVA once for each level of COSTGRP. That is, perform one ANOVA for the subjects with a COSTGRP score of 1, and a separate ANOVA for the subjects with a COSTGRP score of 2.

Interpreting the output. The preceding program would produce 13 pages of output, and would actually perform three ANOVAs. The first would be the omnibus ANOVA, identical to the ANOVA that was reproduced as Output 9.2. The second ANOVA would result from the PROC GLM in which COMMIT was the dependent variable, REWGRP was the independent variable, and the analysis involved only subjects with a score of "1" on COSTGRP (the low-cost group). Finally, the third ANOVA would result from the PROC GLM in which COMMIT was the dependent variable, REWGRP was the independent variable, and the analysis involved only subjects with a score of "2" on COSTGRP (the high-cost group).

Because the omnibus ANOVA (based on all 30 subjects) has already been presented in Output 9.2, it will not be reproduced here again. Instead, here is the output that was created by lines 8-18 of the preceding program (that is, the two one-way ANOVAs). The information appearing in this part of the output is summarized below:

- Page 6 provides class level information and the number of observations in the data set for the low-cost subsample.

- Page 7 provides the ANOVA summary table for the low-cost subsample.

- Page 8 provides the results of the Tukey multiple comparison procedure for the low-cost subsample.

- Page 9 provides the mean commitment scores observed for the various levels of REWGRP for the low-cost subsample.

- Finally, pages 10-13 provide information corresponding to the information appearing on pages 6-9, except that the information on pages 10-13 is based on the analysis of data from the high-cost subsample.

The SAS System   6

---------------------------------- COSTGRP=1 ----------------------------------

General Linear Models Procedure
Class Level Information

Class   Levels   Values

REWGRP   3   1 2 3

Number of observations in by group = 15

                                                                    7

---------------------------------- COSTGRP=1 ----------------------------------

General Linear Models Procedure

Dependent Variable: COMMIT

Source	DF	Sum of Squares	Mean Square	F Value	Pr > F
Model	2	1322.5333333	661.2666667	43.50	0.0001
Error	12	182.4000000	15.2000000		
Corrected Total	14	1504.9333333			

R-Square	C.V.	Root MSE	COMMIT Mean
0.878799	21.34335	3.8987177	18.266667

Source	DF	Type I SS	Mean Square	F Value	Pr > F
REWGRP	2	1322.5333333	661.2666667	43.50	0.0001

Source	DF	Type III SS	Mean Square	F Value	Pr > F
REWGRP	2	1322.5333333	661.2666667	43.50	0.0001

```
                                                                    8
-------------------------------- COSTGRP=1 ----------------------------------

                   General Linear Models Procedure

     Tukey's Studentized Range (HSD) Test for variable: COMMIT

   NOTE: This test controls the type I experimentwise error rate, but
         generally has a higher type II error rate than REGWQ.

               Alpha= 0.05  df= 12  MSE= 15.2
           Critical Value of Studentized Range= 3.773
             Minimum Significant Difference= 6.5781

   Means with the same letter are not significantly different.

          Tukey Grouping           Mean      N  REWGRP

                A               30.800      5  3

                B               15.800      5  2

                C                8.200      5  1
```

```
                                                                    9
-------------------------------- COSTGRP=1 ----------------------------------

                   General Linear Models Procedure

          Level of        ------------COMMIT-----------
          REWGRP     N      Mean              SD

             1       5      8.2000000       3.83405790
             2       5     15.8000000       3.03315018
             3       5     30.8000000       4.65832588
```

```
                                                                   10
------------------------------------ COSTGRP=2 ------------------------------------

                   General Linear Models Procedure
                     Class Level Information

              Class     Levels    Values

              REWGRP        3      1 2 3


          Number of observations in by group = 15
```

```
                                                                          11
---------------------------------- COSTGRP=2 ----------------------------------

                     General Linear Models Procedure

Dependent Variable: COMMIT
                                  Sum of           Mean
Source                  DF        Squares         Square    F Value    Pr > F

Model                    2     36.40000000    18.20000000       1.14    0.3522

Error                   12    191.60000000    15.96666667

Corrected Total         14    228.00000000

             R-Square              C.V.         Root MSE        COMMIT Mean

             0.159649          23.50489        3.9958312          17.000000


Source                  DF       Type I SS    Mean Square    F Value    Pr > F

REWGRP                   2     36.40000000    18.20000000       1.14    0.3522

Source                  DF     Type III SS    Mean Square    F Value    Pr > F

REWGRP                   2     36.40000000    18.20000000       1.14    0.3522
```

```
                                                                          12
---------------------------------- COSTGRP=2 ----------------------------------

                     General Linear Models Procedure

        Tukey's Studentized Range (HSD) Test for variable: COMMIT

NOTE: This test controls the type I experimentwise error rate, but
      generally has a higher type II error rate than REGWQ.


              Alpha= 0.05  df= 12  MSE= 15.96667
          Critical Value of Studentized Range= 3.773
          Minimum Significant Difference= 6.7419


Means with the same letter are not significantly different.

     Tukey Grouping              Mean     N  REWGRP

                   A           19.200     5  3
                   A
                   A           16.000     5  1
                   A
                   A           15.800     5  2
```

```
                                                                    13
------------------------------- COSTGRP=2 ------------------------------

                  General Linear Models Procedure

      Level of        ------------COMMIT-----------
      REWGRP      N        Mean                SD

         1        5     16.0000000         5.52268051
         2        5     15.8000000         3.56370594
         3        5     19.2000000         2.16794834
```

Output 9.3: Results of One-Way ANOVA Procedures Necessary for Testing Simple Effects

Page 7 of Output 9.3 provides the analysis of variance table from the ANOVA in which COMMIT was the dependent variable, REWGRP was the independent variable, and the analysis involved only subjects with a score of "1" on COSTGRP (the low-cost group). Output pages 6-9 are identified with the header "COSTGRP=1" at the top of each page, and this informs you that these pages provide results for only the low-cost group. Information from this output will be used to determine whether there was a simple effect for type of rewards at the low-cost level of the type of costs independent variable.

The last line of page 7 of Output 9.2 provides the F test for the ANOVA in which the independent variable was type of rewards and the analysis was based on only the low-cost subjects. It can be seen that the F value of 43.50 is significant at $p < .0001$. However, this is not the F value for the simple effect of interest. To compute the F for the simple effect, you must take the appropriate mean square from this table, and insert them in the following formula:

$$F = \frac{MS_{simple\ effect}}{Omnibus\ Within-Groups\ MS}$$

In the preceding formula, the $MS_{simple\ effect}$ is the mean square from the last line of page 7 of Output 9.2. In the present case, it can be seen that this mean square is 661.27, and so this value is now inserted in your formula:

$$F = \frac{661.27}{Omnibus\ Within-Groups\ MS}$$

But where will you find the "Omnibus Within-Groups MS" for the preceding formula? This will come from the omnibus two-way ANOVA which was based on the entire sample, and included both type of rewards and type of costs as independent variables. The ANOVA summary table for this analysis was presented earlier on page 2 of Output 9.2. The omnibus MS is simply the

"Mean Square-Error" from Output 9.2. This is on the line labelled "Error", under the heading "Mean Square" from Output 9.2. It can be seen that this Omnibus Within-Groups MS is 15.58, so this term is now inserted in your formula:

$$F = \frac{661.27}{15.58}$$

With both values now in the formula, you may now compute the F ratio that will indicate whether there is a significant simple effect for type of rewards in the low-cost group:

$$F = \frac{MS_{simple\ effect}}{Omnibus\ Within-Groups\ MS} = \frac{661.27}{15.58} = 42.44$$

This is a large value of F, but is it large enough to reject the null hypothesis? To know this, you have to find the critical value of F for this analysis. This, in turn requires knowing how many degrees of freedom are associated with this particular F test. In this case, you had 2 and 24 degrees of freedom. The "2" degrees of freedom for the numerator are the 2 that went into calculating the $MS_{simple\ effect}$. See the bottom of page 7 of Output 9.2, where the row for "REWGRP" intersects with the column for "DF", you see that there are 2 degrees of freedom associated with the type of rewards variable.

The "24" degrees of freedom for the denominator are the 24 degrees of freedom associated with the mean square error term from the omnibus ANOVA. These degrees of freedom may be found in the upper part of page 2 of Output 9.2: look under the heading "DF", to the right of the word "Error".

Now that you have established the degrees of freedom associated with the analysis, you are free to find the critical value of F by referring to the F table in Appendix C at the back of this text. This table shows that, when $p = .05$ and there are 2 and 24 degrees of freedom, the critical value of F is 3.40. Your obtained value of F was 42.44, which was much larger than this critical value. Therefore, you may reject the null hypothesis and conclude that there is a simple effect for type of rewards at the low-cost level of the type of costs factor.

With this done, you will now repeat the procedure to determine whether there is a simple effect for type of rewards with the high-cost group of subjects. The $MS_{simple\ effect}$ necessary to perform this test may be found on page 11 of Output 9.2 (notice that the top of each output page indicates "COSTGRP=2"; this informs you that the results on this page come from the high-cost group).

To find the information necessary for this test, review the bottom of page 11 from Output 9.2, in the section for the type III sum of squares. To find the $MS_{simple\ effect}$ for this subgroup, you look below the heading "Mean Square". It can be seen that, for the high-reward subjects, the $MS_{simple\ effect}$ is equal to 18.20. You may now insert this in your formula:

$$F = \frac{18.20}{Omnibus\ Within-Groups\ MS}$$

The error term for the preceding formula will be the same error term used with the previous test: it will be the Omnibus Within-Groups MS from Output 9.1. With both terms inserted in the formula, you may now compute the F ratio for the simple effect of type of reward in the high-cost group:

$$F = \frac{MS_{\text{simple effect}}}{\text{Omnibus Within-Groups MS}} = \frac{18.20}{15.58} = 1.17$$

This test is also associated with 2 and 24 degrees of freedom (as was the earlier test for a simple effect), so the same critical value of F described earlier (3.40) still applies. Your obtained value of F is 1.17, and this is not greater than the critical value of 3.40. Therefore, you fail to reject the null, and conclude that there is not a significant simple effect for the type of rewards factor at the high-cost level of the type of costs factor.

Formal Description of Results for a Paper

Results from this analysis could be summarized in the following way for a published paper:

> Results were analyzed using two-way ANOVA, with two between-group factors. This revealed a significant Type of Rewards X Type of Costs interaction, F(2, 24) = 15.29, p < .0001, and the nature of this interaction is displayed in Figure 9.8.
>
> Subsequent analyses demonstrated that there was a simple effect for type of rewards at the low-cost level of the type of costs factor, F(2, 24) = 42.44, p < .05. As Figure 9.8 shows, the high-reward group displayed higher commitment scores than the mixed-reward group, which, in turn, demonstrated higher commitment scores than the low-reward group. The simple effect for type of rewards at the high-cost level of the type of costs factor proved to be nonsignificant, F(2, 24) = 1.17, p >.05.

Two Perspectives on the Interaction

The preceding example presented a potential simple effect for the type of rewards factor at two different levels of the type of costs factor. If you had chosen, you could have also investigated this interaction from a different perspective. You could have studied possible simple effects for the type of costs factor at three different levels of the type of rewards factor.

To do this, you would have drawn the preceding figure so that the horizontal axis represented the type of costs factor, and had two midpoints (one for the low-cost group, and one for the high-cost group). Within the body of the figure itself, there would have been three lines, with one line representing the low-reward group, one representing the mixed-reward group, and one representing the high-reward group.

In writing the SAS program, you would have sorted the data set by the REWGRP variable. Then you would have requested an ANOVA in which the criterion was COMMIT and the predictor was COSTGRP. You would add a BY REWGRP statement toward the end of the PROC GLM step, and this would cause one ANOVA to be performed for the low-reward group, one for the mixed-reward group, and one for the high-reward group. The hand calculations to determine the simple effects would have followed in similar fashion.

When a two-factor interaction is significant, you can always view it from these two different perspectives. Furthermore, the interaction is often more interpretable (makes more sense) from one perspective than from the other. Therefore, in many cases you should test for simple effects from both perspectives before interpreting the results.

Conclusion

This chapter, as well as the preceding chapter, dealt with between-groups investigations in which scores were obtained on only one criterion variable. And yet researchers in the social sciences often conduct studies that involve multiple criterion variables. For example, imagine that you are an industrial psychologist who has an hypothesis that some organization-development intervention will positively affect several different aspects of job satisfaction: satisfaction with the work itself, satisfaction with supervision, and satisfaction with pay. When analyzing data from a field experiment that tests this hypothesis, it would be advantageous to use a multivariate statistic that allows you to test the effect of your manipulation on all three criterion variables simultaneously. One statistic that allows this type of test is the multivariate analysis of variance, and this procedure is introduced in the following chapter.

Appendix: Assumptions Underlying Factorial ANOVA with Two Between-Groups Factors

- **Level of measurement**. The criterion variable should be assessed on an interval or ratio level of measurement. Both predictor variables should be nominal-level variables (categorical variables).

- **Independent observations**. A given observation should not be dependent on any other observation in any cell (for a more detailed explanation of this assumption, see Chapter 7: "*t* Tests: Independent-Samples and Paired-Samples").

- **Random sampling**. Scores on the criterion variable should represent a random sample drawn from the populations of interest.

- **Normal distributions**. Each cell should be drawn from a normally distributed population. If each cell contains over 30 subjects, the test is robust against moderate departures from normality.

- **Homogeneity of variance**. The populations represented by the various cells should have equal variances on the criterion. If the number of subjects in the largest cell is no more than 1.5 times greater than the number of subjects in the smallest cell, the test is robust against violations of the homogeneity assumption.

Chapter 10

MULTIVARIATE ANALYSIS OF VARIANCE (MANOVA), WITH ONE BETWEEN-GROUPS FACTOR

Overview. This chapter shows how to key data and prepare SAS programs that will perform a one-way multivariate analysis of variance (MANOVA) using the GLM procedure. You can think of MANOVA as an extension of ANOVA in that it allows for the inclusion of multiple criterion variables in a single test. This chapter focuses on the *between-groups* design, in which each subject is exposed to only one condition under the independent variable. You are shown how to summarize both significant and nonsignificant MANOVA results.

Introduction: The Basics of Multivariate Analysis of Variance

Multivariate analysis of variance (MANOVA) with one between-groups factor is appropriate when the analysis involves

- a single predictor variable measured on a nominal scale

- multiple criterion variables, each of which is measured on an interval or ratio scale.

MANOVA is similar to ANOVA in that it tests for the significance of the difference between two or more groups of subjects. There is an important difference between MANOVA and ANOVA, however: ANOVA is appropriate when the study involves just one criterion variable, but MANOVA is appropriate when the study involves more than one criterion variable. With MANOVA, you can perform a single test that determines whether there is a significant difference between treatment groups when compared on all of the criterion variables simultaneously.

The Aggression Study

To illustrate one possible use of MANOVA, consider the study on aggression that was introduced in Chapter 8 ("One-Way ANOVA with One Between-Groups Factor"). In that study, each of 60 children was assigned to just one of the following treatment groups:

- A group that consumed 0 grams of sugar at lunch

- A group that consumed 20 grams of sugar at lunch

- A group that consumed 40 grams of sugar at lunch

A pair of observers watched each child after lunch, and recorded the number of aggressive acts displayed by that child. The total number of aggressive acts performed by a given child over a two-week period served as that child's score on the "aggression" dependent variable.

It was appropriate to analyze data from the preceding study with ANOVA, because there was a single dependent variable: level of aggression. However, now consider how the study could be modified so that it would instead be appropriate to analyze the data using a multivariate procedure: MANOVA. Imagine that, as the researcher, you wanted to have more than one measure of the children's aggression. After reviewing the literature, you believe that there are at least four different types of aggression that children may display:

- Aggressive acts directed at children of the same sex

- Aggressive acts directed at children of the opposite sex

- Aggressive acts directed at teachers

- Aggressive acts directed at parents

Assume that you now wish to replicate your earlier study, but that this time your observers will note the number of times each child displays an aggressive act in each of the four preceding categories. At the end of the two-week period, you will now have scores for each child on each of the following dependent variables:

- Total number of aggressive acts directed at children of the same sex

- Total number of aggressive acts directed at children of the opposite sex

- Total number of aggressive acts directed at teachers

- Total number of aggressive acts directed at parents

You now have a number of options as to how you will analyze your data. One option is to simply perform four ANOVAs (as described in Chapter 8). In each ANOVA, the independent variable would again be "amount of sugar consumed." In the first ANOVA, the dependent variable would be "number of aggressive acts directed at children of the same sex," in the second ANOVA, the dependent variable would be "number of aggressive acts directed at children of the opposite sex," and so forth.

However, a better alternative to this approach would be to perform a single test that allows you to assess the effect of your independent variable on all four of the dependent variables simultaneously. This is what MANOVA allows you to do. Performing a MANOVA will allow you to test the following null hypothesis:

> In the population, there is no difference between the various treatment groups when they are compared simultaneously on the dependent variables.

Here is another way of stating this null hypothesis:

> In the population, all treatment groups are equal on all dependent variables.

MANOVA will produce a single F statistic that will allow you to test this null hypothesis. If the null hypothesis is rejected, it means that at least two of the treatment groups are significantly different with respect to at least one of the dependent variables. You can then perform follow-up tests to identify the pairs of groups that are significantly different, and the specific dependent variables on which they are different. In doing these follow-up tests, you may find that the groups differ on some dependent variables (such as "aggressive acts directed toward children of the same sex") but not on other dependent variables (such as "aggressive acts directed toward teachers").

A Multivariate Measure of Association

Chapter 8 introduced the R^2 statistic, a measure of association that is often computed when performing ANOVA. Values of R^2 may range 0 to 1, with higher values indicating a stronger relationship between the predictor variable and the criterion variable in the study. If the study is a true experiment, you can view R^2 as an index of the magnitude of the treatment effect.

The current chapter introduces a *multivariate* measure of association: one that can be used when there are multiple criterion variables (as in MANOVA). This multivariate measure of association is called Wilks' lambda. Values of Wilks' lambda may range from 0 to 1, but the way that you interpret lambda is the opposite of the way that you interpret R^2. With lambda, small values (near 0) indicate a relatively strong relationship between the predictor variable and the multiple criterion variables (taken as a group), while larger values (near 1) indicate a relatively weak relationship. The F statistic that tests the significance of the relationship between the predictor and the multiple criterion variables is actually based on Wilks' lambda.

Overview of the Steps Followed in Performing a MANOVA

When you request a multivariate analysis of variance with PROC GLM, the procedure actually produces two sets of results. First are the results from the univariate ANOVAs, with one univariate ANOVA for each criterion variable in the analysis (here, **univariate** means "one criterion variable"). Each of these univariate ANOVAs involves the same type of analysis that was described in Chapter 8. For example, with the present study, the predictor variable ("amount of sugar consumed") will be the same in each analysis. However, one ANOVA will have "aggressive acts directed toward children of the same sex" as the criterion variable, one will have "aggressive acts directed toward children of the opposite sex" as the criterion, and so forth.

The second set of results produced when you request a MANOVA are the results of the multivariate analysis of variance (here, **multivariate** means "multiple criterion variables"). For your purposes, these multivariate results will consist of Wilks' lambda and the F statistic derived from Wilks' lambda.

As the preceding section suggests, there is a specific sequence of steps that you should follow when interpreting these results. First, you should review the multivariate F statistic derived from Wilks' lambda. If this multivariate F statistic is significant, you may reject the null hypothesis of no overall effect for the predictor variable. In other words, you may reject the null hypothesis that, in the population, all groups are equal on all criterion variables. At that point, you may proceed to the univariate ANOVAs and interpret them.

In interpreting the univariate ANOVAs, you will first identify those criterion variables for which the univariate F statistic was significant. If the F statistic is significant for a given criterion variable, you may then go on to interpret the results of the Tukey multiple comparison test, to determine which pairs of groups are significantly different from one another.

However, if the multivariate F statistic that is computed in the MANOVA is nonsignificant, this means that you may not reject the null hypothesis that all groups have equal means on the criterion variables in the population. In most cases, your analysis should terminate at that time;

you generally should not proceed to interpret the univariate ANOVAs, even if one or more of them displays a significant F statistic.

Similarly, even if the multivariate F statistic is significant, you should not interpret the results for any specific criterion variable that did not display a significant univariate F statistic. This is consistent with the general guidelines for univariate ANOVA that were presented in Chapter 8.

Example with Significant Differences between Experimental Conditions

To illustrate MANOVA, assume that you will replicate the study that investigated the effect of rewards on commitment in romantic relationships. However, this time the study will be modified so that you will obtain scores on three different dependent variables, rather than just one.

It was hypothesized that the rewards that people experience in romantic relationships have a causal effect on their commitment to those relationships. In Chapter 8 this hypothesis was tested by conducting a type of role-playing experiment. All 18 subjects in the experiment were asked to engage in a role-playing task: to read the descriptions of 10 potential romantic "partners." For each partner, the subjects imagined what it would be like to date this person, and rated how committed they would be to a relationship with that person. For the first 9 partners, every subject saw exactly the same description. For partner 10, however, the different experimental groups saw a slightly different description of this person. For example, for the 6 subjects in the high-reward condition, the last sentence in their description of partner 10 read as follows:

> This person enjoys the same recreational activities that you enjoy, and is very good-looking.

However, for the 6 subjects in the mixed-reward condition, the last part of the description of partner 10 read as follows:

> Sometimes this person seems to enjoy the same recreational activities that you enjoy, and sometimes he/she does not. Sometimes partner 10 seems to be very good looking, and sometimes he/she does not.

And for the 6 subjects in the low-reward condition, the last sentence in the description of partner 10 read in this way:

> This person does not enjoy the same recreational activities that you enjoy, and is not very good-looking.

In your current replication of the study from Chapter 8, you will manipulate this "type of rewards" independent variable in exactly the same way. The only difference between the present study and the one described earlier involves the number of dependent variables obtained. In the earlier study, you obtained data on just one criterion variable: commitment. **Commitment** was defined as the subjects' rating of their commitment to remain in the relationship. Scores on this variable were created by summing subject responses to four questionnaire items. In the present study, however, you will also obtain two additional dependent variables: subjects' ratings of their satisfaction with their relationship with partner 10, as well as their ratings of how long they intend to stay in the relationship with partner 10. Here, **satisfaction** is defined as the subjects' emotional reaction to partner 10, and the **intention to stay** is defined as the subjects' rating of how long they intend to maintain the relationship with partner 10. Assume that satisfaction and intention to stay are measured with multiple items from a questionnaire, similar to those used to assess commitment.

You can see that you will obtain four scores for each subject in the study. One will simply be a score on a classification variable that indicates whether the subject is in the high-reward group, the mixed-reward group, or the low-reward group. The remaining three scores will be the subject's scores on the measures of commitment, satisfaction, and intention to stay. In conducting the MANOVA, you need to determine whether there is a significant relationship between the type of rewards predictor variable, and the three criterion variables, taken as a group.

Writing the SAS program

Creating the SAS data set. There was one predictor variable in this study, type of rewards. This variable could assume three values: subjects were either in the high-reward group, the mixed-reward group, or the low-reward group. Since this variable simply codes group membership, it is measured on a nominal scale. You give subjects a score of "1" if they were in the low-reward condition, a "2" if they were in the mixed-reward condition, and a score of "3" if they were in the high-reward condition. You will need a short SAS variable name for this variable, so call it REWGRP (for "reward group").

There were three criterion variables in this study. The first criterion variable, commitment, will be given the SAS variable name, COMMIT. The second criterion, satisfaction, will be called SATIS. The third, intention to stay, will be called STAY. With each variable, possible scores could range from a low of 4 to a high of 36.

This is the DATA step of the program that performs the MANOVA. It contains fictitious data from the preceding study:

```
1          DATA D1;
2             INPUT  #1  @1  (REWGRP)  (1.)
3                        @3  (COMMIT)  (2.)
4                        @6  (SATIS)   (2.)
5                        @9  (STAY)    (2.) ;
6          CARDS;
7           1 13 10 14
8           1 06 10 08
9           1 12 12 15
10          1 04 10 13
```

```
11          1 09 05 07
12          1 08 05 12
13          2 33 30 36
14          2 29 25 29
15          2 35 30 30
16          2 34 28 26
17          2 28 30 26
18          2 27 26 25
19          3 36 30 28
20          3 32 32 29
21          3 31 31 27
22          3 32 36 36
23          3 35 30 33
24          3 34 30 32
25          ;
```

The data are keyed so that there is one line of data for each subject. The format used in keying the preceding data is summarized in the following table:

Line	Column	Variable Name	Explanation
1	1	REWGRP	Codes group membership, so that 1 = low-reward condition 2 = mixed-reward condition 3 = high-reward condition
	2	(blank)	(blank)
	3-4	COMMIT	Commitment ratings obtained when subjects rated partner 10
	5	(blank)	(blank)
	6-7	SATIS	Satisfaction ratings obtained when subjects rated partner 10
	8	(blank)	(blank)
	9-10	STAY	Intention to stay ratings obtained when subjects rated partner 10

Testing for significant effects with PROC GLM. In the following example, you write a SAS program to determine whether the overall MANOVA is significant, and follow it up with univariate ANOVAs and Tukey HSD tests. Remember that the results for all of these tests will appear in the output regardless of the significance of the multivariate test; however, you should interpret the univariate ANOVAs and Tukey tests only if the overall MANOVA is significant.

Here is the general form for the SAS program to perform a MANOVA followed by individual ANOVAs and Tukey's HSD tests:

```
PROC GLM DATA=filename;
   CLASS   predictor-variable;
   MODEL   criterion-variables = predictor-variable;
   MEANS   predictor-variable / TUKEY;
   MEANS   predictor-variable;
   MANOVA  H = predictor-variable;
   RUN;
```

Here is the actual program (including the DATA step) that you would use to analyze data from the investment-model study just described:

```
 1            DATA D1;
 2               INPUT  #1  @1   (REWGRP)  (1.)
 3                          @3   (COMMIT)  (2.)
 4                          @6   (SATIS)   (2.)
 5                          @9   (STAY)    (2.) ;
 6            CARDS;
 7            1 13 10 14
 8            1 06 10 08
 9            1 12 12 15
10            1 04 10 13
11            1 09 05 07
12            1 08 05 12
13            2 33 30 36
14            2 29 25 29
15            2 35 30 30
16            2 34 28 26
17            2 28 30 26
18            2 27 26 25
19            3 36 30 28
20            3 32 32 29
21            3 31 31 27
```

```
22          3 32 36 36
23          3 35 30 33
24          3 34 30 32
25          ;
26          PROC GLM DATA=D1;
27             CLASS REWGRP;
28             MODEL COMMIT SATIS STAY = REWGRP;
29             MEANS REWGRP / TUKEY;
30             MEANS REWGRP;
31             MANOVA H = REWGRP;
32             RUN;
```

Notes Regarding the SAS Program

The data are input in lines 1-25 of the preceding program, and the PROC GLM step requesting the MANOVA appears in lines 26-32. In the CLASS statement on line 27, you should specify the name of the nominal-scale predictor variable (REWGRP, in this case). The MODEL statement in line 28 is similar to that described in Chapter 8, except that all of your criterion variables should appear to the left of the "=" sign (COMMIT, SATIS, and STAY in this case). The name of the predictor variable should again appear to the right of the "=" sign.

The MEANS statement on line 29 requests that the Tukey multiple comparison procedure be performed for the REWGRP predictor variable. The second MEANS statement, on line 30, merely requests that the means for the various treatment groups be printed.

The only new statement in the program is the MANOVA statement that appears on line 31. To the right of the term "H =" in this statement, you should specify the name of your study's predictor variable. The present program specifies "H = REWGRP".

Results from the SAS Output

Specifying LINESIZE=80 and PAGESIZE=60 in the OPTIONS statement causes the preceding program to produce 9 pages of output. The following table indicates which specific results appear on each page:

Page	Information
1	Class level information
2	Univariate ANOVA results for COMMIT criterion
3	Univariate ANOVA results for SATIS criterion
4	Univariate ANOVA results for STAY criterion
5	Tukey HSD test results for COMMIT criterion
6	Tukey HSD test results for SATIS criterion
7	Tukey HSD test results for STAY criterion
8	Group means for each criterion variable
9	Results of the multivariate analysis: characteristic roots and vectors, Wilks' lambda, and results of the multivariate *F* test

The output produced by the preceding program is reproduced here as Output 10.1:

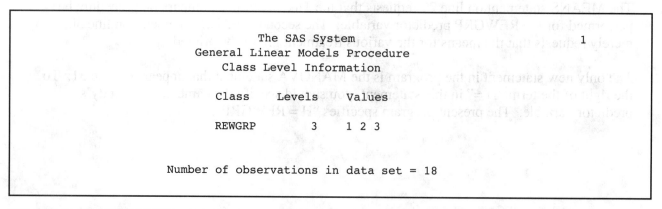

```
                         The SAS System                          1
                 General Linear Models Procedure
                    Class Level Information

            Class     Levels    Values

            REWGRP       3       1 2 3


    Number of observations in data set = 18
```

```
                                                                 2
                General Linear Models Procedure

Dependent Variable: COMMIT
                            Sum of         Mean
Source            DF       Squares        Square     F Value    Pr > F

Model              2     2225.3333333   1112.6666667   122.12    0.0001

Error             15      136.6666667      9.1111111

Corrected Total   17     2362.0000000
```

	R-Square	C.V.	Root MSE	COMMIT Mean
	0.942139	12.40464	3.0184617	24.333333

Source	DF	Type I SS	Mean Square	F Value	Pr > F
REWGRP	2	2225.3333333	1112.6666667	122.12	0.0001

Source	DF	Type III SS	Mean Square	F Value	Pr > F
REWGRP	2	2225.3333333	1112.6666667	122.12	0.0001

3

General Linear Models Procedure

Dependent Variable: SATIS

Source	DF	Sum of Squares	Mean Square	F Value	Pr > F
Model	2	1825.4444444	912.7222222	143.11	0.0001
Error	15	95.6666667	6.3777778		
Corrected Total	17	1921.1111111			

	R-Square	C.V.	Root MSE	SATIS Mean
	0.950202	11.08724	2.5254263	22.777778

Source	DF	Type I SS	Mean Square	F Value	Pr > F
REWGRP	2	1825.4444444	912.7222222	143.11	0.0001

Source	DF	Type III SS	Mean Square	F Value	Pr > F
REWGRP	2	1825.4444444	912.7222222	143.11	0.0001

4

```
                    General Linear Models Procedure

Dependent Variable: STAY
                                 Sum of               Mean
Source                  DF       Squares            Square    F Value    Pr > F

Model                    2    1346.3333333     673.1666667      51.61    0.0001

Error                   15     195.6666667      13.0444444

Corrected Total         17    1542.0000000


              R-Square              C.V.         Root MSE        STAY Mean

              0.873109           15.26074        3.6117094       23.666667


Source                  DF      Type I SS    Mean Square    F Value    Pr > F

REWGRP                   2    1346.3333333    673.1666667      51.61    0.0001

Source                  DF    Type III SS    Mean Square    F Value    Pr > F

REWGRP                   2    1346.3333333    673.1666667      51.61    0.0001
```

5

```
                    General Linear Models Procedure

         Tukey's Studentized Range (HSD) Test for variable: COMMIT

   NOTE: This test controls the type I experimentwise error rate, but
         generally has a higher type II error rate than REGWQ.

              Alpha= 0.05  df= 15  MSE= 9.111111
              Critical Value of Studentized Range= 3.673
              Minimum Significant Difference= 4.5266

   Means with the same letter are not significantly different.

         Tukey Grouping            Mean       N  REWGRP

                      A          33.333       6   3
                      A
                      A          31.000       6   2

                      B           8.667       6   1
```

6

General Linear Models Procedure

Tukey's Studentized Range (HSD) Test for variable: SATIS

NOTE: This test controls the type I experimentwise error rate, but
generally has a higher type II error rate than REGWQ.

Alpha= 0.05 df= 15 MSE= 6.377778
Critical Value of Studentized Range= 3.673
Minimum Significant Difference= 3.7873

Means with the same letter are not significantly different.

Tukey Grouping	Mean	N	REWGRP
A	31.500	6	3
A			
A	28.167	6	2
B	8.667	6	1

7

General Linear Models Procedure

Tukey's Studentized Range (HSD) Test for variable: STAY

NOTE: This test controls the type I experimentwise error rate, but
generally has a higher type II error rate than REGWQ.

Alpha= 0.05 df= 15 MSE= 13.04444
Critical Value of Studentized Range= 3.673
Minimum Significant Difference= 5.4163

Means with the same letter are not significantly different.

Tukey Grouping	Mean	N	REWGRP
A	30.833	6	3
A			
A	28.667	6	2
B	11.500	6	1

8

```
                  General Linear Models Procedure

Level of      ------------COMMIT------------     ------------SATIS------------
REWGRP   N      Mean            SD                  Mean            SD

1        6     8.6666667     3.44480285           8.6666667     2.94392029
2        6    31.0000000     3.40587727          28.1666667     2.22860195
3        6    33.3333333     1.96638416          31.5000000     2.34520788

              Level of      ------------STAY------------
              REWGRP   N      Mean            SD

                1      6    11.5000000     3.27108545
                2      6    28.6666667     4.08248290
                3      6    30.8333333     3.43025752
```

9

```
                  General Linear Models Procedure
                  Multivariate Analysis of Variance

        Characteristic Roots and Vectors of: E Inverse * H, where
     H = Type III SS&CP Matrix for REWGRP    E = Error SS&CP Matrix

Characteristic    Percent           Characteristic Vector  V'EV=1
   Root
                                COMMIT          SATIS          STAY

  31.7043925       99.91        0.05732862     0.07825296    -0.01131767
   0.0276118        0.09       -0.05723078     0.08569473    -0.02621408
   0.0000000        0.00       -0.04299469    -0.02393025     0.08311775

           Manova Test Criteria and F Approximations for
             the Hypothesis of no Overall REWGRP Effect
     H = Type III SS&CP Matrix for REWGRP    E = Error SS&CP Matrix

                   S=2      M=0      N=5.5

Statistic                  Value         F       Num DF   Den DF   Pr > F

Wilks' Lambda            0.02975533   20.7878       6       26     0.0001
Pillai's Trace          0.99629295    4.6322        6       28     0.0022
Hotelling-Lawley Trace 31.73200433   63.4640        6       24     0.0001
Roy's Greatest Root    31.70439252  147.9538        3       14     0.0001

       NOTE: F Statistic for Roy's Greatest Root is an upper bound.
          NOTE: F Statistic for Wilks' Lambda is exact.
```

Output 10.1: Results of the Multivariate Analysis of Variance for the Investment Model Study, Significant Results

Interpretation of pages 1 through 8 (the univariate ANOVA results for the three criterion variables) would proceed in exactly the same fashion as was described in Chapter 8 in the section titled "Steps in Interpreting the Output." Because these steps have already been described in that chapter, they will not be covered again in this chapter. However, you are encouraged to review these results to make sure that everything "looks right" prior to interpreting the multivariate results. You should make sure that all of the subjects were included in the analyses, that the input statements were written correctly, and so forth. Again, remember that these univariate ANOVAs and Tukey tests should be interpreted only if the overall MANOVA is significant.

Steps in Interpreting the Output

1. Review Wilks' lambda, the multivariate *F* statistic, and its associated *p* value. Once you have reviewed the univariate statistics on pages 1-8 to verify that there are no obvious errors in keying data or in writing the program, you may review your MANOVA results on page 9 of the output.

You can state the multivariate null hypothesis for the present study as follows:

> In the population, there is no difference between the high-reward group, the mixed-reward group, and the low-reward group when they are compared simultaneously on commitment, satisfaction, and intention to stay in the relationship.

In other words: In the population, the three groups are equal on all criterion variables. Symbolically, you can represent the null hypothesis this way:

$$\begin{pmatrix} M_{11} \\ M_{21} \\ M_{31} \end{pmatrix} = \begin{pmatrix} M_{12} \\ M_{22} \\ M_{32} \end{pmatrix} = \begin{pmatrix} M_{13} \\ M_{23} \\ M_{33} \end{pmatrix}$$

Each "M" represents a population mean for one of the treatment conditions on one of the criterion variables. With the preceding notation, the first number in each subscript identifies the criterion variable and the second number identifies the experimental group. For example, M_{31} refers to the population mean for the third criterion variable (the intention to stay) in the first experimental group (the low-reward group), while M_{12} refers to the population mean for the first criterion variable (commitment) in the second experimental group (the mixed-reward group).

The *F* statistic appropriate to test this null hypothesis appears on page 9 of output 10.1. The bottom half of this page of output is headed "Manova Test Criteria and F Approximations for the Hypothesis of no Overall REWGRP Effect". The table below this heading actually provides the results from four different multivariate tests, but you will focus only on the first of these: Wilks' lambda.

This table is divided into six columns with the following headings:

- "Statistic"

- "Value"

- "F"

- "Num DF"

- "Den DF"

- "Pr > F"

Below the heading "Statistic," the first subheading you find is "Wilks' Lambda". Read the information from just this row. Where the row headed "Wilks' Lambda" intersects with the column headed "Value", you will find the computed value of Wilks' lambda statistic for this analysis. For the current analysis, lambda is .02975533, which rounds to .03. Remember that small values (closer to 0) indicate a relatively strong relationship between the predictor variable and the multiple criterion variables, and so this obtained value of .03 indicates that there is a very strong relationship between REWGRP and the criterion variables. This is an exceptionally low value for lambda, much lower than you are likely to encounter in actual research.

This value for Wilks' lambda indicates that the relationship between the predictor and the criteria is strong, but is it statistically significant? To learn this, you review the multivariate F statistic. This appears where the row headed "Wilks' Lambda" intersects with the column headed "F." You can see that the multivariate F for this analysis is approximately 20.79. There are 6 and 26 degrees of freedom associated with this test (these appear under the headings "Num DF" and "Den DF", respectively. The probability value for this F appears under the heading "Pr > F", and you can see that this p value is very small at .0001. Because this p value is less than the standard cut off of .05, you may reject the null hypothesis of no differences between groups in the population. In other words, you conclude that there was a significant multivariate effect for type of rewards.

2. Summarize the results of your analyses. This section shows how to summarize just the results of the multivariate test discussed in the previous section. When the multivariate test is significant, you may proceed to the univariate ANOVAs and summarize them using the format presented in Chapter 8.

You can use the following statistical interpretation format to summarize the multivariate results from a MANOVA:

A) Statement of the problem
B) Nature of the variables
C) Statistical test
D) Null hypothesis (H_o)

E) Alternative hypothesis (H_1)
F) Obtained statistic
G) Obtained probability (p) value
H) Conclusion regarding the null hypothesis

You could summarize the preceding analysis in this way:

A) **Statement of the problem:** The purpose of this study was to determine whether there was a difference between people in a low-reward relationship, people in a mixed-reward relationship, and people in a high-reward relationship with respect to their commitment to the relationship, their satisfaction with the relationship, and their intention to stay in the relationship for a long time.

B) **Nature of the variables:** This analysis involved one predictor variable and three criterion variables. The predictor variable was type of rewards, which was measured on a nominal scale and could assume three values: a low-reward condition (coded as 1), a mixed-reward condition (coded as 2), and a high-reward condition (coded as 3). The three criterion variables were commitment, satisfaction, and intention to stay, and all were measured on an interval/ratio scale.

C) **Statistical test:** Wilks' lambda, derived through a one-way MANOVA, between-groups design.

D) **Null Hypothesis (H_0):**

$$
\begin{pmatrix} M_{11} \\ M_{21} \\ M_{31} \end{pmatrix} = \begin{pmatrix} M_{12} \\ M_{22} \\ M_{32} \end{pmatrix} = \begin{pmatrix} M_{13} \\ M_{23} \\ M_{33} \end{pmatrix}
$$

In the population, there is no difference between people in a low-reward relationship, people in a mixed-reward relationship, and people in a high-reward relationship when they are compared simultaneously on commitment, satisfaction, and intention to stay.

E) **Alternative Hypothesis (H_1):** In the population, there is a difference between people in a low-reward relationship, people in a mixed-reward relationship, and people in a high-reward relationship when they are compared simultaneously on commitment, satisfaction, and intention to stay.

F) **Obtained statistic:** Wilks' lambda = .03, corresponding $F = 20.79$.

G) **Obtained probability (p) value:** $p = .0001$.

H) **Conclusion regarding the null hypothesis:** Reject the null hypothesis.

Formal Description of Results for a Paper

You could summarize this analysis in the following way for a scholarly journal:

> Results were analyzed using one-way MANOVA, between-groups design. This analysis revealed a significant multivariate effect for type of rewards, Wilks' lambda = .03, $\underline{F}(6, 26) = 20.79$; $\underline{p} < .001$.

Example with Nonsignificant Differences between Experimental Conditions

Assume that you perform a MANOVA a second time, but that this time the analysis is performed on the following data set:

```
CARDS;
1 16 19 18
1 18 15 17
1 18 14 14
1 16 20 10
1 15 13 17
1 12 15 11
2 16 20 13
2 18 14 16
2 13 10 14
2 17 13 19
2 14 18 15
2 19 16 18
3 20 18 16
3 18 15 19
3 13 14 17
3 12 16 15
3 16 17 18
3 14 19 15
;
```

Results from the SAS Output

The preceding data set was constructed so as to provide nonsignificant results. If you analyze with the program presented earlier, it again results in 9 pages of output, with the same type of information appearing on each page. To conserve space, however, Output 10.2 presents only the results from the multivariate analyses which appear on page 9 of the output:

```
                        The SAS System                        9

                  General Linear Models Procedure
                  Multivariate Analysis of Variance

            Characteristic Roots and Vectors of: E Inverse * H, where
         H = Type III SS&CP Matrix for REWGRP    E = Error SS&CP Matrix

Characteristic    Percent           Characteristic Vector   V'EV=1
    Root
                                 COMMIT        SATIS         STAY

    0.31962691     88.15       -0.07731564   0.06272924    0.11858737
    0.04297906     11.85       -0.03447851   0.06784671   -0.03600286
    0.00000000      0.00        0.08317305   0.03925020    0.00373811


               Manova Test Criteria and F Approximations for
                  the Hypothesis of no Overall REWGRP Effect
         H = Type III SS&CP Matrix for REWGRP    E = Error SS&CP Matrix

                    S=2      M=0      N=5.5

Statistic                     Value        F     Num DF   Den DF  Pr > F

Wilks' Lambda              0.72656295   0.7504      6        26   0.6147
Pillai's Trace             0.28341803   0.7705      6        28   0.5995
Hotelling-Lawley Trace     0.36260596   0.7252      6        24   0.6336
Roy's Greatest Root        0.31962691   1.4916      3        14   0.2599

         NOTE: F Statistic for Roy's Greatest Root is an upper bound.
            NOTE: F Statistic for Wilks' Lambda is exact.
```

Output 10.2: Results of the Multivariate Analysis of Variance for the Investment Model Study, Nonsignificant Results

To the right of the heading "Wilks' Lambda" in Output 10.2, you can see that this analysis resulted in a lambda value of .73. Because this is a relatively large number (closer to 1), it indicates that the relationship between type of rewards and the three criterion variables is substantially weaker with this data set than with the previous data set.

Output 10.2 shows that this analysis produced a multivariate F of only 0.75, which, with 6 and 26 degrees of freedom, was nonsignificant ($p = .615$). In short, this analysis fails to reject the null hypothesis of no group differences in the population. Because the multivariate F is nonsignificant, in most cases your analysis would terminate at this point; you would not go on to interpret the univariate ANOVAs.

Summarizing the Results of the Analysis

Because this analysis tested the same null hypothesis that you tested earlier, you would prepare items A through E in the same manner described before. Therefore, this section presents only items F through H of the statistical interpretation format:

F) Obtained statistic: Wilks' lambda = .73, corresponding $F = 0.75$.

G) Obtained probability (p) value $p = .615$.

H) Conclusion regarding the null hypothesis: Fail to reject the null hypothesis.

Formal Description of Results for a Paper

You could summarize the results of this analysis for a scholarly paper in the following way:

> Results were analyzed using one-way MANOVA, between-groups design. This analysis failed to reveal a significant multivariate effect for type of rewards, Wilks' lambda = .73, $\underline{F}$(6, 26) = 0.75; $\underline{p}$ = .615.

Conclusion

Chapters 8, 9, and 10 of this text have all focused on **between-group** research designs: designs in which each subject is assigned to just one treatment condition, and provides data under that condition only. In some situations, however, it is advantageous to conduct studies in which each subject provides data under *every* treatment condition. This type of design is called a **repeated-measures** design, and requires data analysis techniques that differ from the ones presented in the last three chapters. The next chapter introduces procedures for analyzing data from the simplest type of repeated-measures design.

Appendix: Assumptions Underlying Multivariate ANOVA with One Between-Groups Factor

- **Level of measurement**. Each criterion variable should be assessed on an interval or ratio level of measurement. The predictor variable should be a nominal-level variable (a categorical variable).

- **Independent observations**. Across subjects, a given observation should not be dependent on any other observation in any group. It is acceptable for the various criterion variables to be correlated with one another; however, a given subject's score on any criterion variable should not be affected by any other subject's score on any criterion variable (for a more detailed explanation of this assumption, see Chapter 7: "*t* Tests: Independent Samples and Paired Samples").

- **Random sampling**. Scores on the criterion variables should represent a random sample drawn from the populations of interest.

- **Multivariate normality**. In each group, scores on the various criterion variables should follow a multivariate normal distribution. Under conditions normally encountered in social science research, violations of this assumption have only a very small effect on the type I error rate (the probability of incorrectly rejecting a true null hypothesis). On the other hand, when the data are platykurtic (form a relatively flat distribution), the power of the test may be significantly attenuated (the power of the test is the probability of correctly rejecting a false null hypothesis). Platykurtic distributions may be transformed to better approximate normality (see Rummel, 1970; or Stevens, 1986).

- **Homogeneity of covariance matrices**. In the population, the criterion-variable covariance matrix for a given group should be equal to the covariance matrix for each of the remaining groups. This is the multivariate extension of the "homogeneity of variance" assumption in univariate ANOVA. To illustrate, consider a simple example with just two groups and three criterion variables (V1, V2, and V3). To satisfy the homogeneity assumptions, the variance of V1 in group 1 must equal (in the population) the variance of V1 in group 2. The same must be true for the variances of V2 and V3. In addition, the covariance between V1 and V2 in group 1 must equal (in the population) the covariance between V1 and V2 in group 2. The same must be true for the remaining covariances (between V1 and V3 and between V2 and V3). It becomes clear that the number of corresponding elements that must be equal increases dramatically as the number of groups increases and/or as the number of criterion variables increases. For this reason, the homogeneity of covariance assumption is rarely satisfied in real-world research. Fortunately, the type I error rate associated with MANOVA is relatively robust against typical violations of this assumption as long as the sample sizes are equal. The power of the test, however, tends to be attenuated when the homogeneity assumption is violated.

References

Rummel, R. J. (1970). *Applied factor analysis*. Evanston: Northwestern University Press.

Stevens, J. (1986). *Applied multivariate statistics for the social sciences*. Hillsdale, N.J.: Lawrence Erlbaum Associates.

304

Chapter 11

ONE-WAY ANOVA WITH ONE REPEATED-MEASURES FACTOR

Overview. This chapter shows how to key data and prepare SAS programs that perform a one-way repeated measures ANOVA using the GLM procedure with the REPEATED statement. This chapter focuses on repeated-measures designs, in which each subject is exposed to every condition under the independent variable. This chapter describes the necessary conditions for performing a valid repeated-measures ANOVA, discusses alternative analyses to use when the validity conditions are not met, and reviews strategies for minimizing sequence effects.

Introduction: What is a Repeated-Measures Design?

A one-way repeated-measures ANOVA is appropriate when:

- the analysis involves a single predictor variable measured on a nominal scale

- the analysis also involves a single criterion variable measured on an interval or ratio scale

- each subject is exposed to each condition under the independent variable.

The **repeated-measures design** derives its name from the fact that each subject provides *repeated scores* on the criterion variable. Each subject is exposed to every treatment condition under the study's independent variable, and provides scores on the criterion under each of these conditions. Perhaps the easiest way to understand the repeated-measures design is to contrast it with the **between-groups** design, in which each subject participates in only one treatment condition.

For example, Chapter 8 ("One-Way ANOVA with One Between-Groups Factor") presented a simple experiment that used a between-groups design. In that fictitious study, subjects were randomly assigned to one of three experimental conditions. In each condition, they read descriptions of a number of fictitious romantic partners, and rated their likely commitment to each partner. The purpose of that study was to determine whether the "level of rewards" associated with a given partner affected the subject's rated commitment to that partner. Therefore, the level of rewards was manipulated by varying the description of one specific partner (partner 10) that was presented to the three groups. Level of rewards was manipulated in this way:

- Subjects in the low-reward condition read that partner 10 provides few rewards in the relationship.

- Subjects in the mixed-reward condition read that partner 10 provides mixed rewards in the relationship.

- Subjects in the high-reward condition read that partner 10 provides many rewards in the relationship.

After reading this description, each subject rated how committed he or she would probably be to partner 10.

This study was called a between-groups study because the subjects were divided into different treatment groups and the independent variable was manipulated *between* these groups. In a between-groups design, each subject is exposed to only one level of the independent variable (in the present case, that means that a given subject read either the low-reward description *or* the mixed-reward description *or* the high-reward description, but no subject read more than one of these descriptions of partner 10).

In a repeated-measures design, on the other hand, each subject is exposed to every level of the independent variable, and provides scores on the dependent variable under each of these levels. For example, you could easily modify the preceding study so that it becomes a one-factor repeated-measures design. Imagine that you conduct your study with a single group of 20 subjects, rather than with three treatment groups. You ask each subject to go through a stack of potential romantic partners, and rate his or her commitment to each partner. Imagine further that all three versions of partner 10 appear somewhere in this stack, and that a given subject responds to each of these versions individually.

For example, a given subject may be working her way through the stack, and the third potential partner she comes to happens to be the low-reward version of partner 10 (assume that you have renamed this fictitious partner to be "partner 3"). She rates her commitment to this partner, and moves on to the next partner. Later, the 11th partner she comes to happens to be the mixed-reward version of partner 10 (now renamed as "partner 11"). She rates her commitment, and moves on. Finally, the 19th partner she comes to happens to be the high-reward version of partner 10 (now renamed as "partner 19"). She rates her commitment, and moves on.

Your study now uses a repeated-measures design because each subject has been exposed to all three levels of the independent variable. To analyze these data, you would have to create three SAS variables to include the commitment ratings made under the three different conditions:

- One variable (perhaps named LOW) contains the commitment ratings made for the low-reward version of the fictitious partner.

- One variable (perhaps named MIXED) contains the commitment ratings made for the mixed-reward version of the fictitious partner.

- One variable (perhaps named HIGH) contains the commitment ratings made for the high-reward version of the fictitious partner.

To analyze your data, you would compare the mean scores that are displayed by the three variables. Perhaps you would hypothesize that the mean commitment score contained in HIGH would be significantly higher than the mean commitment scores contained in LOW or MIXED.

Make note of two cautions before moving on. First, remember that you need a special type of statistical procedure to analyze data from a repeated-measures study such as this; you should not analyze these data using the program for a one-way ANOVA with one between-groups factor, as was illustrated in Chapter 8. This chapter shows you the appropriate SAS program for analyzing repeated-measures data.

Second, the fictitious study described here was used merely to illustrate the nature of a repeated-measures research design; do not view it as an example of a *good* repeated-measures research design (in fact, the preceding study suffers from several serious problems). This is because repeated-measures studies are vulnerable to a number of problems that are not experienced with between-groups designs. This means that you must be particularly concerned about design when your investigation includes a repeated-measures factor. Some of the problems associated with this design are discussed later in the section titled "Sequence Effects."

Example: Significant Differences in Investment Size across Time

To demonstrate the use of the repeated measures ANOVA, this chapter presents a new fictitious experiment that investigates a different aspect of the investment model (Rusbult, 1980). You remember from earlier chapters that the investment model is a theory of interpersonal attraction that describes the variables that determine commitment to romantic relationships and other interpersonal associations.

Designing the Study

Some of the earlier chapters have described fictitious investigations of the investment model that involved the use of paper people: written descriptions of potential romantic partners that the subjects responded to as if they were real people. Assume that critics of the previous studies are very skeptical about the use of this type of role-playing in research, and contend that investigations using paper people do not generalize well to how real individuals actually behave in the real world. To address these criticisms, this chapter presents a different fictitious study that you could use to evaluate aspects of the investment model while using actual couples.

This study focuses on the investment size construct from the investment model. **Investment size** refers to the amount of time, effort, and personal resources that an individual has put into his or her relationship with a romantic partner. People report heavy investments in a relationship when they have spent a good deal of time with their romantic partner, when they have a lot of shared activities or friends that they would lose if the relationship were to end, and so forth.

Assume that it is generally desirable for married couples to believe that they have invested a good deal of time and effort in their marriages. Assume that this is desirable because research has shown that couples are more likely to stay together when they feel they have invested a great deal in their marriages.

The "marriage encounter" intervention. Given that higher levels of perceived investment size are generally a good thing, assume that you are interested in finding interventions that are likely to increase perceived investments in a marriage. Specifically, you have read research indicating that a program called "marriage encounter" is likely to increase perceived investments. In a marriage encounter program, married couples spend a weekend together under the guidance of counselors, sharing their feelings, learning to communicate, and engaging in exercises intended to strengthen their marriage.

Based on what you have read, you hypothesize that couples' perceived investments in their marriages will increase immediately after participation in a marriage encounter program. In other words, you hypothesize that, if couples are asked to rate how much they have invested in a marriage both before and immediately after the marriage encounter weekend, the "post" ratings will be significantly higher than the "pre" ratings. This is the primary hypothesis for your study.

However, being something of a skeptic, assume further that you do not expect these increased investment perceptions to last very long. Specifically, you believe that if couples rate their perceived investments at a "follow-up" point some three weeks after the marriage encounter weekend, these ratings will have declined to their previous "pre" level that was observed just before the weekend. In other words, you hypothesize that there will not be a significant difference between investment ratings obtained just before the weekend and those obtained three weeks after. This is the secondary hypothesis for your study.

To test these hypotheses, you conduct a study that uses a single-group experimental design with repeated measures. The design of this study is illustrated in Figure 11.1:

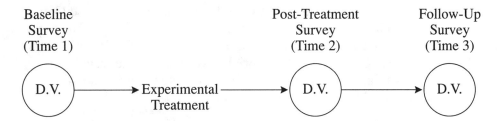

Figure 11.1: Single-Group Experimental Design with Repeated Measures

Specifically, you work with twenty couples, all of whom are about to go through a marriage encounter program. Your criterion variable in this study is perceived investment, and you measure this variable with a multiple-item scale on a questionnaire. The investment variable is such that higher scores on the scale reflect higher levels of perceived investment.

You obtain investment ratings from each couple at three points in time. These points in time are illustrated by the three circles in Figure 11.1 (the "D.V." in each circle stands for "Dependent Variable"). Specifically:

- A "baseline survey" obtains investment scores at time 1, just before the marriage encounter weekend.

- A "post-treatment survey" obtains investment scores at time 2, immediately after the encounter weekend.

- A "follow-up survey" obtains investment scores at time 3, three weeks after the encounter weekend.

Notice that, in Figure 11.1, an "Experimental Treatment" appears between time 1 and time 2. This treatment is the marriage encounter program.

Problems with single-group studies. Before proceeding, be warned that the study described here uses a relatively weak research design. To understand why, remember the main hypothesis that you would like to test, the hypothesis that investment scores would increase significantly from time 1 to time 2 because of the marriage encounter program. Imagine for a moment that you obtain just these results when you analyze your data, that time 2 investment scores are significantly higher than time 1 scores. Does this provide strong evidence that the marriage encounter manipulation caused the increase in investment scores?

Not really. It would be very easy for someone to provide some alternative explanation for the increase. Perhaps someone would argue that investment scores just naturally increase over time among married couples, regardless of whether they participate in a marriage encounter weekend. Perhaps someone would argue that an increase in scores was due to some television program that most of the couples saw, and was not due to the marriage encounter. There is a long list of alternative explanations that could potentially be offered.

The point is simply that you must design repeated-measures studies very carefully to avoid confoundings and other problems, and this study was not designed very carefully (it is used here merely for illustration). A later section in this chapter ("Sequence Effects") discusses some of the problems associated with repeated-measures studies, and reviews strategies for dealing with them. In addition, the following chapter (Chapter 12: "Factorial ANOVA with Repeated-Measures Factors and Between-Groups Factors") shows how you can make the present single-group design much stronger through the addition of a control group.

Predicted results. Remember that your primary hypothesis is that couples' ratings of investment in their relationships increases immediately following the encounter weekend. The secondary hypothesis is that this increase is a transient, or temporary, effect rather than a permanent change. These hypothesized results appear graphically in Figure 11.2. Notice that, in the figure, mean investment scores increase from time 1 to time 2, and then decrease again at time 3.

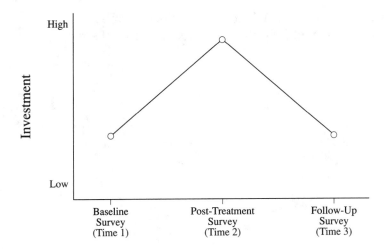

Figure 11.2: Hypothesized Results for the Investment Model Study

You test your primary hypothesis by comparing the investment scores obtained at post-treatment (time 2) to the baseline scores (time 1). By also comparing the follow-up scores (time 3) to the baseline scores (time 1), you will learn whether any changes observed at post-treatment are maintained, and you can use this comparison to test the secondary hypothesis.

Assume that this study is exploratory, because you have not done any studies of this type previously and are therefore uncertain of what methodological problems you may encounter or what the magnitude of changes might be. By providing information on these areas, a pilot study can assist in the design of a more definitive study and the determination of an appropriate sample size. (A follow-up study based on the pilot data from this project is presented in Chapter 12.)

Writing the SAS Program

20 couples participated in this investigation. To keep things simple, imagine that only the investment ratings made by the wife in each couple was actually analyzed. This means that your sample actually consists of data from the 20 women who participated in the marriage encounter program.

The criterion variable in this study is the size of the investments that the subjects (the wives) believe they have made in their relationships. Investment size was measured by a scale on the survey. Assume that these scores are on an interval scale (see Chapter 1, "Basic Concepts in Research and Data Analysis").

Creating the SAS data set. Key the investment scores obtained at the three different points in time in the SAS data set as three separate variables. You will create a new variable named PRE to include investment scores obtained at time 1, a variable named POST to include investment scores obtained at time 2, and a variable named FOLUP to include investment scores obtained at time 3. A variable name ID (for "identification number") denotes the subject number. You can use the following program to create a data set named REP that contains data from the fictitious study:

```
1      DATA REP;
2         INPUT #1 @1  (ID)    (2.)
3                  @5  (PRE)   (2.)
4                  @10 (POST)  (2.)
5                  @15 (FOLUP) (2.);
6      CARDS;
7      01  08  10  10
8      02  10  13  12
9      03  07  10  12
10     04  06  09  10
11     05  07  08  09
12     06  11  15  14
13     07  08  10  09
14     08  05  08  08
15     09  12  11  12
16     10  09  12  12
17     11  10  14  13
18     12  07  12  11
19     13  08  08  09
20     14  13  14  14
21     15  11  11  12
22     16  07  08  07
23     17  09  08  10
24     18  08  13  14
25     19  10  12  12
26     20  06  09  10
27     ;
```

The actual data from the study appear in lines 7-26 of the preceding program. The first column of data (in columns 1-2) simply includes each subject's identification number. The next column of data (in columns 5-6) includes each subject's score on PRE (the investment ratings observed at time 1). The next column of data (in columns 10-11) includes each subject's score on POST (the investment ratings observed at time 2). Finally, the last column of data (in columns 15-16) includes each subject's score on FOLUP (investment ratings from time 3).

Obtaining descriptive statistics with PROC MEANS. After inputting the data set, you should perform a PROC MEANS to obtain descriptive statistics for the three investment variables. This serves two important purposes. First, scanning the sample size, minimum value, and maximum value for each variable provides an opportunity to check for obvious data entry errors. Secondly, you need the means and standard deviations for the variables to interpret significant differences found in the ANOVA. Performing this separate PROC MEANS is necessary because the means for within-subjects variables are not routinely included in the output of the PROC GLM program that performs the repeated-measures ANOVA.

Here are the lines that you can add to the preceding program to obtain simple descriptive statistics for the study's variables:

```
28     PROC MEANS   DATA=REP;
29         RUN;
```

The output from this MEANS procedure appears in Output 11.1. Once you have reviewed the columns headed "N", "Minimum", and "Maximum" to verify that there have been no obvious errors in keying the data, you should review the average investment model scores that appear under the heading "Mean". Where the row headed "PRE" intersects with the column headed "Mean", you can see that the mean investment score observed at time 1 was 8.60. In the row headed "POST", you can see that this average investment score had increased to 10.75 by time 2. Finally, the row headed "FOLUP" shows that the mean score had increased to 11.00 by time 3. Figure 11.3 plots these means graphically:

Variable	N	Mean	Std Dev	Minimum	Maximum
ID	20	10.5000000	5.9160798	1.0000000	20.0000000
PRE	20	8.6000000	2.1373865	5.0000000	13.0000000
POST	20	10.7500000	2.2912878	8.0000000	15.0000000
FOLUP	20	11.0000000	2.0261449	7.0000000	14.0000000

Output 11.1: Results of PROC MEANS, Investment Model Study

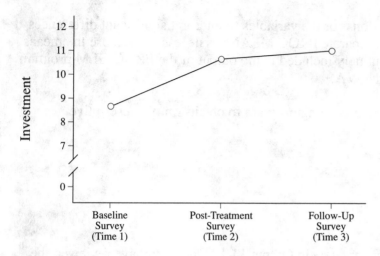

Figure 11.3: Actual Results from the Investment Model Study

A review of the means presented in Figure 11.3 suggests that you may receive support for your study's primary hypothesis, but apparently will not receive support for the study's secondary hypothesis. Notice that mean investment scores seem to increase from the baseline survey (time 1) to the post-treatment survey (time 2). If subsequent analyses show that this increase is statistically significant, this finding would be consistent with your primary hypothesis that perceived investment would increase immediately following the marriage encounter weekend.

However, notice that the mean investment scores remain at a relatively high level at the follow-up survey, three weeks following the program (at time 3). This trend is not consistent with your secondary hypothesis that the increase in perceived investment would be short-lived.

Of course, at this point, you are only "eyeballing" the data, and as yet it is not clear whether any of the differences in means that appear in Figure 11.3 are statistically significant. To determine whether they are significant, you must analyze the data using a repeated-measures ANOVA. The next section shows how to do this.

Testing for significant effects with PROC GLM. The general form for the SAS program to perform a one-way repeated-measures ANOVA is as follows:

```
PROC GLM  DATA=filename;
   MODEL  trial1  trial2  trial3... trialn =  / NOUNI;
   REPEATED  trial-variable-name  #levels  CONTRAST (level#) /
SUMMARY;
   RUN;
```

The actual SAS program that you need to analyze the data set above is as follows:

```
1       PROC GLM  DATA=REP;
2          MODEL PRE POST FOLUP =  / NOUNI;
3          REPEATED TIME 3 CONTRAST (1) / SUMMARY;
4          RUN;
```

Notes Regarding the SAS Program

The repeated-measures ANOVA is similar to the between-groups ANOVA in that both procedures can be performed with PROC GLM. However, notice that you write the MODEL statement differently in a repeated-measures analysis. In the repeated-measures ANOVA, the names of the variables that contain scores on the criterion variable appear to the left of the equals sign in the MODEL statement. In the general form of the program provided here, these variables are represented as "trial1 trial2 trial3...trialn". In the present study, the variable PRE contains investment score obtained at time 1, POST contains investment scores obtained at time 2, and FOLUP contains investment scores obtained at time 3. Therefore, PRE, POST, and FOLUP appear to the left of the equals sign in the MODEL statement.

It should be clear that you need a different criterion variable to include scores obtained under each level of the independent variable. This means that the number of variables appearing to the left of the equals sign in the MODEL statement should equal the number of levels under your independent variable. The present study had three levels under the repeated-measures independent variable (time 1, time 2, and time 3), so three variables appear to the left of the equals sign (PRE, POST, and FOLUP).

In a between-groups study, the name of the predictor variable would normally appear to the right of the equals sign in the MODEL statement. Since there is no between-groups factor in the present study, however, no variable name appears to the right of the equals sign in the preceding program. However, the MODEL statement does include a slash (which signals that options are being requested) followed by the NOUNI option. The NOUNI option suppresses the printing of output relevant to certain univariate analyses that are of no interest with this design. Without the NOUNI option, the SAS program computes and prints a univariate F test for each of the three levels of the trial variable. These tests are not of interest when analyzing within-subjects effects.

The REPEATED statement appears in line 3 of the preceding program. The general form of the program indicates that the first entry in the REPEATED statement should be the "trial-variable-name." This is a name that you supply to refer to your repeated-measures factor. In the present study, the three levels of your repeated-measures factor were "time 1", "time 2", and "time 3". It therefore makes sense to give this repeated-measures factor the name TIME (notice where the name TIME appears on line 3 of the preceding program). Obviously, you could have used any variable name of your choosing, provided that it complies with the usual naming rules for SAS variables.

The general form of the program shows that, to the right of the trial variable name, you are to provide the "#levels." This means that you should key a number that represents the number of levels that appear under your repeated-measures factor. In the present study, the repeated-measures factor included three levels (time 1, time 2, and time 3), and so the number "3" was keyed next to TIME in the REPEATED statement.

The next entry in the REPEATED statement is the "CONTRAST (level#)" option. In a repeated-measures analysis, **contrasts** are planned comparisons between different levels of the repeated-measures variable. The CONTRAST option allows you to choose the types of contrasts that will be made. The number that you specify in the place of "level#" identifies the specific level of the repeated-measures factor against which the other levels will be compared. The preceding program specifies "CONTRAST (1)". A "1" appears in the parentheses with this option, and this means that level 1 under the repeated-measures factor will be contrasted with level 2 and with level 3. In more concrete terms, this requests that the mean investment scores obtained at time 1 will be contrasted with those obtained at time 2, and with those obtained at time 3. Unless otherwise instructed, PROC GLM will automatically perform tests that contrast the last (nth) level of the repeated-measures variable with each of the preceding levels.

The preceding CONTRAST command requests that both the post-treatment (time 2) and follow-up scores (time 3) be compared to the baseline score (time 1). These are the appropriate contrasts for this analysis because these contrasts directly evaluate the two hypotheses of this study. However, remember that you should interpret these contrast tests only if the analysis of variance shows that the effect for TIME (the repeated-measures factor) is significant.

In addition to the planned contrasts described previously, there are a number of post-hoc multiple-comparison tests that are available using SAS/STAT software such as the Tukey test and the Scheffe test. Many of these tests control for the experiment-wise probability of making a type I error (incorrectly rejecting a correct null hypothesis). In Chapter 8 you learned how to use these tests to determine which pairs of groups are significantly different on the criterion variable. Technically, these tests can also be used in a repeated-measures ANOVA. However, these multiple comparison procedures cannot be applied to the repeated-measures variable when you use the REPEATED statement. Use of these procedures is limited to variables that appear in the MODEL statement. If using one of these tests is essential, then you can run the repeated-measures ANOVA according to another method in which you do not use the REPEATED statement. See the section titled "Use of Other Post-Hoc Tests with the Repeated-Measures Variable" in Chapter 12 for a description of this method.

Finally, the REPEATED statement ends with a slash and the SUMMARY option. This SUMMARY option asks for the statistics from the contrasts to appear in the output.

In summary, the complete program (minus the DATA step) that determines means on the criterion variable and performs the repeated-measures ANOVA is as follows:

```
1      PROC MEANS   DATA=REP;
2         RUN;
3
4      PROC GLM   DATA=REP;
```

```
5        MODEL PRE POST FOLUP =  / NOUNI;
6        REPEATED TIME 3 CONTRAST (1) / SUMMARY;
7        RUN;
```

Results from the SAS Output

With LINESIZE=80 and PAGESIZE=60 in the OPTIONS statement, the preceding program (including both PROC MEANS and PROC GLM) produces 5 pages of output. The information that appears on each page is summarized here:

- Page 1 (not shown) provides means and other descriptive statistics for the criterion variables (this was reproduced earlier as Output 11.1).

- Page 2 displays the number of observations included in the analyses performed by PROC GLM.

- Page 3 provides the multivariate significance test for the repeated-measures factor (TIME, in this case).

- Page 4 provides the univariate significance test for TIME, along with information related to the error term used in this F test, and two estimates of the epsilon statistic (discussed later).

- Page 5 provides the results of the planned comparisons requested with the CONTRAST option.

Output 11.2 provides the results of the GLM procedure requested by the preceding program (the results of PROC MEANS appeared earlier as Output 11.1 and are not reproduced here).

```
                        The SAS System                         2

                  General Linear Models Procedure

              Number of observations in data set = 20
```

```
                                                               3


                  General Linear Models Procedure
                  Repeated Measures Analysis of Variance
                  Repeated Measures Level Information

        Dependent Variable      PRE     POST    FOLUP

            Level of TIME         1       2       3



Manova Test Criteria and Exact F Statistics for the Hypothesis of no TIME Effect
```

```
          H = Type III SS&CP Matrix for TIME    E = Error SS&CP Matrix

                         S=1      M=0      N=8

     Statistic                    Value          F      Num DF   Den DF   Pr > F

     Wilks' Lambda             0.30600563    20.4112      2       18     0.0001
     Pillai's Trace            0.69399437    20.4112      2       18     0.0001
     Hotelling-Lawley Trace    2.26791373    20.4112      2       18     0.0001
     Roy's Greatest Root       2.26791373    20.4112      2       18     0.0001
```

```
                                                                              4

                       General Linear Models Procedure
                     Repeated Measures Analysis of Variance
                 Univariate Tests of Hypotheses for Within Subject Effects
     Source: TIME

                                                              Adj  Pr > F
         DF        Type III SS        Mean Square    F Value   Pr > F   G - G    H - F
          2        69.63333333        34.81666667     30.28   0.0001   0.0001   0.0001
     Source: Error(TIME)

         DF        Type III SS        Mean Square
         38        43.70000000         1.15000000
                       Greenhouse-Geisser Epsilon = 0.7593
                           Huynh-Feldt Epsilon = 0.8115
```

```
                                                                              5

                       General Linear Models Procedure
                     Repeated Measures Analysis of Variance
                      Analysis of Variance of Contrast Variables
         TIME.N represents the contrast between the nth level of TIME and the 1st
     Contrast Variable: TIME.2

     Source              DF       Type III SS      Mean Square    F Value     Pr > F

     MEAN                 1       92.45000000      92.45000000     29.01      0.0001

     Error               19       60.55000000       3.18684211
     Contrast Variable: TIME.3

     Source              DF       Type III SS      Mean Square    F Value     Pr > F

     MEAN                 1      115.20000000     115.20000000     43.09      0.0001

     Error               19       50.80000000       2.67368421
```

Output 11.2: Results of PROC GLM, Investment Model Study

Steps in Interpreting the Output

1. Make sure that everything looks right. First check the number of observations listed on page 2 of the output to make certain data from all subjects was used in the analysis. If any data point is missing, then all data for that subject will automatically be dropped from the analysis. Next, check the number of levels assigned to your criterion variable on page 3 of the output (the criterion variable is called "Dependent Variable" in the output).

2. Review the appropriate *F* statistic and its associated probability value. The first step in actually interpreting the results of the analysis is to review the *F* value and associated statistics on page 4 ("Univariate Tests of Hypotheses for Within Subject Effects") of the printout. The *F* value for the trial variable as it was named in the REPEATED statement in the SAS program appears here. This *F* value tells you whether to reject the null hypothesis. In the study, the null hypothesis is that, in the population, there is no difference in the mean investment scores that were obtained at the three points in time. This hypothesis can be represented symbolically in this way:

```
T1 = T2 = T3
```

where T1 is the mean investment score obtained at baseline, T2 is the mean score following a marriage encounter weekend, and T3 is the mean score two weeks after the weekend.

To find the *F* ratio that tests this null hypothesis, look on page 4 of Output 11.2 in the section headed "Source: TIME". Under the heading "F Value", you can see that the *F* statistic for the TIME effect is 30.28. There are 2 and 38 degrees of freedom for this *F* test (find these degrees of freedom on the far left side of the output page).

Notice that there are actually three *p* values associated with this *F* test. The *unadjusted p* value appears under the heading "Pr > F". Two *adjusted p* values appear under the heading "Adj Pr > F". The use of these adjusted *p* values is explained in a later section of this chapter titled "Modified univariate tests."

For the sake of simplicity, consider only the unadjusted *p* value at this point. You can see that this unadjusted *p* value (under "Pr > F") is very small at .0001. Because this *p* value is less than .05, you may reject your null hypothesis of no differences in mean levels of commitment in the population. In other words, you conclude that there is an effect for your repeated-measures variable, TIME.

You may have noticed that page 3 of Output 11.2 provides a "Manova" test for the TIME effect. For the moment, ignore these results and instead focus only on the univariate test for the TIME effect. The multivariate (Manova) approach to conducting a repeated-measures analysis is discussed later in the section titled "Further Notes on Repeated Measures Analyses."

3. Prepare your own version of the ANOVA summary table. As with other ANOVAs, the next step is to formulate the summary table. This is somewhat easier with this analysis as most of the values that you need for the table appear on page 4 of Output 11.2. Table 11.1 illustrates the ANOVA summary table for the analysis just completed:

Table 11.1

ANOVA Summary Table for Study of Investment Using a Repeated Measures Design

Source	df	SS	MS	F
Between Subjects	19	--	--	
Within Subjects	40	113.3		
Treatment	2	69.6	34.82	30.28 *
Residual	38	43.7	1.15	
TOTAL	59			

Note: N = 20.

* p < .0001

4. Review the results of the contrasts. The significant effect for TIME revealed on page 4 of the output simply tells you that the mean investment scores obtained at one point in time are significantly different from scores obtained at some other point in time. You still do not know which means are significantly different from each other. To learn this, you must consult the planned comparisons requested by the CONTRAST option. These appear on page 5 of Output 11.2.

Remember that you specified (in the SAS program with the CONTRAST option) that the mean from trial 1 (baseline) would be compared to each of the other two trials. Results of the analysis comparing trial 1 to trial 2 appear on the upper part of output page 5, below the heading "Contrast Variable: TIME.2." It is this comparison that directly evaluates your primary hypothesis that investment increases significantly at post-treatment (time 2) compared to baseline (time 1). The F ratio for this contrast appears where the "MEAN" row intersects the column headed "F Value". You can see that the obtained F value is 29.01 which, with 1 and 19 degrees of freedom, is significant at $p < .0001$. This tells you that there was in fact a significant increase in investment scores immediately following the marriage encounter program. This is what you may have expected, after you reviewed the mean scores plotted earlier in Figure 11.3. This finding supports your primary hypothesis that investment scores would display a significant increase from time 1 to time 2.

The other contrast appears on the bottom half of page 5 of Output 11.2, beneath the heading "Contrast Variable: TIME.3." This contrast compares baseline scores to the follow-up scores (taken three weeks after the program). The F value for this contrast is also statistically significant ($F[1, 19] = 43.09$, $p < .0001$), indicating that the two treatment means are different. Inspection of the means in Figure 11.3 shows that the follow-up mean is greater than the baseline mean. Your second hypothesis, that the increase in investment would not be sustained, is therefore not supported. The increase in perceived investment size is maintained two weeks after the treatment.

Summarizing the Results of the Analysis

The standard statistical interpretation format used for between-groups ANOVA (as previously described in Chapter 8) is also appropriate for the repeated-measures design. The outline of this format appears again here:

A) Statement of the problem
B) Nature of the variables
C) Statistical test
D) Null hypothesis (Ho)
E) Alternative hypothesis (H1)
F) Obtained statistic
G) Obtained probability (p) value
H) Conclusion regarding the null hypothesis
I) ANOVA summary table
J) Figure representing the results

Since most sections of this format appeared in Chapter 8 or in this chapter (e.g., the ANOVA summary table), they are not repeated here. Instead, the formal description of the results follows.

Formal Description of Results for a Paper

Mean investment size scores across the three trials are displayed in Figure 11.3. Results were analyzed using one-way analysis of variance (ANOVA), repeated-measures design. This analysis revealed a significant effect for the treatment, $F(2,38) = 30.28$; $p <.0001$. Contrasts showed that the baseline measure was significantly lower than the post-treatment trial, $F(1,19) = 29.01$; $p <.0001$, and the follow-up trial, $F(1,19) = 43.09$; $p <.0001$.

Further Notes on Repeated-Measures Analyses

Advantages of the Repeated-Measures Design versus the Between-Groups Design

An alternative to the repeated-measures design is a between-groups design, as described in Chapter 8. For example, you could have followed a between-groups design in which two groups of subjects would be measured at only one point in time: immediately following the weekend program (at time 2, from Figure 11.3). In this between-groups study, one group of couples would attend the weekend encounter, and the other group would not attend. If you conducted the study well, you could then attribute any differences in the group means to the weekend experience.

In both the repeated-measures design and the between-groups design, the sums of squares and mean squares are computed in the same way. However, an advantage of the repeated-measures design is that each subject serves as his or her own control. Since each subject serves in each treatment condition, variability in scores due to individual differences between subjects will not be a factor in determining the size of the treatment effect. The between-subjects variability is removed from the error term in computing the *F* test (see Table 11.1). This computation usually allows for a more sensitive test of treatment effects because the between-subjects variance is typically much larger than the within-subject variance. This is true because multiple observations from the same subject tend to be positively correlated, especially when you obtain measures across time.

An additional advantage with repeated measures is increased efficiency since this design requires only half the number of subjects that you would need in a between-groups design. This may be an important consideration when the targeted study population is limited in number. These statistical and practical differences illustrate the importance of careful planning of the statistical analysis when designing an experiment.

Weaknesses of the One-Way Repeated Measures Design

The primary limitation of the present design is the lack of a control group. Since all subjects receive the treatment in this design, there is no comparison that you can make to evaluate if any observed changes are truly the result of the experimental manipulation. For example, in the study just described, increases in investment scores might occur because of time spent together and have nothing to do with the specific program activities during the weekend (i.e. the treatment). Chapter 12 ("Factorial ANOVA with Repeated-Measures Factors and Between-Groups Factors"), shows how you can remedy this weakness of the single-group repeated measures design with the addition of an appropriate control group.

Another potential problem with this type of design is that subjects might be affected by a treatment in a way that changes subsequent measures. This problem is called a **sequence effect** and is discussed in detail in a section at the end of this chapter.

Validity Conditions for the Univariate One-Way ANOVA, Repeated Measures Design

The analysis described previously was conducted as a conventional univariate repeated-measures ANOVA. This analysis is only valid if certain assumptions about the data hold true. Two assumptions for this test are normality and homogeneity of variance. Statisticians have pointed out that, in many instances, data collected under real world conditions do not meet the second of these assumptions.

The violation of homogeneity of variance is particularly problematic for repeated measures designs, as compared to between-groups designs. In the case of between-groups designs, the analysis still produces a robust F test even when this assumption is not met (provided sample sizes are equal). On the other hand, a violation of this assumption with a repeated measures design leads to an increased probability of a Type I error (i.e. rejection of a true null hypothesis). Therefore, you must take greater care when analyzing repeated measures designs to either prove that the assumptions of the test have been met, or alter the analysis to account for the effects of the violation.

A discussion of the validity conditions for the univariate ANOVA, and alternative approaches to the analysis of repeated measures data appears next. This section merely introduces some of the relevant issues and is not intended as an exhaustive description of the statistical problems inherent with use of repeated measures analyses. For a more detailed treatment, see Barcikowski and Robey (1984) or LaTour and Miniard (1983).

The assumptions underlying a valid application of the conventional F test are that criterion scores from the experimental treatments have a multivariate normal distribution in the population (i.e. normality), and that the common covariance matrix has a sphericity pattern (i.e. homogeneity of covariance). Normality is impossible to prove, but becomes more likely as sample size increases (a rule of thumb is that you can assume normality if the error degrees of freedom statistic is > 20).

Homogeneity of covariance refers to the covariance between subsets of any two treatments. One way to conceptualize this is that subjects should have the same rankings in scores for all pairs of levels of the independent variable. For example, if there are three treatment conditions, the covariance between TX1 and TX2 should be comparable to the covariance between TX2 and TX3, and to the covariance between TX1 and TX3.

NOTE: If there are only two levels of the independent variable, then this assumption is automatically satisfied because there is only one covariance value.

Homogeneity of covariance is sufficient for test validity, but a less specific type of covariance pattern (i.e. sphericity) is a necessary validity condition (Huynh & Mandeville, 1979; Rouanet & Lepine, 1970). SAS performs a test for sphericity if you request the PRINTE option in the REPEATED statement. The general form for this option is as follows:

```
REPEATED trial-variable-name #levels CONTRAST (level#) / SUMMARY PRINTE;
```

The REPEATED statement from the actual program is:

```
3          REPEATED TIME 3 CONTRAST (1) / SUMMARY  PRINTE;
```

Revising the program presented earlier so that it includes the PRINTE option results in seven pages of output. The results requested by the PRINTE option would appear on pages 4 and 5. Those pages appear here as Output 11.3.

```
                              The SAS System                                  4

                        General Linear Models Procedure
                      Repeated Measures Analysis of Variance

        Partial Correlation Coefficients from the Error SS&CP Matrix / Prob > |r|

                    DF = 19          PRE        POST       FOLUP

                    PRE          1.000000   0.677055   0.692736
                                 0.0001     0.0010     0.0007

                    POST         0.677055   1.000000   0.895619
                                 0.0010     0.0001     0.0001

                    FOLUP        0.692736   0.895619   1.000000
                                 0.0007     0.0001     0.0001


                            E = Error SS&CP Matrix

        TIME.N represents the contrast between the nth level of TIME and the 1st

                                 TIME.2           TIME.3

                    TIME.2     60.55000000      45.80000000
                    TIME.3     45.80000000      50.80000000
```

```
                                                                    5


                         General Linear Models Procedure
                       Repeated Measures Analysis of Variance

              Partial Correlation Coefficients from the Error SS&CP Matrix
           of the Variables Defined by the Specified Transformation / Prob > |r|


                        DF = 19         TIME.2      TIME.3


                    TIME.2         1.000000    0.825803
                                   0.0001      0.0001


                    TIME.3         0.825803    1.000000
                                   0.0001      0.0001




              Test for Sphericity: Mauchly's Criterion = 0.3156106
       Chisquare Approximation = 20.758429 with 2 df    Prob > Chisquare = 0.0000


                         Applied to Orthogonal Components:
                 Test for Sphericity: Mauchly's Criterion = 0.6830428
       Chisquare Approximation = 6.8615597 with 2 df    Prob > Chisquare = 0.0324


         Manova Test Criteria and Exact F Statistics for the Hypothesis of no TIME Effect
              H = Type III SS&CP Matrix for TIME    E = Error SS&CP Matrix


                        S=1      M=0      N=8


         Statistic                 Value          F      Num DF    Den DF   Pr > F

         Wilks' Lambda          0.30600563    20.4112       2        18    0.0001
         Pillai's Trace         0.69399437    20.4112       2        18    0.0001
         Hotelling-Lawley Trace 2.26791373    20.4112       2        18    0.0001
         Roy's Greatest Root    2.26791373    20.4112       2        18    0.0001
```

Output 11.3: Results of Test for Sphericity Requested by PRINTE Option

The test performed with orthogonal components is the test of interest. In Output 11.3, this test appears toward the middle of output page 5, to the right of the heading

> Applied to Orthogonal Components:
> Test for Sphericity: Mauchly's Criterion =

In Output 11.3, this test is significant at $p = .0324$. Technically, a significant p value indicates that the data display a significant departure from sphericity. However, be warned that this test is extremely sensitive and any deviation from sphericity results in a significant F test. However, you can compensate for small to moderate deviations from sphericity through use of a modified

F test (discussion follows). If there is a severe departure from sphericity (e.g., $p < .0001$) then another approach to the problem is to use multivariate tests.

Alternative Analyses

If the assumptions of the test are not met, then various alternatives to the conventional univariate ANOVA have been proposed. These alternatives consist of modifications of the univariate ANOVA, or use of the multivariate ANOVA.

Modified univariate tests. As stated above, the primary concern when the sphericity pattern is not present is that the *F* test will be too liberal and lead to inappropriate rejection of the null hypothesis. Therefore, the modifications which are recommended to compensate for non-sphericity are generally aimed at making the test more conservative.

The currently accepted method to modify the *F* test to account for deviations from sphericity is to adjust the degrees of freedom associated with the *F* value. Several correction factors have been developed to accomplish this. The correction factor is named epsilon (Greenhouse & Geisser, 1959). Epsilon varies between a lower limit $[1/(k-1)]$ and 1 depending on the degree to which the data deviate from a sphericity pattern. The degrees of freedom are multiplied by the correction factor to yield a number which is either lower or unchanged. Therefore, a given test typically has fewer degrees of freedom and requires a greater *F* value to achieve a given *p* level. With epsilon at a value of 1 (meaning the assumption has been met), the degrees of freedom are unchanged. To the extent that sphericity is not present, epsilon is reduced and this further decreases the degrees of freedom to produce a more conservative test.

The computations for epsilon are performed routinely as part of the univariate analysis for repeated measures using SAS (see page 4 of Output 11.1). Although the exact procedure to follow is somewhat controversial and may depend on characteristics specific to a given data set, there is some consensus for use of the following general guidelines:

- You should use the modified univariate test when the Greenhouse-Geisser (G-G) epsilon is greater than .75.

- If the G-G epsilon is less than .75, a multivariate analysis (MANOVA) provides a more powerful test.

Multivariate ANOVA. As a repeated-measures design consists of within-subject observations across treatment conditions, the individual treatment measures can be viewed as separate, correlated dependent variables. Thereby the data set is easily conceptualized as multivariate even though the design is univariate, and it can be analyzed with multivariate statistics. In this type of analysis, each level of the repeated factor is treated as a separate variable. The SAS program described earlier in this chapter also automatically computes a multivariate ANOVA, and includes the results in the output. The statistics for the multivariate test appear on page 3 of Output 11.1. SAS computes four test statistics, and the appropriate test to use depends on the characteristics of your data set. For a review of the statistical literature on this topic, see Olson (1976).

The multivariate ANOVA has an advantage over the univariate test in that it requires no assumption of sphericity. Some statisticians recommend that the multivariate ANOVA be used frequently, if not routinely, with repeated measures designs (Davidson, 1972). This argument is made for several reasons.

In selecting a test statistic, it is always desirable to choose the most powerful test. A test has power when it is able to correctly reject the null hypothesis. In many situations, the univariate ANOVA is more powerful than the MANOVA and is therefore the better choice. However, the test to determine if the assumption of sphericity has been met is not very powerful with a small *n*. Therefore, only when the *n* is large (about 20 greater than the number of treatment levels) does the test for sphericity have sufficient power. Remember that the multivariate test becomes just as powerful as the univariate test as the *n* grows larger. Certain statisticians have argued that this creates a sort of catch-22: with a small *n* there is no certainty that the assumptions underlying the univariate ANOVA have been met; with a large *n* the MANOVA is equally if not more powerful than the univariate test.

Others argue that the univariate approach offers a more powerful test for many types of data and should not be so readily abandoned (Tabachnick & Fidell, 1989). In their view, the multivariate ANOVA is reserved for those situations that cannot be analyzed with the univariate ANOVA.

Sequence Effects

Another important consideration in a repeated measures design is the potential for certain experimental confounds. In particular, the experimenter must control for order effects and carry-over effects.

Order effects. **Order effects** result when the ordinal position of the treatments introduces a bias into subject responses. Consider this example. An experimenter studying perception requires subjects to perform a reaction-time task in each of three conditions. Subjects must depress a button on a response pad while waiting for a signal, and after receiving the signal they must depress a different button. The dependent variable is reaction time and the independent variable is the type of signal. The independent variable has three levels: in condition 1 the signal is a flash of light; in condition 2 it is an audio tone; and in condition 3 it is both the light and tone simultaneously. Each test session consists of fifty trials. A mean reaction-time is computed for each session. Assume that these conditions are presented in the same order for all subjects: in the morning, before lunch, and after lunch.

The problem with this research design is that reaction-time scores may be adversely affected after lunch by fatigue. Responses to condition 3 might be more a measure of a fatigue effect than a true treatment effect. For example, suppose the experiment yields mean scores for 10 subjects as shown in Table 11.2. It appears that presentation of both signals (tone and light) causes a delayed reaction-time compared to the other two treatments (tone alone or light alone).

Table 11.2: Mean Reaction-Time (msecs) for All Treatment Conditions

Type of Signal

Tone	Light	Tone and Light
650	650	1125

An alternative explanation for the preceding results is that a fatigue effect in the early afternoon is causing the longer reaction-times. According to this interpretation, you would expect each of the three treatments to have longer reaction-times if presented during the early afternoon period. If you collected the data as described, there is no way for you to determine which explanation is correct.

To control for this problem, you must vary the treatment order. This technique, called **counterbalancing**, is used to present the conditions in different orders to different subjects. A research design that you could use to achieve counterbalancing appears in Table 11.3:

Table 11.3. Counterbalanced Presentation of Treatment Conditions to Control for Sequence Effects

Treatment Order

	AM	Late AM	Early PM
Subject 1	Tone	Light	Both
Subject 2	Both	Tone	Light
Subject 3	Light	Both	Tone
Subject 4	Tone	Both	Light
Subject 5	Light	Tone	Both
Subject 6	Both	Light	Tone

Note that in Table 11.3 each treatment occurs an equal number of times at each time of day. To achieve complete counterbalancing, you must use each combination of treatment sequences for an equal number of subjects.

NOTE: Complete counterbalancing becomes impractical as the number of treatment conditions increases. For example, there are only 6 possible sequences of 3 treatments, but this increases to 24 sequences with 4 treatments, 120 sequences with 5 treatments, and so forth.) Obviously, complete counterbalancing typically is possible only if the independent variable may assume a relatively small number of values.

Carry-over effects. **Carry-over effects** occur when an effect from one treatment changes (carries over to) the subjects' responses in the following treatment condition. For example, suppose you are investigating the sleep-inducing effect of three different drugs. Drug 1 is given on night 1 and sleep onset latency is measured by electroencephalogram. The same measure is collected on nights 2 and 3, when drugs 2 and 3 are administered. If drug 1 has a long half-life, then it may still exert an effect on sleep latency at night 2. This carryover effect would make it impossible to accurately assess the effect of drug 2.

To avoid a potential carry-over effect, the experimenter may decide to separate the experimental conditions by one week. Counterbalancing also provides some control over carry-over effects. If all treatment combinations can be given, then each treatment will be followed (and preceded) by each other treatment with equal frequency. However, carryover effects are not as likely to even out with counterbalancing as are order effects. The advantage of counterbalancing may lie more in enabling the experimenter to measure the extent of carryover effects, and to make appropriate adjustments to the analysis.

Ideally, careful consideration of experimental design will allow the experimenter to avoid significant carryover effects in a study. This is another consideration in choosing between a repeated measures and a between-groups design. In the study of drug effects described previously, the investigator can avoid any possible carryover effects by using a between-groups design. In that design, each subject would only receive one of the drug treatments.

Conclusion

You can use the one-way repeated-measures ANOVA to analyze data from studies in which each subject is exposed to every level of the independent variable. In some cases, this involves a single-group design in which repeated measurements are taken at different points in time. As the present chapter has pointed out, these single-group repeated-measures studies often suffer from a number of problems. Fortunately, some of these problems can be handled successfully by adding a second group of subjects, a control group, to the design. The next chapter shows how to analyze data from that type of study.

Appendix: Assumptions Underlying the One-Way ANOVA with One Repeated-Measures Factor

Assumptions for the Multivariate Test

- **Level of measurement**. Repeated measures designs are so-named because they normally involve obtaining repeated measures on some criterion variable from a single sample of subjects. This criterion variable should be assessed on an interval or ratio level of measurement. The predictor variable should be a nominal-level variable (a categorical variable) which typically codes "time," "trial," "treatment," or some similar construct.

- **Independent observations**. A given subject's score in any one condition should not be affected by any other subject's score in any of the study's conditions. However, it is acceptable for a given subject's score in one condition to be dependent upon his or her own score in a different condition. This is another way of saying, for example, that it is acceptable for subjects' scores in condition 1 to be correlated with their scores in condition 2 or condition 3.

- **Random sampling**. Scores on the criterion variable should represent a random sample drawn from the populations of interest.

- **Multivariate normality**. The measurements obtained from subjects should follow a multivariate normal distribution. Under conditions normally encountered in social science research, violations of this assumption have only a very small effect on the type I error rate (the probability of incorrectly rejecting a true null hypothesis).

Assumptions for the Univariate Test

The univariate test requires all of the preceding assumptions, as well as the following assumption of sphericity:

- **Sphericity**. In order to understand the sphericity assumption, it is necessary to first understand the nature of the difference variables that are created in performing a repeated-measures ANOVA. Assume that a study is conducted in which each subject provides scores on the criterion variable under each of three conditions; the variable V1 includes scores from condition 1, V2 includes scores from condition 2, and V3 includes scores from condition 3.

  It is possible to create a difference variable (called D1) by subtracting each subject's score on V2 from his or her score on V1:

  ```
  D1 = V1 - V2
  ```

  Similarly, it is possible to create a separate difference variable by subtracting each subject's score on V3 from his or her score on V2:

  ```
  D2 = V2 - V3
  ```

  Difference variables are created in this way, by subtracting subjects' scores observed in adjacent conditions (e.g., V1 – V2, V2 – V3). In a given study, the number of difference variables created will be equal to $k-1$, where k = the number of conditions. The present study included three conditions, and therefore will include two difference variables (D1 and D2).

  It is now possible to compute the variances of each of these difference variables, as well as the covariances between the difference variables. You can arrange these values in a variance-covariance matrix. You review this matrix to determine whether its corresponding matrix in the population demonstrates sphericity.

  Two conditions must be satisfied for a variance-covariance matrix to demonstrate sphericity. First, each variance on the diagonal of the matrix should be equal to every other variance on the diagonal. In the present case, this means that the variance for D1 should equal the variance for D2. Second, each covariance off of the diagonal should equal zero (this is analogous to saying that the correlations between the difference variables should be zero). In the present case, this means that the covariance between D1 and D2 should be equal to zero.

PROC GLM performs a test for sphericity by requesting the PRINTE option in the REPEATED statement. When this test indicates that the sphericity assumption is satisfied, you may interpret the univariate test. When the test indicates that the sphericity assumption is not satisfied (and this will often be the case), the situation becomes much more complicated. The options available under these circumstances are discussed in detail in the section "Further Notes on Repeated-Measures Analysis," in this chapter.

References

Barcikowski, R. & Robey, R. (1984). Decisions in single group repeated measures analysis: Statistical tests and three computer packages. *The American Statistician, 38,* 148-150.

Davidson, M. (1972). Univariate versus multivariate tests in repeated-measures experiments. *Psychological Bulletin, 77,* 446-452.

Greenhouse, S. & Geisser, S. (1959). On methods in the analysis of profile data. *Psychometrika, 24,* 95-112.

Huynh, H. & Mandeville, G. (1979). Validity conditions in repeated measures designs. *Psychological Bulletin, 86,* 964-973.

Keselman, H., Rogan, J., Mendoza, J., & Breen, L. (1980). Testing the validity conditions of repeated measures *F* tests. *Psychological Bulletin, 87,* 479-481.

LaTour, S. & Miniard, P. (1983). The misuse of repeated measures analysis in marketing research. *Journal of Marketing Research, Vol. XX,* 45-57.

Olson, C. (1976). On choosing a test statistic in multivariate analysis of variance. *Psychological Bulletin, 83,* 579-586.

Rouanet, H. & Lepine, D. (1970). Comparison between treatments in a repeated-measurement design: ANOVA and multivariate methods. *The British Journal of Mathematical and Statistical Psychology, 23,* 147-163.

Rusbult, C. E. (1980). Commitment and satisfaction in romantic associations: A test of the investment model. *Journal of Experimental Social Psychology, 16,* 172-186.

Tabachnick, B. & Fidell, L. (1980). *Using multivariate statistics.* New York: Harper Collins Publishers.

Chapter 12

FACTORIAL ANOVA WITH REPEATED-MEASURES FACTORS AND BETWEEN-GROUPS FACTORS

Overview. This chapter shows how to key data and prepare SAS programs that perform a two-way mixed-design ANOVA using the REPEATED statement with the GLM procedure. Guidelines for the hierarchical interpretation of the analysis are provided. This chapter shows how to interpret a significant interaction between the repeated-measures factor and the between-groups factor, as well as how to interpret main effects in the absence of an interaction. It also provides an alternative method of performing the analysis that allows for use of a variety of SAS/STAT post-hoc multiple-comparisons tests.

Introduction: The Basics of Mixed-Design ANOVA

This chapter discusses analysis of variance procedures that are appropriate for studies that include both repeated-measures factors and between-groups factors. These research designs are often referred to as **mixed designs**.

A mixed-design ANOVA is similar to the factorial ANOVA discussed in Chapter 9 of this book ("Factorial ANOVA with Two Between-Group Factors"), in that the procedure discussed in Chapter 9 assumed that the criterion variable is assessed on an interval or ratio scale, and that the predictor variables are assessed on a nominal scale. However, a mixed-design ANOVA differs from a factorial ANOVA with two between-group factors with respect to the nature of the predictor variables that are included in the analysis. Specifically, a mixed-designed ANOVA assumes that the analysis will include:

- at least one nominal-scale predictor variable that is a *between-groups* factor (as in Chapter 8: "One-Way ANOVA with One Between-Groups Factor")

- plus at least one nominal-scale predictor variable that is a *repeated-measures* factor (as in Chapter 11: "One-Way ANOVA with One Repeated-Measures Factor").

These designs are called mixed designs because they include a mix of between-groups factors and repeated-measures factors.

Extension of the Single-Group Design

It is useful to think of a factorial mixed design as an extension of the single-group repeated-measures design that was presented in Chapter 11. That chapter stated that a one-factor repeated-measures design involves taking repeated measurements on the criterion variable from just one group of subjects. The occasions on which measurements are taken are called **times** (or **trials**), and there is typically some type of experimental manipulation that occurs between two or more of these occasions. It is assumed that, if there is a change in mean scores on the criterion from one time to another, it is due to the experimental manipulation (although this assumption can easily be challenged, given the many possible confoundings that are associated with this single-group design; more on this later).

Chapter 11 showed how to use a one-factor repeated-measures research design to test the effectiveness of a marriage encounter program in increasing subjects' perceptions of how much they have invested in their romantic (marital) relationships. The concept of investment size was drawn from Rusbult's investment model (Rusbult, 1980). Briefly, **investment size** refers to the amount of time and personal resources that an individual has put into the relationship with his or her romantic partner. In the preceding chapter, it was hypothesized that the subjects' perceived investment in their marriages would increase immediately following the marriage encounter weekend.

Figure 12.1 illustrates the one-factor repeated-measures design that was used to test this hypothesis in Chapter 11. This figure contains three small circles with the initials "D.V." (for "dependent variable"). These circles represent the occasions on which the dependent variable (criterion variable) was assessed. The criterion variable in the study was investment size. You can see that the survey that assessed this criterion variable was administered at three points in time:

- A baseline survey (time 1) was administered immediately before the marriage encounter weekend.

- A post-treatment survey (time 2) was administered immediately after the marriage encounter weekend.

- A follow-up survey (time 3) was administered three weeks after the marriage encounter weekend.

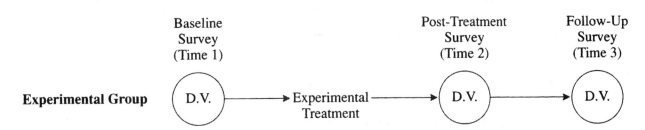

Figure 12.1: Single-Group Experimental Design with Repeated Measures

You could name the predictor variable in this study TIME, and it contains three levels (time 1, time 2, and time 3). Each subject in the study provided data for each of these three levels of the predictor variable, which means that TIME is a repeated-measures factor.

Figure 12.1 shows that an experimental treatment (the marriage encounter program) was positioned between times 1 and 2. You therefore hypothesized that the mean investment scores observed immediately after this treatment (at time 2) would be significantly higher than the mean scores observed just before this treatment (at time 1).

However, Chapter 11 went to some lengths to point out that this single-group repeated-measures design can be a very weak research design, if used inappropriately. The fictitious single-group study that assessed the effectiveness of the marriage encounter program was described as an example of just such a weak design. The reason was simple: even if you obtained evidence consistent with your hypothesis (i.e., time 2 scores were significantly higher than time 1 scores), it would nonetheless provide very weak evidence supporting your hypothesis. This is because there would be so many alternative explanations for your findings, explanations that had nothing to do with the effectiveness of the marriage encounter program.

For example, if perceived investment improved from time 1 to time 2, someone could reasonably argue that this improvement was merely due to the passage of time, rather than the marriage encounter program. This argument would assert that the perception of investments increases over time in all couples, regardless of whether they participate in a marriage encounter program. Because your study included just one group, you have no evidence showing that this alternative explanation is wrong.

As the preceding suggests, data obtained from a single-group experimental design with repeated-measures often provides relatively weak evidence of cause and effect. In order to minimize the weaknesses associated with this design, it is often necessary to expand it into a *two-group* experimental designed with repeated measures (that is, a mixed design).

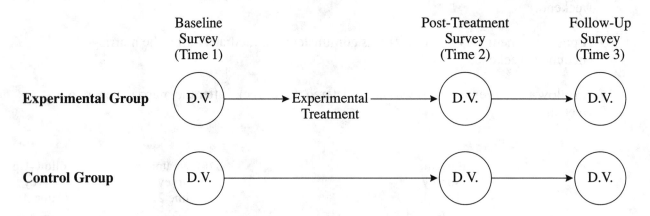

Figure 12.2: Two-Group Experimental Design with Repeated Measures

Figure 12.2 illustrates how to expand the current investment model study into a two-group design with repeated measures. The study would be conducted by starting with a single group of subjects, and randomly assigning each subject to one of two experimental conditions: an experimental group (which would go through the marriage encounter program), or a control group (which would not go through the program).

You would administer the measure of perceived investments to both groups at three points in time:

- A baseline survey (Time 1) immediately before the experimental group went through the marriage encounter program

- A post-treatment survey (Time 2) immediately after the experimental group went through the program

- A follow-up survey (Time 3) three weeks after the experimental group went through the program

Advantages of the Two-Group Repeated-Measures Design

Including the control group makes this a much more rigorous study, compared to the single-group design presented earlier. This is because the control group allows you to test the plausibility of many of the alternative explanations that may be offered for your study's results.

For example, consider a best-case scenario in which you obtain the results that appear in Figure 12.3. The fictitious results of Figure 12.3 show the mean investment scores displayed by the two groups at three points in time. The solid line provides the mean investment scores for the experimental group (the group that experienced the marriage encounter training). The solid line shows that the experimental group displayed a relatively low level of perceived investment at time 1 (mean investment score is approximately 7 on a 12-point scale), but that this increased dramatically following the marriage encounter program at times 2 and 3 (mean investment scores are approximately 11.5 and 11.5, respectively). These findings are consistent with your hypothesis that the marriage encounter program would significantly improve perceptions of investment.

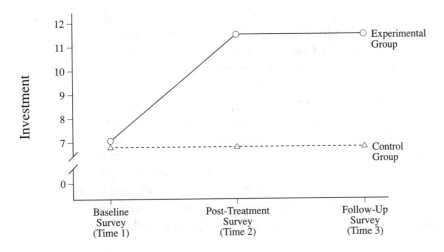

Figure 12.3: A Significant Interaction between TIME and GROUP

In contrast, now consider the broken line of Figure 12.3, which represents the mean scores displayed by the control group (the group that did not receive the marriage encounter program). Notice that the mean investment scores for this group begin relatively low at time 1 (at approximately 6.9 on the 12-point scale), and do not appear to increase at times 2 or 3 (notice that this broken line remains relatively flat). This finding is also consistent with your hypothesis;

since the control group did not receive the training, you would not expect them to demonstrate large improvements in perceived investments over time.

The results of Figure 12.3 are consistent with your hypothesis regarding the effects of the program, and the presence of the control group protects you against many alternative explanations for the results. For example, it would no longer be tenable for someone to argue that the increases in perceived investment were due simply to the passage of time. After all, if that were the case, you would expect to see similar increases in perceived investments in the control group, and these increases are not evident. Similarly, it is not tenable to say the post-treatment scores for the experimental group are significantly higher than those for the control group because of some type of bias in assigning subjects to conditions: Figure 12.3 shows that the two groups demonstrated similar levels of perceived investment at the baseline survey of time 1 (before the experimental treatment). Because this two-group design protects you from these alternative explanations (as well as some others), it is often preferable to the single-group procedure discussed in Chapter 11.

Random Assignment to Groups

It is useful at this point to review the important role played by randomization in the conduct of a mixed-design study. In the experiment just described, it is essential that couples who volunteer for the study be randomly assigned to either the treatment group or control group. In other words, they must be *assigned* to conditions by you (the researcher), and these assignments must be made in a completely *random*, or unsystematic manner.

The importance of random assignment becomes clear when you consider what might happen if subjects are not assigned to conditions in a random fashion. For example, imagine that the experimental group in this study consisted only of people who voluntarily chose to participate in the marriage encounter weekend, and that the control group consisted only of couples who had chosen not to participate in the program. Under these conditions, it would be reasonable to argue that selection bias could affect the outcome of the study. **Selection bias** can occur any time that subjects are assigned to groups in a nonrandom fashion. When this happens, the results of the experiment may reflect pre-existing differences in the subjects rather than treatment effects. For example, in the study just described, couples who volunteer to participate in a marriage encounter weekend may be different in some way from couples who do not volunteer. The volunteering couples may have different concerns about their relationships, different goals, or different views about themselves that may influence their scores on the measure of investment. Such pre-existing differences could render any results from the study meaningless.

One way to rectify this problem in the present study would be to ensure that you recruit all couples from a list of couples who have volunteered to participate in the marriage encounter weekend, and you then randomly assign all couples to treatment conditions. In this way, you are helping to ensure that the couples in both groups are as much alike as possible at the start of the study.

Studies with More Than Two Groups

To keep things simple, this chapter focuses on only *two-group* repeated measures designs. It should be obvious, however, that it is possible to expand these studies to include more than two groups under the between-groups factors. For example, the preceding study included only two groups: a control group and an experimental group. It would have been relatively easy, however, to expand the study so that it included three groups of subjects:

- the control group

- experimental group 1 (which would experience the marriage encounter program)

- experimental group 2 (which would experience traditional marriage counseling).

Obviously, the addition of the third group would allow you to test additional hypotheses. At any rate, the procedures for analyzing the data from such a design would be a logical extension of the two-group procedures described in this chapter.

Some Possible Results from a Two-Way Mixed-Design ANOVA

Before showing how to analyze data from a mixed design, it is instructive to first review some of the results that are possible with this design. This will help illustrate the power of this design, and will lay a foundation for concepts to follow.

A Significant Interaction

In Chapter 9 ("Factorial ANOVA with Two Between-Group Factors") you learned that a **significant interaction** means that the relationship between one predictor variable and the criterion is different at different levels of the second predictor variable (with experimental research, the corresponding definition is "the effect of one independent variable on the criterion variable is different at different levels of the second independent variable"). To better understand this definition, refer back to Figure 12.3, which illustrated the interaction between TIME and GROUP.

In this study, TIME was the variable that coded the repeated-measures factor (time 1 scores versus time 2 scores versus time 3 scores). GROUP, on the other hand, was the variable that coded the between-groups factor (experimental group versus control group). When there is a significant interaction between a repeated-measures factor and a between groups factor, it means that the relationship between the repeated-measures factor and the criterion is different for the different groups coded under the between-groups factor.

This is illustrated by the two lines appearing in Figure 12.3. To understand this interaction, begin by focusing on just the solid line in the figure, which illustrates the relationship between TIME and investment scores for just the experimental group. Notice that the mean for the experimental group is relatively low at time 1, but is significantly higher at times 2 and 3. This shows that there is a significant relationship between TIME and perceived investment for the experimental group.

Next, focus only on the broken line that illustrates the relationship between TIME and perceived investment for just the control group. Notice that this line is flat: There is little change from time 1 to time 2 to time 3. This shows that there is no relationship between TIME and investment size for the control group.

Combined, these results illustrate the definition for an **interaction**: the relationship between one predictor variable (TIME) and the criterion variable (investment size) is different at different levels of the second predictor variable (that is, the relationship between TIME and investment size is significant for the experimental group, but is nonsignificant for the control group).

You will determine whether an interaction is significant by consulting the appropriate statistical test in your SAS output. However, it is also sometimes possible to identify a significant interaction by reviewing a figure that illustrates group means. For example, consider the solid line and the broken line of Figure 12.3, particularly the first segment of each line that goes from time 1 to time 2. Notice that the solid line (for the experimental group) is not parallel to the broken line (for the control group), the solid line has a much steeper angle. This is the hallmark of an interaction: nonparallel lines. Whenever a figure shows that a line segment for one group is not parallel to the corresponding line segment for a different group, it may mean that there is an interaction between the repeated-measures factor and the between-groups factor.

In some (but not all) studies that use a mixed design, your central hypothesis may require that there be a significant interaction between the repeated-measures variable and the between-groups variable. For example, in the present study that assessed the effectiveness of the marriage encounter program, a significant interaction would be required to show that the experimental group displayed a stronger increase in investment size, compared to the control group.

Significant Main Effects

If a given predictor variable is not involved in any significant interactions, you are free to determine whether that variable displays a significant main effect. When a predictor variable displays a significant **main effect**, it means that, in the population, there is a difference between at least two of the levels of that predictor variable with respect to mean scores on the criterion variable.

The number of main effects that are possible in a study is equal to the number of predictor variables. The present investment model study includes two predictor variables, and so two main effects are possible: one for the repeated-measures factor (TIME), and one for the between-groups factor (GROUP). These main effects may take a variety of different forms.

A significant main effect for TIME. For example, Figure 12.4 shows one possible main effect for the TIME variable: an increasing linear time trend. Notice that the investment scores at time 2 are somewhat higher than the scores at time 1, and that the scores at time 3 are somewhat higher than the scores at time 2. Whenever the values of a predictor variable are plotted on the horizontal axis of a figure, a significant main effect for that variable is indicated when the line segments display a relatively steep *angle*.

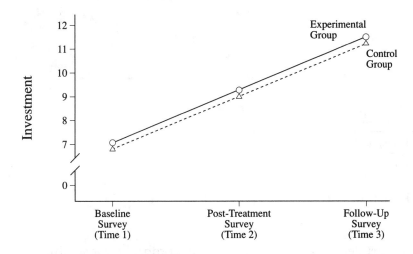

Figure 12.4: A Significant Main Effect for TIME Only

In this case, the values of TIME are plotted on the horizontal axis (these values are identified as "Baseline Survey (Time 1)," "Post-Treatment Survey (Time 2)," and "Follow-Up Survey (Time 3)." There is a relatively steep angle in the line that goes from time 1 to time 2, and also a relatively steep angle in the line that goes from time 2 to time 3. These results will typically indicate a significant main effect (of course, you will always check the appropriate statistical test in the SAS output to verify that the main effect is, in fact, significant).

Remember that the main effect for TIME is averaged over the two groups in the study. In the present case, this means that there is an overall main effect for TIME after collapsing across the experimental group and control group.

A significant main effect for GROUP. You would expect to see a different pattern in a figure if the main effect for the other predictor variable were significant. Earlier, it was said that values of the predictor variable TIME are plotted as three separate points on the horizontal axis of the figure. In contrast, the values of the predictor variable GROUP are coded by drawing separate lines for the two groups under this variable: The experimental group is represented with a solid line, and the control group is represented with a broken line.

When a predictor variable (such as GROUP) is represented in a figure by plotting separate lines for its various levels, a significant main effect for that variable is revealed when at least two of the lines are relatively separated from each other. For example, consider Figure 12.5.

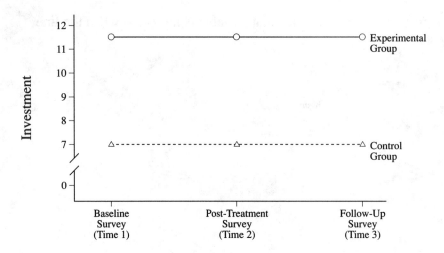

Figure 12.5: A Significant Main Effect for GROUP Only

Begin your review of Figure 12.5 by first determining which effects are probably *not* significant. You can see that all line segments for the experimental group are parallel to their corresponding segments for the control group; this tells you that there is probably not a significant interaction between TIME and GROUP. Next, you can see that none of the line segments in Figure 12.5 display a relatively steep angle; this tells you that there is probably not a significant main effect for TIME.

However, notice that the solid line that represents the experimental group appears to be separated from the broken line that represents the control group. Now look at the individual data points. At time 1, the experimental group displays a mean investment score that appears to be much higher than the one display by the control group. This same pattern of differences appears at times 2 and 3. Combined, these are the results that you would expect to see if there were a significant main effect for GROUP. The actual results in Figure 12.5 suggest that the experimental group consistently demonstrated higher investment scores than the control group.

A significant main effect for both predictor variables. It is possible to obtain significant main effects for both predictor variables simultaneously. Such an outcome appears in Figure 12.6. Notice that the line segments display a relatively steep angle (indicative of a main effect for TIME), and the lines for the two groups are also relatively separated (indicative of a main effect for GROUP).

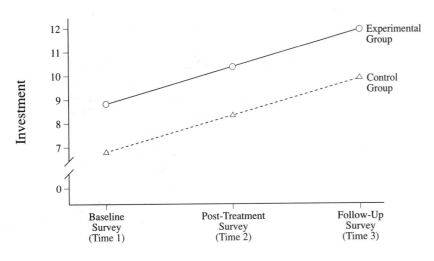

Figure 12.6: Significant Main Effects for Both TIME and GROUP

Nonsignificant Interaction, Nonsignificant Main Effects

Of course, there is no law that says that *any* of your effects have to be significant (as every researcher knows all too well!). This is clear in Figure 12.7. Notice that, in the figure, the lines for the two groups are parallel to one another, indicating a probable nonsignificant interaction. There is also no angle to the line, indicating that the main effect for TIME is nonsignificant. Finally, the line for the experimental group is not really separated from the line for the control group; this likely suggests that the main effect for GROUP is likewise nonsignificant.

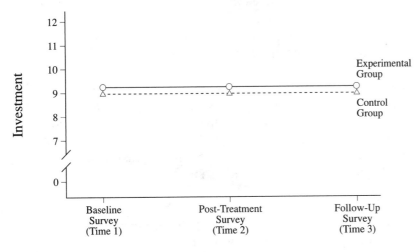

Figure 12.7: A Nonsignificant Interaction, and Nonsignificant Main Effects

Problems with the Mixed-Design ANOVA

An earlier section indicated that the proper use of a control group in a mixed-design investigation can help remedy some of the weaknesses associated with the single-group repeated-measures design. However, there are other problems that may affect a repeated-measures even when it includes a control group.

For example, Chapter 11 ("One-Way ANOVA with One Repeated-Measures Factor") discussed a number of sequence effects that may confound a study with a repeated-measures factor. Specifically, repeated-measures investigations often suffer from **order effects** (effects that occur when the ordinal position of the treatments introduces bias into subject responses) as well as **carry-over effects** (effects that occur when the effect from one treatment changes, or carries over, to the subjects' responses in the following treatment conditions.

You should always be sensitive to the possibility of sequence effects when conducting research with any type of repeated-measures design. In some cases, it is possible to successfully deal with these problems through the proper use of counterbalancing, spacing of trials, additional control groups, or other strategies. Some of these approaches were discussed in the "Sequence Effects" section of Chapter 11.

Example with a Nonsignificant Interaction

The fictitious example of an investigation presented here is a follow-up to the pilot study described in Chapter 11. The results of that pilot study suggest that scores on a measure of perceived investment significantly increase following a marriage encounter weekend. However (as was discussed earlier), you could argue that those investment scores merely increased as a function of time, and not because of the experimental manipulation. In other words, the investment scores could have increased simply because the couples spent time together, and this would have occurred with any activity, not just a marriage encounter experience.

To address concerns about this confounding (as well as some other confoundings inherent in the one-group design), replicate the study as a two-group design. An experimental group once again experiences the marriage encounter program, and a control group does not. Take repeated measures on perceived investment from both groups (the design of this study was illustrated earlier in Figure 12.2). Remember that this two-group design is generally considered to be superior to the design described in Chapter 11, and you would use it in place of that design in most instances.

Your primary hypothesis is that the experimental group will show a greater increase in investment scores at post-treatment and follow-up than the control group. This result would be confirmed by a significant GROUP X TIME interaction in the ANOVA. You also hypothesize (based on the results obtained from the pilot project described in Chapter 11) that the increased investment scores in the treatment group will still be found at follow-up. To determine whether the results are consistent with these hypotheses, it is necessary to check group means, review the results from the "omnibus" test of the interaction, and consult a number of post-hoc tests to be described later.

Writing the SAS Program

The criterion variable in this study is perceived **investment size**: the amount of time and effort that subjects believe they have invested in their relationships (their marriages). Perceived investment will be assessed with a survey, and the overall investment scores obtained with this survey will be created so that higher scores indicate greater levels of investment. Assume that these scores are assessed on an interval scale, and that the scale has been shown to demonstrate acceptable psychometric properties (i.e., it is a valid and reliable measure of investment).

Creating the SAS data set. Because you will obtain investment scores at three points in time (time 1, time 2, and time 3), you must create three SAS variables to contain these scores. Use the following approach:

- A SAS variable named PRE contains investment scores obtained at time 1 (scores from the baseline survey).

- A SAS variable named POST contains investment scores obtained at time 2 (from the post-treatment survey).

- A SAS variable named FOLUP contains investment scores obtained at time 3 (from the follow-up survey).

You need a number of additional variables to complete the analysis. Create the variable named SUBJ to denote each subject's subject number (values will range from 01 through n, where n = the number of subjects). In addition, create a variable named GROUP to designate membership in either the experimental or control groups. Code this variable so that a value of 1 indicates that the subject is in the control group, and a value of 2 indicates that the subject is in the experimental group.

You can use the following program to create a SAS data set call MIXED that contains fictitious data from the mixed-design study:

```
1       DATA MIXED;
2       INPUT #1 @1  (SUBJ)   (2.)
3                @5  (GROUP)  (1.)
4                @10 (PRE)    (2.)
5                @15 (POST)   (2.)
6                @20 (FOLUP)  (2.);
7       CARDS;
8       01  1    08   10   10
9       02  1    10   13   12
10      03  1    07   10   12
11      04  1    06   09   10
12      05  1    07   08   09
```

```
13      06  1    11   15   14
14      07  1    08   10   09
15      08  1    05   08   08
16      09  1    12   11   12
17      10  1    09   12   12
18      11  2    10   14   13
19      12  2    07   12   11
20      13  2    08   08   09
21      14  2    13   14   14
22      15  2    11   11   12
23      16  2    07   08   07
24      17  2    09   08   10
25      18  2    08   13   14
26      19  2    10   12   12
27      20  2    06   09   10
28      ;
```

Lines 8-27 of the preceding program include data from the study. The first column of data includes the subject number variable called SUBJ. You can see that 20 subjects provided data.

The second column of data (in column 4) includes subject scores on GROUP, the variable that indicates which treatment group the subject is in. You can see that data from subjects in the control group appear on lines 8-17 (these subjects were coded with a "1"), while the data from the subjects in the experimental group appear in lines 18-27 (these subjects are identified by a "2").

The third column of data (in columns 10-11) includes perceived investment scores obtained at time 1. These scores were given the SAS variable name PRE. The fourth column of data (columns 15-16) includes the SAS variable POST (investment scores obtained at time 2). Finally, the last column of data (columns 20-21) includes the SAS variable FOLUP (investment scores obtained at time 3).

Obtaining descriptive statistics with PROC MEANS. After inputting the data set, you should perform a PROC MEANS to obtain descriptive statistics from all variables. This serves two important purposes. First, scanning the *n*, minimum value, and maximum value for each variable provides an opportunity to check for obvious data entry errors. Second, you will need the means and standard deviations for the variables to interpret any significant effects observed in the ANOVA results to be reviewed later. Using PROC MEANS is particularly important when analyzing data from a mixed-design study, because the means for within-subjects variables are not routinely included in the output of PROC GLM when it has been used to perform a mixed-design ANOVA.

You will need to have means and other descriptive statistics for all three of your investment score variables: PRE, POST, and FOLUP. You will need to have the overall means (based on the complete sample), as well as the means broken down by GROUP (that is, you will need the means on these three variables that were displayed by the control group, as well as the means that were displayed by the experimental group). You can obtain all of this information by adding the following lines to the preceding SAS program:

```
1      PROC MEANS   DATA=MIXED;
2         RUN;
3
4      PROC SORT   DATA=MIXED;
5         BY GROUP;
6         RUN;
7      PROC MEANS   DATA=MIXED;
8         BY GROUP;
9         RUN;
```

Lines 1-2 of the preceding program requests that PROC MEANS be performed on all variables for the complete sample. Lines 4-6 sort the data set by the variable GROUP, and lines 7-12 request that the MEANS procedure be performed twice: once for the control group, and once for the experimental group.

The output produced by the above program appears here as Output 12.1. The results of the first PROC MEANS (performed on the combined sample) appear on page 1 of this output. It is instructive to review the means from this page of the output to get a sense for any general trends in the data. Remember that the variables PRE, POST, and FOLUP contain investment scores obtained at times 1, 2, and 3, respectively. The PRE variable displays a mean score of 8.60, meaning that the average investment score was 8.60 just before the marriage encounter weekend. The mean score on POST shows that the average investment score increased to 10.75 immediately after the marriage encounter weekend, and the mean score on FOLUP shows that investment scores averaged 11.00 three weeks following the program. These means seem to display a fairly large increase in investment scores from time 1 to time 2, suggesting that you may observe a significant effect for TIME when you later review ANOVA results (presented later).

```
                        The SAS System                              1

     Variable   N        Mean        Std Dev      Minimum       Maximum
     --------------------------------------------------------------------
     SUB       20    10.5000000     5.9160798    1.0000000    20.0000000
     GROUP     20     1.5000000     0.5129892    1.0000000     2.0000000
     PRE       20     8.6000000     2.1373865    5.0000000    13.0000000
     POST      20    10.7500000     2.2912878    8.0000000    15.0000000
     FOLUP     20    11.0000000     2.0261449    7.0000000    14.0000000
     --------------------------------------------------------------------
```

2

```
------------------------------------ GROUP=1 ------------------------------------


    Variable    N        Mean        Std Dev       Minimum        Maximum
    -----------------------------------------------------------------------
    SUB         10      5.5000000    3.0276504     1.0000000     10.0000000
    PRE         10      8.3000000    2.2135944     5.0000000     12.0000000
    POST        10     10.6000000    2.2211108     8.0000000     15.0000000
    FOLUP       10     10.8000000    1.8737959     8.0000000     14.0000000
    -----------------------------------------------------------------------


------------------------------------ GROUP=2 ------------------------------------


    Variable    N        Mean        Std Dev       Minimum        Maximum
    -----------------------------------------------------------------------
    SUB         10     15.5000000    3.0276504    11.0000000     20.0000000
    PRE         10      8.9000000    2.1317703     6.0000000     13.0000000
    POST        10     10.9000000    2.4698178     8.0000000     14.0000000
    FOLUP       10     11.2000000    2.2509257     7.0000000     14.0000000
    -----------------------------------------------------------------------
```

Output 12.1. Results of PROC MEANS

It is important to remember that, in order for your hypotheses to be supported, it is not adequate to merely observe a significant effect for TIME; instead it is necessary that you obtain a significant TIME X GROUP interaction. Specifically, you must find that any increase in investment scores over time is greater among subjects in the experimental group than it is among subjects in the control group. To see whether such an interaction has occurred, it is necessary to prepare a figure that plots data for the two groups separately, and consult the appropriate statistical analyses. You can prepare the necessary figure by referring to the group means that appear on page 2 of Output 12.1 (a later section presents the appropriate statistical analyses).

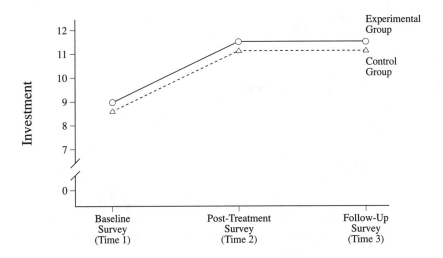

Figure 12.8: Mean Investment Scores from Output 12.8

In Figure 12.8, the broken line illustrates mean investment scores from the control group. These mean scores were obtained from the PRE, POST, and FOLUP variables that appeared on the part of Output 12.1 labeled "GROUP=1". The solid line in the figure illustrates mean scores for the experimental group, and these scores were obtained from the section of Output 12.1 labeled "GROUP=2" (for a review of how to prepare figures such as Figure 12.8 from a table of means, see Chapter 9).

The general pattern of means that are plotted in Figure 12.8 does not appear to show an interaction between TIME and GROUP. When two variables are involved in an interaction, the lines that represent the various groups tend not to be parallel to one another. So far, the lines for the control group and experimental group of Figure 12.8 do appear to be parallel. This may mean that the interaction is nonsignificant. However, the only way to be sure is to actually analyze the data and consult the appropriate statistical test. The next section shows how to do this.

Testing for significant effects with PROC GLM. The general form for the SAS program to perform a factorial ANOVA with one repeated-measures factor and one between-groups factor is as follows:

```
PROC GLM   DATA=filename;
   CLASS   group-variable-name;
   MODEL   trial1  trial2  trial3... trialn = group-variable-name   /
NOUNI;
   REPEATED   trial-variable-name   #levels   CONTRAST (level#) /
SUMMARY;
   RUN;
```

The actual SAS program needed to analyze this data set is:

```
1       PROC GLM  DATA=MIXED;
2          CLASS GROUP;
3          MODEL PRE POST FOLUP = GROUP / NOUNI;
4          REPEATED TIME 3 CONTRAST (1) / SUMMARY;
5          RUN;
```

Notes Regarding the SAS Program

The analysis begins with the PROC GLM statement on line 1. The CLASS statement on line 2 identifies the variable that codes the between-groups factor (that is, the variable that codes the experimental group versus the control group). In this study, the between-groups factor has the SAS variable name GROUP.

In the MODEL statement on line 3, the variables that contain the criterion variable scores appear to the left of the equals sign. The number of variables will equal the number of levels of the repeated-measures variable (these levels are represented as "trial1 trial2... trialn" in the general form). In this study, the repeated-measures variable had three levels (time 1, time 2, and time 3), so the variables that represent these levels (PRE, POST, and FOLUP) appear to the left of the equals sign.

Also in the MODEL statement, the variable that codes the between-groups factor should appear to the right of the equals sign (this will be the same variable name listed in the CLASS statement). In the present study, this between-groups factor is GROUP.

The last entries in the MODEL statement are a slash (which indicates that options are to follow) and the NOUNI option. The NOUNI option suppresses the printing of certain univariate statistics which are of no interest in this analysis.

The REPEATED statement appears next in the program, and in this statement you must list a "trial-variable-name." That is, you must create a new variable name to represent your repeated-measures factor. In this study, the levels of the repeated-measures factor were time 1, time 2, and time 3 (represented as PRE, POST, and FOLUP in the MODEL statement). It therefore follows that an appropriate name for the repeated-measures variable in this study might be TIME. Note that variable name TIME appears as the first entry on the REPEATED statement on line 4 of the preceding program.

The general form for the program shows that the next entry in the REPEATED statement should be "#levels", a number that indicates how many levels are coded under the repeated-measures factor. In the present study, the repeated-measures variable has three levels (time 1, time 2, and time 3), so the number 3 appears to the right of TIME in the REPEATED statement.

The next entry in the REPEATED statement is the "CONTRAST (level#)" option. In a repeated-measures analysis, **contrasts** are planned comparisons between different levels of the repeated-measures variable. The CONTRAST option allows you to choose the types of contrasts that will be made. The number that you specify in the place of "level#" identifies the specific level of the repeated-measures factor against which the other levels will be compared. The preceding program specifies "CONTRAST (1)". A "1" appears in the parentheses with this option, and this means that level 1 under the repeated-measures factor will be contrasted with level 2 and with level 3. In more concrete terms, this means that the mean investment scores obtained at time 1 will be contrasted with those obtained at time 2, and with those obtained at time 3. Unless otherwise instructed, PROC GLM automatically performs tests that contrast the last (n^{th}) level of the repeated-measures variable with each of the preceding levels.

The preceding CONTRAST command requests that both the post-treatment and follow-up scores be compared to the baseline score. However, remember that you should interpret these tests only if the interaction effect is not significant and the TIME effect is significant. If the interaction effect is significant, then other post-hoc procedures will be necessary.

Finally, the REPEATED statement ends with a slash and the SUMMARY option. This SUMMARY option asks for the statistics from the contrasts to appear in the output.

Results from the SAS Output

With LINESIZE=80 and PAGESIZE=60 in the OPTIONS statement, the preceding program would produce 5 pages of output. This output appears here as Output 12.2. The information that appears on each page is summarized here:

- Page 1 provides level information for the between-groups factor (GROUP, in this case).

- Page 2 provides:

    - level information for the repeated-measures factor (TIME, in this case)

    - the results of the multivariate significance test for the main effect of TIME

    - the results of the multivariate significance test for the TIME X GROUP interaction.

- Page 3 provides the results of the significance test for the main effect of GROUP.

- Page 4 provides:

    - the results of the univariate significance tests for the main effect for TIME, and the for the TIME X GROUP interaction

    - information related to the error term in the univariate significance tests that involve the repeated-measures factor (the error degrees of freedom, the type III error sum of squares, and the error mean square)

    - two estimates of the epsilon statistic.

- Page 5 provides the results of the planned comparisons requested with the CONTRAST option.

```
                        The SAS System                           1

                 General Linear Models Procedure
                 General Linear Models Procedure
                    Class Level Information

              Class     Levels     Values

              GROUP        2         1 2


         Number of observations in data set = 20
```

```
                                                                 2

                 General Linear Models Procedure
              Repeated Measures Analysis of Variance
              Repeated Measures Level Information

         Dependent Variable     PRE     POST    FOLUP

            Level of TIME          1       2        3


Manova Test Criteria and Exact F Statistics for the Hypothesis of no TIME Effect
     H = Type III SS&CP Matrix for TIME     E = Error SS&CP Matrix

                    S=1      M=0     N=7.5

 Statistic                 Value        F      Num DF   Den DF   Pr > F

 Wilks' Lambda          0.30518060   19.3524      2        17    0.0001
 Pillai's Trace         0.69481940   19.3524      2        17    0.0001
 Hotelling-Lawley Trace 2.27674828   19.3524      2        17    0.0001
 Roy's Greatest Root    2.27674828   19.3524      2        17    0.0001

              Manova Test Criteria and Exact F Statistics for
                 the Hypothesis of no TIME*GROUP Effect
        H = Type III SS&CP Matrix for TIME*GROUP     E = Error SS&CP Matrix

                    S=1      M=0     N=7.5

 Statistic                 Value        F      Num DF   Den DF   Pr > F

 Wilks' Lambda          0.99234386   0.0656       2        17    0.9368
 Pillai's Trace         0.00765614   0.0656       2        17    0.9368
 Hotelling-Lawley Trace 0.00771521   0.0656       2        17    0.9368
 Roy's Greatest Root    0.00771521   0.0656       2        17    0.9368
```

3

General Linear Models Procedure
Repeated Measures Analysis of Variance
Tests of Hypotheses for Between Subjects Effects

Source	DF	Type III SS	Mean Square	F Value	Pr > F
GROUP	1	2.81666667	2.81666667	0.23	0.6355
Error	18	218.03333333	12.11296296		

4

General Linear Models Procedure
Repeated Measures Analysis of Variance
Univariate Tests of Hypotheses for Within Subject Effects

Source: TIME

					Adj Pr > F	
DF	Type III SS	Mean Square	F Value	Pr > F	G - G	H - F
2	69.63333333	34.81666667	28.84	0.0001	0.0001	0.0001

Source: TIME*GROUP

					Adj Pr > F	
DF	Type III SS	Mean Square	F Value	Pr > F	G - G	H - F
2	0.23333333	0.11666667	0.10	0.9081	0.8568	0.8818

Source: Error(TIME)

DF	Type III SS	Mean Square
36	43.46666667	1.20740741

Greenhouse-Geisser Epsilon = 0.7605
Huynh-Feldt Epsilon = 0.8623

5

General Linear Models Procedure
Repeated Measures Analysis of Variance
Analysis of Variance of Contrast Variables

TIME.N represents the contrast between the nth level of TIME and the 1st

Contrast Variable: TIME.2

Source	DF	Type III SS	Mean Square	F Value	Pr > F
MEAN	1	92.45000000	92.45000000	27.69	0.0001
GROUP	1	0.45000000	0.45000000	0.13	0.7178
Error	18	60.10000000	3.33888889		

```
Contrast Variable: TIME.3

Source                 DF      Type III SS      Mean Square    F Value    Pr > F

MEAN                    1     115.20000000     115.20000000      40.98    0.0001
GROUP                   1       0.20000000       0.20000000       0.07    0.7927

Error                  18      50.60000000       2.81111111
```

Output 12.2: Results of the Two-Way Mixed-Design ANOVA with a Nonsignificant Interaction

Steps in Interpreting the Output

1. Make sure that everything looks right. As is always the case, you should review the output for possible signs of problems before interpreting the results. Most of these steps with a mixed-design ANOVA are similar to those used with between-groups designs (e.g., check the number of observations listed on page 1 to make certain data from all subjects were used in the analysis, and check the number of levels that appear under each predictor variable). Because most of these steps were already discussed in earlier chapters, they are not reviewed here.

2. Determine whether the interaction term is statistically significant. As was discussed in Chapter 11, when an analysis included a repeated-measures factor, the SAS output includes results of univariate, modified univariate, and multivariate ANOVAs. The section "Further Notes On Repeated-Measures Analyses" from that chapter reviews some of the basic issues to consider when choosing between univariate versus multivariate statistics.

Interpretation of the current study is somewhat more complicated than the interpretation of the one-factor design described in Chapter 11, because the current mixed-design requires that you interpret the effects of both a between-groups factor and an interaction, in addition to the effect of the repeated-measures factor. To simplify matters, this chapter follows the same general procedure recommended in Chapter 9, in which you first check for interactions before proceeding to test for main effects and post-hoc analyses.

As discussed in Chapter 9, the first step in interpreting a two-factor ANOVA is to check the interaction effect. If the interaction effect is not statistically significant, then you may proceed with interpretation of main effects. You should interpret the univariate test of the interaction effect first, and this univariate test appears on page 4 of Output 12.2. On the left side of page 4, find the heading "Source: TIME*GROUP"; the information relevant to the interaction appears in this section. Under the heading "F Value", you can see that the univariate F for the TIME X GROUP interaction is 0.10. With 2 and 36 degrees of freedom, this F has an associated p value of .91, and so is clearly nonsignificant.

The next step is to check the multivariate test for the interaction. In most analyses, the univariate and multivariate tests yield tests with similar *p* values. The results of these two approaches are likely to vary only if the assumptions for the univariate test are grossly violated, or possibly if the time variables are highly intercorrelated. The results of the multivariate test for the interaction appear on page 2 of Output 12.2. Find the section on this page headed "Manova Test Criterion and Exact *F* Statistics for the Hypothesis of no TIME*GROUP Effect". To the right of the heading "Wilks' Lambda", you can see that the MANOVA yielded an *F* value of 0.0656, and a corresponding *p* value of approximately .94. Once again, you fail to reject the null hypothesis of a TIME*GROUP interaction.

The primary hypothesis for this study required a significant interaction, but you now know that the present data do not support the existence of such an interaction. If you were actually conducting this research project, your analyses might terminate at this point. However, in order to illustrate additional steps in the analysis of data from a mixed-design, this section will instead proceed with the tests for main effects.

3. Determine if the group effect is statistically significant. In this chapter, the term **group effect** is used to refer to the effect of the between-groups factor. In the present study, the SAS variable named GROUP represented this effect.

The group effect is of no real interest in the present investment-model investigation, since support for the study's central hypothesis required a significant interaction. Nonetheless, it is still useful to plot group means and review the statistic for the group effect in order to validate the methodology used to assign subjects to groups. For example, if the effect for GROUP proved to be significant, and if the means for one of the treatment groups were consistently higher than the corresponding mean for the other group (particularly at time 1) it could indicate that the two groups were not equivalent at the beginning of the study. This might suggest that there was some type of bias in the selection process. Such a finding could invalidate any other results from the study.

The significance test for the group effect appears on page 3 of Output 12.2. You can see that the obtained *F* value for the GROUP effect is only 0.23, which, with 1 and 18 degrees of freedom, is nonsignificant (the *p* value for this *F* is quite large at 0.6355). This indicates that there was not an overall difference between experimental and control groups with respect to their mean investment scores. This finding is also illustrated by Figure 12.8, which shows that there is very little separation between the line for the experimental group and the line for the control group.

4. Determine if the time effect is statistically significant. In this chapter, the term **time effect** is used to refer to the effect of the repeated-measures factor. Remember that the SAS variable named TIME was used to code this factor. A main effect for TIME would suggest that there was a significant difference between investment scores obtained at one time, and the investment scores obtained at least one other time during study (i.e., that the scores obtained at time 2 were significantly higher than those obtained at time 1).

The univariate test for the TIME effect appears on page 4 of Output 12.2, under the section headed "Source: TIME". Under the heading "F Value", you can see that the univariate F for the TIME effect is 28.84. With 2 and 36 degrees of freedom, this F is significant at $p < .0001$.

The multivariate test for the TIME effect appears on page 2 of Output 12.2, under the heading "Manova Test Criteria and Exact F Statistics for the Hypothesis of no TIME Effect". To the right of "Wilks' Lambda", you can see that the multivariate F for the TIME effect is 19.35, which, with 2 and 17 degrees of freedom, is also significant at $p < .0001$. Clearly, there is a significant effect for the TIME variable.

The group means plotted in Figure 12.8 are helpful in interpreting this TIME effect. The trend displayed by the means suggests that time 2 scores may be significantly higher than time 1 scores, and time 3 scores may also be significantly higher than time 1 scores. A later section shows how to interpret the results requested by the CONTRAST option to see if these differences are statistically significant.

5. Prepare your own version of the ANOVA summary table. Table 12.1 summarizes the preceding analysis of variance:

Table 12.1

ANOVA Summary Table for Study Investigating Changes in Investments
Following an Experimental Manipulation (Nonsignificant Interaction)

Source	df	SS	MS	F
Between subjects	19	220.85		
Group (A)	1	2.82	2.82	0.23
Residual between	18	218.03	12.11	
Within subjects	40	113.33		
Time (B)	2	69.63	34.82	28.84 *
A X B Interaction	2	0.23	0.12	0.10
Residual within	36	43.47	1.21	
Total	59	334.18		

Note: N = 20.
* p < .001

6. Review the results of the contrasts. The program presented earlier included the following REPEATED statement:

```
4          REPEATED TIME 3 CONTRAST (1) / SUMMARY;
```

The keyword CONTRAST in this statement was followed by a "1" in parentheses. This requests that level 1 under the TIME variable be contrasted with the other levels under TIME. In other words, it requests that the mean investment score observed at time 1 be contrasted with the mean investment score at time 2, and that time 1 also be contrasted with time 3.

The resulting contrast analyses appear on page 5 of Output 12.2. The analysis that compares time 1 investment scores with time 2 scores appears under the heading "Contrast Variable: TIME.2". The information of interest appears to the right of the heading "MEAN". You can see that this comparison results in an F ratio of 27.69, which is significant at $p < .0001$. You may therefore reject the null hypothesis that there is no difference between time 1 investment scores and time 2 investment scores in the population. The nature of the means displayed in Figure 12.8 show that time 2 scores were significantly higher than time 1 scores.

The analysis that compares time 1 to time 3 appears under the heading "Contrast Variable: TIME.3". With an F ratio of 40.98, it is clear that investment scores at time 3 are also significantly higher than time 1 scores ($p < .0001$).

Summarizing the Results of the Analysis

The results of this mixed-design analysis could be summarized using the standard statistical interpretation format presented earlier in this text:

A) Statement of the problem
B) Nature of the variables
C) Statistical test
D) Null hypothesis (H_0)
E) Alternative hypothesis (H_1)
F) Obtained statistic
G) Obtained probability (p) value
H) Conclusion regarding the null hypothesis
I) ANOVA summary table
J) Figure representing the results

This summary could be performed three times: once for the null hypothesis of no interaction in the population, once for the null hypothesis of no main effect for GROUP, and once for the null hypothesis of no main effect for TIME. As this format has been already described, it does not appear again here.

Formal Description of Results for a Paper

Below is one way that you could summarize the present results for a published paper. Notice that the names of the independent variables (time and group) are not capitalized, although the first letter of each variable's name is capitalized in the expression "Group X Time interaction".

> Results were analyzed using a two-way ANOVA with repeated measures on one factor. The Group X Time interaction was not significant, $F(2,36) = 0.10$, $p = .91$. The main effect of group also was not significant, $F(1,18) = 0.23$, $p = .63$. This analysis did reveal a significant effect for time, $F(2,36) = 28.84$, $p < .001$. Post-hoc contrasts found that investment scores at the post-treatment and follow-up times were significantly higher than the scores observed at baseline (time 1) ($p < .001$).

Example with a Significant Interaction

Remember that your initial hypothesis was that the investment scores would increase more for the experimental group than for the control group, and that, to be supported, this hypothesis required a significant TIME X GROUP interaction. This section presents the results of an analysis of a different set of fictitious data: data that will provide the needed interaction. You will see that it is necessary to perform a number of different follow-up analyses when you obtain a significant interaction in a mixed-design ANOVA.

Output 12.3 presents the results of an analysis in which the TIME X GROUP interaction is significant. The following section shows how to interpret the output and perform the necessary tests for simple effects.

```
                        The SAS System                              1

                General Linear Models Procedure
                   Class Level Information

                Class     Levels    Values

                GROUP        2       1 2


            Number of observations in data set = 20
```

2

General Linear Models Procedure
Repeated Measures Analysis of Variance
Repeated Measures Level Information

Dependent Variable	PRE	POST	FOLUP
Level of TIME	1	2	3

Manova Test Criteria and Exact F Statistics for the Hypothesis of no TIME Effect
H = Type III SS&CP Matrix for TIME   E = Error SS&CP Matrix

S=1   M=0   N=7.5

Statistic	Value	F	Num DF	Den DF	Pr > F
Wilks' Lambda	0.57520118	6.2774	2	17	0.0091
Pillai's Trace	0.42479882	6.2774	2	17	0.0091
Hotelling-Lawley Trace	0.73852217	6.2774	2	17	0.0091
Roy's Greatest Root	0.73852217	6.2774	2	17	0.0091

Manova Test Criteria and Exact F Statistics for
the Hypothesis of no TIME*GROUP Effect
H = Type III SS&CP Matrix for TIME*GROUP   E = Error SS&CP Matrix

S=1   M=0   N=7.5

Statistic	Value	F	Num DF	Den DF	Pr > F
Wilks' Lambda	0.72221432	3.2694	2	17	0.0629
Pillai's Trace	0.27778568	3.2694	2	17	0.0629
Hotelling-Lawley Trace	0.38463054	3.2694	2	17	0.0629
Roy's Greatest Root	0.38463054	3.2694	2	17	0.0629

3

General Linear Models Procedure
Repeated Measures Analysis of Variance
Tests of Hypotheses for Between Subjects Effects

Source	DF	Type III SS	Mean Square	F Value	Pr > F
GROUP	1	2.40000000	2.40000000	0.20	0.6634
Error	18	220.66666667	12.25925926		

4

General Linear Models Procedure
Repeated Measures Analysis of Variance
Univariate Tests of Hypotheses for Within Subject Effects

Source: TIME

DF	Type III SS	Mean Square	F Value	Pr > F	Adj Pr > F G - G	H - F
2	20.63333333	10.31666667	8.38	0.0010	0.0030	0.0019

Source: TIME*GROUP

DF	Type III SS	Mean Square	F Value	Pr > F	Adj Pr > F G - G	H - F
2	9.70000000	4.85000000	3.94	0.0284	0.0414	0.0352

Source: Error(TIME)

DF	Type III SS	Mean Square
36	44.33333333	1.23148148

Greenhouse-Geisser Epsilon = 0.7625
Huynh-Feldt Epsilon = 0.8650

5

General Linear Models Procedure
Repeated Measures Analysis of Variance
Analysis of Variance of Contrast Variables

TIME.N represents the contrast between the nth level of TIME and the 1st

Contrast Variable: TIME.2

Source	DF	Type III SS	Mean Square	F Value	Pr > F
MEAN	1	24.20000000	24.20000000	7.03	0.0163
GROUP	1	9.80000000	9.80000000	2.85	0.1089
Error	18	62.00000000	3.44444444		

Contrast Variable: TIME.3

Source	DF	Type III SS	Mean Square	F Value	Pr > F
MEAN	1	36.45000000	36.45000000	12.99	0.0020
GROUP	1	18.05000000	18.05000000	6.43	0.0207
Error	18	50.50000000	2.80555556		

```
                                                                          6
------------------------------ GROUP=1 ------------------------------------


   Variable   N        Mean        Std Dev      Minimum       Maximum
   ---------------------------------------------------------------------
   SUB       10     5.5000000     3.0276504    1.0000000    10.0000000
   PRE       10     9.8000000     2.2509257    7.0000000    14.0000000
   POST      10    10.2000000     2.3944380    7.0000000    15.0000000
   FOLUP     10    10.2000000     1.6865481    8.0000000    12.0000000
   ---------------------------------------------------------------------



------------------------------ GROUP=2 ------------------------------------


   Variable   N        Mean        Std Dev      Minimum       Maximum
   ---------------------------------------------------------------------
   SUB       10    15.5000000     3.0276504   11.0000000    20.0000000
   PRE       10     9.1000000     2.0248457    6.0000000    13.0000000
   POST      10    10.9000000     2.4698178    8.0000000    14.0000000
   FOLUP     10    11.4000000     2.3664319    7.0000000    14.0000000
   ---------------------------------------------------------------------
```

Output 12.3: Results of Two-Way Mixed Design ANOVA with a Significant Interaction

Steps in Interpreting the Output

1. Determine whether the interaction term is statistically significant. Once you have scanned the results in the usual manner to verify that there are no obvious errors in the program or data set, you should check the appropriate statistics to see whether the interaction between the between-groups factor and the repeated-measures factor is significant. The univariate results appear on page 4 of Output 12.3, in the section headed "Source: TIME*GROUP". The F value for this interaction term is 3.94. With 2 and 36 degrees of freedom, the unadjusted p value for this F is .0284, and the adjusted p value is .0414 (Greenhouse-Geisser adjustment). The interaction is therefore significant.

This finding is consistent with the hypothesis that the relationship between the TIME variable and investment scores is different for the two experimental groups. To determine whether the experimental group shows greater increases in investments than the control group (as hypothesized), you must plot the interaction.

2. Plot the interaction. To plot the interaction, you once again need to obtain mean investment scores for each of the two groups at each level of TIME. You can obtain these means by using PROC MEANS with a BY GROUP statement, as follows:

```
1     PROC SORT DATA=MIXED;
2         BY GROUP;
3         RUN;
4
5     PROC MEANS DATA=MIXED;
6         BY GROUP;
7         RUN;
```

Chapter 9 shows how you can use the results from this MEANS procedure to plot an interaction. The means from the present data set appear on page 6 of Output 12.3, and are plotted in Figure 12.9.

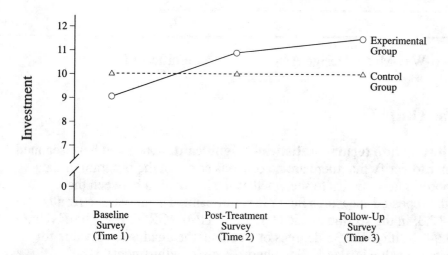

Figure 12.9: Significant TIME X GROUP Interaction Obtained in the Analysis of the Investment Model Data

Notice that the line for the experimental group in Figure 12.9 (the solid line) is not perfectly parallel to the line for the control group (the broken line). This is what you would expect with a significant TIME X GROUP interaction. You can see that the line for the control group is relatively flat. There does not appear to be much of an increase in perceived investment from time 1 to time 2 to time 3. In contrast, notice the angle that is displayed by the line for the experimental group. There is a relatively large increase in investment size from time 1 to time 2, and another slight increase from time 2 to time 3.

These findings are consistent with the hypothesis that there would be a bigger increase in investment scores in the experimental group than in the control group. But to have more confidence in this conclusion, you must test for simple effects.

3. Test for simple effects. When you test for **simple effects**, you determine whether there is a significant relationship between one predictor variable and the criterion for subjects at one level of the second predictor variable. The concept of simple effects first appeared in Chapter 9.

For example, in the present study you might be interested in seeing whether there is a significant relationship between TIME and the investment variable among those subjects in the experimental group. If there is, you could state that there is a simple effect for TIME at the experimental group level of GROUP.

To understand the meaning of this, consider just the solid line in Figure 12.9 (the line that represents the experimental group). This line plots investment scores for the experimental group at three points in time. If there is a simple effect for TIME in the experimental group, it means that investment scores obtained at one point in time are significantly higher than investment scores obtained at at least one other point in time. If the marriage encounter program really is effective, you would expect to see a simple effect for TIME in the experimental group: mean investment scores should improve over time in this group. You would not expect to see a simple effect for TIME in the control group, since they did not experience the program.

Testing for simple effects following a mixed-design ANOVA is relatively straightforward. To test for the simple effects of the repeated-measures factor (TIME, in this case), it is necessary to

- divide the subjects into subgroups, based on their classification under the group variable (GROUP, in this case)

- perform a one-way ANOVA with one repeated-measures factor on just those subjects in the first treatment group

- repeat this repeated-measures ANOVA for each of the remaining subgroups.

For the present study, this means that you first divide the subjects into experimental and control groups. Next, using data from just the experimental group, you perform a one-way repeated measures ANOVA in which investment scores are the criterion and TIME is the predictor variable. You then repeat this analysis using data from the control group. You would compute and interpret these ANOVAs according to the procedures described in Chapter 11.

Now for the specifics: the first step in this process is to divide subjects into the experimental group and the control group. You do this with the following statements:

```
1       DATA CONTROL;
2          SET MIXED;
3          IF GROUP=1 THEN OUTPUT;
4          RUN;
```

```
5
6       DATA EXP;
7          SET MIXED;
8          IF GROUP=2 THEN OUTPUT;
9          RUN;
```

Lines 1-4 of the preceding program create a new data set called CONTROL. It begins by setting the data set equal to the MIXED data set, but retains only those subjects whose score on GROUP is equal to 1 (see line 3). Therefore, the data set called CONTROL will contain only data from the control group. In the same way, you can see that lines 6-9 create a new data set called EXP that contain only data from subjects in the experimental group (i.e., those subjects with a score on GROUP equal to 2).

Later in the same program, you will add the lines to test the simple effect for TIME in the control group. The following lines accomplish this.

```
1       PROC GLM  DATA=CONTROL;
2          MODEL PRE POST FOLUP =  / NOUNI;
3          REPEATED TIME 3 CONTRAST (1) / SUMMARY;
4          RUN;
```

In line 1 of the preceding program, the DATA=CONTROL option requests that the analysis be performed using the data set that contains only data from the control group. To test this simple effect in the experimental group, it is necessary only to change the data set that is named in this line:

```
1       PROC GLM  DATA=EXP;
2          MODEL PRE POST FOLUP =  / NOUNI;
3          REPEATED TIME 3 CONTRAST (1) / SUMMARY;
4          RUN;
```

Therefore, the complete program (minus data input) that creates the two new data sets and performs the two tests for simple effects is as follows:

```
1       DATA CONTROL;
2          SET MIXED;
3          IF GROUP=1 THEN OUTPUT;
4          RUN;
5
6       DATA EXP;
7          SET MIXED;
```

```
8      IF GROUP=2 THEN OUTPUT;
9      RUN;
10
11    PROC GLM  DATA=CONTROL;
12       MODEL PRE POST FOLUP =  / NOUNI;
13       REPEATED TIME 3 CONTRAST (1) / SUMMARY;
14       RUN;
15
16    PROC GLM  DATA=EXP;
17       MODEL PRE POST FOLUP =  / NOUNI;
18       REPEATED TIME 3 CONTRAST (1) / SUMMARY;
19       RUN;
```

The results of these two ANOVAs would constitute tests of the simple effects of TIME for each level of GROUP. See Chapter 11 for guidelines in interpreting the results. The results of this analysis for the current study are reproduced here as Ouput 12.4.

```
                         The SAS System                          7

                   General Linear Models Procedure

               Number of observations in data set = 10
```

```
                                                                 8

                   General Linear Models Procedure
                   Repeated Measures Analysis of Variance
                   Repeated Measures Level Information

         Dependent Variable        PRE     POST    FOLUP

             Level of TIME           1       2       3


Manova Test Criteria and Exact F Statistics for the Hypothesis of no TIME Effect
      H = Type III SS&CP Matrix for TIME    E = Error SS&CP Matrix

                      S=1      M=0      N=3

   Statistic                 Value         F      Num DF    Den DF  Pr > F

   Wilks' Lambda           0.91884058    0.3533      2         8    0.7128
   Pillai's Trace          0.08115942    0.3533      2         8    0.7128
   Hotelling-Lawley Trace  0.08832808    0.3533      2         8    0.7128
   Roy's Greatest Root     0.08832808    0.3533      2         8    0.7128
```

9

General Linear Models Procedure
Repeated Measures Analysis of Variance
Univariate Tests of Hypotheses for Within Subject Effects

Source: TIME

DF	Type III SS	Mean Square	F Value	Pr > F	Adj Pr > F G - G	Adj Pr > F H - F
2	1.06666667	0.53333333	0.47	0.6302	0.6012	0.6302

Source: Error(TIME)

DF	Type III SS	Mean Square
18	20.26666667	1.12592593

Greenhouse-Geisser Epsilon = 0.8498
Huynh-Feldt Epsilon = 1.0270

10

General Linear Models Procedure
Repeated Measures Analysis of Variance
Analysis of Variance of Contrast Variables

TIME.N represents the contrast between the nth level of TIME and the 1st

Contrast Variable: TIME.2

Source	DF	Type III SS	Mean Square	F Value	Pr > F
MEAN	1	1.60000000	1.60000000	0.51	0.4945
Error	9	28.40000000	3.15555556		

Contrast Variable: TIME.3

Source	DF	Type III SS	Mean Square	F Value	Pr > F
MEAN	1	1.60000000	1.60000000	0.78	0.3994
Error	9	18.40000000	2.04444444		

11

General Linear Models Procedure

Number of observations in data set = 10

12

General Linear Models Procedure
Repeated Measures Analysis of Variance
Repeated Measures Level Information

Dependent Variable	PRE	POST	FOLUP
Level of TIME	1	2	3

Manova Test Criteria and Exact F Statistics for the Hypothesis of no TIME Effect
H = Type III SS&CP Matrix for TIME   E = Error SS&CP Matrix

S=1   M=0   N=3

Statistic	Value	F	Num DF	Den DF	Pr > F
Wilks' Lambda	0.35571178	7.2451	2	8	0.0160
Pillai's Trace	0.64428822	7.2451	2	8	0.0160
Hotelling-Lawley Trace	1.81126482	7.2451	2	8	0.0160
Roy's Greatest Root	1.81126482	7.2451	2	8	0.0160

13

General Linear Models Procedure
Repeated Measures Analysis of Variance
Univariate Tests of Hypotheses for Within Subject Effects

Source: TIME

DF	Type III SS	Mean Square	F Value	Pr > F	Adj Pr > F G - G	H - F
2	29.26666667	14.63333333	10.94	0.0008	0.0043	0.0031

Source: Error(TIME)

DF	Type III SS	Mean Square
18	24.06666667	1.33703704

Greenhouse-Geisser Epsilon = 0.6519
Huynh-Feldt Epsilon = 0.7170

```
                                                                        14
                    General Linear Models Procedure
                  Repeated Measures Analysis of Variance
                  Analysis of Variance of Contrast Variables

      TIME.N represents the contrast between the nth level of TIME and the 1st

Contrast Variable: TIME.2

Source                  DF      Type III SS     Mean Square    F Value     Pr > F

MEAN                     1      32.40000000     32.40000000       8.68     0.0163

Error                    9      33.60000000      3.73333333

Contrast Variable: TIME.3

Source                  DF      Type III SS     Mean Square    F Value     Pr > F

MEAN                     1      52.90000000     52.90000000      14.83     0.0039

Error                    9      32.10000000      3.56666667
```

Output 12.4: Results of Tests for Simple Effects of TIME among Subjects in the Control Group (Output Pages 7-10) and Subjects in the Experimental Group (Output Pages 11-14)

The test of the simple effect of TIME at the control group level of GROUP appears on pages 7-10 of Output 12.4. The results of the univariate test appear on output page 9, which shows an F value of 0.47. With 2 and 18 degrees of freedom, the simple effect for TIME in the control group is nonsignificant ($p = .601$).

The test of the simple effect of TIME at the experimental group level of GROUP appears on pages 11-14 of Output 12.4. The results for the univariate test appear on output page 13, which shows an F value of 10.94. With 2 and 18 degrees of freedom, the simple effect for TIME in the experimental group is significant ($p < .005$).

Since the simple effect for TIME was significant in the experimental group, you could now go on to interpret the results of the planned contrasts that appear on page 14 of Output 12.4. These contrasts show that the there was a significant difference between mean scores obtained at time 1 versus those obtained at time 2, $F(1, 9) = 8.68$, $p > .02$, and that there was also a significant difference between mean scores obtained at time 1 versus time 3, $F(1, 9) = 14.83$, $p > .004$.

Although the preceding seems fairly straightforward, there are actually two complications in the interpretation of these results. First, you are now performing multiple tests (one test for each level under the group factor), and this means that the significance level you have initially chosen will have to be adjusted so that your experimentwise probability of making a type I error does not get out of hand. Looney and Stanley (1989) have recommended dividing the initial alpha

(.05 in the present study) by the number of tests to be conducted, and using the result as the required significance level for each test. For example, assume that in this investigation your alpha is initially set at .05. You are performing two tests for simple effects, and so this initial alpha must be divided by 2, resulting in an actual alpha of .025. When you conduct your tests for simple effects, you conclude that an effect is significant only if the *p* value that appears in the output is less than .025. This approach to adjusting alpha is viewed as a very rigorous adjustment, and you may want to consider alternative approaches for protecting the experiment-wise error rate.

The second complication involves the error term used in the analyses. With the preceding approach, the error term used in computing the *F* ratio for a simple effect is the mean square error from the one-way ANOVA based on data from just one group. An alternative approach is to use the mean square error from the "omnibus" test that includes the between-groups factor, the repeated-measures factor, and the interaction term (from Output 12.3). This second approach has the advantage of using the same yardstick (the same mean square error) in the computation of both simple effects, and some authors recommend it when the mean squares for the various groups are homogeneous. On the other hand, the approach just presented in which different error terms are used in the different tests has the advantage (or disadvantage, depending upon your perspective), of providing a slightly more conservative *F* test, since it involves fewer degrees of freedom for the denominator. For a discussion of the alternative approaches for testing simple effects, see Keppel (1982, pp. 428-431), and Winer (1971, pp. 527-528).

So far, this section has discussed simple effects for only the TIME factor. It is also possible to perform tests for simple effects for the GROUP factor. You can test three simple effects for GROUP in the present study. Specifically, you may determine whether there is a significant difference between the experimental group and the control group with respect to

* investment scores obtained at time 1

* investment scores obtained at time 2

* investment scores obtained at time 3.

To test a simple effect for GROUP, you simply perform a one-way ANOVA with one between-groups factor. In this analysis, the criterion variable is the SAS variable that includes investment scores at a specific point in time (such as time 1). The predictor variable is GROUP.

For example, assume that you want to test the simple effect for GROUP with respect to investment scores taken at time 1. The investment scores obtained at time 1 are contained in a variable named PRE (as discussed earlier). The following program tests this simple effect:

```
1       PROC GLM DATA=MIXED;
2           CLASS GROUP;
3           MODEL PRE = GROUP ;
4           RUN;
```

To test the simple effect for GROUP with respect to investment scores observed at time 2, it is only necessary to change the MODEL statement in the preceding program so that the variable PRE is replaced with the variable POST (which includes the time 2 scores). Similarly, you may test the simple effect at time 3 by using FOLUP as the criterion variable. These lines perform these analyses:

```
5       PROC GLM DATA=MIXED;
6           CLASS GROUP;
7           MODEL POST = GROUP ;
8           RUN;
9
10      PROC GLM DATA=MIXED;
11          CLASS GROUP;
12          MODEL FOLUP = GROUP ;
13          RUN;
```

The results produced by the preceding lines appear here as Output 12.5.

                              The SAS System   15

                    General Linear Models Procedure
                        Class Level Information

                    Class   Levels   Values

                    GROUP   2   1 2

            Number of observations in data set = 20

                                                                                16

                    General Linear Models Procedure

Dependent Variable: PRE

| | | Sum of | Mean | | |
Source	DF	Squares	Square	F Value	Pr > F
Model	1	2.45000000	2.45000000	0.53	0.4741
Error	18	82.50000000	4.58333333		
Corrected Total	19	84.95000000			

	R-Square	C.V.	Root MSE	PRE Mean
	0.028840	22.65473	2.1408721	9.4500000

Source	DF	Type I SS	Mean Square	F Value	Pr > F
GROUP	1	2.45000000	2.45000000	0.53	0.4741

Source	DF	Type III SS	Mean Square	F Value	Pr > F
GROUP	1	2.45000000	2.45000000	0.53	0.4741

17

General Linear Models Procedure
Class Level Information

Class	Levels	Values
GROUP	2	1 2

Number of observations in data set = 20

18

General Linear Models Procedure

Dependent Variable: POST

Source	DF	Sum of Squares	Mean Square	F Value	Pr > F
Model	1	2.45000000	2.45000000	0.41	0.5280
Error	18	106.50000000	5.91666667		
Corrected Total	19	108.95000000			

	R-Square	C.V.	Root MSE	POST Mean
	0.022487	23.05611	2.4324199	10.550000

Source	DF	Type I SS	Mean Square	F Value	Pr > F
GROUP	1	2.45000000	2.45000000	0.41	0.5280

Source	DF	Type III SS	Mean Square	F Value	Pr > F
GROUP	1	2.45000000	2.45000000	0.41	0.5280

19

```
                  General Linear Models Procedure
                     Class Level Information

                  Class     Levels     Values

                  GROUP        2        1 2


         Number of observations in data set = 20
```

20

```
                  General Linear Models Procedure

Dependent Variable: FOLUP
                               Sum of            Mean
Source               DF       Squares          Square    F Value    Pr > F

Model                 1    7.20000000      7.20000000       1.71    0.2080

Error                18   76.00000000      4.22222222

Corrected Total      19   83.20000000


            R-Square            C.V.        Root MSE           FOLUP Mean

            0.086538         19.02597       2.0548047           10.800000


Source               DF     Type I SS    Mean Square    F Value    Pr > F

GROUP                 1    7.20000000     7.20000000       1.71    0.2080

Source               DF   Type III SS    Mean Square    F Value    Pr > F

GROUP                 1    7.20000000     7.20000000       1.71    0.2080
```

Output 12.5: Results of Tests for Simple Effects of GROUP for Data Gathered at Time 1 (Output pages 15-16), Time 2 (Output pages 17-18), and Time 3 (Output pages 19-20)

You can assess the simple effects for GROUP at the time 1 level of TIME by reviewing pages 15-16 of Output 12.5. These pages show the results of the analysis in which PRE was the criterion variable. In the section for the type III sum of square at the bottom of output page 16, you can see that the F for this simple effect is only 0.53 which, with 1 and 18 degrees of freedom, is nonsignificant. In other words, the simple effect for GROUP at the the time 1 level of TIME is nonsignificant. By the same token, you can see that the simple effect for GROUP is also nonsignificant at time 2 ($F = 0.41$, $p = .528$ from output page 18), and at time 3 ($F = 1.71$, $p = .208$ from output page 20).

To step back and get the big picture concerning GROUP X TIME interaction discovered in this analysis, it becomes clear that the interaction is due to a simple effect for TIME at the experimental group level of GROUP. On the other hand, there is no evidence of a simple effect for GROUP at any level of TIME.

4. Prepare your own version of the ANOVA summary table. Table 12.2 presents the ANOVA summary table from the analysis.

Table 12.2

ANOVA Summary Table for Study Investigating the Change
in Investment Following an Experimental Manipulation (Significant
Interaction)

Source	df	SS	MS	F
Between subjects	19	223.07		
Group (A)	1	2.40	2.40	0.20
Residual between	18	220.67	12.26	
Within subjects	40	74.66		
Time (B)	2	20.63	10.32	8.38 **
A X B Interaction	2	9.70	4.85	3.94 *
Residual within	36	44.33	1.23	
Total	59	297.73		

Note: N = 20.

* p<.05, ** p<.01

Formal Description of Results for a Paper

>   Results were analyzed using a two-way ANOVA with
> repeated measures on one factor. The Group X Time
> interaction was significant, $F(2,36) = 3.94$, $p < .05$.
> Tests for simple effects showed that the mean investment
> scores for the control group displayed no significant
> differences across time, $F(2,18) = 0.47$, $p > .60$. However,
> the experimental group did display significant increases
> in perceived investment across time, $F(2,18) = 10.94$, $p <
> .005$. Post-hoc contrasts showed that the experimental
> group has significantly higher scores at post-test
> ($F[1,9] = 8.68$, $p < .02$) and follow-up ($F[1,9] = 14.83$,
> $p < .004$) compared to baseline.

Use of Other Post-Hoc Tests with the Repeated-Measures Variable

In some instances the contrasts described above will not be ideal and you will need other multiple comparison tests will for the interpretation of the analysis. For example, if there were ten levels of the repeated-measures factor, and this factor was significant in the overall analysis, you might need to perform a multiple comparison procedure to determine which levels are different from each other. Although you could do this by using a large number of CONTRAST statements, this approach would be undesirable because each contrast is equivalent to a paired-samples *t* test. A multiple comparison procedure that controls for experiment-wise error rate would be preferable.

Several such tests are available in SAS/STAT for this situation (e.g., the Bonferroni test, the Scheffe test, the Tukey test). However, you cannot use these tests with the repeated-measures factor when you use the REPEATED statement. To utilize these tests, you must name the variable being analyzed in the MODEL statement. Fortunately, SAS can compute the ANOVA in a way that allows for use of these multiple comparison tests in analyzing a repeated factor. Essentially, this approach requires that the analysis be performed without use of the REPEATED statement. This procedure for conducting a repeated-measures analysis is somewhat more cumbersome than the approach described previously, and requires that the data set be restructured.

Restructuring the Data Set

To perform an ANOVA with a repeated-measures factor without using the REPEATED statement, you must create a new variable. This variable will function in the same way as the variable named in the REPEATED statement. In the example just presented, the new variable would most appropriately be named TIME. Each subject would have three observations, one with TIME=PRE, one with TIME=POST, and one with TIME=FOLUP. A value for a variable named INVEST would be paired with each level of TIME for every subject. In other words, instead of coding the three values of the criterion variable by using three variables (i.e., PRE, POST, FOLUP), each value will need two variables to code it. One variable describes the level under the repeated-measures factor (TIME), and the other gives the specific value on the criterion (INVEST).

For purposes of illustration, assume that you have created a data set in the manner that was illustrated in the earlier sections of this chapter. That is, you have one line of data for each subject. The data for one fictitious subject appear here (the subject's data appear below the corresponding variable names):

SUBJ	GROUP	PRE	POST	FOLUP
1	1	8	10	10

To use SAS/STAT multiple comparison procedures on the repeated-measures variable (TIME), you must restructure this subject's data so that they instead appear in the following way:

SUBJ	GROUP	TIME	INVEST
1	1	PRE	8
1	1	POST	10
1	1	FOLUP	10

If you were actually to go into a file and restructure the data set in this way by hand, it would be a tedious chore that would take a very long time. Fortunately, it is possible to restructure the data very easily by instead including the appropriate data manipulation statements as part of your SAS program. The program lines that would restructure the current data set are:

```
1     DATA MIXED1;
2        SET MIXED;
3        TIME='PRE';
4        INVEST=PRE;
5        OUTPUT;
6        TIME='POST';
7        INVEST=POST;
8        OUTPUT;
9        TIME='FOLUP';
10       INVEST=FOLUP;
11       OUTPUT;
12       RUN;
```

These lines create a restructured data set called MIXED1 (see line 1 from above). Because the data set has been restructured, it is necessary to write a very different PROC GLM program to analyze it. The following section shows how to do this.

An Alternative SAS Program to Perform the Analysis

Once you have created the restructured data set, you can analyze it with the following SAS program:

```
1    PROC GLM DATA=MIXED1;
2       CLASSES SUBJ GROUP TIME;
3       MODEL INVEST = GROUP SUBJ(GROUP) TIME GROUP*TIME
4       TIME*SUBJ(GROUP);
5       TEST H=GROUP      E=SUBJ(GROUP);
6       TEST H=TIME GROUP*TIME     E=TIME*SUBJ(GROUP);
7       MEANS TIME / TUKEY;
8       RUN;
```

Because this is a mixed design with both between-subjects factors and repeated-measures factors, different error terms are needed to compute the various effects. The REPEATED statement (described earlier) automatically used the appropriate error term in the computation of these effects. However, since the new program does not use the REPEATED statement, you must specifically request the appropriate error term in the program itself. This is why the TEST statements appear. The between-subjects error term is "SUBJ(GROUP)", and this is used in the test of the GROUP effect (see line 5). The within-subject error term is "TIME*SUBJ(GROUP)", and this is used for the TIME effect and the TIME X GROUP interaction effect (see line 6).

The MEANS statement requests the TUKEY multiple comparison procedure to analyze differences among the levels of TIME. This statement is provided as an example, and you may request other tests instead. Ordinarily, investigators do not know in advance which post-hoc tests they need.

Conclusion

In summary, the two-way mixed design ANOVA is appropriate for a type experimental design that is frequently used in behavioral research. In the most common form of this design, subjects are divided on a group factor, and provide repeated measures on the criterion variable at various time intervals. This analysis is easily handled by PROC GLM. Conducting the analysis with the REPEATED statement offers the advantage that the error terms for the various effects are automatically selected by the program, while conducting the analysis without the REPEATED statement allows you to request a number of post-hoc multiple comparison procedures.

Appendix: Assumptions Underlying Factorial ANOVA with Repeated-Measures Factors and Between-Groups Factors

All of the statistical assumptions associated with a one-way ANOVA, repeated-measures design are also required for a factorial ANOVA with repeated-measures factors and between-groups factors. In addition, the latter design also requires a homogeneity of covariances assumption for the multivariate test, and the homogeneity assumption as well as two symmetry conditions for the univariate test. This section reviews the assumptions for the one-way repeated measures ANOVA, and introduces the new assumptions for the factorial ANOVA, mixed design.

Assumptions for the Multivariate Test

- **Level of measurement**. The criterion variable should be assessed on an interval- or ratio-level of measurement. The predictor variables both should be a nominal-level variables (categorical variables). One predictor codes the within-subjects variable, and the second codes the between-subjects variable.

- **Independent observations**. A given subject's score in any one condition should not be affected by any other subject's score in any of the study's conditions. However, it is acceptable for a given subject's score in one condition to be dependent upon his or her own score in a different condition (under the within-subjects predictor variable).

- **Random sampling**. Scores on the criterion variable should represent a random sample drawn from the populations of interest.

- **Multivariate normality**. The measurements obtained from subjects should follow a multivariate normal distribution. Under conditions normally encountered in social science research, violations of this assumption have only a very small effect on the type I error rate (the probability of incorrectly rejecting a true null hypothesis).

- **Homogeneity of covariance matrices**. In the population, the criterion-variable covariance matrix for a given group (under the between-subject's predictor variable) should be equal to the covariance matrix for each of the remaining groups. This assumption was discussed in greater detail in Chapter 10: "Multivariate Analysis of Variance (MANOVA) with One Between-Groups Factor."

Assumptions for the Univariate Test

The univariate test requires all of the preceding assumptions, as well as the following assumptions of sphericity and symmetry:

- **Sphericity**. Sphericity is a characteristic of a difference-variable covariance matrix that is obtained in performing a repeated-measures ANOVA (the concept of sphericity was discussed in greater detail in Chapter 11. Briefly, two conditions must be satisfied for the covariance matrix to demonstrate sphericity. First, each variance on the diagonal of the matrix should be equal to every other variance on the diagonal. Second, each covariance off of the diagonal should equal zero (this is analogous to saying that the correlations between the difference variables should be zero). Remember that, in a study with a between-subjects factor, there will be a separate difference-variable covariance matrix for each group under the between-subjects variable.

- **Symmetry conditions**. There are two symmetry conditions, and the first of these is the sphericity condition just described. The second condition is that the difference-variable covariance matrices obtained for the various groups (under the between-subjects factor) should be equal to one another.

For example, assume that a researcher has conducted a study that includes a repeated-measures factor with three conditions, and a between-subjects factor with two conditions. Subjects assigned to condition 1 under the between-subjects factor are designated here as "group 1", and those assigned to condition 2 are designated as "group 2". With this research design, one difference-variable covariance matrix will be obtained for group 1, and a second for group 2 (the nature of these difference-variable covariance matrices was discussed in Chapter 11). The symmetry conditions are met if both matrices demonstrate sphericity, and each element in the matrix for group 1 is equal to its corresponding element in the matrix for group 2.

References

Keppel, G. (1982). *Design and analysis: A researcher's handbook, second edition*. Englewood Cliffs, NJ: Prentice Hall.

Looney, S. & Stanley, W. (1989). Exploratory repeated measures analysis for two or more groups. *The American Statistician*, *43*, 220-225.

Rusbult, C. E. (1980). Commitment and satisfaction in romantic associations: A test of the investment model. *Journal of Experimental Social Psychology, 16*, 172-186.

SAS Institute Inc. (1989). *SAS/STAT user's guide, version 6, fourth edition, volume 2*. Cary, NC: SAS Institute Inc.

Winer, B. J. (1971). *Statistical principles in experimental design (second edition)*. New York: Mcgraw-Hill.

Chapter 13

MULTIPLE REGRESSION

Overview. This chapter shows how to perform multiple regression analysis to investigate the relationship between a continuous criterion variable and multiple continuous predictor variables. It describes the different components of the multiple regression equation, and discusses the meaning of R^2 and other results from a multiple regression analysis. It shows how bivariate correlations, multiple regression coefficients, and uniqueness indices may be reviewed to assess the relative importance of predictor variables. Fictitious data are examined using PROC CORR and PROC REG to show how the analysis can be conducted and to illustrate how the results can be summarized in tables and in text.

Introduction: Answering Questions with Multiple Regression

Multiple regression is a highly flexible procedure that allows researchers to address many different types of research questions with many different types of data. Perhaps the most common multiple regression analysis involves a single continuous criterion variable measured on an interval or ratio scale, and multiple continuous predictor variables also assessed on an interval or ratio scale.

For example, you may be interested in determining the relative importance of variables that are believed to predict adult income. To conduct your research, you obtain information for 1,000 U.S. adults. The criterion variable in your study is annual income for these subjects. The predictor variables are age, years of education, IQ, and income of parents. In this study, the criterion variable as well as the predictor variables are all continuous and are all assessed on an interval or ratio scale. Because of this, multiple regression is the appropriate data analysis procedure.

Analysis with multiple regression allows you to answer a number of research questions. For example, it allows you to determine

- whether there is a significant relationship between the criterion variable and the multiple predictor variables, when taken as a group

- whether the multiple regression coefficient for a given predictor variable is statistically significant (this coefficient represents the amount of weight given to a specific predictor, while holding constant the other predictors)

- whether a given predictor accounts for a significant amount of variance in the criterion, beyond the variance accounted for by the other predictors.

By conducting the preceding analyses, you will learn something about the relative importance of the predictor variables that are included in your multiple regression equation. Researchers conducting nonexperimental research in the social sciences are very often interested in learning about the relative importance of their naturally occurring predictor variables. This chapter shows you how to perform these analyses.

Because multiple regression is such a flexible procedure, however, there are many other types of regression analyses that are beyond the scope of this chapter. For example, in the study dealing with annual income that was discussed earlier, all predictor variables were continuous variables on an interval or ratio scale. In practice, nominal (classification) variables may also be used as predictors in a multiple regression analysis, provided that they have been appropriately transformed using dummy-coding or effect-coding. Because this chapter provides only an introduction to multiple regression, it will not cover circumstances in which nominal-scale variables are included as predictors. In addition, this chapter covers only those situations in which you explore a linear relationship between the predictor variables and the criterion; curvilinear and interactive relationships are not discussed.

Once you have learned the basics of multiple regression from this chapter, you can learn more about advanced regression topics (such as dummy-coding nominal variables or testing curvilinear relationships) in Cohen and Cohen (1975) and Pedhazur (1982). To learn about how to perform these more-advanced procedures using the SAS System, see Freund and Littell (1991) and Littell, Freund, and Spector (1991).

Multiple Regression versus ANOVA

Chapters 8 through 12 of this text presented analysis of variance (ANOVA) procedures that are often used to analyze data from **experimental research**: research in which one or more categorical independent variables (such as "experimental condition") are manipulated to determine how they affect the study's dependent variable.

For example, imagine that you were interested in studying **prosocial behavior**: actions intended to help others. Examples of prosocial acts might include donating money to the poor, donating blood, doing volunteer work at a hospital, and so forth. You may have developed an experimental treatment that you believe will increase the likelihood that people will engage in prosocial acts. To investigate this, you conduct an experiment in which you manipulate the independent variable (half of your subjects are given the experimental treatment, and half are given a placebo treatment). You then assess your dependent variable, the number of prosocial acts that the subjects later perform. It would be appropriate to analyze data from this study using one-way ANOVA, because you had a single criterion variable assessed on an interval/ratio scale (number of prosocial acts), and you had a single predictor variable measured on a nominal scale (experimental group).

Multiple regression is similar to ANOVA in at least one important respect: with both procedures, the criterion variable should be continuous and should be assessed on either an interval- or ratio-level of measurement. Chapter 1 indicated that a **continuous** variable is a variable that may assume a relatively large number of values. For example, the "number of prosocial acts performed over a six-month period" may be a continuous variable, provided that subjects demonstrate a wide variety of scores (such as 0, 4, 10, 11, 20, 25, 30, and so forth).

However, multiple regression also differs from ANOVA in some ways. The most important difference involves the nature of the predictor variables. When data are analyzed with ANOVA, the predictor variable is a categorical variable: that is, a variable that simply codes group membership. In contrast, the predictor variables in multiple regression are generally continuous variables.

As an illustration, assume that you conduct a study in which you administer a questionnaire to a group of subjects that assesses the number of prosocial acts each has performed. You may then go on to obtain scores for the same subjects on each of the following predictor variables:

- age

- income

- a questionnaire-type scale that assesses level of moral development.

Perhaps you have a hypothesis that the number of prosocial acts performed is causally determined by these three predictor variables, as illustrated by the model in Figure 13.1.

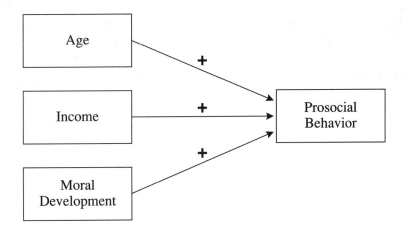

Figure 13.1: A Model of the Determinants of Prosocial Behavior

You can see that each of the predictor variables in your study (age, income, and moral development) are continuous, and are assessed on an interval or ratio scale. This, combined with the fact that your criterion variable is also a continuous variable assessed on an interval/ratio scale, means that you may analyze your data using multiple regression.

This is a most important distinction between the two statistical procedures: with ANOVA, the predictor variables are always categorical; with multiple regression, they are generally continuous ("generally" because categorical variables are sometimes used in multiple regression provided they have been dummy-coded or effect-coded; for more information, see Cohen and Cohen [1975], or Pedhazur [1982]).

Multiple Regression and Naturally Occurring Variables

Multiple regression is particularly well suited for studying the relationship between **naturally occurring** predictor and criterion variables; that is, variables that are not manipulated by the researcher, but rather are simply measured as they naturally occur in the real world. The preceding prosocial behavior study provides good examples of naturally occurring predictor variables: age, income, and level of moral development.

This is what makes multiple regression such an important tool in the social sciences: it allows researchers to study variables that cannot be experimentally manipulated. For example, assume that you have a hypothesis that domestic violence (an act of aggression against a domestic partner) is caused by

- childhood trauma experienced by the abuser

- substance abuse

- low self-esteem.

The model illustrating this hypothesis appears in Figure 13.2. It is obvious that you would not want to experimentally manipulate the predictor variables of the model, and then later observe the subjects as adults to see if the manipulation affected their incidence of domestic violence. However, it is possible to simply measure these variables as they naturally occur and determine whether they are related to one another in the predicted fashion. Multiple regression allows you to do this.

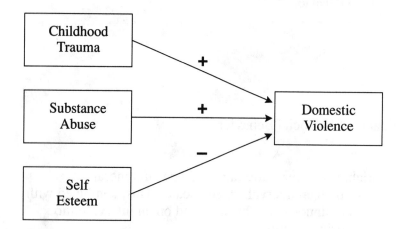

Figure 13.2: A Model of the Determinants of Domestic Violence

Does this mean that ANOVA is only for the analysis of manipulated predictor variables, while multiple regression is only for the analysis of naturally occurring variables? Not necessarily, because naturally occurring variables can be predictor variables in an ANOVA, provided they are categorical. For example, ANOVA can be used to determine whether subject sex (a naturally occurring predictor variable) is related to relationship commitment (a criterion variable). In addition, a categorical manipulated variable (such as "experimental condition") may be used as a predictor variable in multiple regression, provided that it has been dummy-coded or effect-coded. The main distinction to remember is this: with ANOVA, the predictor variables may only be categorical variables; with multiple regression, the predictor variables may be either categorical or continuous.

How large must my sample be? Multiple regression is a large-sample procedure; unreliable results may be obtained if the sample does not include at least 100 observations, preferably 200. The greater the number of predictor variables included in the multiple regression equation, the greater the number of subjects that will be necessary to obtain reliable results. Most experts recommend at least 15-30 subjects per predictor variable.

"Proving" Cause and Effect Relationships

Multiple regression can determine whether a given set of variables is useful in predicting a criterion variable. Among other things, this means that multiple regression can be used to determine:

- whether the relationship between the criterion variable and predictors variables (taken as a group) is statistically significant

- how much variance in the criterion is accounted for by the predictors

- which predictor variables are relatively important predictors of the criterion.

However, although the preceding section often refers to causal models, it is nonetheless important to remember that the procedures discussed in this chapter do not provide relatively strong evidence concerning cause and effect relationships between predictor variables and the criterion. For example, consider the causal model presented in Figure 13.2. Assume that naturally occurring data for these four variables are gathered and analyzed using multiple regression. Assume further that the results are significant: that multiple regression coefficients for all three of the predictor variables are significant and in the predicted direction. Although these findings are consistent with your theoretical model, they do not "prove" that these predictor variables have a causal effect on domestic violence. Because the data are correlational, there is probably more than one way to interpret the observed relationships between the four variables. The most that you would be justified in saying is that your findings are *consistent* with the causal model portrayed in Figure 13.2; it would be going too far to say that the results "prove" that the model is correct.

Then why analyze correlational data with multiple regression at all? There are a number of reasons. Very often, researchers are not really interested in testing a causal model. Perhaps the purpose of the study is simply to understand the predictive relationships between a set of variables.

However, even when the research is based on a causal model, multiple regression can still be useful. For example, if you obtained correlational data relevant to the domestic violence model of Figure 13.2, analyzed it, and found that none of the multiple regression coefficients were significant, this would still be useful information. It would be useful because it showed that the model failed to survive a test; it failed to survive an analysis that investigated the predictive relationships between the variables.

If the model does survive an analysis with multiple regression (i.e., if significant results are obtained), this is useful as well. You may prepare a research report indicating that the results were consistent with the hypothesized model; in other words, the model survived an attempt at disconfirmation. If you are dealing with predictor variables that can be ethically manipulated, you may choose next to perform an actual experiment to determine whether the predictors actually have a causal effect on the criterion variable under controlled circumstances. If it is not possible to perform a true experiment, you may plan a more ambitious correlational study to be analyzed with path analysis: a somewhat more sophisticated procedure that allows the testing of causal models.

In summary, it is important to remember that the multiple regression procedures discussed in this chapter provide relatively weak evidence of cause and effect relationships. However, they are extremely useful for determining whether one set of variables can predict variation in a criterion.

Background: Predicting a Criterion Variable from Multiple Predictors

The criterion, or predicted, variable in multiple regression is represented with the symbol Y, and is therefore often referred to as the "Y variable." The predictor variables are represented as X_1, X_2, X_3, and so forth, and are referred to as the "X variables." The purpose of multiple regression is to understand better the relationship between the Y variable and the X variables, when taken as a group.

A Simple Predictive Equation

For example, consider again the model of the determinants of prosocial behavior, which was presented in Figure 13.1. This model hypothesizes that the number of prosocial acts performed by an individual in a given period of time may be predicted by three variables:

- the subject's age

- the subject's income

- the subject's level of moral development.

Notice that each arrow (each causal path) in the figure is identified with either a "+" sign or a "–" sign. A plus sign indicates that you expect the relevant predictor variable to demonstrate a positive relationship with the criterion; a minus sign indicates that you expect the predictor to demonstrate a negative relationship. The nature of these signs in Figure 13.1 shows that you expect

- a positive relationship between age and prosocial behavior, meaning that older subjects will perform more prosocial acts

- a positive relationship between income and prosocial behavior, meaning that wealthier people will perform more prosocial acts

- a positive relationship between moral development and prosocial behavior, meaning that subjects who score higher on the paper-and-pencil measure of moral development will perform more prosocial acts.

Assume that you have administered a questionnaire to a sample of 100 subjects that assesses the subjects' level of moral development (scores on this scale may range from 10 to 100, and higher scores reflect higher levels of development). From the same subjects, you have also obtained information regarding their age and their income. You now want to use this information to predict the number of prosocial acts the subject will perform in the next six months. More specifically, you want to create a new variable, Y', that represents your best guess of how many prosocial acts the subjects will perform. Y' represents your prediction of the subjects' standing on the criterion variable (as distinguished from Y, which is the subjects' *actual* standing on the criterion variable).

Assume that the three predictor variables really are positively related to prosocial behavior. To arrive at a prediction of how many prosocial behaviors the subjects will engage in, one of your options is to simply add together the subjects' scores on the three X variables, and allow the sum to be your best guess of how many prosocial acts they will perform. You could do this using the following equation:

$$Y' = X_1 + X_2 + X_3$$

where

Y' = the subjects' predicted scores on "prosocial behavior"

X_1 = the subjects' actual scores on "age"

X_2 = the subjects' actual scores on "income" (in thousands)

X_3 = the subjects' actual scores on the moral development scale.

To make this more concrete, consider the fictitious data presented in Table 13.1. This table presents actual scores for four of the study's subjects on the three predictor variables.

Table 13.1

<u>Fictitious Data, Prosocial Behavior Study</u>

Subject	Age (X_1)	Income (in thousands) (X_2)	Moral Development (X_3)
1. Bob	19	15	12
2. Sally	24	32	28
3. Jim	33	45	50
.			
.			
.			
100. Sheila	55	60	95

To arrive at an estimate of the number of prosocial behaviors the first subject (Bob) will engage in, you could insert his scores on the three X variables into the preceding equation:

$$Y' = X_1 + X_2 + X_3$$

$$Y' = 19 + 15 + 12$$

$$Y' = 46$$

So your best guess is that the first subject, Bob, will perform 46 prosocial acts in the next six months. By repeating this process for each subject, you could go on to compute their scores on

Y' in the same way. Table 13.2 presents the predicted scores on the prosocial behavior variable for some of the study's subjects:

Table 13.2

Predicted Scores on the Prosocial Behavior Variable Using a Simple Predictive Equation

Subject	Predicted Scores On Prosocial Behavior (Y')	Age (X_1)	Income (in thousands) (X_2)	Moral Development (X_3)
1. Bob	46	19	15	12
2. Sally	84	24	32	28
3. Jim	128	33	45	50
.				
.				
.				
100. Sheila	338	55	60	95

Notice the general relationships between Y' and the X variables in table 13.2. Because of the way Y' was created, if subjects have low scores on age, income, and moral development, your equation predicts that they will engage in relatively few prosocial behaviors; if subjects have high scores on these X variables, your equation predicts that they will engage in a relatively large number of prosocial behaviors. For example, Bob had relatively low scores on these X variables, and as a consequence, the equation predicts that he will perform only 46 prosocial acts over the next six months. In contrast, Sheila displayed relatively high scores on age, income, and moral development; as a consequence, your equation predicts that she will engage in 338 prosocial acts.

So, in effect, you have created a new variable, Y'. Imagine that you now go out and gather data regarding the actual number of prosocial acts that these subjects engage in over the following six months. This variable would be represented with the symbol Y, because it represents the subjects' *actual* scores on the criterion (and not their predicted scores, Y').

Once you have determined the actual number of prosocial acts performed by the subjects, you could list them in a table alongside of the subjects' predicted scores on prosocial behavior, as in Table 13.3:

Table 13.3

<u>Actual Scores and Predicted Scores on the Prosocial Behavior Variable</u>

Subject	Actual Scores On Prosocial Behavior (Y)	Predicted Scores On Prosocial Behavior (Y')
1. Bob	10	46
2. Sally	40	84
3. Jim	70	128
.		
.		
.		
100. Sheila	130	338

Notice that, in some respects, your predictions of the subjects' scores on Y are not terribly accurate. For example, your equation predicted that Bob would engage in 46 prosocial activities, but in reality he engaged in only 10. Similarly, it predicted that Sheila would engage in 338 prosocial behaviors, while she actually engaged in only 130.

Despite this, you should not lose sight of the fact that your new variable Y' does appear to be correlated with the actual scores on Y. Notice that those subjects with low scores on Y' (such as Bob) also tend to have low scores on Y; notice that subjects with high scores on Y' (such as Sheila) also tend to have high scores on Y. If you computed a product-moment correlation (r) between Y and Y', you would probably observe a moderately large correlation coefficient. This trend is supportive of your model; it suggests that there really is a relationship between Y and the three X variables, when taken as a group.

The procedures (and the predictive equation) described in this section have been somewhat crude in nature, and do not describe the way that multiple regression is actually performed. However, they do illustrate some important basic concepts in multiple regression analysis. For example, in multiple regression analysis, you create an artificial variable, Y', to represent your best guess of the subject's standings on the criterion variable. The relationship between this variable and the subject's actual standing on the criterion (Y) is assessed to indicate the strength of the relationship between Y and the X variables when taken as a group.

However, multiple regression as it is actually performed has many important advantages over the crude practice of simply adding together the X variables, as was illustrated in this section. With true multiple regression, the various X variables are multiplied by optimal weights before they are added together to create Y'. This generally results in a more accurate estimate of the subjects' standing on the criterion variable. In addition, you can use the results of a true multiple regression procedure to determine which of the X variables are relatively important, and which are relatively unimportant predictors of Y. These issues are discussed in a following section.

An Equation with Weighted Predictors

In the preceding section, each predictor variable was given approximately equal weight in computing scores on Y'. You did not, for example, give twice as much weight to income as you gave to age in computing Y' scores. Assigning equal weights to the various predictors may make sense in some situations, especially when all of the predictors are equally predictive of the criterion.

However, what if some of the X variables in a model are better predictors of Y than others? For example, what if your measure of moral development displayed a strong correlation with prosocial behavior (r = .70), income demonstrated a moderate correlation with prosocial behavior (r = .40), and age demonstrated only a very weak correlation (r = .20)? In a situation such as this, it would make sense to assign different weights to the different predictors. For example, you might assign a weight of 1 to age, a weight of 2 to income, and a weight of 3 to moral development. The predictive equation that reflects this weighting scheme is:

$$Y' = (1)\ X_1 + (2)\ X_2 + (3)\ X_3$$

In this equation, once again X_1 = age, X_2 = income, and X_3 = moral development. In calculating a given subject's score on Y', you would multiply his or her score on each X variable by the appropriate weight, and sum the resulting products. For example, Table 13.2 showed that the subject Bob had a score of 19 on X1, a score of 15 on X2, and a score of 12 on X_3. His predicted prosocial behavior score, Y', could be calculated in the following way:

```
Y' = (1) X₁ + (2) X₂ + (3) X₃
Y' = (1) 19 + (2) 15 + (3) 12
Y' =      19 +     30 +     36
Y' = 85
```

This weighted equation predicts that Bob will engage in 85 prosocial acts over the next six months. You could use the same weights to compute the remaining subjects' scores on Y' in the same way. Although this example has again been somewhat crude in nature, it is this concept of optimal weighting that is at the heart of multiple regression analysis.

The Multiple Regression Equation

Regression coefficients and intercepts. In linear multiple regression as performed by the SAS System's REG procedure, optimal weights of the sort described in the preceding section are automatically calculated in the course of the analysis. The following symbols are used to represent the various components of an actual multiple regression equation:

$$Y' = b_1 X_1 + b_2 X_2 + b_3 X_3 \ldots + b_k X_k + a$$

where

Y' = subject's predicted scores on the criterion variable

b_k = the nonstandardized multiple regression coefficient for the kth predictor variable

X_k = the kth predictor variable

a = intercept constant.

Some of the components of this equation, such as Y', have already been discussed in the preceding section. However, some new components require additional explanation.

The term "b_k" represents the nonstandardized multiple regression coefficient for an X variable. A **multiple regression coefficient** for a given X variable represents the average change in Y that is associated with a one-unit change in that X variable, while holding constant the remaining X variables. This somewhat technical definition for a regression coefficient will be explained in more detail in a later section; for the moment, however, it is useful to think of a regression coefficient as revealing the amount of *weight* that the X variable is given in computing Y'. For this reason, these are sometimes referred to as **b weights**.

The symbol "a" represents the **intercept constant** of the equation. The intercept is a fixed value that is either added to or subtracted from the weighted sum of X scores in computing Y'. The inclusion of this constant in the regression equation improves the accuracy of prediction.

To develop a true multiple regression equation using PROC REG, it necessary to gather data on both the Y variable and the X variables in a sample of subjects. Assume that you do this in a sample of 100 subjects. You analyze the data, and the results of your analyses indicate that the relationship between prosocial behavior and the three predictor variables can be described by the following equation:

```
Y' = b₁ X₁     + b₂ X₂     + b₃ X₃     + a

Y' = (.10) X₁ + (.25) X₂ + (1.10) X₃ + (-3.25)
```

The preceding equation indicates that your best guess of a given subject's score on prosocial behavior may be computed by multiplying his or her score on age by .10, multiplying his or her score on income by .25, multiplying his or her score on moral development by 1.10, summing these products, and subtracting the intercept of 3.25 from this sum. This process is illustrated by inserting Bob's scores on the X variables in the equation:

```
Y' = (.10) 19 + (.25) 15 + (1.10) 12 + (-3.25)

Y' = 1.9      + 3.75      + 13.2      + (-3.25)

Y' = 18.85    + (-3.25)

Y' = 15.60
```

Your best guess is that Bob will perform 15.60 prosocial acts over the next six months. You can calculate the Y' scores for the remaining subjects in Table 14.2 by inserting their X scores in this same equation.

The principle of least squares. At this point it is reasonable to ask, "How did the REG procedure determine that the 'optimal' b weight for X_1 was .10? How did it determine that the 'optimal' weight for X_2 was .25? How did it determine that the 'optimal' intercept ("a" term) was –3.25?"

The answer is that these values are "optimal" in the sense that they minimize a function of the errors of prediction. An **error of prediction** refers to the difference between a subject's actual score on the criterion (Y), and his or her predicted score on the criterion (Y'). This difference may be illustrated as follows:

```
Y - Y'
```

Remember that you must gather actual scores on Y in order to perform multiple regression, so it is in fact possible to compute the error of prediction (the difference between Y and Y') for each subject in the sample. For example, Table 13.4 reports the actual score for several subjects on Y, their predicted scores on Y, based on the optimally weighted regression equation above, and their errors of prediction.

Table 13.4

<u>Errors of Prediction Based on an Optimally Weighted Multiple Regression Equation</u>

Subject	Actual Scores On Prosocial Behavior (Y)	Predicted Scores On Prosocial Behavior (Y')	Errors of Prediction (Y − Y')
1. Bob	10	15.60	−5.60
2. Sally	40	37.95	2.05
3. Jim	70	66.30	3.70
.			
.			
.			
100. Sheila	130	121.75	8.25

For Bob, the actual number of prosocial acts performed was 10, while your multiple regression equation predicted that he would perform 15.60 acts. The error of prediction for Bob was therefore 10 − 15.60 = −5.60. The errors of prediction for the remaining subjects were calculated in the same fashion.

Now, back to the initial point. Earlier it was stated that the b weights and intercept calculated by PROC REG are optimal in the sense that they minimize errors of prediction. More specifically, these b weights and intercept are computed according to the principle of least squares. The **principle of least squares** says that Y' values should be calculated so that the sum of the squared errors of prediction are a minimal value. The sum of the squared errors of prediction can be calculated using this formula:

$$\Sigma \, (Y - Y')^2$$

To compute the sum of the squared errors of prediction according to this formula, it is necessary only to

- compute the error of prediction (Y – Y') for a given subject

- square this error

- repeat this process for all remaining subjects

- sum the resulting squares. (The purpose of squaring the errors before summing them is to eliminate the minus sign that some of the difference scores will display.)

When a given data set is analyzed using multiple regression, PROC REG applies a set of formulas that calculates the optimal b weights and the optimal intercept for that data set. The formulas that do this calculate the b weights and intercept that best minimize these squared errors of prediction. That is why we say that multiple regression calculates "optimal" weights and intercepts. They are optimal in the sense that no other set of b weights or intercepts could do a better job of minimizing squared errors of prediction for the current data set.

With these points established, it is finally possible to summarize what multiple regression actually allows you to do:

> *Multiple regression allows you to investigate the relationship between a single criterion variable and an optimally weighted linear combination of predictor variables.*

In the preceding statement, "optimally weighted linear combination of predictor variables" refers to Y'. The expression "linear combination" refers to the fact that the various X variables are combined, or added together (using the formula for a straight line), to arrive at Y'. The words "optimally weighted" refer to the fact that the various X variables are assigned weights that satisfy the principle of least squares.

Therefore, although we normally think of multiple regression as a procedure that investigates the relationship between single criterion and multiple predictor variables, it also possible to view it in somewhat more simple terms: as a procedure that investigates the relationship between just two variables, Y and Y'.

The Results of a Multiple Regression Analysis

The Multiple Correlation Coefficient

The **multiple correlation coefficient**, symbolized as R, represents the strength of the relationship between a criterion variable and an optimally weighted linear combination of predictor variables. Its values may range from .00 through 1.00, and it is interpreted in the same way a Pearson product-moment correlation coefficient (r) is interpreted (except that R can only assume positive values). Values near zero indicate little relationship between the criterion and the predictors, values near 1.00 indicate strong relationships.

Conceptually, R should be viewed as the product-moment correlation between Y and Y'. This can be symbolized in the following way:

$$R = r_{YY'}$$

In other words, if you were to obtain data from a sample of subjects that included their scores on Y as well as a number of X variables, computed Y' scores for each subject, and then correlated predicted criterion scores (Y') with actual scores (Y), the resulting bivariate correlation coefficient would be equivalent to R.

With bivariate regression, it is possible to estimate the amount of variance in Y that is accounted for by X by simply squaring the correlation between the two variables. The resulting product is sometimes referred to as the **coefficient of determination**. For example, if r = .50 for a given pair of variables, then their coefficient of determination can be computed as

$$\text{Coefficient of determination} = r^2$$
$$= (.50)^2$$
$$= .25$$

Therefore, in this situation it can be said the X variable accounts for 25% of the variance in the Y variable.

An analogous coefficient of determination may also be computed in multiple regression by simply squaring the observed multiple correlation coefficient, R. The resulted **R^2 value** (often referred to simply as R-squared) represents the percentage of variance in Y that is accounted for by the linear combination of predictor variables. The concept of "variance accounted for" is an extremely important one in multiple regression analysis, and is therefore given detailed treatment in the following section.

Variance Accounted for by Predictor Variables: The Simplest Models

In multiple regression analyses, researchers often speak of "variance accounted for." By this, they mean the percent of variance in the criterion variable accounted for by the linear combination of predictor variables.

A single predictor variable. This concept is perhaps easier to understand by beginning with a simple bivariate example. Assume that you compute the correlation between prosocial behavior and moral development, and find that r = .50 for these two variables. As was previously discussed, you can determine the percentage of variance in prosocial behavior that is accounted for by moral development by squaring this correlation coefficient:

$$r^2 = (.50)^2$$

$$= .25$$

25% of the variance in prosocial behavior is accounted for by moral development. This can be illustrated graphically by using a Venn diagram in which the total variance in a variable is represented with a circle. The Venn diagram representing the correlation between prosocial behavior and moral development is in Figure 13.3:

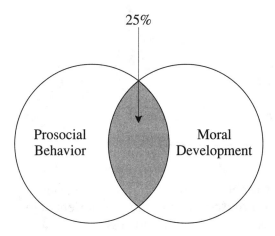

Figure 13.3: Venn Diagram: Variance in Prosocial Behavior Accounted for by Moral Development

Notice that the circle representing moral development overlaps the circle representing prosocial behavior; this represents the fact that the two variables are correlated. More specifically, the figure shows that 25% of the area of the prosocial behavior circle is overlapped by the moral development circle, meaning that moral development accounts for 25% of the variance in prosocial behavior.

Multiple predictor variables with intercorrelations of zero. It is now possible to expand the discussion to the situation in which there are multiple X variables. Assume that you obtain data on prosocial behavior, age, income, and moral development in a sample of 100 subjects, and observe correlations between the four variables as summarized in Table 13.5:

Table 13.5

Correlation Matrix: Zero Correlations between X Variables

Variable	Y	X_1	X_2	X_3
Y Prosocial behavior	1.00			
X_1 Age	.30	1.00		
X_2 Income	.40	.00	1.00	
X_3 Moral development	.50	.00	.00	1.00

When all possible correlations are computed for a set of variables, these correlations are usually presented in a published article in the form of a **correlation matrix** such as the one presented in Table 13.5. To find the correlation between two variables, you simply find the row for one variable, and the column for the second variable. Where the row and column intersect, the correlation between the two variables is reproduced. For example, where the row for X_1 (age) intersects with the column for Y (prosocial behavior), you can see a correlation of .30; this means that the correlation between age and prosocial behavior is .30.

You can use the preceding correlations to determine how much variance in Y is accounted for by the three X variables. For example, the correlation between age and prosocial behavior is .30; squaring this results in .09 (because .30 X .30 = .09). This means that age accounts for 9% of the variance in prosocial behavior. Following the same procedure, you learn that income accounts for 16% of the variance in Y (because .40 X .40 = .16), while moral development continues to account for 25% of the variance in Y.

Notice another (somewhat unusual) fact concerning the correlations in this table: Each of the X variables demonstrates a correlation of zero with all of the other X variables. For example, where the row for X_2 (income) intersects with the column for X_1 (age), you can see a correlation coefficient of .00. In the same way, Table 13.5 also shows correlations of .00 between X_2 and X_3, and between X_1 and X_3.

The correlations between the variables of Table 13.5 may be illustrated with the Venn diagram of Figure 13.4:

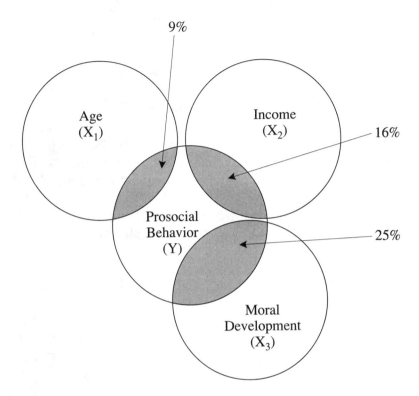

Figure 13.4: Venn Diagram: Variance in Prosocial Behavior Accounted for by Three Noncorrelated Predictors

Notice two important points concerning the Venn diagram in Figure 13.4: each X variable accounts for some variance in Y, but no X variable accounts for any variance in any other X variable. The second point is important; because the preceding table showed that the X variables were uncorrelated with each other, it was necessary to draw the Venn diagram so that no X variable overlapped with any other X variable.

How much variance in Y is accounted for by the three predictors of Figure 13.4? This is easily determined by simply adding together the percent of variance accounted for by each of the three predictors individually:

```
Total variance accounted for = .09 + .16 + .25
                             = .50
```

The linear combination of $X_1, X_2,$ and X_3 accounts for 50% of the variance in prosocial behavior. In most areas of research in the social sciences, this would be considered a fairly large percentage of variance.

One word of warning: in the preceding example, the total variance in Y accounted for by the X variables was determined by simply summing the squared bivariate correlations between Y and the individual X variables. It is important to remember that you can use this procedure to determine the total variance accounted for in Y only when the X variables are completely uncorrelated with one another. When there is any degree of correlation between the X variables themselves, this approach is likely to give very misleading results. The reasons for this are discussed in the next section.

Variance Accounted for by Intercorrelated Predictor Variables

The preceding shows that it is simple to determine the percent of variance in a criterion that is accounted for by a set of predictor variables when the predictor variables display zero correlation with one another: In that situation, the total variance accounted for will be equal to the sum of the squared bivariate correlations (that is, the sum of $r_{Y1}{}^2$, $r_{Y2}{}^2$, and so forth). The situation becomes much more complex, however, when the predictor variables are correlated with one another. In this situation, it is not possible to make simple, blanket statements about how much variance will be accounted for by a set of predictors.

In part, this is because multiple regression equations with correlated predictors behave one way when the predictors include a suppressor variable, and they behave a very different way when the predictors do not contain a suppressor variable. A later section will explain just what a suppressor variable is, and will describe the complexities that are introduced by this somewhat rare phenomenon. First, consider the (relatively) simpler situation that exists when the predictors included in a multiple regression equation are intercorrelated but do not contain a suppressor variable.

When intercorrelated predictors do not include a suppressor variable. The preceding example was fairly unrealistic in that each X variable was said to have a correlation of zero with all of the other X variables. In nonexperimental research in the social sciences, you will almost never observe a set of predictor variables that are mutually uncorrelated in this way. Remember that nonexperimental research involves measuring naturally occurring (nonmanipulated) variables, and naturally occurring variables will almost always display some degree of intercorrelation.

For example, consider the nature of the variables studied here. Given that people tend to earn higher salaries as they grow older, is it not likely that subject age would be positively correlated with income? Similarly, is it not possible that people with higher incomes will demonstrate higher levels of moral development, since they do not experience the deprivation and related stresses of poverty? If this speculation is correct (and please remember that this is only speculation!), you might expect to see a correlation of perhaps .50 between age and income, as well as a correlation of .50 between income and moral development. These new correlations are displayed in Table 13.6. Notice that this table is similar to the preceding table in that all X variables display the same correlations with Y as were displayed earlier, and age and moral development are still uncorrelated.

Table 13.6

Correlation Matrix: Nonzero Correlations between X Variables

	Variable	Y	X_1	X_2	X_3
Y	Prosocial behavior	1.00			
X_1	Age	.30	1.00		
X_2	Income	.40	.50	1.00	
X_3	Moral development	.50	.00	.50	1.00

The X variables of Table 13.6 display the same correlations with Y as were displayed earlier in Table 13.5. Does this mean that the linear combination of the three X variables will still account for the same total percentage of variance in Y? In most cases, the answer will be no. Remember that, with Table 13.5, the X variables were not correlated with one another, while in Table 13.6 there is now a substantial correlation between age and income, and between income and moral development; these correlations can decrease the total variance in Y that is accounted for by the X variables. The reasons for this are illustrated in the Venn Diagram of Figure 13.5.

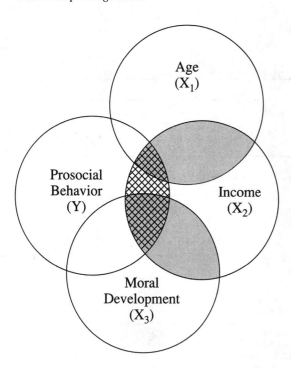

Figure 13.5: Venn Diagram: Variance Accounted for by Three Correlated Predictors

In Figure 13.5, the area shaded in with dots represents variance in income that is accounted for by age and moral development. The area shaded in with cross-hatching, on the other hand, represents variance in prosocial behavior that is accounted for by income.

Notice that each X variable individually still accounts for the same percentage of variance in prosocial behavior: Age still accounts for 9%, income still accounts for 16%, and moral development still accounts for 25%. In this respect, Figure 13.5 is similar to Figure 13.4.

However, there is one important respect in which the two figures are different. Figure 13.5 shows that some of the X variables are now correlated with one another: The area of overlap between age and income (shaded in with dots) represents the fact that age and income now share about 25% of their variance in common (because the correlation between these variables was .50, and $.50^2 = .25$). In the same way, the area of overlap between income and moral development (also shaded in with dots) represents the fact that these variables share about 25% of their variance in common.

There is an important consequence of the fact that some of the X variables are now correlated with one another: Some of the variance in Y that is accounted for by one X variable is now also accounted for by another X variable. For example, consider the X_2 variable, income. By itself, income accounted for 16% of the variance in prosocial behavior. But notice how the circle for age overlaps part of the variance in Y that is accounted for by income (this area is shaded in with both dots and cross-hatching). This means that some of the variance in Y that is accounted for by income is also accounted for by age. In other words, because age and income are correlated, this has decreased the amount of variance in Y that is accounted for *uniquely* by income.

The same is true when one considers the correlation between income and moral development. The circle for moral development overlaps part of the variance in Y that is accounted for by income (again, this area is shaded in with both dots and cross-hatching). This shows that some of the variance in Y that was accounted for by income is now also accounted for by moral development.

In short, there is some redundancy between age and income in the prediction of Y, and there is also some redundancy between income and moral development in the prediction of Y. The result of this redundancy (or correlation) between the predictor variables is a net decrease in the total amount of variance in Y that is accounted for by the linear combination of X variables. Compare the Venn diagram for the situation in which the X variables were uncorrelated (Figure 13.4) to the Venn diagram for the situation in which there was some correlation between the X variables (Figure 13.5). When the X variables were not correlated among themselves, they accounted for 50% of the variance in Y. Now notice the area in Y that overlaps with the X variables in Figure 13.5: Clearly, the area of overlap is smaller in the second figure, showing that the X variables account for less of the total variance in Y when they are correlated with one another.

This is because X variables usually make a smaller unique contribution to the prediction of Y when they are correlated with one another; the greater the correlation between the X variables, the smaller the amount of unique variance in Y that is accounted for by each individual X variable, and hence the smaller the total variance in Y that is accounted for by the combination of X variables.

The meaning of unique variance can be understood with reference to the cross-hatched area in the Venn diagram of Figure 13.5. In the figure, the area shaded in with both dots and cross-hatching identifies the variance in Y that is accounted for by both income and age. Dots and cross-hatching are also used to identify the variance in Y accounted for by both income and moral development. The remaining variance in Y accounted for by income is the variance that is uniquely accounted for by income. In the figure, this is the area of overlap between income and prosocial behavior that is shaded in with only cross-hatching (not with dots and cross-hatching). Obviously, this area is quite small, indicating that income accounts for very little variance in prosocial behavior that is not already accounted for by age and moral development.

There are a number of practical implications arising from this state of affairs. The first implication is that, in general, the amount of variance accounted for in a criterion variable will be larger to the extent that the following two conditions hold:

- the predictor variables demonstrate relatively strong correlations with the criterion variable

- the predictor variables demonstrate relatively weak correlations with each other.

These will hold true "in general," because they will not apply to the special case of a suppressor variable (more on this in the following section).

The second implication is that there will generally be a point of diminishing returns when it comes to adding new X variables to a multiple regression equation. Because so many predictor variables in social science research are correlated with one another, only the first few predictors added to a predictive equation are likely to account for meaningful amounts of unique variance in a criterion; variables that are subsequently added will tend to account for smaller and smaller percentages of unique variance. At some point, predictors added to the equation will account for only negligible amounts of unique variance. For this reason, most multiple regression equations in published social science studies contain a relatively small number of variables, usually 2-10.

When intercorrelated predictors do include a suppressor variable. The preceding section describes the kinds of results that you can normally expect to observe when regressing a criterion variable on multiple intercorrelated predictor variables. However, there is a special case in which the preceding generalizations will not hold: that is the special case of the suppressor variable. Although reports of genuine suppressor variables are somewhat rare in the social sciences, it is important that you understand the concept, so that you will recognize a suppressor variable when you encounter one.

Briefly, a **suppressor variable** is a predictor variable that improves the predictive power of a multiple regression equation by controlling for unwanted variation that it shares with other predictors in the equation. Suppressor variables typically display the following characteristics:

- Zero or near-zero correlations with the criterion

- Moderate-to-strong correlations with at least one other predictor variable

Suppressor variables are interesting because, even though they may display a bivariate correlation with the criterion variable of zero, adding them to a multiple regression equation can result in a meaningful increase in R^2 for the model. This of course, violates the generalizations drawn in the preceding section.

To understand how suppressor variables work, consider this fictitious example. Imagine that you want to identify variables that can be used to predict the success of firefighters. To do this, you conduct a study with a group of 100 firefighters. For each subject, you obtain a "Firefighter Success Rating" that indicates how successful this person has been as a firefighter. These ratings are on a scale of 1-100, with higher ratings indicating greater success.

To identify variables that might be useful in predicting these success ratings, you have each firefighter complete a number of "paper-and-pencil" tests. One of these is a paper-and-pencil "Firefighter Knowledge Test." High scores on this test indicate that the subject possesses the knowledge needed to operate a fire hydrant, enter a burning building safely, and perform other tasks related to firefighting. A second test is a "Verbal Ability Test." This test has nothing to do with firefighting; high scores simply indicate that the subject has a good vocabulary and other verbal skills.

The three variables in this study could be represented with the following symbols:

Y = Firefighter Success Ratings (the criterion variable)

X_P = Firefighter Knowledge Test (the predictor variable of interest)

X_S = Verbal Ability Test (the suppressor variable)

Imagine that you perform some analyses to understand the nature of the relationship between these three variables. First, you compute the Pearson correlation between the Firefighter Knowledge Test and the Verbal Ability Test, and find that r = .40. This is a moderately strong correlation, and it only makes sense that these two tests would be moderately correlated. This is because both firefighter knowledge and verbal ability are assessed by the same method: a paper-and-pencil testing method. To some extent, getting a high score on either of these tests requires that the subject be able to read instructions, read questions, read possible responses, and perform other verbal tasks. This means that the two tests are correlated because scores on both tests are influenced by the subject's verbal ability.

Next, you perform a series of regressions in which Firefighter Success Ratings (Y) is the criterion to determine how much variance in this criterion is accounted for by various regression equations. This is what you learn:

- When the regression equation contains only the Verbal Ability Test, it accounts for 0% of the variance in Y.

- When the regression equation contains only the Firefighter Knowledge Test, it accounts for 20% of the variance in Y.

- When the regression equation contains both the Firefighter Knowledge Test and the Verbal Ability test, it accounts for 25% of the variance in Y.

The finding that the Verbal Ability Test accounts for none of the variance in Firefighter Success Ratings makes sense, because it (presumably) does not require a good vocabulary or other verbal skills to be a good firefighter.

The second finding that the Firefighter Knowledge Test accounts for a respectable 20% of the variance in Firefighter Success Ratings also makes sense, as it is reasonable to expect more knowledgeable firefighters to be rated as better firefighters.

However, you run into a real problem when trying to make sense of the third finding: the finding that the equation that contains both the Verbal Ability Test and the Firefighter Knowledge Test accounts for 25% of the variance in Y. How is it possible that the combination of these two variables accounts for 25% of the variance in Y when one accounted for only 20% and the other accounted for 0%?

The answer is that, in this situation, the Verbal Ability Test is serving as a suppressor variable. It is suppressing irrelevant variance in scores on the Firefighter Knowledge Test, thus "purifying" the relationship between the Firefighter Knowledge Test and Y. Here is how it works. Subject scores on the Firefighter Knowledge Test are influenced by at least two factors: their actual knowledge about firefighting, and their verbal ability (ability to read instructions, etc.). Obviously, the first of these two factors is relevant for predicting Y, and the second is irrelevant. Because scores on the Firefighter Knowledge Test are to some extent "contaminated" by the effects of the subject's verbal ability, the actual correlation between the Firefighter Knowledge

Test and Firefighter Success Ratings is somewhat lower than it would be if you could somehow purify Knowledge Test scores of this unwanted verbal factor. That is exactly what a suppressor variable does.

In most cases, a suppressor variable is given a negative regression weight in a multiple regression equation (these weights will be discussed in more detail later in this chapter). Partly because of this, including the suppressor variable in the equation adjusts each subject's predicted score on Y so that it comes closer to the subject's actual score on Y. In the present case, this means that, if a subject scores above the mean on the Verbal Ability Test, his or her predicted score on Y will be adjusted downward to penalize the subject for scoring high on this irrelevant predictor. Alternatively, if a subject scores below the mean on the Verbal Ability Test, his or her predicted score on Y will be adjusted upward. Another way of thinking about this is to say that a person applying for a firefighter's job who has a high score on the Firefighter's Knowledge Test but a low score on the Verbal Ability Test would be preferred over an applicant with a high score on the Knowledge Test and a high score on the Verbal Test (this is because the second candidate's score on the Knowledge Test was probably inflated due to his or her good verbal skills).

The net effect of these corrections is improved accuracy in predicting Y. This is why you earlier found that R^2 is .25 for the equation that contains the suppressor variable, but only .20 for the equation that does not contain it.

The possible existence of suppressor variables has implications for how you should conduct multiple regression analyses. For example, when attempting to identify variables that would make good predictors in a multiple regression equation, it is clear that you should not base the selection exclusively on the bivariate (Pearson) correlations between the variables. For example, even if two predictor variable are moderately or strongly correlated with one another, it does not necessarily mean that they are always providing redundant information; if one of them is a suppressor variable, then the two variables are not entirely redundant.

In the same way, a predictor variable should not be eliminated from consideration as a possible predictor just because it displays a zero or near-zero bivariate correlation with the criterion. This is because a suppressor variable may display a bivariate correlation with Y of zero, even though it could substantially increase R^2 if added to a multiple regression equation. When starting with a set of possible predictor variables, it is generally safer to begin the analysis with a multiple regression equation that contains all predictors, on the chance that one of them is serving as a suppressor variable (the topic of choosing an "optimal" subset of predictor variables from a larger set is a complex one that is beyond the scope of this text; for a helpful discussion, see Chapter 4 of Freund and Littell [1991]).

To provide some sense of perspective, however, you should take comfort in knowing that true suppressor variables are somewhat rare in social science research. In most cases, you can expect your data to behave according to the generalizations made in the preceding section (the one that dealt with regression equations that do not contain suppressors). That is to say that, in most cases, you will find that R^2 is larger to the extent that the X variables are more strongly correlated with Y, and less strongly correlated with one another. To learn more about suppressor variables, see Pedhazur (1982).

The uniqueness index. A **uniqueness index** represents the percentage of variance in a criterion that is accounted for by a given predictor variable, above and beyond the variance accounted for by the other predictor variables in the equation. A uniqueness index is one measure of an X variable's importance as a predictor: the greater the amount of unique variance accounted for by a predictor, the greater its usefulness.

The concept of a uniqueness index can be illustrated with reference to Figure 13.6, which illustrates the uniqueness index for the predictor variable, income. Figure 13.6 is identical to Figure 13.5 with respect to the correlations between income and prosocial behavior, and the correlations between the three X variables. In Figure 13.6, however, only the area that represents the uniqueness index for income has been shaded in. It can be seen that this area is consistent with the definition given earlier, which stated that the uniqueness index for a given variable represents the percentage of variance in the criterion (prosocial behavior) that is accounted for by the predictor variable (income) above and beyond the variance accounted for by the other predictors in the equation (age and moral development, in this case).

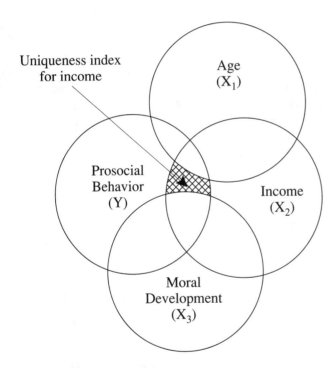

Figure 13.6: Venn Diagram: Uniqueness Index for Income

When performing multiple regression, it is often useful to compute the uniqueness index for each X variable in the equation. These indices, along with other information, can be useful in more completely understanding the nature of the relationship between the criterion and the predictors.

Computing the uniqueness index for a given X variable actually requires estimating two multiple regression equations. The first equation should include all of the X variables of interest. This can be referred to as the **full equation**, because it contains the full set of predictors.

In contrast, the second multiple regression equation should include all of the X variables except for the X variable of interest. For this reason, this second equation can be called the **reduced equation**.

To calculate the uniqueness index for the X variable of interest, you subtract the R^2 value for the reduced equation from the R^2 value for the full equation. The resulting difference is the uniqueness index for the X variable of interest.

This procedure can be illustrated by calculating the uniqueness index for income. Assume that two multiple regression equations are estimated, and that prosocial behavior is the criterion variable in both. With the full equation, the predictor variables include age, income, and moral development. With reduced equation, the predictors include only age and moral development (income was dropped because you wish to calculate the uniqueness index for income). Assume that the following R^2 values are obtained for the two equations:

$$R^2_{Full} = .40$$
$$R^2_{Reduced} = .35$$

These R^2 values show that, when all three predictor variables were included in the equation, they accounted for 40% of the variance in prosocial behavior. However, when income was dropped from this equation, the reduced equation accounted for only 35% of the variance in prosocial behavior. The uniqueness index for income (symbolized as U) can now be calculated by subtracting the reduced-equation R^2 from the full-equation R^2:

$$U = R^2_{Full} - R^2_{Reduced}$$
$$U = .40 - .35$$
$$U = .05$$

The uniqueness index for income was .05, meaning that income accounts for only 5% of the variance in prosocial behavior, beyond the variance accounted for by age and moral development.

To compute the uniqueness index for age, you would have to estimate yet another multiple regression equation: one in which age had been dropped from the full equation (in other words, an equation containing only income and moral development). The R^2 for the new reduced equation would be calculated, and would be subtracted from the R^2 for the full equation to arrive at the U for age. A similar procedure would then be performed to compute the U for moral development. A later section of this chapter (titled "Computing Uniqueness Indices with PROC REG") shows how the results of the SAS System's REG procedure can be used to compute uniqueness indices for a set of predictors.

Testing the Significance of the Difference between Two R^2 Values

The preceding section showed that you can calculate a uniqueness index by

- estimating two R^2 values: one for a full equation with all X variables included, and one for a reduced equation with all X variables except for the X variable of interest

- subtracting the R^2 for the reduced model from the R^2 for the full model.

The difference between the two R^2 values is the uniqueness index for the dropped X variable.

Once a uniqueness index has been calculated, however, the next logical question is, "Is this uniqueness index significantly different from zero?" In other words, does the predictor variable represented by this index account for a significant amount of variance in the criterion, beyond the variance accounted for by the other predictors? To answer this question, it is necessary to test the significance of the difference between the R^2 value for the full equation versus the R^2 for the reduced equation. This section will show how this is done.

One of the most important procedures in multiple regression analysis involves testing the significance of the difference between two R^2 values. This test is conducted when you have estimated two multiple regression equations, and wish to know whether the R^2 value for one equation is significantly larger than the R^2 for the other equation.

There is one important condition for performing this test, however: The two multiple regression equations must be nested. Two equations are said to be **nested** when they include the same criterion variable, and the X variables included in the smaller equation are a subset of the X variables included in the larger equation.

To illustrate this concept, we refer again to the study in which

```
Y  = Prosocial behavior
X₁ = Age
X₂ = Income
X₃ = Moral development
```

The following two multiple regression equations are nested:

```
Full equation:     Y = X₁ + X₂ + X₃

Reduced equation:  Y = X₁ + X₂
```

It can be said that the reduced equation is nested within the full equation, because the predictors for the reduced equation (X_1 and X_2) are a subset of the predictors in the full equation (X_1, X_2, and X_3).

However, the following two multiple regression equations are not nested:

> Full equation: $Y = X_1 + X_2 + X_3$
>
> Reduced equation: $Y = X_1 + X_4$

Even though the "reduced" equation in the preceding example contains fewer X variables than the "full" equation, it is not nested within the full equation. This is because the reduced equation contains the variable X_4, which does not appear in the full equation. The X variables of the reduced equation are therefore not a subset of the X variables in the full equation.

When two equations are in fact nested, it is possible to test the significance of the difference between the R^2 values for the equations. This is sometimes referred to as "testing the significance of variables added to the equation." To understand this expression, think about the situation in which the full equation contains X_1, X_2, and X_3, and the reduced equation contains only X_1 and X_2. The only difference between these two equations is the fact that the full equation contains X_3 while the reduced equation does not. By testing the significance of the difference between the R^2 values for the two equations, you are determining whether adding X_3 to the reduced equation results in a significant increase in R^2.

Here is the equation for the *F* ratio that tests the significance of the difference between two R^2 values:

$$F = \frac{(R^2_{Full} - R^2_{Reduced}) / (K_{Full} - K_{Reduced})}{(1 - R^2_{Full}) / (N - K_{Full} - 1)}$$

where

R^2_{Full} =   the obtained value of R^2 for the full multiple regression equation; that is, the equation containing the larger number of predictor variables

$R^2_{Reduced}$ =   the obtained value of R^2 for the reduced multiple regression equation; that is, the equation containing the smaller number of predictor variables

K_{Full} =   the number of predictor variables in the full multiple regression equation

$K_{Reduced}$ =   the number of predictor variables in the reduced multiple regression equation

N =   the total number of subjects in the sample

The preceding equation can be used to test the significance of any number of variables added to a regression equation. The examples in this section will involve testing the significance of adding just one variable to an equation. This section focuses on the one-variable situation because of its relevance to the concept of the uniqueness index, as discussed above. Remember that a uniqueness index represents the percentage of variance in a criterion that is accounted for by a single X variable, above and beyond the variance accounted for by the other X variables.

Earlier, it was stated that a uniqueness index is calculated by estimating a full equation with all X variables included, along with a reduced equation in which one X variable has been dropped. The difference between the two resulting R^2 values is the uniqueness index for the dropped X variable.

The relevance of the preceding formula to the concept of the uniqueness index should now be obvious. This formula allows you to test the statistical significance of a uniqueness index; it allows you to test the statistical significance of the variance in Y accounted for by a given X variable, beyond the variance accounted for by the other X variables. For this reason, the formula is helpful in determining which predictors are relatively important, and which are relatively unimportant.

To illustrate the formula, imagine that you conduct a study in which you use age, income, and moral development to predict prosocial behavior in a sample of 104 subjects. You now wish to calculate the uniqueness index for the predictor, moral development. To do this you estimate two multiple regression equations: a "full model" that includes all three X variables as predictors, and a "reduced model" that includes all predictors except for moral development. Here are the R^2 values obtained for the two models:

Table 13.7

Variance Accounted for by Full and Reduced Models, Prosocial Behavior Study

R^2 Obtained for this model	Predictor variables included in the equation
.30	Age, income, moral development (full model)
.20	Age, income (reduced model)

Note: N = 104.

The preceding table shows that the reduced equation (including only age and income) accounts for only 20% of the variance in prosocial behavior. However, adding moral development to this equation increases R^2 to .30. The uniqueness index for moral development is therefore $.30 - .20 = .10$.

To compute the F test that tests the significance of the difference between these two R^2 values, you simply insert the appropriate figures in the following equation:

$$F = \frac{(R^2_{Full} - R^2_{Reduced}) / (K_{Full} - K_{Reduced})}{(1 - R^2_{Full}) / (N - K_{Full} - 1)}$$

$$F = \frac{(.30 - .20) / (3 - 2)}{(1 - .30) / (104 - 3 - 1)}$$

$$F = \frac{(.10) / (1)}{(.70) / (100)}$$

$$F = \frac{(.10)}{(.007)}$$

$$F = 14.29$$

The F ratio for this test is 14.29. To determine whether this F is significant, you turn to the table of critical values of F that appears as Appendix C in the back of this text. To find the appropriate critical value of F, it is necessary to first establish the degrees of freedom for the numerator and the degrees of freedom for the denominator that are associated with the current analysis. When comparing the significance of the difference between two R^2 values, the degrees of freedom for the numerator are equal to $K_{Full} - K_{Reduced}$ (which appears in the numerator of the preceding equation). In the present analysis, the number of predictors in the full equation is 3 and the number in the reduced equation is 2, and so the degrees of freedom for the numerator is $3 - 2 = 1$.

The degrees of freedom for the denominator of this F test is $N - K_{Full} - 1$ (which appears in the denominator of the preceding equation). The sample size in the present study was 104, so the degrees of freedom for the denominator is $104 - 4 - 1 = 100$.

The table of F values shows that, with 1 df for the numerator and 100 df for the denominator, the critical value of F ($p < .05$) is approximately 3.94. The preceding formula produced an observed F value of 14.29, which of course is much larger than this critical value. You may therefore reject the null hypothesis of no differences, and conclude that there is a significant difference between the two R^2 values that were compared. In other words, adding moral development to an equation already containing age and income resulted in a significant increase in variance accounted for. In still other words, the uniqueness index for moral development was proven to be statistically significant.

Multiple Regression Coefficients

The b weights discussed earlier in this chapter were referred to as nonstandardized multiple regression coefficients. It was said that a **multiple regression coefficient** for a given X variable represents the average change in Y that is associated with a one-unit change in that X variable, while holding constant the remaining X variables. "Holding constant" means that the multiple regression coefficient for a given predictor variable is an estimate the average change in Y that would be associated with a one-unit change in that X variable if all subjects had exactly the same scores on the remaining X variables.

When conducting multiple regression analyses, researchers are often interested in determining which of the X variables are relatively important predictors of the criterion, and which are relatively unimportant. In doing this, you may be tempted to review the multiple regression coefficients estimated in the analysis, and use these as indicators of importance. According to this logic, a regression coefficient represents the amount of *weight* that is given to a given X variable in the prediction of Y; if a variable is given much weight, it must be an important predictor.

Nonstandardized versus standardized coefficients. However, great caution must be exercised when using multiple regression coefficients in this fashion. There are at least two reasons for this. First, you must remember that two types of multiple regression coefficients are produced in the course of an analysis: nonstandardized coefficients and standardized coefficients. **Nonstandardized multiple regression coefficients** (sometimes called b weights and symbolized with a lowercase b or *b*) are the coefficients that are produced when the data analyzed are in raw score form. "Raw score" form mean s that the variables have not been standardized in any way: the different variables may have very different means and standard deviations. For example, the standard deviation for X_1 may be 1.35, while the standard deviation for X_2 may be 584.20.

Generally speaking, it is not appropriate to use the relative size of nonstandardized regression coefficients in assessing the relative importance of predictor variables. This is because the relative size of a nonstandardized coefficient for a given predictor variable is very much influenced by the size of that predictor's standard deviation: With other things equal, the variables with larger standard deviations will tend to have smaller nonstandardized regression coefficients, while variables with smaller standard deviations will tend to have larger regression coefficients. Because of this, the size of nonstandardized coefficients generally tell us nothing about which variables were relatively important predictors.

If this is the case, then for what are the nonstandardized coefficients useful? They are most frequently used to calculate subjects' predicted scores on Y. For example, an earlier section presented a multiple regression equation for the prediction of prosocial behavior, in which X_1 = age, X_2 = income, and X_3 = moral development. That equation is reproduced here:

$$Y' = (.10) X_1 + (.25) X_2 + (1.10) X_3 + (-3.25)$$

In this equation, the nonstandardized multiple regression coefficient for X_1 was .10, the coefficient for X_2 was .25, and so forth. If you had a subject's raw scores on the three predictor variables, these values could be inserted in the preceding formula to compute that subject's estimated score on Y. The resulting Y' value would also be in raw score form. It would be an estimate of the number of prosocial acts you expect the subject to perform over a six-month period.

In summary, you should not refer to the nonstandardized regression coefficients to assess the relative importance of predictor variables. A better alternative (although still not perfect) is to refer to the standardized coefficients. **Standardized multiple regression coefficients** (sometimes called beta weights or B weights and symbolized with the uppercase B or ß) are the coefficients that would be produced if the data analyzed were in standard score form. "Standard score" form (or "z-score form") means that the variables have been standardized so that each has a mean of zero and a standard deviation of 1. This is important because all variables (Y variables and X variables alike) now have the same standard deviation (a standard deviation of 1); they are now measured on the same scale of magnitude. You no longer have to worry that some variables will display large regression coefficients simply because they have small standard deviations. To some extent, the size of standardized regression coefficients does reflect the relative importance of the various predictor variables; these coefficients should therefore be among the results that are consulted when interpreting the results of a multiple regression analysis.

For example, assume that the analysis of the prosocial behavior study produced the following multiple regression equation with standardized coefficients:

$$\texttt{Y' = (.70) X}_1 \texttt{ + (.20) X}_2 \texttt{ + (.20) X}_3$$

In the preceding equation, X_1 displayed the largest standardized coefficient; this could be interpreted as evidence that it was a relatively important predictor variable, compared to X_2 and X_3.

You can see that the preceding equation, like all regression equations with standardized coefficients, does not contain an intercept constant. This is because the intercept is always equal to zero in a standardized equation. This is a useful fact to know; if a researcher has presented a multiple regression equation in a research article but has not indicated whether it is a standardized or a nonstandardized equation, simply look for the intercept constant. If an intercept is included in the equation, it is almost certainly a nonstandardized equation; if there is no intercept, it is probably a standardized equation. Remember also that the lowercase symbol b or *b* is typically used to represent nonstandardized regression coefficients, while the uppercase symbol B or ß is typically used to represent standardized coefficients.

The reliability of multiple regression coefficients. The preceding section noted that standardized coefficients reflect the importance of predictors only to some extent. The qualification is necessary because of the unreliability that is often demonstrated by multiple regression weights. In this case, unreliability refers to the fact that, when multiple regression using the same variables is performed on data from more than one sample, very different estimates of the multiple regression coefficients are often obtained in the different samples. This is the case for standardized as well as nonstandardized coefficients.

For example, assume that you draw a sample of 50 subjects from a given population, measure the variables discussed in the preceding section (prosocial behavior, age, income, moral development), and estimate a multiple regression equation in which prosocial behavior is the criterion and the remaining variables are predictors (assume that age, income, and moral development are X_1, X_2, and X_3, respectively). With the analysis completed, it is possible that your output would reveal the following standardized regression coefficients for the three predictors:

$$Y' = (.70) X_1 + (.20) X_2 + (.20) X_3$$

The relative size of the coefficients in the preceding equation suggest that X_1 (with a beta weight of .70) is the most important predictor of Y, while X_2 and X_3 (each with beta weights of .20) are much less important.

However, what if you were then to repeat your study with a different group of 50 subjects? It is unfortunately possible (if not likely) that would obtain very different beta weights for the X variables. For example, you might obtain the following:

$$Y' = (.30) X_1 + (.50) X_2 + (.10) X_3$$

In the second equation, X_2 has emerged as the most important predictor of Y, followed by X_1 and X_3.

This is what is meant by the unreliability of standardized regression coefficients: When the same study is performed on different samples, researchers sometimes obtain coefficients of very different sizes. This means that the interpretation of these coefficients must always be made with caution.

This problem of unreliability is more likely in some situations than in others. Specifically, multiple regression coefficients become increasingly unreliable as the analysis is based on increasingly smaller samples, and as the X variables become increasingly correlated with one another. Unfortunately, much of the research that is carried out in the social sciences involves the use of small samples and correlated X variables. For this reason, the standardized regression coefficients (beta weights) are only some of the pieces of information that should be reviewed when assessing the relative importance of predictor variables. The use of these coefficients should be supplemented with a review of the simple bivariate correlations between the X variables and Y, and the uniqueness indices for the X variables. The following sections will show how to do this.

Example: A Test of the Investment Model

The statistical procedures of this chapter will be illustrated by analyzing fictitious data from a correlational study based on the investment model (Rusbult, 1980a, 1980b). You will remember that the investment model was used to illustrate the use of a number of other statistical procedures earlier in this book (e.g., in Chapters 7-12).

The investment model identifies a number of variables that are believed to predict a person's level of commitment to a romantic relationship (as well as to other types of relationships). **Commitment** refers to the individual's intention to maintain the relationship and remain with the current partner. One version of the investment model asserts that commitment will be affected by the following four variables:

Rewards:	The number of "good things" that the subject associates with the relationship; The positive aspects of the relationship
Costs:	The number of "bad things" or hardships associated with the relationship
Investment Size:	The amount of time and personal resources that the subject has put into the relationship
Alternative Value:	The attractiveness of the subject's alternatives to the relationship (e.g., the attractiveness of alternative romantic partners)

The hypothesized relationship between commitment and these four predictor variables is presented in Figure 13.7.

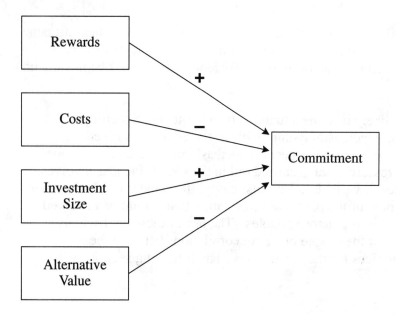

Figure 13.7: One Version of the Investment Model

If these four variables actually have a causal effect on commitment, it is reasonable to assume that they should also be useful for *predicting* commitment in a simple correlational study. Therefore, the present study will be correlational in nature, and will use multiple regression procedures to assess the nature of the predictive relationship between these variables. If the model survives this test, you may then wish to follow it up by performing a new study that is more capable of testing the proposed causal relationships between the variables: perhaps a true experiment, or perhaps a more ambitious correlational study to be analyzed using path analysis. The present chapter, however, will focus only on the somewhat less ambitious (and less complicated) multiple regression procedures.

Overview of the Analysis

To understand better the nature of the relationship between the five variables presented in Figure 13.7, the data will be analyzed using two SAS System procedures. First, PROC CORR will be used to compute Pearson correlations between the variables. This is useful for understanding the big picture: the simple bivariate relations between the variables.

Next, PROC REG will be used to perform a multiple regression in which commitment is simultaneously regressed on the four predictor variables. This will provide a number of important pieces of information. First, you will learn whether there is a significant relationship between commitment and the linear combination of predictors (that is, whether there is a significant relationship between commitment and the four variables taken as a group). In addition, you will review the multiple regression coefficients for each of the four predictors to determine which are statistically significant, and which standardized coefficients are relatively large.

Finally, the SELECTION=RSQUARE option will be used with PROC REG in a separate analysis to determine the amount of variance in commitment that is accounted for by every possible combination of predictor variables. Results from this analysis will be used to determine the uniqueness index for each of the four predictors. The formula for testing the significance of the difference between two R^2 values will then be used to determine which of the uniqueness indices are significantly different from zero.

Gathering and Inputting Data

The Questionnaire

Assume that you conduct a study in which the subjects are 50 college students, each of whom are currently involved in a romantic relationship. Each subject completes a 24-item questionnaire designed to assess the six investment model constructs: commitment, satisfaction, rewards, costs, investment size, and alternative value (one construct, satisfaction, is not included in the version of the investment model to be tested in this study, and will therefore not be referred to again in this chapter).

Each investment model construct is assessed with four questions. For example, the four items that assess the "commitment" construct are reproduced here:

---

21. **How committed are you to your current relationship?**

Not at all   1 2 3 4 5 6 7 8 9   Extremely
committed   Committed

22. **How long do you intend to remain in your current relationship?**

A very   1 2 3 4 5 6 7 8 9   A very
short time   long time

23. **How often do you think about breaking up with your current partner?**

Frequently   1 2 3 4 5 6 7 8 9   Never

24. **How likely is it that you will maintain your current relationship for a long time?**

Extremely   1 2 3 4 5 6 7 8 9   Extremely
unlikely   Likely

Notice that, with each item, circling a higher response number (such as 8 or 9) indicates a higher level of commitment, and circling a lower response number (such as 1 or 2) indicates a lower level of commitment. A given subject's responses to these four items are summed to arrive at a single score that reflects that subject's overall level of commitment. This summed score will serve as the commitment variable in your analyses. Scores on this variable may range from 4 to 36, with higher values indicating higher levels of commitment.

Each of the remaining investment model constructs are assessed in the same way, with responses to four survey items being summed to create a single overall measure of the construct. With each variable, scores can range from 4 to 36, and higher scores always indicate higher levels of the construct being assessed.

Inputting the Data

Analyzing raw data. In practice, the easiest way to create these summed scores would probably involve keying the raw data and then using data manipulation statements in the SAS program to create the summed scores needed for each subject. Raw data in this sense refers to the subject's responses to the 24 items on the questionnaire. You could prepare a single SAS program that would input these raw data, create new variables (overall scale scores) from existing variables, and perform the regression analyses on the new variables.

For example, imagine that you have keyed the raw data so that there was one line of data for each subject, and this line contained the subjects' responses to questions 1-24. Assume that items 1-4 assessed the rewards construct, items 5-8 assessed the costs construct, and so forth. The following program would input these data and create the necessary summed scores:

```
1       DATA D1;
2          INPUT   #1    @1    (V1-V24)    (1.)    ;
3
4              REWARD = V1  + V2  + V3  + V4;
5              COST   = V5  + V6  + V7  + V8;
6              INVEST = V9  + V10 + V11 + V12;
7              ALTERN = V13 + V14 + V15 + V16;
8              SATIS  = V17 + V18 + V19 + V20;
9              COMMIT = V21 + V22 + V23 + V24;
10
11             IF REWARD NE . AND COST   NE . AND INVEST NE . AND
12                ALTERN NE . AND COMMIT NE . ;
13
14      CARDS;
15      343434346465364735748234
16      867565768654544354865767
17      434325524243536435366355
18      .
19      .
20      .
21      874374848763747667677467
22      534232343433232343524253
23      979876768968789796868688
24      ;
25
26      Place PROC statements here
```

Lines 1-2 of the preceding program tell the system that there is one line of data for each subject, variables V1 through V24 begin at column 1, and each variable is one column wide.

Line 4 of the program tells the system to create a new variable called REWARD, and a given subject's score on REWARD should be equal to the sum of his or her score on variables V1, V2, V3, and V4 (questionnaire items 1-4). Lines 5 though 9 of the program create the study's remaining variables in the same way.

Lines 11-12 contain a subsetting IF statement that eliminates from the data set any subject with missing data on any of the five variables to be analyzed. This ensures that each analysis will be performed on exactly the same subjects: you will not have to worry that some analyses may be based on 50 subjects while others are performed on only 45 due to missing data (Chapter 4 deals with the use of subsetting IF statements).

Notice that SATIS (the satisfaction variable) is not listed in this subsetting IF statement. This is because SATIS will not be included in any of the analyses (SATIS will not be listed as a predictor variable or a criterion variable in any analysis). Including SATIS in the subsetting IF statement may have unnecessarily eliminated some subjects from your data set. For example, if a subject named Bob Smith had missing data on SATIS, and SATIS were in fact included in this subsetting IF statement, then Bob Smith would have been dropped from the data set and each analysis would have been based on 49 observations rather than 50. But dropping Bob Smith in this case would have been pointless, because SATIS was not going to be used as a predictor or criterion variable in any analysis anyway. To summarize, only variables that are to be used in your analyses should be listed in the subsetting IF statement that eliminates subjects with missing data.

The CARDS statement and some fictitious data are presented on lines 14-24. Line 26 shows where the PROC statements (discussed later) would be placed in the program.

How this program handles missing data in creating scale scores. With the preceding program, if a subject left blank any one of the four questions that constitute a scale, that subject will receive score of "missing" ("."), on that scale. For example, if Bob Smith completes items 1, 2, and 3 of the REWARDS scale, but leaves blank item 4, he will be assigned a missing value on REWARDS. If the data set were printed using PROC PRINT, his value on REWARDS would appear as ".".

This is fortunate for your purposes; just consider the problems that would arise if the system did not assign missing values in this way. What if the system simply summed each subject's responses to the items that they did complete, even when some had been left blank? Remember that Bob Smith completed only 3 items on the 4-item response scale. In his case, the highest score he could possibly receive on REWARDS would be 27 (this is because the 3 items use a 9-point response scale, and 3 X 9 = 27). For those subjects who completed all 4 items in the REWARDS scale, the highest score possible is 36 (because 4 X 9 = 36). Obviously, under these circumstances the scores from subjects with incomplete responses would not be directly comparable to scores from subjects with complete data. It is therefore best that subjects with incomplete responses be assigned missing values when scale scores are computed.

Analyzing pre-calculated scale scores. A second option available to you is to compute each subject's score on each of the six constructs by hand, and then prepare a SAS program that inputs and analyzes these pre-calculated scores. In other words, you could review the questionnaire completed by subject 1, sum the responses to items 1 through 4 (perhaps by using a hand calculator) record this sum on a summary sheet, repeat this process for the remaining scales, and repeat the entire process for all subjects.

Later, the summed scores could be keyed as data in a SAS program. This data set would consist of 50 lines of data (one line for each subject). Instead of raw data, a given subject's summed score on each of the six variables would appear on his or her data line. Scores on the commitment variable might be keyed in columns 1-2, scores on the satisfaction variable might be keyed in columns 4-5, and so forth. The guide used in keying these data is presented here:

Line	Column	Variable Name	Explanation
1	1-2	COMMIT	Scores on commitment variable.
	3	(blank)	(blank)
	4-5	SATIS	Scores on the satisfaction variable.
	6	(blank)	(blank)
	7-8	REWARD	Scores on rewards variable.
	9	(blank)	(blank)
	10-11	COST	Scores on costs variable.
	12	(blank)	(blank)
	13-14	INVEST	Scores on investment size variable.
	15	(blank)	(blank)
	16-17	ALTERN	Scores on the alternative value variable.

Fictitious data from the 50 subjects in your study have been keyed according to these guidelines and are presented in Appendix B. The analyses discussed in this chapter will be performed on this data set.

Following is the SAS program that will input these data. Lines 9-10 again include a subsetting IF statement that would eliminate from the data set any subject with missing data on any of the variables to be analyzed (as was explained in the preceding section). A few lines of the actual data are presented as lines 13-22. Line 25 indicates the position where the PROC statements (to be discussed later) would be placed in this program.

```
1         DATA D1;
2           INPUT   #1    @1   (COMMIT)   (2.)
3                         @4   (SATIS)    (2.)
4                         @7   (REWARD)   (2.)
5                         @10  (COST)     (2.)
6                         @13  (INVEST)   (2.)
7                         @16  (ALTERN)   (2.)    ;
8
9           IF REWARD NE . AND COST   NE . AND INVEST NE . AND
10             ALTERN NE . AND COMMIT NE . ;
11
12        CARDS;
13        34 30 25 13 25 12
14        32 27 27 14 32 13
15        34 23 24 21 30 14
16        .
17        .
18        .
19        .
20        36 32 28 13 15  5
21        32 29 30 21 32 22
22        30 32 33 16 34  9
23        ;
24
25        Place PROC statements here
```

Computing Bivariate Correlations with PROC CORR

In most studies in which data are analyzed using multiple regression, it is appropriate to begin the analysis by computing all possible correlations between the study's variables. Reviewing these correlations will help you understand the big picture concerning the simple relationships between the criterion variable and the four predictor variables, as well as between the four predictor variables themselves. When the results of the study are ultimately published, many journals require that the first table in the results section present these correlations, along with variable means and standard deviations.

Writing the Program

Following is the general form for the SAS statements that will compute all possible correlations between the variables being investigated (because detailed information concerning use of the

CORR procedure was provided in Chapter 6 of this text, most of that information will not be repeated here).

```
PROC CORR    DATA=data-set-name;
   VAR  criterion-variable-and-predictor-variables ;
   RUN;
```

Technically, the variables may be presented in any sequence desired, although there are some advantages to (a) listing the criterion variable first, and (b) then listing the predictor variables in the same order that they will be discussed in the text. This often makes it easier for reader to interpret the results of the correlation matrix when it is published in a journal article.

Below is the entire program (including a portion of the fictitious data) that would compute all possible correlations between the five variables of interest in the current study. Output 13.1 presents the results produced by this program.

```
1       DATA D1;
2          INPUT    #1    @1   (COMMIT)   (2.)
3                          @4   (SATIS)    (2.)
4                          @7   (REWARD)   (2.)
5                          @10  (COST)     (2.)
6                          @13  (INVEST)   (2.)
7                          @16  (ALTERN)   (2.)   ;
8
9          IF REWARD NE . AND COST   NE . AND INVEST NE . AND
10            ALTERN NE . AND COMMIT NE . ;
11
12      CARDS;
13      34 30 25 13 25 12
14      32 27 27 14 32 13
15      34 23 24 21 30 14
16      .
17      .
18      .
19      .
20      36 32 28 13 15  5
21      32 29 30 21 32 22
22      30 32 33 16 34  9
23      ;
24
25      PROC CORR    DATA=D1;
26         VAR  COMMIT  REWARD   COST  INVEST   ALTERN;
27         RUN;
```

```
                            The SAS System                              1

                          Correlation Analysis

            5 'VAR' Variables:   COMMIT   REWARD   COST   INVEST   ALTERN


                            Simple Statistics

Variable        N         Mean      Std Dev        Sum      Minimum      Maximum

COMMIT         48     27.70833     10.19587       1330      4.00000     36.00000
REWARD         48     26.64583      5.05076       1279      9.00000     33.00000
COST           48     16.58333      5.49597   796.00000     5.00000     26.00000
INVEST         48     25.33333      6.08218       1216     11.00000     34.00000
ALTERN         48     16.60417      7.50529   797.00000     4.00000     34.00000


     Pearson Correlation Coefficients / Prob > |R| under Ho: Rho=0 / N = 48

                 COMMIT        REWARD         COST         INVEST        ALTERN

COMMIT          1.00000       0.57597      -0.24826       0.61403      -0.72000
                0.0           0.0001        0.0889        0.0001        0.0001

REWARD          0.57597       1.00000      -0.45152       0.57117      -0.46683
                0.0001        0.0           0.0013        0.0001        0.0008

COST           -0.24826      -0.45152       1.00000       0.02143       0.27084
                0.0889        0.0013        0.0           0.8851        0.0626

INVEST          0.61403       0.57117       0.02143       1.00000      -0.44776
                0.0001        0.0001        0.8851        0.0           0.0014

ALTERN         -0.72000      -0.46683       0.27084      -0.44776       1.00000
                0.0001        0.0008        0.0626        0.0014        0.0
```

Output 13.1: Results of the CORR Procedure

Interpreting the Results of PROC CORR

1. Make sure that the numbers look right. Before interpreting the meaning of the correlation coefficients, it is important to review descriptive statistics to help verify that no errors were made in keying data or writing the INPUT statement. Most of this information is presented in a table of simple statistics that appears at the top of the output page.

The simple statistics table at the top of Output 13.1 provides means, standard deviations, and other descriptive statistics for the five variables analyzed. Note that N = 48 for all six variables, meaning that there must have been missing data for 2 of the 50 subjects in the original data set (the 2 with missing data were deleted by the subsetting IF statement discussed earlier; review the actual data set in Appendix B to verify that 2 subjects did in fact have missing data).

The rest of the descriptive statistics should also be reviewed to verify that all of the figures are reasonable. In particular, check the "Minimum" and "Maximum" columns for evidence of problems. The lowest score that a subject could possibly receive on any variable was 4; if any variable displays a minimum score below 4, an error must have been made either in keying the data or in the program. Similarly, no score in the "Maximum" column should exceed 36.

2. Determine the size of the sample producing the correlations. When all correlations are based on the same number of subjects, the sample size for the correlations should appear on the line just below the table of simple statistics. In Output 13.1, this line reads

```
Pearson Correlation Coefficients / Prob > |R| under Ho:  Rho=0 / N = 48
```

The final entry in this line tells us that N = 48 for the analysis. If the various correlations had instead been based on different sample sizes, then the N associated with each coefficient would appear within the table of correlations coefficients, just below the *p* value for the corresponding correlation.

3. Review the correlation coefficients. The correlations between the five variables appear in the 5 X 5 matrix in the bottom half of Output 13.1. In this matrix, where the row for one variable intersects with the column of a second variable, you find the cell that provides information about the correlation between these variables. The top figure in the cell is the Pearson correlation between the variables; the bottom figure is the *p* value associated with this correlation.

For example, consider the vertical column under the "COMMIT" heading. Where the column headed "COMMIT" intersects with the row headed "REWARD", you find that the correlation between commitment and rewards is .57597 (which rounds to .58). The *p* value associated with this correlation is .0001, meaning that there is less than 1 chance in 10,000 of obtaining a sample correlation of this size if the population correlation were zero. In other words, this correlation of .58 is statistically significant at the .0001 level.

Reviewing the correlations in the COMMIT column tells you something about the pattern of simple bivariate correlations between commitment and the four predictors. Notice that COMMIT demonstrates a positive correlation with REWARD and INVEST. This is as you would expect: the subjects who report higher levels of rewards and investment size also report higher levels of commitment. It can also be seen that COMMIT demonstrates negative relationships with COST and ALTERN. This is also as you would expect: subjects who report higher levels of costs and alternative value report lower levels of commitment. Each of these correlations are in the direction predicted by the investment model (see Figure 13.7).

However, notice that some predictors are more strongly related to COMMIT than are others. Specifically, ALTERN displays the strongest correlation at –.72, followed by INVEST (.61) and REWARD (.58). Each of these correlations are statistically significant at the .0001 level.

The correlation between COMMIT and COST is much weaker at −.25. In fact, this correlation is not statistically significant; the *p* value associate with it is .0889, just above the traditional significance level of .05. Based on these results, you could not reject the null hypothesis that commitment and costs are uncorrelated in the population.

The correlations in Output 13.1 also provide important information about the correlations among the four predictor variables. When using multiple regression, an ideal predictive situation is typically one in which each predictor variable displays a relatively strong correlation with the criterion, while the predictor variables display relatively weak correlations among themselves (the reasons for this were discussed in an earlier section).

With this in mind, the correlations presented in Output 13.1 show that the predictive situation obtained with the current data set is something less than ideal. It is true that three of the predictors display relatively strong correlations with commitment , but it is unfortunately also true that most of the predictors display relatively strong correlations with each other. Notice that r = −.45 for the correlation between REWARD and COST, that r = .57 for REWARD and INVEST, and r = −.47 for REWARD and ALTERN. These correlations are moderately large, as is the correlation between INVEST and ALTERN. Moderate intercorrelations of this sort sometimes result in nonsignificant multiple regression coefficients for at least some predictor variables when the data are analyzed with multiple regression; the analyses reported in the following section should bear this out.

Estimating the Full Multiple Regression Equation with PROC REG

There are a number of different SAS System procedures that allow one to perform multiple regression analyses. The basic multiple regression procedure, however, is PROC REG. This procedure estimates multiple regression coefficients for the various predictors, calculates R^2 and tests it for significance, and prints additional information relevant to the analysis.

Writing the Program

Here is the general form for using PROC REG to request a basic multiple regression analysis with standardized multiple regression coefficients:

```
PROC REG    DATA=data-set-name       options;
   MODEL   criterion = predictor-variables  /  STB   options;
   RUN;
```

Predictor variables in the preceding MODEL statement should be separated by at least one space. The name of the last predictor variable should be followed by a slash and a list of options, if any are desired. You should always specify STB in the options field of the MODEL statement, as this requests that the standardized multiple regression coefficients be printed. These coefficients will almost always be useful in interpreting results.

Here are some options for the REG statement that may be particularly useful in social science research; additional options may be found in the Chapter 36 ("The REG Procedure") of the *SAS/STAT user's guide, version 6, fourth edition, volume 2* (1989):

`CORR`

requests that the correlation matrix for all variables in the MODEL statement be printed.

`SIMPLE`

requests simple statistics for all variables in the analysis (mean, variance, standard deviation, and uncorrected sum of squares).

These are some options for the MODEL statement that may be prove particularly useful; more are listed in Chapter 36 of the *SAS/STAT user's guide, volume 2* (1989). The notes appearing here that refer the reader to the *SAS/STAT user's guide* are similarly referring to Chapter 36.

`COLLIN`

prints diagnostics regarding collinearity among the predictor variables. See the section on collinearity diagnostics in the PROC REG chapter of the *SAS/STAT user's guide* for details.

`INFLUENCE`

prints diagnostics regarding the influence of each observation on the parameter estimates and on the predicted Y values. See the section on influence diagnostics in the PROC REG chapter of the *SAS/STAT user's guide* for details.

`P`

prints actual Y scores, predicted Y scores, and residual scores (errors of prediction) for each observation. See the section on predicted and residual values in the PROC REG chapter of the *SAS/STAT user's guide* for details.

`R`

requests a detailed analysis of the residuals, including Cook's D statistic, which assesses the influence of each observation on the parameter estimates. See the section on predicted and residual values in the PROC REG chapter of the *SAS/STAT user's guide* for details.

`SELECTION`=model-selection-method

requests a specific model-selection method. Model-selection methods are used to select an "optimal" group of predictor variables from a larger set. Keywords for available methods are FORWARD, BACKWARD, STEPWISE, MAXR, MINR, RSQUARE, ADJRSQ, CP, and NONE. This chapter will show how to use the SELECTION=RSQUARE option to obtain information that is necessary for computing uniqueness indices. For information on model-selection methods, see the PROC REG chapter in the *SAS/STAT user's guide*, or Chapter 4 ("Multicollinearity: Detection and Remedial Measures") of Freund and Littell, (1991).

STB

requests the printing of the standardized multiple regression coefficient (beta weight) for each predictor variable.

In the present analysis, it was necessary to estimate a multiple regression equation in which the criterion variable was commitment, and the predictor variables were rewards, costs, investment size, and alternative value. Here are the statements that requested this model; the STB option in the MODEL statement requests the standardized regression coefficients:

```
PROC REG    DATA=D1;
     MODEL COMMIT = REWARD   COST   INVEST   ALTERN / STB;
     RUN;
```

The SAS output created by these statements is reproduced as Output 13.2.

```
                             The SAS System                              2
Model: MODEL1
Dependent Variable: COMMIT
                          Analysis of Variance
                             Sum of        Mean
      Source        DF      Squares       Square    F Value    Prob>F

      Model          4    3154.83928    788.70982    19.592    0.0001
      Error         43    1731.07738     40.25761
      C Total       47    4885.91667

          Root MSE        6.34489     R-square      0.6457
          Dep Mean       27.70833     Adj R-sq      0.6127
          C.V.           22.89885
                          Parameter Estimates
                        Parameter      Standard     T for H0:
      Variable  DF      Estimate        Error     Parameter=0    Prob > |T|

      INTERCEP   1     20.038127     8.73670776      2.294       0.0268
      REWARD     1      0.279372     0.27330885      1.022       0.3124
      COST       1     -0.105747     0.20800295     -0.508       0.6138
      INVEST     1      0.523465     0.21037217      2.488       0.0168
      ALTERN     1     -0.679430     0.14670404     -4.631       0.0001
                       Standardized
      Variable  DF       Estimate

      INTERCEP   1      0.00000000
      REWARD     1      0.13839348
      COST       1     -0.05700182
      INVEST     1      0.31226487
      ALTERN     1     -0.50013618
```

Output 13.2: Results of the REG Procedure with the STB Option

Interpreting the Results of PROC REG

1. Make sure that everything looks right. Near the top left section of the page, verify that the name of the criterion variable is listed to the right of "Dependent Variable". In this case, the criterion is COMMIT. In the "Analysis of Variance" section, one of the headings is "DF" for "degrees of freedom." Where this DF column intersects with the row headed "C Total", you will find the corrected total degrees of freedom. Verify that this number is equal to N – 1, where N = the total number of subjects who provided usable data for the analysis. In the present case, the total size of the sample was 50, but 2 of these subjects did not provide usable data (as was discussed in the section on PROC CORR), leaving usable data from 48 subjects. Output 13.2 shows that corrected total degrees of freedom are 47, which of course is equal to N – 1 (where N = 48). These degrees of freedom therefore appear to be correct.

2. Review the obtained value of R^2. Toward the center of the page you will find the heading "R-square". The value to the right of this is the observed R^2 for this multiple regression equation. Earlier it was said that this R^2 value indicates the percent of variance in the criterion variable that is accounted for by the linear combination of predictor variables. In the present case, $R^2 = 0.6457$, which may be rounded to .65. This indicates that the linear combination of REWARD, COST, INVEST, and ALTERN accounts for about 65% of the variance in COMMIT.

There is a significance test associated with this R^2 which tests the null hypothesis that $R^2 = 0$ in the population. To test this null hypothesis, look in the "Analysis of Variance" section, under the heading "F Value". In this case, you see an *F* value of 19.59. Under the heading "Prob>F" is the *p* value associated with this F. Remember that the *p* value gives us the probability that you would obtain an *F* this large or larger if the null hypothesis were true. In this case, the *p* value is very small (.0001), so you reject the null hypothesis, and conclude that the obtained value of R^2 is statistically significant. In other words, you conclude that R^2 is probably greater than zero in the population.

The preceding analysis determines whether the linear combination of predictor variables accounts for a significant amount of variance in the criterion, and this test should be reviewed each time one conducts a multiple regression. However, in addition to determining whether the predictors account for a significant amount of variance, you should also determine whether your predictors account for a *meaningful* amount of variance; that is, a relatively large amount of variance. How large must an R^2 value be to be considered meaningful? That will depend, in part, on what has been found in prior research concerning the criterion variable being investigated. If, for example, predictor variables in earlier investigations have routinely accounted for 50% of the variance in the criterion, but the predictors in your study have accounted for only 10%, your findings may not be viewed as being very important. On the other hand, if the predictors of earlier studies have routinely accounted for only 5% of the variance, but the variables of your study have accounted for 10%, this may be considered a meaningful amount of variance.

This issue of "statistical significance" versus "percentage of variance accounted for" is an important one, because it is possible to obtain an R^2 value that is very small (say, .03), but is still statistically significant. This often occurs when analyzing data from very large samples. Therefore, always review both the statistical significance of the equation, as well as the total amount of variance accounted for, in assessing the substantive importance of your findings.

3. Review the adjusted value of R^2. Below the heading R-square is the heading "Adj R-sq", which stands for "adjusted R^2." To the right of "Adj R-sq" appears a version of R^2 which has been adjusted for degrees of freedom. This is provided because the actual value of R^2 obtained with a given sample often overestimates the population value of R^2. The adjusted R^2, however, has been adjusted downward to more closely approximate the population value. For this reason, the value to the right of "Adj R-sq" is normally smaller than the value to the right of "R-square".

4. Review the intercept and nonstandardized regression coefficients. The bottom half of the output page provides information about the parameter estimates. These parameter estimates are the terms that constitute the multiple regression equation: the intercept and the nonstandardized multiple regression coefficients for the predictor variables.

To begin, notice that the first column of information (on the left) is headed "Variable". Below this heading are the names of the terms in the regression equation: the intercept, and the names of the four predictor variables (REWARD, COST, INVEST, and ALTERN). The third column from the left is headed "Parameter Estimate". This provides the intercept estimate, along with the nonstandardized multiple regression coefficients for the predictors. In this case, the intercept is 20.038, the nonstandardized regression coefficient for REWARD is .279, the nonstandardized coefficient for COST is –.106, and so forth. Based on these estimates, you may write the multiple regression equation in this way:

```
Y' =    0.279(REWARD) - 0.106(COST) + 0.523(INVEST)
      - 0.679(ALTERN) + 20.038
```

Remember that the multiple regression coefficient for a given predictor indicates the amount of change in Y that is associated with a one-unit change in that predictor, while holding constant the remaining predictors. Nonstandardized coefficients represent the change that would be observed when the variables are in nonstandardized, "raw score" form (i.e., the different variables have different means and standard deviations). The nonstandardized regression equation would be used to predict subjects scores on COMMIT so that the resulting scores would be on the same scale of magnitude as was observed with the raw data. However, the coefficients in this equation should not be used to assess the relative importance of the predictor variables.

5. Review the significance of the regression coefficients. Researchers are often interested in determining whether regression coefficients for the various predictor variables are significantly different from zero. When given coefficients are statistically significant, this may be seen as evidence that the corresponding predictor variable is a relatively important predictor of the criterion.

For each predictor variable, the output of PROC REG provides a *t* test that tests the null hypothesis that, in the population, the regression coefficient is equal to zero. The obtained *t* value may be found in the column headed "T for HO: Parameter=0". The *p* value corresponding to this value of *t* may be found in the next column, headed "Prob > |T|".

For example, in the present case, the nonstandardized regression coefficient for REWARD was 0.279. In testing the significance of this coefficient, the obtained value of *t* was 1.022, which had a corresponding *p* value of .312. Because this *p* value is greater than .05, you could not reject the null hypothesis, and were forced to tentatively conclude that the regression coefficient for REWARDS is not significantly different from zero. A different finding is obtained for the predictor INVEST, however, which had a nonstandardized regression coefficient of .523. The *t* value for this coefficient was 2.488, with a corresponding *p* value of .0168. Because this value was less than .05, you reject the null hypothesis, and tentatively conclude that the coefficient for INVEST is significantly different from zero.

The first paragraph of this subsection indicated that the statistical significance of a regression coefficient may be seen as evidence of that variable's importance as a predictor. This statement includes a qualification to emphasize that great caution should be used in interpreting statistical significance as evidence of predictor's importance. There are at least two reasons for this.

First, an earlier section in the chapter has discussed the fact that multiple regression coefficients are often unreliable, especially under the conditions that are often encountered in social science research. Second, a multiple regression coefficient may prove to be statistically significant even when the standardized coefficient is relatively small in absolute magnitude, and hence is of little predictive value. This is especially likely to be the case when sample sizes are very large. For these reasons, the statistical significance of regression coefficients should be viewed as only one indicator of a variable's importance, and should always be combined with additional information, such as the size of the standardized regression coefficients and uniqueness indices.

6. Review the standardized regression coefficients (beta weights). An earlier section in this chapter indicated that nonstandardized regression coefficients often tell very little about which variables are relatively important predictors. This is because the different predictors normally have different standard deviations, and these differences affect the size of the nonstandardized coefficients. To avoid this difficulty, it is necessary to instead review the standardized multiple regression coefficients, which are also called beta weights. Beta weights are the regression coefficients that would be obtained if all the variables were standardized, so that they had the same standard deviations. It is therefore more appropriate to review the beta weights when you wish to compare the relative importance of predictor variables (in many textbooks, beta weights are represented by the symbol B or ß, while nonstandardized regression coefficients are represented by the symbol b or *b*).

In the preceding program, you requested standardized regression coefficients (beta weights) by specifying STB in the options section of the MODEL statement. These beta weights appear toward the bottom of Output 13.2, below the "Standardized Estimate" heading. Note that the intercept for this equation is zero, as will always be the case with a standardized regression equation.

The results of Output 13.2 show that the beta weight for REWARD is .138, the beta for COST is −.057, the beta for INVEST is .312, and the beta for ALTERN is −.500. Based on these results, you could rank the predictors from most to least important as follows: ALTERN, INVEST, REWARD, and COST.

This interpretation should be made with caution, however, because multiple regression coefficients, whether standardized or nonstandardized, tend to be somewhat unreliable under the conditions normally encountered in social science research. A more cautious approach to understanding the relative importance of predictor variables would involve combining information from a variety of sources, including bivariate correlations, standardized regression coefficients, and uniqueness indices.

You can see that Output 13.2 does not report significance tests for the standardized regression coefficients. This is because the significance of the nonstandardized coefficients has already been reported, and a separate test for the standardized coefficients is not necessary: If the *t* test for the nonstandardized coefficient is significant, then the corresponding standardized coefficient for that variable is also significantly different from zero.

Computing Uniqueness Indices with PROC REG

When the SELECTION=RSQUARE option is included in the MODEL statement of PROC REG, it requests that all possible multiple regression equations be created, given the predictor variables that are specified in the MODEL statement. This means that it creates every possible regression equation that could be created by taking the predictors one at a time, every possible equation that could be created by taking the predictors two at a time, and so forth. The last equation it creates is the full equation: the equation that includes all predictor variables listed in the MODEL statement.

Output from this procedure reports only the R^2 obtained for each of these equations (and not information concerning the regression coefficients, sum of squares, and so forth). The SELECTION=RSQUARE option is therefore useful for quickly and efficiently determining the percentage of variance in a criterion that is accounted for by every possible combination of predictor variables.

Although this information may be used for a number of purposes, this chapter shows how to use it to determine the uniqueness index for each predictor, and how to test the significance of each uniqueness index. Earlier, it was said that the uniqueness index for a given predictor indicates the percentage of variance in the criterion that is accounted for by this predictor, above and beyond the variance accounted for by the other predictors. It can also be defined as the squared semipartial correlation between a criterion variable and the predictor variable of interest, after statistically controlling for the variance that the predictor shares with the other predictors.

Writing the Program

Here is the general form for the program statements that request the SELECTION=RSQUARE option with PROC REG:

```
PROC REG   DATA=data-set-name;
   MODEL  criterion  =  predictor-variables  /  SELECTION=RSQUARE;
   RUN;
```

The names of the predictor variables in the MODEL statement should be separated by at least one space. The SELECTION=RSQUARE option computes and prints the R^2 value for every possible regression equation that can be created from these variables. First, it will print R^2 for a series of 1-predictor models, in which each predictor variable is the sole X variable in its own equation. Next, a series of 2-predictor models is printed, in which the various equations represent every possible combination of predictors taken two at a time. The procedure continues in this fashion, until a single equation containing all of the predictor variables is printed.

These are the program statements that request the REG procedure necessary for the current analysis. Notice that the MODEL statement is identical to that used with the previous REG procedure, except that the STB option has now been replaced with the SELECTION=RSQUARE option:

```
PROC REG   DATA=D1;
   MODEL COMMIT = REWARD COST INVEST ALTERN / SELECTION=RSQUARE;
   RUN;
```

The results produced by these statements appear as Output 13.3.

```
                     The SAS System                              3

      N = 48     Regression Models for Dependent Variable: COMMIT


          Number in     R-square    Variables in Model
            Model


              1         0.51840263   ALTERN
              1         0.37703521   INVEST
              1         0.33173693   REWARD
              1         0.06163135   COST
          ---------------------------------------
              2         0.62478663   INVEST ALTERN
              2         0.59195945   REWARD ALTERN
              2         0.52146251   COST ALTERN
              2         0.45233976   REWARD INVEST
              2         0.44540421   COST INVEST
              2         0.33191194   REWARD COST
          ---------------------------------------
```

```
        3      0.64357098    REWARD INVEST ALTERN
        3      0.63709144    COST INVEST ALTERN
        3      0.59468518    REWARD COST ALTERN
        3      0.46897158    REWARD COST INVEST
   ----------------------------------------------------
        4      0.64570059    REWARD COST INVEST ALTERN
   ----------------------------------------------------
```

Output 13.3: Results of the REG Procedure with the SELECTION=RSQUARE Option

Interpreting the Results of PROC REG with SELECTION=RSQUARE

1. Make sure that everything looks right. The first line of output near the top of the page should present the number of subjects who provided usable data for the analysis, as well as the name of the criterion variable (called "Dependent Variable" in the output). In Output 13.3, this line indicates that the criterion variable is COMMIT, and that the analysis was based on 48 cases. Given that two of the subjects were dropped due to missing data, this appears to be correct.

The table of results created by the SELECTION=RSQUARE option includes three columns of information. The first column (on the left) indicates the number of predictor variables included in a given multiple regression equation. The second column (in the middle) provides the R^2 for that equation (the percent of variance in the criterion variable accounted for by this set of predictors). Finally, the third column provides the names of the predictor variables included in this equation.

In the first section of this table (the section containing the 1-predictor models), you can see that the equation that includes only the predictor ALTERN has an R^2 of 0.51840263 (meaning that ALTERN accounts for approximately 52% of the variance in COMMIT). In the second section of the table (the section containing 2-predictor models), you can see that the model containing INVEST and ALTERN account for about 62% of the variance in COMMIT.

2. Determine the uniqueness index for the predictor variables of interest. The formula for determining the uniqueness index for a predictor variable is as follows:

$$U = R^2_{Full} - R^2_{Reduced}$$

where

U = The uniqueness index for the predictor variable of interest

R^2_{Full} = The obtained value of R^2 for the full multiple regression equation; that is, the equation containing all predictor variables

$R^2_{Reduced}$ = The obtained value of R^2 for the reduced multiple regression equation; that is, the equation containing all predictor variables except for the predictor variable of interest

For example, assume that you want to determine the uniqueness index for the predictor, ALTERN. First, you identify the observed value of R^2 for the full regression equation. This is the equation that contains all four predictors: REWARD, COST, INVEST, and ALTERN. In Output 13.3, you first look under the heading "Variables in the Model" to find the single entry that contains the names of all four variables. This is the last entry on the page, and under the heading "R-square", you see that the R^2 for this 4-variable model is .64570059, which may be rounded to .646

Next, you find the R^2 for the reduced model: the model that includes all variables except for the variable of interest, ALTERN. Under "Variables in the Model", you find the model containing only REWARD, COST, and INVEST. To the left, the R^2 for this model (the reduced model) is .46897158, which may be rounded to .469. It is now possible to calculate the uniqueness index for ALTERN by inserting these values in the formula:

$$U = R^2_{Full} - R^2_{Reduced}$$

$$U = .646 - .469$$

$$U = .177$$

The uniqueness index for ALTERN is 0.177. There are a number of ways that this finding could be stated in a published report; a few of these are now presented:

- "Alternative value accounted for approximately 18% of the variance in commitment, beyond the variance accounted for by the other three predictor variables."

- "Alternative value accounted for approximately 18% of the incremental variance in commitment."

- "The squared semi-partial correlation between alternative value and commitment was .177, while partialling variance that commitment shared with the other three predictors."

Once the uniqueness index has been determined, it may be tested for statistical significance. This means testing the null hypothesis that, in the population, the uniqueness index for the variable of interest is equal to zero. This can be done by using the formula for testing the significance of the difference between two R^2 values. This formula is again reproduced here:

$$F = \frac{(R^2_{Full} - R^2_{Reduced}) \ / \ (K_{Full} - K_{Reduced})}{(1 - R^2_{Full}) \ / \ (N - K_{Full} - 1)}$$

where

R^2_{Full} = the obtained value of R^2 for the full multiple regression equation; that is, the equation containing the larger number of predictor variables

$R^2_{Reduced}$ = the obtained value of R^2 for the reduced multiple regression equation; that is, the equation containing the smaller number of predictor variables

K_{Full} = the number of predictor variables in the full multiple regression equation

$K_{Reduced}$ = the number of predictor variables in the reduced multiple regression equation

N = the total number of subjects in the sample.

Begin by testing the significance of the uniqueness index for ALTERN. Remember that the "full equation" in this analysis is the equation that contains all four predictor variables and produced an R^2 of .646. The "reduced equation" contains only three variables (all variables except ALTERN), and produced an R^2 of .469. These analyses were based on a sample of 48 usable responses. Here, these figures are paired with the appropriate symbols from the formula:

R^2_{Full} = .646

$R^2_{Reduced}$ = .469

K_{Full} = 4

$K_{Reduced}$ = 3

N = 48

These values are now inserted in the appropriate locations in the formula, and the *F* ratio is calculated:

$$F = \frac{(R^2_{Full} - R^2_{Reduced}) / (K_{Full} - K_{Reduced})}{(1 - R^2_{Full}) / (N - K_{Full} - 1)}$$

$$F = \frac{(.646 - .469) / (4 - 3)}{(1 - .646) / (48 - 4 - 1)}$$

$$F = \frac{(.177) / (1)}{(.354) / (43)}$$

$$F = \frac{(.177)}{(.00823)}$$

$$F = 21.51$$

The obtained *F* for this test was 21.51. To determine whether this *F* is large enough to reject the null hypothesis, you must first find the critical value of *F* appropriate for the test. To do this, you turn to the table of *F* found in Appendix C in the back of the text. You need to locate the critical value of *F* that is appropriate when $p = .05$, and corresponds to the following degrees of freedom:

$$\text{df for the numerator} = K_{Full} - K_{Reduced}$$

$$\text{df for the denominator} = N - K_{Full} - 1$$

Notice that these degrees of freedom have already been calculated in the preceding *F* formula: the df for the numerator ($K_{Full} - K_{Reduced}$) appeared in the numerator of the *F* formula, and the df for the denominator ($N - K_{Full} - 1$) appeared in the denominator of the formula. There, it was determined that the df statistic for the numerator was $4 - 3 = 1$, and the df statistic for the denominator was $48 - 4 - 1 = 43$.

A table of *F* shows that the critical value of *F* with 1 and 43 degrees of freedom is approximately 4.07 ($p < .05$). Your obtained *F* value of 21.51 is clearly larger than this critical value, so you may reject the null hypothesis that the population uniqueness index was zero. Apparently, ALTERN accounts for a significant amount of variance in COMMIT, beyond the variance accounted for by the remaining X variables.

At this point, you would proceed to test the uniqueness index for each of the remaining X variables in the equation. In each case, calculating the uniqueness index for a given variable involves simply finding the percentage of variance in COMMIT that was accounted for by the equation that excluded that predictor (from Output 13.3), and subtracting this value from the R^2 value for the 4-variable model (.646). Here, the uniqueness index for each of the remaining three X variables is calculated:

```
REWARD:    .646 - .637 = .009

COST:      .646 - .644 = .002

INVEST:    .646 - .595 = .051
```

The preceding shows that REWARD accounts for less than 1% of the variance in COMMIT, beyond the variance accounted for by the other three variables. The same is true for COST. INVEST, on the other hand, has a somewhat larger uniqueness index, accounting for approximately 5% of the incremental variance in COMMIT.

Testing the statistical significance of the remaining three uniqueness indices is relatively straightforward, because most of the necessary calculations have already been performed in testing the significance of ALTERN. Here, again, is the formula:

$$F = \frac{(R^2_{Full} - R^2_{Reduced}) / (K_{Full} - K_{Reduced})}{(1 - R^2_{Full}) / (N - K_{Full} - 1)}$$

Notice that most of the components of this formula remain unchanged when you test the significance of the uniqueness index of a different predictor variable. For example, regardless of which predictor variable's uniqueness index is being tested,

- $(K_{Full} - K_{Reduced})$ will be equal to $4 - 3 = 1$

- $(1 - R^2_{Full})$ will be equal to $1 - .646 = .354$

- $(N - K_{Full} - 1)$ will be equal to $48 - 4 - 1 = 43$.

This means that the only component of the equation that will be different for different predictor variables is the quantity $(R^2_{Full} - R^2_{Reduced})$. Therefore, for the current regression equation, the F formula simplifies in the following way:

$$F = \frac{(R^2_{Full} - R^2_{Reduced}) / (K_{Full} - K_{Reduced})}{(1 - R^2_{Full}) / (N - K_{Full} - 1)}$$

$$F = \frac{(R^2_{Full} - R_{Reduced}) / (4 - 3)}{(1 - .646) / (48 - 4 - 1)}$$

$$F = \frac{(R^2_{Full} - R_{Reduced}) / (1)}{(.354) / (43)}$$

$$F = \frac{(R^2_{Full} - R_{Reduced})}{(.00823)}$$

Remember that $(R^2_{Full} - R^2_{Reduced})$ is simply the formula for the uniqueness index for the variable of interest. Therefore, the preceding shows that, for the current regression equation, the F ratio that tests the significance of the uniqueness index for a given X variable may be calculated by simply dividing that uniqueness index by .00823. The degrees of freedom for each of these tests will continue to be 1 and 43, which means that the critical value of F will continue to be 4.07.

You can now use this simplified formula to test the significance of the uniqueness indices for the remaining X variables.

For REWARD:

$$F = \frac{(R^2_{Full} - R^2_{Reduced})}{(.00823)} = \frac{(.646 - .637)}{(.00823)} = \frac{(.009)}{(.00823)}$$

$$F = 1.09$$

For COST:

$$F = \frac{(R^2_{Full} - R^2_{Reduced})}{(.00823)} = \frac{(.646 - .644)}{(.00823)} = \frac{(.002)}{(.00823)}$$

$$F = 0.24$$

For INVEST:

$$F = \frac{(R^2_{\text{Full}} - R^2_{\text{Reduced}})}{(.00823)} = \frac{(.646 - .595)}{(.00823)} = \frac{(.051)}{(.00823)}$$

$$F = 6.20$$

Remember that, with 1 and 43 df, the critical value of F ($p < .05$) is 4.07 for all of these F tests. It can be seen that only the obtained F ratio for INVEST (at 6.20) exceeds this critical value. Therefore, only INVEST demonstrated a statistically significant uniqueness index. These findings make sense when you consider the size of the uniqueness indices. INVEST accounted for approximately 5% of the unique variance in COMMIT, but REWARD accounted for less than 1%, as did COST.

In summary, only ALTERN and INVEST accounted for significant amounts of variance in COMMIT beyond the variance accounted for by the other predictors. ALTERN demonstrated a uniqueness index of .177, while INVEST demonstrated a uniqueness index of .051.

An earlier section of this chapter indicated that it is important to determine both whether your linear combination of predictor variables accounts for a statistically significant amount of variance in the criterion, as well as whether this combination of predictors accounts for a meaningful (relatively large) amount of variance in the criterion. The same concern should be shown when reviewing the results of these tests of the significance of uniqueness indices. With a large sample, it is possible to obtain a uniqueness index that is statistically significant even though the predictor variable accounts for only 2 % or 3% of the unique variance in the criterion. When reviewing your results, it is important to assess whether a significant uniqueness index is large enough to be of substantive importance.

How large is "large enough?" That will depend, in part, on what earlier research with your criterion variable has found. When doing research with a criterion variable that traditionally has been difficult to predict, a uniqueness index of .05 (and possibly even smaller) may be viewed as being of substantive importance. When researching a criterion that is relatively easy to predict, the uniqueness index may have to be larger to be considered important.

Summarizing the Results in Tables

There are a number of different ways to summarize the results of a multiple regression analysis in a paper. When preparing a research report for a specific journal, the best strategy is to review recent issues of that publication, locate articles that report multiple regression analyses similar to yours, and follow their format. Summarized results of the present analyses follow, using table formats that are fairly representative of those appearing in journals of the American Psychological Association.

The Results of PROC CORR

It is usually desirable to present simple descriptive statistics, such as means and standard deviations, along with the correlation matrix. If reliability estimates (such as coefficient alpha estimates) are available for the predictors, they should be included on the diagonal of the correlation matrix, in parentheses. The results for the present fictitious study are summarized in Table 13.8:

Table 13.8

<u>Means, Standard Deviations, Intercorrelations, and Coefficient Alpha
Reliability Estimates</u>

			Intercorrelations				
Variable	<u>M</u>	<u>SD</u>	1	2	3	4	5
1. Commitment	27.71	10.20	(84)				
2. Rewards	26.65	5.05	58**	(75)			
3. Costs	16.58	5.50	-25	-45*	(72)		
4. Investment size	25.33	6.08	61**	57**	02	(83)	
5. Alternative value	16.60	7.50	-72**	-47**	27	-.45*	(91)

<u>Note</u>. <u>N</u> = 48. Decimals omitted from correlations and reliability estimates. Reliability estimates appear on the diagonal.

*<u>p</u> < .01., **<u>p</u> < .001

The Results of PROC REG

Depending on the nature of the research problem, it is sometimes possible to combine the results concerning the standardized regression coefficients (beta weights) with the results concerning the uniqueness indices in a single table. This is done in Table 13.9:

Table 13.9

<u>Beta Weights and Uniqueness Indices Obtained in Multiple Regression Analyses
Predicting Commitment</u>

Predictor	Beta Weights [a]		Uniqueness Indices [b]	
	Beta	t [c]	Uniqueness Index	F [d]
1. Rewards	.14	1.02	.009	1.09
2. Costs	-.06	-0.51	.002	0.24
3. Investment size	.31	2.49*	.051	6.20*
4. Alternative value	-.50	-4.64**	.177	21.51**

<u>Note</u>. <u>N</u> = 48.

[a] Beta weights are standardized multiple regression coefficients obtained when commitment was regressed on all four predictors. [b] Uniqueness indices indicate the percentage of variance in commitment scores accounted for by a given predictor variable beyond the variance accounted for by the other three predictors. [c] For <u>t</u> tests that tested the significance of the beta weights <u>df</u> = 43. [d] For <u>F</u> test that tested the significance of the uniqueness indices <u>df</u> = 1, 43.

*<u>p</u> < .05, **<u>p</u> < .001

Getting the Big Picture

It is instructive to pause and reflect on the big picture concerning your findings before moving on to summarize them in text form. First, notice the bivariate correlations from Table 13.8. The correlations between commitment and rewards, between commitment and investment size, and between commitment and alternative value are both significant and in the predicted direction.

Only the correlation between commitment and costs was nonsignificant. These findings provide partial support for the investment model.

A somewhat similar pattern of results can be seen in Table 13.9, which shows that the beta weights and uniqueness indices for investment size and alternative value are both significant and in the predicted direction. However, unlike the case for the correlations, Table 13.9 shows that neither the beta weight nor the uniqueness index for rewards is statistically significant. This may come as a surprise, because the correlation between commitment and rewards was moderately strong at .58. With such a strong correlation, how could the multiple regression coefficient and uniqueness index for rewards be nonsignificant?

A possible answer may be found in the correlations of Table 13.8. Notice that the correlation between commitment and rewards is somewhat weaker than the correlation between commitment and either investment size or alternative value. In addition, it can be seen that the correlations between rewards and both investment size and alternative value are fairly substantial at .57 and –.47, respectively. In short, REWARDS shares a great deal of variance in common with investment size and alternative value and is a poorer predictor of commitment. In this situation, it is unlikely that a multiple regression equation that already contains investment size and alternative value would need a variable like REWARDS to improve the accuracy of prediction; any variance in commitment that is accounted for by REWARDS has probably already been accounted for by investment size and alternative value. As a result, the REWARDS variable is redundant, and consequently displays a nonsignificant beta weight and uniqueness index.

Was this a real test of the investment model? It must be emphasized again that the results concerning the investment model presented here are entirely fictitious, and should not be viewed as legitimate tests of that conceptual framework. Most published studies of the investment model have, in fact, been very supportive of its predictions; for representative examples of this research, interested readers are referred to Rusbult (1980a, 1980b), Rusbult and Farrell (1983), and Rusbult, Johnson and Morrow (1986).

Formal Description of Results for a Paper

Again, there are a number of ways to summarize the results of these analyses within the text of the paper. The amount of detail provided in describing the analyses should be dictated by the statistical sophistication of your audience; less detail is needed if the audience is likely to be familiar with the use of multiple regression. The following format is fairly typical:

Results were analyzed using both bivariate correlation and multiple regression. Means, standard deviations, Pearson correlations and coefficient alpha reliability estimates appear in Table 13.8. The bivariate correlations revealed three predictor variables that were significantly related to commitment: rewards (r = .58), investment size (r = .61), and alternative value (r = -.72). All of these correlations were significant at p < .001, and all were in the predicted direction. The correlation between costs and commitment, on the other hand, was nonsignificant with r = -.25.

Using multiple regression, commitment scores were then regressed on the linear combination of rewards, costs, investment size, and alternative value. The equation containing these four variables accounted for 65% of the variance in commitment, F(4, 43) = 19.60, p < .001, adjusted R^2 = .61.

Beta weights (standardized multiple regression coefficients) and uniqueness indices were then reviewed to assess the relative importance of the four variables in the prediction of commitment. The uniqueness index for a given predictor is the percentage of variance in the criterion accounted for by that predictor, beyond the variance accounted for by the other predictor variables. Beta weights and uniqueness indices are presented in Table 13.9.

The table shows that only investment size and alternative value displayed significant beta weights. Alternative value demonstrated the somewhat larger beta weight at -.50 (p < .001), while the beta weight for investment size was .31 (p < .05). Both coefficients were in the predicted direction.

The findings regarding uniqueness indices matched those for beta weights, in that only investment size and alternative value displayed significant indices. Alternative value accounted for approximately 18% of the variance in commitment, beyond the variance accounted for by the other three predictors, F(1, 43) = 21.51, p < .001. In contrast, investment size accounted for only 5% of the unique variance in commitment, F(1, 43) = 6.20, p < .05.

The preceding tables and text make reference to the degrees of freedom for the statistical tests that assessed the significance of the model R^2 as well as the significance of the individual regression coefficients. It may be helpful to summarize how these degrees of freedom are calculated.

The second paragraph indicates that "The equation containing these four variables accounted for 65% of the variance in commitment, $F(4, 43) = 19.60$, $p < .001$, adjusted $R^2 = .61$." The information from this passage may be found in the results of PROC REG using the STB option, which appeared as Output 13.2. The F value that tests the significance of the model R^2 may be found in the analysis of variance section, under the heading "F Value". The p value associated with this test appears to the right of the F value. The degrees of freedom for the test may be found the second column, headed "DF" for "degrees of freedom." The degrees of freedom for the numerator in the F ratio (4, in this case) may be found to the right of "Model"; the degrees of freedom for the denominator (43, in this case) may be found to the right of "Error".

The beta weights and their corresponding t values appear in the lower half of Output 13.2. The beta weights themselves appear under the heading "Standardized Estimate", while the t values appear under "T for H0: Parameter = 0)". The degrees of freedom for these t tests are equal to

$$N - K_{Full} - 1$$

in which N = total sample size and K_{Full} = number of predictor variables in the full equation. In this case, df = $48 - 4 - 1 = 43$.

Conclusion: Learning More about Multiple Regression

This chapter has provided only an elementary introduction to multiple regression, one of the most flexible and powerful research tools in the social sciences. It has discussed only the situation in which a criterion variable is being predicted from continuous predictor variables, all of which display a linear relationship with the criterion. At this time, you may be ready to move on to a more comprehensive treatment of the topic, one that deals with curvilinear relationships, interactions between predictors, dummy coding, effect coding, and regression equations that contain both continuous and categorical predictor variables. Cohen and Cohen (1975) and Pedhazur (1982) provide authoritative treatments of these and other advanced topics in multiple regression. SAS System users will find Freund and Littell's (1991) *SAS system for regression* to be particularly helpful for learning more about multiple regression. Freund and Littell's text covers many essential topics that are seldom discussed in other books on regression; of particular importance are sections that explain how SAS System procedures can be used for testing assumptions, detecting multicollinearity, and identifying influential outliers.

Appendix: Assumptions Underlying Multiple Regression

• **Level of measurement**. For multiple regression, both the predictor variables and the criterion variable should be assessed on an interval or ratio level of measurement. Nominal-level predictor variables may be used if they have been appropriately dummy-coded or effect-coded.

• **Random sampling**. Each subject in the sample will contribute one score on each predictor variable, and one score on the criterion variable. These sets of scores should represent a random sample drawn from the population of interest.

• **Normal distribution of the criterion variable**. For any combination of values on the predictor variables, the criterion variable should be normally distributed.

• **Homogeneity of variance**. For any combination of values of the predictor variables, the criterion variable should demonstrate a constant variance.

• **Independent observations**. A given observation should not be affected by (or related to) any other observation in the sample. For example, this assumption would be violated if the various observations represented repeated measurements taken from a single subject. It would also be violated if the study included multiple subjects, but some subjects contributed more that one observation to the data set (i.e., some subjects contributed more than one set of scores on the criterion variable and predictor variables).

• **Linearity**. The relationship between the criterion variable and each predictor variable should be linear. This means that, in the population, the mean criterion scores at each value of a given predictor should fall on a straight line.

• **Errors of prediction**: The errors of prediction should be normally distributed, and the distribution of errors should be centered at zero; the error of prediction associated with a given observation should not be correlated with the errors associated with the other observations; the errors of prediction should demonstrate a constant variance; the errors of prediction should not be correlated with the predictor variables.

• **Absence of measurement error**. The predictor variables should be measured without error. Violation of this assumption may lead to underestimation of the regression coefficient for the corresponding predictor.

• **Absence of specification errors**. The term **specification error** generally refers to situations in which the model represented by the regression equation is not theoretically tenable. In multiple regression, specification errors most frequently result from omitting relevant predictor variables from the equation, or including irrelevant predictor variables in the equation. Specification errors also result when researchers posit a linear relationship between variables that are actually involved in a curvilinear relationship.

It is infrequent that all of these assumptions will be perfectly satisfied in applied research. Fortunately, regression analysis is generally robust against minor violations of most of these assumptions. However, it is not robust against violations of the assumptions involving independent observations, measurement error, or specification errors (Pedhazur, 1982).

In addition to considering the preceding assumptions, researchers are also advised to inspect their data sets for possible problems involving outliers or multicollinearity. An **outlier** is an unusual observation that does not fit the regression model well. Outliers are often the result of mistakes made in keying data, and can profoundly bias parameter estimates (such as regression coefficients). **Multicollinearity** exists when two or more predictor variables demonstrate a high degree of correlation with one another. Multicollinearity can cause regression coefficient estimates to fail to demonstrate statistical significance, be biased, or even demonstrate the incorrect sign. Freund and Littell (1991) discuss these problems, and show how to detect outliers, multicollinearity, and other problems sometimes encountered in regression analysis.

References

Cohen, J. & Cohen, P. (1975). *Applied multiple regression/correlation analysis for the behavioral sciences.* New York: Wiley.

Freund, R. J. & Littell, R. C. (1991). *SAS system for regression, second edition.* Cary, NC: SAS Institute Inc.

Littell, R. C., Freund, R. J., & Spector, P. C. (1991). *SAS system for linear models, third edition.* Cary, NC: SAS Institute Inc.

Pedhazur, E. J. (1982), *Multiple regression in behavioral research (2nd edition).* New York: Holt, Rinehart, and Winston.

Rusbult, C. E. (1980a). Commitment and satisfaction in romantic associations: A test of the investment model. *Journal of Experimental Social Psychology, 16,* 172-186.

Rusbult, C. E. (1980b). Satisfaction and commitment in friendships. *Representative Research in Social Psychology, 11,* 96-105.

Rusbult, C. E. & Farrell, D. (1983). A longitudinal test of the investment model: The impact on job satisfaction, job commitment, and turnover of variations in rewards, costs, alternatives, and investments. *Journal of Applied Psychology, 68,* 429-438.

Rusbult, C. E., Johnson, D. J., & Morrow, G. D. (1986). Predicting satisfaction and commitment in adult romantic involvements: An assessment of the generalizability of the investment model. *Social Psychology Quarterly, 49,* 81-89.

SAS Institute Inc. (1989). *SAS/STAT user's guide, version 6, fourth edition, volume 2.* Cary, NC: SAS Institute Inc.

Chapter 14

PRINCIPAL COMPONENT ANALYSIS

Overview. This chapter provides an introduction to principal component analysis: a
variable-reduction procedure similar to factor analysis. It provides guidelines regarding
the necessary sample size and number of items per component. It shows how to determine
the number of components to retain, interpret the rotated solution, create factor scores, and
summarize the results. Fictitious data from two studies are analyzed to illustrate these
procedures. The present chapter deals only with the creation of orthogonal (uncorrelated)
components; oblique (correlated) solutions are covered in Chapter 2 ("Exploratory Factor
Analysis") from *A Step-by-Step Approach to Using the SAS System for Factor Analysis
and Structural Equation Modeling* (Hatcher, 1994), a companion volume from the *SAS
System for the Social Sciences* series.

Introduction: The Basics of Principal Component Analysis

Principal component analysis is appropriate when you have obtained measures on a number of
observed variables and wish to develop a smaller number of artificial variables (called principal
components) that will account for most of the variance in the observed variables. The principal
components may then be used as predictor or criterion variables in subsequent analyses.

A Variable Reduction Procedure

Principal component analysis is a variable reduction procedure. It is useful when you have
obtained data on a number of variables (possibly a large number of variables), and believe that
there is some redundancy in those variables. In this case, redundancy means that some of the
variables are correlated with one another, possibly because they are measuring the same
construct. Because of this redundancy, you believe that it should be possible to reduce the

observed variables into a smaller number of principal components (artificial variables) that will account for most of the variance in the observed variables.

Because it is a variable reduction procedure, principal component analysis is similar in many respects to exploratory factor analysis. In fact, the steps followed when conducting a principal component analysis are virtually identical to those followed when conducting an exploratory factor analysis. However, there are significant conceptual differences between the two procedures, and it is important that you do not mistakenly claim that you are performing factor analysis when you are actually performing principal component analysis. The differences between these two procedures are described in greater detail in a later section titled "Principal Component Analysis is *Not* Factor Analysis."

An Illustration of Variable Redundancy

A specific (but fictitious) example of research will now be presented to illustrate the concept of variable redundancy introduced earlier. Imagine that you have developed a 7-item measure of job satisfaction. The instrument is reproduced here:

Please respond to each of the following statements by placing a rating in the space to the left of the statement. In making your ratings, use any number from 1 to 7 in which 1 = "strongly disagree" and 7 = "strongly agree."

_____ 1. My supervisor treats me with consideration.

_____ 2. My supervisor consults me concerning important decisions that affect my work.

_____ 3. My supervisors give me recognition when I do a good job.

_____ 4. My supervisor gives me the support I need to do my job well.

_____ 5. My pay is fair.

_____ 6. My pay is appropriate, given the amount of responsibility that comes with my job.

_____ 7. My pay is comparable to the pay earned by other employees whose jobs are similar to mine.

Perhaps you began your investigation with the intention of administering this questionnaire to 200 or so employees, and using their responses to the seven items as seven separate variables in subsequent analyses (for example, perhaps you intended to use the seven items as seven separate predictor variables in a multiple regression equation in which the criterion variable was "intention to quit the organization.")

There are a number of problems with conducting the study in this fashion, however. One of the more important problems involves the concept of redundancy that was mentioned earlier. Take a close look at the content of the seven items in the questionnaire. Notice that items 1-4 all deal with the same topic: the employees' satisfaction with their supervisors. In this way, items 1-4 are somewhat redundant to one another. Similarly, notice that items 5-7 also all seem to deal with the same topic: the employees' satisfaction with their pay.

Empirical findings may further support the notion that there is redundancy in the seven items. Assume that you administer the questionnaire to 200 employees and compute all possible correlations between responses to the 7 items. The resulting fictitious correlations are reproduced in Table 14.1:

Table 14.1

<u>Correlations among Seven Job Satisfaction Items</u>

Correlations

Variable	1	2	3	4	5	6	7
1	1.00						
2	.75	1.00					
3	.83	.82	1.00				
4	.68	.92	.88	1.00			
5	.03	.01	.04	.01	1.00		
6	.05	.02	.05	.07	.89	1.00	
7	.02	.06	.00	.03	.91	.76	1.00

<u>Note</u>: <u>N</u> = 200.

When correlations among several variables are computed, they are typically summarized in the form of a **correlation matrix**, such as the one reproduced in Table 14.1. This is an appropriate opportunity to review just how a correlation matrix is interpreted. The rows and columns of

Table 14.1 correspond to the seven variables included in the analysis: Row 1 (and column 1) represents variable 1, row 2 (and column 2) represents variable 2, and so forth. Where a given row and column intersect, you will find the correlation between the two corresponding variables. For example, where the row for variable 2 intersects with the column for variable 1, you find a correlation of .75; this means that the correlation between variables 1 and 2 is .75.

The correlations of Table 14.1 show that the seven items seem to hang together in two distinct groups. First, notice that items 1-4 show relatively strong correlations with one another. This could be because items 1-4 are measuring the same construct. In the same way, items 5-7 correlate strongly with one another (a possible indication that they all measure the same construct as well). Even more interesting, notice that items 1-4 demonstrate very weak correlations with items 5-7. This is what you would expect to see if items 1-4 and items 5-7 were measuring two different constructs.

Given this apparent redundancy, it is likely that the seven items of the questionnaire are not really measuring seven different constructs; more likely, items 1-4 are measuring a single construct that could reasonably be labelled "satisfaction with supervision," while items 5-7 are measuring a different construct that could be labelled "satisfaction with pay."

If responses to the seven items actually displayed the redundancy suggested by the pattern of correlations in Table 14.1, it would be advantageous to somehow reduce the number of variables in this data set, so that (in a sense) items 1-4 are collapsed into a single new variable that reflects the employees' satisfaction with supervision, and items 5-7 are collapsed into a single new variable that reflects satisfaction with pay. You could then use these two new artificial variables (rather than the seven original variables) as predictor variables in multiple regression, or in any other type of analysis.

In essence, this is what is accomplished by principal component analysis: it allows you to reduce a set of observed variables into a smaller set of artificial variables called principal components. The resulting principal components may then be used in subsequent analyses.

What is a Principal Component?

How principal components are computed. Technically, a **principal component** can be defined as a linear combination of optimally-weighted observed variables. In order to understand the meaning of this definition, it is necessary to first describe how subject scores on a principal component are computed.

In the course of performing a principal component analysis, it is possible to calculate a score for each subject on a given principal component. For example, in the preceding study, each subject would have scores on two components: one score on the satisfaction with supervision component, and one score on the satisfaction with pay component. The subject's actual scores on the seven questionnaire items would be optimally weighted and then summed to compute their scores on a given component.

Below is the general form for the formula to compute scores on the first component extracted (created) in a principal component analysis:

$$C_1 = b_{11}(X_1) + b_{12}(X_2) + \ldots b_{1p}(X_p)$$

where

C_1 = the subject's score on principal component 1 (the first component extracted)

b_{1p} = the regression coefficient (or weight) for observed variable p, as used in creating principal component 1

X_p = the subject's score on observed variable p.

For example, assume that component 1 in the present study was the "satisfaction with supervision" component. You could determine each subject's score on principal component 1 by using the following fictitious formula:

$$C_1 = \quad .44\ (X_1) + .40\ (X_2) + .47\ (X_3) + .32\ (X_4)$$
$$+\ \ .02\ (X_5) + .01\ (X_6) + .03\ (X_7)$$

In the present case, the observed variables (the "X" variables) were subject responses to the seven job satisfaction questions; X_1 represents question 1, X_2 represents question 2, and so forth. Notice that different regression coefficients were assigned to the different questions in computing subject scores on component 1: Questions 1-4 were assigned relatively large regression weights that range from .32 to 44, while questions 5-7 were assigned very small weights ranging from .01 to .03. This makes sense, because component 1 is the satisfaction with supervision component, and satisfaction with supervision was assessed by questions 1-4. It is therefore appropriate that items 1-4 would be given a good deal of weight in computing subject scores on this component, while items 5-7 would be given little weight.

Obviously, a different equation, with different regression weights, would be used to compute subject scores on component 2 (the satisfaction with pay component). Below is a fictitious illustration of this formula:

$$C_2 = \quad .01\ (X_1) + .04\ (X_2) + .02\ (X_3) + .02\ (X_4)$$
$$+\ \ .48\ (X_5) + .31\ (X_6) + .39\ (X_7)$$

The preceding shows that, in creating scores on the second component, much weight would be given to items 5-7, and little would be given to items 1-4. As a result, component 2 should account for much of the variability in the three satisfaction with pay items; that is, it should be strongly correlated with those three items.

At this point, it is reasonable to wonder how the regression weights from the preceding equations are determined. The SAS System's PROC FACTOR solves for these weights by using a special type of equation called an **eigenequation**. The weights produced by these eigenequations are optimal weights in the sense that, for a given set of data, no other set of weights could produce a set of components that are more successful in accounting for variance in the observed variables. The weights are created so as to satisfy a principle of least squares similar (but not identical) to the principle of least squares used in multiple regression. Later, this chapter will show how PROC FACTOR can be used to extract (create) principal components.

It is now possible to better understand the definition that was offered at the beginning of this section. There, a principal component was defined as a linear combination of optimally weighted observed variables. The words "linear combination" refer to the fact that scores on a component are created by adding together scores on the observed variables being analyzed. "Optimally weighted" refers to the fact that the observed variables are weighted in such a way that the resulting components account for a maximal amount of variance in the data set.

Number of components extracted. The preceding section may have created the impression that, if a principal component analysis were performed on data from the 7-item job satisfaction questionnaire, only two components would be created. However, such an impression would not be entirely correct.

In reality, the number of components extracted in a principal component analysis is equal to the number of observed variables being analyzed. This means that an analysis of your 7-item questionnaire would actually result in seven components, not two.

However, in most analyses, only the first few components account for meaningful amounts of variance, so only these first few components are retained, interpreted, and used in subsequent analyses (such as in multiple regression analyses). For example, in your analysis of the 7-item job satisfaction questionnaire, it is likely that only the first two components would account for a meaningful amount of variance; therefore only these would be retained for interpretation. You would assume that the remaining five components accounted for only trivial amounts of variance. These latter components would therefore not be retained, interpreted, or further analyzed.

Characteristics of principal components. The first component extracted in a principal component analysis accounts for a maximal amount of total variance in the observed variables. Under typical conditions, this means that the first component will be correlated with at least some of the observed variables. It may be correlated with many.

The second component extracted will have two important characteristics. First, this component will account for a maximal amount of variance in the data set that was not accounted for by the first component. Again under typical conditions, this means that the second component will be correlated with some of the observed variables that did not display strong correlations with component 1.

The second characteristic of the second component is that it will be *uncorrelated* with the first component. Literally, if you were to compute the correlation between components 1 and 2, that correlation would be zero.

The remaining components that are extracted in the analysis display the same two characteristics: each component accounts for a maximal amount of variance in the observed variables that was not accounted for by the preceding components, and is uncorrelated with all of the preceding components. A principal component analysis proceeds in this fashion, with each new component accounting for progressively smaller and smaller amounts of variance (this is why only the first few components are usually retained and interpreted). When the analysis is complete, the resulting components will display varying degrees of correlation with the observed variables, but are completely uncorrelated with one another.

What is meant by "total variance" in the data set? To understand the meaning of "total variance" as it is used in a principal component analysis, remember that the observed variables are standardized in the course of the analysis. This means that each variable is transformed so that it has a mean of zero and a variance of one. The "total variance" in the data set is simply the sum of the variances of these observed variables. Because they have been standardized to have a variance of one, each observed variable contributes one unit of variance to the "total variance" in the data set. Because of this, the total variance in a principal component analysis will always be equal to the number of observed variables being analyzed. For example, if seven variables are being analyzed, the total variance will equal seven. The components that are extracted in the analysis will partition this variance: Perhaps the first component will account for 3.2 units of total variance; perhaps the second component will account for 2.1 units. The analysis continues in this way until all of the variance in the data set has been accounted for.

Orthogonal versus Oblique Solutions

This chapter will discuss only principal component analyses that result in orthogonal solutions. An **orthogonal solution** is one in which the components remain uncorrelated (orthogonal means "uncorrelated").

It is possible to perform a principal component analysis that results in correlated components. Such a solution is called an **oblique solution**. In some situations, oblique solutions are superior to orthogonal solutions because they produce cleaner, more easily-interpreted results.

However, oblique solutions are also somewhat more complicated to interpret, compared to orthogonal solutions. For this reason, the present chapter will focus only on the interpretation of orthogonal solutions. To learn about oblique solutions, see Hatcher (1994). The concepts discussed in this chapter will provide a good foundation for the somewhat more complex concepts discussed in that text.

Principal Component Analysis is *Not* Factor Analysis

Principal component analysis is sometimes confused with factor analysis, and this is understandable, because there are many important similarities between the two procedures: Both are variable reduction methods that can be used to identify groups of observed variables that tend to hang together empirically. Both procedures can be performed with the SAS System's FACTOR procedure, and they sometimes even provide very similar results.

Nonetheless, there are some important conceptual differences between principal component analysis and factor analysis that should be understood at the outset. Perhaps the most important deals with the **assumption of an underlying causal structure**: Factor analysis assumes that the covariation in the observed variables is due to the presence of one or more latent variables (factors) that exert causal influence on these observed variables. A example of such a causal structure is presented in Figure 14.1:

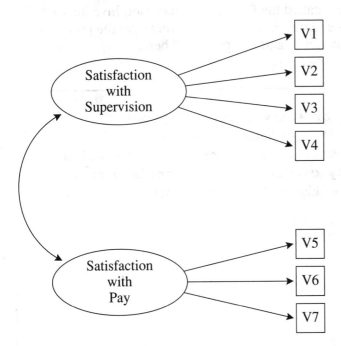

Figure 14.1: Example of the Underlying Causal Structure that is Assumed in Factor Analysis

The ovals in Figure 14.1 represent the latent (unmeasured) factors of "satisfaction with supervision" and "satisfaction with pay." These factors are latent in the sense that they are assumed to actually exist in the employee's belief systems, but cannot be measured directly. However, they do exert an influence on the employee's responses to the seven items that constitute the job satisfaction questionnaire described earlier (these seven items are represented as the squares labelled V1-V7 in the figure). It can be seen that the "supervision" factor exerts influence on items V1-V4 (the supervision questions), while the "pay" factor exerts influence on items V5-V7 (the pay items).

Researchers use factor analysis when they believe that certain latent factors exist that exert causal influence on the observed variables they are studying. Exploratory factor analysis helps the researcher identify the number and nature of these latent factors.

In contrast, principal component analysis makes no assumption about an underlying causal model. Principal component analysis is simply a variable reduction procedure that (typically) results in a relatively small number of components that account for most of the variance in a set of observed variables.

In summary, both factor analysis and principal component analysis have important roles to play in social science research, but their conceptual foundations are quite distinct. The similarities and differences between these procedures are discussed in greater detail in Hatcher (1994).

Example: Analysis of the Prosocial Orientation Inventory

Assume that you have developed an instrument called the Prosocial Orientation Inventory (POI) that assesses the extent to which a person has engaged in helping behaviors over the preceding six-month period. The instrument contains six items, and is reproduced here.

Instructions: Below are a number of activities that people sometimes engage in. For each item, please indicate how frequently you have engaged in this activity over the preceding six months. Make your rating by circling the appropriate number to the left of the item, and use the following response format:

```
7 = Very Frequently
6 = Frequently
5 = Somewhat Frequently
4 = Occasionally
3 = Seldom
2 = Almost Never
1 = Never
```

```
1 2 3   5 6 7    1.   Went out of my way to do a favor for a
                      coworker.

1 2 3 4 5 6 7    2.   Went out of my way to do a favor for a
                      relative.
```

```
1 2 3 4 5 6 7    3.   Went out of my way to do a favor for a
                      friend.

1 2 3 4 5 6 7    4.   Gave money to a religious charity.

1 2 3 4 5 6 7    5.   Gave money to a charity not associated with
                      a religion.

1 2 3 4 5 6 7    6.   Gave money to a panhandler.
```

When you developed the instrument, you originally intended to administer it to a sample of subjects and use their responses to the six items as six separate predictor variables in a multiple regression equation. However, you have recently learned that this would be a questionable practice (for the reasons discussed earlier), and have now decided to instead perform a principal component analysis on responses to the six items to see if a smaller number of components can successfully account for most of the variance in the data set. If this is the case, you will use the resulting components as the predictor variables in your multiple regression analyses.

At this point, it may be instructive to review the content of the six items that constitute the POI to make an informed guess as to what you are likely to learn from the principal component analysis. Imagine that, when you first constructed the instrument, you assumed that the six items were assessing six different types of prosocial behavior. However, inspection of items 1-3 shows that these three items share something in common: they all deal with the activity of "going out of one's way to do a favor for an acquaintance." It would not be surprising to learn that these three items will hang together empirically in the principal component analysis to be performed. In the same way, a review of items 4-6 shows that all of these items involve the activity of "giving money to the needy." Again, it is possible that these three items will also group together in the course of the analysis.

In summary, the nature of the items suggests that it may be possible to account for the variance in the POI with just two components: An "acquaintance helping" component, and a "financial giving" component. At this point, we are only speculating, of course; only a formal analysis can tell us about the number and nature of the components measured by the POI.

(Remember that the preceding fictitious instrument is used for purposes of illustration only, and should not be regarded as an example of a good measure of prosocial orientation; among other problems, this questionnaire obviously deals with very few forms of helping behavior).

Preparing a Multiple-Item Instrument

The preceding section illustrates an important point about how *not* to prepare a multiple-item measure of a construct: Generally speaking, it is poor practice to throw together a questionnaire, administer it to a sample, and then perform a principal component analysis (or factor analysis) to see what the questionnaire is measuring.

Better results are much more likely when you make a priori decisions about what you want the questionnaire to measure, and then take steps to ensure that it does. For example, you would have been more likely to obtain desirable results if you:

- had begun with a thorough review of theory and research on prosocial behavior

- used that review to determine how many types of prosocial behavior probably exist

- wrote multiple questionnaire items to assess each type of prosocial behavior.

Using this approach, you could have made statements such as "There are three types of prosocial behavior: acquaintance helping, stranger helping, and financial giving." You could have then prepared a number of items to assess each of these three types, administered the questionnaire to a large sample, and performed a principal component analysis to see if the three components did, in fact, emerge.

Number of Items per Component

When a variable (such as a questionnaire item) is given a great deal of weight in constructing a principal component, we say that the variable **loads** on that component. For example, if the item "Went out of my way to do a favor for a coworker" is given a lot of weight in creating the acquaintance helping component, we say that this item loads on the acquaintance helping component.

It is highly desirable to have at least three (and preferably more) variables loading on each retained component when the principal component analysis is complete. Because some of the items may be dropped during the course of the analysis (for reasons to be discussed later), it is generally good practice to write at least five items for each construct that you wish to measure; in this way, you increase the chances that at least three items per component will survive the analysis. Note that we have unfortunately violated this recommendation by apparently writing only three items for each of the two a priori components constituting the POI.

One additional note on scale length: the recommendation of three items per scale offered here should be viewed as an absolute minimum, and certainly not as an optimal number of items per scale. In practice, test and attitude scale developers normally desire that their scales contain many more than just three items to measure a given construct. It is not unusual to see individual scales that include 10, 20, or even more items to assess a single construct. Other things held constant, the more items in the scale, the more reliable it will be. The recommendation of three items per scale should therefore be viewed as a rock-bottom lower bound, appropriate only if practical concerns (such as total questionnaire length) prevent you from including more items. For more information on scale construction, see Spector (1992).

Minimally Adequate Sample Size

Principal component analysis is a large-sample procedure. To obtain reliable results, the minimal number of subjects providing usable data for the analysis should be the larger of 100 subjects or five times the number of variables being analyzed.

To illustrate, assume that you wish to perform an analysis on responses to a 50-item questionnaire (remember that, when responses to a questionnaire are analyzed, the number of variables is equal to the number of items on the questionnaire). Five times the number of items on the questionnaire equals 250. Therefore, your final sample should provide usable (complete) data from at least 250 subjects. It should be remembered, however, that any subject who fails to answer just one item will not provide usable data for the principal component analysis, and will therefore be dropped from the final sample. A certain number of subjects can always be expected to leave at least one question blank (despite the most strongly worded instructions to the contrary!). To ensure that the final sample includes at least 250 usable responses, you would be wise to administer the questionnaire to perhaps 300-350 subjects.

These rules regarding the number of subjects per variable again constitute a lower bound, and some have argued that they should apply only under two optimal conditions for principal component analysis: when many variables are expected to load on each component, and when variable communalities are high. Under less optimal conditions, even larger samples may be required.

What is a communality? A **communality** refers to the percent of variance in an observed variable that is accounted for by the retained components (or factors). A given variable will display a large communality if it loads heavily on at least one of the study's retained components. Although communalities are computed in both procedures, the *concept* of variable communality is more relevant in a factor analysis than in principal component analysis.

SAS Program and Output

You may perform a principal component analysis using either the PRINCOMP or FACTOR procedures. This chapter will show how to perform the analysis using PROC FACTOR since this is a somewhat more flexible SAS System procedure (it is also possible to perform an exploratory factor analysis with PROC FACTOR). Because the analysis is to be performed using the FACTOR procedure, the output will at times make references to factors rather than to principal components (i.e., component 1 will be referred to as FACTOR1 in the output, component 2 as FACTOR2, and so forth). However, it is important to remember that you are nonetheless performing a principal component analysis.

This section will provide instructions on writing the SAS program, along with an overview of the SAS output. A subsequent section will provide a more detailed treatment of the steps followed in the analysis, and the decisions to be made at each step.

Writing the SAS Program

The DATA step. To perform a principal component analysis, data may be input in the form of raw data, a correlation matrix, a covariance matrix, as well as other some other types of data (for details, see Chapter 21 on "The FACTOR Procedure" in the *SAS/STAT user's guide, version 6, fourth edition, volume 1* [1989]). In this chapter's first example, raw data will be analyzed.

Assume that you administered the POI to 50 subjects, and keyed their responses according to the following keying guide:

Line	Column	Variable Name	Explanation
1	1-6	V1-V6	Subjects' responses to survey questions 1 through 6. Responses were made using a 7-point "frequency" scale.

Here are the statements that will input these responses as raw data. The first three and the last three observations are reproduced here; for the entire data set, see Appendix B.

```
1       DATA D1;
2          INPUT    #1    @1    (V1-V6)    (1.)   ;
3       CARDS;
4       556754
5       567343
6       777222
7       .
8       .
9       .
10      767151
11      455323
12      455544
13      ;
```

The data set in Appendix B includes only 50 cases so that it will be relatively easy for interested readers to key the data and replicate the analyses presented here. However, it should be remembered that 50 observations will normally constitute an unacceptably small sample for a principal component analysis. Earlier it was said that a sample should provide usable data from the larger of either 100 cases or 5 times the number of observed variables. A small sample is being analyzed here for illustrative purposes only.

The PROC FACTOR statement. The general form for the SAS program to perform a principal component analysis is presented here:

```
PROC FACTOR    DATA=data-set-name
               SIMPLE
               METHOD=PRIN
               PRIORS=ONE
               MINEIGEN=p
               SCREE
               ROTATE=VARIMAX
               ROUND
               FLAG=desired-size-of-"significant"-factor-loadings ;
   VAR  variables-to-be-analyzed ;
   RUN;
```

Options used with PROC FACTOR. The PROC FACTOR statement begins the FACTOR procedure, and a number of options may be requested in this statement before it ends with a semicolon. Some options that may be especially useful in social science research are:

FLAG
>   causes the printer to flag (with an asterisk) any factor loading whose absolute value is greater than some specified size. For example, if you specify

>   FLAG=.35

>   an asterisk will appear next to any loading whose absolute value exceeds .35. This option can make it much easier to interpret a factor pattern. Negative values are not allowed in the FLAG option, and the FLAG option should be used in conjunction with the ROUND option.

METHOD=factor-extraction-method
>   specifies the method to be used in extracting the factors or components. The current program specifies METHOD=PRIN to request that the principal axis (principal factors) method be used for the initial extraction. This is the appropriate method for a principal component analysis.

`MINEIGEN=p`

> specifies the critical eigenvalue a component must display if that component is to be retained (here, p = the critical eigenvalue). For example, the current program specifies

`MINEIGEN=1`

> This statement will cause PROC FACTOR to retain and rotate any component whose eigenvalue is 1.00 or larger. Negative values are not allowed.

`NFACT=n`

> allows you to specify the number of components to be retained and rotated, where *n* = the number of components.

`OUT=name-of-new-data-set`

> creates a new data set that includes all of the variables of the existing data set, along with factor scores for the components retained in the present analysis. Component 1 is given the varible name FACTOR1, component 2 is given the name FACTOR2, and so forth. It must be used in conjunction with the NFACT option, and the analysis must be based on raw data.

`PRIORS=prior-communality-estimates`

> specifies prior communality estimates. Users should always specify PRIORS=ONE to perform a principal component analysis.

`ROTATE=rotation-method`

> specifies the rotation method to be used. The preceding program requests a varimax rotation, which results in orthogonal (uncorrelated) components. Oblique rotations may also be requested; oblique rotations are discussed in Hatcher (1994).

`ROUND`

> causes all coefficients to be limited to two decimal places, rounded to the nearest integer, and multiplied by 100 (thus eliminating the decimal point). This generally makes it easier to read the coefficients because factor loadings and correlation coefficients in the matrices printed by PROC FACTOR are normally carried out to several decimal places.

`SCREE`

> creates a plot that graphically displays the size of the eigenvalue associated with each component. This can be used to perform a scree test to determine how many components should be retained.

`SIMPLE`

> requests simple descriptive statistics: the number of usable cases on which the analysis was performed, and the means and standard deviations of the observed variables.

The VAR statement. The variables to be analyzed are listed in the VAR statement, with each variable separated by at least one space. Remember that the VAR statement is a *separate* statement, not an option within the FACTOR statement, so don't forget to end the FACTOR statement with a semicolon before beginning the VAR statement.

Example of an actual program. The following is an actual program, including the DATA step, that could be used to analyze some fictitious data from your study. Only a few sample lines of data appear here; the entire data set may be found in Appendix B.

```
1     DATA D1;
2        INPUT    #1    @1    (V1-V6)    (1.)  ;
3     CARDS;
4     556754
5     567343
6     777222
7     .
8     .
9     .
10    767151
11    455323
12    455544
13    ;
14    PROC FACTOR    DATA=D1
15                   SIMPLE
16                   METHOD=PRIN
17                   PRIORS=ONE
18                   MINEIGEN=1
19                   SCREE
20                   ROTATE=VARIMAX
21                   ROUND
22                   FLAG=.40    ;
23       VAR V1 V2 V3 V4 V5 V6;
24       RUN;
```

Results from the Output

If printer options are set so that LINESIZE=80 and PAGESIZE=60, the preceding program would produce four pages of output. Here is a list of some of the most important information provided by the output, and the page on which it appears:

- Page 1 includes simple statistics.

- Page 2 includes the eigenvalue table.

• Page 3 includes the scree plot of eigenvalues.

• Page 4 includes the unrotated factor pattern and final communality estimates.

• Page 5 includes the rotated factor pattern.

The output created by the preceding program is reproduced here as Output 14.1:

```
                        The SAS System                         1

           Means and Standard Deviations from 50 observations

                  V1        V2        V3        V4        V5        V6
Mean            5.18       5.4      5.52      3.64      4.22       3.1
Std Dev   1.39518121 1.10656667 1.21621695 1.79295674 1.66953495 1.55511008
```

```
                                                               2


Initial Factor Method: Principal Components

              Prior Communality Estimates: ONE

      Eigenvalues of the Correlation Matrix:   Total = 6  Average = 1

                              1         2         3
              Eigenvalue    2.2664    1.9746    0.7973
              Difference    0.2918    1.1773    0.3581
              Proportion    0.3777    0.3291    0.1329
              Cumulative    0.3777    0.7068    0.8397

                              4         5         6
              Eigenvalue    0.4392    0.2913    0.2312
              Difference    0.1479    0.0601
              Proportion    0.0732    0.0485    0.0385
              Cumulative    0.9129    0.9615    1.0000

      2 factors will be retained by the MINEIGEN criterion.
```

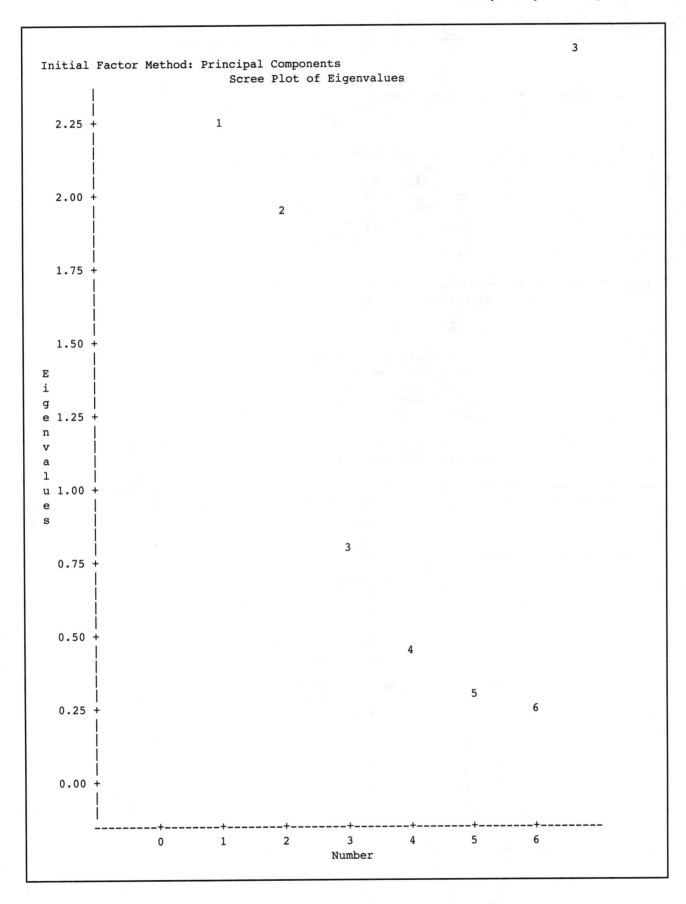

Initial Factor Method: Principal Components
Scree Plot of Eigenvalues

4

Initial Factor Method: Principal Components

Factor Pattern

	FACTOR1	FACTOR2
V1	58 *	70 *
V2	48 *	53 *
V3	60 *	62 *
V4	64 *	−64 *
V5	68 *	−45 *
V6	68 *	−46 *

NOTE: Printed values are multiplied by 100 and rounded to the nearest integer.
Values greater than 0.4 have been flagged by an '*'.

Variance explained by each factor

FACTOR1	FACTOR2
2.266436	1.974615

Final Communality Estimates: Total = 4.241050

V1	V2	V3	V4	V5	V6
0.823418	0.508529	0.743990	0.822574	0.665963	0.676575

The SAS System

5

Rotation Method: Varimax

Orthogonal Transformation Matrix

	1	2
1	0.76914	0.63908
2	−0.63908	0.76914

Rotated Factor Pattern

	FACTOR1	FACTOR2
V1	0	91 *
V2	3	71 *
V3	7	86 *
V4	90 *	−9
V5	81 *	9
V6	82 *	8

```
NOTE: Printed values are multiplied by 100 and rounded to the nearest integer.
      Values greater than 0.4 have been flagged by an '*'.

                      Variance explained by each factor

                          FACTOR1   FACTOR2
                          2.147248  2.093803


          Final Communality Estimates: Total = 4.241050

             V1        V2        V3        V4        V5        V6
          0.823418  0.508529  0.743990  0.822574  0.665963  0.676575
```

Output 14.1: Results of the Initial Principal Component Analysis of the Prosocial Orientation Inventory (POI) Data

Page 1 from Output 14.1 provides simple statistics for the observed variables included in the analysis. Once the SAS log has been checked to verify that no errors were made in the analysis, these simple statistics should be reviewed to determine how many usable observations were included in the analysis and to verify that the means and standard deviations are in the expected range. The top line of Output 14.1, page 1, says "Means and Standard Deviations from 50 Observations", meaning that data from 50 subjects were included in the analysis.

Steps in Conducting Principal Component Analysis

Principal component analysis is normally conducted in a sequence of steps, with somewhat subjective decisions being made at many of these steps. Because this is an introductory treatment of the topic, it will not provide a comprehensive discussion of all of the options available to you at each step. Instead, specific recommendations will be made, consistent with practices often followed in applied research. For a more detailed treatment of principal component analysis and its close relative, factor analysis, see Kim and Mueller (1978a; 1978b), Rummel (1970), or Stevens (1986).

Step 1: Initial Extraction of the Components

In principal component analysis, the number of components extracted is equal to the number of variables being analyzed. Because six variables are analyzed in the present study, six components will be extracted. The first component can be expected to account for a fairly large amount of the total variance. Each succeeding component will account for progressively smaller amounts of variance. Although a large number of components may be extracted in this way, only the first few components will be important enough to be retained for interpretation.

Page 2 from Output 14.1 provides the eigenvalue table from the analysis
(this table appears just below the heading "Eigenvalues of the Correlation Matrix: Total = 6
Average = 1"). An **eigenvalue** represents the amount of variance that is accounted for by a given
component. In the row headed "Eignenvalue" (running from left to right), the eigenvalue for
each component is presented. Each column in the matrix (running up and down) presents
information about one of the six components: The column headed "1" provides information
about the first component extracted, the column headed "2" provides information about the
second component extracted, and so forth.

Where the row headed EIGENVALUE intersects with the columns headed "1" and "2," it can be
seen that the eigenvalue for component 1 is 2.27, while the eigenvalue for component 2 is 1.97.
This pattern is consistent with our earlier statement that the first components extracted tend to
account for relatively large amounts of variance, while the later components account for
relatively smaller amounts.

Step 2: Determining the Number of "Meaningful" Components to Retain

Earlier it was stated that the number of components extracted is equal to the number of variables
being analyzed, necessitating that you decide just how many of these components are truly
meaningful and worthy of being retained for rotation and interpretation. In general, you expect
that only the first few components will account for meaningful amounts of variance, and that the
later components will tend to account for only trivial variance. The next step of the analysis,
therefore, is to determine how many meaningful components should be retained for
interpretation. This section will describe four criteria that may be used in making this decision:
the eigenvalue-one criterion, the scree test, the proportion of variance accounted for, and the
interpretability criterion.

A. The eigenvalue-one criterion. In principal component analysis, one of the most commonly
used criteria for solving the number-of-components problem is the eigenvalue-one criterion, also
known as the Kaiser criterion (Kaiser, 1960). With this approach, you retain and interpret any
component with an eigenvalue greater than 1.00.

The rationale for this criterion is straightforward. Each observed variable contributes one unit of
variance to the total variance in the data set. Any component that displays an eigenvalue greater
than 1.00 is accounting for a greater amount of variance than had been contributed by one
variable. Such a component is therefore accounting for a meaningful amount of variance, and is
worthy of being retained.

On the other hand, a component with an eigenvalue less than 1.00 is accounting for less variance
than had been contributed by one variable. The purpose of principal component analysis is to
reduce a number of observed variables into a relatively smaller number of components; this
cannot be effectively achieved if you retain components that account for less variance than had
been contributed by individual variables. For this reason, components with eigenvalues less than
1.00 are viewed as trivial, and are not retained.

The eigenvalue-one criterion has a number of positive features that have contributed to its popularity. Perhaps the most important reason for its widespread use is its simplicity: You do not make any subjective decisions, but merely retain components with eigenvalues greater than one.

On the positive side, it has been shown that this criterion very often results in retaining the correct number of components, particularly when a small to moderate number of variables are being analyzed and the variable communalities are high. Stevens (1986) reviews studies that have investigated the accuracy of the eigenvalue-one criterion, and recommends its use when less than 30 variables are being analyzed and communalities are greater than .70, or when the analysis is based on over 250 observations and the mean communality is greater than or equal to .60.

There are a number of problems associated with the eigenvalue-one criterion, however. As was suggested in the preceding paragraph, it can lead to retaining the wrong number of components under circumstances that are often encountered in research (e.g., when many variables are analyzed, when communalities are small). Also, the mindless application of this criterion can lead to retaining a certain number of components when the actual difference in the eigenvalues of successive components is only trivial. For example, if component 2 displays an eigenvalue of 1.001 and component 3 displays an eigenvalue of 0.999, then component 2 will be retained but component 3 will not; this may mislead you into believing that the third component was meaningless when, in fact, it accounted for almost exactly the same amount of variance as the second component. In short, the eigenvalue-one criterion can be helpful when used judiciously, but the thoughtless application of this approach can lead to serious errors of interpretation.

With the SAS System, the eigenvalue-one criterion can be implemented by including the MINEIGEN=1 option in the PROC FACTOR statement, and not including the NFACT option. The use of MINEIGEN=1 will cause PROC FACTOR to retain any component with an eigenvalue greater than 1.00.

The eigenvalue table from the current analysis appears on page 2 of Output 14.1. The eigenvalues for components 1, 2, and 3 were 2.27, 1.97, and 0.80, respectively. Only components 1 and 2 demonstrated eigenvalues greater than 1.00, so the eigenvalue-one criterion would lead you to retain and interpret only these two components.

Fortunately, the application of the criterion is fairly unambiguous in this case: The last component retained (2) displays an eigenvalue of 1.97, which is substantially greater than 1.00, and the next component (3) displays an eigenvalue of 0.80, which is clearly lower than 1.00. In this analysis, you are not faced with the difficult decision of whether to retain a component that demonstrates an eigenvalue that is close to 1.00, but not quite there (e.g., an eigenvalue of .98). In situations such as this, the eigenvalue-one criterion may be used with greater confidence.

B. The scree test. With the scree test (Cattell, 1966), you plot the eigenvalues associated with each component and look for a "break" between the components with relatively large eigenvalues and those with small eigenvalues. The components that appear *before* the break are assumed to be meaningful and are retained for rotation; those apppearing *after* the break are assumed to be unimportant and are not retained.

Sometimes a scree plot will display several large breaks. When this is the case, you should look for the *last* big break before the eigenvalues begin to level off. Only the components that appear before this last large break should be retained.

Specifying the SCREE option in the PROC FACTOR statement causes the SAS System to print an eigenvalue plot as part of the output. This appears as page 3 of Output 14.1.

You can see that the component numbers are listed on the horizontal axis, while eigenvalues are listed on the vertical axis. With this plot, notice that there is a relatively small break between component 1 and 2, and a relatively large break following component 2. The breaks between components 3, 4, 5, and 6 are all relatively small.

Because the large break in this plot appears between components 2 and 3, the scree test would lead you to retain only components 1 and 2. The components appearing after the break (3-6) would be regarded as trivial.

The scree test can be expected to provide reasonably accurate results, provided the sample is large (over 200) and most of the variable communalities are large (Stevens, 1986). However, this criterion has its own weaknesses as well, most notably the ambiguity that is often displayed by scree plots under typical research conditions: Very often, it is difficult to determine exactly where in the scree plot a break exists, or even if a break exists at all.

The break in the scree plot on page 3 of Output 14.1 was unusually obvious. In contrast, consider the plot that appears in Figure 14.2.

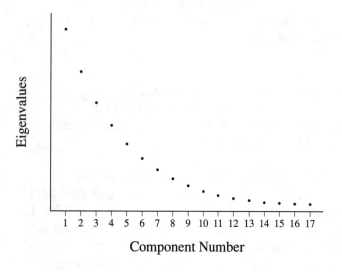

Figure 14.2: A Scree Plot with No Obvious Break

Figure 14.2 presents a fictitious scree plot from a principal component analysis of 17 variables. Notice that there is no obvious break in the plot that separates the meaningful components from the trivial components. Most researchers would agree that components 1 and 2 are probably meaningful, and that components 13-17 are probably trivial, but it is difficult to decide exactly where you should draw the line.

Scree plots such as the one presented in Figure 14.2 are common in social science research. When encountered, the use of the scree test must be supplemented with additional criteria, such as the variance accounted for criterion and the interpretability criterion, to be described later.

Why do they call it a "scree" test? The word "scree" refers to the loose rubble that lies at the base of a cliff. When performing a scree test, you normally hope that the scree plot will take the form of a cliff: At the top will be the eigenvalues for the few meaningful components, followed by a break (the edge of the cliff). At the bottom of the cliff will lie the scree: eigenvalues for the trivial components.

In some cases, a computer printer may not be able to prepare an eigenvalue plot with the degree of precision that is necessary to perform a sensitive scree test. In such cases, it may be best to prepare the plot by hand. This may be done simply by referring to the eigenvalue table on output page 2. Using the eigenvalues from this table, you can prepare an eigenvalue plot following the same format used by the SAS System (component numbers on the horizontal axis, eigenvalues on the vertical). Such a hand-drawn plot may make it easier to identify the break in the eigenvalues, if one exists.

C. Proportion of variance accounted for. A third criterion in solving the number of factors problem involves retaining a component if it accounts for a specified proportion (or percentage) of variance in the data set. For example, you may decide to retain any component that accounts for at least 5% or 10% of the total variance. This proportion can be calculated with a simple formula:

$$\text{Proportion} = \frac{\text{Eigenvalue for the component of interest}}{\text{Total eigenvalues of the correlation matrix}}$$

In principal component analysis, the "total eigenvalues of the correlation matrix" is equal to the total number of variables being analyzed (because each variable contributes one unit of variance to the analysis).

Fortunately, it is not necessary to actually compute these percentages by hand, since they are provided in the results of PROC FACTOR. The proportion of variance accounted for by each component is printed in the eigenvalue table from output page 2, and appears to the right of the "Proportion" heading.

The eigenvalue table for the current analysis appears on page 2 of Output 14.1. From the "Proportion" line in this eigenvalue table, you can see that the first component alone accounts for 38% of the total variance, the second component alone accounts for 33%, the third component accounts for 13%, and the fourth component accounts for 7%. Assume that you have decided to retain any component that accounts for at least 10% of the total variance in the data set. For the present results, using this criterion would cause you to retain components 1, 2, and 3 (notice that use of this criterion would result in retaining more components than would be retained with the two preceding criteria).

An alternative criterion is to retain enough components so that the *cumulative* percent of variance accounted for is equal to some minimal value. For example, remember that components 1, 2, 3, and 4 accounted for approximately 38%, 33%, 13%, and 7% of the total variance, respectively. Adding these percentages together results in a sum of 91%. This means that the *cumulative* percent of variance accounted for by components 1, 2, 3, and 4 is 91%. When researchers use the "cumulative percent of variance accounted for" as the criterion for solving the number-of-components problem, they usually retain enough components so that the cumulative percent of variance accounted for at least 70% (and sometimes 80%).

With respect to the results of PROC FACTOR, the "cumulative percent of variance accounted for" is presented in the eigenvalue table (from page 2), to the right of the "Cumulative" heading. For the present analysis, this information appears in the eigenvalue table on page 2 of Output 14.1. Notice the values that appear to the right of the heading "Cumulative": Each value in this line indicates the percent of variance accounted for by the present component, as well as all preceding components. For example, the value for component 2 is .7068 (this appears at the intersection of the row headed "Cumulative" and the column headed "2"). This value of .7068 indicates that approximately 71% of the total variance is accounted for by components 1 and 2 combined. The corresponding entry for component 3 is .8397, meaning that approximately 84% of the variance is accounted for by components 1, 2, and 3 combined. If you were to use 70% as the "critical value" for determining the number of components to retain, you would retain components 1 and 2 in the present analysis.

The proportion of variance criterion has a number of positive features. For example, in most cases, you would not want to retain a group of components that, combined, account for only a minority of the variance in the data set (say, 30%). Nonetheless, the critical values discussed earlier (10% for individual components and 70%-80% for the combined components) are obviously arbitrary. Because of these and related problems, this approach has sometimes been criticized for its subjectivity (Kim & Mueller, 1978b).

D. The interpretability criteria. Perhaps the most important criterion for solving the "number-of-components" problem is the **interpretability criterion**: interpreting the substantive meaning of the retained components and verifying that this interpretation makes sense in terms of what is known about the constructs under investigation. The following list provides four rules to follow in doing this. A later section (titled "Step 4: Interpreting the Rotated Solution") shows how to actually interpret the results of a principal component analysis; the following rules will be more meaningful after you have completed that section.

1. **Are there at least three variables (items) with significant loadings on each retained component?** A solution is less satisfactory if a given component is measured by less than three variables.

2. **Do the variables that load on a given component share the same conceptual meaning?** For example, if three questions on a survey all load on component 1, do all three of these questions seem to be measuring the same construct?

3. **Do the variables that load on different components seem to be measuring different constructs?** For example, if three questions load on component 1, and three other questions load on component 2, do the first three questions seem to be measuring a construct that is conceptually different from the construct measured by the last three questions?

4. **Does the rotated factor pattern demonstrate "simple structure?"** Simple structure means that the pattern possesses two characteristics: (a) Most of the variables have relatively high factor loadings on only one component, and near zero loadings on the other components, and (b) most components have relatively high factor loadings for some variables, and near-zero loadings for the remaining variables. This concept of simple structure will be explained in more detail in a later section titled "Step 4: Interpreting the Rotated Solution."

Recommendations. Given the preceding options, what procedure should you actually follow in solving the number-of-components problem? We recommend combining all four in a structured sequence. First, use the MINEIGEN=1 options to implement the eigenvalue-one criterion. Review this solution for interpretability, and use caution if the break between the components with eigenvalues above 1.00 and those below 1.00 is not clear-cut (i.e., if component 2 has an eigenvalue of 1.001, and component 2 has an eigenvalue of 0.998).

Next, perform a scree test and look for obvious breaks in the eigenvalues. Because there will often be more than one break in the scree plot, it may be necessary to examine two or more possible solutions.

Next, review the amount of common variance accounted for by each individual component. You probably should not rigidly use some specific but arbitrary cutoff point such as 5% or 10%. Still, if you are retaining components that account for as little as 2% or 4% of the variance, it may be wise to take a second look at the solution and verify that these latter components are of truly substantive importance. In the same way, it is best if the combined components account for at least 70% of the cumulative variance; if less than 70% is accounted for, it may be wise to consider alternative solutions that include a larger number of components.

Finally, apply the interpretability criteria to each solution that is examined. If more than one solution can be justified on the basis of the preceding criteria, which of these solutions is the most interpretable? By seeking a solution that is both interpretable and also satisfies one (or more) of the other three criteria, you maximize chances of retaining the correct number of components.

Step 3: Rotation to a Final Solution

Factor patterns and factor loadings. After extracting the initial components, PROC FACTOR will create an unrotated **factor pattern matrix**. The rows of this matrix represent the variables being analyzed, and the columns represent the retained components (these components are referred to as FACTOR1, FACTOR2 and so forth in the output).

The entries in the matrix are factor loadings. A **factor loading** is a general term for a coefficient that appears in a factor pattern matrix or a factor structure matrix. In an analysis that results in oblique (correlated) components, the definition for a factor loading is different depending on whether it is in a factor *pattern* matrix or in a factor *structure* matrix. However, the situation is simpler in an analysis that results in orthogonal components (as in the present chapter): In an orthogonal analysis, factor loadings are equivalent to bivariate correlations between the observed variables and the components.

For example, the factor pattern matrix from the current analysis appears on page 4 of Output 14.1. Where the rows for observed variables intersect with the column for FACTOR1, you can see that the correlation between V1 and the first component is .58; the correlation between V2 and the first component is .48, and so forth.

Rotations. Ideally, you would like to review the correlations between the variables and the components and use this information to *interpret* the components; that is, to determine what construct seems to be measured by component 1, what construct seems to be measured by component 2, and so forth.   Unfortunately, when more than one component has been retained in an analysis, the interpretation of an unrotated factor pattern is usually quite difficult. To make interpretation easier, you will normally perform an operation called a rotation. A **rotation** is a linear transformation that is performed on the factor solution for the purpose of making the solution easier to interpret.

PROC FACTOR allows you to request several different types of rotations. The preceding program that analyzed data from the POI study included the statement

```
ROTATE=VARIMAX
```

which requests a **varimax rotation**. A varimax rotation is an orthogonal rotation, meaning that it results in uncorrelated components. Compared to some other types of rotations, a varimax rotation tends to maximize the variance of a column of the factor pattern matrix (as opposed to a row of the matrix). This rotation is probably the most commonly used orthogonal rotation in the social sciences. The results of the varimax rotation for the current analysis appear on page 5 of Output 14.1.

Step 4: Interpreting the Rotated Solution

Interpreting a rotated solution means determining just what is measured by each of the retained components. Briefly, this involves identifying the variables that demonstrate high loadings for a given component, and determining what these variables have in common. Usually, a brief name is assigned to each retained component that describes its content.

The first decision to be made at this stage is to decide how large a factor loading must be to be considered "large." Stevens (1986) discusses some of the issues relevant to this decision, and even provides guidelines for testing the statistical significance of factor loadings. Given that this is an introductory treatment of principal component analysis, however, simply consider a loading to be "large" if its absolute value exceeds .40.

The rotated factor pattern for the POI study appears on page 5 of Output 14.1. The following text provides a structured approach for interpreting this factor pattern.

A. Read across the row for the first variable. All "meaningful loadings" (i.e., loadings greater than .40) have been flagged with an asterisk ("*"). This was accomplished by including the FLAG=.40 option in the preceding program. If a given variable has a meaningful loading on more than one component, scratch that variable out and ignore it in your interpretation. In many situations, researchers want to drop variables that load on more than one component, because the variables are not pure measures of any one construct. In the present case, this means looking at the row headed "V1", and reading to the right to see if it loads on more than one component. In this case it does not, so you may retain this variable.

B. Repeat this process for the remaining variables, scratching out any variable that loads on more than one component. In this analysis, none of the variables have high loadings on more than one component, so none will have to be dropped.

C. Review all of the surviving variables with high loadings on component 1 to determine the nature of this component. From the rotated factor pattern, you can see that only items 4, 5, and 6 load on component 1 (note the asterisks). It is now necessary to turn to the questionnaire itself and review the content of the questions in order to decide what a given component should be named. What do questions 4, 5, and 6 have in common? What common construct do they seem to be measuring? For illustration, the questions being analyzed in the present case are reproduced here. Remember that question 4 was represented as V4 in the SAS program, question 5 was V5, and so forth. Read questions 4, 5, and 6 to see what they have in common.

```
1 2 3   5 6 7     1.   Went out of my way to do a favor for a
                       coworker.

1 2 3 4 5 6 7     2.   Went out of my way to do a favor for a
                       relative.

1 2 3 4 5 6 7     3.   Went out of my way to do a favor for a
                       friend.
```

```
1 2 3 4 5 6 7     4.  Gave money to a religious charity.

1 2 3 4 5 6 7     5.  Gave money to a charity not associated with a
                      religion.

1 2 3 4 5 6 7     6.  Gave money to a panhandler.
```

Questions 4, 5, and 6 all seem to deal with "giving money to the needy." It is therefore reasonable to label component 1 the "financial giving" component.

D. Repeat this process to name the remaining retained components. In the present case, there is only one remaining component to name: component 2. This component has high loadings for questions 1, 2, and 3. In reviewing these items, it becomes clear that each seems to deal with helping friends, relatives, or other acquaintances. It is therefore appropriate to name this the "acquaintance helping" component.

E. Determine whether this final solution satisfies the interpretability criteria. An earlier section indicated that the overall results of a principal component analysis are satisfactory only if they meet a number of interpretability criteria. In the following list, the adequacy of the rotated factor pattern presented on page 5 of Output 14.1 is assessed in terms of these criteria.

1. **Are there at least three variables (items) with significant loadings on each retained component?** In the present example, three variables loaded on component 1, and three also loaded on component 2, so this criterion was met.

2. **Do the variables that load on a given component share some conceptual meaning?** All three variables loading on component 1 are clearly measuring giving to the needy, while all three loading on component 2 are clearly measuring prosocial acts performed for acquaintances. Therefore, this criterion is met.

3. **Do the variables that load on different components seem to be measuring different constructs?** The items loading on component 1 clearly are measuring the respondents' financial contributions, while the items loading on component 2 are clearly measuring helpfulness toward acquaintances. Because these seem to be conceptually very different constructs, this criterion seems to be met as well.

4. **Does the rotated factor pattern demonstrate "simple structure?"** Earlier, it was said that a rotated factor pattern demonstrates simple structure when it has two characteristics. First, most of the variables should have high loadings on one component, and near-zero loadings on the other components. It can be seen that the pattern obtained here meets that requirement: items 1-3 have high loadings on component 2, and near-zero loadings on component 1. Similarly, items 4-6 have high

loadings on component 1, and near-zero loadings on component 2. The second characteristic of simple structure is that each component should have high loadings for some variables, and near-zero loadings for the others. Again, the pattern obtained here also meets this requirement: component 1 has high loadings for items 4-6 and near-zero loadings for the other items, while component 2 has high loadings for items 1-3, and near-zero loadings on the remaining items. In short, the rotated component pattern obtained in this analysis does seem to demonstrate simple structure.

Step 5: Creating Factor Scores or Factor-Based Scores

Once the analysis is complete, it is often desirable to assign scores to each subject to indicate where that subject stands on the retained components. For example, the two components retained in the present study were interpreted as a financial giving component and an acquaintance helping component. You may want to now assign one score to each subject to indicate that subject's standing on the financial giving component, and a different score to indicate that subject's standing on the acquaintance helping component. With this done, these component scores could be used either as predictor variables or as criterion variables in subsequent analyses.

Before discussing the options for assigning these scores, it is important to first draw a distinction between factor scores versus factor-based scores. In principal component analysis, a **factor score** (or **component score**) is a linear composite of the optimally-weighted observed variables. If requested, PROC FACTOR will compute each subject's factor scores for the two components by

- determining the optimal regression weights

- multiplying subject responses to the questionnaire items by these weights

- summing the products.

The resulting sum will be a given subject's score on the component of interest. Remember that a separate equation, with different weights, is developed for each retained component.

A **factor-based score**, on the other hand, is merely a linear composite of the variables that demonstrated meaningful loadings for the component in question. For example, in the preceding analysis, items 4, 5, and 6 demonstrated meaningful loadings for the financial giving component. Therefore, you could calculate the factor-based score on this component for a given subject by simply adding together his or her responses to items 4, 5, an 6. Notice that, with a factor-based score, the observed variables are not multiplied by optimal weights before they are summed.

Computing factor scores. Factor scores are requested by including the NFACT and OUT options in the PROC FACTOR statement. Here is the general form for a SAS program that uses the NFACT and OUT option to compute factor scores:

```
PROC FACTOR    DATA=data-set-name
               SIMPLE
               METHOD=PRIN
               PRIORS=ONE
               NFACT=number-of-components-to-retain
               ROTATE=VARIMAX
               ROUND
               FLAG=desired-size-of-"significant"-factor-loadings
               OUT=name-of-new-SAS-data-set    ;
  VAR  variables-to-be-analyzed ;
  RUN;
```

Here are the actual program statements (minus the DATA step) that could be used to perform a principal component analysis and compute factor scores for the POI study.

```
1       PROC FACTOR    DATA=D1
2                      SIMPLE
3                      METHOD=PRIN
4                      PRIORS=ONE
5                      NFACT=2
6                      ROTATE=VARIMAX
7                      ROUND
8                      FLAG=.40
9                      OUT=D2    ;
10      VAR V1 V2 V3 V4 V5 V6;
11      RUN;
```

Notice how this program differs from the original program presented earlier in the chapter (in the section titled "SAS Program and Output"): the MINEIGEN=1 option has been dropped, and has been replaced with the NFACT=2 option; and the OUT=D2 option has been added.

Line 9 of the preceding programs asks that an output data set be created and given the name D2. This name was arbitrary; any name consistent with SAS System requirements would have been acceptable. The new data set named D2 will contain all of the variables contained in the previous data set (D1), as well as new variables named FACTOR1 and FACTOR2. FACTOR1 will contain factor scores for the first retained component, and FACTOR2 will contain scores for the second component. The number of new "FACTOR" variables created will be equal to the number of components retained by the NFACT statement.

The OUT option may be used to create component scores only if the analysis has been performed on a raw data set (as opposed to a correlation or covariance matrix). The use of the NFACT statement is also required.

Having created the new variables named FACTOR1 and FACTOR2, you may be interested in seeing how they relate to the study's original observed variables. This can be done by appending PROC CORR statements to the SAS program, following the last of the PROC FACTOR statements. The full program (minus the DATA step) is now reproduced:

```
1      PROC FACTOR    DATA=D1
2                     SIMPLE
3                     METHOD=PRIN
4                     PRIORS=ONE
5                     NFACT=2
6                     ROTATE=VARIMAX
7                     ROUND
8                     FLAG=.40
9                     OUT=D2    ;
10        VAR V1 V2 V3 V4 V5 V6;
11        RUN;
12
13     PROC CORR    DATA=D2;
14        VAR FACTOR1 FACTOR2;
15        WITH V1 V2 V3 V4 V5 V6 FACTOR1 FACTOR2;
16        RUN;
```

Notice that the PROC CORR statement on line 13 specifies DATA=D2. This data set (D2) is the name of the output data set created on line 9 in the PROC FACTOR statement. The PROC CORR statements request that the factor score variables (FACTOR 1 and FACTOR2) be correlated with the subjects' responses to questionnaire items 1-6 (V1-V6), as well as with themselves (FACTOR1 and FACTOR2).

With printer options of LINESIZE=80 and PAGESIZE=60, the preceding program would again produce four pages of output. Pages 1-2 provide simple statistics, the eigenvalue table, and the unrotated factor pattern, identical to those produced with the first program. Page 3 provides the rotated factor pattern and final communalities (same as before), along with the standardized scoring coefficients used in creating the factor scores. Finally, page 4 provides the correlations requested by the CORR procedure. Pages 3 and 4 of the output created by the preceding program are reproduced here as Output 14.2.

The SAS System   3

Rotation Method: Varimax

Orthogonal Transformation Matrix

	1	2
1	0.76914	0.63908
2	-0.63908	0.76914

Rotated Factor Pattern

	FACTOR1	FACTOR2
V1	0	91 *
V2	3	71 *
V3	7	86 *
V4	90 *	-9
V5	81 *	9
V6	82 *	8

NOTE: Printed values are multiplied by 100 and rounded to the nearest integer.
Values greater than 0.4 have been flagged by an '*'.

Variance explained by each factor

FACTOR1	FACTOR2
2.147248	2.093803

Final Communality Estimates: Total = 4.241050

V1	V2	V3	V4	V5	V6
0.823418	0.508529	0.743990	0.822574	0.665963	0.676575

Scoring Coefficients Estimated by Regression
Squared Multiple Correlations of the Variables with each Factor

FACTOR1	FACTOR2
1.000000	1.000000

Standardized Scoring Coefficients

	FACTOR1	FACTOR2
V1	-0.03109	0.43551
V2	-0.00726	0.34071
V3	0.00388	0.41044
V4	0.42515	-0.07087
V5	0.37618	0.01947
V6	0.38020	0.01361

```
                                                                    4
                        Correlation Analysis

    8 'WITH' Variables:   V1      V2      V3      V4      V5      V6
                          FACTOR1 FACTOR2
    2 'VAR'  Variables:   FACTOR1 FACTOR2


                          Simple Statistics

Variable        N      Mean     Std Dev       Sum     Minimum    Maximum

V1             50    5.18000    1.39518   259.00000   1.00000    7.00000
V2             50    5.40000    1.10657   270.00000   3.00000    7.00000
V3             50    5.52000    1.21622   276.00000   2.00000    7.00000
V4             50    3.64000    1.79296   182.00000   1.00000    7.00000
V5             50    4.22000    1.66953   211.00000   1.00000    7.00000
V6             50    3.10000    1.55511   155.00000   1.00000    7.00000
FACTOR1        50       0       1.00000       0      -1.87908    2.35913
FACTOR2        50       0       1.00000       0      -2.95892    1.58951


     Pearson Correlation Coefficients / Prob > |R| under Ho: Rho=0 / N = 50

                            FACTOR1         FACTOR2

            V1            -0.00429         0.90741
                           0.9764          0.0001

            V2             0.03328         0.71234
                           0.8185          0.0001

            V3             0.06720         0.85993
                           0.6429          0.0001

            V4             0.90274        -0.08740

                           0.0001          0.5462

            V5             0.81055         0.09474
                           0.0001          0.5128

            V6             0.81834         0.08303
                           0.0001          0.5665

       FACTOR1            1.00000         0.00000
                           0.0            1.0000

       FACTOR2            0.00000         1.00000
                           1.0000          0.0
```

Output 14.2: Output Pages 3 and 4 from the Analysis of POI Data in Which Factor Scores Were Created

The simple statistics for the CORR procedure appear at the top of page 4 in Output 14.2. Notice that the simple statistics for the observed variables (V1-V6) are identical to those that appeared at the beginning of the FACTOR output discussed earlier (at the top of Output 14.1, page 1). In contrast, note the simple statistics for FACTOR1 and FACTOR2 (the factor score variables for components 1 and 2, respectively): both have means of 0 and standard deviations of 1. Obviously, these variables were constructed in such a way as to be standardized variables.

The correlations between FACTOR1 and FACTOR2 and the original observed variables appear on the bottom half of page 4. You can see that the correlations between FACTOR1 and V1-V6 on page 4 of Output 14.2 are identical to the factor loadings of V1-V6 on FACTOR1 on page 5 of Output 14.1, under "Rotated Factor Pattern". This makes sense, as the elements of a factor pattern (in an orthogonal solution) are simply correlations between the observed variables and the components themselves. Similarly, you can see that the correlations between FACTOR2 and V1-V6 from page 4 of Output 14.2 are also identical to the corresponding factor loadings from page 5 of Output 14.1.

Of special interest is the correlation between FACTOR1 and FACTOR2, as computed by PROC CORR. This appears on page 4 of Output 14.2, where the row for FACTOR2 intersects with the column for FACTOR1. Notice the observed correlation between these two components is zero. This is as expected: the rotation method used in the principal component analysis was the varimax method, which produces orthogonal, or uncorrelated, components.

Computing factor-based scores. A second (and less sophisticated) approach to scoring involves the creation of new variables that contain factor-based scores rather than true factor scores. A variable that contains factor-based scores is sometimes referred to as a **factor-based scale**.

Although factor-based scores can be created in a number of ways, the following method has the advantage of being relatively straightforward and is commonly used:

1. To calculate factor-based scores for component 1, first determine which questionnaire items had high loadings on that component.

2. For a given subject, add together that subject's responses to these items. The result is that subject's score on the factor-based scale for component 1.

3. Repeat these steps to calculate each subject's score on the remaining retained components.

Although this may sound like a cumbersome task, it is actually made quite simple through the use of data manipulation statements contained in a SAS program. For example, assume that you have performed the principal component analysis on your survey responses, and have obtained the findings reported in this chapter. Specifically, you found that survey items 4, 5, and 6 loaded on component 1 (the financial giving component), while items 1, 2, and 3 loaded on component 2 (the acquaintance helping component).

You would now like to create two new SAS variables. The first variable, called FINANCE, will include each subject's factor-based score for financial giving. The second variable, called ACQUAINT, will include each subject's factor-based score for acquaintance helping. Once these variables are created, you can use them as criterion variables or predictor variables in subsequent analyses. To keep things simple in the present example, assume that you are simply interested in determining whether there is a significant correlation between FINANCE and ACQUAINT.

At this time, it may be useful to review Chapter 4 on "Working with Variables and Observations in SAS Data Sets," particularly the section on creating new variables from existing variables. Such a review should make it easier to understand the data manipulation statements used here.

Assume that earlier statements in the SAS program have already input subject responses to the six questionnaire items. These variables are included in a data set called D1. The following are the subsequent lines that would go on to create a new data set called D2. The new data set will include all of the variables in D1, as well as the newly created factor-based scales called FINANCE and ACQUAINT.

```
14
15      DATA D2;
16         SET D1;
17
18      FINANCE   = (V4 + V5 + V6);
19      ACQUAINT  = (V1 + V2 + V3);
20
21      PROC CORR   DATA=D2;
22         VAR FINANCE ACQUAINT;
23         RUN;
```

Lines 15 and 16 request that a new data set called D2 be created, and that it be set up as a duplicate of existing data set D1. In line 18, the new variable called FINANCE is created. For each subject, his or her responses to items 4, 5, and 6 are added together. The result is the subjects' score on the factor-based scale for the first component. These scores are stored in a variable called FINANCE. The component-based scale for the acquaintance helping component is created on line 19, and these scores are stored in the variable called ACQUAINT. Line 21-23 request the correlations between FINANCE and ACQUAINT be determined. FINANCE and ACQUAINT may now be used as predictor or criterion variables in subsequent analyses.

To save space, the results of this program will not be reproduced here. However, note that this output would probably display a significant correlation between FINANCE and ACQUAINT. This may come as a surprise, because earlier it was shown that the factor scores contained in FACTOR1 and FACTOR2 (counterparts to FINANCE and ACQUAINT) were completely uncorrelated.

The reason for this apparent contradiction is simple: FACTOR1 and FACTOR2 are true principal components, and true principal components (created in an orthogonal solution) are always created with optimally weighted equations so that they will be mutually uncorrelated.

In contrast, FINANCE and ACQUAINT are not true principal components that consist of true factor scores; they are merely artificial varibles that were *based* on the results of a principal component analysis. Optimal weights (that would ensure orthogonality) were not used in the creation of FINANCE and ACQUAINT. This is why factor-based scales will often demonstrate nonzero correlations with one another, while true principal components (from an orthogonal solution) will not.

Recoding reversed items prior to analysis. It is generally best to recode any reversed items before conducting any of the analyses described here. In particular, it is essential that reversed items be recoded prior to the program statements that produce factor-based scales. For example, the three questionnaire items that assess financial giving appear again here:

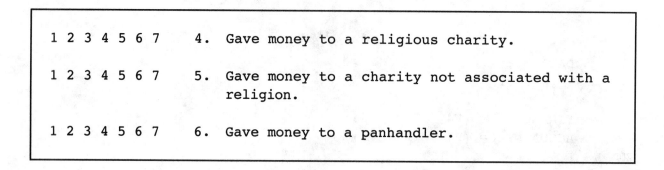

None of these items are reversed; with each item, a response of "7" indicates a high level of financial giving. In the following, however, item 4 is a reversed item: with item 4, a response of "7" indicates a *low* level of giving:

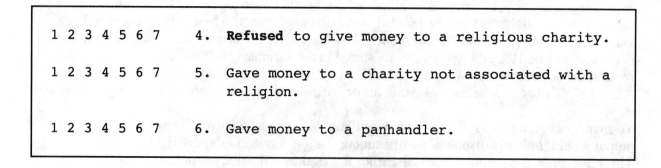

If you were to perform a principal component analysis on responses to these items, the factor loading for item 4 would most likely have a sign that is the opposite of the sign of the loadings for items 5 and 6 (e.g., if items 5 and 6 had positive loadings, item 4 would have a negative loading). This would complicate the creation of a component-based scale: with items 5 and 6, higher scores indicate greater giving; with item 4, lower scores indicate greater giving. Clearly, you would not want to sum these three items as they are presently coded. First, it will be necessary to reverse item 4. Notice how this is done in the following program (assume that the data have already been input in a SAS data set named D1):

```
15      DATA D2;
16         SET D1;
17
18      V4 = 8 - V4;
19
20      FINANCE    = (V4 + V5 + V6);
21      ACQUAINT   = (V1 + V2 + V3);
22
23      PROC CORR    DATA=D2;
24         VAR FINANCE ACQUAINT;
25         RUN;
```

Line 18 of the preceding program created a new, recoded version of variable V4. Values on this new version of V4 will be equal to the quantity 8 minus the value of the old version of V4. Therefore, for subjects whose score on the old version of V4 was 1, their value on the new version of V4 will be 7 (because $8 - 1 = 7$); for subjects whose score on the old version of V4 was 7, their value on the new version of V4 will be 1 (because $8 - 7 = 1$); and so forth.

The general form of the formula used when recoding reversed items is

```
Variable-name  =  constant  -  variable-name ;
```

In this formula, the "constant" is the following quantity:

The number of points on the response scale used with the questionnaire item plus 1

Therefore if you are using the 4-point response format, the constant is 5; if using a 9-point scale, the constant is 10.

If you have prior knowledge about which items are going to appear as reversed items (with reversed component loadings) in your results, it is best to place these recoding statements early in your SAS program, before the PROC FACTOR statements. This will make interpretation of the components a bit more straightforward because it will eliminate significant loadings with opposite signs from appearing on the same component. In any case, it is essential that the statements that recode reversed items appear before the statements that create any factor-based scales.

Step 6: Summarizing the Results in a Table

For published articles that summarize the results of your analysis, it is generally desirable to prepare a table that presents the rotated factor pattern. When the variables being analyzed contain responses to questionnaire items, it can be helpful to actually reproduce the questionnaire items themselves within this table. This is done in Table 14.2:

Table 14.2

<u>Rotated Factor Pattern and Final Communality Estimates from</u>
<u>Principal Component Analysis of Prosocial Orientation Inventory</u>

Component

1	2	$\underline{h}^2$		Items
.00	.91	.82	1.	Went out of my way to do a favor for a coworker.
.03	.71	.51	2.	Went out of my way to do a favor for a relative.
.07	.86	.74	3.	Went out of my way to do a favor for a friend.
.90	−.09	.82	4.	Gave money to a religious charity.
.81	.09	.67	5.	Gave money to a charity not associated with a religion.
.82	.08	.68	6.	Gave money to a panhandler.

<u>Note</u>: $\underline{N}$ = 50. Communality estimates appear in column headed $\underline{h}^2$.

The final communality estimates from the analysis are presented under the heading "$\underline{h}^2$" in the table. These estimates appear in the SAS output following the "Rotated Factor Pattern" and "Variance explained by each factor" (page 3 of Output 14.2).

Very often, the items that constitute the questionnaire are so lengthy, or the number of retained components is so large, that it is not possible to present both the factor pattern, the communalities, and the items themselves in the same table. In such situations, it may be preferable to present the factor pattern and communalities in one table, and the items in a second (or in the text of the paper). Shared item numbers may then be used to associate each item with its corresponding factor loadings and communality.

Step 7: Preparing a Formal Description of the Results for a Paper

The preceding analysis could be summarized in the following way for a published paper:

> Responses to the 6-item questionnaire were subjected to a principal component analysis using ones as prior communality estimates. The principal axis method was used to extract the components, and this was followed by a varimax (orthogonal) rotation.
>
> Only the first two components displayed eigenvalues greater than 1, and the results of a scree test also suggested that only the first two components were meaningful. Therefore, only the first two components were retained for rotation. Combined, components 1 and 2 accounted for 71% of the total variance.
>
> Questionnaire items and corresponding factor loadings are presented in Table 14.2. In interpreting the rotated factor pattern, an item was said to load on a given component if the factor loading was .40 or greater for that component, and was less than .40 for the other. Using these criteria, three items were found to load on the first component, which was subsequently labelled the financial giving component. Three items also loaded on the second component, which was labelled the acquaintance helping component.

An Example with Three Retained Components

The Questionnaire

The next example involves a piece of fictitious research that investigates the investment model (Rusbult, 1980). As has been stated in earlier chapters, the investment model identifies variables that are believed to affect a person's commitment to a romantic relationship. In this context, **commitment** refers to the person's intention to maintain the relationship and stay with the current romantic partner.

One version of the investment model predicts that commitment will be affected by three antecedent variables: satisfaction, investment size, and alternative value. **Satisfaction** refers to the subject's affective response to the relationship; among other things, subjects report high levels of satisfaction when their current relationship comes close to their ideal relationship. **Investment size** refers to the amount of time, energy, and personal resources that an individual has put into the relationship. For example, subjects report high investments when they have spent a lot of time with their current partner and have developed a lot of mutual friends that may be lost if the relationship were to end. Finally, **alternative value** refers to the attractiveness of one's alternatives to the current partner; a subject would score high on alternative value if, for example, it would be attractive to date someone else or perhaps to not be dating at all.

Assume that you wish to conduct research on the investment model, and are in the process of preparing a 12-item questionnaire that will assess levels of satisfaction, investment size, and alternative value in a group of subjects involved in romantic associations. Part of the instrument used to assess these constructs is reproduced here:

Indicate the extent to which you agree or disagree with each of the following statements by writing the appropriate response number in the space to the left of the statement. Please use the following response format in making these ratings:

```
7 = Strongly Agree
6 = Agree
5 = Slightly Agree
4 = Neither Agree Nor Disagree
3 = Slightly Disagree
2 = Disagree
1 = Strongly Disagree
```

_____ 1. I am satisfied with my current relationship.

_____ 2. My current relationship comes close to my ideal relationship.

_____ 3. I am more satisfied with my relationship than is the average person.

_____ 4. I feel good about my current relationship.

_____ 5. I have invested a great deal of time in my current relationship.

_____ 6. I have invested a great deal of energy in my current relationship.

_____ 7. I have invested a lot of my personal resources (e.g., money) in developing my current relationship.

_____ 8. My partner and I have developed a lot of mutual friends which I might lose if we were to break up.

_____ 9. There are plenty of other attractive people around for me to date if I were to break up with my current partner.

_____ 10. It would be attractive for me to break up with my current partner and date someone else.

_____ 11. It would be attractive for me to break up with my partner and just be alone for a while.

_____ 12. It would be attractive for me to break up with my partner and "play the field" for a while.

In the preceding questionnaire, items 1-4 were designed to assess satisfaction, items 5-8 were designed to assess investment size, and items 9-12 were designed to assess alternative value. Assume that you administer this questionnaire to 300 subjects, and now want to perform a principal component analysis on their responses.

Writing the Program

Earlier, it was mentioned that it is possible to perform a principal component analysis on a correlation matrix as well as on raw data; this section shows how this is done. The following program inputs the correlation matrix that provides all possible correlations between responses to the 12 items on the questionnaire, and performs a principal component analysis on these responses (these correlations are based on fictitious data):

```
1    DATA D1(TYPE=CORR) ;
2       INPUT    _TYPE_    $
3                _NAME_    $
4                V1-V12    ;
5    CARDS;
6    N      .    300  300  300  300  300  300  300  300  300  300  300  300
7    STD    .    2.48 2.39 2.58 3.12 2.80 3.14 2.92 2.50 2.10 2.14 1.83 2.26
8    CORR V1     1.00  .    .    .    .    .    .    .    .    .    .    .
9    CORR V2      .69 1.00  .    .    .    .    .    .    .    .    .    .
10   CORR V3      .60  .79 1.00  .    .    .    .    .    .    .    .    .
11   CORR V4      .62  .47  .48 1.00  .    .    .    .    .    .    .    .
12   CORR V5      .03  .04  .16  .09 1.00  .    .    .    .    .    .    .
13   CORR V6      .05 -.04  .08  .05  .91 1.00  .    .    .    .    .    .
14   CORR V7      .14  .05  .06  .12  .82  .89 1.00  .    .    .    .    .
15   CORR V8      .23  .13  .16  .21  .70  .72  .82 1.00  .    .    .    .
16   CORR V9     -.17 -.07 -.04 -.05 -.33 -.26 -.38 -.45 1.00  .    .    .
17   CORR V10    -.10 -.08  .07  .15 -.16 -.20 -.27 -.34  .45 1.00  .    .
18   CORR V11    -.24 -.19 -.26 -.28 -.43 -.37 -.53 -.57  .60  .22 1.00  .
19   CORR V12    -.11 -.07  .07  .08 -.10 -.13 -.23 -.31  .44  .60  .26 1.00
20   ;
21   PROC FACTOR    DATA=D1
22                  METHOD=PRIN
23                  PRIORS=ONE
```

```
24                    MINEIGEN=1
25                    SCREE
26                    ROTATE=VARIMAX
27                    ROUND
28                    FLAG=.40   ;
29        VAR  V1-V12;
30        RUN;
```

The PROC FACTOR statement in the preceding program follows the general form recommended for the initial analysis of a data set. Notice that the MINEIGEN=1 statement requests that all components with eigenvalues greater than one be retained, and the SCREE option requests a scree plot of the eigenvalues. These options are particularly helpful for the initial analysis of the data, as they can help determine the correct number of components to retain. If the scree test (or the other criteria) suggests retaining some number of components other than what would be retained using the MINEIGEN=1 option, that option may be dropped and replaced with the NFACT option.

Results of the Initial Analysis

The preceding program produced four pages of output, with the following information appearing on each page:

- Page 1 includes the eigenvalue table.

- Page 2 includes the scree plot of eigenvalues.

- Page 3 includes the unrotated factor pattern and final communality estimates.

- Page 4 includes the rotated factor pattern.

The eigenvalue table from this analysis appears on page 1 of Output 14.3. The eigenvalues themselves appear in the row to the right of the "Eigenvalue" heading. From the values appearing in this row, you can see that components 1, 2, and 3 demonstrated eigenvalues of 4.47, 2.73, and 1.70, respectively. Further, you can see that only these first three components demonstrated eigenvalues greater than one. This means that three components will be retained by the MINEIGEN criterion. Notice that the first nonretained component (component 4) displays an eigenvalue of approximately 0.85 which, of course, is well below 1.00. This is encouraging, as you can have more confidence in the eigenvalue-one criterion when the solution does not contain components with "near-miss" eigenvalues of , say, .98 or .99.

```
                        The SAS System                              1

Initial Factor Method: Principal Components

              Prior Communality Estimates: ONE

    Eigenvalues of the Correlation Matrix:   Total = 12   Average = 1

                           1          2          3          4
        Eigenvalue     4.4706     2.7306     1.7017     0.8463
        Difference     1.7400     1.0289     0.8555     0.2256
        Proportion     0.3725     0.2276     0.1418     0.0705
        Cumulative     0.3725     0.6001     0.7419     0.8124

                           5          6          7          8
        Eigenvalue     0.6206     0.4110     0.3450     0.3029
        Difference     0.2096     0.0660     0.0421     0.0701
        Proportion     0.0517     0.0343     0.0288     0.0252
        Cumulative     0.8642     0.8984     0.9272     0.9524

                           9         10         11         12
        Eigenvalue     0.2328     0.1869     0.1062     0.0453
        Difference     0.0460     0.0806     0.0609
        Proportion     0.0194     0.0156     0.0089     0.0038
        Cumulative     0.9718     0.9874     0.9962     1.0000

      3 factors will be retained by the MINEIGEN criterion.
```

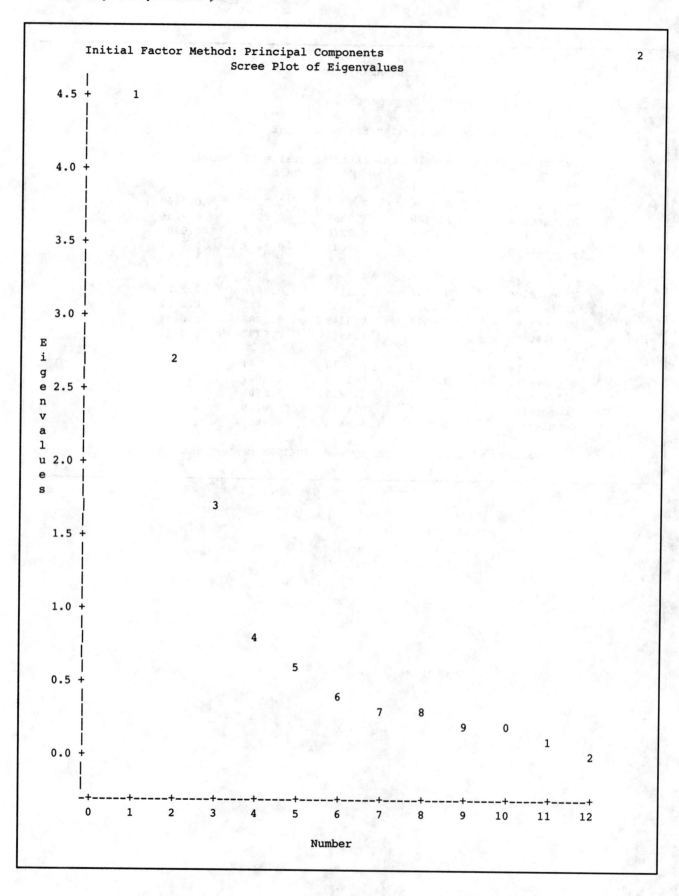

The SAS System   3

Initial Factor Method: Principal Components

Factor Pattern

	FACTOR1	FACTOR2	FACTOR3
V1	39	76 *	-14
V2	31	82 *	-12
V3	34	79 *	9
V4	31	69 *	15
V5	80 *	-26	41 *
V6	79 *	-32	41 *
V7	87 *	-27	26
V8	88 *	-14	9
V9	-61 *	14	47 *
V10	-43 *	23	68 *
V11	-72 *	-6	12
V12	-40	19	72 *

NOTE: Printed values are multiplied by 100 and rounded to the nearest integer.
Values greater than 0.4 have been flagged by an '*'.

Variance explained by each factor

FACTOR1	FACTOR2	FACTOR3
4.470581	2.730623	1.701734

Final Communality Estimates: Total = 8.902938

V1	V2	V3	V4	V5	V6
0.755221	0.782123	0.747982	0.598878	0.871668	0.899804

V7	V8	V9	V10	V11	V12
0.899918	0.796680	0.611250	0.694877	0.532084	0.712453

The SAS System   4

Rotation Method: Varimax

Orthogonal Transformation Matrix

	1	2	3
1	0.83139	0.34426	-0.43620
2	-0.29475	0.93866	0.17902
3	0.47107	-0.02026	0.88186

```
                   Rotated Factor Pattern

                FACTOR1     FACTOR2     FACTOR3

         V1         3         85 *       -16
         V2        -4         88 *       -10
         V3         9         86 *         8
         V4        13         75 *        12
         V5        93 *        2          -3
         V6        95 *       -4          -4
         V7        93 *        4         -19
         V8        81 *       17         -33
         V9       -32        -9          71 *
         V10      -11         6          82 *
         V11      -52 *      -30         41 *
         V12       -5         3          84 *
```

NOTE: Printed values are multiplied by 100 and rounded to the nearest integer.
      Values greater than 0.4 have been flagged by an '*'.

```
             Variance explained by each factor

              FACTOR1     FACTOR2     FACTOR3
             3.704983    2.936412    2.261543
```

```
        Final Communality Estimates: Total = 8.902938

          V1         V2         V3         V4         V5         V6
       0.755221   0.782123   0.747982   0.598878   0.871668   0.899804

          V7         V8         V9        V10        V11        V12
       0.899918   0.796680   0.611250   0.694877   0.532084   0.712453
```

Output 14.3: Results of the Initial Principal Component Analysis of the Investment Model Data

The eigenvalue table in Output 14.3 also shows that the first three components combined account for approximately 74% of the total variance (this variance value can be observed at the intersection of the row headed "Cumulative" and column headed "3"). According to the "percentage of variance accounted for" criterion, this once again suggests that it may be appropriate to retain three components.

The scree plot from this solution appears on page 2 of Output 14.3. This scree plot shows that there are several large breaks in the data following components 1, 2, and 3, and then the line begins to flatten out beginning with component 4. The last large break appears after component 3, suggesting that only components 1-3 account for meaningful variance. This indicates that only these first three components should be retained and interpreted. Notice how it is almost possible to draw a straight line through components 4-12? The components that lie along a semi-straight line such as this are typically assumed to be measuring only trivial variance (components 4-12 constitute the "scree" of your scree plot!).

So far, the results from the eigenvalue-one criterion, the variance accounted for criterion, and the scree plot have converged in suggesting that a three-component solution may be appropriate. It is now time to review the rotated factor pattern to see if such a solution is interpretable. This matrix is presented on page 4 of Output 14.3.

Following the guidelines provided earlier, you begin your interpretation by looking for factorially complex items; that is, items with meaningful loadings for more than one component. A review shows that item 11 (variable V11) is a complex item, loading on both components 1 and 3. Item 11 is therefore scratched out. Except for this item, the solution is otherwise fairly clean.

To interpret component 1, you read down the column for FACTOR1 and see that items 5-8 display significant loadings for this component (remember that item 11 has been scatched out). These items are:

_____ 5.   I have invested a great deal of time in my current relationship.

_____ 6.   I have invested a great deal of energy in my current relationship.

_____ 7.   I have invested a lot of my personal resources (e.g., money) in developing my current relationship.

_____ 8.   My partner and I have developed a lot of mutual friends which I might lose if we were to break up.

All of these items deal with the investments that subjects have made in their relationships, so it makes sense to label this the "investment size" component.

The rotated factor pattern shows that items 1-4 displayed meaningful loadings for component 2. These items are:

_____ 1.   I am satisfied with my current relationship.

_____ 2.   My current relationship comes close to my ideal relationship.

_____ 3.   I am more satisfied with my relationship than is the average person.

_____ 4.   I feel good about my current relationship.

Given the content of the preceding items, it seems reasonable to label component 2 the "satisfaction" component.

Finally, component 3 displayed large loadings for items 9, 10, and 12 (again, remember that item 11 has been scratched out). These items are:

```
_____  9.   There are plenty of other attractive people around for me to date
            if I were to break up with my current partner.

_____ 10.   It would be attractive for me to break up with my current partner
            and date someone else.

_____ 12.   It would be attractive for me to break up with my partner and
            "play the field" for a while.
```

These items all seem to deal with the attractiveness of one's alternatives to the current relationship, so it makes sense to label this the "alternative value" component.

You may now step back and determine whether this solution satisfies the interpretability criteria presented earlier:

1. Are there at least three variables with meaningful loadings on each retained component?

2. Do the variables that load on a given component share the same conceptual meaning?

3. Do the variables that load on different components seem to be measuring different constructs?

4. Does the rotated factor pattern demonstrate "simple structure"?

In general, the answer to each of the preceding questions is "yes," indicating that the current solution is in most respects satisfactory. There was, however, a problem with item 11, which loaded on both components 1 and 3. This problem prevented the current solution from demonstrating a perfectly "simple structure" (criterion 4 from above). To eliminate this problem, it may be desirable to repeat the analysis, this time analyzing all of the items *except* for item 11. This will be done in the second analysis of the investment model data, to be described below.

Results of the Second Analysis

To repeat the current analysis with item 11 deleted, it is necessary only to modify the VAR statement of the preceding program. This may be done by changing the VAR statement so that it appears as follows:

```
VAR V1-V10 V12;
```

All other aspects of the program would remain as they were previously. The eigenvalue table, scree plot, the unrotated factor pattern, the rotated factor pattern, and final communality estimates obtained from this revised program appear in Output 14.4:

```
                              The SAS System                              1

Initial Factor Method: Principal Components

                  Prior Communality Estimates: ONE

      Eigenvalues of the Correlation Matrix:   Total = 11   Average = 1

                         1          2          3          4
        Eigenvalue    4.0241     2.7270     1.6898     0.6838
        Difference    1.2970     1.0372     1.0060     0.1274
        Proportion    0.3658     0.2479     0.1536     0.0622
        Cumulative    0.3658     0.6137     0.7674     0.8295

                         5          6          7          8
        Eigenvalue    0.5564     0.3963     0.3074     0.2668
        Difference    0.1601     0.0889     0.0406     0.0798
        Proportion    0.0506     0.0360     0.0279     0.0243
        Cumulative    0.8801     0.9161     0.9441     0.9683

                         9         10         11
        Eigenvalue    0.1869     0.1131     0.0486
        Difference    0.0739     0.0645
        Proportion    0.0170     0.0103     0.0044
        Cumulative    0.9853     0.9956     1.0000

        3 factors will be retained by the MINEIGEN criterion.
```

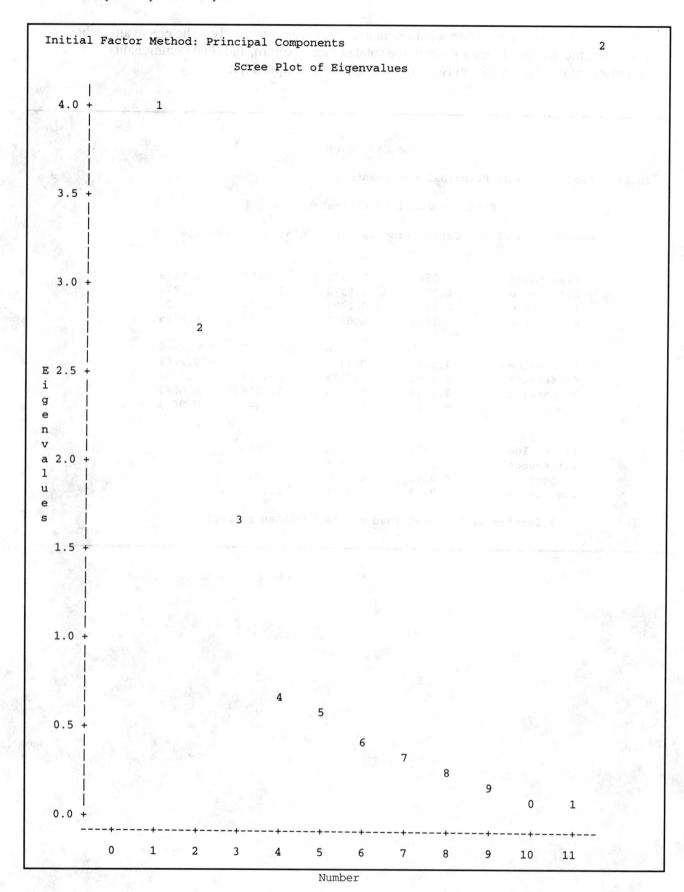

The SAS System   3

Initial Factor Method: Principal Components

                              Factor Pattern

                        FACTOR1   FACTOR2   FACTOR3

            V1   38   77 *   -17
            V2   30   83 *   -15
            V3   32   80 *   8
            V4   29   70 *   15
            V5   83 *   -23   38
            V6   83 *   -30   38
            V7   89 *   -24   24
            V8   88 *   -12   7
            V9   -56 *   13   47 *
            V10   -44 *   22   70 *
            V12   -40   18   74 *

NOTE: Printed values are multiplied by 100 and rounded to the nearest integer.
      Values greater than 0.4 have been flagged by an '*'.

                    Variance explained by each factor

                    FACTOR1   FACTOR2   FACTOR3
                    4.024086   2.727039   1.689791

          Final Communality Estimates: Total = 8.440916

        V1   V2   V3   V4   V5   V6
     0.772386   0.798289   0.748233   0.591921   0.882544   0.921349

        V7   V8   V9   V10   V12
     0.904096   0.796623   0.553800   0.736193   0.735482

The SAS System   4

Rotation Method: Varimax

                    Orthogonal Transformation Matrix

                          1   2   3

              1   0.84709   0.32928   -0.41715
              2   -0.27787   0.94351   0.18051
              3   0.45303   -0.03699   0.89073

```
                    Rotated Factor Pattern

                   FACTOR1      FACTOR2      FACTOR3

          V1          3           86 *        -17
          V2         -4           89 *        -11
          V3          8           86 *          8
          V4         12           75 *         14
          V5         94 *          4           -4
          V6         96 *         -2           -6
          V7         93 *          5          -20
          V8         81 *         18          -33
          V9        -30           -8           68 *
          V10       -12            4           85 *
          V12        -5            1           86 *
```

NOTE: Printed values are multiplied by 100 and rounded to the nearest integer.
      Values greater than 0.4 have been flagged by an '*'.

```
                 Variance explained by each factor

                   FACTOR1      FACTOR2      FACTOR3
                   3.444866     2.866255     2.129795
```

```
        Final Communality Estimates: Total = 8.440916

          V1         V2         V3         V4         V5         V6
       0.772386   0.798289   0.748233   0.591921   0.882544   0.921349

          V7         V8         V9         V10        V12
       0.904096   0.796623   0.553800   0.736193   0.735482
```

Output 14.4: Results of the Second Analysis of the Investment Model Data

The results obtained when item 11 was dropped from the analysis are very similar to those obtained when it was included. The eigenvalue table of Output 14.4 shows that the eigenvalue-one criterion would again result in retaining three components. The first three components account for 77% of the total variance, which means that three components would also be retained if you used the variance-accounted-for criterion. Finally, the scree plot from page 2 of Output 14.4 is just a bit cleaner than had been observed with the initial analysis: The break between components 3 and 4 is now slightly more distinct, and the eigenvalues again level off after this break. This means that three components would also likely be retained if the scree test were used to solve the number-of-components problem.

The biggest change can be seen in the rotated factor pattern, which appears on page 4 of Output 14.4. The solution is now cleaner, in the sense that no item now loads on more than one component. In this sense, the current results demonstrate a somewhat simpler structure than had been demonstrated by the initial analysis of the investment model data.

Conclusion

Principal component analysis is a powerful tool for reducing a number of observed variables into a smaller number of artificial variables that account for most of the variance in the data set. It is particularly useful when you need a data reduction procedure that makes no assumptions concerning an underlying causal structure that is responsible for covariation in the data. When it is possible to postulate the existance of such an underlying causal structure, it may be more appropriate to analyze the data using exploratory factor analysis. This topic is covered in Hatcher (1994).

Both principal component analysis and factor analysis are often used to construct multiple-item scales from the items that constitute questionnaires. Regardless of which method is used, once these scales have been developed it is often desirable to assess their reliability by computing **coefficient alpha**: an index of internal consistency reliability. The following chapter shows how this can be done using the SAS System's PROC CORR.

Appendix: Assumptions Underlying Principal Component Analysis

Because a principal component analysis is performed on a matrix of Pearson correlation coefficients, the data should satisfy the assumptions for this statistic. These assumptions were described in detail in Chapter 6 "Measures of Bivariate Association", and are briefly reviewed here:

- **Interval-level measurement**. All analyzed variables should be assessed on an interval or ratio level of measurement.

- **Random sampling**. Each subject will contribute one score on each observed variable. These sets of scores should represent a random sample drawn from the population of interest.

- **Linearity**. The relationship between all observed variables should be linear.

- **Normal distributions**. Each observed variable should be normally distributed. Variables that demonstrate marked skewness or kurtosis may be transformed to better approximate normality (see Rummel, 1970).

- **Bivariate normal distribution**. Each pair of observed variables should display a bivariate normal distribution; e.g., they should form an elliptical scattergram when plotted. However, the Pearson correlation coefficient is robust against violations of this assumption when the sample size is greater than 25.

References

Cattell, R. B. (1966). The scree test for the number of factors. *Multivariate Behavioral Research, 1,* 245-276.

Hatcher, L. (1994). *A step-by-step approach to using the SAS system for factor analysis and structural equation modeling.* Cary, NC: SAS Institute Inc.

Kaiser, H. F. (1960). The application of electronic computers to factor analysis. *Educational and Psychological Measurement, 20,* 141-151.

Kim, J. O. & Mueller, C. W. (1978a). *Introduction to factor analysis: What it is and how to do it.* Beverly Hills, CA: Sage.

Kim, J. O. & Mueller, C. W. (1978b). *Factor analysis: Statistical methods and practical issues.* Beverly Hills, CA: Sage.

Rummel, R. J. (1970). *Applied factor analysis.* Evanston, IL: Northwestern University Press.

Rusbult, C.E. (1980). Commitment and satisfaction in romantic associations: A test of the investment model. *Journal of Experimental Social Psychology, 16,* 172-186.

SAS Institute Inc. (1989). *SAS/STAT user's guide, version 6, fourth edition, volume 1.* Cary, NC: SAS Institute Inc.

Spector, P.E. (1992). *Summated rating scale construction: An introduction.* Newbury Park, CA: Sage.

Stevens, J. (1986). *Applied multivariate statistics for the social sciences.* Hillsdale, NJ: Lawrence Erlbaum Associates.

Chapter 15

ASSESSING SCALE RELIABILITY
WITH COEFFICIENT ALPHA

> **Overview**. This chapter shows how to use PROC CORR to compute the coefficient alpha reliability index for a multiple-item scale. It reviews basic issues regarding the assessment of reliability, and describes the circumstances under which a measure of internal consistency reliability is likely to be high. Fictitious questionnaire data are analyzed to demonstrate how you can use the results of PROC CORR to perform an item analysis, thereby improving the reliability of the scale.

Introduction: The Basics of Scale Reliability

You may compute coefficient alpha when you have administered a multiple-item, summated rating scale to a group of subjects and want to determine the internal consistency reliability of the scale. The items constituting the scale may be scored dichotomously (scored as "right" or "wrong"), or they may use a multiple-point rating format (e.g., subjects may respond to each item using a 7-point "agree-disagree" rating scale).

This chapter shows how to use the SAS System's PROC CORR to easily compute coefficient alpha for the types of scales that are often used in social science research. However, this chapter will not show how to actually *develop* a multiple-item scale for use in research. To learn about recommended approaches for creating summated rating scales, see Spector (1992).

Example of a summated rating scale. A **summated rating scale** usually consists of a short list of statements, questions, or other items that a subject responds to. Very often, the items that constitute the scale are statements, and subjects indicate the extent to which they agree or disagree with each statement by circling or checking some response on a rating scale (perhaps a 7-point rating scale in which 1 = "Strongly Disagree" and 7 = "Strongly Agree"). The scale is called a *summated* scale because the researcher typically sums the response numbers circled by a subject to create an overall score on the scale for that subject. These scales are often referred to as **Likert scales** or **Likert-type scales**.

For example, imagine that you are interested in measuring job satisfaction in a sample of employees. To do this, you might develop a 10-item scale that includes items such as "In general, I am satisfied with my job." Employees respond to these items using a 7-point response format in which 1 = "Strongly Disagree" and 7 = "Strongly Agree."

You administer this scale to 200 employees and compute a job satisfaction score for each individual by summing his or her responses to the 10 items. Scores may range from a low of 10 (if the employee circled "Strongly Disagree" for each item) to a high of 70 (if the employee circled "Strongly Agree" for each item). Given the way these scores were created, higher scores indicate higher levels of job satisfaction. With the job satisfaction scale now developed and administered to a sample, you hope to use it as a predictor variable or criterion variable in research. However, the people who later read about your research are going to have questions about the psychometric properties of your scale; at the very least, they will want to see empirical evidence that the scale is reliable. This chapter discusses the meaning of scale reliability, and shows how to use the SAS System to obtain an index of internal consistency reliability for summated rating scales.

True scores and measurement error. Most observed variables assessed in the social sciences (such as scores on your job satisfaction scale) actually consist of two components: a **true score** component (which indicates where the subject actually stands on the variable of interest), along with a **measurement error** component. Almost all observed variables in the social sciences contain at least some measurement error, even the variables that seem to be objectively measured.

For example, imagine that you assess the observed variable "Age" in a group of subjects by asking the subjects to write down their age in years. To a large extent, this observed variable (what the subjects wrote down) is influenced by the true score component: To a large extent, what they write will be influenced by how old they actually are. Unfortunately, however, this observed variable will also be influenced by measurement error: some subjects will write down the wrong age because they don't know how old they are; some will write the wrong age because they don't want the researcher to know how old they are; some will write the wrong age because they didn't understand the question. In short, it is likely that there will not be a perfect correlation between the observed variable (what the subjects write down) and their true scores on the underlying construct (their actual age).

And remember that the preceding "Age" variable was relatively objective and straightforward. If a question such as this is going to be influenced by measurement error, imagine how much more error is likely to be displayed by responses to subjective questionnaire items (such as the items that constitute your job satisfaction scale).

Underlying constructs versus observed variables. In conducting research, it is also useful to draw a distinction between underlying constructs versus observed variables. An **underlying construct** is the hypothetical variable that you actually want to measure. For example, in the job satisfaction study just described, you wanted to measure the underlying construct of job satisfaction in a group of employees. The **observed variable**, on the other hand, consists of the measurements that you actually obtained. In that example, the observed variable consisted of scores on the 10-item measure of job satisfaction. These scores may or may not be a good measure of the underlying construct.

Reliability defined. With this foundation laid, it is now possible to provide some definitions. Technically, a **reliability coefficient** may be defined as the percent of variance in an observed variable that is accounted for by true scores on the underlying construct. For example, imagine that in the study just discussed, you were able to obtain two scores for the 200 employees in the sample: their observed scores on the job satisfaction questionnaire, and their true scores on the underlying construct of job satisfaction. Assume that you compute the correlation between these two variables. The square of this correlation coefficient represents the reliability of your job satisfaction scale; it is the percent of variance in observed job satisfaction scores that is accounted for by true scores on the underlying construct of job satisfaction.

The preceding was a technical definition for reliability, and this definition is of little use in practice because it is generally not possible to obtain true scores on a variable. For this reason, reliability is usually defined in practice in terms of the **consistency** of the scores that are obtained on the observed variable; an instrument is said to be reliable if it is shown to provide consistent scores upon repeated administration, upon administration by alternate forms, and so forth. A variety of methods of estimating scale reliability are actually used in practice.

Test-retest reliability. For example, assume that you administer your measure of job satisfaction to a group of 200 employees at two points in time: once in January, and again in March. If the instrument is indeed reliable, you would expect that the subjects who displayed high scores in January will also tend to display high scores in March, and that those who displayed low scores in January will also display low scores in March. These results will support the test-retest reliability of the scale. Test-retest reliability is assessed by administering the same instrument to the same sample of subjects at two points in time, and computing the correlation between the two sets of scores.

Internal consistency reliability. One problem with the test-retest reliability procedure is the time that it requires. What if you do not have time to perform two administrations of the scale? In such situations, you are likely to turn to reliability indices that may be obtained with only one administration. In research that involves the use of questionnaire data, the most popular of these are the internal consistency indices of reliability. Briefly, **internal consistency** is the extent to which the individual items that constitute a test correlate with one another or with the test total. In the social sciences, one of the most widely-used indices of internal consistency reliability is coefficient alpha (Cronbach, 1951).

Coefficient Alpha

Formula. Coefficient alpha is a general formula for scale reliability based on internal consistency. It provides the lowest estimate of reliability that can be expected for an instrument.

The formula for coefficient alpha is as follows:

$$r_{xx} = \left(\frac{N}{N-1} \right) \left(\frac{S^2 - \Sigma S_i^2}{S^2} \right)$$

where

r_{xx} = Coefficient alpha.

N = Number of items constituting the instrument.

S^2 = Variance of the summated scale scores (for example, assume that you compute a total score for each subject by summing each subject's responses to the items that constitute the scale; the variance of this total score variable would be S^2).

ΣS_i^2 = The sum of the variances of the individual items that constitute this scale.

When will coefficient alpha be high? Other factors held constant, coefficient alpha will be high to the extent that many items are included in the scale, and the items that constitute the scale are highly correlated with one another.

To understand why coefficient alpha is high when the items are highly correlated with one another, consider the second term in the preceding formula:

$$\left(\frac{S^2 - \Sigma S_i^2}{S^2} \right)$$

This term shows that the variance of the summated scales scores is (essentially) divided by itself to compute coefficient alpha. However, the combined variance of the individual items is first subtracted from this variance before the division is performed. This part of the equation shows that, if combined variance of the individual items is a small value, then coefficient alpha will be a relatively larger value.

This is important because (once again, with other factors held constant), the stronger the correlations between the individual items, the smaller the term ΣS_i^2 will be. This is why coefficient alpha for a given scale is likely to be large to the extent that the variables constituting that scale are strongly correlated with one another.

Assessing Coefficient Alpha with PROC CORR

Imagine that you have conducted research in the area of prosocial behavior, and have developed an instrument designed to measure two separate underlying constructs: acquaintance helping and financial giving. **Acquaintance helping** refers to prosocial activities performed to help coworkers, relatives, and friends. **Financial giving**, on the other hand, refers to giving money to charities or panhandlers (see Chapter 14: "Principal Component Analysis," for a more detailed description of these constructs). In the following questionnaire, items 1-3 were designed to assess acquaintance helping, and items 4-6 were designed to assess financial giving.

```
Instructions:  Below are a number of activities that people
sometimes engage in.  For each item, please indicate how
frequently you have engaged in this activity over the preceding
six months.  Make your rating by circling the appropriate number
to the left of the item, and use the following response format:

     7 = Very Frequently
     6 = Frequently
     5 = Somewhat Frequently
     4 = Occasionally
     3 = Seldom
     2 = Almost Never
     1 = Never
```

```
1 2 3   5 6   7      1.   Went out of my way to do a favor for a
                          coworker.

1 2 3 4 5 6 7        2.   Went out of my way to do a favor for a
                          relative.

1 2 3 4 5 6 7        3.   Went out of my way to do a favor for a
                          friend.

1 2 3 4 5 6 7        4.   Gave money to a religious charity.

1 2 3 4 5 6 7        5.   Gave money to a charity not associated with
                          a religion.

1 2 3 4 5 6 7        6.   Gave money to a panhandler.
```

Assume that you have administered this 6-item questionnaire to 50 subjects. For the moment, we are concerned only with the reliability of the scale that includes items 1-3 (the items that assess acquaintance helping).

Let us further assume that you have made a mistake in assessing the reliability of this scale. Assume that you erroneously believed that the acquaintance helping construct was assessed by items 1-4 (whereas, in reality, of course, the construct was assessed by items 1-3). It will be instructive to see what you learn when you mistakenly include item 4 in the analysis.

General form. Here is the general form for the SAS statements that estimate coefficient alpha reliability for a summated rating scale:

```
PROC CORR    DATA=data-set-name    ALPHA    NOMISS;
   VAR   list-of-variables;
   RUN;
```

In the preceding program, the ALPHA option requests that coefficient alpha be computed for the group of variables included in the VAR statement. The NOMISS option is required to compute coefficient alpha. The VAR statement should list only the variables (items) that constitute the scale in question. You must perform a separate CORR procedure for each scale whose reliability you want to assess.

A 4-item scale. Here is an actual program, including the DATA step, that you could use to analyze some fictitious data from your study. Only a few sample lines of data appear here; the complete data set appears in Appendix B.

```
1      DATA D1;
2         INPUT    #1    @1    (V1-V6)      (1.)  ;
3      CARDS;
4      556754
5      567343
6      777222
7      .
8      .
9      .
10     767151
11     455323
12     455544
13     ;
14     PROC CORR    DATA=D1    ALPHA    NOMISS;
15        VAR V1 V2 V3 V4;
16        RUN;
```

The results of this analysis appear as Output 15.1. Page 1 of these results provides the means, standard deviations, and other descriptive statistics that you should review to verify that the analysis proceeded as expected. Page 2 provides the results pertaining to the reliability of the scale.

```
                         The SAS System                           1

                      Correlation Analysis

        4 'VAR' Variables:  V1      V2      V3      V4


                        Simple Statistics

Variable     N      Mean     Std Dev       Sum    Minimum    Maximum

V1          50    5.18000    1.39518   259.00000   1.00000    7.00000
V2          50    5.40000    1.10657   270.00000   3.00000    7.00000
V3          50    5.52000    1.21622   276.00000   2.00000    7.00000
V4          50    3.64000    1.79296   182.00000   1.00000    7.00000
```

```
                        Correlation Analysis

                    Cronbach Coefficient Alpha

                for RAW variables          :   0.490448
                for STANDARDIZED variables:    0.575912
```

	Raw Variables			Std. Variables	
Deleted Variable	Correlation with Total	Alpha		Correlation with Total	Alpha
V1	0.461961	0.243936		0.563691	0.326279
V2	0.433130	0.318862		0.458438	0.420678
V3	0.500697	0.240271		0.546203	0.342459
V4	-0.037388	0.776635		-0.030269	0.773264

```
    Pearson Correlation Coefficients / Prob > |R| under Ho: Rho=0 / N = 50
```

	V1	V2	V3	V4
V1	1.00000	0.49439	0.71345	-0.10410
	0.0	0.0003	0.0001	0.4719
V2	0.49439	1.00000	0.38820	0.05349
	0.0003	0.0	0.0053	0.7122
V3	0.71345	0.38820	1.00000	-0.02471
	0.0001	0.0053	0.0	0.8648
V4	-0.10410	0.05349	-0.02471	1.00000
	0.4719	0.7122	0.8648	0.0

Output 15.1: Simple Statistics and Coefficient Alpha Results for Analysis of Scale that Includes Items 1-4, Prosocial Behavior Study

On page 2 of Output 15.1, to the right of the heading "Cronbach Coefficient Alpha for RAW variables" you see that the reliability coefficient for the scale that includes items 1-4 is only .490448, which rounds to .49 (reliability for raw variables is normally reported in published articles).

But how large must a reliability coefficient be to be considered acceptable? A widely used rule of thumb of .70 has been suggested by Nunnally (1978): For scales used in research, reliability coefficients less than .70 are generally seen as inadequate. However, you should remember that this is only a rule of thumb, and the social science literature does sometimes report studies employing variables with coefficient alpha reliabilities under .70 (and sometimes even under .60!).

The coefficient alpha of .49 reported in Output 15.1 is not acceptable; obviously, it should be possible to significantly improve the reliability of this scale. But how?

In some situations, the reliability of a multiple-item scale is improved by dropping from the scale those items that demonstrate poor item-total correlations. An **item-total correlation** is the correlation between an individual item, and the sum of the remaining items that constitute the scale. If an item-total correlation is small, this may be seen as evidence that the item is not measuring the same construct that is measured by the other items in the scale. This may mean that you should drop an item demonstrating a small item-total correlation from the scale.

Consider Output 15.1. Under the "Correlation with Total" heading, you can see that items 1-3 each demonstrate reasonably strong correlations with the sum of the remaining items on the scale. However, item V4 demonstrates an item-total correlation of approximately –.04. This suggests that item V4 is probably not assessing the same construct that is assessed by items V1–V3.

In Output 15.1 under the "Alpha" heading you find an estimate of what alpha would be if a given variable (item) were deleted from the scale. To the right of "V4", PROC CORR estimates that alpha would be approximately .78 if V4 were deleted (this value appears where the row headed "V4" intersects with the column headed "Alpha" in the "Raw Variables" section). This makes sense, because variable V4 demonstrates a correlation with the remaining scale items of only –.04. Obviously, you could substantially improve this scale by removing the item that is clearly not measuring the same construct that is assessed by the other items.

A 3-item scale. Output 15.2 reveals the results of PROC CORR when coefficient alpha is requested for just variables V1–V3 (this is done by specifying only V1–V3 in the VAR statement).

```
                           The SAS System                              3

                        Correlation Analysis

             3 'VAR' Variables:   V1        V2        V3


                         Simple Statistics

Variable        N       Mean     Std Dev       Sum    Minimum   Maximum

V1             50     5.18000     1.39518   259.00000   1.00000   7.00000
V2             50     5.40000     1.10657   270.00000   3.00000   7.00000
V3             50     5.52000     1.21622   276.00000   2.00000   7.00000
```

4

```
                         Correlation Analysis

                      Cronbach Coefficient Alpha

               for RAW variables         :   0.776635
               for STANDARDIZED variables:   0.773264


                    Raw Variables                    Std. Variables

   Deleted       Correlation                     Correlation
   Variable      with Total        Alpha         with Total          Alpha
   ------------------------------------------------------------------------
   V1             0.730730        0.557491         0.724882         0.559285
   V2             0.480510        0.828202         0.476768         0.832764
   V3             0.657457        0.649926         0.637231         0.661659


       Pearson Correlation Coefficients / Prob > |R| under Ho: Rho=0 / N = 50


                          V1               V2               V3


           V1          1.00000          0.49439          0.71345
                         0.0             0.0003           0.0001


           V2          0.49439          1.00000          0.38820
                        0.0003            0.0             0.0053


           V3          0.71345          0.38820          1.00000
                        0.0001           0.0053            0.0
```

Output 15.2: Simple Statistics and Coefficient Alpha Results for Analysis of Scale that Includes Items 1-3, Prosocial Behavior Study

Page 4 of Output 15.2 provides a raw-variable coefficient alpha of .78 for the three variables included in this analysis (this value appears to the right of the heading "Cronbach Coefficient Alpha for RAW variables"). This coefficient exceeds the minimum value of .70 recommended by Nunnally (1978). Obviously, the acquaintance-helping scale demonstrates a much higher level of reliability with item V4 deleted.

Summarizing the Results

Summarizing the results in a table. Researchers typically report the reliability of a scale in a table that reports simple descriptive statistics for the study's variables, such as means, standard deviations, and intercorrelations. In these tables, coefficient alpha reliability estimates are usually reported on the diagonal of the correlation matrix, within parentheses. Such an approach appears in Table 15.1.

Table 15.1

Means, Standard Deviations, Intercorrelations, and Coefficient Alpha Reliability Estimates for the Study's Variables

Variables	Mean	SD	1	2	3
1. Authoritarianism	13.56	2.54	(.90)		
2. Acquaintance helping	15.60	3.22	.37	(.78)	
3. Financial giving	12.55	1.32	.25	.53	(.77)

Note: N = 200. Reliability estimates appear on the diagonal.

In the preceding table, information for the authoritarianism variable is presented in both the row and the column that is headed "1". Where the row headed "1" intersects with the column headed "1", you will find the coefficient alpha reliability index for the authoritarianism scale. You can see that this index is .90. In the same way, you can find coefficient alpha for acquaintance helping where row 2 intersects with column 2 (alpha = .78), and you can find coefficient alpha for financial giving where row 3 intersects with column 3 (alpha = .77).

Preparing a formal description of the results for a paper. When reliability estimates are computed for a relatively large number of scales, it is common to report them in a table (such as Table 15.1), and make only a global reference to them within the text of the paper. For example, within the section on instrumentation, you might indicate:

Coefficient alpha reliability estimates (Cronbach, 1951) all exceeded .70, and are reported on the diagonal of Table 15.1.

When reliability estimates are computed for only a small number of scales, it is possible to instead report these estimates within the body of the text itself. Here is an example of how this might be done:

```
      Scale reliability was assessed by calculating
coefficient alpha (Cronbach, 1951).  Reliability estimates
were .90, .78, and .77 for the authoritarianism,
acquaintance helping, and financial giving scales,
respectively.
```

Conclusion

Assessing scale reliability with coefficient alpha (or some other reliability index) should be one of the first tasks you complete when conducting questionnaire research; if the scales you use are not reliable, there is no point performing additional analyses. You can often improve a single scale demonstrating poor reliability by deleting items with poor item-total correlations, according to the procedures just discussed. When several scales on a questionnaire display poor reliability, you may be better advised to perform a principal component analysis or an exploratory factor analysis on responses to all items on the questionnaire, to determine which items tend to group together empirically. If **many items load on each retained factor, and if the factor pattern** obtained from such an analysis displays simple structure, chances are good that the resulting scales will demonstrate adequate internal consistency reliability estimates.

References

Cronbach, L. J. (1951). Coefficient alpha and the internal structure of tests. *Psychometrika, 16,* 297-334.

Nunnally, J. (1978). *Psychometric theory.* New York: McGraw-Hill.

Spector, P. E. (1992). *Summated rating scale construction: An introduction.* Newbury Park, CA: Sage.

Appendix A

CHOOSING THE CORRECT STATISTIC

Overview

This appendix provides a structured approach for choosing the correct statistical procedure to use when analyzing data. With this approach, the choice of a specific statistic is based on the number and scale of the criterion (dependent) variables in the study, considered in conjunction with the number and scale of the predictor (independent) variables. Commonly used statistics are grouped into three tables, based on the number of criterion and predictor variables in the analysis.

Introduction: Thinking about the Number and Scale of Your Variables

Researchers are often confused by the task of choosing the correct statistical procedure for analyzing a given data set. There are so many procedures from which to choose that it is easy to become frustrated, not even knowing where to begin. This appendix addresses this problem by providing a relatively simple system for classifying statistics. It provides a structured approach that should make it easier to find the appropriate statistical procedure for a wide variety of circumstances.

In a sense, most statistical procedures involve investigating the relationship between two variables (or two sets of variables). In a given study, the outcome variable that you are interested in is called either a **criterion variable** (in nonexperimental research) or a **dependent variable** (in experimental research). In nonexperimental research, you study the relationship between the criterion variable and some **predictor variable**, whose values are used to predict scores on the criterion (in experimental research, a manipulated **independent variable** is the counterpart to this predictor variable). In general, nonexperimental research involves understanding the relationship between a criterion variable and a predictor variable, while experimental research involves understanding the relationship between a dependent variable and an independent variable. To simplify matters, this appendix blurs the distinction between nonexperimental versus experimental research, and uses "criterion variable" to represent criterion variables as well as dependent variables, and uses "predictor variable" to represent predictor variables as well as independent variables.

Thinking about your criterion variables. Two of the factors that determine the correct statistic for a data set are the number and the scale of the criterion variables. The **number**, of course, merely refers to how many criterion variables appear in the data set, while the **scale** refers to the level of measurement used in assessing these criterion variables (i.e., nominal, ordinal, ratio, or interval).

For example, assume that you want to conduct a study to learn about variables that predict success in college. In your study, you may choose to use just one criterion variable as an index of college success, such as college grade point average (GPA). Alternatively, you may instead choose to use several criterion variables so that you will have multiple indices of success: college GPA, college class rank, and whether or not the subject was inducted into some college honorary society (yes versus no). Here, you can see the *number* of criterion variables varies: In the first case there was only one criterion variable, in the second their were three.

Notice, however, that the *scale* used to assess college success also varies. The criterion variable college GPA was assessed on an interval scale, college class rank was assessed on an ordinal scale, and induction into an honorary society was assessed on a nominal scale. The number of criterion variables used in the analysis, as well as the scale used to measure those variables, help determine which statistic you should use to analyze your data.

Thinking about your predictor variables. However, you still do not have enough information to choose the appropriate statistic. Two additional factors that determine the correct statistic are the number and scale of the *predictor* variables. For example, again consider the college success study. Assume that you are interested in learning about the variables that predict college success. Assume that you have decided to use just one criterion variable as a measure of success: college GPA. You may choose to design a study that also includes just one predictor variable: high school GPA. Alternatively, you may instead design a study that includes multiple predictor variables such as high school GPA, scores on the Scholastic Assessment Test (SAT), high school rank, and whether the student received a scholarship (yes versus no).

Notice that, in the above paragraph, the number of predictor variables that may be included in a study varies. The first study included just one predictor, while the second included multiple predictors. Note that the scale used to assess these predictors also varies. Predictors were assessed on an interval scale (high school GPA, SAT scores), an ordinal scale (high school rank), and a nominal scale (whether the student received a scholarship). The number of predictor variables included in your study, as well as their scale, also help determine the appropriate statistic.

Putting it together. The preceding discussion has provided a foundation for the following recommendation. In choosing the appropriate statistic for an analysis, always consider

- the number and scale of the criterion variables, in conjunction with

- the number and scale of the predictor variables.

For example, imagine that, in your study, you used only one measure of college success (GPA) and one predictor variable (SAT scores). Since you have a single criterion variable assessed on an interval scale, and a single predictor variable also on an interval scale, you know that the appropriate statistic is the Pearson correlation coefficient (assuming that a few additional assumptions are met). But what if you modified your study so that it still contained only one criterion variable, but now contains two predictor variables, both assessed on an interval scale (specifically, SAT scores and high school GPA)? In the latter case, it would be more appropriate to analyze your data using multiple regression.

This is the approach recommended in this appendix: to select the right statistic, you must consider the number and nature of both your criterion and predictor variables. To facilitate this decision-making process, the appendix includes three tables: one that lists statistics for studies that involve a single criterion variable and a single predictor, one for studies that involve a single criterion variable and multiple predictors, and a final table for studies with multiple criterion variables.

A few words of caution are in order before presenting the tables. First, these tables were not designed to present an *exhaustive* list of statistical procedures. They focus only on the tests that are probably the most commonly reported in the social sciences. A good number of statistical procedures that did not fit neatly into this format (such as principal component analysis or path analysis) do not appear. Second, these tables do not necessarily provide you with *all* of the information that you need to make the final selection of a statistical procedure. Many statistical procedures require that a number of assumptions concerning the data be met for the procedure to be appropriate, and these assumptions are often too numerous to include in a short appendix such as this. The purpose of this appendix is to help you locate the statistic that may be correct for your situation, given the nature of the variables. It is then up to you to learn more about the assumptions for that statistic, to determine whether your data satisfy those assumptions.

Guidelines for Choosing the Correct Statistic

Studies with a single criterion variable and a single predictor variable. These are among the simplest (and most common) studies conducted in the social sciences. Some of the statistics appropriate for this type of investigation are listed in Table A.1:

Table A.1

Studies with a *Single* Criterion Variable and a *Single* Predictor Variable

Criterion/ Dependent Variable	Predictor/ Independent Variable	Analysis
Nominal	Nominal	**Chi-square test of independence.***
Ordinal; Interval; Ratio	Nominal	**Kruskal-Wallis test.** Typically-used with an ordinal-scale criterion; also used with interval/ratio scale criterion if markedly non-normal.
Interval; Ratio	Nominal	***t* test.*** Appropriate only if predictor variable consists of no more than two values.
Interval; Ratio	Nominal	**One-way analysis of variance (ANOVA).***
Ordinal; Interval; Ratio	Ordinal; Interval; Ratio	**Spearman correlation coefficient.*** Typically used if at least one variable is ordinal-scale. Also used with interval/ratio variables if markedly non-normal.
Interval; Ratio	Interval; Ratio	**Pearson correlation coefficient.***

* Statistics covered in this text

Table A.1 consists of three columns. The first column describes the nature of the criterion or dependent variable in the study, the second describes the predictor or independent variable, and the third describes the statistic that may be appropriate for that study. For example, the first entry indicates that, if your predictor variable is assessed on a nominal scale, and your criterion is also assessed on a nominal scale, it may be appropriate to assess the relationship between these variables using the chi-square test of independence. To understand this, assume that in your study you use one index of college success, and it is assessed on a nominal scale. You may have chosen "graduation" as this criterion (the graduation variable may have been coded with the value "Yes" if the student did graduate from college, and "No" if he or she did not). Assume further that you have used one nominal-scale predictor variable in your study: scholarship status. You have coded this scholarship status variable so that the value "Ath" represents students who received athletic scholarship, "Acad" represents students who received academic scholarships, and "None" represents students who received no scholarship. You analyze your data set with a chi-square test of independence to determine whether there is a significant relationship between scholarship status and graduation. This may result in a significant value of chi-square, and inspection of the cells of your classification table may show that students in the academic scholarship group were more likely to graduate than students in the athletic scholarship or no scholarship groups.

Notice that in the Analysis column the entry "Chi-square test of independence" is flagged with an asterisk (*). Tests that are flagged with an asterisk in this way are described in this text. However, rest assured that even the procedures that are not flagged can still be analyzed with the SAS System. For help with these procedures, consult Littell, Freund, & Spector (1991), the *SAS/STAT ® user's guide, volumes 1 and 2* (1989), and Schlotzhauer and Littell (1987).

The first row of Table A.1 dealt with the chi-square test. The next row down describes the appropriate conditions for a Kruskal-Wallis test. Notice that the entry in the Criterion/Dependent Variable column is "Ordinal; Interval; Ratio". This entry indicates that the Kruskal-Wallis test may be appropriate if you have a single criterion variable that is assessed on *either* an ordinal scale, an interval scale, or a ratio scale (obviously, it is *not* meant to suggest that you should have three criterion variables, each assessed with different scales!).

Studies with a single criterion variable and multiple predictor variables. Table A.2 lists some procedures that are appropriate when the analysis includes a single criterion variable and multiple predictors. Notice that each entry in the Predictor/Independent Variable column is flagged with the symbol "(M)". This symbol stands for "multiple," as in "multiple predictor variables." It simply indicates that the analysis should include more than one predictor variable, regardless of the scale on which the variables are measured.

For example the last row of the table is for multiple regression. The entry in the predictor variable column is "Nominal; Interval; Ratio (M)", which means that the predictor variables may be assessed on *either* a nominal scale, an interval scale, or a ratio scale (or some combination thereof) as long as you include more than one predictor variable. Earlier, we indicated that it would be appropriate to use multiple regression to analyze data that included college GPA as the criterion variable, and SAT scores and high school GPA as predictors. Note how this is consistent with the guidelines of Table A.2: there is a single criterion variable assessed on an interval scale (college GPA), and there are multiple predictor variables, both assessed on an interval scale (SAT scores and high school GPA).

Table A.2

Studies with a *Single* Criterion Variable and *Multiple* Predictor Variables

Criterion/ Dependent Variable	Predictor/ Independent Variables	Analysis
Nominal; Ordinal	Nominal; Interval; Ratio (M)	**Logistic regression.** If the criterion variable is on a nominal scale, it may consist of no more than two values; for more values, consider discriminant analysis. If used, nominal-scale predictor variables must be dummy-coded or effect coded.
Nominal	Interval; Ratio (M)	**Discriminant analysis.**
Interval; Ratio	Nominal (M)	**Factorial analysis of variance (ANOVA).***
Interval; Ratio	Nominal; Interval; Ratio (M)	**Analysis of covariance (ANCOVA).** Used when predictors include at least one nominal-scale variable and at least one interval/ratio-scale variable.
Interval; Ratio	Nominal; Interval; Ratio (M)	**Multiple regression.*** If used, nominal-scale predictor variables must be dummy-coded or effect coded.

* Statistics covered in this text
(M) = Multiple variables

Studies with multiple criterion variables. The "(M)" symbol in the criterion variable column of Table A.3 shows that all of the procedures in this table are appropriate for studies that include multiple criterion variables. However, note that only the last three analytic procedures (factorial MANOVA, MANCOVA, and canonical correlation) involve multiple *predictor* variables; the first procedure (one-way MANOVA) requires only a single predictor variable on a nominal scale.

Table A.3

Studies with *Multiple* Criterion Variables

Criterion/ Dependent Variables	Predictor/ Independent Variable(s)	Analysis
Interval; Ratio (M)	Nominal	**One-way multivariate analysis of variance (MANOVA).** *
Interval; Ratio (M)	Nominal (M)	**Factorial multivariate analysis of variance (MANOVA).**
Interval; Ratio (M)	Nominal; Interval; Ratio (M)	**Multivariate analysis of covariance (MANCOVA).** Used when predictors include at least one nominal-scale variable and at least one interval/ratio-scale variable.
Interval; Ratio (M)	Interval; Ratio (M)	**Canonical Correlation.**

* Statistics covered in this text
(M) = Multiple variables

Conclusion

As stated earlier, this appendix is intended to serve as a starting place for choosing appropriate statistics. You can use the preceding tables to identify procedures that may be appropriate for your research design. It is then up to you, however, to learn more about the assumptions associated with the statistic: whether it requires data drawn from a normal population, whether it requires independent observations, and so forth. These tables, when used in conjunction with the "Assumptions" sections included in the earlier chapters of this text (as well as the additional references provided below) should help you find the right procedure for analyzing the types of data that are most frequently encountered in social science research.

References

Littell, R. C., Freund, R. J. & Spector, P. C. (1991). *SAS system for linear models, third edition.* Cary, NC: SAS Institute Inc.

SAS Institute Inc. (1989). *SAS/STAT user's guide, version 6, fourth edition, volume 1.* Cary, NC: SAS Institute Inc.

SAS Institute Inc. (1989). *SAS/STAT user's guide, version 6, fourth edition, volume 2.* Cary, NC: SAS Institute Inc.

Schlotzhauer, S. D.& Littell, R. C. (1987). *SAS system for elementary statistical analysis.* Cary, NC: SAS Institute Inc.

Appendix B

DATA SETS

Overview. This appendix provides data sets that were used in analyses reported in Chapter 13: "Multiple Regression", Chapter 14: "Principal Component Analysis", and Chapter 15: "Assessing Scale Reliability with Coefficient Alpha". The data sets appear here rather than in the chapters in which they were discussed because they are longer than most data sets used in the text.

Data Set from Chapter 13: Multiple Regression

```
CARDS;
34 30 25 13 25 12
32 27 27 14 32 13
34 23 24 21 30 14
26 26 22 18 27 19
 4 17 25 10 11 34
31 26 30 22 31 13
22 29 31 18 27 14
32 29 27  9 31  8
33 36 31 14 28 13
36 32 26 14 19 12
19 24 22 23 23  4
36 35 31 14 34  4
30 30 30 20 30 23
35 21 22 20 24 19
36 27 33  7 31  4
35 31 30 20 29  8
 4 20 20 22 14 28
36 35 29 14 34  8
36 32 28 14 28 15
19 18 17 25 18 20
20 30 26 20 23 28
36 34 31 21 32 18
```

```
29 27 24 19 19 13
 9 36 30  5 18 24
28 24 27 15 22 20
10 26 24 24 27 27
34 31 29  9 29 17
 7 12 16 26 20 33
35 36 33 13 27 16
36 33 30  5 29 13
 6 19 27 21 24 26
35  . 30 18 24 21
35 34 32 18 28 16
24 24 23 17 17 20
36 24 31 14 30 20
28 24 19 24 24 17
33 33 28 16 19 11
 5 12  9 15 11 32
21 24 20 24 22 14
16  9 12 30  . 15
36 34 32  6 20  9
29 27 27 20 30 21
 .  7 12 23 13 26
34 34 32 20 31 13
35 27 23 21 31 18
25 26 29  7 23 18
36 25 25 16 29 11
36 32 28 13 15  5
32 29 30 21 32 22
30 32 33 16 34  9
;
```

Data Set from Chapter 14: Principal Component Analysis

```
CARDS;
556754
567343
777222
665243
666665
353324
767153
666656
```

```
334333
567232
445332
555232
546264
436663
265454
757774
635171
667777
657375
545554
557231
666222
656111
464555
465771
142441
675334
665131
666443
244342
464452
654665
775221
657333
666664
545333
353434
666676
667461
544444
666443
676556
676444
676222
545111
777443
566443
767151
455323
455544
;
```

Data Set from Chapter 15: Assessing Scale Reliability
with Coefficient Alpha

The data set described in Chapter 15 is identical to the data set from Chapter 14, which appears in the previous section.

Appendix C

CRITICAL VALUES OF THE
F DISTRIBUTION

Upper 5% points

ν_1 / ν_2	1	2	3	4	5	6	7	8	9	10	12	15	20	24	30	40	60	120	∞
1	161.4	199.5	215.7	224.6	230.2	234.0	236.8	238.9	240.5	241.9	243.9	245.9	248.0	249.1	250.1	251.1	252.2	253.3	254.3
2	18.51	19.00	19.16	19.25	19.30	19.33	19.35	19.37	19.38	19.40	19.41	19.43	19.45	19.45	19.46	19.47	19.48	19.49	19.50
3	10.13	9.55	9.28	9.12	9.01	8.94	8.89	8.85	8.81	8.79	8.74	8.70	8.66	8.64	8.62	8.59	8.57	8.55	8.53
4	7.71	6.94	6.59	6.39	6.26	6.16	6.09	6.04	6.00	5.96	5.91	5.86	5.80	5.77	5.75	5.72	5.69	5.66	5.63
5	6.61	5.79	5.41	5.19	5.05	4.95	4.88	4.82	4.77	4.74	4.68	4.62	4.56	4.53	4.50	4.46	4.43	4.40	4.36
6	5.99	5.14	4.76	4.53	4.39	4.28	4.21	4.15	4.10	4.06	4.00	3.94	3.87	3.84	3.81	3.77	3.74	3.70	3.67
7	5.59	4.74	4.35	4.12	3.97	3.87	3.79	3.73	3.68	3.64	3.57	3.51	3.44	3.41	3.38	3.34	3.30	3.27	3.23
8	5.32	4.46	4.07	3.84	3.69	3.58	3.50	3.44	3.39	3.35	3.28	3.22	3.15	3.12	3.08	3.04	3.01	2.97	2.93
9	5.12	4.26	3.86	3.63	3.48	3.37	3.29	3.23	3.18	3.14	3.07	3.01	2.94	2.90	2.86	2.83	2.79	2.75	2.71
10	4.96	4.10	3.71	3.48	3.33	3.22	3.14	3.07	3.02	2.98	2.91	2.85	2.77	2.74	2.70	2.66	2.62	2.58	2.54
11	4.84	3.98	3.59	3.36	3.20	3.09	3.01	2.95	2.90	2.85	2.79	2.72	2.65	2.61	2.57	2.53	2.49	2.45	2.40
12	4.75	3.89	3.49	3.26	3.11	3.00	2.91	2.85	2.80	2.75	2.69	2.62	2.54	2.51	2.47	2.43	2.38	2.34	2.30
13	4.67	3.81	3.41	3.18	3.03	2.92	2.83	2.77	2.71	2.67	2.60	2.53	2.46	2.42	2.38	2.34	2.30	2.25	2.21
14	4.60	3.74	3.34	3.11	2.96	2.85	2.76	2.70	2.65	2.60	2.53	2.46	2.39	2.35	2.31	2.27	2.22	2.18	2.13
15	4.54	3.68	3.29	3.06	2.90	2.79	2.71	2.64	2.59	2.54	2.48	2.40	2.33	2.29	2.25	2.20	2.16	2.11	2.07
16	4.49	3.63	3.24	3.01	2.85	2.74	2.66	2.59	2.54	2.49	2.42	2.35	2.28	2.24	2.19	2.15	2.11	2.06	2.01
17	4.45	3.59	3.20	2.96	2.81	2.70	2.61	2.55	2.49	2.45	2.38	2.31	2.23	2.19	2.15	2.10	2.06	2.01	1.96
18	4.41	3.55	3.16	2.93	2.77	2.66	2.58	2.51	2.46	2.41	2.34	2.27	2.19	2.15	2.11	2.06	2.02	1.97	1.92
19	4.38	3.52	3.13	2.90	2.74	2.63	2.54	2.48	2.42	2.38	2.31	2.23	2.16	2.11	2.07	2.03	1.98	1.93	1.88
20	4.35	3.49	3.10	2.87	2.71	2.60	2.51	2.45	2.39	2.35	2.28	2.20	2.12	2.08	2.04	1.99	1.95	1.90	1.84
21	4.32	3.47	3.07	2.84	2.68	2.57	2.49	2.42	2.37	2.32	2.25	2.18	2.10	2.05	2.01	1.96	1.92	1.87	1.81
22	4.30	3.44	3.05	2.82	2.66	2.55	2.46	2.40	2.34	2.30	2.23	2.15	2.07	2.03	1.98	1.94	1.89	1.84	1.78
23	4.28	3.42	3.03	2.80	2.64	2.53	2.44	2.37	2.32	2.27	2.20	2.13	2.05	2.01	1.96	1.91	1.86	1.81	1.76
24	4.26	3.40	3.01	2.78	2.62	2.51	2.42	2.36	2.30	2.25	2.18	2.11	2.03	1.98	1.94	1.89	1.84	1.79	1.73
25	4.24	3.39	2.99	2.76	2.60	2.49	2.40	2.34	2.28	2.24	2.16	2.09	2.01	1.96	1.92	1.87	1.82	1.77	1.71
26	4.23	3.37	2.98	2.74	2.59	2.47	2.39	2.32	2.27	2.22	2.15	2.07	1.99	1.95	1.90	1.85	1.80	1.75	1.69
27	4.21	3.35	2.96	2.73	2.57	2.46	2.37	2.31	2.25	2.20	2.13	2.06	1.97	1.93	1.88	1.84	1.79	1.73	1.67
28	4.20	3.34	2.95	2.71	2.56	2.45	2.36	2.29	2.24	2.19	2.12	2.04	1.96	1.91	1.87	1.82	1.77	1.71	1.65
29	4.18	3.33	2.93	2.70	2.55	2.43	2.35	2.28	2.22	2.18	2.10	2.03	1.94	1.90	1.85	1.81	1.75	1.70	1.64
30	4.17	3.32	2.92	2.69	2.53	2.42	2.33	2.27	2.21	2.16	2.09	2.01	1.93	1.89	1.84	1.79	1.74	1.68	1.62
40	4.08	3.23	2.84	2.61	2.45	2.34	2.25	2.18	2.12	2.08	2.00	1.92	1.84	1.79	1.74	1.69	1.64	1.58	1.51
60	4.00	3.15	2.76	2.53	2.37	2.25	2.17	2.10	2.04	1.99	1.92	1.84	1.75	1.70	1.65	1.59	1.53	1.47	1.39
120	3.92	3.07	2.68	2.45	2.29	2.17	2.09	2.02	1.96	1.91	1.83	1.75	1.66	1.61	1.55	1.50	1.43	1.35	1.25
∞	3.84	3.00	2.60	2.37	2.21	2.10	2.01	1.94	1.88	1.83	1.75	1.67	1.57	1.52	1.46	1.39	1.32	1.22	1.00

$F = \frac{s_1^2}{s_2^2} = \frac{S_1/\nu_1}{S_2/\nu_2}$, where $s_1^2 = S_1/\nu_1$ and $s_2^2 = S_2/\nu_2$ are independent mean squares estimating a common variance σ^2 and based on ν_1 and ν_2 degrees of freedom, respectively.

Table C.1 Critical Values of the *F* Distribution with Alpha Level of .05

Upper 1% points

ν_1 / ν_2	1	2	3	4	5	6	7	8	9	10	12	15	20	24	30	40	60	120	∞
1	4052	4999.5	5403	5625	5764	5859	5928	5981	6022	6056	6106	6157	6209	6235	6261	6287	6313	6339	6366
2	98.50	99.00	99.17	99.25	99.30	99.33	99.36	99.37	99.39	99.40	99.42	99.43	99.45	99.46	99.47	99.47	99.48	99.49	99.50
3	34.12	30.82	29.46	28.71	28.24	27.91	27.67	27.49	27.35	27.23	27.05	26.87	26.69	26.60	26.50	26.41	26.32	26.22	26.13
4	21.20	18.00	16.69	15.98	15.52	15.21	14.98	14.80	14.66	14.55	14.37	14.20	14.02	13.93	13.84	13.75	13.65	13.56	13.46
5	16.26	13.27	12.06	11.39	10.97	10.67	10.46	10.29	10.16	10.05	9.89	9.72	9.55	9.47	9.38	9.29	9.20	9.11	9.02
6	13.75	10.92	9.78	9.15	8.75	8.47	8.26	8.10	7.98	7.87	7.72	7.56	7.40	7.31	7.23	7.14	7.06	6.97	6.88
7	12.25	9.55	8.45	7.85	7.46	7.19	6.99	6.84	6.72	6.62	6.47	6.31	6.16	6.07	5.99	5.91	5.82	5.74	5.65
8	11.26	8.65	7.59	7.01	6.63	6.37	6.18	6.03	5.91	5.81	5.67	5.52	5.36	5.28	5.20	5.12	5.03	4.95	4.86
9	10.56	8.02	6.99	6.42	6.06	5.80	5.61	5.47	5.35	5.26	5.11	4.96	4.81	4.73	4.65	4.57	4.48	4.40	4.31
10	10.04	7.56	6.55	5.99	5.64	5.39	5.20	5.06	4.94	4.85	4.71	4.56	4.41	4.33	4.25	4.17	4.08	4.00	3.91
11	9.65	7.21	6.22	5.67	5.32	5.07	4.89	4.74	4.63	4.54	4.40	4.25	4.10	4.02	3.94	3.86	3.78	3.69	3.60
12	9.33	6.93	5.95	5.41	5.06	4.82	4.64	4.50	4.39	4.30	4.16	4.01	3.86	3.78	3.70	3.62	3.54	3.45	3.36
13	9.07	6.70	5.74	5.21	4.86	4.62	4.44	4.30	4.19	4.10	3.96	3.82	3.66	3.59	3.51	3.43	3.34	3.25	3.17
14	8.86	6.51	5.56	5.04	4.69	4.46	4.28	4.14	4.03	3.94	3.80	3.66	3.51	3.43	3.35	3.27	3.18	3.09	3.00
15	8.68	6.36	5.42	4.89	4.56	4.32	4.14	4.00	3.89	3.80	3.67	3.52	3.37	3.29	3.21	3.13	3.05	2.96	2.87
16	8.53	6.23	5.29	4.77	4.44	4.20	4.03	3.89	3.78	3.69	3.55	3.41	3.26	3.18	3.10	3.02	2.93	2.84	2.75
17	8.40	6.11	5.18	4.67	4.34	4.10	3.93	3.79	3.68	3.59	3.46	3.31	3.16	3.08	3.00	2.92	2.83	2.75	2.65
18	8.29	6.01	5.09	4.58	4.25	4.01	3.84	3.71	3.60	3.51	3.37	3.23	3.08	3.00	2.92	2.84	2.75	2.66	2.57
19	8.18	5.93	5.01	4.50	4.17	3.94	3.77	3.63	3.52	3.43	3.30	3.15	3.00	2.92	2.84	2.76	2.67	2.58	2.49
20	8.10	5.85	4.94	4.43	4.10	3.87	3.70	3.56	3.46	3.37	3.23	3.09	2.94	2.86	2.78	2.69	2.61	2.52	2.42
21	8.02	5.78	4.87	4.37	4.04	3.81	3.64	3.51	3.40	3.31	3.17	3.03	2.88	2.80	2.72	2.64	2.55	2.46	2.36
22	7.95	5.72	4.82	4.31	3.99	3.76	3.59	3.45	3.35	3.26	3.12	2.98	2.83	2.75	2.67	2.58	2.50	2.40	2.31
23	7.88	5.66	4.76	4.26	3.94	3.71	3.54	3.41	3.30	3.21	3.07	2.93	2.78	2.70	2.62	2.54	2.45	2.35	2.26
24	7.82	5.61	4.72	4.22	3.90	3.67	3.50	3.36	3.26	3.17	3.03	2.89	2.74	2.66	2.58	2.49	2.40	2.31	2.21
25	7.77	5.57	4.68	4.18	3.85	3.63	3.46	3.32	3.22	3.13	2.99	2.85	2.70	2.62	2.54	2.45	2.36	2.27	2.17
26	7.72	5.53	4.64	4.14	3.82	3.59	3.42	3.29	3.18	3.09	2.96	2.81	2.66	2.58	2.50	2.42	2.33	2.23	2.13
27	7.68	5.49	4.60	4.11	3.78	3.56	3.39	3.26	3.15	3.06	2.93	2.78	2.63	2.55	2.47	2.38	2.29	2.20	2.10
28	7.64	5.45	4.57	4.07	3.75	3.53	3.36	3.23	3.12	3.03	2.90	2.75	2.60	2.52	2.44	2.35	2.26	2.17	2.06
29	7.60	5.42	4.54	4.04	3.73	3.50	3.33	3.20	3.09	3.00	2.87	2.73	2.57	2.49	2.41	2.33	2.23	2.14	2.03
30	7.56	5.39	4.51	4.02	3.70	3.47	3.30	3.17	3.07	2.98	2.84	2.70	2.55	2.47	2.39	2.30	2.21	2.11	2.01
40	7.31	5.18	4.31	3.83	3.51	3.29	3.12	2.99	2.89	2.80	2.66	2.52	2.37	2.29	2.20	2.11	2.02	1.92	1.80
60	7.08	4.98	4.13	3.65	3.34	3.12	2.95	2.82	2.72	2.63	2.50	2.35	2.20	2.12	2.03	1.94	1.84	1.73	1.60
120	6.85	4.79	3.95	3.48	3.17	2.96	2.79	2.66	2.56	2.47	2.34	2.19	2.03	1.95	1.86	1.76	1.66	1.53	1.38
∞	6.63	4.61	3.78	3.32	3.02	2.80	2.64	2.51	2.41	2.32	2.18	2.04	1.88	1.79	1.70	1.59	1.47	1.32	1.00

$F = \dfrac{s_1^2}{s_2^2} = \dfrac{S_1}{S_2} \Big/ \dfrac{S_2}{\nu_2}$, where $s_1^2 = S_1/\nu_1$ and $s_2^2 = S_2/\nu_2$ are independent mean squares estimating a common variance σ^2 and based on ν_1 and ν_2 degrees of freedom, respectively.

Table C.2 Critical Values of the *F* Distribution with Alpha Level of .01

Upper 0·1 % points

ν_2 \ ν_1	1	2	3	4	5	6	7	8	9	10	12	15	20	24	30	40	60	120	∞
1	4053*	5000*	5404*	5625*	5764*	5859*	5929*	5981*	6023*	6056*	6107*	6158*	6209*	6235*	6261*	6287*	6313*	6340*	6366*
2	998.5	999.0	999.2	999.2	999.3	999.3	999.4	999.4	999.4	999.4	999.4	999.4	999.4	999.5	999.5	999.5	999.5	999.5	999.5
3	167.0	148.5	141.1	137.1	134.6	132.8	131.6	130.6	129.9	129.2	128.3	127.4	126.4	125.9	125.4	125.0	124.5	124.0	123.5
4	74.14	61.25	56.18	53.44	51.71	50.53	49.66	49.00	48.47	48.05	47.41	46.76	46.10	45.77	45.43	45.09	44.75	44.40	44.05
5	47.18	37.12	33.20	31.09	29.75	28.84	28.16	27.64	27.24	26.92	26.42	25.91	25.39	25.14	24.87	24.60	24.33	24.06	23.79
6	35.51	27.00	23.70	21.92	20.81	20.03	19.46	19.03	18.69	18.41	17.99	17.56	17.12	16.89	16.67	16.44	16.21	15.99	15.75
7	29.25	21.69	18.77	17.19	16.21	15.52	15.02	14.63	14.33	14.08	13.71	13.32	12.93	12.73	12.53	12.33	12.12	11.91	11.70
8	25.42	18.49	15.83	14.39	13.49	12.86	12.40	12.04	11.77	11.54	11.19	10.84	10.48	10.30	10.11	9.92	9.73	9.53	9.33
9	22.86	16.39	13.90	12.56	11.71	11.13	10.70	10.37	10.11	9.89	9.57	9.24	8.90	8.72	8.55	8.37	8.19	8.00	7.81
10	21.04	14.91	12.55	11.28	10.48	9.92	9.52	9.20	8.96	8.75	8.45	8.13	7.80	7.64	7.47	7.30	7.12	6.94	6.76
11	19.69	13.81	11.56	10.35	9.58	9.05	8.66	8.35	8.12	7.92	7.63	7.32	7.01	6.85	6.68	6.52	6.35	6.17	6.00
12	18.64	12.97	10.80	9.63	8.89	8.38	8.00	7.71	7.48	7.29	7.00	6.71	6.40	6.25	6.09	5.93	5.76	5.59	5.42
13	17.81	12.31	10.21	9.07	8.35	7.86	7.49	7.21	6.98	6.80	6.52	6.23	5.93	5.78	5.63	5.47	5.30	5.14	4.97
14	17.14	11.78	9.73	8.62	7.92	7.43	7.08	6.80	6.58	6.40	6.13	5.85	5.56	5.41	5.25	5.10	4.94	4.77	4.60
15	16.59	11.34	9.34	8.25	7.57	7.09	6.74	6.47	6.26	6.08	5.81	5.54	5.25	5.10	4.95	4.80	4.64	4.47	4.31
16	16.12	10.97	9.00	7.94	7.27	6.81	6.46	6.19	5.98	5.81	5.55	5.27	4.99	4.85	4.70	4.54	4.39	4.23	4.06
17	15.72	10.66	8.73	7.68	7.02	6.56	6.22	5.96	5.75	5.58	5.32	5.05	4.78	4.63	4.48	4.33	4.18	4.02	3.85
18	15.38	10.39	8.49	7.46	6.81	6.35	6.02	5.76	5.56	5.39	5.13	4.87	4.59	4.45	4.30	4.15	4.00	3.84	3.67
19	15.08	10.16	8.28	7.26	6.62	6.18	5.85	5.59	5.39	5.22	4.97	4.70	4.43	4.29	4.14	3.99	3.84	3.68	3.51
20	14.82	9.95	8.10	7.10	6.46	6.02	5.69	5.44	5.24	5.08	4.82	4.56	4.29	4.15	4.00	3.86	3.70	3.54	3.38
21	14.59	9.77	7.94	6.95	6.32	5.88	5.56	5.31	5.11	4.95	4.70	4.44	4.17	4.03	3.88	3.74	3.58	3.42	3.26
22	14.38	9.61	7.80	6.81	6.19	5.76	5.44	5.19	4.99	4.83	4.58	4.33	4.06	3.92	3.78	3.63	3.48	3.32	3.15
23	14.19	9.47	7.67	6.69	6.08	5.65	5.33	5.09	4.89	4.73	4.48	4.23	3.96	3.82	3.68	3.53	3.38	3.22	3.05
24	14.03	9.34	7.55	6.59	5.98	5.55	5.23	4.99	4.80	4.64	4.39	4.14	3.87	3.74	3.59	3.45	3.29	3.14	2.97
25	13.88	9.22	7.45	6.49	5.88	5.46	5.15	4.91	4.71	4.56	4.31	4.06	3.79	3.66	3.52	3.37	3.22	3.06	2.89
26	13.74	9.12	7.36	6.41	5.80	5.38	5.07	4.83	4.64	4.48	4.24	3.99	3.72	3.59	3.44	3.30	3.15	2.99	2.82
27	13.61	9.02	7.27	6.33	5.73	5.31	5.00	4.76	4.57	4.41	4.17	3.92	3.66	3.52	3.38	3.23	3.08	2.92	2.75
28	13.50	8.93	7.19	6.25	5.66	5.24	4.93	4.69	4.50	4.35	4.11	3.86	3.60	3.46	3.32	3.18	3.02	2.86	2.69
29	13.39	8.85	7.12	6.19	5.59	5.18	4.87	4.64	4.45	4.29	4.05	3.80	3.54	3.41	3.27	3.12	2.97	2.81	2.64
30	13.29	8.77	7.05	6.12	5.53	5.12	4.82	4.58	4.39	4.24	4.00	3.75	3.49	3.36	3.22	3.07	2.92	2.76	2.59
40	12.61	8.25	6.60	5.70	5.13	4.73	4.44	4.21	4.02	3.87	3.64	3.40	3.15	3.01	2.87	2.73	2.57	2.41	2.23
60	11.97	7.76	6.17	5.31	4.76	4.37	4.09	3.87	3.69	3.54	3.31	3.08	2.83	2.69	2.55	2.41	2.25	2.08	1.89
120	11.38	7.32	5.79	4.95	4.42	4.04	3.77	3.55	3.38	3.24	3.02	2.78	2.53	2.40	2.26	2.11	1.95	1.76	1.54
∞	10.83	6.91	5.42	4.62	4.10	3.74	3.47	3.27	3.10	2.96	2.74	2.51	2.27	2.13	1.99	1.84	1.66	1.45	1.00

* Multiply these entries by 100.
This 0·1% table is based on the following sources: Colcord & Deming (1935); Fisher & Yates (1953, Table V) used with the permission of the authors and of Messrs Oliver and Boyd; Norton (1952).

Table C.3 Critical Values of the *F* Distribution with Alpha Level of .001

Index

An Array of Challenges — Test Your SAS® Skills
by **Robert Virgile**..................................Order No. A55625

Applied Multivariate Statistics with SAS® Software
by **Ravindra Khattree**
and **Dayanand N. Naik**........................Order No. A55234

Applied Statistics and the SAS® Programming Language, Fourth Edition
by **Ronald P. Cody**
and **Jeffrey K. Smith**..........................Order No. A55984

Beyond the Obvious with SAS® Screen Control Language
by **Don Stanley** ....Order No. A55073

Carpenter's Complete Guide to the SAS® Macro Language
by **Art Carpenter** ....Order No. A56100

The Cartoon Guide to Statistics
by **Larry Gonick**
and **Woollcott Smith**............................Order No. A55153

Categorical Data Analysis Using the SAS® System
by **Maura E. Stokes, Charles S. Davis,**
and **Gary G. Koch** ....Order No. A55320

Common Statistical Methods for Clinical Research with SAS® Examples
by **Glenn A. Walker**..............................Order No. A55991

Concepts and Case Studies in Data Management
by **William S. Calvert**
and **J. Meimei Ma**.................................Order No. A55220

Efficiency: Improving the Performance of Your SAS® Applications
by **Robert Virgile**..................................Order No. A55960

Essential Client/Server Survival Guide, Second Edition
by **Robert Orfali, Dan Harkey,**
and **Jeri Edwards**.................................Order No. A56285

Extending SAS® Survival Analysis Techniques for Medical Research
by **Alan Cantor**.....................................Order No. A55504

A Handbook of Statistical Analyses using SAS®
by **B.S. Everitt**
and **G. Der**..Order No. A56378

The How-To Book for SAS/GRAPH® Software
by **Thomas Miron** ....Order No. A55203

In the Know ... SAS® Tips and Techniques From Around the Globe
by **Phil Mason** ....Order No. A55513

Integrating Results through Meta-Analytic Review Using SAS® Software
by **Morgan C. Wang** and
Brad J. Bushman ....Order No. A55810

Learning SAS® in the Computer Lab
by **Rebecca J. Elliott** ....Order No. A55273

The Little SAS® Book: A Primer
by **Lora D. Delwiche** and
Susan J. Slaughter ....Order No. A55200

The Little SAS® Book: A Primer, Second Edition
by **Lora D. Delwiche** and
Susan J. Slaughter ....Order No. A56649
(updated to include Version 7 features)

Mastering the SAS® System, Second Edition
by **Jay A. Jaffe** ....Order No. A55123

The Next Step: Integrating the Software Life Cycle with SAS® Programming
by **Paul Gill** ....Order No. A55697

Painless Windows 3.1: A Beginner's Handbook for SAS® Users
by **Jodie Gilmore** ....Order No. A55505

Painless Windows: A Handbook for SAS® Users
by **Jodie Gilmore** ....Order No. A55769

Professional SAS® Programmers Pocket Reference, Second Edition
by **Rick Aster** ....Order No. A56646

Professional SAS® Programming Secrets, Second Edition
by **Rick Aster**
and **Rhena Seidman** ....Order No. A56279

Professional SAS® User Interfaces
by **Rick Aster** ....Order No. A56197

Programming Techniques for Object-Based Statistical Analysis with SAS® Software
by **Tanya Kolosova**
and **Samuel Berestizhevsky** ....Order No. A55869

Quick Results with SAS/GRAPH® Software
by **Arthur L. Carpenter**
and **Charles E. Shipp** ....Order No. A55127

Quick Start to Data Analysis with SAS®
by **Frank C. Dilorio**
and **Kenneth A. Hardy**........................Order No. A55550